Aging, Society, and the Life Course

Fourth Edition

Leslie A. Morgan, PhD, is Associate Dean at the Erickson School of Aging Studies, Co-director of the Gerontology Doctoral Program, and Professor in the Department of Sociology and Anthropology at the University of Maryland, Baltimore County. Dr. Morgan has 27 years of experience in teaching and research in aging and has published on a variety of topics, from economic well-being and family relationships to assisted living. She has authored or coauthored three books and numerous articles. Dr. Morgan has been principal or coprincipal investigator on several NIH-funded studies of life in assisted living, examining the quality of resident experience and transitions among residents.

Suzanne R. Kunkel, PhD, is the director of Scripps Gerontology Center and Professor in the Department of Sociology and Gerontology at Miami University. Dr. Kunkel has 20 years of experience in research and teaching in gerontology. She is the recipient of the 2006 Outstanding Gerontology Educator Award from the Ohio Association of Gerontology in Higher Education. She has authored or coauthored more than 35 articles, book chapters, and research monographs, and has coedited, with Valerie Wellin, *Consumer Voice and Choice in Long-Term Care* (Springer Publishing Company, 2006). Her research focuses primarily on demography of aging, health and disability, and innovations and quality in long-term care systems.

Aging, Society, and the Life Course

Fourth Edition

Leslie A. Morgan, PhD, and
Suzanne R. Kunkel, PhD

SPRINGER PUBLISHING COMPANY

New York

Springer Publishing Company, LLC
11 West 42nd Street
New York, NY 10036
www.springerpub.com

Acquisitions Editor: Sheri W. Sussman
Senior Editor: Rose Mary Piscitelli
Cover design: Mimi Flow
Composition: Jennifer Boelter/Apex CoVantage

ISBN: 978-0-8261-1937-7
E-book ISBN: 978-0-8261-1938-4

12 13/ 5 4 3

The author and the publisher of this Work have made every effort to use sources believed to be reliable to provide information that is accurate and compatible with the standards generally accepted at the time of publication. The author and publisher shall not be liable for any special, consequential, or exemplary damages resulting, in whole or in part, from the readers' use of, or reliance on, the information contained in this book. The publisher has no responsibility for the persistence or accuracy of URLs for external or third-party Internet Web sites referred to in this publication and does not guarantee that any content on such Web sites is, or will remain, accurate or appropriate.

Library of Congress Cataloging-in-Publication Data

Morgan, Leslie A.
    Aging, society & the life course / Leslie A. Morgan and Suzanne R. Kunkel. — 4th ed.
        p. cm.
    Rev. ed. of: Aging : aging, society and life course. 3rd ed. 2006.
    Includes bibliographical references and index.
    ISBN 978-0-8261-1937-7 (alk. paper) — ISBN 978-0-8261-1938-4 (ebook)
1. Older people—United States. 2. Aging—United States. 3. Gerontology—United States.
I. Kunkel, Suzanne. II. Morgan, Leslie A. Aging. III. Title. IV. Title:
Aging, society and the life course.
    HQ1064.U5M6818   2011
    305.26—dc22   2011002333

Special discounts on bulk quantities of our books are available to corporations, professional associations, pharmaceutical companies, health care organizations, and other qualifying groups.

If you are interested in a custom book, including chapters from more than one of our titles, we can provide that service as well.

For details, please contact:

Special Sales Department, Springer Publishing Company, LLC
11 West 42nd Street, 15th Floor, New York, NY 10036-8002
Phone: 877-687-7476 or 212-431-4370; Fax: 212-941-7842
Email: sales@springerpub.com

Printed in the United States of America by Bang Printing

Contents

Preface

Each new edition of a textbook provides authors new opportunities to sharpen, update, and extend the material and to include issues that have come to the forefront in recent years. This edition reflects a major reorganization of material and addition of significant new topics, while retaining its focus on the social and sociological aspects of aging. In rethinking our organization of content, we recast some pairs of chapters (relating to families, health and employment/retirement) into single chapters, creating space for the addition of chapters focusing on two important new topics, the baby boomers and global aging. The resulting 12-chapter book is well attuned to most academic schedules for a "one chapter a week" reading assignment.

Continuing Themes

In presenting knowledge about aging in social context, we focus on five majors themes. The first theme is emphasizing the diversity of the older population; this *stereotype-busting* focus carries throughout all of the chapters, emphasizing how notably the experience of aging is affected by social characteristics. Material highlights diversity by gender, social class, race/ethnicity, and even age differences among older adults. A second major theme is the *micro/macro distinction* in understanding aging as a social phenomenon. Aging of individuals occurs within layers of social context from the family to the political and economic systems. Understanding the complex dynamics among these multiple levels is key to a deep understanding of aging processes and outcomes. The third key theme is *social construction*. With this approach, which is described in Chapter 1, we hope to highlight how aging is much more than an individual journey through time; aging is a complex social process that influences each of us on the journey and is, in turn, influenced collectively by those making the journey. The fourth distinguishing characteristic of this text is the focus on the *life course*. This perspective informs our discussions of the movement of people and cohorts through age-related stages and transitions in all major social institutions and provides an organizing theme for new research and theoretical developments in the field of gerontology.

The final key theme is *integrating the learning of theory with content about aging*. Reading theories without much substance attached is challenging for many students. Instead, scattered throughout our chapters are "Applying Theory" segments that describe a particular theory as it relates to content such as health care, family caregiving, or retirement. In this way the theory is grounded with some application that makes it more relevant and memorable.

Pedagogical Features

We have continued three features from earlier editions. First, we have updated our "Web Wise" listings at the end of each chapter. Students will find these selected sites useful complements to the material presented in the chapter. A second feature that is designed to help students relate to the material and deepen their understanding of abstract concepts is the inclusion of questions for thought and discussion. Finally, key terms that are useful for review and discussion are highlighted within the text and listed at the end of each chapter. The terms are presented in bold, with a definition within the body of the book, and are among the essential elements of understanding the content presented.

In our teaching experience, most students relate easily to aging through their personal or family experiences. Seldom do they come to a course understanding the implications of an aging society for major social institutions. On the basis of the fundamental expansion of the *sociological imagination* into the *gerontological imagination,* we hope to expand students' perspectives to a bigger picture of aging as a social phenomenon that will reshape their lives well before they themselves are older adults. One way that we attempt to expand one's view of aging is through our third continued feature, a series of five Topical Essays, which are scattered between chapters throughout the book. Our intention with these is to take the lens of aging and look at an array of contemporary issues, reflecting a more engaging way to "think outside the box" regarding the implications of aging for persons and the larger society. Interesting ideas, such as the role of music in the life course and antiaging medicine, are employed to provide opportunities for discussion, take a further step with knowledge gained in the prior chapters, and connect concepts to our shared real-world experiences.

Our original and continued purpose in writing this book has been to provide a new type of textbook on the social aspects of human aging—one that is neither encyclopedic in its coverage of research findings nor overly weighted down with jargon. We hope that we have more closely approached these goals in this fourth edition.

Acknowledgments

With any project of this scope, there are many people who make important contributions to its completion. We would like to acknowledge the technical support provided by the staff at Springer Publishing Company. We also need to thank our support systems on our campuses. For Leslie Morgan this includes the Department of Sociology and Anthropology at UMBC, most especially the support of Shoshana Ballew, former PhD student in Gerontology. For Suzanne Kunkel, appreciation is extended to a long list of colleagues, graduate assistants, and undergraduate student assistants at Miami University's Scripps Gerontology Center. Special thanks to Lisa Grant for overseeing the production of exhibits for the manuscript. E. J. Hanna and Mike Payne contributed the great majority of the photos in the book; an added thanks to Mike Payne for preparing photo captions.

We would also like to acknowledge our mentors and colleagues (both proximate and remote) who have shaped our professional lives and perspectives. These include Robert Atchley, Vern Bengtson, Kevin Eckert, William Feinberg, Joe Hendricks, Norris Johnson, Matilda White Riley, Neal Ritchey, Mildred Seltzer, and Judith Treas, among others. Finally we would like to acknowledge our families and closest friends; these are the people who give us our roots and our wings, help us keep perspective, and remind us of the importance of balance in our lives.

Aging, Society, and the Life Course

Fourth Edition

Aging and Society

The individual does not act alone, although conscious beings will do and act as if they had control over their lives and could do what best pleased them. . . . No person really acts independent of the influences of our fellow human beings. Everywhere there is a social life setting limitations and influencing individual action. People cooperate, compete, combine, and organize for specific purposes, so that no one lives to him/herself.

(Blackmar, 1908, pp. 3–4)

Aging is something that happens to all of us. It is a natural and virtually inevitable process. Even so, older people are often the subject of bad jokes and negative stereotypes, and many people in our society dread growing old. A quick visit to the birthday card section of your local card shop will confirm our preoccupation with negative views of, and jokes about, aging. Despite this preoccupation, our ideas about what aging really means and why it matters are notably diverse. Consider:

- At age 40, people in the labor force are legally defined as "older workers" by the Age Discrimination in Employment Act.
- Most of us know, or know about, people who became grandparents in their 40s; we also know people who became parents in their 40s.
- A 70-year-old woman in India gave birth in 2010, becoming the oldest new mother in the world. The event sparked extensive scientific and ethical debate about when a woman is too old to have a baby, but there was little discussion about when a man might be too old to become a father.
- In 2009, a US Airways pilot was credited with saving the lives of 150 people when he landed a plane in the Hudson River after a flock of birds flew into the engines. Captain Sullenberger was the pilot of what was dubbed the "Miracle on the Hudson." He was about a week shy of his 58th birthday, and his years of experience were cited as a factor in his ability to respond so effectively to the emergency. He retired the following year.
- "Until the mid-sixteenth century. . . . few people knew exactly how old they were" (Cole, 1992, p. 5).
- Most people who are age 75 do not think they belong in the "old" age category.
- At age 16, people are "old enough" to be licensed drivers, at age 18 they are "old enough" to vote, and at age 21 they are "old enough" to drink alcohol.
- In some states, an older driver seeking to renew a license must pass a series of tests to demonstrate his or her fitness to drive. For example, in New Hampshire, renewal applicants age 75 and older must take a road test. Georgia, Virginia, and South Carolina are among the states that require vision tests for older applicants.
- In the 2010 NBA playoffs, commentators predicted that the Boston Celtics, who had the highest average age of any team in the league, would be "too old" to win the championship. Others predicted the team's years of experience would ensure their victory.
- Members of the armed forces can retire as early as age 37.
- At age 90, Ludwig Magener won the national swimming championship in six masters' swimming events.

The authors would like to acknowledge Robert C. Atchley for the contributions he made to some sections in the earliest version of this chapter.

■ The human genome project could potentially extend life expectancy significantly. What will it mean to be 75 if life expectancy is 200? What will happen to our ideas about education, careers, and grandparenthood?

These examples illustrate two very important points. First, we have many different formal and informal social definitions of age and aging. Second, the meanings, definitions, and experiences of aging vary across situations, cultures, and time. So, questions about when aging begins, what it is, and why it matters can only be answered by paying attention to the social contexts in which aging takes place.

Dimensions of Aging

If you ask someone to define *aging,* she might reasonably respond that it means growing older. But, what does growing older mean? Is it simply the passage of time, or having another birthday? Increasingly, scholars argue that chronological age is a relatively meaningless variable (see Ferraro, 2007; Maddox & Lawton, 1988). Age is only a way of marking human events and experiences; these events and experiences are what matters, not time itself. Time's passing is of concern only because it is connected, however loosely, with other changes: physical, psychological, and social.

Physical Aging

The passage of time for human organisms is related to maturation; there are developmental timetables for the predictable changes that take place as we age, including growth charts for infants and language acquisition for children. In later life, the passage of time is related to a large number of specific physical alterations, such as gray hair, wrinkling of skin, and changes in reproductive capacity, immune system response, and cardiovascular functioning. An interesting question about these physical changes is whether they are inevitable, natural consequences of growing older. In fact, research shows that some of the changes we think of as normal aspects of aging are modifiable, preventable, and related to lifestyle choices and cultural practices. For example, while some wrinkling of the skin and some loss of arterial elasticity appear to be related to physical aging processes, the magnitude of change and speed of deterioration are affected by lifestyle choices and culture. We know that wrinkling of the skin is accelerated and accentuated by sun exposure and by smoking, and some of the changes over time in cardiovascular functioning are related to diet, exercise, and smoking. Similarly, most of us know 70-year-olds who are as active, healthy, and vigorous as an average 40-year-old. Increasing evidence shows enormous variability in physical aging across individuals; this growing evidence of variability has resulted in new ways of thinking about aging.

In earlier eras of gerontology, researchers searched for the *normal* changes that accompanied aging; an important part of this search was to distinguish normal age changes from pathological or disease processes that became more prevalent with age but were not caused by aging. Knowledge about the modifiability and variability of physical aging processes resulted in a new perspective about aging. Rowe and Kahn (1998) offered us the concept of successful aging, drawing distinctions among usual, optimal, and pathological aging. *Optimal* aging is characterized by minimal loss of physical function and a healthy, vigorous body; *pathological* aging is aging accompanied by multiple chronic diseases and negative environmental influences. *Usual* aging refers to the typical or average experience, somewhere between pathological and optimal. Exhibit 1.1 illustrates this view of the variability of physical aging (Machemer, 1992). The concept of successful aging is undergoing continual refinement (c.f. Dillaway & Byrnes, 2009; Kahn, 2002), and research about successful aging—how it is defined and measured, who achieves it, how it is attained—is still in its early years (Blazer, 2006). Even with continuing debate and the

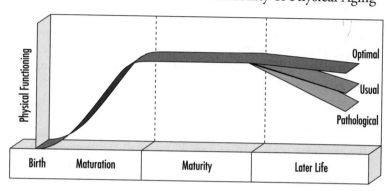

EXHIBIT 1.1
Variability of Physical Aging

Adapted from Machemer, 1992.

need for further research, the distinctions among usual, successful, and pathological aging reflect new ways of thinking about physical aging—as a variable and sometimes modifiable set of processes that often have important social components.

As we continue to find that the changes we call physical aging are merely age-linked and not age-caused and that many are, in fact, modifiable, we are forced to reconsider the question of what aging means as a physical process. The ever-increasing evidence that individuals vary greatly in their experience of physical aging suggests that few (if any) of the significant aspects of aging are purely or even primarily physical.

Psychological Aging

Psychological aging processes include changes in personality, mental functioning, and sense of self during our adult years. Some changes are considered a normal part of adult development, some are the result of physiological changes in the way the brain functions, and some psychological dimensions show little change at all in later years. As in the case of physical aging, a wealth of research has explored the complexities of these processes and ways to distinguish distinct disease processes, such as Alzheimer's disease, from normal aging changes.

For our purposes, several generalizations are important. First, human beings do continue to develop and grow throughout their lives. Some researchers in gerontology are very interested in the unique nature of human development in the later years—the tasks, growth, and adaptations that typically take place through time. Much of this work focuses on opportunities for personal development and contributions to the world around us that can emerge in later life. Concepts such as *gerotranscendence* (Tornstam, 1997, 2005), serving from spirit (Atchley, 2004), *sageing* (Schachter-Shalomi & Miller, 1995), and *elderhood* (Thomas, 2004) offer a glimpse into the positive developmental stages that may characterize late life. We explore these ideas further in Chapter 4. For now it is sufficient to recognize that human development occurs throughout our entire lives; it does not end with adolescence or early adulthood.

A second broad statement related to psychological aspects of aging is that personality does not undergo profound changes in later life; most personality traits, self-concept, and self-esteem remain fairly stable from mid-life onward. For example, people do not become wise, grumpy, or rigid in their thinking as a result of growing older; the grumpy old man was very likely a grumpy young man. Although the developmental challenges and opportunities vary through life, the strategies people use to adapt to change, to refine and reinforce a sense of self, to work toward realizing full human potential are practiced throughout adulthood. The simple passage of time seldom requires or causes fundamental changes to these basic personality structures and strategies.

Similarly, loss of cognitive functioning is not an inevitable result of aging. Just as significant loss of physical function is not inevitable or universal, so, too, memory and other cognitive skills may remain stable or even improve with age. However, it is important to be accurate here about changes with age. One recent study on the prevalence of dementia shows that 5% of people aged 71 to 79 had dementia, compared to 37.4% of those aged 90 and older (Plassman et al., 2007). Based on this pattern, it is fair to say that advanced age is a marker for increased likelihood of dementia, but it is misleading to say that aging causes the impairment.

Social Aging

If aging brings only relatively small universal and inevitable changes in physical or cognitive functioning, in the basic structure of personality, and in the trajectory of adult development, why does it matter in people's lives? In this book, we argue that age is significant primarily because of the social meanings, structures, and processes attached to it. Gray hair, wrinkles, longer reaction time, and even some short-term memory loss matter only because the social world in which we live has defined those characteristics as meaningful. Much of the social meaning of aging is tied to erroneous beliefs about the effects of aging on physical and mental capabilities. Aging does not inevitability cause us to become rigid in our thinking, forgetful, or unable to carry out our favorite physical or intellectual activities. For most people aging is a process of change that is so gradual that we compensate for most of it so that it has little impact on our everyday lives.

However, society uses age to assign people to roles, to channel people into and out of positions within the social structure, as a basis for allocation of resources, and as a way to categorize individuals. In its most benevolent form, using age to allocate opportunities is a reasonable mechanism. For example, our society has rules about the minimum age for employment; these laws were designed to protect young people from being exploited and, according to some, they are good for the labor force because they control the flow of new workers into the labor market. In a more constraining way, however, age artificially and unevenly limits the opportunities of people. Gray hair and wrinkles, perhaps the most visible signs of aging, and the chronological age of 65—the most often-used criterion of old age—have no effect on physical functioning or cognitive capability. They do, however, have profound effects on social interactions and opportunities for individuals in the social world. Whether we would seriously consider someone as a possible candidate for a job or as an interesting partner in social interaction is, in fact, influenced by our assessment of the age of that person and what that person's age symbolizes to us. Again, it is not because age 65 or gray hair is symptomatic of competence or incompetence or of a boring or dazzling personality, or even that visible signs of aging are inherently unattractive or attractive. We make these assessments because we live in a society that has constructed the meaning of aging in particular (primarily negative) ways.

It is important to think about the extent to which the very same processes work at other ages and stages of life. In our culture, it is possible to be "too young" just as it is possible to be "too old" for certain roles and opportunities. We have very clear social prescriptions, often in the form of federal and state laws, about when a person is old enough to drive a car, get married, and be President of the United States. In these examples, "old enough" seems to imply the window of opportunity between legally too young and socially too old.

Social aging, then, refers to the ways in which society helps to shape the meanings and experiences of aging. Social aging includes the expectations and assumptions of those around us about how we should behave, what we are like, what we can do, and what we should be doing at different ages. The concept of social aging also refers to the ways in which those expectations influence what opportunities are open to us as we grow older. Later chapters in the book apply the concepts of social aging to the major dimensions of our social lives.

Social Construction of Aging

The preceding discussion about the ways in which the experiences of aging are largely constructed by society is an example of an important sociological idea introduced by Berger and Luckmann (1966): the *social construction* of reality. This concept suggests that reality does not exist out there, waiting to be measured and understood by us. Rather, reality is created out of interactions among humans and by the social institutions in which people live their lives. For an illustration of the gap between physical reality and peoples' lived experience of aging, think about witnesses to an unusual event, such as an auto accident. While we know that there are facts in such a situation—for example, the color of the cars, the direction and speed they were traveling—eyewitness accounts often vary greatly on even these details. Human beings pay attention to different things, remember different things, and report different things. If one of the people in the accident is an older person, the witness might be motivated (consciously or unconsciously) to notice and report details based on their assumptions about that driver's capabilities. You can probably think of many examples from your everyday life in which a conversation, phrase, or gesture has been interpreted very differently, depending on the perspectives of the people involved.

Societal Aging

Beyond the social construction of aging, social forces influence the experience of aging in another important way. Societies themselves experience aging. As the proportion of population in the "older" age categories increases, profound changes in the social structure take place. Societal aging—these demographic, structural, and cultural transformations—affects every aspect of social life, from social institutions to the experiences of aging individuals. We can define **societal aging** as the demographic, structural, and cultural transformations a society undergoes as the proportion of its population that is aging increases. Education and the economy are good examples of social organizations and institutions that are affected greatly by the growth of the older population. The impact of population changes on the educational system in the United States can be seen in the growing number of attempts to address the needs of mature learners and in the growing number of college and university programs targeting the older population. Some of you may have summer Elderhostel or Exploritas programs at your institutions, or free tuition available for students over age 65. The University of Massachusetts at Boston has a certificate program in gerontology; more than half of the hundreds of people who have earned that certificate are over the age of 60. The impact of population aging on our society is discussed in greater detail in the later chapters of this book.

Another impact of the growth of the older population is the increased visibility of aging, which results in increased exposure of the general population to the diversity and uniqueness among older individuals. As older people become more numerous and visible, stereotypical attitudes and discriminatory practices that disadvantage older people are more likely to be challenged. For example, in comparing magazine advertisements in the year 2010 to those from 1980, we see a marked increase in both the number of ads that feature older people and in the average age of many models (other than the supermodels, who are very young). While most people in ads are still young, our images of aging are changing along with heightened awareness of the aging of society.

The aging of a population influences how aging itself is socially constructed. As groups of people born at different times (**cohorts**) move through the stages of aging, they are affected by, but also have an impact on, the experience of being older. The baby boomers will experience aging in a very different way than the current generation of older people. Negative stereotypes are being challenged, age discrimination is illegal, and there is growing recognition of the expanding mature market for goods and services. All of these changes were set into motion by earlier groups of people as they grew older, but are picking up speed as the very large baby boom cohorts approach later life. When these social changes combine with the political activism that has historically characterized the baby boomers, and with their potential power in the marketplace and in the polling booths, the experiences and definitions of aging are being altered.

When cohorts born at different time periods move into later life, they also have an impact on social institutions such as the economy and health care. For example, the current generation of older people grew up during the Great Depression. Their investment, purchasing, and savings habits have been shaped by that experience (Elder, 1974); they tend to save at higher rates than other groups of adults, especially the baby boomers, and they are less likely to make risky investments or purchases. The baby boomers grew up during relatively comfortable economic times, are not good savers, and are more likely to make nonessential purchases (McKinsey Global Institute, 2008). During the past two decades we have seen tremendous growth in the "games for adults" industry; a walk down the games aisle at your neighborhood toy store will reveal a very large number of board games designed for adults, far beyond the number available just 10 years ago. This trend is related to the purchasing power, leisure preferences, and buying habits of baby boomers. You can use your imagination to think about new leisure, health care, cosmetics, or convenience products for aging baby boomers. Thus, the aging of cohorts, as a dimension of population aging, has an impact on the economy—on product and service development, on savings, and on consumer demand patterns.

With these examples we do not mean to oversimplify societal aging, or social change in institutions such as the economy. Rather, these examples are intended to illustrate how the experiences of aging, and the social contexts in which they take place, change over time as a result of the aging of unique cohorts. As new groups of people go through stages of growing older, they bring with them a unique historical profile, and they alter the meanings and values associated with growing older. The movement of new and larger groups into old age also places new demands on the social system. Changes to the social structure emerge in response to the size, characteristics, and demands of each new group of older people. The intricacies of this dynamic between cohorts and social change are discussed in further detail in later chapters. For our purposes at this point it is important to acknowledge that societal aging is a significant dimension of the social processes of aging.

Ways of Categorizing People by Age

As we consider the many dimensions of social aging, we need a way to mark or measure the age of individuals. Most often people are categorized in one of three ways: using *chronological age, functional status,* or life stage. Each way of expressing age has advantages and disadvantages, and the decision to use any one of them should be based on the goals of examining age. Keep in mind that whether we use chronological age, functional status, or life stages, we are applying socially constructed labels and definitions, which allow us to treat people as members of meaningful social categories. We use these definitions in many ways. We sometimes make implicit judgments about whether we are likely to have anything in common with someone based on the age group they appear to belong to, and we explicitly use age to select a specific target for social action or policy, or to define a subject of study. Remember, all these definitions, including chronological age, are human creations. In selecting definitions of aging or age categories, we need to be conscious of our underlying purpose and select our definitions accordingly.

Chronological Age

Chronological age is one of the simplest assessments of age, and thus, it reduces administrative complexity. Chronological age is used in our society as the basis for determining many social roles (voting, driving, marrying, holding public office), for eligibility in social programs (such as Social Security, AARP membership, or Older Americans Act services), and for inclusion in research about aging.

The use of chronological age to mark major life transitions is taken for granted in modern urban societies. However, it is a relatively recent development coinciding with the rise of large-scale industrialism in the early 20th century (Moody, 1993). The industrial economy required that human lives be ordered efficiently so that work years coincided with the years assumed to be associated with peak productivity. Chronological age was adopted as a simple way to define a worker's life stage.

The meaningfulness of chronological age is questioned in many ways today, however. The number of birthdays an individual has had tells us little in and of itself. The fluidity and multiplicity of today's lifestyles defy the use of

Like most cultures, ours places a big emphasis on chronological age—for both young and old alike. (Credit: M. Payne)

rigid boundaries, such as numerical age (Moody, 1993). When it is possible to have two career peaks—one at age 40 in your first career, and a second at age 60 in your second career—and when it is increasingly common to find people having children when they are 40—about the age at which others are becoming grandparents—the usefulness of chronological age as a life stage marker is indeed questionable.

In the world of social policy and programs, the validity of chronological age is being questioned at another level. Even though "age has long stood as a formidable proxy for demonstrable need and, in turn, the receipt of support from the larger society" (Hudson, 2005, p. 1), there are political and ideological debates about the usefulness of age-based policies. The age for eligibility for full benefits under Social Security is gradually being raised so that by the year 2027 you will need to be 67 to retire with your full benefit. Services established by the Older Americans Act, for which people become eligible at age 60, are increasingly being targeted to groups within the older population with the greatest need—frail, low-income, and minority groups. In general, policies seem to be moving away from a central focus on chronological age. We discuss these policy issues in greater detail in Chapter 9. For now, it is important to recognize that these policy shifts are further examples of the challenges to the meaningfulness of chronological age.

Functional Age

What marker of age will we use if chronological age continues to lose its significance and usefulness? There is considerable difference (on average) between 65-year-olds and 95-year-olds, yet all are considered to be older adults. In the case of policies and programs, *targeting* of services to specific subgroups is increasingly common, not simply on the basis of age, but also on the basis of need. For example, if we are interested in identifying people who have physical limitations that require regular assistance, we can use measures of functional status, such as *activities of daily living,* a generic term for several scales that measure an individual's ability to accomplish, without assistance, routine personal care activities such as bathing, eating, dressing, and getting in and out of bed. Such measures are useful if we are interested in targeting home care programs to those who need them because of physical frailty.

When we use chronological age as a convenient way to determine eligibility for benefits such as Medicare, we are assuming that age is a proxy for the need for those services. Functional

*Advancing age does not prevent engagement in many positive aspects of life.
(Credit: U.S. Census Bureau, Public Information Office [PIO])*

status is a way to move beyond that generalized assumption about age, but it is obviously a much more complicated way to grant access to programs and services.

Life Stage

As lives progress, people tend to reach certain plateaus of stability (life stages) punctuated by periods of change or transition. Thus, people can be categorized as being in roughly comparable circumstances, such as adolescence, young adulthood, middle age, and later maturity. We can assume that people going through the *empty nest* transition have living adult children and are in the process of launching these children into lives as independent adults. We can assume that people in very old age (sometimes called *old-old* age, referring to people 85 and above) are probably physically frail and live simple lives. Therefore, **life stages** are broad social categories that describe particular times of life involving new social roles (such as grandparenthood), physical changes (such as physical frailty), or transitions (such as leaving one's job to retire).

Life stages roughly correspond to chronological age ranges but are much more socially constructed and culturally based than chronological age. For example, when is someone an adult? When they move out of their parents' home, reach age 18 or age 21, have a child, have a full-time job, or act mature? Life stages rely on some information about physical changes but are much more attentive to other traits such as the roles (e.g., parent, employee) that people play. For example, the empty nest described previously implies something about chronological age, but derives its meaning from the new family roles and relationships emerging during that stage. The complexity of the concept of life stage is also well-illustrated by new research on our changing timetables for entry into adulthood and the subjective definitions that come into play (Settersten, Furstenberg, & Rumbaut, 2005; Shanahan, Porfeli, Mortimer, & Erickson, 2005). These topics are discussed further in Chapter 4, when we explore the sequences of roles people move into and out of as we age. We specifically discuss life stages within the family and within the economy, emphasizing the shared expectations about what roles we should be playing at what ages.

Ageism

With all of the possible ways to assess and define age, and the limitations of any single approach, it is fair to ask why we continue to use age in so many aspects of social life. In part, we use social categories to help organize our world so that every situation is not completely new and confusing. Unfortunately, our use of social characteristics such as age, gender, and race to categorize people often leads to stereotypes, prejudice, and discrimination. **Ageism** is "a systematic stereotyping

of and discrimination against people because they are old, just as racism and sexism accomplish this with skin color and gender" (Butler, 1989, p. 243). At the heart of any kind of *-ism* (ageism, racism, sexism, classism) is the creation of an *other*, that is, grouping together people identified as different from ourselves because of some characteristic they do or do not possess (e.g., gender, race, class, or age). Ageism and other -isms make us more comfortable in making sweeping generalizations about members of that other category, stereotyping them (often incorrectly) as sharing common traits or attitudes. These stereotypes often extend to excluding the others from aspects of participation in social life or limiting their opportunities. We are all familiar with the views of older people as lonely, frail, poor, and deserving of our help. This "compassionate ageism" (discussed further in a later chapter) (Binstock, 1991a) now exists side by side with other stereotypical views: older people are cute and interesting; older people are wise and funny; older people are greedy and selfish and economically more advantaged than any other group. While the content of these ageist views does vary considerably, the impact is the same. Older people are seen as *other*, in either positive or negative light; they are different from us, but all like each other.

We often use visual, informal assessments to decide if a person is *old* or not. Be aware, however, that such categorizations limit the opportunities available, both for formal social participation and for informal interaction, to the person assigned to the *older* category. For example, think about your reactions to someone who seems old and strikes up a conversation with you as you wait to cross the street. If you have any kind of automatic negative reaction to that person, you may unconsciously limit the possibilities for interaction. As further illustration of the power of these visual assessments, we can think about why it is considered such a compliment to say to someone, "You don't look 50 (or 30 or 80)!" Why is it so desirable to look younger than your age? And what should 50 look like?

The Rise of Old Age as a Social Category

We tend to take for granted the idea of categorizing people by age. We aren't often conscious of the many ways in which this categorization takes place, or of its impacts. It is often difficult to take a step back from our everyday lives in order to reflect on why we organize our social lives the way we do. Social science, especially sociology, helps us to gain this more reflective attitude. The notion of systematically studying society and its dynamics developed at the time of the industrialization of Western Europe in the mid- to late 19th century. The era's grand masters of social theory—Comte, Spencer, Durkheim, Weber, and Marx—focused on the ideological and cultural shifts that transformed Europe from agricultural, small-scale societies to urban, mass societies. They also observed the shift from the family as the basic economic unit to individual achievement and performance in a complex division of the labor market. They either said nothing at all about age, aging, or generations, or referred to these topics only in passing, perhaps because they were more interested in society as a whole than in the details of individual life structure. Populations in these societies were much younger then, before the significant changes that brought about societal aging (discussed in Chapter 3).

Generational Consciousness

By the 1950s social theorists began thinking and writing about age, aging, generations, and the life course. Their work remains relevant today. The first serious attempt to look at the social importance of age groups was made by the German sociologist Karl Mannheim in an essay titled "The Problem of Generations," which was first published in 1927 (see Mannheim, 1952b). Mannheim defined **generation** as a category of people born within a specific historical era or time period. For Mannheim, a generation was also characterized by a common worldview that distinguished it from other generations. Mannheim was keenly aware that accident of birth timing did not automatically create these common understandings and worldviews; he observed that social and psychological processes led some members of a generation to develop an identity and consciousness with peers of the same age. Mannheim suggested that generational consciousness arose not from merely being born at the same time but from being exposed to the same kinds of experiences and historical events in a common social and political environment. According to Mannheim then, belonging to a generation is a combination of a *state of mind* and an age grouping.

Each generation reacts to their social and historical time, and sharing these experiences gives each generation a unique *character*. In today's workplace, it is not unusual to have three or four generations working side by side. There is a growing industry of books, organizations, and consultants who help businesses understand the differences in motivations, behaviors, and attitudes across the generations in their workplace. The idea that each generation has its own identity is intuitively appealing, but it is easy (and dangerous) to overgeneralize. Today's young adults are categorized as technologically savvy, cynical about the materialistic values of preceding

There is often a very special, loving bond between grandparents and their grandchildren that immensely enriches both generations. (Credit: E. J. Hanna)

generations, and jaded by growing up in a world of violence; but there are certainly different subgroups within this generation. Mannheim suggested that each generation may comprise a number of specific units, each with a unique consciousness.

The Aging Population as a Social Force

Warren Thompson and P. K. Whelpton (1933), like Mannheim, drew attention to issues related to aging in the late 1920s and early 1930s. However, Thompson and Whelpton used a demographic perspective to ponder the effects of population aging on society. As a student, Thompson became interested in the interplay between population and social structure. In 1930, the President's Research Committee on Social Trends gave Thompson and Whelpton the assignment of projecting the population of the United States from 1930 to 1980 and identifying significant population trends that should be taken into account in national planning.

The rapid growth of the older population and societal aging (discussed further in Chapter 3) were identified by Thompson and Whelpton (1933) as perhaps the most fundamental expected change in the population of the United States. Exhibit 1.2 shows how dramatically Thompson and Whelpton expected the population age structure to change in what, for a large population, was a very short period of time. Even though Thompson and Whelpton had no way to anticipate the post–World War II baby boom, their projections concerning growth in the proportion of the older population were very much on target. The actual proportion of people age 65 and over in the United States in 1980 was 11.9% compared to their projection of 12.1%.

Thompson and Whelpton assumed that retirement would continue to occur at age 65 and speculated that funding retirement pensions would be a major social challenge for the future. "The problem of old-age pensions is one thing in 1930 with 5.4 percent of the population over 65 years of age but will be a different thing in 1980 when the proportion over 65 years of age will probably be more than twice this large (over 12 percent)" (Thompson & Whelpton, 1933, p. 165). Writing before Social Security was enacted, they were understandably concerned about the

EXHIBIT **1.2**

Distribution of the Population by 5-Year Age Periods: 1880–1930 and 1930–1980

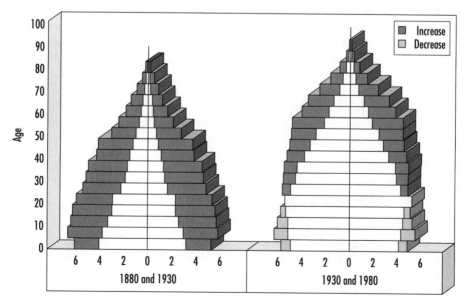

Source: Thompson & Whelpton, 1933.

potential social disruption that might come when a large proportion of the population would be retired but with no broad-based programs in place to provide continued retirement income. They were also concerned that poverty at older ages could be even greater than they anticipated "if, as is quite commonly believed, industry and commerce are scrapping men at earlier ages than formerly and if they hire older men only at very low wages" (p. 170). (The use of "men" in this quote reflects a very different era. In the 1930s, the vast majority of middle-class workers were, indeed, men.)

Making an assumption that elders are more politically and socially conservative than the average American, Thompson and Whelpton (1933) suggested that an increase in the proportion of older adults in the population might lead to stronger defense of the status quo in politics and less innovation and risk taking in business. Older people would, they argued, be less ready to abandon outdated social policies and business practices. To their credit, however, Thompson and Whelpton pointed out that social innovation could still be fostered through intentional planned effort by middle-aged and older members of society to search for creative and more efficient business methods.

In their discussions of employment and income problems for an aging population, Thompson and Whelpton (1933) tended to portray the growing population of older Americans as an imminent social problem. However, social problems refer to difficulties that categories of people encounter not because of their own qualities but because of the way they fare in the operation of the social system. C. Wright Mills (1959) spoke of the distinction between *private troubles* that arise from accidents of personal history and *social problems* that arise from inequities built into the concepts, laws, rules, and procedures we live by. Thompson and Whelpton were writing specifically about the social problem of poverty arising from the practice at that time of compulsory retirement at age 65 in the absence of retirement pensions. In an entirely different vein, however, they noted that the processes of adult development could have a beneficial influence on social cultural trends:

> Youth is more concerned with doing things, forging ahead, and making a place in the world. Age is apt to be more reflective, perhaps because the spur of poverty is less sharp, the inner drive is weaker, or time and thought have brought about a change of ideas as to the goal of life. The mere shift in age distribution, therefore, may lead to more interest in cultural activities and increased support for the arts. Such developments in turn will influence the outlook and taste of the whole population. (Thomas & Whelpton, 1933, p. 168)

Here they acknowledged that elders were not simply a social problem or a category toward which policy might be directed, but also people who were continuously evolving and could become social resources and agents for change. This potential role for the older population sounds very similar to an idea that is currently receiving a great deal of attention. **Civic engagement** refers to the involvement by people of all ages in actions and efforts designed to make a difference in our communities; it is both an activity and a value. As a social value, civic engagement implies a commitment to solving problems and making a difference (Ehrlich, 2000). Recognizing and encouraging the many ways that older people can contribute skills, knowledge, and energy to the common good is a growing topic of research, advocacy, and public policy in gerontology. Thompson and Whelpton foreshadowed this new movement with their observation that aging populations might benefit from the unique contributions that older people can make to civic life.

The Life Course and Old Age

A further key step in the development of old age as a social category came through the comparative, cross-cultural work of anthropologist Ralph Linton (1942). *Social anthropology* is concerned with identifying cultural universals, patterns that appear in all human cultures, as well as links between culture and personality. Linton advanced the thesis that all known societies have been stratified by at least two human characteristics: age and sex. The definitions of age and age categories, the number of age categories, and the rules governing transitions from one age to another have varied considerably across societies, but in all societies old men and old women have been differentiated from one another and from adult men, adult women, boys, girls, and infants. Linton's very simple and basic statement of fact still appears to be true more than 60 years later.

Another important concept that permeated Linton's (1942) work is the idea of a **life course**, formed by a succession of age–sex categories. In all societies, males who survive infancy go on to experience boyhood, ascend to adult manhood, and then are either elevated to or relegated to the position of old man, depending on whether the society was accepting or rejecting in its treatment of old men. A parallel sequence exists for females.

Linton (1942) believed that these life course age–sex categories are arranged in a hierarchy of social influence. In most societies, the adult males have been the most influential, although occasionally Linton discovered cases where elder men have had the most influence. He found another kind of variability: in many cases, elder women experienced increased freedom and status when they went through the transition from adult to older woman. "Even in societies which are strongly patriarchal in theory it will be found that a surprisingly large number of families are ruled by strong willed mothers and grandmothers . . . [Among the Comanche] old women . . . could acquire and use 'power' on exactly the same terms as men and were treated as equals by male 'power' holders" (Linton, p. 594).

In addition to looking at life stages and age–sex categories, Linton (1942) discussed transitions from one age–sex category to the next. He was impressed with the capacity of humans to make sometimes quite abrupt and substantial changes without showing signs of mental distress. Linton suggested that the transition from adulthood to old age was a particularly difficult one because the loss of power is not satisfactorily offset by a decline in obligations and because formal values about respect and authority granted to older people may not be carried out in actual practice.

Linton's work has been an extremely important resource for the social perspective on aging. He drew attention to the process that connects age to social position and influence and used the sociological concepts of status and role to explicate a complex social structure made up of interconnected role obligations and opportunities. Linton's work presented the life course as a progression of age grades, thus linking the issue of aging with life stages. The life course perspective is, in fact, one of the most important frameworks in social gerontology today. Finally, Linton drew our attention to the importance of life course transitions and hinted at a human adaptive capacity to deal with life changes.

Social Perspectives on Aging

The work of the social scientists described in this chapter provides excellent illustrations of understanding age as a social category. Throughout our discussion of old age and aging, we have referred to the way society creates and perpetuates our ideas about who is old, how they should act, and how we treat them. We will continually return to the ideas of social construction as we discuss the many aspects of aging. While many fields of study discuss society, social changes, and people's lives, two perspectives in particular are helpful frameworks from which to understand the social context of aging: social gerontology and the sociology of aging.

Social Gerontology

Many social gerontology courses are taught in departments of sociology by sociologists, and much of the material included in social gerontology courses consists of research on aging by sociologists. However, social gerontology has a broader range of interests than the sociology of aging. **Social gerontology** is a multidisciplinary field that includes research, policy, and practice information from all of the social sciences and the humanities (see Exhibit 1.3). A specific example helps us describe its scope.

EXHIBIT 1.3

In Social Gerontology, the Sociology of Aging Is But One of Many Disciplines

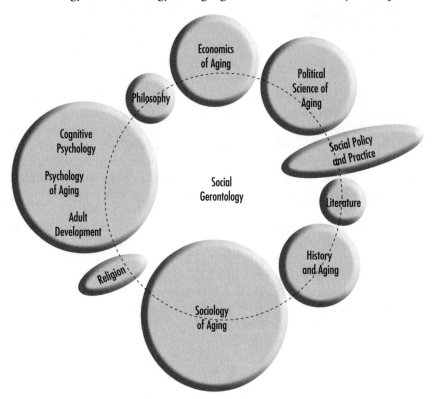

More and more families are facing the challenge of deciding about long-term care arrangements for relatives or friends who need increasing amounts of help throughout each day. Decision making about long-term care has implications for individuals, families, health care systems, and public policy. How, when, by whom, and with what outcome are some of the different issues related to the long-term care decision. Each of these topics can be approached from many different angles, with many different disciplinary perspectives. Psychologists might be interested in the communication and cognitive processes that are involved in negotiations and decisions of this type. Sociologists might consider the hierarchy or differences in power that come into play as family members, the older person, and professionals negotiate the decision. Professionals from the world of long-term care practice might be interested in ways to more effectively describe options to families; they might also be concerned about making sure that the older person whose life is being discussed has a say in the planning and decisions. Researchers interested in public policy might focus on how the timing of long-term care decisions might be affected by the service options available and have an effect on costs to themselves or the long-term care system. Social gerontologists draw on all of these perspectives to fully understand the processes and outcomes of decisions about long-term care.

Both social gerontology and the sociology of aging share an interest in sociological work applied to aging. The **sociology of aging** is concerned with understanding aging from sociological perspectives and applying that understanding to sociology in general. Social gerontology is concerned with understanding aging from a variety of perspectives and integrating information from various social science and humanities disciplines to achieve an understanding of aging, in general, and to apply that understanding to resolving problems and creating policy. Increasingly, social gerontologists are seeking to more fully benefit from the multiple disciplinary perspectives that can be brought to bear on any topic related to age, aging, and the life course by moving to an **interdisciplinary** approach. While social gerontology is, by definition, multidisciplinary (drawing on multiple perspectives), interdisciplinary research would involve more than working together with respect for, and being somewhat conversant in, each others' disciplines. Interdisciplinary research would mean active collaboration and new ways of formulating the questions we are asking, and new methods for exploring those questions. The study of the genetic, behavioral, social, and cultural factors that contribute to longevity could be an example of interdisciplinary research. Does this mean that every member of the research team must be trained in all of these specialties, or does it mean that the team works together with new methods and techniques? This question does not have a clear answer yet. In the meantime, social gerontology is continuing to develop as a truly productive, multidisciplinary field.

Although the sociology of aging and other disciplinary perspectives, such as biology of aging, can be differentiated from social gerontology, in the actual study of aging the boundaries among disciplines are often blurry. Often studies focus on a topic that falls both within the domain of social gerontology and within the traditional domain of sociology and economics or psychology. However, as a field, sociology has not been particularly interested in the sociology of aging. Until recently, aging has generally been seen as a fringe topic rather than a serious area of scholarship dealing with one of the most important social trends societies will confront throughout the next 50 years. By contrast, the field of aging (gerontology) has been very interested in the sociology of aging. Some of the unique contributions of sociology are presented in the chapters here.

The Sociological Imagination

The promise of the sociological perspective has been powerfully and eloquently expressed in C. Wright Mills's (1959) classic presentation of the **sociological imagination.** He suggests that the promise and the responsibility of sociology lies in giving individuals the tools to make the distinction between, and see the connections between, concerns we face in our own lives and problems that are rooted in society. Mills advises, "Know that many personal troubles cannot be solved merely as troubles, but must be understood in terms of public issues—and in terms of the problems of history. Know that the human meaning of public issues must be revealed by relating them to personal troubles—and to the problems of the individual" (p. 226). We can make this distinction if we have a social context and a sense of history from which to understand their personal experiences. The ability to shift perspectives, to analyze an experience or an issue from many levels of analysis (e.g., personal, family, community, societal), and to see the intersection of these many levels of mutual influence is the fruit of the sociological imagination. If you develop a new understanding of your own attitudes about older people because of what you learn about how societies construct meanings of age, you will have experienced the sociological imagination. If you understand how an older individual's situation of economic disadvantage is a product of social forces rather than simply personal choice or chance, you are applying the sociological imagination.

"No social study that does not come back to the problems of biography, of history, and of their intersections within a society has completed its intellectual journey" (Mills, 1959, p. 5). Mills suggests that there are three basic questions we must continually ask in exercising our sociological imagination. First, what is the structure of this particular society as a whole? How does it differ from other varieties of social order? Second, where does this society stand in human history? What are the essential features of this period? Third, what varieties of people prevail in this society and in this period? How are these types "selected and formed, liberated and repressed, made sensitive and blunted" (p. 7)?

Note, particularly, Mills's third question, which suggests that social order and historical period actually select in favor of certain kinds of people. This is a profoundly different view of human nature than those most familiar to us. Yet, armed with this understanding, we can go on to understand how, "by the fact of our living, we contribute, however minutely, to the shaping of our society and to the course of its history, even as we are made by society and its historical push" (Mills, 1959, p. 4). Also, defining an issue as *public* creates new ways to seek answers, beyond adopting an "every person for him/herself" approach. Age-based policies initially developed as a consequence of seeing aging as a public rather than simply a personal issue. Social Security developed as a consequence of the Great Depression, when poverty became viewed as a public matter, not an individual problem.

Micro and Macro Perspectives

Mills's discussion of history, society, and biography draws our attention to the intersection of individual life experience and broad social forces, including social changes around us, and in doing so points to the micro-to-macro range of perspectives on any topic. A **micro** perspective focuses on the individual level, while a **macro** perspective focuses more broadly on society. Likely, most of us agree that our behaviors, attitudes, and even our feelings are shaped partly by our personalities and partly by the social situation in which we live. There is an interplay between individual responses to social influences (*micro* concerns) and the social structures—organizations and institutions—that create the conditions requiring a response from individuals (*macro* concerns). The camera lens is in many ways an apt metaphor. A standard lens depicts a modest visual field and a modest amount of close detail. The wide-angle lens captures a much wider visual field, but the images of specific objects within the field usually show less visible detail compared to images produced by the standard lens. The telephoto lens allows the camera to focus on distant objects in greater detail, but the width of the visual field is very narrow. If we look at three photographs of the same general visual field taken with different lenses, we can see that none of the photographs captures everything that the human eye is capable of seeing. Which photograph is the most useful depends on the purpose to which the photograph is to be put. Similarly, different questions about the social context, meanings, and experiences of aging require different perspectives along the micro–macro continuum.

Several major streams of research are concerned with understanding micro-level issues, such as the adaptation of individuals to the changes that accompany aging. This work considers the individual's adjustment to changes in his or her social situation, such as retirement. A more macro perspective seeks to understand, explain, and predict the social construction of those conditions to which the individual must respond: What is the status attached to being retired? What provisions does society make to support economic and other needs of retirees? What are corporate rules regarding eligibility to retire? Other questions look at the larger scale (macro level) questions without considering the individual (micro level). How does retirement affect companies? How is retirement related to overall societal patterns of employment and unemployment? How does retirement reflect and affect the overall productivity of a society?

This micro–macro distinction is one of the energizing tensions in the study of aging; each perspective enriches the other and can push the other to greater clarity and applicability. There are many ways of classifying and organizing our experiences of the social world. The micro–macro distinction is one important way of categorizing ideas and information, directing us to different, but equally important, questions about aging in the social world.

Patterning of Experience: Diversity and Heterogeneity

Looking more deeply and critically at the ways in which society influences the meanings and experiences of aging, some sociologists have focused on how, why, and to what extent the experiences of aging are different for different groups of people—looking for a **patterning of experience.** For example, poverty is substantially more prevalent among older Black women who live alone than among any other group of older people. Why does this pattern exist? What social forces have produced this structured disadvantage for older Black women?

Many scholars have warned against using averages to describe the older population because there is often more variation among older people than among younger people on some variables. This heterogeneity is very often acknowledged but not thoroughly examined. Arguing for the need to really analyze patterns of difference, Dannefer (1988) suggests that research should begin to look for the extent, nature, and patterns of heterogeneity on a wide range of variables. Is the older population as heterogeneous on life satisfaction as they are on income? Are the political attitudes of older people as varied as their health status in later life? Does the amount of heterogeneity on health status change as people grow older? What is the pattern of that change? Does heterogeneity increase, decrease, or fluctuate over time? Finding out more about how much heterogeneity exists among the older population, on which variables, and in what pattern are important first steps in understanding the different experiences people have as they age.

However, we need to go even further than that to really understand the many different realities of aging. Dannefer (1988) suggests that the next step is to analyze the sources of heterogeneity. How is heterogeneity produced, and what should be done about it? Calasanti (1996b) further refines this position by distinguishing between heterogeneity as variation among individuals and diversity. *Heterogeneity,* the extent to which older individuals are different from each other, is what we have discussed in the preceding paragraph and might also be called individuality. **Diversity** refers to patterns of difference across *groups of people* in different social locations. The most common indicators of these social locations are gender, race, ethnicity, and social class. Contemporary scholarship on diversity searches for the nature, extent, and causes of differences among groups of older people. In doing so, we acknowledge that the realities of aging are not the same across all groups. Throughout this text we present information and ideas about the diverse experiences of aging, focusing on race, ethnicity, gender, and social class. Race and ethnicity are extremely complex and personal identities. In the most recent U.S. Census (2010), respondents could choose one race or more than one race; six separate race categories were listed and people could check more than one. In addition, there were questions about Latino or Hispanic identity. Hispanic/Latino respondents can be of any race, so many combinations of race and ethnicity are possible. The complexities and implications of race and ethnicity are far-reaching. For the purposes of this book, we focused on two major categories of race and Hispanic or Latino for ethnicity. You will see that we use "Black" and "White" for much of the race data and Hispanic/non-Hispanic in the discussion of ethnicity. Studying diversity can take one of two directions. We can compare groups to try to understand their different experiences of aging. There is a fair amount of research that takes this approach, and some of it will be referred to in later chapters. This is a useful but limited approach. The disadvantage of the *comparison* model for studying diversity is that there is always a reference group to whom everyone else is compared. For example, we can say that women have higher rates of diabetes than men, or that older Black women have the highest rates of poverty among adults. While this information is instructive, the implicit use of a dominant group as a point of comparison reinforces the reference group's experience as normal and minimizes the different social reality inhabited by the "other" groups (Calasanti, 1996b). Most typically the comparison group has been White males, even though women outnumber men at later ages because of the differential in life expectancy by sex.

The limits of the comparison approach are well-illustrated by the fact that such analyses often categorize people as White/non-White, or male/not-male. This approach assumes that the complexities of life in a particular social category (Black, female, working class) are somehow captured by not being a member of the reference group. But it is very clear that being female is not the same as not being male (Kunkel & Atchley, 1996).

By focusing on groups of people in particular social locations we can better understand the different worlds of aging. We would ask different questions that delve more deeply into the lives of the members of the group in which we are interested. Instead of comparing men's and women's rates of diabetes, we might ask how the rates of diabetes vary among women, by social class and race; or we might attempt to specify exactly how social forces affect the lives of members of a particular group. Listening to the voices of those groups better illuminates their situation than focusing on how they are different from the dominant group. The questions we ask, the concerns we attend to, and even the items we include on a survey will be more insightful if we begin with a conviction that reality itself is different for groups in different social positions. For example, Gibson (1996) introduced the idea of "unretired-retired" status to describe individuals who are 55 or older and not working but who do not consider themselves retired. This status is most common among poor Blacks. They do not meet traditional criteria for retirement and, therefore, are never included in studies of retirement. This example clearly illustrates how using the experiences and meanings that are relevant for one dominant group completely undermines our ability to understand the experiences of other groups. Some of the new work on successful aging, mentioned earlier in this chapter, is raising questions about the definitions and meanings of success for different groups of older people.

As social research on diversity in aging matures, there is more attention given to diversity as an approach to reality rather than a kind of comparative perspective on various topics of interest; that is, diversity in the aging experience should be understood more deeply and holistically than a simple comparison of one group to another. Calasanti (1996b) argues for an acknowledgment of the constructed and contextual nature of social reality in all theorizing and research: "Being inclusive requires acknowledging the unique configuration of a group within the matrix of power relations, being sensitive to the importance of these cross-cutting relations, and not making undue generalizations" (p. 15).

Summary

Aging is a broad and diverse field of study. In recent decades, as the population has aged, the topic of aging has become part of the agenda for many different disciplines and perspectives. It is a very exciting time to be using sociology and social gerontology to study age, aging, and the life course. Enormous social changes are underway, changes that both affect older people and are affected by the aging of our society. Public policy, families, health care, education, and the economy are all changing as our society ages.

The very large baby boom is joining the ranks of the older population; the oldest baby boomers began turning 65 in January 2011. The sheer size of this group, and its unique generational experience, will doubtless change the meanings and experiences of aging for those to follow. Two publications suggest the transformations that are underway: *Reinventing Aging* (Center for Health Communication, Harvard School of Public Health, 2004) describes the opportunities for, and promise of, the baby boom generation to continue to be involved in society well into old age. The second report, *Reimagining America* (AARP, 2005), summarizes the challenges that our nation faces as baby boomers enter old age and offers suggestions for innovative solutions to those challenges.

Our goal in this book is to illustrate the kinds of work leading to a new understanding of the social context and social constructions of aging. How social theorists and researchers think about, analyze, critique, and investigate questions related to aging is our major focus. In the process, we note areas that have not received adequate attention and offer some suggestions about why some questions and issues have remained unasked and unexamined. This latter course requires some speculation on our part, but we decided it would be challenging and interesting and might inspire some of you to fill in the gaps in our understanding of aging.

In the chapters that follow, we delve much more deeply into the social aspects of aging at both the micro and macro levels, focusing on the changing face of later life within the dynamic context of the social world. Because aging is reshaping the future for us all, we expect you will find compelling issues for yourself, your family, and for the larger society.

Web Wise

At the end of each chapter we present a number of Web sites that may be relevant to further investigation of select topics presented in that chapter. Some are oriented toward research, while others focus on policy or practice. For each site we provide the address (current as of the time of publication) and a brief description of what is included or tips on links you may wish to pursue. To get you started, we have included here a few "how to" Web sites, describing how to access, use, and cite information from the Web. Another included site encompasses a directory to many other Web sites that you may find useful if you are interested in a topic for which we did not list a particular site.

AARP Research Center   http://www.aarp.org/research/
This page provides links to a large array of sites related to specific topics and original sources for data and research. Topics range from individual health, mobility, and housing to public policy and law. The page includes links to the AARP Public Policy Institute, Surveys and Statistics, and external links to worldwide data on older adults, and a directory of more than 1,000 sites for and about older adults.

ChangingAging.org   http://changingaging.org/
This Web site compiles current information from various news and media sources and provides video clips and links to those sources and a blog for people to react to the stories. Dr. Bill Thomas, a well-known geriatrician and gerontologist, gives his insights about the attitudes and stereotypes that underlie some of these stories. The purpose of the organization is to provide "a platform to attach conventional attitudes towards aging and to provide positive, growth-oriented alternatives for a life worth living." Blogs are posted very frequently; content is updated every month.

OWL Purdue Online Writing Lab   http://owl.english.purdue.edu/owl/resource/560/10/
This site provides guidelines and specific examples for all kinds of online references, including electronic journals, newspaper articles, sections of web documents, and online encyclopedias. Other pages on the main site include guidelines for in-text citations, footnotes and endnotes, and links to additional style guides.

Key Terms

ageism	life course	social gerontology
civic engagement	life stages	societal aging
cohorts	macro	sociological imagination
diversity	micro	sociology of aging
generation	patterning of experience	
interdisciplinary	social aging	

Questions for Thought and Discussion

1. Browse through a birthday card selection, taking note of cards that are designed for different ages. What is your reaction? How are the messages of the cards different based on the age group for whom they are intended? What makes a birthday card funny?

2. Senator and former astronaut John Glenn completed a much-publicized return to space in 1998. His age (he was 77) was a major topic of conversation. Why is the American public so amazed by, and possibly wary of, a 77-year-old astronaut?

3. Respond to the statement "You are only as old as you feel." Do you agree or disagree? What are some of the things that influence how old we "feel"?

4. What are some of the causes, consequences, and solutions to ageism? Do you speak up if you hear ageist remarks? Why or why not?

Studying Aging

2

[N]ever begin a sentence with "The elderly are . . ." or "The elderly do. . . ." No matter what you are discussing, some are, and some are not; some do, and some do not. The most important characteristic of the aged is their diversity. The average can be very deceptive, because it ignores the tremendous dispersion around it. Beware of the mean.

(Quinn, 1987, p. 64)

Despite the perennial desire to understand how and why people age in a physical sense, the study of the social aspects of aging is a relatively recent phenomenon; the vast bulk of research has been done in the past 50 years. The research techniques that were initially applied to the study of the social and life course aspects of aging were borrowed from the research traditions of sociology, economics, history, psychology, and other fields and applied to the study of processes and products of aging, primarily focusing on individual outcomes. The traditions and assumptions of these transplanted analytical approaches both shaped the types of questions that were asked and the manner in which we have sought answers to them. More recently, however, the study of aging has matured and developed its own, unique approaches to answering the key questions. These new approaches, based in the life course perspective and the bio/psycho/social approach to aging, were necessary because of the growing complexity of questions that research on aging seeks to answer and because of the interdisciplinary nature of the field. The innovations in research approaches and the unique questions and challenges of social gerontology research are the subject of this chapter.

Mainstream social science research has dealt with *age* for years as a secondary variable in research, often grouped together with other *status* variables, such as race, ethnicity, socioeconomic status (social class), and gender. The study of aging, however, redirects our attention to age as one of the central variables of interest, with the correlates and consequences of aging the focus of attention. The earliest research on social aspects of aging focused on the aged as a group, considering their circumstances (such as poverty or ill health) as social problems and examining ways to intervene on both the individual and the societal level. More recently, however, the focus has shifted from studying "the aged" as a population category to studying *aging* as a social process (Campbell & O'Rand, 1985). This shift has prompted a move away from research methods that focused on analysis of a static group (e.g., everyone over age 65) to studies of dynamic processes in society or within individual people as they move through the life course's various stages to reach later life. In short, the recent shift was from a focus on *the aged* to focusing on the process of aging. This shift, closely aligned with emergence of the life course perspective (discussed in greater detail in Chapter 4), has raised a whole range of new questions and prompted the development of new research techniques to answer them.

Why Do We Conduct Research?

There are a number of important reasons to conduct research on our social world. The most central motive is a deep curiosity about how our social world works. Social research helps us to understand how the various facets of our social world interact to shape the lives of individuals, groups, and major social institutions such as the economy, contributing to the stream of social change that we all encounter as we move through our lives (Schutt, 2004). Thus, the first impulse of researchers is to generate accurate knowledge about the social world in which we live.

The interest in research goes deeper than a simple curiosity or desire for knowledge of facts. Social scientists, like all scientists, are committed to a fuller understanding of how and why things work the way they do; in our case, this interest is aging people and the larger social world. This understanding requires us to build theories that both explain and predict social behavior on the micro level of the individual, on the macro level of the social institution or society, or on any level between these two extremes (Hendricks, Applebaum, & Kunkel, 2010). The second major purpose of doing research, then, is to generate, test, and refine theories. Ironically, the purpose of any specific piece of research is not to validate a theory but to refute it. Because most theories are created and promoted because they seem logical and plausible, it is often easy for us to accept their propositions as sensible and appealing. But sometimes common sense is wrong. As with other fields, the study of aging has had theories that seemed intuitively appealing but were subsequently proved to be inadequate or false. Some examples of both successful and unsuccessful theories are described in subsequent chapters. Scientific method requires that we do as much as we can to test a theory by trying to prove it to be wrong, thereby invalidating it and prompting us to move on to develop stronger, alternative theories to better explain what we see. In this way, progress is made toward understanding many social phenomena, including aging.

A third and increasingly compelling reason for conducting research on aging is to provide input for public policy and intervention. This *applied* research or *evaluation* research uses scientific methods to identify ways to intervene in problems of policy and practice (Hendricks et al., 2010; McAuley, 1987). For example, researchers could evaluate a particular service-delivery program for family caregivers of older adults to see if it improved their care, reduced their stress, or brought about other desired outcomes. Some applied research looks at the effects of programs, services, and policies or tries to identify causes for problems, such as later-life poverty, to reduce its frequency or severity (Rossi, Lipsey, & Freeman, 2004). In these areas of policy and practice, the demonstrated effectiveness of an intervention (such as a special program for educationally at-risk students or a falls-prevention program for older adults) helps to decide whether it should be refined, funded, and continued (or not). Applied and evaluation research has always been a focus for researchers interested in aging, given the field's early focus on social problems. More emphasis has been placed recently on translating research findings to make them more quickly useful to practitioners, policy makers, aging individuals, and their families (National Institutes of Health, 2006).

In an aging society and an aging world, the conditions affecting individuals and groups as they grow older become inextricably linked to the well-being of the overall society. For example, older women are much more likely to be poor in later life, with many of them relying on modest Social Security survivor benefits as their sole source of income (Beedon & Wu, 2005). As society changes and more women are employed throughout adulthood, however, the plight of this group may improve as more aging women have their own private pensions, savings, and Social Security benefits (Morgan, 1991). Making plans and policies based on conditions we see among older adults today, without including research insights on elders of the future, might lead to serious mistakes. More and more aging research is applied in the sense that its findings are directly translatable to strategies for intervention in the lives of older persons or policy recommendations on the local, state, or federal level.

Each of these goals—generating knowledge, refining and testing theory, and shaping policy—requires research that is systematic and rigorous. Social research represents a significant improvement over everyday observations that can be affected by errors such as selective perception (only seeing part of the picture), or overgeneralization (assuming that what we are observing is true for all people or in all similar situations) (Schutt, 2004). Research that is carefully designed and rigorously executed will give us knowledge that is more valid and an understanding that is richer and more trustworthy than the casual observation each of us does in daily life.

The design of social science research involves many detailed decisions that are beyond the scope of this chapter. Designing good research about aging involves some unique challenges that we explore in this chapter. As a starting point, let us consider the link between theory and research. This link is important for all types of research.

The Role of Theory

Theories are often described as the driving force behind research, dictating both the specific questions that need to be asked and the most appropriate analytical techniques to use in answering them. For example, during the 1960s and 1970s, the theoretical contention between disengagement and activity theories (discussed in Chapter 6) led to considerable research on the concept of life satisfaction among the elderly. Today, while these theories are discussed infrequently, contemporary research gives continued attention to subjective well-being, a concept closely related to life satisfaction, in contemporary research (George, 2010).

Research methods in social gerontology are sometimes viewed simply as tools to enable the testing of theoretical propositions, allowing them to be supported or refuted. But, the relationship between theory and methods is more complex than that. Both theory and methods are shaped by dominant ideas about what kinds of questions are interesting and appropriate and what scientific tools are appropriate to answer them. This argument is compellingly presented by Thomas Kuhn (1996), who describes the ways in which our views of the world are necessarily limited. We cannot consider, see, or explore every possible aspect of reality, and what we do see is shaped by our experiences in the social world. The work of other researchers and scholars provides a map toward our destination and possible paths to get there; that is, a model of the questions we are trying to answer and the methods we use to explore them. Kuhn called these maps paradigms. *Paradigms* are conceptual frameworks or models in existence during the training of a new scientist that influence what she or he defines as important research questions and what are considered as the best approaches to solve those research questions. "In learning a paradigm, the scientist acquires theory . . . and methods together, usually in an inextricable mixture" (Kuhn, 1996, p. 109). To illustrate, we can return to the tension between disengagement and activities theories mentioned earlier. These theories propose opposing explanations for adaptation of individuals who are aging. Disengagement theory suggests that aging individuals and society mutually withdraw, while activity theory proposes that maintaining activity levels and involvement in social roles results in high life satisfaction in later years. Even though these theories propose different solutions to the so-called problem of aging, they both focus on how individuals should and do adapt with time/age. The methods we used to examine these competing theories involve the measurement of individual circumstances, attitudes, and adaptation. A different paradigm might shift our focus to very different questions: Why does aging require adaptation? What are the sources of the challenges that people adapt to as they age? This paradigm would lead us to theories and methods that consider the ways in which societies and social institutions contribute to the problems of aging individuals, rather than focusing just on the ways in which individuals might cope on their own.

Given their common roots in paradigms, the relationship between theory and methods is very dynamic (Campbell & O'Rand, 1985). By constraining what the researcher is able to do, the methods available often stimulate the development of theory in certain areas while blocking it in others. A theory that cannot be tested through research, although it may be intriguing, is not scientifically viable (Achenbaum & Bengtson, 1994). Again, a good example is disengagement theory (discussed in detail in Chapter 6). The theory was compelling when first presented, but it was untestable and therefore not useful to research. For this and other reasons, interest in the theory soon waned, and researchers looked to other theories that provided more productive avenues for advancing knowledge (Achenbaum & Bengtson, 1994). Although theory shapes methodology, the relationship is actually a reciprocal one, with feedback from methodology to further theory development, as shown in Exhibit 2.1. Theory can be "research-driven"

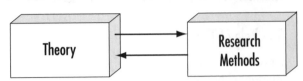

Synergy Between Theory and Research Methods

(Campbell & O'Rand, 1985), just as research is often "theory-driven." Theory can arise from research, as in the case of grounded theory (Glaser & Strauss, 1967). The link between research and theory is further discussed later in this chapter when we present qualitative and quantitative approaches to understanding our social world.

How Do We Conduct Research on Aging?

Research on aging can be driven by theories, curiosity about the world around us, or questions left unanswered by other research. One of the interesting features in aging research is that it seeks to answer a dazzling array of questions, covering topics related to the aging of cells to the variations in the aging of the world's populations. What is it like to be old? What does aging *do* to us physically, emotionally, or socially? How do different cultures or societies treat people differently on the basis of their age? How, why, and in what ways does age make a difference in our lives? What are the costs and impacts of programs and policies serving older people? How do families adjust to the changes throughout the life course, including the onset of disability and need for help from older family members? Each of these broad areas of curiosity could lead to a seemingly endless list of possible research questions.

The range of research questions we might explore in aging relates to the micro/macro continuum discussed in Chapter 1. To some extent, the kind of question a researcher chooses to investigate is influenced by her or his academic background and life experiences. For example, biologists may examine aging in units as small as chemical compounds and components of the cell, whereas the macro level for a biologist may include entire complex organisms, such as mice or human beings. Within the social sciences the continuum also differs by discipline. Psychologists move from within-individual phenomena, such as changes in cognitive or sensory functioning (micro), to the complex behavior of the person in social interaction (macro); sociologists take the *individual* as the micro end of their disciplinary continuum and *entire societies* as the macro end.

Often the same topic can be addressed using many different levels of analysis to examine different aspects. For example, the social dimensions of retirement can be examined with the individual as the unit of analysis (addressing questions such as the effects of retirement on economic well-being, friendship patterns, or marital satisfaction), on the company level (How does retirement affect the quality of the company's labor force?), or on the societal level (How do the economies of Western societies fare when there is large-scale retirement or large numbers of retirees?).

The first step in any research process is to think through exactly what we want to explore. Before researchers can work through the details of how to design and conduct a study, they must be very clear about the scope, level, and unit of analysis implied in their question. One of the unique challenges in aging research is specifying exactly why and how we are including age in our study.

Age as a Variable

As was discussed in Chapter 1, age can have many different meanings. Similarly, when we say that we want to study aging, we can be referring to very different kinds of questions related to the aged, aging, or the life course. Consider these three related examples: (1) a study of the impact of aging on physical health, (2) a study of effectiveness of training older people through a structured exercise program, and (3) a study asking whether an exercise program has the same effects for older people as for younger people. While all of these topics are similar, the role that age would play in the research would be very different. In the first study, where we want to know about the ways in which age affects health, we are treating age as an independent variable. An **independent variable** is assumed to cause, or have an impact on, another variable (the **dependent variable**). In the second study, we want to see if participating in an exercise program has a positive effect on the health of older people. In this case, age is simply a selection variable—we are choosing to study older adults, in particular. The independent variable in this second study is not age; it is participation in the exercise program, and the dependent variable is health. In the third study, we are again treating the exercise program as the independent variable, looking for the impact it has on physical health. However, in this research, we want to see if the effects of the exercise program are the same for people of all ages. In this case, we are treating age as a **control variable,** a variable that might influence the findings of our study; for example, the exercise program might work better for older rather than younger participants in improving fitness.

The role that age will play in our study—as an independent variable, a control variable, or a selection variable (among others)—is an important conceptual decision that has implications for the way we will measure age in our research. This might seem like quite a simple matter; we can just ask people how old they are, or when they were born. In fact, much research on aging does just that. However, it is important to consider whether we want to know about the impact of every single year of age, or whether the age group of the person is most important (e.g., old vs. not old; middle age vs. old age; member of the baby boom generation or another identifiable age group).

It is essential to go through the formal process of conceptualization in our research on aging. **Conceptualization** refers to the process of generalizing or grouping ideas into a category. In research, this term refers to specifying exactly what we mean by an abstract concept, such as age. The conceptualization of age directs us back to the issue of why we think age matters for the topic we want to study. Depending on the particular research question, age may be referring to the passage of time, as in the case of our first study discussed previously, which focused on the impact of aging on health. In this situation, we might indeed want to track changes by single years of age. Age may also be used to define membership in a group—a generation such as the baby boom, or a target population for a service or program such as Medicare—or to mark the boundaries of a life stage, such as retirement. In these cases, a person's exact age does not matter, and our research will not be focusing on the impact of every passing year. Conceptualization thus has implications for how we should measure age in our research.

Although age is often a significant factor in social research, many older persons soar above and beyond stereotypes based on their years. (Credit: E. J. Hanna)

Sorting Out Age, Period, and Cohort Effects

Thinking through what we mean by *age* as a variable in our research is the first very important step in designing a study. Once we have achieved some clarity about why and how we think age matters in our research, it is necessary to pay attention to one of the most challenging issues in research on aging—the age-period-cohort problem. When a researcher studying political participation, such as voting behavior, finds that the percentage of the population that votes is higher in upper age groups (see Binstock, 2009), what exactly does that tell us? (See Exhibit 2.2.) Does it mean that advancing years or changes resulting from aging make us more politically active or involved? Not necessarily. There are, in fact, three related influences that shape changes across age groups and over time: aging, period, and cohort effects. Understanding these three forces is central to understanding the complexity of aging in a social context.

Many researchers are interested in learning about the **aging effects**—that is, the changes that occur as individuals accumulate years and move through the life course. When most people think of the effects of aging, they think first of the physical effects, such as wrinkling of skin or graying of hair. Yet, there is clearly a social side to aging as well. As we discussed earlier, chronological age can be a proxy for life stages and can also be an indicator of social and psychological maturation. Therefore, we may have questions about the effects of aging on our social as well as physical lives. For example, we may want to know whether and how aging influences individuals' productivity at work, happiness in marriage, choices in saving or spending money, or religious participation. But answering these questions is not as simple as it first appears. Our initial inclination would be to observe, for example, workers of various ages to learn how productive they are at a specific task and then draw comparisons by age. But would any differences that appear from this observation be *only* the result of aging?

It is very difficult to isolate the effects of aging in research because human aging or maturation does not occur in a vacuum. Instead, the process of aging is surrounded by social, economic, and historical events that influence the lives of individuals and groups differently as they age. Beyond aging, a second force that is sometimes responsible for differences between age groups derives from historical events and trends. **Period effects** emerge from the major events or trends that occur in the social world while we are studying aging. For example, if we surveyed a sample of adults 35 years ago and repeated the survey today and found that the same people knew much more about AIDS now than they did before, should we conclude that their increased knowledge is a result of aging? Of course not. The period effect of growing public awareness of AIDS has

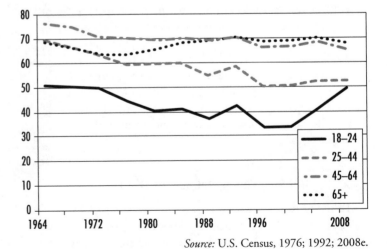

EXHIBIT **2.2**

Percentage Voting in Presidential Elections, 1964–2008

Source: U.S. Census, 1976; 1992; 2008e.

influenced individuals of all ages over that time period (a period effect)—at the same time that the adults were aging 35 years. Because individual aging and period effects are tied together by time, it is important to attempt to separate period effects from those of aging. The time at which we measure knowledge of AIDS, not the fact that the respondents are older, is the real issue with period effects. Often we think of major wars, economic booms or busts, and dramatic modifications in the social norms of society as shaping people's experiences as they age (Schuman & Scott, 1989). It is important to recognize, however, that more "everyday" period effects—for example, the introduction of new technologies such as personal computers and social networking—can also have profound period effects.

Third, birth cohorts—groups of individuals born at approximately the same time and sharing historical life experiences (period effects)—often differ from each other in important ways. These **cohort effects**—differences between groups sharing major life events (such as birth, marriage, college entry) at different points in historical time—are the third piece of this puzzle. For example, if a research study found that appreciation of the music of the Rolling Stones was higher among some birth cohorts than others, would it mean that you would come to like that particular music when you reach the same age? Again, this difference is not an aging effect. Instead, the baby boomers, some of whom came of age during the heyday of the Rolling Stones, have continued to like that music as they have aged. Their preference is a cohort effect: the preference was not "caused" by aging, it has moved with them as they aged.

Norman Ryder (1965) identified the critical nature of the cohort in understanding aging in society. Paralleling some of Mannheim's (1952a, 1952b) ideas about *generation* discussed in Chapter 1, Ryder identified the flow of birth cohorts through society as both creating and institutionalizing change in society over time. "Each cohort has a distinctive composition and character reflecting the circumstances of its unique origination and history" (p. 845). Members of a cohort share a slice of history and the social and cultural influences of their time, differentiating them from cohorts who preceded them or those that follow. Thus, each cohort has a lifetime of its own. Cohort traits, such as its size or its ethnic or gender composition, influence outcomes for the larger society and shape the life chances of individuals within the cohort (Easterlin, 1987).

The diagram in Exhibit 2.3 is a graphic representation by Riley (1987, 1994) of the triple forces of aging, period, and cohort. In this diagram, time is represented by the movement from left to right on the horizontal axis, and age is represented on the vertical axis. The diagram shows three birth cohorts (A, B, and C), each born at a different point in history. For each cohort, we can move from the year of birth on the horizontal axis diagonally upward as two things happen simultaneously: time/history passes and each group ages. Thus, the diagonal black bars represent the aging component. The white vertical bars represent period effects, the first being World War II, the second perhaps the Vietnam War, and the third could be the widespread integration of personal computers into daily life. The fourth could represent the economic downturn that started in 2008, although this graphic predates that particular event.

You can see that most of the cohorts intersect several of these period events, but they do so at different ages and stages of their lives. For members of the oldest cohort, World War II occurred when they were in their 50s, the age to be parents of soldiers. Members of the next cohort, born in 1920, were young adults, likely to be heavily involved in actual fighting or war work on the home front. The 1950 cohort did not experience that war directly but was undoubtedly influenced by its aftermath. For them the second event, the Vietnam War, fell at about the same time in their life spans (their early 20s), as World War II did for the 1920 cohort. In contrast, the Vietnam War was too late to have much effect on the surviving members of the cohort born in 1890, who were by then about 80. Thus, different cohorts encounter these same historical events (period effects) at different stages of the life course and, therefore, relate to them differently. Such period effects may influence these cohorts as a collectivity in ways that may persist throughout their lifetimes (Elder, 1974; Riley, 1987).

Any large-scale event, such as a lengthy war or a significant economic downturn, is likely to have an impact on everyone in the society, but the effects are differential based on membership

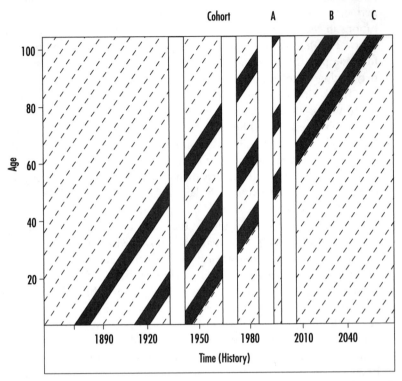

EXHIBIT 2.3

Changing Lives and Sociocultural Change

Source: Riley, 1994.

in different cohorts. Young adult cohorts, those most likely to be called upon to fight in the event of war or most negatively impacted when jobs are scarce, are more likely to experience a life-changing effect from the period effect. At the same time, older cohorts, while doubtless affected by these events, are less likely to feel the same magnitude of effect on their lives (Pavalko & Elder, 1990). More mundane examples also apply. Certainly being a teenager in the 2010s is different from having been one in the 1940s, even though many of the issues of aging/maturation faced by teenagers remain the same. These sorts of accumulated differences throughout life may make the two cohorts very different when they reach their third or eighth decade of life.

Because they are so closely interrelated, these three factors (aging, period, and cohort) are extremely difficult to disentangle in research (Firebaugh & Chen, 1995). In fact, age, period, and cohort are "exact linear functions of each other because Age = Period – Cohort" (Winship & Harding, 2004, p. 3). In other words, an individual's age can be known by subtracting their year of birth (cohort) from the year of the study (period). Because it is so important to sort out the empirical and conceptual distinctions among these three factors, scholars continue to develop research designs and statistical models to untangle their influences. More complicated research designs, such as some described later in this chapter, can often assist in separating one type of effect (for example, a cohort effect) from the other two, but currently available statistical techniques are only starting to enable us to distinguish the relative inputs from each of these three factors (Schaie & Hertzog, 1982; Winship & Harding, 2008). We still have a great deal of progress to make in systematically addressing this vexing puzzle (George, 1995).

To return to our initial example in Exhibit 2.2, when we see variations by age in voting behavior, it is not apparent from a comparison across age group whether aging, period, or cohort effects, or some combination of them, is at work. If we make the assumption that it is all from aging, we commit what is called a **life course fallacy**—interpreting age differences in data collected at one time as if the differences were *caused by* the process of aging, without ruling out other possibilities, such as cohort differences (Riley, 1987). Although it may be the case that adults do become more politically aware with the accumulation of experience (aging), and therefore act upon that awareness in the voting booth, this interpretation is not the only possibility. A second explanation for differences by age may relate to cohorts and their experience. Older cohorts today, raised at a time when patriotism was more emphasized and having experienced World War II, may feel a greater duty to vote and may have voted at higher rates all of their lives when compared with later cohorts of baby boomers. The age difference in voting, therefore, could also be a cohort effect. A third possibility is a period effect, where a political event, issue or candidate could increase or decrease the voter turnout or voter registration rates (Firebaugh & Chen, 1995). Some contend that the increased voting rate among young adults in 2008 represented a specific, positive reaction to the Obama campaign. Finally, it is quite possible that the pattern of voting behavior is a result of some combination of aging, cohort, and period effects. Despite the research difficulties in disentangling these three forces in the complexities of social life, some research has succeeded in doing so. By way of illustration, we will describe three research examples in which one of the three factors was successfully distinguished from the other two.

Aging Effects: Criminal Behavior by Age

Research has clearly established that not all citizens are equally likely to commit crimes. As Exhibit 2.4 shows, many of the crimes of concern to society are committed by adolescents and young adults. Further, peak ages for commission of these crimes have remained consistent or declined since the 1940s (Steffensmeier, Allan, Harer, & Streifel, 1989; U.S. Department of Justice, 2007). Teenagers and young adults commit (and are arrested for) substantially more crimes than children or more mature adults. Why do we think this is an aging effect? In large measure the answer rests on the fact that similar age-related patterns of criminal behavior have been reported in many different societies and in different historical periods, diminishing the potency of explanations based on period or cohort effects. Although the amount of age difference in criminal behavior and the size of the decline with advancing age vary, many crimes show similar patterns of variation by age (Steffensmeier et al., 1989). When a pattern as apparently consistent as this appears, then we cautiously conclude that there is an aging effect on both committing crime and being arrested.

EXHIBIT 2.4

Peak Ages for Arrests for Various Crimes

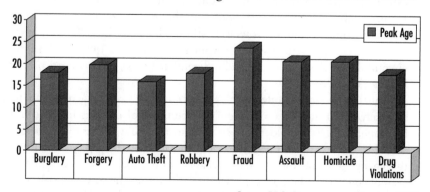

Source: U.S. Department of Justice, 2007.

But how is aging implicated in crime? Certainly criminal activity may be somewhat related to physical aging, in that some crimes require strength, speed, or agility. More plausible, however, are the social explanations for crime: "Society at large is faced perennially with an invasion of barbarians . . . [and] every adult generation is faced with the task of civilizing those barbarians" (Ryder, 1965, p. 845). The barbarians to whom Ryder refers are, of course, the youthful cohorts being socialized into the ways of society and their roles as responsible adults. With limited integration into the social world (few links or responsibilities toward work or family) and with incomplete socialization and maturation, teenagers and young adults face fewer constraints against committing crimes than do their older counterparts. This explanation suggests that as people mature and gain more responsibilities and linkages to the social order (that is, increase their **social integration**), the personal costs of committing a crime rapidly grow to outweigh the benefits, discouraging participation (Laub, Nagin, & Sampson, 1998; Steffensmeier et al., 1989).

Cohort Effects: The Case of Voting Among Women After the Nineteenth Amendment

Although it is typically very difficult to sort out age, period, and cohort effects, sometimes social life provides a "natural experiment" enabling researchers to clearly identify the consequences of cohort membership. In one such study, Firebaugh and Chen (1995) examined the changes in voting behavior of women in conjunction with passage of the 19th Amendment to the Constitution, giving women the right to vote. The researchers noted that the voting rates of women just after passage of the amendment were much lower than those for men but that this gap gradually narrowed over the years and then disappeared. Why didn't women immediately vote at the same rate as men?

To examine the issue, the researchers compared the voting behavior of three 10-year birth cohorts of White women: those born before 1896, who were still denied the right to vote in young adulthood; those born between 1896 and 1905, who spent their childhoods before women could vote, but could vote by the time they came of age; and those born between 1906 and 1915, who became aware of politics after the enactment of the 19th amendment. Firebaugh and Chen (1995) hypothesized that the experience of lacking the franchise (the right to vote) would have a lasting cohort effect on the first group, and that each of the later two cohorts would be more likely to vote than the first cohort, because this oldest group had been socialized to think that women should not vote and had themselves been prohibited from voting in their youth.

To make the test even more stringent, the voting behavior the researchers examined was from much later: national elections between 1952 and 1988. The analysis revealed a true and enduring cohort effect from the passage of the 19th Amendment. Women from the earliest cohort, who had been kept from voting as young women, were less likely than either of the subsequent two cohorts to vote throughout their lives. Even though they did get to vote as soon as they reached adulthood, the women in the second cohort, who were socialized during the era when women could not vote, were still less likely to do so 30 years later than their younger counterparts, who were raised after women had the right to vote. Thus, the critical experience of youth lasted throughout life and differentiated these three cohorts of women in their voting behavior even decades later.

Finally, the authors offered an explanation as to why the gender gap in voting rates shrank gradually over time. This reduction was the result of changes in the composition of the voting population. As the older cohorts of women, who were less likely to vote, died and were replaced by women of later cohorts more likely to vote, the gap systematically diminished. Thus, this change probably did not reflect changes in the voting behavior of particular individuals or even of cohorts. Rather, the explanation derives from the so-called **cohort composition effect**. As cohorts age and their members die, they are replaced in the population (here, the voting-age population) by younger cohorts whose behaviors and attitudes may differ. This gradual shift in the composition of the voting population, then, accounts for the disappearance of the voting gap between women and men.

Period Effects: A Hypothetical Example of Consumer Spending Over the Life Course

As businesses anticipate the needs and desires of aging baby boomers, they might want to track consumer expenditures, looking for changes in the way people spend their money as they age. Imagine that hypothetical Company T (a travel and resort company) conducts some research on this topic, wanting to know how these patterns might change with age. Remember, age effects are not just physical; we can be interested in physical, psychological, or social maturation. Company T assumes that consumer expenditures may change because of life stage, hypothesizing that middle and later life will be marked by greater availability of discretionary income and leisure time. To test this question of change with age, they conduct a longitudinal study, tracking the same people over time as they age. Exhibit 2.5 shows the hypothetical data resulting from this study.

As anticipated, the participants were gradually increasing the amount of money they were spending on travel as they moved into and through middle age. The increase continued until a precipitous drop in 2001. There was a subsequent modest growth in spending, but not a rapid return to earlier spending patterns. Was this an aging effect? Did these study participants suddenly reduce the money they spent on travel when they retired or began receiving Social Security? Was there some other age-based event resulting in change? Unlikely! Two major period effects occurred during the time of this study—the 2001 attacks on the World Trade Center and the Pentagon, and the major economic downturn starting in 2008. It is much more likely that the pattern of rapid drop in consumer spending on travel was due to this period effect, not the effects of aging or life stage of participants in the study. It is widely known that the travel industry suffered tremendous losses following the 9/11 attacks and again during the recession. These examples of period effects illustrate how a significant historical event or social change can

EXHIBIT **2.5**

Hypothetical Traveling Spending

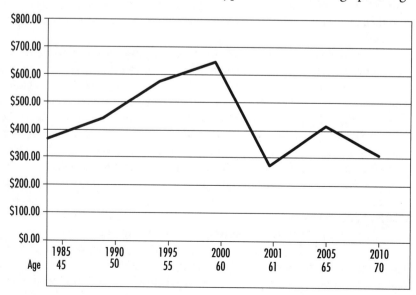

influence the results of a study that might be designed to help us understand aging. Without doubt, studies of all types of consumers, not just aging baby boomers, would also show this period effect of a drop in travel spending. In this case, period effects made it especially difficult for Company T to project behaviors of baby boomers, whose behaviors were being reshaped as they aged through period effects.

Designs and Methods Targeted to Research on Aging

As you can see, research on aging includes many unique challenges, including the conceptualization and measurement of age/aging, and sorting out age, period, and cohort effects. There are some research designs that are especially suited to these special concerns. These designs focus on who is studied, how data are collected, and how the influences of age, period, and cohort can be distinguished.

Longitudinal/Panel Studies

Longitudinal studies, also called panel studies, attempt to isolate aging from cohort or period effects by following a sample of units of analysis (cells, individuals, states, corporations, or societies) over time to observe how they remain stable or change. The most often used type of longitudinal study is one in which individuals in a sample are repeatedly surveyed about their lives over a period of years or even decades. Longitudinal designs are contrasted with **cross-sectional studies**, in which data are collected at one point in time, generating a snapshot of differences between cohorts/age groups. Cross-sectional studies can tell us how age groups may differ from each other, but they cannot tell us the extent to which those differences are due to the effects of aging. Cross-sectional studies often entangle aging effects with cohort or period effects. To illustrate, consider a question about whether people become more religious as they grow older. A cross-sectional study would allow us to compare the religiosity of today's 80-year-olds with today's 60-, 40-, and 20-year olds. If we see that the older groups are more religious (e.g., attend church or pray more often), we cannot be sure how much of that difference is due to aging processes and how much might be due to the fact that different cohorts grew up in eras with different emphasis on elements of religiosity, such as church attendance. Longitudinal designs, following people over time, help us to sort out aging effects from cohort effects; because we follow a sample over time, as they age, we are comparing individuals' religiosity at later ages to their own earlier behavior, allowing us to avoid confusing aging effects with cohort differences or period effects.

Although it is not a panacea for all of the analytical problems we have been discussing (Campbell, 1988), the use of longitudinal data drawn from the study of a sample over time is generally touted as a necessity in the study of social processes of aging. However, the design has drawbacks. Because the commitment in time, financial resources, and effort involved in collecting significant longitudinal data can be staggering, the benefits sometimes are not seen for years (Campbell & O'Rand, 1985). In addition, researchers face challenges in conducting longitudinal studies that are not characteristic of cross-sectional work. It is difficult to keep participants involved in a study that spans years or decades; researchers may find that some of the questions do not work very well and be tempted to change them; and new ideas critical to the topic being studied may emerge while the research is in progress, leaving researchers frustrated about their lack of information in earlier years' surveys (Lawton & Herzog, 1989).

Yet, longitudinal data are critical to disentangling the effects of age, cohort, and period on processes of individual aging and social change over time. In recent years, researchers have begun to make more active use of long-span panel data, finding effects of early life influences on specific outcomes in later life. For example, Hatch, Feinstein, Link, Wadsworth, and Richards (2007), studying a sample from the 1946 birth cohort in England, found that adult education was associated with cognitive ability years later, with benefits that extend to several health-related areas. Spanning an even longer time period, Zhang, Gu, and Hayward (2008) reported that childhood circumstances of Chinese elders aged 80 or older were connected to their cognitive performance. Older Chinese who lived in urban areas and had more education (indicative of higher socioeconomic status) as children performed better than their less advantaged peers. Kasper and her collaborators (2008) found that long-term stress and poverty over several decades was associated with poorer functional health among older Black women. Bernburg (2003) found that arrest as a teenager results in lower educational attainment and job stability and higher odds of subsequent criminal behavior—outcomes connected with higher risks of lifetime disadvantage. Such results encourage us to take a very long view of what may influence outcomes in later life (Settersten, 1999).

Longitudinal studies that follow more than one cohort as they age—a **cohort sequential design**—are especially useful. Exhibit 2.6 shows a hypothetical sequential design, following three cohorts over four time periods. Each group is reinterviewed at 5-year intervals. This design makes it possible to compare cohorts as they age. For example, we can compare the age changes that cohort 1 and cohort 2 go through as they move from ages 40 to 50; even though they will go through these ages at slightly different historical times, knowing whether an age change observed for one cohort holds true for another gives us greater confidence in our conclusions about the effect of aging. Following more than one cohort longitudinally enables some separation of the effects of aging, period, and cohort. One study, for example, included 15 birth cohorts (every 3 years between 1916 and 1958) and collected data annually for 11 years, providing a substantial amount of information to sort out age and cohort effects for disease and disability (Reynolds, Crimmins, & Saito, 1998). In the earlier example of women's voting patterns following ratification of the 19th Amendment, by focusing on a span of behavior (voting patterns from 1952 to 1988) with three distinct cohorts, the researchers used a cohort-sequential design to clearly isolate cohort effects.

Secondary Analysis

One way around the time constraints and costs for research in aging is to use existing data. **Secondary analysis** "refers to the study of existing data initially collected for another purpose" (Liang & Lawrence, 1989, p. 31). Although secondary analyses need not use longitudinal data or even survey data (for example, secondary analysis of medical records) (Palmore, 1989), many of the most valuable contributions to our knowledge of aging have involved secondary analysis of longitudinal surveys.

EXHIBIT *2.6*

Cohort Sequential Design

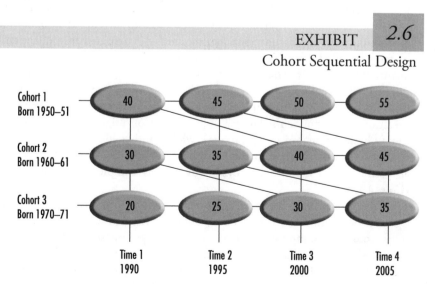

| Cohort 1 Born 1950–51 | 40 | 45 | 50 | 55 |

| Cohort 2 Born 1960–61 | 30 | 35 | 40 | 45 |

| Cohort 3 Born 1970–71 | 20 | 25 | 30 | 35 |

| | Time 1 1990 | Time 2 1995 | Time 3 2000 | Time 4 2005 |

A growing number of large, national longitudinal analyses of datasets originally designed to examine specific issues (such as economic status, employment, utilization of health services, and family relationships) have been employed by aging researchers in secondary analyses to answer questions beyond those envisioned by their original designers. Many such data sets are available from computerized archives, making them readily accessible to researchers for secondary analyses (Liang & Lawrence, 1989; National Archive of Computerized Data on Aging, 2010). You can locate examples of such datasets through Web sites listed at the end of this chapter. These studies have been used to dramatically expand knowledge in a number of areas about aging, despite having been designed with other goals in mind. One long-standing study is the Panel Study of Income Dynamics (PSID, 2009), which sampled a set of nationally representative families in 1968 and has followed them (and new households established by their children) throughout 40 or more years, providing key data on employment, health, housing, family, and other topics of interest to aging researchers. Newer longitudinal studies, including the Health and Retirement Survey initiated in 1992 with large samples of women and men, will update and expand upon the knowledge provided by panels initiated in the 1960s and 1970s (Juster & Suzman, 1995). Without a doubt, these longitudinal studies used for secondary analysis have added considerably to our store of knowledge about aging.

The growth in these large, national data sources available to researchers for secondary analysis is a mixed blessing. As Kasl (1995) points out, although these studies provide both a longitudinal design and a large, national sample, which would probably otherwise be unavailable to most researchers on aging, they offer information on a limited number of variables. Researchers may not be able to measure concepts of interest (such as health status, family cohesiveness, or political involvement) in ways that are ideal; essentially they must work within constraints of what the original study provided. If a key measurement is missing, then the researcher must choose between not using the data at all and attempting to work around this limitation.

Qualitative, Quantitative, or Combined Methods

Most of the techniques drawn from other social science traditions that have been applied to the study of aging are **quantitative approaches**. These approaches include experiments, surveys, and much of the applied and evaluation research that we discussed earlier in this chapter. Even though these specific designs are different from each other, they share one central feature: they examine numerical data using statistical techniques. The numerical data may be derived from medical records, the census, an experiment, or from a survey of individuals, states, or companies. The data are then analyzed with the presumption that numbers are meaningful reflections of reality. For example, a person reporting limitations in five activities of daily living (ADLs)— a common measure of functional health status—is assumed in a quantitative approach to be more disabled than a person reporting only two such limitations. Although widely used, quantitative approaches have limitations. Because of the focus on numerically valid data that can be used to make general statements about the larger population, or about the causal connections between variables of interest, quantitative research attends less to subjective interpretations by respondents. For example, one person might identify themselves "limited" in some physical function (e.g., walking), while another individual, whose health is the same based on a medical exam, might not report themselves as limited. Quantitative research is also criticized for inhibiting theorizing by turning complex social life into a set of numbers (Cole, 1995).

Complementing quantitative approaches are numerous **qualitative analysis** techniques designed to deal with the very issues that quantitative research cannot address. "Qualitative research starts from the assumption that one can obtain a profound understanding about persons and their worlds from ordinary conversations and observations" (Sankar & Gubrium, 1994, p. vii). Qualitative research is thus based not on numbers but on words, meanings, and symbols. Key to the qualitative approach are the acknowledgment of (1) people's inherent ability to know and communicate things about their own lives and their respective worlds, (2) the researcher's role in obtaining the facts of experience, and (3) the importance of seeking to understand the multi-faceted and complex nature of human experience from the perspective of subjects (Sankar & Gubrium, 1994). Thus, instead of using questions with multiple-choice answers, which construct the meaning of the social situation for the respondent in advance (e.g., your health is either excellent, good, fair, or poor), qualitative researchers tend to focus their research efforts on in-depth interviewing, life-history collection, and observation, sometimes as a participant in a social setting. The goal is to represent the participant's reality as faithfully as possible from his or her point of view (e.g., my overall health is good, except for severe arthritis) (Sankar & Gubrium, 1994). The researcher, rather than being only minimally present for the administration of a questionnaire asking yes/no questions or for numerical ratings of the subject's health, is an active participant in eliciting meanings from the informants, whose reality is often recorded on audio or videotape for later analysis.

For example, Gay Becker (1993) analyzed the aftermath of stroke in a sample of 100 victims. Her analysis was based on repeated interviews with the sample, participant observation in a stroke rehabilitation ward of a hospital, and observation of patient–practitioner interactions over a 5-year period. The interviews, once transcribed, were used to identify central themes that appeared throughout the data. Those themes became the basis of theoretical explanations and hypotheses for further consideration. Among her key conclusions was that victims viewed stroke as a major life-course disruption, requiring victims to reconstruct their lives with new expectations and patterns of behavior. In this case, Becker examined the event (stroke) from the perspective of those going through it to learn how they, not physicians or researchers, socially constructed the major issues. As an observant outsider, the qualitative researcher may see aspects of the situation that are missed or taken for granted by those in the situation. The hallmark of qualitative research is looking at the meanings central to social actors, not those that may be imposed by the perspective and goals of the researcher.

When we are exploring topics about which we have very little information, qualitative research is often the most appropriate design. It is important to point out that these two approaches—qualitative and quantitative—represent two different, not necessarily opposing, frames of reference for examining the social world and are sometimes combined in research studies to enhance results. For example, if we want to develop a new measure that will eventually be used in a large-scale survey, it would be wise to begin with a qualitative phase. In this phase, we can ask people to tell us in-depth about their experiences of participating at a senior center, becoming a grandparent, or relocating to assisted living so that the measure we develop will capture what is meaningful to those we will survey.

At the beginning of any research project, we should consider whether qualitative, quantitative, or a combined approach will be best suited for what we want to understand. This research decision is part of some of the challenging but essential work that must take place before we begin to collect or analyze data. Some of those all-important initial decisions are summarized in Exhibit 2.7.

Event History Analysis

One of the specialized tools in the study of aging is called event history analysis. In aging research we are often interested in when a particular life event happens or in the social forces that trigger its occurrence. Event history analysis attempts to address these issues. This frame of reference draws our attention to a particular event of interest, such as retirement, enactment of a new social policy, entry into a nursing home, or divorce.

As its name suggests, **event history analysis** focuses on when and how particular events happen to the persons or group of interest. Based in longitudinal data, this technique explores

EXHIBIT 2.7

Designing a Study: Critical Questions

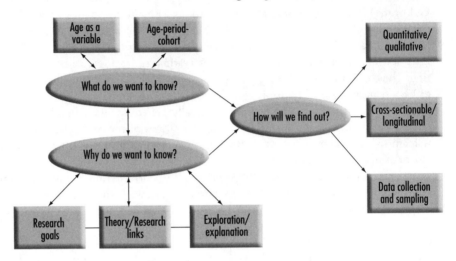

how much time passes before the event of interest occurs, the rates of occurrence of particular events (e.g., widowhood within a population), and how these rates change with the passage of time (Does the rate of widowhood increase as women age?) (Campbell & O'Rand, 1985). This type of analysis allows us to answer questions related not only to when something occurs, but also to the relationships, if any, between events—for example, marriage and childbirth, or passage of a new retirement policy and changes in the behavior of persons or groups affected by it.

Although event history analysis is most frequently used on the individual level, examining the impact of specific life events, it can also be applied to large-scale (macro) events. For example, it would be equally valid to look cross-nationally at how changes in eligibility age for retirement influence when workers retire in various countries, using the country as the unit of analysis. Regardless of the unit of analysis, it is essential that the unit under study have the potential to undergo a particular change that may have identifiable consequences of interest.

One key to event history analyses is being able to pinpoint the timing of the event of interest (Campbell & O'Rand, 1985). Current longitudinal studies often enable us to know only that the event took place between the third and fourth round of interviews, but not the specific date of the event in question. A second complication in this type of analysis is known as censoring. If we are following a large sample to examine the timing and rate of a particular event—say the onset of dementia for those age 70 or older, which occurs at widely different ages—this event would already have occurred for some people, not yet occurred for others, and will never occur for some others. In the cases where the event doesn't occur or the study ends before we know its timing, the event is considered *censored,* not available for analysis. Therefore, unless we can wait 40 years to ensure that everyone in the sample has either shown signs of dementia or died without doing so, event history analyses are always dealing with censoring. Censoring simply means that we lack knowledge of when those remaining people will experience the event of interest, if ever. Fortunately, statistical techniques are available to assist in dealing with the problems of censoring.

As a specific example of event history analysis, Moen, Dempster-McClain, and Williams (1989) conducted a study of women's mid-life role involvement and longevity. They used a sample of married mothers (originally ages 25–50 in 1956) who were reinterviewed in 1986, at ages 55–80. The event of interest was mortality. Most women in the sample (76%) had survived and were therefore censored as to the timing of their eventual deaths. Another 5% could not be located and were also considered censored as to time of mortality; 19% of the sample had died during the 30 years between interviews. Knowing the dates of death for the women who died, however, enabled the researchers to utilize complex statistical techniques to evaluate the relationship between longevity and the number of social roles that women in the sample had held earlier in life.

The researchers were interested in whether the number of social roles (aside from being a wife and mother) in 1956 was related to longevity. They found that, after controlling for social class and age, social roles did help to predict longevity. Women who were more involved earlier in their lives, especially those who belonged to clubs or organizations, had greater longevity than those who did not. The authors concluded that social integration of midlife women has beneficial effects that translate into greater life expectancy. The event history approach enables researchers to examine a variety of life course events that are of considerable interest.

Life History and Reminiscence

Some researchers choose to address questions of time, aging, and social change at a more individual level, asking older persons to look back over their lives, emphasizing the transitions and events that served as turning points. This **life history** or reminiscence approach is used not only for research purposes but is also considered by many to be therapeutic for older persons themselves (Parker, 1995). Review of past life events may occur spontaneously by an older person alone or in conversation, through a structured interview process or in a group workshop. It is these latter two settings that have been involved in research and therapeutic activities. As a research tool, life history interviewing is somewhat controversial. Many methodologists argue that retrospection (looking back) involves a mental reconstruction of the past that is subject to bias (Hagburg, 1995). You might not accurately remember the order of events or how you reacted to them, for example. This very act of reconstruction, however, may be what is of interest, rather than an accurate recounting of the events precisely as they happened. For example, what is of interest to a researcher today may not be the exact realities of the Great Depression of the 1930s or World War II but how those events and times are recalled over the course of many years, and how they influence those who experienced them today.

Bo Hagburg (1995), in a life history study focusing on close personal relationships throughout the life cycle, examined satisfaction with the events surrounding retirement. Hagburg found that positive recollections of relationships in childhood and adolescence were associated with a positive reaction to the experience of retirement. Retirees remembering earlier life stages and the significant people in them most positively were most likely also to be satisfied in retirement. Neither the current mental status nor the cognitive ability of the retiree explained this relationship. Instead, satisfaction with retirement was linked to a positive report of relationships to significant others during childhood and adolescence. Was this positive tie to significant others the way these relationships were viewed at the time (i.e., during childhood and teen years)? It is hard to say, but Hagburg's findings suggest that how they are recalled now remains influential.

Other Special Issues in Studying Aging

Separating Normal From Pathological Aging

In Chapter 1 we mentioned the difficulty in separating out the *normal* aging of the body from diseases that are age-related but not caused by age. Similar problems arise in studying the social phenomena associated with aging. If people typically experience a decline in response time at the wheel of a car or in purchasing power in the marketplace as they age, can we say that these factors are part of the normal process of aging? Often we cannot. Although some social phenomena are clearly age-related (e.g., the probability of widowhood for women is clearly related to the ages of their husbands), many times the chain of causation is indirect at best. The decline in response time may result from illness, rather than age. A decline in income at higher ages, though common, is a consequence of the manner in which society constructs the systems for income-maintenance for older people who have retired and the fact that women, with fewer economic resources in current older cohorts, outlive men. Because we have institutionalized retirement and developed income-replacement strategies that do not always keep up with inflation, many people see their purchasing power erode. A majority of these survivors are older women. Therefore, just as physical pathology is hard to separate from the biological components of aging, social effects are intertwined with individual processes of growing older.

There is nothing natural or inevitable about providing retirement income this way—age systems are socially constructed in societies. In agricultural economies, where the ownership of land often remains in the hands of the oldest generation, their power and economic security may endure until death. We must remain vigilant to avoid assumptions that because something is common or typical it is somehow *normal.* This critical eye enables us to identify and address, through policies and programs, problems of older persons that are not inevitable parts of the aging process but that could in some instances be thought of as social pathologies in need of treatment through policy intervention.

The late Mel Harder, a former All-Star pitcher with the Cleveland Indians, knew a thing or two about life's curveballs and longevity on and off the mound, living to the age of 93. He pitched in the major leagues for 19 years and stayed in the game for 21 more seasons as a coach with the Indians and other major league teams. (Credit: Mike Payne, courtesy of the Ohio Department of Aging)

Increasing Variability With Age

Dale Dannefer (1988) points out another difficulty related to the study of aging. He argues that there is now an ample body of both psychological and sociological research demonstrating that individuals in a cohort become more differentiated (or, in sociological terms, **heterogeneous**) as age increases. "Older people have been thought to be more dissimilar from one another than are younger people in terms of physical health status, intellectual capacity, and psychological functioning, material resource availability and life-style. Although such comparisons are often used to contrast different age groups or strata at one point in time, they also implicitly connote a life-course pattern toward greater heterogeneity among age peers" (p. 360).

The processes involved in creating this increased variability are complex, and the growing differentiation with advancing age creates challenges for research. Dannefer (1988) argues that neither our theories nor our research methods are well equipped to deal with this pattern. Adequate study of variability with aging would require both very large samples and longitudinal data (collected on the same individuals over long periods of time), studies that are costly in terms of both time and money.

Many of our current approaches to describing age-related changes focus on **measures of central tendency,** such as averages (means or medians) that define how a *typical* older person is doing. We then compare these averages across age groups to find differences associated with age. Measures of central tendency ignore the variability within each cohort, making such measures less adequate to describe older groups than younger groups. It is this average or *mean* that Quinn (1987) warns us about in the quote that begins this chapter. Alternative measures are available, and Dannefer (1988) urges their use in the study of aging populations.

Sampling Adequately

In most research, we cannot study every person who is a member of the population of interest. So, we use *samples.* As Nesselroade (1988) so simply put it, "A sample is a small part of anything (or a few of a larger number of somethings) that is (are) used to show the nature of the whole"

(p. 13). In most social science research, a **sample** is a few units of analysis (people, families, businesses, city governments, states, or countries) out of all of the possible pertinent units of analysis (the population) that you wish to study. The units in the sample reflect the location along the macro/micro continuum that has been selected as appropriate for the question at hand, with the number of units in any given sample being highly variable (depending on the study) and the number of samples potentially to be drawn from any large population infinite. The goal is to have a sample that represents the entire population, because it is too costly in time and money to reach every member of that population, and good estimates of results for the total population can be developed from a good quality sample. The sampling process is especially challenging given the diversity among older adults, discussed previously.

A study of the entire population of the United States is conducted every decade when a census is taken. The U.S. Census, by not using a sample, is more the exception than the rule, by including the full population in its data collection. Because it is impossible to interview every person for most studies, researchers select a sample believed to represent in most critical ways the larger population from which it was selected (e.g., all new recipients of Medicare benefits).

A wide variety of sampling techniques can be applied to various types of quantitative and qualitative research (McAuley, 1987). Many of these techniques are directly applicable to studies of aging, where attention is often focused on constructing samples based on age (e.g., a survey studying how attitudes toward Social Security vary by age). Sampling is often a difficult task because there is no simple way to identify or reach large and representative groups of people of interest for your particular study. For example, there is no full roster of retirees or persons over age 65 from which we can easily draw samples (McAuley, 1987). Although the Social Security system has information about most older adults, their information is confidential and not typically available to researchers to use in developing research samples.

The study of aging encompasses more than just age in selecting participants for research. Sometimes researchers are interested in locating individuals from more specific groups or *rare populations:* daughters providing at-home care for a frail parent, older adults who have maintained high levels of creative productivity in the arts, or African American business owners anticipating retirement in the next few years. Efforts to examine specific groups require additional attention to sampling and sometimes the use of special sampling techniques (Kalton & Anderson, 1989). Not only may these groups be statistically rare, but they may also be hesitant to participate in research for a variety of reasons (McAuley, 1987). To develop a high-quality sample in these cases requires considerable resourcefulness.

Studies that focus attention on the oldest individuals in society, who are often frail or cognitively impaired, raise additional concerns. Researchers are ethically bound to use extreme caution in conducting interviews or observations with such samples, given the relatively higher risks of stress, fatigue, and health impacts from upsetting a normal routine. Gatekeepers, such as relatives or health care providers, are often reluctant to give permission for frail persons in their care to participate in research studies. Special protections, including detailed reviews of research methods for risk factors when older subjects are involved, work to minimize problems for such vulnerable samples. In addition, the more advanced the age of the sample, the more selective it is due to mortality. If one is sampling centenarians, for example, they are an elite group of survivors who doubtless differ in important ways from those who did not survive to age 100.

Early research on aging was plagued by samples that were small, local, and unrepresentative of the larger population (Cutler, 1995). Researchers could draw limited conclusions only because there was no certainty that their results pertained to the population beyond the city or state where they did the study. Until fairly recently, most studies underrepresented certain groups, such as minority populations (LaViest, 1995; Markides, Liang, & Jackson, 1990) and women. In fact, many studies were conducted using convenience samples that tended to overrepresent White, middle-class individuals. The development in large, nationally representative samples that enable researchers to examine many issues of concern in aging has marked a major advancement in the field (Cutler, 1995; Kasl, 1995).

Ethical Issues in Research on Aging

All researchers have an obligation to avoid harm to anyone who participates in their studies. All universities and governments, and most agencies or organizations that serve the public, have mechanisms to protect research participants. In many organizations, the group charged with this oversight is called an Institutional Review Board (IRB). This group reviews research before it even begins to make sure that any proposed study will not cause undue distress and that people do not feel that they are coerced into participating. The protection of human subjects is of concern to everyone involved in research. There are special concerns that arise when we wish to study the older population. In particular, older people who are living in nursing homes or receiving home-care services need to be assured that their participation is voluntary and that they can be honest in their answers. You can imagine that individuals in these situations might worry that they will disappoint the researcher or the agency if they choose not to participate; in addition, they might be concerned about giving any negative feedback, fearing possible repercussions. For example, a home care recipient might not be willing to say that her worker shows up late sometimes because of worry that the worker might lose her job and not show up at all. Addressing such concerns are all part of ensuring that human subjects are protected. The integrity of both the researcher and the research process are equally essential to the ethical conduct of research.

Cohort-Centrism, Dynamism, and Limits of Current Knowledge

As we have already noted, the scientific study of aging is a relatively recent development. For example, early research on topics like later-life families and retirement began in the 1950s and grew dramatically in the decades that followed. Most of what we know about how retirement affects individuals, families, the labor market, and the overall economy is drawn on research from the 1970s through today. The same could be said about a wide range of other topics associated with aging. As a result, our knowledge of these topics is limited to cohorts experiencing them during these particular historic periods, with all of their related cohort-based traits and experiences. They represent a truly narrow slice of history upon which to build a knowledge base. Riley (1987) warns against the **fallacy of cohort-centrism,** whereby an erroneous assumption is made that future (or past) cohorts will age (have aged) in the same fashion as current cohorts under study. We should expect research findings to change as new cohorts, with vastly different experiences in health care, the labor market, education, the family, and in other domains of their lives, approach and enter later life. These newer groups will experience later life in a global economy where family life, social norms and technology, among other things, have changed dramatically.

In studying aging, part of the problem is that we attempt to study a moving target. Matilda White Riley (1987) describes this dynamic aspect of the study of aging from her perspective of examining cohort flow through the age structure of society over time. She describes two, interrelated dynamisms as underlying this interplay of individual aging and social change. The first process is the *aging of people* in successive cohorts who grow up, grow old, die, and are replaced by people in subsequent cohorts. Because the members of these successive cohorts age in different ways, they contribute to social change. "When many individuals in the same cohort are affected by social change in similar ways, the change in their collective lives can produce changes in social structure" (p. 9).

For example, Riley (1987) explains the rising economic well-being of older adults using the *cohort composition* explanation described earlier. The reduction in the poverty level of the older population has been brought about by deaths among the oldest cohorts, who were the least financially secure, and the movement into older ages of their replacement cohorts, more of

SIPRESS

"Wait a minute—this can't be me.
I'm a much younger woman."

whom retired with pensions and assets to combine with Social Security benefits. Thus, according to Riley, the fates of particular elderly persons have not improved over the past decades. Instead, the movement of cohorts into and out of (through death) the older population has changed the composition of, and thus society's view of, the economic security of the older population.

Second, there is constant *change in society* as people of different ages pass through the social institutions organized by age. As society changes members of different cohorts age differently. The economic boom following World War II and the increased availability of pensions has enabled more of the older people today to retire at earlier ages. Early retirement, in turn, created a boom in housing, travel, and leisure pursuits for this economically advantaged group, to which the economy has had to react by providing products and services. "The key to this understanding lies in the *interdependence* of aging and social change, as each transforms the other" (Riley, 1987, p. 2).

The problem, according to Riley (1987), is that we are attempting to study the process of aging within the context of constant change in the social world. Social changes, in turn, modify the process of and the adaptations to aging among successive cohorts, making it more difficult to determine what, if anything is caused by aging at either the macro or micro level. One such dynamic, described later, is change in the size and composition of birth cohorts, which, according to economist Richard Easterlin (1987), may have important, and unrecognized, influences on the lives of various cohorts.

Sociology of Knowledge and Research Activism

Most of us take the information we get, especially from authoritative sources, for granted. We assume that the information is factual and unbiased. But there are many questions that we can, and perhaps should, ask about it. How do certain ideas come to the forefront in a society? Why do particular theories become popular and taken for granted or actively opposed by researchers

Cohort Size and Life Chances: The Easterlin Hypothesis

Do you believe that your personal fate and your opportunities are entirely in your own hands? Is it only your individual abilities and choices that determine how your life will turn out? Economist Richard Easterlin (1987) has formulated a very interesting and controversial theoretical argument about the opportunities individuals get in society (what sociologists call **life chances**). His premise is a simple one: The life chances of individuals are influenced to a significant degree by the size of the cohort (which he calls a *generation*) into which they are born. "For those fortunate enough to be members of a small generation, life is—as a general matter—disproportionately good; the opposite is true for those who are members of a large generation" (p. 3). Prompted by the obvious impact of the baby boom birth cohorts, and recognizing an apparently cyclical movement between large and small generations, Easterlin argues that cohort size affects the well-being and outcomes experienced by a cohort's individual members. Members of large cohorts must compete for attention in families, schools, and the labor market; members of smaller cohorts see their fortunes advance relatively easily by comparison. Large cohort members must work harder and accumulate benefits from their efforts more slowly than their peers in small cohorts. When the members of larger cohorts are unable to achieve their high aspirations, Easterlin argues, they react by such actions as having fewer children, and they experience higher rates of unemployment, divorce, suicide, crime, and political alienation. In short, their opportunities for success over the life course are not equal, simply due to the number of births that are proximate to theirs.

Although Easterlin (1987) has presented a compelling case in his book *Birth and Fortune,* other researchers have demonstrated its limitations. To test one of Easterlin's predicted negative outcomes for large cohorts, Kahn and Mason (1987) analyzed survey data on political alienation from 1952 through 1980. They found that period effects (such as the Vietnam War or Watergate) had more to do with political alienation than did birth cohort size. Political alienation fluctuated over time in similar patterns for all cohorts, rather than differentially for cohorts of different sizes.

In other studies examining cohort size and crime, findings are mixed. One analysis showed that larger cohort size was related to the commission of homicide (O'Brien, Stockard, & Isaacson, 1999), but others showed, contrary to Easterlin's prediction, that larger cohorts were not especially prone to crime (Steffensmeier, et al., 1987). These authors argued that looking only at cohort size is too simplistic and that prediction of criminal behavior needs to take into account the larger social and economic climate as well.

As the debate on the validity of Easterlin's hypothesis on cohort size continues, it may be important for you to consider the size of your cohort (either your birth cohort or the cohort with which you entered school, job, or marriage) and to contemplate whether the size of that group, and the resulting degree of competition you face, is likely to shape your opportunities and, as a result, your life chances as you move through your life course.

or the public? Why do certain discoveries get coverage in popular media, whereas others disappear from view? We often assume that experts know what they are talking about and use appropriate means to determine and present facts without the influence of political or ideological slants. But these assumptions are not necessarily true. One subfield of sociology, the **sociology of knowledge**, has made knowledge its subject matter, assuming that we need to question how we know what we know and to examine the social influences on sources of information that most of us take for granted. Science is, in fact, a social enterprise and a human activity that is shaped by the setting and the historical context in which it is performed. Researchers bring their personal frames of reference, including ideologies, expectations, interests, and experiences, to the research setting, sometimes unwittingly confounding what they find in their studies with what they wish to see.

These problems of potential bias are much more pertinent in the social sciences than they are in physics, for example, where the topics the scientist is studying are more removed from personal values. When scientists study people and society and how they operate, however, they touch upon topics in which all social scientists have a strong vested interest. It becomes more difficult to maintain the objectivity that scientists are supposed to have regarding their subject matter when the processes under study affect them and all of the people important to them. Because we are all aging and have family and friends who are aging, these issues become very personal.

Not only do forces internal to the individual scientist shape the kinds of questions being asked and the ways answers are sought; external forces, too, can influence the situation. Research, like fashion, has trends shaped by a variety of external forces, including political trends, the availability of research funding targeted to particular topics, and the popularity of specific research methodologies. Conflicts regarding research priorities, including actions of political or advocacy groups, may also shape what is studied and how it is studied. A good example of these external forces is the dramatic increase in funding from the mid-1980s to the 1990s for research on both the physical and social aspects of Alzheimer's disease (Adelman, 1995). Although the disease itself has been identified since 1906, it was "re-discovered" by the public during the 1980s with the assistance of advocacy groups stressing dire projections of the number of the oldest old who would eventually face this disease. Funding for Alzheimer's disease research grew tremendously, resulting in increasing knowledge about the disease, its impact on the health care delivery system, and its effects on family members who provide care and support to its victims (Adelman, 1995). Although most diseases receive research funding that reflects their burden on the population, Alzheimer's disease is not alone because both AIDS and breast cancer research receive greater funding than would seem warranted by the number of people affected and the lethality of the diseases (Gross, Anderson, & Powe, 1999). This differential treatment may represent an active social construction (for the benefit of legislators and those funding research) as to the relative seriousness of diseases and their priority for funding. In another social/political context, research funding might have been allocated in an entirely different fashion. Thus, rather than being a neutral force, knowledge is both created and shared in a socially constructed context that has overtones of economics, politics, and personal interest of scientists and their sponsors. The sociology of knowledge perspective emphasizes the importance of looking at research on aging with a critical eye for implicit assumptions, potential biases, and alternative conclusions.

A second major critique has to do with the issue of **activism** among researchers versus the objectivity expected by the scientific method. It is difficult for researchers studying aging, as in most other fields focusing on human behavior or society, to separate themselves completely from the topic they study and remain objective. One ongoing dispute about the scientific method has to do with whether science should even attempt to be objective, value-free, or value neutral, as the scientific method suggests. The opposing viewpoint argues that researchers should be activists, taking a stand on critical social issues of importance and providing applied research findings oriented toward solving these problems. There are compelling arguments on both sides of the debate. Those espousing an objective approach to science suggest that it is critical for researchers to acknowledge and work to overcome any biases or preconceptions they may have. In this way, the research may be more valid, reflecting viewpoints not influenced by those of the researcher, and may have more credibility with audiences. A study finding beneficial effects of nursing home placement, for example, would be more credible if conducted by an independent researcher with no vested interest than if conducted by a research group funded by the nursing home industry. Those on the other side argue that it is fundamentally impossible for us to put aside our personal frames of reference in conducting research. Rather, we ought to acknowledge the assumptions and biases that have directed us to select particular topics for study and our approaches to studying them. Instead of pretending value neutrality, researchers should acknowledge and work with their biases to achieve applied research that is oriented toward improving the circumstances of some group or solving some problem. They may carry their activism to testifying before legislative bodies or lobbying on behalf of the causes they choose, combining research with individual political activism.

Summary

Researchers studying social aspects of aging and the life course have a growing number of techniques and approaches at their disposal. Not only can they draw from techniques developed by several disciplines (such as economics and psychology), but the field has added some specific methodologies, such as expanding use of longitudinal and event history analyses, to the methodological arsenal. Increasingly, data are available on selected topics following multiple cohorts over 20 or more years, allowing us to disentangle some of the changing nature of individuals and cohorts as they age. The growing number of nationally representative samples, including lengthy panels focusing on a wide range of topics, has increased researchers' abilities to address important issues without trying to collect their own data in an era of limited research funding. The recent rise in popularity of qualitative techniques has enriched the information on many subjects in which statistical analyses, though useful, can lose the flavor and meaning of the results.

The quality of research on aging has improved substantially in recent decades, but numerous challenges remain (Cutler, 1995). Researchers continue to compete for financial support to perform research on aging, and the knowledge builds selectively as research funding for biomedical concerns outstrips that for the social sciences. The need for high-quality applied research on aging escalates as the population ages and we seek solutions to many related social issues (Singer & Ryff, 2001). The main challenge for researchers is to clearly identify their research problem, its appropriate unit of analysis, the population from which a sample is to be drawn, the best way in which to collect information (surveys, observations, review of historical records), and specific techniques for analyzing that information in order to answer the original question. Only then can we be confident that our base of knowledge about aging in a social context is sound. Many studies on aging show failings in one or more of these steps, in part because of the "youth" of the field, and in part because of the practical constraints on research. It is the skill to match methodology to the problem that is the hallmark of important research to advance our knowledge of aging.

Web Wise

AgingStats.gov   http://www.agingstats.gov/agingstatsdotnet/main_site/default.aspx
The AgingStats Web site is intended to provide users with easy access to government statistics on a wide range of topics, drawn from a range of federal agencies. The site organizes and provides access to information that is collected and made available online or through publications. It is a "one-stop shopping" site and allows you to search for information on demographic traits,

issues relating to retirement, or for data sources that may be relevant to your interests across a range of governmental agencies. The site provides an overview of key indicators of well-being of older adults.

HRS Study   http://hrsonline.isr.umich.edu
The University of Michigan Health and Retirement Study (HRS) surveys more than 22,000 Americans over the age of 50 every 2 years. Supported by the National Institute on Aging, the study paints a portrait of an aging America's physical and mental health, insurance coverage, financial status, family support systems, labor market status, and retirement planning. Data are available for use at no cost to researchers.

National Archive of Computerized Data on Aging (NACDA)
http://www.icpsr.umich.edu/NACDA/
The National Archive of Computerized Data on Aging, located at the University of Michigan's Interuniversity Consortium for Political and Social Research (ICPSR), has been a substantial resource for researchers interested in secondary analysis of large databases. NACDA archives and maintains a large number of datasets that can be retrieved by individuals who teach or study at ICPSR member institutions. They also provide a database of publications generated from their databases, which is searchable.

National Institute on Aging   http://www.nih.gov/nia
The National Institute on Aging (NIA), part of the federally funded National Institutes of Health, is involved with both basic and applied research on physical, social, and psychological aspects of health as people age. Their Web site provides information on their research agenda, including extramural research (funding to outside groups, such as university-based researchers) on biology of aging, behavioral and social research, neurosciences and neuropsychology, and geriatrics. In addition, NIA funds its own research labs (internal programs) and provides a number of online publications and research information by topics. To find out what is "hot" in aging research, one good place to look is the NIA Web site.

Key Terms

activism	event history analysis	period effects
aging effects	fallacy of cohort-centrism	qualitative analysis
cohort composition effect	heterogeneous	quantitative approaches
cohort effects	independent variable	sample
cohort sequential design	life chances	secondary analysis
conceptualization	life course fallacy	social integration
control variable	life history	sociology of knowledge
cross-sectional studies	longitudinal studies	
dependent variable	measures of central tendency	

Questions for Thought and Discussion

1. The literature on aging is growing by leaps and bounds. Look at one or two published articles, and try to decipher how the authors were using age as a variable. Were they looking at age as a cause of something, or as a marker for group membership? Or were they investigating something about the older population? Were they clear about why they included age as a variable and why they expected age to matter to their topic?

2. Conducting research is always complicated. Taking a question or topic that interests you, go through the questions posed in Exhibit 2.7 to consider how you might begin to shape a strategy to answer your question.

3. Examining your own life, identify some events or historical transitions that you think might influence your aging to make it different from that of your parents or grandparents.

4. Think about the lives of yourself and one of your grandparents. What are the commonalities that you expect to find in the childhood and adolescence of these two lives? What differences do you expect in later life stages? What causes these potential differences between you and your grandparent?

Will They Play the Rolling Stones at the Nursing Home?

What kinds of music do you listen to now? Rock, classical, bluegrass, hip hop, jazz, or some other genre? Is it the same music you listened to 5 or 10 years ago? Do you like the music of your parents' generation or that of your grandparents'? Can you imagine what the music of your children or grandchildren is going to sound like? One thing is certain—it probably will be very different from what you listen to today.

Analyzing the social aspects of music is in some ways like analyzing the social aspects of age—both are elements of daily life that most of us approach with a "taken-for-granted" attitude (Martin, 1995). Music, like growing older, just seems to *happen* and to be part of everyday existence, rather than some puzzle to be solved. Although age has not been dealt with in a very extensive fashion in connection with music (Martin, 1995), there are some interesting questions that we can pose. Although most attention in the sociology of music has focused on classical music (perhaps because it has been the music of powerful elites in many Western societies), some contemporary analysts also examine class, race, and age as elements of musical preferences (LeBlanc, Sims, Silvola, & Obert, 1996; Martin, 1995; VonEijck, 2001). Issues such as *how* and *when* musical preferences are formed, whether and when they change, as well as how trends in popular music evolve over time have also been addressed in a preliminary fashion by researchers. Here we examine some possible connections of music with the concepts of age, period, and cohort.

Do Popular Music Styles Have a Life Cycle?

Music, like many aspects of our culture, evolves with the passage of time. Every era has its *sound* as well as its sights, smells, and tastes that evoke the ambiance and events of the day. In 1995 the 50th anniversary of the end of World War II brought back not only the events of the day, but also a nostalgic visit with the music and performers that evoke that historical period. In a sense, the music is connected in our memories with the events (period effects) that shaped peoples' lives during that time; this may be especially important for the young adults most affected by the war. Many people from later cohorts might think of this music as being *old*, both by virtue of being out of date compared to the newest contemporary styles and by recalling a bygone historical era.

Perhaps musical styles and songs could be described as going through life stages. Many musical styles make their entries as brash youth, breaking the rules and often raising the ire of older generations. Parents in the 1920s were concerned with the moral decay implicit in the fast-paced music behind the dances in vogue, such as the Charleston. The same issues arose with the birth of rock and roll, where parents thought the music and dancing led to inappropriate sexual stimulation. Today's parental chagrin with youthful musical trends is anything but new!

With the passage of time, some of the new musical forms become institutionalized and accepted as part of the musical marketplace. As the musical style matures, we may hear versions

47

of these songs converted into muzak for elevators or shopping mall background music. By this point in their life cycle the songs, their performers, and the styles have become an accepted part of the culture, even though some people will favor music of other types. Emphasizing the motivation of youth to separate their music from that of older cohorts, Epstein, speaking about rock music, claims that,

> As generations of rock fans grow up, and have families of their own, they bring their music with them into adulthood. This makes it necessary for rock music to change, to mutate . . . Once a music is co-opted into the mass culture, it can no longer be considered confrontational, as is demonstrated by the Beatles song 'Revolution.' Revolution was once considered a controversial song about radical political change; now it is used in television commercials to sell shoes. (Epstein, 1994, p. xvii)

The once-shocking Rolling Stones passed this milestone when one of their hits became the anthem for a major software advertising campaign in 1995; their appearance as the halftime entertainment for the 2006 Super Bowl is an even stronger illustration of Epstein's mainstreaming argument.

Artists age along with their audiences. New performers may rocket to stardom, often to fade from the scene after a few years (Bennett, 2006; Martin, 1995). Just remember that the most innovative, cutting edge musical artists of today will, if you wait long enough and their music has continued popularity, become established oldies, both musically and chronologically!

Do Cohorts Have Fixed Musical Preferences?

Especially compelling for each cohort seems to be the music associated with the events of young adulthood and coming of age. Couples may have their song to mark their romance and marriage; young adults recall their passage to maturity with the songs they heard as they surmounted major milestones toward adulthood. Perhaps Mannheim (1952a, 1952b) was right in suggesting that the strongest influences upon us are those we encounter in late adolescence and young adulthood because they form the standards against which we evaluate whatever comes later. In music, at least, this would mean each cohort's tastes become set in young adulthood. If this hypothesis is true, then no music could have greater impact on us than the music of our youth.

Setting of musical tastes in late adolescence and demographic trends go a long way to explain why many major cities now have at least one "oldies" station, playing the hits of the 1960s and 1970s aimed at a baby boomer audience. Radio station managers have come to believe that each cohort's tastes are fixed in young adulthood so that baby boomers will continue to listen to the music of that era throughout their lives. The large size of the cohorts of the baby boom, and their current location in their high-earning years, makes them a very valuable market for advertisers. In past years, radio advertisers pushed fast cars and the newest fashions to the boomer market, but now products marketed to this group include insurance, minivans, and "relaxed fit" jeans. So what if Mick Jagger is past 65 and the surviving Beatles are grandfathers? The logical outcome of this fixing of musical tastes, of course, is that eventually they will need to play the Rolling Stones in nursing homes.

In contemporary nursing homes, of course, one may hear at least two kinds of music. For afternoon sing-alongs or performances the most favored music comprises the "old songs," reflecting the youthful period of the residents (Note: Take the current year and subtract about 60–70 years for a good estimate of the musical era in question). Even those residents with cognitive impairment seem to recall the words of and to be buoyed by the old songs that are so familiar. The other music to be heard in nursing homes, however, is leaking out of the earbuds of the staff, reflecting a younger generation and their tastes in music. Although it may satisfy the workers to hear more contemporary music, we might guess that the musical tastes of most

The music we listen to in adolescence will likely be the music we play in our later years. (Credit: Courtesy of the U.S. Administration on Aging)

workers, who may also differ in social class and race/ethnicity as well as age from those in their care, would not win many converts among the residents.

But do we all become fixed in our musical tastes in young adulthood? Is musical preference really a cohort-related trait? Probably not completely. There are those who cultivate a taste for other types of music as they mature. A fan of hip-hop may eventually cultivate a taste for jazz or the classics. There once was a *maturation hypothesis* regarding music, the absolute opposite of the cohort hypothesis derived from Mannheim. The maturation hypothesis argued that musical tastes routinely changed as we matured. Musical preferences, like our bodies, were thought to change in a predictable way. "Easy listening" radio stations once hoped for a major market boost, expecting that the baby boomers, once they achieved middle age, would convert from the music of their youth to the style and performers of music that had been favored by their parents in mid-life. Instead of a high decibel level and a heavy beat, they hoped that mature boomers would be more interested in a milder and more settled sound. That change failed to materialize in large enough numbers to maintain the "easy listening" format in many radio markets, and some of these stations converted to talk radio or "oldies" rock formats.

Just to throw our neat musical cohort scheme into chaos, there are occasional aberrations. An example is the mid-1990s resurgence of 1950s singer Tony Bennett with a new, young adult audience. Bennett is a singing star closer to their grandparents' than their parents' generation; he has not altered his pop style to accommodate his youthful fans. Unlike stars of most generations, Bennett, having already become "chronologically advantaged" relative to this new audience, will not have the luxury of growing older with them for too many years in the future.

An Aging World: Demographic Perspectives

*Population aging may be seen as a human success story . . . But the worldwide phenom-
enon of aging [brings] many challenges . . . concerning the ability of [nations], states
and communities to provide for aging population.*

(Kinsella & Phillips, 2005, p. 5)

The challenges presented by an aging world are hinted at in the opening quote. New reports and articles appear almost weekly, describing the issues facing many aging societies. Work, housing, retirement, transportation, technology, health care, and intergenerational relationships are being transformed by population aging. No doubt, you can see signs of these changes all around you. Baby boomer aging is discussed on news programs, reflected in a seemingly endless array of new products, and is even the subject of a growing number of Web sites. An aging workforce, with a short supply of younger workers, will cause us to rethink our attitudes about older workers and retirement. Our health care system is currently undergoing significant overhaul, and some of those changes will help to meet the needs of our burgeoning older population for long-term care and prescription drugs.

Concerns about the long-range solvency of the Social Security system are directly related to the aging of our population (particularly the ubiquitous baby boomers). You may be worried about whether Social Security will be there for your generation and about how much you will have to pay in taxes to keep it going. The battle lines in the debate are drawn by political processes and societal values, and the future of the program will be resolved as a matter of public policy and public sentiment, as we will see in Chapter 9. However, the demographics of our aging society are also at work in framing the Social Security debate. The number of beneficiaries receiving Social Security and the number of workers contributing to the system have a direct impact on the amount of taxes workers will have to pay to keep Social Security viable. The size of the older population ahead of you in line for Social Security helps to determine how much you will have to pay in taxes during your prime working years. The crisis of Social Security, then, is driven partly by demography. The numbers are the starting point.

Many aspects of culture and social life, including those that help shape the experiences of aging, are affected by the size, structure, and composition of a society's population. Therefore, as we begin this discussion of the demography of aging, put aside any preconceived ideas you may have about demography as thinly disguised math that is ultimately irrelevant to you. As in the case of Social Security, demography is shaping public policy and your future. Even the number and kinds of jobs available to you when you enter (or re-enter) the job market will be determined in part by demography, especially the size of the generations just ahead of you.

The Aging of Societies

One of the most important worldwide trends is societal aging. **Societal aging** refers to the social and demographic processes that result in the aging of a population—the transition to an age structure with increasing numbers and proportions of older people and decreasing proportions at the youngest ages. The specific forces involved in, and measures of, societal aging are discussed later in this chapter. For now, our focus is on the general impact of population aging on a society.

The size and composition of the older population influence the most basic features of social life; for example, the aging of the baby boomers has sparked the emergence of more and more active adult communities, widespread marketing campaigns for lifestyle pharmaceuticals, and ethical debates about end-of-life medical treatment. Families, the labor market, education, government, media, and consumer goods are all affected by the age of a population. Two brief examples will help to illustrate this point.

First, consider the number of advertisements and commercials that deal in some way with age and aging. Some of these ads present negative messages about aging and try to sell products that slow down or alter the signs of aging. Others use a positive message, such as the sporting goods commercial that talks about "94-year-old swimmers, 89-year-old weightlifters . . . . People who forgot to retire . . . and never got old." Analyzing the effectiveness and purposes of negative versus positive age-based advertising is interesting. For our purposes, however, the main point of these ads is their mere existence. Advertisements featuring aging in some way, the appearance of middle-aged and older characters on television, and the design of new products for midlife people are all recent developments. They are related to the increasing average age of our population. As a large proportion of our population enters middle and later life, marketers and advertisers are responding to this shift by including a new range of images, messages, and products. The use of 1970s music in advertisements for financial services is clearly targeted to the maturing baby boomers. As a result of the aging of the U.S. population, "in one way or another, every social institution in American society has had to accommodate to older people's needs, court their favor, or mobilize their resources and contributions" (Treas, 1995, p. 2).

For another example of the impact of population aging on social life, think about the differences between India and the United States. India is a relatively young society: only 5% of its population is age 65 or older, and average life expectancy is about 64. The United States is considered to be an *aging* society, with more than 12% of its population in the age 65 or older category and an average life expectancy of 77. As we will see in our discussion of population pyramids, young societies have high birth rates (fertility) and high death rates (mortality), whereas aging societies have low fertility and low mortality. Many aspects of social life (such as the type and availability of housing, the level of economic development, and the status of women) are related to these patterns of birth and death that produce population aging. For example, health care in India is focused largely on maternal and child health, family planning, and immunization. In contrast, the United States spends its health care dollars very differently; Medicare, the government-sponsored health insurance for older people, is the nation's largest health insurer (U.S. Department of Health and Human Services, n.d.).

The availability of public education, access to safe water and sufficient food, and the demands that compete for limited government resources are very different in the two countries. In the United States, we take clean water for granted (though there is increasing evidence that perhaps we shouldn't), education through age 18 is guaranteed as a basic right of all citizens, and nearly 90% of the older population is eligible for a public pension (Social Security). In India, all of the major causes of death in children are directly linked to the lack of clean water and food, two-thirds of older men and more than 90% of older women are illiterate, there is no national policy of health care for older people, and there is virtually no public pension system. Older adults live with and are economically dependent on kin to meet their needs. Although the different age of the two populations does not fully explain these basic and profound differences, the age of a population is a contributing factor. One Indian scholar summarizes the significance of population aging this way: "The aging of society reflects the triumph of civilization over illness, poverty, and misery, and the decline in human fertility" (Goyal, 1989, p. 10).

In this chapter, we present the aging of societies as an important demographic process that affects our everyday lives, even though it may seem (at a macro level) distant from us. We discuss how societies age, how we can tell they are aging, and why it matters. We also present an overview of the demographic characteristics of the older population in the United States, focusing on the uses of such information for policy and planning.

Demographic Transition Theory

The *demographic transition* is a set of inter-related social and demographic changes that result in both rapid growth and aging of the population. The prototypical transition pattern occurred throughout Western Europe in the 19th and early 20th centuries. The first stage of the transition is related to mortality (the rate of death in a society). During the transition, the economies of these countries went through enormous shifts, changing from an agricultural base to an industrial mode of production. At the same time, these countries experienced mortality decline as a by-product of economic development. They gained control over infectious diseases, improved the availability of clean water, and saw the emergence of more advanced medical technology. This shift from high and somewhat variable mortality (variable because of epidemics) to lower mortality is shown in Exhibit 3.1.

As you can also see in Exhibit 3.1, fertility remained high longer than did mortality as these societal changes unfolded, but then it began to decline. This second transition phase, the lag between mortality decline and fertility decline, set the stage for rapid population growth. Mortality was not removing nearly as many people from the population as before, and continued high fertility was adding many additional people. Finally, with sustained low mortality and low fertility, population aging occurs. Exhibit 3.1 shows the curves for population growth and for growth in the aged population that results from the demographic transition.

Thus far we have been discussing the demographic transition as a pattern of change in mortality and fertility that accompanied industrialization. Yet, we have referred to the demographic transition *theory*. As you know, a theory goes beyond description to

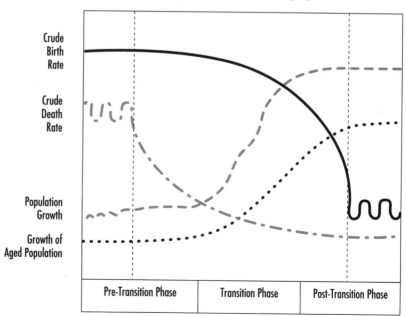

EXHIBIT **3.1**

A Simplified Diagram of the Demographic Transition

| Pre-Transition Phase | Transition Phase | Post-Transition Phase |

Source: Myers, 1990; Yaukey, 1985.

search for explanations and ultimately to make predictions. *Why* did mortality and fertility decline accompany economic development in Western Europe? Is the pattern of decline consistent? What will happen in nations that are just beginning to enter the transition phase? Data on the consistency of the prototypical pattern suggest that even in Western Europe there were variations in the timing of fertility and mortality declines.

More importantly, *causal* connections between the demographic trends and industrialization are not well established. In Western Europe, the stages of the demographic transition are related to, "and in part caused by, industrialization, urbanization, and the spread of literacy and education" (Matras, 1990, p. 27). An industrial economy created, for the first time, an economic surplus; all members of a society could be supported by a smaller number of workers. For this reason, it was not necessary for families to have large numbers of children as workers or to ensure that at least some survived. It may seem unusual to imagine that people decide how many children to have based on such a rational calculation. However, there is an extensive literature in demography about the many factors, including the cost and benefits of having children, that go into such a personal and emotional decision. Keep in mind as well that the means of birth control were limited and unreliable prior to the past six decades.

We can understand more about the strengths and weaknesses of the demographic transition theory by looking at how well the pattern and predictions are holding for the developing regions of the world that are still young. The declining mortality rates in some of these countries are characteristic of the beginning of the second stage of the demographic transition. Whether, when, and how quickly declining birth rates will follow mortality declines remains to be seen. Matras (1990) points out that Mexico, Nicaragua, and Jordan have all experienced dramatic mortality declines, but these countries show little evidence of downward trends in birth rates. Such a decline is necessary, however, for these and other developing nations to move into the third (post-transition) stage, characterized by an older population, a lower rate of population growth, a stable low mortality, and a fluctuating but low fertility.

When and how any given country reaches the post-transition stage depends on an array of cultural and social factors that are not thoroughly understood. In developing nations there is some evidence to suggest that mortality is having a greater impact on population aging than it did in developed nations. This departure from the classic demographic transition model (Coale, 1964), in which fertility has the primary impact on population aging, points to the caution we must exercise in applying existing models of change to developing nations. Furthermore, in the United States, Western Europe, and Japan, population aging proceeded along with economic development. In developing nations today, partly because of the rapid importation of technology to control fertility and mortality, population aging can occur ahead of economic development. These forces will very likely have an impact on the timing and nature of population aging in the developing regions of the world.

How Do Populations Age?

The simple answer to the question of how populations age is that they grow older when both the fertility and mortality rates are low. In short, population aging occurs when large numbers of people survive into old age and relatively few children are born. In such societies life expectancies are high, and the proportion of the population age 65 and older is high. But how does mortality decline? Under what circumstances does a whole society of people decide to have fewer children, lowering the fertility rate? An important framework for understanding these changes is the demographic transition theory, explained in the "Applying Theory" section of this chapter.

Measures of Population Aging

The importance of population's age is far-reaching. Mederios-Kent and Haub (2005) describe the "demographic divide" between countries with low birth rates and high life expectancies (aging/slow or no growth populations) and those with high birth rates and relatively low life expectancies (young/high growth) populations. They point out that the divide is important because of "the disparities associated with the demographic trends—disparities in living standards, personal health, well-being, and future prospects" (pp. 2–3).

How can we show whether a population is aging? The five commonly used indicators of population aging are *population pyramids, proportion aged, median ages, dependency ratios, the aging index,* and *life expectancy.* Each of these measures tells part of the story of a society's age, and each is described and compared in the following sections.

Population Pyramids

A **population pyramid** is a graphic illustration of the age and sex structure of a population. It shows the percentage or number of people within a total population that fit into selected age and sex categories. Population pyramids truly are pictures worth a thousand words. They capture and illustrate at a glance many past, present, and future demographic trends. Only three demographic forces directly determine the shape of a pyramid: fertility, mortality, and migration. The numbers of people being born, dying, and moving into or out of a location will affect the relative size of all of the age and sex groupings for that population, whether it is a town or a country. You can see the impact of fertility, mortality, and migration in shaping a population structure in the examples of population pyramids discussed throughout this section.

Exhibit 3.2a shows the population pyramid for the United States in 2010. The "bulge" of people in the 45- to 65-year-old range is the infamous baby boom (the large number of people born after World War II, between 1946 and 1964). Thus, we see the powerful impact of a past fertility trend reflected in the shape of our pyramid today. We can also see the slightly lopsided top of the pyramid, which shows the greater number of older women than men. This imbalance is a manifestation of past and current trends in mortality: women live longer than men do. We discuss this phenomenon in greater detail later in this chapter.

Based on the age/sex structure illustrated in the 2010 pyramid, we can make some predictions about the shape of our population pyramid in the future. The most significant feature of that shape will be the movement upward of the baby boom generation. Demographers sometimes refer to this as the "pig-in-the-python," conjuring up the earthy image of watching a whole pig move slowly through the digestive tract of a large snake. So, too, the baby boom bulge moves slowly upward through the population pyramid of the United States. The midlife baby boomers of today are the older generations of tomorrow, and young adults today are the middle-aged of the near future! Exhibit 3.2b shows this very phenomenon, with projections for the population in 2050.

EXHIBIT   *3.2a*

Population Pyramid for the United States, 2010

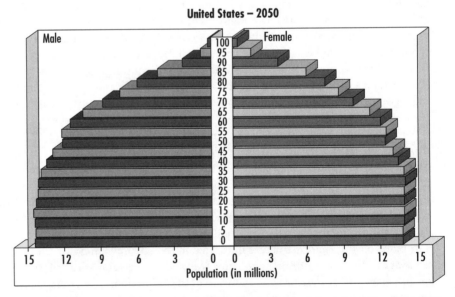

EXHIBIT   *3.2b*

Population Pyramid for the United States, 2050

Source: U.S. Census Bureau International Data Base, 2010.

Contrasting the U.S. pyramids, the population pyramid for the United Arab Emirates (Exhibit 3.3) has a very unusual shape. Working-age men far outnumber women of the same age. Why would this be so? We know that there are only three possible influences on the shape of a pyramid: fertility, mortality, and migration. In this case, the imbalance in the numbers of working-age men and women is due to the immigration of thousands of people from Asia and

EXHIBIT **3.3**

United Arab Emirates Population Pyramid, 2010

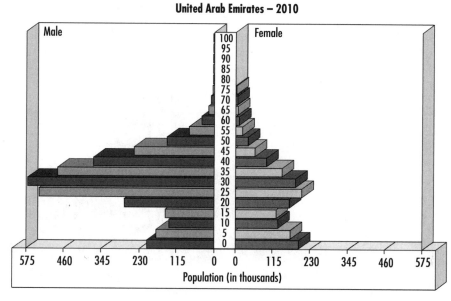

Source: U.S. Census Bureau International Data Base, 2010.

other parts of the Middle East to work in the oil fields. These workers are nearly always men who migrate into the UAE without their families (McFalls, 1998), skewing the sex distribution in these age ranges.

For most countries, migration does not currently play such a big role in the age and sex structure; fertility and mortality are by far the more powerful influences. However, for smaller geographic units, such as states and counties within the United States, migration can be an important factor. Think about what the population pyramid would look like for a small county that builds a 500-unit, state-of-the-art, low-cost retirement community that can accommodate 1,000 older people. This desirable location would attract people from all around the area, including neighboring counties; the relative size of the older population for the "receiving" county would be affected immediately and significantly. If the receiving county had a small, rural population, a large number of new, older residents could create a T-shaped population pyramid with a concentration at the top age ranges.

The shape of a population pyramid thus tells us something about the past, present, and future of a society—not only the fertility, mortality, and migration trends, but also something about life in that society. Population pyramids often take on one of three basic shapes; each stylized shape distinguishes, in a general way, demographic patterns and other aspects of social life, such as a stage in the demographic transition and level of economic development. Exhibit 3.4 shows two of the three basic shapes. The true pyramid, or fast-growth shape, is characteristic of young countries with high fertility and high mortality, such as Kenya. The rectangular, or no-growth, pyramid shows the effects of sustained very low fertility and very low mortality, as in Denmark.

The third classic pyramid shape is a slow-growth, beehive-shaped pyramid; it represents a transition between the true pyramid and a rectangle. We saw this shape for the United States in Exhibit 3.2a, reflecting a pattern of low mortality and fertility. Some demographers have suggested a fourth pattern: the collapsing or inverted pyramid, which is narrowest at the base. The bottom half of the pyramid for Denmark (in Exhibit 3.4) has this shape, and it is possible that Denmark will eventually have an inverted pyramid, if current levels of extremely low fertility continue.

EXHIBIT   *3.4*

Examples of Classic Population Pyramid Shaped: Kenya and Denmark, 2010

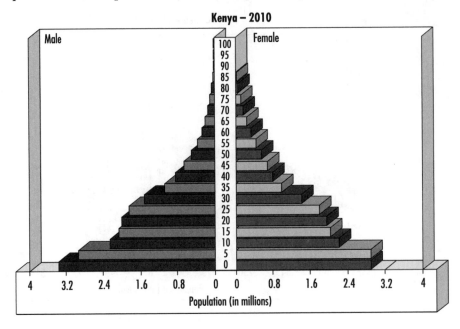

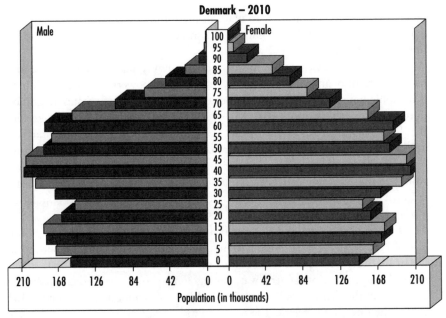

Source: U.S. Census Bureau International Data Base, 2010.

Students are often curious about which pyramid is most desirable for a society. That question has no simple answer; each of these pyramid shapes represents a different set of challenges. For example, a pyramid with a wide base and narrow apex describes a society with lots of children, large families, and high rates of mortality. In such a society, the major focus of public policy will probably be on maternal and child health, schools, and family planning. In a society with a rectangular pyramid, it is fairly certain that significant public policy and tax resources will be devoted to caring for older people. There is no best shape for a population pyramid; our views on which set of challenges we find most acceptable are determined by political and economic development, as well as cultural and social values.

Population pyramids are elegant, informative, intuitively useful representations of the age and sex structure of a society. They give information about how old or young a society is and provide an indication of the level of economic development, the state of advancement in medical technology, and the nature of the resource allocation dilemmas faced by a society.

Proportion Aged

A very straightforward measure of population aging is the proportion of a society that is older. "Older than what?" you might ask. Good question! Most reports of *proportion aged* use 65 as the marker, but some, especially those comparing countries around the world, use age 60 as a cutoff point. Therefore, it is wise to be attentive to the precise definition of proportion aged. The first column in Exhibit 3.5 shows the proportion of population that is age 65 and over for a broad selection of countries. These proportions range from a low of 2.2% to a high of 17.4%. The average proportion of the population 65 and over for the more developed world is 14.3%; for less developed nations, it is 5.1% (United Nations, 2002).

The proportion aged is easily used to make comparisons among nations or across historical time periods within a country, state, or city. Proportions aged are both less complicated and less informative than population pyramids, which give a more detailed picture of the age structure of the population. Nonetheless, trends in the proportion aged in a society are a very important and easily compared indicator of population aging.

Median Ages

Like the proportion aged, **median ages** are single numbers that are often used in conjunction with other measures of population aging. The *median* is the midpoint of a range of numbers—the point at which half the cases fall above and half below. The second and third columns of Exhibit 3.5 show quite a range of median ages. Sweden, by many measures the oldest country in the world, has a median age of almost 40. Nigeria, one of the youngest countries in the world,

	EXHIBIT							*3.5*

Measures of Population Aging in Selected Countries, 2000 and 2050

	%65+		Median Age		Life Expectancy at Birth		Aging Index	
	2000	2050	2000	2050	2000	2050	2000	2050
Kuwait	2.2	17.8	22.2	39.2	76.5	81.1	14.1	130.4
Nigeria	3.0	6.8	17.2	29.6	52.1	69.3	10.6	41.2
Nepal	3.7	8.3	19.4	31.8	59.8	70.5	14.4	52.7
India	5.0	14.8	23.7	31.3	64.2	75.4	22.7	105.0
China	6.9	22.7	30.0	43.8	71.2	79.0	40.7	183.3
United States	12.3	21.1	35.5	40.7	77.5	82.6	74.4	144.9
Japan	17.2	36.4	41.2	53.0	81.5	88.0	157.9	338.2
Italy	18.1	35.9	40.2	54.0	78.7	82.5	168.5	369.2
Sweden	17.4	30.4	39.7	51.2	80.1	84.6	123.0	270.1

Source: United Nations, 2002.

has an amazingly low median age of 17.2; half of the people in Nigeria are under the age of 17.2! Curiosity about these patterns would lead us to investigate the recent history, fertility patterns, political turmoil, natural disasters, and food shortages that might have befallen a country with an unusual demographic pattern.

Aging Index

The **aging index** is the ratio of older people (60 and older) to children under the age of 15. It is a straightforward measure of the age structure of a population, telling us how many older people there are for every 100 children under age 15. By 2030, nearly all of the more developed countries of the world will have an aging index of 100 or more (Kinsella & Phillips, 2005), indicating that there will be one older person for every child under age 15. As you might expect, more developed countries have a much higher aging index than less developed countries. In 2000, Europe had an aging index of 116, more than 10 times higher than that of Africa. In Africa, the aging index of 12 per 100 describes a very young population. The fourth section of Exhibit 3.5 further illustrates the differences among nations around the world on the aging index. Nigeria has fewer than 11 older people for every 100 children, while Italy has 168 older people for every 100 children. The aging index is an indicator of the pressures that societies may face in allocation of resources.

Dependency Ratios

Dependency ratios are, as the term suggests, measures of the proportion of a population that falls within age categories traditionally thought to be economically dependent: traditionally those under age 15 (the youth dependency ratio) and over age 64 (the aged dependency ratio). We can take issue with the definition of anyone under 15 or over 64 as automatically being economically dependent, especially in countries where people work long before age 15 and sometimes long after age 65. In some calculations of dependency ratios, age 18 is used instead of age 15, but international comparisons still use age 15. Other scholars have challenged the dependency assumption by pointing out that some older people fuel economic growth through their taxes and income and that some working-age people may be unemployed (Kinsella & Phillips, 2005). Despite this limitation, however, dependency ratios are useful as comparative indicators of the relative proportions of working-age versus non–working-age people. As such, they point to different patterns of demand on economic and social resources across states or nations, such as health care, tax dollars, and the educational system.

Growing life expectancy means make older adults more visible in society. (Credit: U.S. Census Bureau, Public Information Office [PIO])

The aged dependency ratio is similar to proportion aged and to the aging index, but it is calculated and interpreted in a different way. The proportion aged in a society is simply the number of older people divided by the total population. The aged dependency ratio is the number of older people divided by the number of people ages 15 to 64. It is interpreted as the number of older people for every working-age person (sometimes stated as the number of older people per 100 working-age people).

Exhibit 3.6 shows the youth, aged, and total dependency ratios for the same selection of countries as Exhibit 3.5. Of these, the country with the highest total dependency ratio in the

EXHIBIT 3.6

Dependency Ratios for Selected Countries, 2000

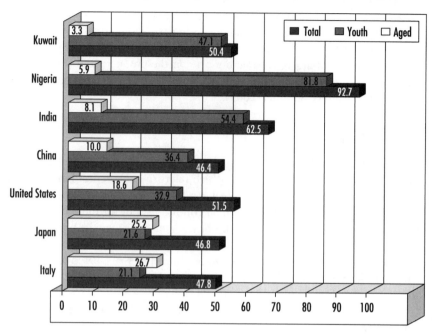

Source: United Nations, 2002.

list is Nigeria, which has almost 93 younger and older citizens for every 100 working-age citizens. Countries such as the United States, Japan, and Italy have roughly two working-age people for every dependent person. If you look at the two components (aged and youth) of the total dependency ratio for countries with very high total dependency ratios and those with relatively low ones, you see that most often the youth dependency ratio contributes disproportionately to high overall ratios. This pattern would be predicted by the demographic transition theory. As you will recall, high fertility and high mortality are typical of a country in the pretransition or early transition phase. Lots of children are being born, and lots of people are dying, producing a low proportion of older people and a high proportion of children relative to the working-age population. The relative sizes of the youth and aged dependency ratios are also demonstrated by the shape of a country's population pyramid.

One final point about dependency ratios is important to keep in mind. Although the numbers and patterns may be (to some of us) interesting in and of themselves, they are most often used to make an argument, defend a position, or influence public policy. In the United States, the increasing proportion of older persons, and the accompanying increase in the aged dependency ratio, has "prompted concern and even alarm about society's capacity to pay for pensions, to finance health care, and to provide the personal assistance that disabled older adults need in their daily lives" (Treas, 1995, p. 6).

It is certainly reasonable to debate the nation's ability, obligation, and strategies to provide these important programs and services; however, these issues have been used to fuel a political agenda built on the rhetoric of burden. Using "voodoo demographics" (Schulz, 1986), proponents of the burden perspective present data such as the aged dependency ratio to conclude that the number of workers will be insufficient to support age-based entitlement programs for the huge baby boom generation lurking just around the bend. They argue that the economic burden of an aging population will become unfair and unbearable in the near future; their proposed solution is to cut programs and alter eligibility criteria for those programs. Although we may decide to take such action, the demographics of our aging society are not the driving force behind either the problem or the solution. Interestingly, while the aged dependency ratio in the United States is increasing steadily, the youth dependency ratio has been declining, so that our current total dependency ratio is lower than it was in the 1960s and 1970s (Treas, 1995). The ability of a society to meet the needs of its aging population depends not only on numbers of old people in relation to working-age people but also on the productivity of the economy, the continued contributions of older adults, and on conscious decision making on the part of politicians and voters (Friedland & Summer, 2005).

Life Expectancy

Life expectancy refers to the average length of time the members of a population can expect to live. It is not the same as **life span**, which refers to a theoretical biological maximum length of life that could be achieved under ideal conditions. We have calculations of the life span of species that can be raised in those optimal conditions, but for humans it is not ethically viable or possible to control the environment. For humans, we gauge the maximum possible life span by using the most recent reliable data on how long a single individual has actually lived. Currently, the life span for humans is estimated to be about 120 years, based on the experience of a French woman, Jeanne Louise Calment, who died in 1997 at the age of 122 (Gerontology Research Group, 2006; Russell & McWhirter, 1987).

Life expectancy, then, is the *average* experience of a population. It is calculated from actual mortality data from a single year and looks at what would happen to a hypothetical group of people if they moved through their lives experiencing the mortality rates observed for the country as a whole during the year in question. The last column in Exhibit 3.5 shows the different life expectancies for the sample of countries we have been discussing. It is probably not surprising that those countries with the lowest percentages of aged persons, lowest median and mean ages, and age/sex structures most resembling pyramids are also those countries with the lowest life expectancies. These various measures of societal aging are all related.

Because life expectancy (also termed *longevity*) reflects so many biological and social processes, it deserves further consideration. Exhibit 3.7 gives more detail about average length of life in the United States; it shows the average number of years of life remaining for people of different age, sex, and race categories in the United States in 2006. To use the table, look at the leftmost column to find a target age, then read across to the race and gender category that is of interest to you. Find the number of years in the appropriate cell of the table, and add those years to the age in the leftmost column to obtain the life expectancy for someone of that age, gender, and race. For example, the life expectancy for a 40-year-old Black female in 2006 was 78.9 (40 plus 38.9).

Calculating life expectancies from this table reveals some interesting sources of variation. Average length of life varies depending on age, race, and sex. Life expectancy at birth (all races, both sexes) in 2006 was 77.7; but life expectancy at age 75 is an additional 11.6 years (to almost 87). For every year of life a person survives, his/her life expectancy goes up. Therefore, the longer you live, the longer you can expect to live (and you can quote us on that)!

The race differential in life expectancy is evident in Exhibit 3.7. Black men of all ages have the lowest life expectancies. Black women have lower life expectancies than White women but higher life expectancies than White men. Notice, however, that the differences between Blacks and Whites (within gender categories) become smaller and smaller as age increases. The difference in life expectancy at birth for Black and White boys is 6 years. Black males who make it to age 80, however, have life expectancies almost equal to those of White males (7.7 and 7.8 years, respectively), and Black females at age 85 have life expectancies that exceed those of White females of the same age. This decrease in the Black/White difference in life expectancy is called

EXHIBIT **3.7**

Abridged Expectancy Table by Race and Sex: United States, 2006

Age	All Races, Both Sexes	White Males	White Females	Black Males	Black Females
0	77.7	75.7	80.6	69.7	76.5
5	73.3	71.2	76.1	65.8	72.6
10	68.4	66.3	71.1	60.9	67.7
15	63.4	61.3	66.1	56.0	62.7
20	58.6	56.6	61.3	51.3	57.8
25	53.9	51.9	56.4	46.8	53.0
30	49.2	47.3	51.5	42.4	48.2
35	44.4	42.6	46.7	37.9	43.5
40	39.7	37.9	41.9	33.5	38.9
45	35.2	33.4	37.2	29.2	34.5
50	30.7	29.0	32.6	25.2	30.2
55	26.5	24.9	28.2	21.6	26.1
60	22.4	20.9	23.8	18.2	22.2
65	18.5	17.1	19.8	15.1	18.6
70	14.9	13.6	15.9	12.3	15.1
75	11.6	10.5	12.3	9.8	12.0
80	8.7	7.8	9.3	7.7	9.3
85	6.4	5.7	6.7	5.9	7.1

Source: Arias, 2010.

convergence; the eventual reversal (at the oldest ages) of the difference in remaining years of expected life by race is called the **crossover effect**.

These observations suggest two questions: why is there a race differential in life expectancy at all, and why does it diminish and even reverse itself at the oldest ages? In answer to the first question, much of the race differential in mortality is explained by differences in socioeconomic status (Queen, Pappas, Harden, & Fisher, 1994). Blacks in the United States have historically been economically disadvantaged and continue to have unequal access to educational and occupational opportunity; the health disadvantages that derive from lack of access to important opportunities, such as employer-based health insurance, show up in higher mortality. We discuss these racial differences in health status, prevalence of diseases, and causes of death in greater detail in Chapter 8.

The second question—regarding the convergence in the race differential in life expectancy—has received some attention, but no definitive answer. One suggested explanation is that the data are unreliable. Among the current generation of older Blacks, the lack of official date-of-birth information may be responsible for some misreporting of age (Preston, Elo, & Rosenwaike, 1996).

Another hypothesis for the convergence effect is that because Blacks who make it to the oldest ages do so in spite of many disadvantages and long odds, they may be survivors. In other words, the survivor group may have some complex set of physiological and social psychological advantages resulting in greater life expectancy once they reach advanced ages.

A final variation in life expectancy that is readily apparent in Exhibit 3.8 is the gender difference. At every age, for both races, females have higher life expectancies than do males. How can we explain this excess male mortality? You probably have some ideas on the subject. Whenever we present this question in classes, in talks, or in casual conversation, we never wait long for responses. Explanations for the sex differential fall into two major categories: biological and social/behavioral. Biological explanations are based on the premise that females have a physiological advantage that results in greater longevity, whereas social/behavioral explanations focus on lifestyle choices, socialization, risk taking, stress, and occupational hazards. There is evidence supporting both kinds of explanations.

One example of empirical support for the biological basis for the sex differential in mortality comes from the sex ratio. About 120 males are conceived for every 100 females conceived, but by the time of birth that ratio is down to about 105 males for every 100 females. Assuming that social and behavioral factors do not play a prenatal role, we might conclude that male fetuses are slightly less viable than female fetuses. Another bit of evidence for the physiological basis is heart disease. Prior to menopause, women have significantly lower rates of heart disease than men do, but after menopause, women's rates increase to approximate those of men. Apparently estrogen (which is high during the childbearing years but low after menopause) provides some protection against at least this one major cause of death.

The superior biological viability argument does not tell the whole story, though. Waldron (1993) found that as much as 50% of the sex differential in mortality could be explained by risk-taking and other unhealthy behaviors such as smoking. Men in U.S. culture are socialized to drive fast, drink alcohol, and smoke; they are also less likely to see a physician on a regular basis and less likely to use social support networks to deal with stress. All of these factors help to explain men's shorter life expectancies.

No doubt the life expectancy difference between men and women is explained by some combination of biological, lifestyle, and social influences. Sorting out the explanations is interesting but also has important implications for health promotion and enhancement. The longevity differential had been consistently widening from 1900 until 1972 in the United States, but it has been narrowing since the late 1970s (Kochanek, Murphy, Anderson, & Scott, 2004), primarily as a result of greater gains in life expectancy for men (Vincent & Velkoff, 2010). For many decades, everyone's life expectancy has been improving, but the rate of improvement varies. AIDS is having a dampening effect on the extension of longevity in the United States, especially for some groups within the society.

The same pattern of excess male mortality holds true for most other countries around the world, although the difference between men's and women's life expectancies is often not as great in the developing nations. For the United States and the European Community, females live on average about 6 years longer than males; in less developed regions, the difference is less than 2 years (United Nations, 2002). In a handful of countries, the difference is in the opposite direction. For example, in Nepal in 2000, life expectancy at birth was 60.1 for men and 59.6 for women. The smaller or reversed gender difference in longevity in the developing nations is due primarily to maternal mortality—deaths among women during pregnancy and childbearing. We saw this same pattern in the United States in the late 19th century, when knowledge and medical care for childbirth were less advanced and not widely available.

Thus far, we have seen that life expectancy varies by age, by race, by gender, and by economic development of a nation. Many other factors help to determine how long any individual is likely to live. To get a sense of these other influences and how they can affect an average expectation of life, spend a few minutes taking the "life expectancy test" in Exhibit 3.8. After you have answered all of the questions, sum up your added and subtracted years of life. Take your

EXHIBIT   *3.8*

The Abridged Life Expectancy Test

Have any of your grandparents lived to age 80 or beyond? If so, add one year for each grandparent living beyond that age. Add one-half year for each grandparent surviving beyond the age of 70.   _____

If any parent, grandparent, sister, or brother died of a heart attack, stroke, or arteriosclerosis before the age of 50, subtract four years for each incidence. If any of those close relatives died of the above before the age of 60, subtract two years for each incidence.   _____

Do you prefer vegetables, fruits, and simple foods to foods high in fat and sugar, and do you always stop eating before you feel really full? If your honest answer to both questions is yes, add one year.   _____

How much do you smoke? If you smoke two or more packs of cigarettes a day, subtract twelve years. If you smoke less than a pack a day, subtract two years. If you have quit smoking, congratulations, you subtract no years at all.   _____

How much do you exercise? Add three years if you exercise at least three times a week at one of the following: jogging, bike riding, swimming, taking long, brisk walks, dancing, or skating. Just exercising on weekends does not count.   _____

If you enjoy regular sexual activity, having intimate sexual relations once or twice a week, add two years.   _____

If you are married and living with your spouse, add one year.   _____

If you are a separated or divorced man living alone, subtract nine years, and if you are a widowed man living alone, subtract seven years. If, as a separated, divorced, or widowed man, you live with other people such as family members, subtract only half the years given above. Living with others is beneficial for formerly married men.   _____

Women who are separated or divorced should subtract four years, and widowed women should subtract three and a half years. The loss of a spouse through divorce or death is not as life-shortening to a woman, and she lives about as long whether she lives alone or with family, unless she is the head of the household. Divorced or widowed women who live with family as the head of their household should subtract two years for the formerly married status.   _____

If you are a woman who has never married, subtract one year for each unmarried decade past the age of 25. If you live with a family or friends as a male single person, you should also subtract one year for each unmarried decade past the age of 25. However, if you are a man who has never married and are living alone, subtract two years for each unmarried decade past the age of 25.   _____

Do you generally like people and have at least two close friends in whom you can confide almost all the details of your life? If so, add one year.   _____

total number, find yourself on the life expectancy table (Exhibit 3.7), and calculate how long you are likely to live. Obviously, this is not a scientific prediction of your life expectancy, but it should be interesting for you to consider how long your life might be and how you feel about it. Does it seem too long or too short?

The life expectancy test shows the importance of genetics, lifestyle, social factors, and other social traits, such as marital status. For many of these influences on longevity, their impact is apparent, but perhaps the relationship between marriage and life expectancy was a surprise to you. This relationship is quite well established; it has been observed consistently in our country and in other nations as well (Hu & Goldman, 1990). Married people live longer than unmarried people do. There are two major explanations for this phenomenon (Weeks, 2005). First is the selectivity hypothesis (that healthy people are more likely to get married and remain married). The second is that marriage is good for your health. Having a stable intimate relationship is argued to be conducive to good health, and the availability of caregiving support is an important health advantage. The numerous influences on life expectancy are relevant to all of us as individuals. They are also part of the complex picture of how, why, and when a population ages.

Prospective Age

As a final note in this section on measures of population aging, consider the expression that "50 is the new 40." This statement makes some intuitive sense—the average 50-year-old today seems as young as the 40-year-old of earlier times. We are likely thinking about overall health and vitality when we make such an observation. Some very innovative demographers are shedding scientific light on the notion that "50 is the new 40" by analyzing prospective age rather than chronological age (Sanderson & Scherbov, 2008). Prospective age, based on life expectancy, is the average number of years of life a person has left. They suggest that this measure can be more meaningful for understanding population aging than chronological age—how many years a person has already lived. Sanderson and Scherbov illustrate this idea by comparing data on French women born in 1922 and those born in 1975. The 1922 cohort has a life expectancy of 74.7, while the younger group has a life expectancy of 84.4 years. If we focus on how many years of life each cohort has left, we see that the older group had 44.7 years left by the time they reached age 30, but the younger group will be 40 before their remaining life expectancy is 44.7. For this younger group, we can use their prospective age to say that "40 is the new 30." These scholars go on to show the significant implications of using prospective age for some of the measures of population age that we have discussed in this chapter. Their work offers us a scientific and provocative look at new ways to measure, think about, and respond to population aging.

Global Aging

Why does the aging of a population matter to individuals or to societies as a whole? In many ways, this entire book is about the effects of population aging—on social institutions such as work, the family, the economy, and the health care system. In Chapter 4 we will see that the social construction of life stages is partly a result of how long people in a society live. For example, *adolescence* is a fairly new life stage in historical terms; in earlier eras, when people married and had children in their early teens and only lived to their thirties, there was no preparatory stage of life. Now we take adolescence as an established and essential stage of human development, especially in societies with long life expectancies.

One of the most far-reaching consequences of population aging is that the entire world is aging. The world's elderly population is increasing by about 880,000 persons *per month* (Kinsella & He, 2009)! If you look back at Exhibit 3.5, you can see some of the dramatic

"GOOD NEWS, MENOPAUSE IS THE NEW PUBERTY."

The proportion of older people in the population is expected to increase in several Asian countries as well as in the United States and across most of Europe. (Credit: E. J. Hanna)

changes that will be taking place in countries around the world over the next 40 years. For all of the countries in the table, the minimum increase we see is a near doubling of the older population by 2050. In the United States, the proportion aged will go from 12.3% in 2000 to more than 20%. Other countries will have significantly higher growth. India's proportion aged will nearly triple, and Kuwait will experience a nine-fold increase in the proportion of its population that is 65 or above. Italy and Japan will have median ages of 54 and 53, respectively. The aging index for every country will increase significantly by 2050, signaling a greater number of older people per 100 children than was the case in 2000. China will change dramatically over these 50 years, from 40 older people per 100 children to 183 older persons per 100 children. Japan and Italy will have more than three times as many older people as children under age 15. "This trend may lead to compelling demands for changes in the way society's resources are shared between generations" (United Nations, 2002, p. 16). The demographics of global aging and the specific ways in which population aging is affecting life in every society around the world have never been of greater importance. Chapter 10 further explores these momentous issues of global aging.

The causes, consequences, and measurement of population aging are large-scale issues. Powerful forces, such as fertility and mortality; alarmist warnings about the consequences of global aging; and assumption-laden measures of dependency ratios may seem far distant from your life. However, we hope that you have begun to see that population aging affects us as individuals and our families; on a more macro level it affects government, public policy, health care systems, and the economy. A description of the older population in the United States will help bring this picture into sharper focus.

Demographic Characteristics of the U.S. Aging Population

The purpose of this section is not to provide extensive detail about every possible demographic characteristic, but to provide a general description of the older population. This overview provides a better idea of the kinds of information available and encourages thinking about how such information is useful. Among the many population characteristics that we could describe are labor force participation, living arrangements, ethnic diversity, geographic distribution, education, and sex ratios. Some of the most important demographic characteristics, such as health, income, and marital status, are discussed in greater detail in later chapters. The major disadvantage of not including them here is that these characteristics provide some of the best illustrations of the great variation among older persons in the population—a point that is always important to keep in mind. The major advantage to leaving certain demographic characteristics until later in the book is that we do not want to press our luck in convincing you that demography provides a fascinating, lively, and useful perspective on the issues of aging. Therefore, this discussion focuses on three demographic variables and their interpretations.

Living Arrangements

Information about the *living arrangements* of older people is important for community planners, housing designers, researchers interested in social support networks, and those of us curious about the validity of prevailing societal images. Contrary to a common stereotype, the majority of older people do not live in nursing homes or other "seniors only" housing settings. As you can see from the graph in Exhibit 3.9, only a very small proportion live in nursing homes—about 5% of all people 65 and over in 2005. This percentage does increase considerably by age; 17% of the 85 and older population lives in nursing homes, but it is still not anywhere near a majority.

The chart in Exhibit 3.9 also shows that living arrangements for noninstitutionalized older people vary by sex. Older men are much more likely to live with a spouse than older women; the most common living situation for women 65 and older is living alone. This pattern reflects differences in marital status. Because women live longer than men and tend to marry men who are about 3 years older, women are much more likely than men to become widowed in later life. This gender difference in marital status is discussed further in Chapter 5.

As with many aspect of aging, there are some interesting racial and ethnic differences in living arrangements of older people. He, Sengupta, Velkoff, and DeBarros (2005) found the following patterns among older people in the United States in 2003: Black men are more likely than other groups of older men to live alone (nearly 30% do so, compared to about 19% for Whites, and less than 10% for Asian or Hispanic older men). Asian, Hispanic, and Black older women are much more likely than White women 65 and older to live with other relatives (about 35% do so, compared to less than 14% of White older women). Information about where and with whom older people live is useful for a host of reasons. For example, the statistics about nursing home residence are useful in dispelling the stereotype that Americans

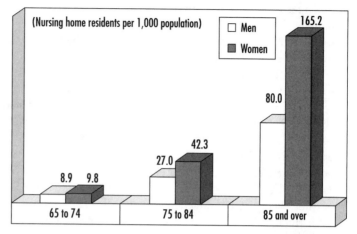

EXHIBIT   *3.9*

Rate of Nursing Home Residence Among People Aged 65
and Over by Age and Sex: 2004

Source: Federal Interagency Forum on Aging-Related Statistics, 2008.

abandon their elders by warehousing them in nursing homes. Most older people do not live in nursing homes, and as you'll see in chapter 5, families provide most of the long-term care that older people receive. The data about gender, age, racial, and ethnic patterns in living arrangements is useful context for thinking about target populations for services and programs.

Geographic Distribution

How are the households in which older people reside distributed geographically? This question may appear to be of interest to a limited number of people, but the **geographic distribution** of the older population (across states, among cities and suburbs, across counties) actually has far-reaching consequences for a location's tax base, educational system, demand on transportation services, and voting patterns. The numbers of older people, their percentage in a given community or state, and how they got there (by growing older in the same community or by migration) are all related to outcomes of interest.

It is not surprising to learn that many of the states with large numbers of older people happen to be states with large overall populations. California, New York, Texas, and Pennsylvania are examples of states with both large populations and large numbers of older people (Administration on Aging, 2010). The *proportion* of older people in any given location can be a different story; the proportion of older people in a geographic area is affected by the three key demographic forces of fertility, mortality, and selective migration, regardless of its overall population size. California has a large number of older people but a lower proportion of older adults than the United States as a whole (11.2% compared to 12.8% in 2009), partly because of high rates of international and interstate migration of younger people into the state. In contrast, Florida has a large number of older people and the highest proportion of older people in the nation (17.4% in 2009), largely because of in-migration of retirees seeking a "sun belt" locale. Even though Florida receives a lot of older people from elsewhere, it is not the case that everybody moves to Florida when they retire. Although a large proportion of the older people who do relocate tend to move to Florida or other warm-climate states, older people are much less likely to move than people under the age of 65. Less than 4% of the older population moved at all between 2007 and 2008; of this small proportion who did move, only 20% moved across state lines (Administration on Aging, 2010). States and other locations that receive large numbers of older people have to factor in increased (and sometimes seasonal) demands for housing, food, retail, and other services and amenities.

A number of other interesting trends and issues relate to the distribution and redistribution of the older population through migration. Longino (1990) has described a model for understanding the causes and consequences of multiple moves by older people. He distinguishes an initial relocation that is motivated by the attractiveness of a particular destination to later moves, motivated by the desire to be closer to kin or the need for long-term care. Investigations into seasonal migration are also increasing in number. The presence of "snowbirds" (seasonal migrants to a warmer climate during the winter months) in a given location has important consequences for the economy and daily life; imagine what a seasonal growth of 20% or 30% might mean to retailers, traffic, and housing in a sunbelt community.

In addition to where people live geographically and with whom they live, information about where they are housed is also of interest. Housing availability, affordability, and quality are of major concern to all of us. For older people with fixed incomes and increased likelihood of health problems, appropriate housing options are more challenging. More than 60% of older homeowners have lived in their current homes for 20 years or more, speaking to an emotional as well as financial investment in a place and a community. Deciding how and when to make a housing change and finding desirable and affordable options are complex and difficult processes. Even though three-quarters of older people own their own homes (a higher proportion than any other age group), reduced income and frailty can place at risk their many years of financial, physical, and emotional investment in home and neighborhood (Callis, 2003). Housing represents a public policy and planning challenge; it is also a matter of personal and family concern, encompassing an array of issues such as independence, autonomy, security, and the meaning of home. While those with ample financial resources have a wide range of choices, those with more moderate incomes may find relatively few attractive choices in the housing market. The current economic crisis in the United States is having an impact on housing options for a much bigger segment of the older population than ever before.

Gender Composition

The **sex ratio** is a measure used by demographers to summarize the gender composition of a population. Traditionally, the sex ratio is presented as the number of men for every 100 women; calculated by dividing the number of men by the number of women. It has also been called the "masculinity ratio" (see, e.g., Yaukey, 1985). In the United States in 2000, the overall ratio of men to women was 96 men for every 100 women. For the older population, however, the sex ratio is less balanced, and it makes more sense to talk about a "femininity ratio"—the number of older women for every 100 older men. For the population age 65 and older in 2010, the ratio was 132 women for every 100 men; among those 85 and older, it was 230 women for every 100 men (Vincent & Velkoff, 2010). These ratios capture the differential impact of mortality on men and women. The imbalance has implications for remarriage possibilities following widowhood, for the economic well-being of the oldest old, for living arrangements, and for patterns of social interaction.

Increasing Diversity

Another important aspect of our demographic future is the increasing racial and ethnic diversity of the United States as a whole and the older population in particular. There is evidence for a substantial shift in the racial and ethnic composition of the U.S. resident population. Exhibit 3.10 shows the changes between 2010 and 2050 in the proportion of the older population that identifies as a particular race/ethnicity group. The proportion of the older population that is non-Hispanic White will decrease from 80% to 58.5% by 2050, while the proportion

EXHIBIT   *3.10*

Proportion of Older Population (65 and older) in Racial and Ethnic Groups:
United States, 2010 and 2050

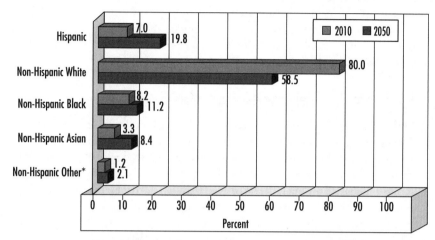

*Non-Hispanic Other includes: American Indians, Alaskan Natives, Native
Hawaiians, Pacific Islanders, and persons with two or more races.

Source: Administration on Aging, n.d.

identifying with every other racial and ethnic group will increase. The proportion that identifies as Hispanic will increase from 7% to 19.8%. This trend of increasing diversity in the older population is of great importance for everyone trying to understand and describe the experiences of aging in the United States. Because ethnic and racial identities often play a central role in shaping those experiences, we need to be aware of this diversity among the older population. Racial and ethnic diversity is also a significant factor in planning for programs and services and for the cultural training that might enhance the ability of aging-services workers to meet the needs of their clients.

Centenarians

Centenarians—people aged 100 and older—are another important part of our demographic profile. In 1980, there were only about 15,000 centenarians in the United States; that number had almost doubled by 1990, and in 2009 the estimated number was 104,754 (U.S. Census Bureau, 2010a). The number of centenarians is projected to grow to around 834,000 by the year 2050 (Velkoff, 2000). These centenarians have experienced incredible social change and major historical events throughout their lives. There is growing interest in studying centenarians for the many contributions they can make to our understanding of aging, as well as how lives connect to history and social/technological change. In addition, scientists speculate that the study of centenarians may provide clues to factors that influence longevity (New England Centenarian Study, 2010; Velkoff, 2000).

Interpreting and Using Demographic Data

In describing select demographic characteristics of the older population, we have illustrated some important uses for demographic data. Such information is the foundation for a wide range of professional endeavors, including product design and development, community planning, market research, education about aging, and public policy development. You can also use demographic information to support a position you are taking in a term paper, debate, or presentation. We all use such data to help us understand the realities of aging. Throughout this chapter we have been encouraging you to see the importance and usefulness of demographic information. We make those same points in the final section of this chapter.

In using such data about the older population, it is extremely important not to overgeneralize—not to make blanket statements about all older people or about the *typical* older person. Therefore, while we encourage use of demographic data as a valuable tool, we caution you to see it as a way to uncover the complexities and varieties of aging.

The Fallacy of the Demographic Imperative

One key to avoiding errors in interpretation is to keep in mind that demography is not destiny. Friedland and Summer (1999, 2005) illustrate various interpretations of even commonly accepted demographic wisdom. You have heard and read a lot about the baby boomers and what their aging will mean to you and to society. Friedland and Summer point out that we can get a different sense of the magnitude of the "baby boom problem" if we consider not only the total number of people in that birth cohort but also the additional people born solely because of the higher birth rate. The higher birth rate during the 18 years of the baby boom era added about 12 million additional children beyond the number that would have been born if the pre–World War II birth rates had continued. During the peak year of the baby boom, 4.3 million babies were born; in 2008, 4.25 million babies were born in the United States—very nearly the same number (Hamilton, Martin, & Ventura, 2010). If we think about it this way, the baby boom does not seem as large. These authors also clearly demonstrate how economics and policy issues play roles at least equal to demography in shaping our destiny.

Although the numbers in demographic projections may seem compelling, we have illustrated several times throughout this chapter that numbers are only part of the picture. This point will be further illustrated in the chapter on global aging. What any society decides to do about the aging of its population depends not simply on how many older people there are but also on the political, social, and moral values of the society.

The warning against invoking the demographic imperative can apply to the uses of the dependency ratio to foretell impending economic disaster for U.S. society. The implication of the

Willard Scott will find no shortage of centenarians to salute in the coming years, with the number of those living to be 100 and beyond expected to soar from approximately 50,000 in the year 2000 to 834,000 by the year 2050. (Credit: Mike Payne, courtesy of the Ohio Department of Aging)

numbers is a matter of interpretation. Critical choices about which numbers authors or speakers choose to present are often very ideological decisions because some facts better support a particular policy agenda than others. Therefore, while we encourage you to consider demographic information as a useful resource, it is important to be aware of the social and political contexts that generate the numbers and direct their uses. For example, someone interested in raising the retirement age may choose to present dependency ratios in one way, but the same statistics can also be shaped to support those opposing that change. Keep this warning in mind as you use demographic facts and as you critically analyze anything you read that uses such information.

While demographic information provides an essential framework from which to understand the aging of societies, it is equally important to remain aware of the overarching impact of other social institutions (the economy, politics, family systems) as we consider how best to deal with the challenges of aging. "We need not believe ourselves to be at the mercy of blind forces such as demographic and economic imperatives, as if these existed outside the realm of public discussion and debate" (Robertson, 1991, p. 147).

Summary

This chapter has illustrated that the increase in the size and proportion of our older population has an impact on every aspect of social life. In the United States, the number of older people is projected to exceed 70 million by the year 2030, at which time all of the baby boomers will have reached age 65; older people will represent about 20% of our population by then—one in every five people you see on the sidewalks and in the grocery store will be 65 or older!

When populations age, the labor force is profoundly affected. As large numbers of people retire and come to be supported by company pensions and health insurance, the cost of doing business escalates. Some of this demand can be accommodated by increased productivity from technological improvements. Companies worry that their competitive edge is dulled by the weight of retirees, resulting in recent trends to end private pension systems, converting them to annuities that provide lower benefits than promised.

Around the world, the increase in the size of the older population is equally dramatic and consequential. As we saw earlier in this chapter, a large proportion of all older people will live in developing nations by the year 2020. Those nations will have seen their older populations grow by an average of 160% between 1991 and 2020. The challenges facing the nations where rapid population aging will compete with maternal and child health concerns are enormous. Of equal magnitude are the challenges for the global community to plan for their aging societies and to propose and implement culturally relevant solutions to the challenges of health care and economic security. As we proceed with our look at the social dimensions of aging, the demographic frame of reference will continually direct our attention to the distinct yet diverse characteristics, situations, and needs of the older population; to the aging of our society; and to global aging. Societal aging; patterns of fertility, mortality, and migration; and the demographic composition of the older population may at first glance seem to be remote and irrelevant, but they have a major impact on your life, your family, the country, and the planet of which you are a citizen.

Web Wise

Following is a list of sites that can provide you with information on demography of the aging population in the United States and in various countries around the world. Note that not all of the information is free and that some of it refers you to published (hard copy) materials.

Age Data   http://www.census.gov/population/www/socdemo/age.html
This is a linked Web site maintained by the U.S. Census Bureau. It provides access to national, state, or local sources of information on demography from the Census Bureau. International data are also available. In general, the census provides both statistics on current populations and projections for population change/growth through these sites and their printed publications.

Agingstats Site   www.agingstats.gov
The Federal Interagency Forum on Aging-Related Statistics (Forum) was initially established in 1986 with the goal of bringing together Federal agencies that share a common interest in improving aging-related data. The Forum has played a key role by critically evaluating existing data resources and limitations, stimulating new database development, encouraging cooperation and data sharing among Federal agencies, and preparing collaborative statistical reports. In addition to the original three core agencies (National Institute on Aging, National Center for Health Statistics and Census Bureau), the organizing members of the Forum now include senior officials from the Administration on Aging, Agency for Healthcare Research and Quality, Bureau of Labor Statistics, Centers for Medicare and Medicaid Services, Department of Veterans Affairs, Environmental Protection Agency, Office of Management and Budget, Office of the Assistant Secretary for Planning and Evaluation in HHS, Social Security Administration, and the Substance Abuse and Mental Health Services Administration.

International Data Base (IDB) from the U.S. Census Bureau
http://www.census.gov/ipc/www/idbnew.html
If you ever want to know what population pyramids will look like for Albania, Guatemala, or Sierra Leone in 2025, this is the Web site for you. Visiting the IDB site provided by the U.S. Census Bureau enables you to look at projections for population and detailed characteristics of various countries or regions of the world. Choose from a large number of countries and look at the aging rates of the populations (via population pyramids) or at statistics in tables. It is also possible to download IDB data, but review the requirements in advance and be prepared for a large data set!

Population Reference Bureau   http://www.prb.org
The Population Reference Bureau, funded by government agencies, foundations, universities, and nonprofit organizations, makes available a range of demographic data, including a page on "Aging." Articles, reports and datasheets change over time but focus on the size, diversity, and characteristics of the older population and the baby boomers in the United States and the world.

United Nations Statistics Division
http://unstats.un.org/unsd/methods/inter-natlinks/sd_natstat.htm
The UNSD provides a Web page that links to selected national statistics offices. Each of the country's statistical information is unique but may be useful for international comparisons on aging issues. Nations are organized alphabetically by continent.

U.S. Bureau of Statistics: FactFinder
http://factfinder.census.gov/home/saff/main.html?_lang=en&_ts=
The FactFinder is an excellent resource for accessing information that is amassed by the Census Bureau on a wide range of individual characteristics, housing, and business issues. Using the system, users can find customized information on a wide array of topics, including many up-to-date statistics regarding aging, family, health and related topics. Much information on older adults can be found under the "people" tab.

Key Terms

aging index

centenarians

convergence

crossover effect

dependency ratios

geographic distribution

life expectancy

life span

median ages

population pyramid

sex ratio

societal aging

Questions for Thought and Discussion

1. How does the age structure of a society affect the kinds of decisions that must be made by national policy makers? Can you think of examples from the United States where the aging of our society has influenced political agendas?

2. Find some examples in newspapers or magazines of the ways in which demographic information about the older population is used to convey messages of alarm or optimism. Is the information being presented in an accurate and balanced way? How might the same information, presented differently, be used to convey a different message?

3. If your local senior center wanted to revamp their services for the upcoming baby boom generations, what kind of demographic information would you advise them to look at?

4. How does the life expectancy in a country affect the way life is organized—for example, number of years spent in school, age at marriage, and age at retirement?

The Aging Individual in Social Context

4

> *Like gender or height or the presence/absence of ear lobes, age itself is not a cause of anything. Rather, it is . . . a socially significant title that covers complex sociocultural formulations, including some which are directly implicated in personal and collective identities.*
>
> (Hazelrigg, 1997, p. 96)

Aging is a very complex social phenomenon because it involves interrelationships among biological, psychological, social, and cultural processes. At another level, aging is also a very personal experience. Most of us care about aging because we are aware that it is happening to us and to people around us. All of us, if we are lucky, will grow old and all of us continue to age, regardless of where we are today within the life course. Thus, aging is a more universal experience than any other. Most of us will grow old, but few of us will change our status in other social categories such as gender or race. Even changes in marital status or religion are far less predictable than changes in age status. Because aging is something that happens to everyone at a personal level, it is helpful to discuss what happens to individuals as they grow older, and then to put those insights into a larger context—the social context of aging.

Setting the Stage: Psychology of Aging

The psychology of aging is a well-developed field of study, with a wide range of questions in its scope. The topics covered within the psychology of aging include changes in cellular processes in the brain, the relationship between psychology and physical processes of health and illness, changes in cognitive performance, and complex social psychological concepts, such as the self and identity. In all of these diverse domains the psychology of aging focuses on the stability and change in how humans operate psychologically at various ages and stages of life. To describe the breadth of the research and theory included in the psychology of aging, Salthouse (2006) offered a taxonomy of "what, when, why, where, and how" questions that guide the field. Topics covered by this taxonomy include: the psychological ways in which people of different ages vary, the ages at which these changes occur, where they occur (specifically, what structures of the brain might be involved in changes), and why they occur. Because the field is so broad, scholars who study the psychology of aging have different areas of specialization. Some focus on cognitive psychology and neuroscience, which includes the physiology of cognitive impairments; the impact of aging on memory, intelligence, information processing, and learning; and changes in sensory functioning. Other psychologists of aging are interested in aging and behavior such as problem solving and decision making; some focus on the impact of aging on personality and the self; still others look at the intersection of internal psychological processes with social aspects of life. The breadth and depth of theory and research in the psychology of aging are far beyond the scope of this text. Students interested in a fuller picture of the psychology of aging will find a vast array of resources, including the *Handbook of the Psychology of Aging* (Birren & Schaie, 2006).

The psychology of aging is obviously an important and well-developed dimension of the field of gerontology. Because this book uses a sociological perspective on aging and the life course, an in-depth exploration of psychology is not reasonable. However, some aspects of the psychology of aging help to set the stage. First, while the sociological perspective emphasizes the social forces that shape the realities of aging, it is vital to recognize that aging-related changes and experiences occur for and within individuals. The psychology of aging furnishes knowledge about these internal changes and experiences. Second, there are areas of overlap between the psychological and sociological frameworks for the study of aging. In particular, the science of human development provides a foundation for linking individual actions and experiences to the social context in which decisions, behaviors, and outcomes take place.

Human Development and Aging

The study of human development has roots in psychology, but also has a significant interdisciplinary focus and strong ties to sociology and social gerontology. As a broad field of study, **human development** examines progressive and systematic changes across the life span in cognitive, emotional, interpersonal, personality, and self-concept processes. One of the central concepts in the sociology of aging—the life course—also explores the way that individuals lives change with time, as is discussed later in this chapter. Both perspectives—life course and life span human development—refer to the growth and change that people experience over their lives. Both perspectives place some importance on internal psychological processes as well as external social processes in shaping the way that individual lives unfold over time. The difference between a psychological focus on life span and a sociological focus on life course is the amount of attention given to the internal aspects of development (for the former) compared to the social influences on human development (for the latter). However, the overlap between life span human development and sociology of the life course creates rich possibilities for connections between sociology and psychology of aging (Settersten, 2005a), as we see later in this chapter.

For many years the focus of human development was on the changes that take place in infancy, childhood, and adolescence; topics such as language acquisition, emergent cognitive abilities, moral development, and problem solving were researched extensively. More recently, attention has been given to questions about the growth and change that take place throughout the human life span, including adulthood and aging. A pioneer in this area was Erik Erikson, who proposed that adults face development tasks, just as children and adolescents do. His initial work on this topic identified two developmental stages for later life. **Generativity**—learning how to look outside oneself and focus on passing on a legacy to future generations—was described as the major developmental task of middle age. For older people, self-reflection and coming to terms with one's life is the developmental challenge Erikson identified; a successful resolution of this stage of life was termed **ego-integrity**. Erikson further refined these stages, offering more detail about the developmental challenges that we face as we age (Erikson, Erikson, & Kivnick, 1986). Erikson's work was vital in drawing attention to the fact that human beings do continue to grow, develop, and change throughout their lives. His writing set the stage for research on the major questions identified by Salthouse (2006): what developmental changes take place in later life, and why do they occur?

Scholars continue to explore the nature of human development in later life and to understand the unique characteristics of the later stages of life. Tornstam (1997, 2005) proposes that later life offers the opportunity for **gerotranscendence**; he describes this transformation as "a shift from materialistic and pragmatic view of the world to a more cosmic and transcendent one, normally accompanied by a contemplative dimension" (1977, p. 143). His ideas are based on interviews with older people, who described a gradual change involving self-reflection, refinement of personal qualities they sought to enhance or to modify, and a deeper investment in select important social relationships. Atchley (2004) describes a similar focus on an inner journey of self-reflection, but he also suggests that service to one's community can be the outcome of this path; "serving from spirit" is the concept he offers to express the unique contributions that can be made by spiritually grounded elders. *Elderhood* is the phase in later life that William Thomas (2004) describes as moving from doing to being; one of the greatest challenges to achieving this state is our fondness for adult supremacy—for the phase of life where success is defined in terms of activity and striving. Schachter-Shalomi and Miller (1995) summarize many of these ideas in their call for "a new paradigm of aging with emphasis on lifelong learning, brain-mind development, and consecrated service to humanity" (p. 244). Schachter-Shalomi's "sage-ing," Atchley's "serving from spirit," Thomas's "elderhood," and Tornstam's "gerotranscendence" all build on, and expand, Erikson's early ideas about the unique challenges and opportunities of human development in later life.

Social Context and Individual Aging

As the study of human development suggests, the passage of time signals physiological and psychological development and changes that happen *within* individuals as they age. However, such changes do not happen in a vacuum. Goals, values, preferences, and actions that characterize later life are shaped by a lifetime of individual experiences and by social circumstances. For example, the desire and the opportunity to continue to work past the typical age of retirement vary considerably by the kind of jobs that people have, their economic needs, and the policies that their employers have in place. Working in later life is not simply the result of individual choice; social forces play an essential role. In an economic downturn, competition for jobs is heightened, and older people may be disadvantaged in such a market because of outright age discrimination, or because the kinds of jobs they might be seeking are no longer readily available. People respond to, and are affected by, both the social context and the physical environment in which they live.

The importance of surroundings is clear from the literature on the role of social support in later life. Social support can include the network of people with whom we have contact, the amount of contact we have with them, the kinds of support and help that we get from those around us, or the confidence that we can count on others when needed. There is growing evidence that strong social support has a positive effect on health and well-being in later life and that it is "a key determinant of successful aging" (Antonucci & Akiyama, 1987; Krause, 2001).

Environmental Gerontology

Physical environments can also have significant impact on the aging individual, as eloquently described and empirically verified by Lawton and his colleagues. In his influential work on this topic, Lawton suggests that the fit between a person and his or her environment can actually have an impact on how competently individuals can get by in their everyday lives. Lawton's classic model of the relationship between behavior and the environment visually depicts the optimal fit between environmental press that encourages maximum performance by the individual, as well as potential negative outcomes for the person if the environment demands too much or too little (see Lawton, 1986). If the environment demands more of the person than they can accomplish, maladaptive behavior and negative affect can result; similarly, if the environment is not challenging enough, an individual may not be motivated to maximize their competence.

This eloquent and intuitively appealing formulation can be applied to a host of questions and circumstances. For example, *environment* can refer to a private home environment or a planned environment such as a retirement community, and even to a larger community such as a neighborhood or a city (Wahl & Weisman, 2003). A burgeoning global movement to design cities, neighborhoods, and villages that are aging-friendly is linked to Lawton's (1986) ideas. The World Health Organization (WHO) has undertaken an initiative to address environmental issues that can hinder or promote healthy aging. According to their *Age-Friendly Environments Programme,* "an age-friendly city is an inclusive and accessible urban environment that promotes active ageing" (WHO, 2010a). This straightforward statement acknowledges Lawton's major premise: that environments can be designed or adapted to maximize the independence, engagement, health, and competence of older people.

Lawton's (1986) groundbreaking work has given rise to the field of **environmental gerontology**, which seeks to "understand the behavioral and psychological implications of encounters between elders and their environments" (Scheidt & Windley, 2006, p. 105). This specialized area within gerontology involves a wide range of disciplines and professionals, including psychology, sociology, architecture, community planning, and public policy. The research agenda for environmental gerontology is broad, but it is particularly well-suited to evaluate the impact of interventions (such as modifications to the home environment) on the health and well-being of older adults. Gitlin (2003) describes the growing interest in and research about "environmental and behavioral adjustments to support family caregiving or physical and cognitive functioning of frail older people" (p. 631).

Social Context

Environmental gerontology is an excellent illustration of the importance of built environments and social contexts for aging individuals. For sociologists who study aging, the social context within which a person ages is the major focus of their work. This is the unique contribution sociology makes to the study of aging. *Sociology* examines the ways in which social life is organized and the ways in which it affects individual actions and behaviors at all ages. Chapter 3 describes the ways that demographic forces (fertility, mortality, and migration) help to shape social institutions, and at least indirectly have an influence on individual lives. Recall the discussion of the role of population aging in the challenges facing Social Security and the current high level of competition for jobs that is partially related to the large number of baby boomers in the work force. As an example of the sociological perspective, demography takes the essentially individual events of birth, death, and relocation and sums them up, describes large-scale patterns and trends, and considers the causes and consequences of these events from a macro-level point of view. One of the great values of sociology is to lend a broader perspective—what Mills (1959) called exercising the sociological imagination. This perspective places personal experiences in a broader social and historical context and gives us a frame of reference for understanding individual experiences. The sociological imagination is invaluable for understanding the experiences of aging.

There is a tendency in U.S. society to focus on the individual. We are enamored of the concept of free will and autonomy—that individuals can control or shape their futures through their actions. We value independence, and our nation is built on ideas about individual choice and individual responsibility. We are curious about the various circumstances in which people find themselves and often take some comfort in attributing success or failure to a person's choices and actions, rather than external forces. Such thinking allows us to believe that good fortune will come to us if we work hard and position ourselves correctly and that ill fortune will not befall us because we have done the right thing. The sociological imagination makes possible a richer understanding of the power of social structures and contexts that influence individual lives.

One of the most important concepts for understanding the ways in which social factors help to shape the experience of aging is the life course. The life course is a socially constructed road map that influences the individual choices we make about moving into and out of important social roles such as marriage, parenthood, employment, and retirement. The life course is a fundamental feature of the societal framework within which individual aging takes place.

The Life Course

All societies use age in some way to organize social life—to assign people to roles, to regulate interaction, or as a basis for division of labor. The United States has laws about minimum ages for drinking, driving, voting, and holding public offices. We also have some expectations about what ages are appropriate for people to marry, enter the job market, and retire. Many people thought that the 66-year-old woman who had a baby in 2005 with the aid of in vitro fertilization was definitely too old to have a child. Most of us plan to retire sometime in our 60s. In addition to ideas about appropriate ages for entry into and exit from important social roles, we also share some general expectations about age-appropriate behavior. The dictum to "act your age" is a clear illustration that we do have some underlying ideas about what we should be doing at various stages in our lives. "Expectations regarding age-appropriate behavior form an elaborated and pervasive system of norms governing behavior and interaction, a network of expectations that is imbedded throughout the cultural fabric of adult life" (Neugarten, Moore, & Lowe, 1965, pp. 22–23). These expectations are part of our culture; they are taught to us as we grow up and continually reinforced throughout adulthood. They also sometimes shift, as we have seen over recent decades, when ages for having children have extended and ages at which individuals seek higher education have come to include mid-life and older adults. These expectations are reflected in our laws, policies, and organizational rules; they are also part of a general timetable we use for major life events. Neugarten and her colleagues observed that people "are aware not only of the social clocks that operate in various areas of their lives, but they are aware also of their own timing and readily describe themselves as 'early,' 'late,' or 'on-time' with regard to family and occupational events" (p. 23). This social clock is the life course (Settersten, 1999).

The **life course** is a sequence of stages people move through as they age; movement out of one stage and into another is typically marked by a significant event or social transition. Some, like adolescence, are marked by chronological age. Other stages of the life course are less defined and may be entered at varying ages. The clearest example is the lengthy stage of adulthood. At what point and by which criteria do we determine that someone is an adult? There are legal definitions of adulthood, and there are social roles that can indicate movement into adulthood (such as employment, completion of education, marriage, or parenthood). Some of these markers do not occur at a single point in time, and not all of them occur for every person, making many life course transitions fuzzy or gradual. Settersten (2007) suggests that extended life expectancy and recent dramatic changes to the economy, work, and family have significantly altered the roles and expectations that traditionally defined adulthood: "the straight and narrow road into and through adulthood has all but disappeared" (p. 250).

The life course is generally delineated by the roles we are expected to play in particular sequences or within particular age ranges. Atchley (1994) defines the life course as "a cultural ideal consisting of an age-related progression or sequence of roles and group memberships that individuals are expected to follow as they mature and move through life" (p. 154). The life course can be applied to many domains of social life, including the family, education, and work. We can talk about the timing of events in the occupational domain and whether they fit well or poorly with the expectations at the same ages for the family domain. For example, career building comes at an age when many are actively involved in parenting small children, and the reduction of time demands at retirement occurs when society demands few other contributions from older adults.

Events and social roles early in life may shape the entire life course. (Credit: U.S. Census Bureau, Public Information Office [PIO])

Because the life course is subject to social change over time, issues of asynchrony (aspects or their timing not fitting together well) regularly appear.

Indeed, many people feel some pressure to achieve milestones at fairly specific ages. Deciding on a college major and finding a job after graduation are two milestones that many college students feel pressured to accomplish within a certain time frame. Think about the following questions as further evidence of the existence of a life course: Why don't more people work past the age of 65? Why don't people wait until they are in their late thirties to get married? Would you feel comfortable announcing to your family, friends, and professors that you have decided to delay your entry into the job market until you are in your mid-40s and, in the meantime, you will enjoy your leisure and pick up some odd jobs here and there? Why not plan for a period of middle-aged "retirement" followed by a return to the labor force? The life course carries fairly influential ideas about what we are supposed to do and how we are supposed to behave at various stages of life. It is one of the ways in which society shapes our opportunities, decisions, and behaviors at various ages throughout life. Because it is so thoroughly embedded in our culture, the life course remains largely invisible to and unquestioned by us; we do notice, however, when someone does things out of order or at atypical ages.

Social Time

The concept of **social time** (Neugarten & Datan, 1973) refers to the expectations and definitions that society gives to stages of the life course. These stages, and their timing, are not natural or immutable. They are sometimes linked to natural processes, such as physiological development, most clearly from infancy to adolescence. But the roles accessible to us, and their links to age expectations, are malleable and are primarily determined by society. For example, childhood did not exist as a distinct stage of life until industrialization made child labor unnecessary (and countries made it illegal), and formal education became a social institution in the 17th and 18th centuries (Aries, 1962). Similarly, retirement is a fairly recent life stage; life expectancy had to increase sufficiently for enough people to grow old enough to retire, and income support systems generated by higher productivity were created after industrialization (see Chapter 6).

In summary, the life course is a socially constructed, culturally and historically specific sequence of stages, often with connected social roles, that people are expected to move through as they mature and grow older. The life course is closely linked with age/stage-specific social roles, and the entry and exit from those roles are influenced by age norms. These two building blocks of the life course require further examination.

Social Roles

The concept of social role is one of the fundamental building blocks of the life course (and of sociology). It is the mechanism through which real people are linked to the more nebulous structures of social groups and institutions. There are actually two dimensions of the linkage between social roles and people in social structures. First, roles entail socially recognized positions (e.g., father, employee, student) within established social networks; second, role occupants behave in certain ways (i.e., according to specific expectations) when they are in those positions. A **social role** is a set of expected activities and responsibilities that go along with a position we hold in a social network. Conveniently, this important concept has an everyday referent; the term *role* conjures up theatrical images of parts to be played. In fact, a social role is essentially that— a part to be played in social life (Goffman, 1969). A role includes a set of expectations about how people who occupy a particular position will behave—what they will do, what they should do, and what they should not do. For example, you may simultaneously occupy the social roles of sister and employee. Each of these positions is understood to have certain rights and duties, and you are expected to behave differently when you are acting as a sister than you do when you are behaving as an employee. Roles exist in relationship to other roles; that is, each role has a counterpart. Some examples of reciprocal roles are mother/child, teacher/student, friend/friend. Because roles exist in relation to each other, having shared expectations about what each person will do (or not do) in a given role is essential for social interaction and social order. If we had no idea at all about what to expect when we enter a classroom—that is, no idea what the teacher will do or what the students should do—it would be very difficult to accomplish anything. Instead, you have learned that to enact the role of a student you should take a seat rather than stand in front of the room, be quiet until appropriate moments during class, look to what is happening at the front of the room, and take notes on what is presented. Teachers, however, undertake their roles by fulfilling the reciprocal actions. For our purposes, it is sufficient to understand that role implies a more or less organized set of interrelated functions, activities, and behaviors associated with a given social position. Remember the theatrical reference; a role is a script.

A central figure in U.S. social psychology, George Herbert Mead, used the idea of a baseball game to explain the reciprocity of social roles and their importance for social interaction (see Turner, 1956). Mead points out that every player in a baseball game has to learn how to play her own position, but she also has to learn what the responsibilities of the other positions are as well. A good player has to understand the function of every position on the team in order to effectively play her own position. Similarly, role players in society have to understand how their position relates to other roles in the social structure in order to fully participate in society—as an employee how do you behave relative to your coworkers, your boss, or your clients? Role behaviors are structured, but not completely. There is room for variation in how we enact a particular role, such as student, worker, or daughter. Age norms help to define which roles we should undertake at various stages of life and how we should play them.

Sociologist Irving Rosow (1985) raised the question of whether social roles are always attached to a particular position in a social network and vice versa. Often we have clearly defined roles (a well-written script; clear expectations about behavior) attached to a well-defined position in a social structure, including clear interrelationships with other statuses. "Grandmother" is an example of this situation; we have fairly clear (albeit fairly limited) expectations about how someone should and should not behave in that role. And it is a well-defined position in relation to another social position (grandchild). However, Rosow suggests that there are situations where either the role is not clearly defined, or the position is not very specific. "Retired worker" is an example of ill-defined expectations about essential activities. The past connection to the work place help define the position rather than any current social position or linked position. But what is one expected to do or not do as a retired worker? Being a retiree indicates who a person is not, rather than who he is. Rosow questions whether old age itself, because of the multiple

**"I don't know how to act my age.
I've never been my age before!"**

role losses associated with growing older, is a position without substantial role expectations—a "roleless role."

Age Norms

Have you ever seen a small child dressed in a suit and acting very mature, or someone in his or her seventies playing hopscotch? Do these images strike you as remarkable in any way—either positive or negative? Reactions to such incongruities can include amusement, discomfort, or disapproval. Any response whatsoever to someone not "acting their age" is explained by the existence of age norms. The ideas and expectations shared by members of a culture about how a person of a certain age should behave are age norms. **Age norms** are a subset of all social norms, which tell us how to act in various circumstances or toward particular others (e.g., how to act in a museum versus a party, or toward a peer compared to a police officer). These shared rules guide the behavior of members of a society by specifying what behavior and activities are expected, appropriate, and inappropriate. **Norms** are broader and more intangible than social roles; they are the ideas we have deeply learned that are collectively shared by members of a culture. Norms enable us to predict much of a person's behavior while they are playing a role. Later in this chapter we discuss the dangers of overapplication of age norms, which can lead to stereotyping and ageism.

Age norms are "socially governed expectations and sanctions concerning the appropriateness of role acquisitions and behaviors as a function of chronological age" (Burton, 1996, p. 199). For example, we have age norms about entry into roles (driving, voting, marrying, or working) and exit from roles (retirement, graduation). Sometimes these age norms are formalized into law and policy, but sometimes they remain simply *understood* among people who share a common culture. We also share age-related expectations about behavior, dress, and speech. To explore your own age norms about behavior and dress, think about how you would react to an 80-year-old woman wearing a very short skirt, a 70-year-old couple kissing passionately, a 50-year-old man who has never held a full-time job, an 80-year-old woman going to college, or a 17-year-old male who drives very slowly.

There are three important components of age norms: (1) they prescribe and proscribe behavior (i.e., tell us what to do and what not to do), (2) they are shared by some social group (such as society, a work organization, or a subculture), and (3) they carry with them some element of social control or sanction (there are consequences of failing to behave according to the social expectations). Some sociologists would add a fourth key feature: they must actually constrain peoples' behavior to qualify as age norms (see Lawrence, 1996; Settersten & Hagestaad, 1996a, 1996b).

These four components of age norms raise conceptually challenging questions. If age norms must meet these four standards, how do we know if these criteria are met? Who do we ask, and what do we ask them to find out if a particular age norm exists, in particular, whether it constrains behavior? A number of researchers have attempted to answer this question with research on age norms and their operation in society.

A basic dilemma in the study of age norms and the life course is what should be measured: what people typically *do* or what people say they think they (and others) *should do*. Both approaches have been used by researchers. The former strategy—looking at what people typically do—is well-illustrated by the work of Paul Glick (1977), who calculated the median age at major life events for women (such as marriage, birth of first child, marriage of last child, and death of spouse) from the 1900s to the 1970s. His findings, summarized in Exhibit 4.1, showed very little change in women's median age at marriage, but dramatic increases in the number of years spent in marriage until the death of a spouse (not surprising given life expectancy improvements), and a substantial decline in the length of time spent in the childbearing stage as family size declined. Similarly, Matras (1990) documented the "compression of employment" into a smaller proportion of the life span, and Uhlenberg (1996) analyzed the impact of increased life expectancy on opportunity for intergenerational relationships throughout the life course. These demographic patterns speak to typical behaviors, relatively predictable timetables, and to the

EXHIBIT *4.1*

Demographic Description of the Family Life Cycle
in the United States, 1880s–1950s

	Birth of Wife	1880s	1890s	1910s	1920s	1930s	1940s	1950s
Family Life Cycle Stage	Approximate Period of First Marriage	1900s	1910s	1930s	1940s	1950s	1960s	1970s
Median age at								
First marriage		21.4	21.2	21.4	20.7	20.0	20.5	21.2
Birth of first child		23.0	22.9	23.5	22.7	21.4	21.8	22.7
Birth of last child		32.9	32.0	32.0	31.5	31.2	30.1	29.6
Marriage of last child		55.4	54.8	53.2	53.2	53.6	52.7	52.3
Death of one spouse		57.0	59.6	63.7	64.4	65.1	65.1	65.2
Difference between								
Ages at birth of first and last children		9.9	9.1	8.5	8.8	9.8	8.3	6.9
Ages at birth of first and marriage of last child		22.5	22.6	21.2	21.7	22.4	22.6	22.7
Ages at marriage of last child and death of spouse (empty nest)		1.6	4.8	10.5	11.2	11.5	12.4	12.9

Source: Adapted from Glick, 1977; Matras, 1990.

evolution of new or altered life stages. They also indicate social changes, as patterns of family and work life shifted during the 20th century.

The second approach to measuring age norms—asking people what they think are appropriate ages for life events—has been adopted in a number of studies. Exhibit 4.2 presents results from one of the classic studies on this topic (Neugarten et al., 1965). These findings show a high degree of consensus among respondents on appropriate ages for various life stages and events (some of the interesting variations by gender are discussed in our section on modifiers of the life course). Researchers asked respondents about both their own timetables and about what other people expected for timing of life events. There was a difference between personal attitudes and attitudes attributed to others—age norms were consistently acknowledged to exist in other peoples' minds, but were not always accepted as personally valid or constraining (Neugarten et al., 1965). At a later time and in a different culture (New Zealand), other researchers concluded that the degree of consensus and overall pattern of age norms had remained fairly consistent since the Neugarten study (Byrd & Breuss, 1992).

Settersten and Hagestad (1996a) found that age norms are still perceived to be relevant for most major life events for both men and women. Exhibit 4.3 shows the percentages of people who perceived deadlines for major family transitions and the average deadlines for those transitions. A strong majority perceived deadlines for all family transitions except for grown children returning home, a nonnormative event until recent years. The average ages for these deadlines varied for women and for men. Women are expected to marry and complete childbearing earlier than men. While the averages were interesting, the variations are also important. There was

EXHIBIT 4.2

Consensus in a Middle-Class, Middle-Aged Sample Regarding Various Age-Related Characteristics

	Age Range Designated as Appropriate or Expected	Percent Who Concur	
		Men (N=50)	Women (N=43)
Best age for a man to marry	20–25	80	90
Best age for a woman to marry	19–24	85	90
When most people should become grandparents	45–50	84	79
Best age for most people to finish school and go to work	20–22	86	82
When most men should be settled on a career	24–26	74	64
When most men should hold their top jobs	45–50	71	58
When most people should be ready to retire	60–65	83	86
A young man	18–22	84	83
A middle-aged man	40–50	86	75
An old man	65–75	75	57
A young woman	18–24	89	88
A middle-aged woman	50–59	87	77
An old woman	60–75	83	87
When a man has the most responsibilities	35–50	86	80
When a man accomplishes most	40–50	82	71
The prime of life for a man	35–50	86	80
When a woman has the most responsibilities	25–40	93	91
When a woman accomplishes most	30–45	94	92
A good-looking woman	20–35	92	92

Source: Neugarten, Moore, and Lowe, 1965.

a lot of variation in the ages given for completion of childbearing for men (more than 7 years), and for grandparenthood (more than 7 years), but less diversity for the acceptable age for young adults leaving home. This important study suggests that there is a perceived timetable but that there is some flexibility in the timing of some family events.

Settersten and Hagestad (1996a) also found that, although most respondents perceive age norms, they did not perceive any negative outcomes for violating these deadlines. "Being late" did not carry with it significant consequences. Lashbrook (1996) found fairly consistent age norms for promotions in work organizations but little relationship between being "off time" (either early or late in relation to the social timetable) and job well-being for middle-aged men. The lack of sanction for being off time and the flexibility in timing led Settersten and Hagestad (1996a) to conclude that cultural timetables and age norms "may be an important force shaping the life course, but their influence may instead be secondary . . . and may be much more flexible in individuals' minds than researchers have assumed" (p. 187).

Age Norms and Life Course Flexibility

People seem to subscribe to ideas about the ages at which it is appropriate to be at certain stages in one's life, but they do not feel particularly pressured to conform to those expectations. These two facts seem inconsistent. This apparent inconsistency can be explained in several ways. Foner (1996) suggests that perhaps age norms are only part of the age structuring of society, and age norms are flexible across social contexts. Settersten and Hagestad (1996a, 1996b) offer the idea that cultural timetables—age norms that we perceive for everyone—can be different from personal timetables that individuals use to construct their life courses.

EXHIBIT **4.3**

Perceived Age Deadlines for Major Family Transitions

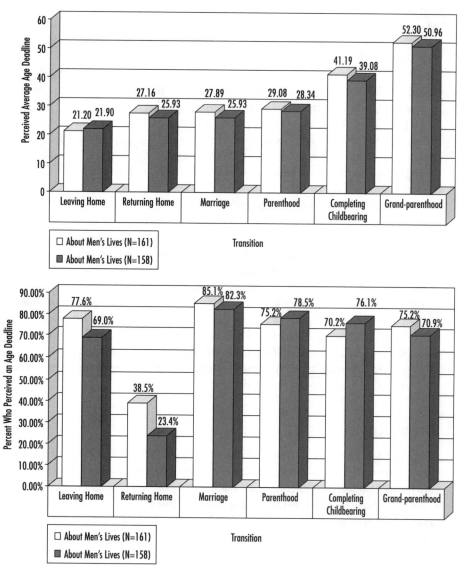

Source: Settersten & Hagestad, 1996a.

This latter explanation reminds us that age structures and other social forces are not totally deterministic. Humans do take some active role in the structuring of their own lives. In fact, people have an impact on social structures and social forces. Individuals are not merely reactive; they are, to some extent, "proactive architects" of their own life course trajectories (George, 1996, p. 254). One of the interesting questions in the study of the life course is the interplay between individual choice and constraints imposed by society. Settersten (2003) summarizes this reciprocal influence as "agency with structure" and identifies a major challenge for researchers to "conceptualize the life course as *actively created by individuals and groups, but within the confines of the social world in which they exist*" (p. 30).

Age Norms and Ageism

As we discussed previously, age norms are shared expectations for how a person should behave or what they should do based on their age. Earlier in this discussion we asked you to think about your reactions to how people were dressed and how they acted (e.g., playing hopscotch). These are examples of general age norms; they are not specifically related to a role. Our expectations about how people should behave and what kinds of roles they should be engaged in because of their age provide some level of social order and organization.

However, an overapplication of these expectations can lead to ageism. **Ageism,** as we discussed in Chapter 1, is "a systematic stereotyping of and discrimination against people because they are old, just as racism and sexism accomplish this with skin color and gender" (Butler, 1989, p. 243). While ageism may be related to society's use of age to organize social life and expectations for behavior, it is not a necessary by-product of age norms. In other cultures and at other times in history, older people were valued differently. Ageism is a product of complicated demographic, political, ideological, and economic forces (see Scrutton, 1996, for a discussion of the foundations of ageism).

Ageism is alive and well in U.S. society. Reflecting on his 30 years of research on this topic, gerontologist Erdman Palmore (2005) expressed optimism that ageism can be overcome in our society, but he concluded that, "ageism makes a great difference in our society and culture . . . It is a social disease much like racism and sexism" (p. 90). In an intriguing exposé of our discrimination against older people, author Patricia Moore used makeup and dress to "disguise" herself as an older woman. Her book *Disguised* (1985) documents the experiences she had traveling as an old woman and presenting herself in various situations. She encountered both negative and positive forms of ageism; she was ignored, patronized, deferred to, ridiculed, and offered assistance. These were not the reactions she received when she presented herself as a young woman. Even participants at conferences on aging treated Ms. Moore differently depending on the age she portrayed, often excluding her from conversation or treating her as if she were invisible when she was dressed as an older woman (Ferraro, 2007).

Structural Lag

Although age norms are important influences, Matilda Riley (1996) eloquently argues against "life-course reductionism," which treats social structures, such as age norms, as simply the context for individual lives. She urges an examination of how changes come about in norms and social structures. "As lives change, new norms develop and become widely accepted and institutionalized in structural transformations" (Riley, 1996, p. 258). But, changes in norms do not always occur at the same time as changes in other aspects of society. Structural lag is the term used to describe this mismatch between changing expectations about aging (among other social phenomena) and the inertia of social institutions, laws, and organizations. Structural lag is based on Riley's age stratification theory, which pulls together some of the most important concepts (such as cohort flow, age graded opportunity structures, and the aging of society) in the sociology of aging. Because this idea captures so well the power, fluidity, and evolution of the life course, we present it in further detail.

In their discussion of the concept, Riley, Kahn, and Foner (1994) clarify the link between real human lives and the more formal, less tangible structure of social roles. They define **structural lag** as the tendency for the social structure of roles, norms, and social institutions to change more slowly, and thus lag behind, changes in peoples' lives. For example, the majority of people retire around age 65. Because of increases in life expectancy, most people will live an average of 15 to 20 years in retirement. But what roles or opportunities exist for people after retirement? As Rosow (1985) asked decades ago, what exactly do we expect a retired person to do? What links do retirees have to the life of the larger society? Society has not kept up with the increase in life expectancy by building opportunities and responsibilities for the new stage of life. Society has lagged behind the changes in peoples' lives—structural lag.

Older persons have much to offer via volunteerism in schools and other areas where others may benefit from the wealth of their accumulated knowledge. Society should work on expanding the ways it taps into the vast resource of the older population's wisdom and experience. (Credit: Mike Payne, courtesy of the Ohio Department of Aging)

Another example of the mismatch between society and peoples' lives is the persistence of age norms about the timing for completion of education at a relatively young age. The notion that education and career training should be complete by age 25 or 30 "lags behind individual need for continual retraining in the workplace over the person's whole life; these norms are not in accord with the capabilities of older people and their motivations" (Foner, 1996, p. 222). These education and work examples illustrate the gaps that have emerged between peoples' longer (and changing) lives and the timing of opportunities, roles, and rewards in the life course.

Structural lag occurs, according to Riley and her colleagues (1994), because human lives, including the timing of life course events, change more rapidly than do the corresponding social structures and institutions. Riley and Riley (1994) argue that we currently organize social life in a very age-segregated way. Young people are involved in education, middle-aged people are focused on work, and older people are immersed in the world of leisure. A more flexible, age-integrated arrangement would open up these three areas of social life for people of all ages. Exhibit 4.4 illustrates these two different arrangements of activity through lifetimes. The Rileys suggest that we should be moving to an age-integrated structure to accommodate the needs, interests, abilities, and contributions of people of all ages. These scholars are optimistic that "age will lose its current power to determine when people should enter or leave these basic social structures (work, education, retirement); nor will age any longer constrain expectations as to how people should perform" (Riley & Riley, 1994, p. 110). Whether or not we reach such a state where age is truly irrelevant in the near future, there are some changes in age structures that reflect the Rileys' position. Lifelong learning programs (such as the Institute for Learning in Retirement, and Exploritas) and over-60 audit policies at many institutions of higher education have opened up the opportunity for continued learning for many older people. Increasing numbers of adults are returning to seek more advanced degrees to benefit the development of their careers, or in response to changing tides in the labor market. The integration of service learning, internships or community service into the curriculum at many colleges, also acknowledges the importance of crossing the artificial work/education barrier that is implied by classroom-only curricula. More flexible career trajectories, including protected time off for child or elder care, suggest a loosening of the boundary between work and leisure.

This idea can be used to support a position of advocacy for older adults. One of the clear messages in the discussion of structural lag is the unfulfilled potential of a large proportion of the older population due to lack of formal outlets and recognized positions in which they can

EXHIBIT   *4.4*

Two Idealized Age Structures

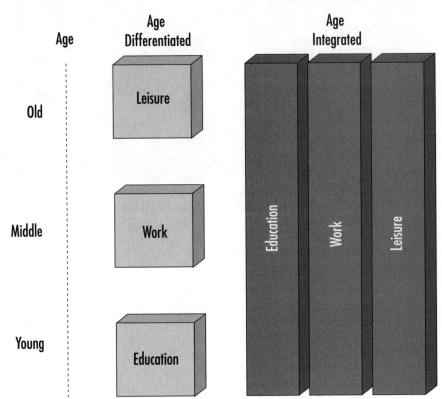

Source: Riley & Riley, 1994.

make their contributions. This attention to the costly lack of opportunities for contribution is the backdrop for the growing body of work on **productive aging**—the recognition that older people sometimes want to and often can continue to be involved in volunteer or paid work. This important area of research is discussed further in Chapter 11.

Life Course Perspective in Gerontology

The concept of the life course is essential for understanding how individual lives unfold as people age. History, economics, and social forces affect individuals throughout their lives, and early experiences shape later ones. Extensive scholarly attention to this complex interplay of human agency, individual biographies, and social structures has elevated the life course from a useful idea to one of the most influential theoretical frameworks in the field of gerontology. As one eminent scholar notes, "For all those who wish to analyze social structure at the level of individual action and thus at the level where its impact is most visible and where it is reproduced, the life course approach has become indispensable" (Kohli, 2007, p. 253).

The life course perspective is comprehensive; it encompasses and generates a broad array of research questions, from micro to macro. But it is also grounded in well-established and accepted principles. As discussed earlier in this chapter, some of the most important guiding principles of the life course perspective are that human development is a lifelong process, individuals construct their own life course within the constraints of history and social circumstance, and the life course of individuals is shaped by historical times and places they experience over their lifetime (Elder, Johnson, & Crosnoe, 2007). These assumptions underlie all of the questions and interpretations generated by life course research; this common foundation aids in the accumulation of knowledge about the unfolding of human lives across time, history, and social context.

The utility and adaptability of the life course perspective is evident in the growing array of empirical and theoretical questions it addresses. Scholars are questioning the extent to which the life course is becoming more flexible and less chronologically standardized (Kohli, 2007; Settersten, 2003). The traditional tripartitioned life course based on work (preparing to work, working, retiring from work) is no longer the only model for understanding the patterning of roles across life stages (Henretta, 2003; Kohli, 2007). Variability in the life course across culture, gender, race, ethnicity, and social class is another fruitful direction for gerontology research based in the life course perspective. For example, Dannefer (2005) suggests that future studies should consider global differences in life course patterns and opportunities. In sum, the life course perspective is helping to chart a new course for research in social gerontology.

Summary

Society shapes life stages and individual experiences of aging. Americans place high value on a sense of individual achievement and responsibility, and so it is often difficult for us to embrace the notion that our destinies are not completely the product of our individual actions and choices. Having a sociological imagination helps us to better understand our own and others' social experiences. We can see that our personal circumstances arise, at least in part, from a particular social and historical context. The ways in which experiences in later life are patterned by gender, race, and social class provide examples of the impact and constraints of social location.

Some sociologists take a purely deterministic view and argue that there is no such thing as personal choice; they suggest that all action and experience are the result of social location and social influences. Others argue that social influences do indeed have an impact but that human beings retain free will and are never truly completely socialized. While this debate is ongoing, many scholars are more interested in the interplay between social constraints and individual actions. The idea of reciprocal influence has been presented a few times in this chapter; people are influenced by social forces such as age norms, but they also, collectively, can have an impact on age norms and social structures. "People's lives can only be fully understood as they influence, and are influenced by, the surrounding social structure of roles, groups, nation states, and other social and cultural institutions" (Riley, 1996, p. 256).

In our society is it very popular to focus on individual attitudes, the power of positive thinking, and individual responsibility. Comments such as "Aging is all in your mind," or "You're only as old as you feel" reflect those values. Now that you have been thinking about the ways in which society shapes our lives, we ask you to reconsider such statements. Is it really so simple? Is personal attitude all that matters? Or are there age-related social forces that do have an impact on whether we can find a job and how young we can possibly feel?

Web Wise

American Psychological Association—Division 20: Adult Development and Aging
http://apadiv20.phhp.ufl.edu/
Division 20 is the section of the American Psychological Association that is devoted to the study of human development throughout the adult years, including old age. The Web page offers links to recent research on topics such as Alzheimer's disease, depression, behavioral health, and emotional health. A recent visit to this Web page offered links to articles on the genetic components of Alzheimer's disease and the role of social networks in protecting against the effects of Alzheimer's disease.

The Emergence of Developmental Science

Social theories about aging attempt to explain a wide range of phenomena, from individual adaptation through life to societal changes driven by cohorts. As you know, *theories* are frameworks that help us to organize information and understand our world. Many of the major social theories about aging are presented in detail in various chapters in this book. In this chapter we discuss human development in later life, the ways in which social forces shape our lives across the life course, and the interplay between individual agency and social structure. Adequate conceptualization and careful investigation of the complex questions related to the many dimensions of aging requires interdisciplinary theory and methods. Settersten (2005a, 2005b) terms this emerging perspective **developmental science** and makes the case for "a new social studies of old people and old age." This approach is taking shape in conceptual and empirical work on the life course in the areas of leisure (Hendricks & Cutler, 2003), work (Henretta, 2003), health (George, 2003), and families (Hagestad, 2003). This emerging scientific framework represents a new stage for gerontology. Where do new theories come from, and how are they developed? How can we understand the way that new questions and new framework develop in our field? Theories reflect historically grounded views of what the appropriate questions are for us to ask about age or aging, as well as what should be the focal subject matter (Ferraro, 2007). For example, questions about how people adapt to retirement received a lot of attention in the 1970s and 1980s. During this era, the attention of researchers, policy makers, and the general public was turned to the experiences of aging individuals, partly because we were beginning to recognize the tremendous growth of the older population. In this era more people were retired than ever before. Today, in contrast to the focus on individuals' retirements, the research on retirement tends to focus more on larger-scale political and economic questions, including how to finance retirement and regulate employer pensions.

Theories "furnish the boundaries for what we know . . . A theoretical orientation becomes a habit of the mind . . . and does not easily recognize contradictory evidence" (Hendricks, 1992, pp. 32–33). Theories create competing explanations, or even raise different kinds of questions that might be asked about a particular subject, such as retirement, housing, or lengthy marriages. To understand how a given theory reflects the historical period during which it evolved, Hendricks discusses "generations of theory." He suggests that there are three generations of theory on the social dimensions of aging. The first generation of theory focused on individual adaptation and adjustment—how individuals react to (or do not react to) changes and continuities in their lives over time. In the second generation, theories began to focus on structural processes and the social organization that surround cohorts of aging individuals, directing attention to such questions as how the labor force responds to retirement or how groups such as the family adapt to more long-lived members. In the third generation, theories of aging synthesized these individual- and structural-level emphases of the earlier generations, examining questions relating multiple levels from micro to macro (continuum from individual to societal, as we discuss in Chapter 1). In this phase, theories became more "dynamic and political . . . recognizing the important of structure . . . but also seeing people as intentional actors involved in creating social situation and their lives" (Hendricks, 1992, p. 37). In turning our attention to the ways in which theory development is a product of a particular historical and social context, Hendricks (1992) and Ferraro (2007) are pointing out that knowledge itself is a social construction—a product of dominant ideas and assumptions. The emerging "developmental science" of the life course is a well-articulated example of a new generation of theory, full of promise. "This cluster of ideas, old and new, will bring opportunities to reflect on what the field of gerontology now is, reclaim some of what it once was, and dream about what it might one day become" (Settersten, 2005b, p. S179).

As you encounter more detailed presentations of many sociological theories of aging in this text, you can deepen your understanding of those theories by comparing and contrasting them. Does it focus on individual actions and adaptations, the social structure, or both? To what "generation" does the theory belong? What assumptions does a theory make about the appropriate topics to explore? What exactly does the theory try to explain, and where does it look for answers? These questions can help you analyze and categorize the variety of social gerontological theories of aging.

American Sociological Association—Section on Aging and the Life Course
http://www.asanet.org/sectionaging/
Just as the psychologists have a specialized division focusing on aging and the life course, the American Sociological Association also has a membership section addressing issues related to aging. This home page gives you access to recent newsletters, membership information, data resources, and a description of sociology's role in the study of aging and life course issues. Included are links to other aging organizations.

Brave Old World   http://columbia.news21.com/2010/about.html
As part of a project supported by the Carnegie-Knight Initiative on the Future of Journalism Education, students at Columbia University filmed interviews with older people and their families, gerontologists, and advocacy groups to "portray the aging America of today and tomorrow." The Web site provides links to those interviews, as well as short summaries about very current and sometimes controversial topics in gerontology, including telemedicine, senior housing options, and saving for retirement.

Key Terms

ageism	generativity	productive aging
age norms	gerotranscendence	social role
developmental science	human development	social time
ego-integrity	life course	structural lag
environmental gerontology	norms	

Questions for Thought and Discussion

1. To what extent do you feel constrained by age norms and life course expectations? How aware are you and your friends of these expectations?
2. Informally interview a handful of people and ask them some specific age norm questions, such as the age at which a person should be settled into a career, or the age at which they expect to marry (if at all). What do these findings tell you about the power of age norms?
3. Do you think that the stages of human development in later life (such as gerotranscendence and elderhood) are possible to achieve only when we are old? Why or why not?
4. How do societies "use" age? Why does chronological age make any difference whatsoever in our lives? Give some examples of the ways in which social definitions of age, including ageism, have affected your life (or someone you know well).

Love, Sex, and Longevity

A old song from the 1950s said, "Love and marriage . . . go together like a horse and carriage." Perhaps, but which comes first? If you are a thoroughly socialized product of U.S. culture, you probably feel strongly that people should get married after they fall in love. However, in other cultures people assume that love will grow within marriage. Love is not a necessary condition to their decision to marry. Researchers asked college students from 11 countries whether they would marry someone they did not love. Only about 5% of the students in the United States and Australia said they would marry someone with the right qualities even if they did not love him or her. About 50% of the students from India and Pakistan said they would marry without love (Levine, Sato, Hashimoto, & Verma, 1995). The cultural practice of arranged marriages still prevails in countries such as India, helping to explain the acceptability of marrying first, then letting love develop later. In India, people still use the term *love marriages* to describe the small but growing proportion of Indian couples who decide to marry on their own, without parental arrangements, approval, and decision making.

Although love may not be the basis for all decisions to marry in India, it is still highly valued. However, cultural definitions of love vary. In India, love is based on long-term commitment and devotion to the family. In contrast, U.S. culture highly prizes romantic love—an idealized view of partners and relationships—based on passion, erotic attraction, and media images of ever-growing ardor and tenderness.

Where do these different cultural definitions of love come from? There are a lot of factors that contribute to this ephemeral (and culturally-based) concept. We suggest that one of those factors is a quite unromantic, somewhat prosaic demographic element: the average life expectancy in a society. In young countries, such as India, where life expectancy is relatively low, romance may be a luxury. In such societies, people marry younger and begin childbearing earlier because life is shorter. Older societies, like the United States where people live longer, are more likely to place cultural value on romance and to favor falling in love before marriage.

We discuss elsewhere the emergence of childhood as a differentiated stage of life. Changes in life expectancy were part of the conditions necessary for that new stage of life to develop. People had to live long enough for there to be time in life devoted to education and learning how to become an adult. Similarly, we can argue intuitively that living long enough is a necessary precondition for having the time to search for a desirable partner and to enjoy courtship and engagement prior to marriage. These stages prior to marriage are devoted to romance—the search for the ideal partner; the excitement, passion, and the anticipation of the new relationship; getting to know each other; and making plans for a life together—all of which fuel a romantic view of love and marriage. When we marry in our 20s or 30s and live until our 80s, we have the luxury of time to search for the perfect partner, therefore, we have the opportunity to sustain the ideal of romantic love. We are also confronted with the prospect of five or six decades with our marriage partners, so our choices in this matter have quite an impact on our lives. The adage "marry in haste, repent at leisure" alludes to the care that one should take in this decision, given the potential length of time spent in marriage.

Longer life expectancy can provide the basis for cultural values about romantic love to develop. These two factors together—longevity and preference for romantic love—are also linked to divorce patterns. "Our culture emphasizes romantic love as a basis for marriage, rendering relationships vulnerable to collapse as sexual passion subsides. There is now widespread support for the notion that one may end a marriage in favor of a new relationship simply to renew excitement and romance" (Macionis, 1997, p. 471). And, because we live long enough, we have time to pursue, develop, and sustain more than one romance-based marital relationship. Serial monogamy—having more than one spouse sequentially but not simultaneously—is a phenomenon unique to societies with long life expectancies. Just as an extended life course provides opportunities for second careers in the job market, it also provides for second and third chances at love relationships. Having the time to spend in search of new and improved relationships makes it possible to sustain the illusion of an ideal partner, one with the most important elements in romantic love.

Obviously there are factors in addition to longevity that shape a society's values about love and marriage. Other cultural values play important roles. The importance of extended family, the value placed on independence, and the primacy of parental authority are all cultural values that can influence attitudes toward love and marriage. Simmons, Vom Kolke, and Hideko (1986) compared the attitudes of students toward love and marriage. They found that Japanese students, who live in a culture that highly values respect toward parental decisions and the importance of the family, placed a significantly lower value on romantic love than did students in the United States or West Germany. The predominance of arranged marriages in India reflects the very strong familial system (Gupta, 1976), while in the United States the emphasis on independence and autonomy of individuals would preclude such a practice.

Countries with higher life expectancies thus have the demographic foundation for romanticized views of love and marriage. The life course in these societies is long enough and differentiated enough for time to be spent in the search for at least one perfect partner and in the development of those love relationships. But is there a time in the life course when people lose interest in this vital endeavor? Do people lose interest in love, romance, and sex as they grow older? According to the stereotypes, they do. According to older people, they do not. The Association of Reproductive Health Professionals (2002) has designed a continuing medical education program titled "Mature Sexuality" to improve the awareness of health care professionals about older people's sexuality. In one of the most extensive studies on sexuality and aging, Wiley and Bortz (1996) found that more than two-thirds of the middle-aged and older adults in their study were sexually active. While 60% reported a decrease in frequency of sexual activity over the past decade, 32% reported no change, and 8% reported an increase—and this research predates the availability of prescription drugs for the treatment of erectile dysfunction, such as sildenafil citrate (Viagra®). About 50% of the women and 70% of the men in this study stated a desire for increased sexual activity. Availability of a partner is, obviously, one significant factor influencing sexual activity. One study found that more than 80% of married people in their 70s were still sexually active (Brecher reported in Hillier & Barrow, 1999). Summarizing findings from a number of studies of sexuality in later life, Hillier and Barrow (1999) report additional findings that challenge stereotypes about sex, love, and aging. Overall, patterns of sexual activity are established in mid-life and remain fairly continuous throughout old age, barring serious illness or disability. Studies also show that nursing home residents often retain their interest in sexuality. Research also reports that three-fourths of older people said their lovemaking had improved with time; 15% of people aged 60 and older reported increased sexual activity over the course of a 10-year longitudinal study. The rate of masturbation increases for women as they get older, partly related to the lack of available sexual partners. Some people have a first homosexual experience in later life. Therefore, sexuality does not cease in later life.

It is not uncommon to respond to the idea of love, romance, and sex among older people in an ageist, stereotypical way. We may find continued sexual activity hard to believe and even distasteful, or we may label it as touching and "cute." Both responses discriminate against older people by treating them as different and by presuming that age brings with it a fundamental change in our interest in and ability to be sexual. However, according to older people themselves, interest in sexuality and need for intimacy persist throughout the life course.

Aging and the Family: Personal and Institutional Contexts 5

The Family as an Institution

Families, the cornerstone of all human societies, have been discovered in every human culture in history. **Family** is the social institution that is perhaps closest to us; we immediately see its influence in our everyday lives. Everyone has a common sense understanding of what is meant when we say *family,* yet there is difficulty coming to a social consensus on its definition. Most attention focuses on the concept of the family as the group socially responsible for bearing and rearing children, rather than on the family relationships that continue as an important organizing force throughout our lives. Contemporary Western societies have a wide variety of family forms, but most also had different family structures in the past (Hareven, 1995); family structures and norms are both culturally and historically specific. The contemporary family structure has been described as the **modified extended family** (Litwak, 1960). The modified extended family acknowledges that although kin may reside in separate households, often at great distance, strong bonds of affection, identity, and support remain.

Research on *later-life families*—those families beyond the child-rearing years (Brubaker, 1990)—began in the 1960s as a reaction to the neglect of families beyond early marriage and child-bearing (Parsons, 1959; Parsons & Bales, 1955; Sussman & Burchinal, 1968). Family researchers, however, quickly remedied this limited view of kinship by demonstrating both the active interchanges of support and the bonds of affection that exist among extended kin (Hill, 1965; Litwak, 1965; Shanas, 1967; Sussman & Burchinal, 1968). Families are, in fact, some of the most important age-integrating organizations in society. While many other social contexts segregate us by age, families necessarily bring together individuals of various ages and generations in social groups sharing mutual interests, experiences, cultures, and values. It is through family membership that many of us develop our initial interest in and knowledge of other stages of the life course.

Nonetheless, the centrality of the family as an organizing force in societies cannot be overemphasized.

While many other social contexts segregate us by age, families necessarily bring together individuals of various ages and generations. (Credit: Mike Payne, courtesy of the Ohio Department of Aging)

Many of our closest, most enduring social linkages in life are located in the family. In this chapter we first examine the macro view of family as a key social institution and then focus on the inter-personal aspects of families that we experience in everyday life.

The Meanings of Generation

Linking various ages in the family are the biological generations that are key to the family's structure. Although the term **generation** has multiple meanings, its meaning within the family is clear and familiar to most of us. In this context generations are "lineage descent positions within families" (Bengtson, Cutler, Mangen, & Marshall, 1985, p. 305). Grandparent, parent, and child generations in family systems form clearly recognizable social linkages connecting individuals of various ages and cohorts into one family. The popularity of genealogical research and the development of family trees reflect our interest in better understanding these generational linkages to our historical predecessors in earlier generations.

In studying family relationships, we encounter a great deal of difficulty in distinguishing the effects of cohort membership from those of aging, especially because most of the research on later-life families has been conducted only since the 1970s, showing the aging of only a few family cohorts. When we generalize from the experience of such historically limited cohorts we are risking *cohort centrism*. For example, our knowledge of later-life marriage is currently based on the experiences of couples from cohorts born between approximately 1885 and 1945, but both marriage and gender norms have changed greatly in recent years. This makes it difficult to predict whether future cohorts of married couples and families will age in the same ways. Cohort-centrism remains a limitation in our knowledge about aging in families.

Aspects of Family Variation

Not all families are alike. Not only do they vary by size, composition, and closeness, but researchers also have identified several social dimensions of diversity on which families vary. One is the family's stage of development, reflecting the size of the family, the ages of its members, and the types of challenges it faces. (See the "Applying Theory" section on family life cycle theory later in this chapter). Other differences identified by researchers relate to race/ethnicity and social class.

A considerable body of research has examined the differences by race or ethnicity in how families address the aging of their members. Much of the research has focused on Blacks, but recently more attention has been paid to families in other cultural groups, particularly Hispanic and Asian groups (see Aboderin, 2004; Agree, Biddlecom, Chang, & Perez, 2002; Coleman, Ganong, & Rothrauff, 2006; Han, Choi, Kim, Lee, & Kim, 2008; Laumann, Leitsch, & Waite, 2008). The bulk of research on Black families suggests that kin relationships demonstrate more interdependence among family members and close others (such as church members) (Shuey & Hardy, 2003; Sussman, 1985). For example, Black elders are more often cared for at home by relatives, rather than by formal service providers or nursing homes, when their health fails (Miller, McFall, & Campbell, 1994). However, such differences may reflect not only cultural variations in family norms (Shuey & Hardy, 2003) but also experiences of economic disadvantage or discrimination in access to health care services.

Differences among middle-class Whites, Blacks, and Hispanics are sometimes attributed to stronger norms of familism in the latter groups, a cultural emphasis on communal sharing of resources directed toward those most in need, and a greater emphasis on family responsibilities. Some researchers have emphasized the apparently greater flexibility in kinship roles among Black families in particular, including a greater likelihood of establishing **fictive kinship** (granting someone who is unrelated the title and rights of a family member—"She is like a sister to me") and **surrogate family relationships**, whereby family members or others take on an active role responsibility by replacing an absent parent, child, or caregiver (Burton & DeVries, 1995; Johnson, 1995).

Although some research indicates African Americans are more apt to establish fictive kinship roles with nonrelatives, supportive relationships engendering the closeness of family occur among those in all ethnic groups. (Credit: Mike Payne, courtesy of the Ohio Department of Aging)

Most research has shown a higher level of intergenerational exchange and support in Black families than in White families (Mitchell & Register, 1984; Mutran, 1985; Shuey & Hardy, 2003), but efforts to identify the distinct influences of race or ethnicity in families are often obscured by their connections with income and social class. When researchers compare families across race or ethnicity, they have often unavoidably included the effects of income or class differences as well (Mitchell & Register, 1984; Mutran, 1985). Separating these factors can be difficult, but it is more possible today with a growing middle class in the Hispanic and Black populations. In an early study, Mitchell and Register found that slightly more Black elders shared a residence with a child or a grandchild, but the major finding of the research was that race makes only a very small difference in family relationships and that social class is more important in explaining family patterns. Shuey and Hardy (2003), however, demonstrated that Black and Hispanic couples were still more likely than White couples to provide assistance to parents or parents-in-law even when the effects of economic differences are taken into account.

In terms of social class, the great majority of research has focused attention on middle-class families. Early research on working-class households showed extended kin living in closer proximity than middle-class families, substantial exchanges of support and assistance, and that marital relationships were less central to family life (Bengtson, Rosenthal, & Burton, 1990; Lopata, 1979; Townsend, 1968).

Core Norms and Expectations of Family Relationships

Family relationships are often thought of simply as bonds based on caring and love. These critical social linkages are, however, more complex than simply the affection that is characteristic of some, but not all, kinship ties. What keeps family members together when relationships are stressed? Why do adult siblings often assist each other in many ways but seldom help each other financially? Why is it often stressful if an adult child moves back in with his parents following a divorce? What structures the separations between kin and households in such a way as to promote privacy and autonomy?

Clearly family relationships are governed by culturally based rules and social norms (discussed in Chapter 4) regarding how members should act toward one another. These cultural

EXHIBIT 5.1

Dynamics of Family Norms

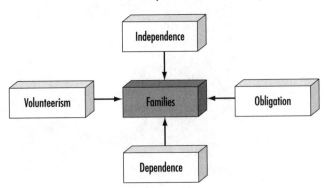

norms for families are specialized in three ways. First, they are specific to particular role relationships. For example, the issue of privacy may be very different between a teenager and a parent than between a husband and a wife; yet both relationships operate under some social norms regarding privacy. Second, these variations in familial norms may be systematically related to social class, race, ethnicity, religion, or region. One example, noted previously, is the stronger emphasis on mutual help in Black families reported by many researchers. Third, the norms may vary across individual families, so that particular families, besides sharing a joint history and membership in other social groups, may have their own unique family norms (traditions) to add to the basic cultural norms.

These rules, the social norms governing family life, include two major dynamics, portrayed in Exhibit 5.1. These dimensions include the degree of **independence** or **dependence** of bonds among members and the extent to which relationships are ruled by voluntarism or obligation. These two underlying themes, though certainly not exhaustive in terms of family norms, are central to understanding the social issues faced by families as aging changes them and their individual members.

Independence and Dependence

Central to the relationships within the family are issues of *independence* and *dependence*. Young children are physically and emotionally dependent on their parents, and we expect spouses to have dependencies on each other throughout their marriage. Yet, we do not expect children to remain dependent on their parents forever, nor is a high level of economic, social, or emotional interdependence anticipated among adult siblings (Suitor, Pillemer, Keeton, & Robison, 1994). These norms may be violated, as when unmarried adult children remain in the home of their parents or return there following a divorce or employment disruption (White & Peterson, 1995). Fears of violating norms of independence in adulthood and later life also shape the relationships between older adults and their adult offspring. The vigor of such norms is indicated by the fact that dependency of an elderly parent, often termed "being a burden to the children," is a concern often voiced by middle-class Americans (Sussman, 1985).

Living arrangements are indicative of the norm of generational independence in the United States. Significant numbers of both sexes—but especially women—live alone in later life; relatively few women or men live in "other" arrangements, which include, among other options, living with relatives (see Exhibit 5.2). These data also show notable gender differences in the majority of men living with spouses, compared to less than half of women. However, as these U.S. data clearly show, neither men nor women, except those in cultural groups with norms

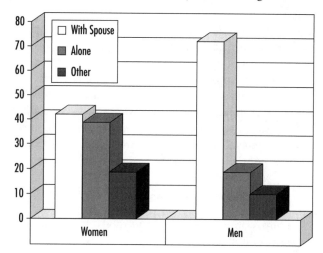

EXHIBIT 5.2

Living Arrangements of Older Americans by Sex and Age, 2008

Source: Federal Interagency Forum on Aging-Related Statistics, 2008.

supporting this behavior, plan to live with relatives in later life. Instead, a majority of older Americans prefer to live independently (Federal Interagency Forum on Aging-Related Statistics, 2008). With adequate finances, health, and housing, the majority of older adults prefer to live independently of their adult children, although some may prefer to live in close proximity (in line with the modified extended family). This pattern of proximity in separate households has been called **intimacy at a distance** (Rosenmayr & Kockeis, 1963), where emotional and social bonds between parents and children are maintained across modest distances. This household autonomy underpins the independence of each of the generations because neither generation is subject to the rule of the other as household head.

Norms about interdependence of family members have changed over time as families have moved from shared economic activity (such as a family farm or business) toward relationships based more on social and emotional bonds among kin (Hareven, 1995). Cohler (1983) suggests that the core values of industrial capitalism—self-reliance and autonomy—inhibit the expression of mutual dependency among two or more generations of adults. Instead, there is pressure to maintain at least the guise of independence between related adults linked by familial bonds other than marriage.

Generational independence is also reflected in the norm of reciprocity, which operates in most social relationships, to provide an acceptable way of managing dependency. In family relationships, as in the larger society, the **norm of reciprocity** dictates that individuals who are recipients of benefits from others have a debt or obligation until a comparable favor can be returned (Silverstein, 2006). The common statement "I owe you a favor" is an expression of this norm in everyday life.

Although reciprocity is generally expected, families often exhibit some flexibility in how the obligation is fulfilled. In some cases, reciprocity may be direct and involve exactly equivalent goods or services, as when siblings take turns helping each other move from one home to another. In others, reciprocity may involve exchanges of goods or services deemed equivalent, as when parents give their adult children money for a down payment on a home in exchange for assistance with household repairs. Finally, the exchange may be indirect, with support received from one family member paid back in the form of support to another. For example, reciprocity norms may be deemed as fulfilled when parents provide for their children, who, when grown, pay the debt back by caring well for the grandchildren of the original givers (Antonucci, 1990). In this case, the indirect repayment of the obligation fulfills an assumption that ultimately all members of the family group benefit through the ongoing assistance passed down through the generations.

There is evidence from longitudinal research that reciprocity has an influence on relationships between adults and their aging parents. In a study of multiple generations (the youngest age 16–20) started in 1971, follow-ups in 1985 and 1997 showed that the adults who had received more support as teens returned more support to their aging parent(s) compared to those who received less. Mothers received more support than fathers, and support levels increased over time among those parents who survived to 1997 (Silverstein, Conroy, Wang, Giarrusso, & Bengtson, 2002). Even in families where there was little support to teenagers, advancing parental age generated some support from adult children, perhaps from a sense of filial obligation, a social norm discussed in the next section (Silverstein et al., 2002).

Voluntarism and Obligation

Family relationships differ from those between friends in that kinship carries with it a higher degree of **obligation**. "Family are supposed to perform in times of need, friends are not so obligated" (Antonucci, 1990, p. 215). Expectations of mutual responsibility and support have been at the heart of most family systems across cultures and throughout history (Antonucci, 1990; Jarrett, 1985), but the degree of **voluntarism** in these relationships (the extent to which individuals have choices regarding whether and when to meet individual versus family needs) has varied widely.

The extent to which *obligation* drives family relationships has changed. Since the 19th century, families in the United States and many other Western cultures have moved toward greater voluntarism, with families held together more by sentiment compared with past eras where family ties were more strongly based on obligation or duty (Hareven, 1994; Hess & Waring, 1978). While parental duties remain strong obligations, one area of change that has been studied is that of adult children's obligations toward their aging parents. **Filial obligation** (or filial duty) refers to the responsibility that children have toward their parents, particularly in later life. As with other norms, filial obligation varies across cultures and historical periods. In some societies and locations, including many U.S. states, filial obligation is mandated by laws, but many of these provisions are not actively enforced.

Until World War II, norms for White families in the United States dictated that one child, most typically a younger daughter, would forgo or delay marriage in order to provide care for her aged parents until their deaths (Hareven, 1995). Although this practice has largely disappeared, contemporary U.S. society still has strong filial support expectations for older parents requiring help (Finley, Roberts, & Banahan, 1988; Hareven, 1995). But instead of living with the older relative, a son or daughter will more commonly provide a combination of emotional, practical, and financial support to enable the parent to live independently or in supportive housing.

Not all adult children feel these obligations equally, creating potential strain in the parent–child and sibling relationships (Jarrett, 1985). While both males and females claimed to accept responsibility toward their mothers, the level of responsibility varied by the degree of affection the child felt toward the parent and their residential proximity (Finley et al., 1988). For fathers, however, the sense of obligation was also diminished if there had been prior conflicts for daughters but not among sons.

Family Life Cycle Theory and Individual Dependency in the Family

Family life cycle theory is one theoretical "lens" that has been especially pertinent to the study of families as they age. Originated by Evelyn Duvall and her colleagues in the 1950s, when the focus in family research was on the nuclear family unit, **family life cycle theory** focuses attention on the systematic changes that occur in family life over time in conjunction with the maturation of its members. "Families, like individual persons, progress from birth to death in the steps and patterns inherent in the human condition" (Duvall & Miller, 1985, p. 20). According to this developmental approach, family relationships, goals, and routines are differentiated by stages of development. Families with preschool-age children, for example, are quite different in their concerns than are families with teenagers moving toward adulthood or *postparental families,* whose children have left the household for college, jobs, or marriage. The theory recognizes these stage differences and focuses on the patterns of change expected as members of the nuclear family mature.

Because the original theory was developed after World War II in a time of high fertility, births clustered fairly closely together, and low divorce rates, it emerged with a set of stages that were driven by the maturation of the oldest child. For example, when the oldest child started school or became an adolescent, according to this formulation, the family moved into a new stage. This emphasis on stages has been criticized for focusing attention on a traditional, idealized, nuclear family in which family events occur on time and without disruption (Cohler & Altergott, 1995). It fails to recognize the contemporary variations in family life (e.g., families may have both teenagers and preschoolers at the same time) or to account for nonnormative patterns, such as childlessness, divorce and remarriage, or single parenthood.

More recently, attention to this theory has turned to understanding the transitions experienced by the family or its members rather than assigning them to particular stages. This emphasis on family dynamics rather than on stages opens the theory to greater flexibility in examining the life course of the family (Cohler & Altergott, 1995). The family life cycle theory has accomplished one vital goal—it focused attention on the fact that family life is dynamic over time, involving predictable changes. It has also moved our attention beyond just the start of family life to include postparental and later-life families.

One key area of change, mirrored in stages of family development, has to do with the development of children and their dependence on the family. Your own experience is probably one of moving from a high degree of dependence as a baby to greater independence as you moved toward and into adulthood. Later, others may be reliant on you, if you become a partner or parent, and even later you may have a second phase of dependency, should you experience failing health in advanced old age. Those changes in dependency also shaped your relationships with others in myriad ways. Family life cycle theory points out that our relationships are not static. Just as individuals grow and change with the passage of time, so too does each nuclear family unit.

Families as a Personal Network

Beyond its macro-level influences as a social institution, the family is also a very personal group with which we interact throughout our lifetimes. Early gerontological theorists hypothesized that the family's importance to individuals increased as they aged and as other social roles and statuses (such as employment) fell away through disengagement (Cumming & Henry, 1961). Whatever *life space* remained to the older individual was believed to be reallocated to remaining roles, including familial roles (Neugarten, Moore, & Lowe, 1968). We have since learned that families carry importance to individuals throughout their lives, with the family's span now expanding through increasing longevity to permit many shared decades with parents, spouses, siblings, and children.

Because of gendered views of family roles, early gerontologists also believed that women experienced aging with more ease than men. Women were thought to have two family based advantages. First, their primary identity with the family, as opposed to employment, guaranteed a strong source of continuity throughout life. Second, because family roles involve continual changes with the addition, maturation, and departures of family members, women were thought to be more accustomed to change than men. Male identity, presumed to be anchored in employment rather than the family, would, in contrast, be suddenly interrupted at retirement (Maddox, 1968). We now recognize that these ideas are overly simplistic stereotypes. Women and men hold core identities both in family and employment; these gender-based assumptions, however, shaped the questions of early studies of later-life families.

Of the aging topics studied from a social perspective, perhaps the largest body of research is associated with family relationships and their impact on the older individual. Because the material in this area is so extensive, the information presented in this section is necessarily selective.

Strengths in Later-Life Families

Families are resilient and resourceful groups that connect us to the past and to the future in meaningful ways. In addition, families provide a close network of emotional and practical support, which shifts over time as members and their capacities and involvements change. Family members are key to the *convoys of support* that provide continuity in the social networks of individuals as they move through time (Antonucci & Akiyama, 1987). Typically, individuals hold high expectations for the roles that the family members play in meeting their emotional, social, and personal needs (Cherlin, 2004).

As discussed in Chapter 4, the American focus on individualism is relatively new in historical terms and characterizes Westernized cultures rather than family systems everywhere in the world (Cherlin, 2004). In earlier historical periods in the United Sates, families in the largely agricultural economy were units of basic survival for their members (see Giarrusso, Feng, & Bengtson, 2004). Today most children seek education and employment independent of their families and may move far away to pursue careers, fundamentally changing the linkages of the family from ones of obligation and economic interdependence to bonds that are more voluntary and emotional (Hess & Waring, 1978).

Despite the strengths and positive connotations of family bonds, kin relationships are not all close and affectionate, including those involving older adults. Just as supportive relationships can have a positive impact on the lives of older adults, negative ones may add to psychological distress and increase risks of chronic illness (Finch & Graziano, 2001; Wolff & Agree, 2004). Some kin bonds may remain distant or hostile over many decades as a result of earlier conflicts. For example, if a father and teenage son had a difficult relationship, punctuated by serious conflict, it is unlikely that this conflicted history will evaporate without a trace in later decades or that they will develop unambiguously warm and affectionate bonds (Suitor et al., 1994). Negative aspects of family relationships may coexist simultaneously with positive ones in the same relationship, reminding us not to stereotype family relationships of older adults as being either purely positive or purely negative (Pillemer & Suitor, 2004). The normative obligations for family relationships also mean that relatives, even those with some negative feelings, will often provide some level of family support (Krause & Rook, 2003). Regardless of these changes and limitations, the value of the family remains pivotal to the vast majority of people of all ages.

Continuity and Change in Later-Life Families

Brubaker (1990) defines a *later-life family* as one that is moving through the child-launching phase and into the postparental phase, in which couples may eventually experience retirement, health limitations, and widowhood. Spousal, parental, and sibling relationships are well established by this stage and typically exhibit considerable continuity in how they operate. One approach to understanding family relationships in later life is to examine these continuities.

Family members are typically involved to some degree with one another's lives, providing advice and emotional support and sometimes giving or seeking assistance both across and within generations. This mutual exchange is such an ongoing routine that it is hardly noticed as anything special or important by members of the family. It is these regular, ongoing activities and traditions that constitute the bulk of family relationships over the years (Matthews, 2002). At times, however, a crisis, such as a divorce or serious illness, intervenes to upset the routine operation of established kin relationships. In these circumstances, family relationships may change, with shifts in living arrangements, patterns of assistance, or interaction. Major transition events may call for at least a temporary and sometimes a permanent modification of the established patterns that have characterized family relationships up to that time. Keep in mind that, while the attention of the research literature focuses on change and crisis, the great majority of time that families share is based in the routine, not extraordinary, patterns of family relations.

For most of the adult years, later-life families are governed by the norm of independence. Despite continuing patterns of relationships with both positive and negative elements and ongoing support exchanged in the modified extended family, two contrasting myths have characterized discussions about these families. The first, and perhaps most persistent, myth is that adult children neglect and abandon their older parents (Shanas, 1979a, 1979b). This persistent theme of abandonment was described in the quotation that opens this chapter. The second mythic theme is that of family solidarity, support, and affection as universally descriptive of parent–child bonds in later life. Although these themes have traded places in terms of prominence over time, both probably reflect unrealistic stereotyping of parent–child relationships as completely positive or negative. As is often the case, the truth (and considerable diversity) lies somewhere in between these extremes.

There has been a good deal of research on the levels and types of interactions between adult generations in a family. This research shows that older persons are not isolated from their families and that a majority of interactions across the generations are positive (Bengtson et al., 1985). Interestingly, it is often assumed that *more* interaction is always *better* for the elderly family members, ignoring the possibility of prior conflict in familial relationships (Antonucci, 1990). Among such families a majority recognize some conflicts in their relationship along with prominent positive aspects (Antonucci, 1990; Clarke, Preston, Raksin, & Bengtson, 1999; Lueschler & Pillemer, 1998). In an effort to overcome the myth of family abandonment of the elderly, researchers may have gone too far in emphasizing support and consensus within the family.

Key Familial Roles and Relationships

Despite being a group, families have largely been studied from the perspective of an individual member. Research studies tend to survey or interview single family members as units of analysis, not **dyads** (two-person relationships) or the complete family network. Therefore, in most research we see the family through the eyes of only one of its participants, a limited view for such a complex system of roles and linkages. Consequently, much of the research in this section focuses on views of the individual about dyadic or multiperson relationships within the family. Further, some relationships, including those between siblings and parent–child relationships (except when it relates to caregiving), are seldom studied. Consequently, most of these *normal* exchanges, whether supportive or tense or some combination of the two, are not well represented in research. We focus here on the more studied relationships between spouses and between grandparents and grandchildren.

Spouses/Aging Couples

The majority of older men (almost 80% of those age 65–74 and 66% of those age 75 and older) were listed as "currently married" in 2008 (U.S. Census Bureau, 2010b). For women the picture is quite different, with 56.8% of women age 65–74, but only 30.8% of women age 75 or older, currently married. Instead, the growing category of older women is the widowed, reflecting women's higher life expectancy as well as having married slightly older men. Fewer women or men in today's older cohorts were divorced or never married—reflecting the experience of those cohorts where most people were married and remained so; these figures will change in the future (see Exhibit 5.3). Data on marital status overlook older individuals who are part of long-term couples without being married (Huyck, 1995). These uncounted individuals are often erroneously presumed to be without an intimate partner because they are not legally married.

For persons born in the United States at the turn of the past century marriage was much shorter than today. Given average life expectancies of about 51 years for White women and

EXHIBIT **5.3**

Marital Status by Sex and Age, 2008

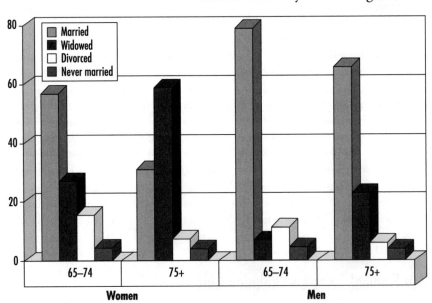

Source: U.S. Census Bureau, 2010b.

48 years for White males (35 and 32.5 years, respectively, for Black women and men) in 1900, it is not surprising that many persons were widowed before their children were grown (National Center for Health Statistics, 1989; U.S. Census Bureau, 1991a). More recently, couples who marry at older ages (28 is the median for males, 26 for females) can, because of increased life expectancy, expect to be married for 50 or more years (Infoplease, 2009). Of course, about half of first marriages do not make it to that landmark, but the reason today is primarily divorce rather than death of a spouse (Cherlin, 2004). This increasing potential duration of marriage has led to suggestions, only half humorous, that higher divorce rates may be one outcome of greater longevity. Couples who might tolerate a problematic marital relationship for 20 years may choose not to endure it for 50 years, instead opting for divorce.

Marriage does not remain static over the second half of adult life because the roles and responsibilities of the partners change with the launching of children, the deaths of older kin, and the addition of grandparent roles (Huyck, 1995). Important differences also exist between marriage cohorts (groups married at different times in history) as to how household labor is divided and how gender relations are structured. Here it is possible to confuse the effects of aging with cohort differences. Many of today's middle-class retiree couples had wives who were homemakers and continue to do much of the household work in retirement years; baby boomer couples will reach retirement with more two-earner couples who have pursued a more equal division of household chores. One type of chore that remains in the female domain is the work involved in maintaining family relationships (called **kin-keeping**) (Bengtson et al., 1990; Rogers, 1995). Women do more than men to plan birthdays, holiday parties, fulfill traditions of culture and religion, and other work to keep family members connected through time.

Marital Satisfaction Throughout the Life Course

Among the earliest and most persistent themes in the study of couples in later life is that of **marital satisfaction**—the degree to which couples are satisfied with their partners and marital relationships. In an early study on marital satisfaction, with a sample of 400 couples married in the early 1930s, Pineo (1961) reported decline in marital satisfaction between the honeymoon and the 20-year mark, a change that Pineo dubbed *marital disenchantment.* Other studies have confirmed a decline in satisfaction over the first years of marriage (Lee, 1988). Later cross-sectional data for different marital cohorts suggested that marital satisfaction follows a curvilinear path— from a peak during the honeymoon to a valley during the rearing of children, followed by an improvement as couples move through child launching and into later life. Gary Lee (1988) contends that role overload (e.g., conflicting demands of employment and parenting) might explain lower marital satisfaction in midlife and better scores for couples in later life. Couples who experienced their golden wedding anniversary, elite marital survivors, were asked to recall their levels of marital satisfaction at various times during the family life cycle. Their results, interestingly, showed the U-shaped pattern for both men and women, but with wives reporting a deeper decline in marital happiness than men (Condie, 1989).

This research has been criticized for concluding that individual couples go through this curvilinear pattern because the researchers (1) compared across cohorts with very different marital experiences; (2) relied on the average marital satisfaction score to describe this highly variable trait of marriages; (3) ignored the survivorship effect (as time passes, many of the unhappiest couples get divorced, leaving behind a pool of marital survivors who were probably among the happiest all along); or (4) relied on a recall of happiness decades earlier (see Vaillant & Vaillant, 1993; Weishaus & Field, 1988). We also must be cautious not to generalize beyond these cohorts of married couples (cohort-centrism); ultimately, longitudinal studies will help to better define whether and how marital satisfaction changes through time.

Many married couples observe that their love grows stronger in the later years. (Credit: Mike Payne, courtesy of the Ohio Department of Aging)

Termination of Marriage: Widows and Widowers

The sex difference in average life expectancy dictates that more women than men will survive their spouses (Kinsella & Taeuber, 1993). Past age 75, widows outnumbered widowers 4 to 1 in the United States in 2008 (U.S. Census Bureau, 2010b). As Exhibit 5.4 shows, the incidence of widowhood increases overall with age, but the gender gap remains. Added to the life-expectancy differential are the facts that: (1) women tend to marry men older than themselves, and (2) widowers have ample opportunity to remarry, should they wish to do so (Bengtson et al., 1990). Both because of their larger numbers and more pressing problems (e.g., higher rates of poverty), most widowhood research has focused on women rather than men.

The transition from married to widowed is one of the most stressful in life, removing a central role as wife or husband and the relationship to the late spouse, changing social relationships with friends, collapsing the division of labor in the household, modifying relationships with kin and friends, and often diminishing economic well-being. Marital roles are highly salient to individuals of all ages, structuring much of their identity and social activities. Even an unhappy marriage influences one's self-concept and activities. The loss of this relationship has both expected and unexpected consequences. Widowed women, for example, experience a disruption in their friendship networks, which are (at least for the middle class) based on couples that socialized together. Upon being widowed, a widow/widower becomes a "fifth wheel," creating social discomfort in the former friendship group of couples (Lopata, 1979). Gradually, most widowed persons modify their friendships, spending less time with married friends and more with peers who are widowed. In addition, widowhood has been connected with social and physical vulnerability, increasing the mortality rate and risk of nursing home placement over time for both sexes (Elwert & Christakis, 2008; Nihtila & Martikainen, 2008).

In earlier cohorts the gender-based task division in marriage was more strict, such that many newly widowed women and men were unfamiliar with (and thus unable to successfully perform) the tasks delegated to their partners. Among the oldest cohorts of women, these unfamiliar tasks often included driving, managing finances, or overseeing household repairs (Lund, Caserta, Dimond, & Shaffer, 1989). Among males, who often went from the home of their parents into marriage, many never learned how to cook or manage a household or a social network. That strict division of labor meant that the surviving spouse was vulnerable in terms of the other spouse's tasks; widowers might not eat properly and widows might manage their

EXHIBIT   *5.4*

Numbers of Men and Women Widowed by Age, 2008 (in Thousands)

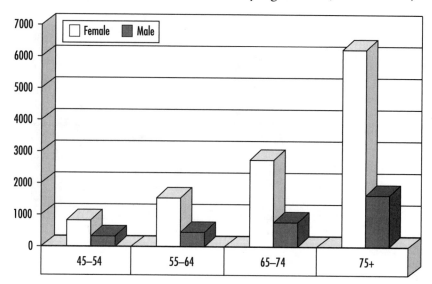

Source: U.S. Census Bureau, 2010.

money poorly. In more recent cohorts of couples, this strict division attenuates, until we reach young cohorts of today, who typically spend some time living on their own, learning basic survival skills once divided into strict male or female duties. While tasks still are typically divided between the couple during their marriage, fewer enter widowhood without some experience in these tasks.

Changes in family relationships following widowhood include intensified relationships with adult children as sons and daughters assist the surviving parent in the period following the death (Lopata, 1979). This increased volume of interaction with children is permanent for widows; widowers' volume of contact with adult children returns to lower levels after a period of mourning (Morgan, 1984). Why this difference? One possible explanation is the emotionally closer relationships with mothers (Finley et al., 1988) or a concern that widows are more vulnerable following the loss of their spouses (Morgan, 1984). In either case, widowed persons in the United States, conforming to norms of independence and "intimacy at a distance," seldom move in with adult children if they are healthy and have adequate income, unless their culture or religion dictates otherwise.

As Exhibit 5.5 shows, rates of poverty are significantly higher for widowed women than men and are greater among those older than age 75. Because the poverty threshold is very low ($10,326 for a single person age 65 and older), researchers also often examine the "near poor," those within 125% or 150% of these levels, who may not be quite poor enough to be eligible for some programs but struggle to afford daily living. Economic security is especially tenuous for widows, in part because of the rules for Social Security and private pensions (see Chapter 7 for further details). Because both systems were established primarily to protect workers (male), Social Security, upon the death of the beneficiary, reduces the benefits to a dependent spouse to 66% of the couple's benefit, although research suggests that the survivor needs 80% of the couple's previous income to maintain her standard of living (Burkhauser & Smeeding, 1994). In addition, until recently many pensions did not provide survivor benefits. Thus, many widows were forced to adjust economically from sharing a Social Security benefit *plus* private pension to having only two-thirds of the prior Social Security benefit. In addition, movement over recent decades to greater reliance on 401(k)-type pension programs (see Chapter 6)

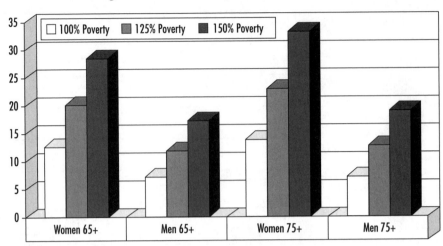

EXHIBIT 5.5

Risks of Being Poor/Near Poor by Household Status and Sex: 2007

Source: U.S. Census Bureau, 2008d.

increases widowed persons' risk of becoming poor because many exclude spouse protection (Johnson, Uccello, & Goldwyn, 2005). Under these conditions, is it any wonder that poverty among older, widowed women has been among the most persistent social problems in America (Burkhauser & Smeeding, 1994)?

Grandparents

What pictures come to mind when thinking about grandparents? Typically, we carry mental images (fostered by advertisers) that feature advanced age, gray hair, leisure and hobbies, kindness, and celebration of family rituals and holiday traditions. Do grandparents really fit this image? What exactly do grandparents do?

A majority of older adults are parents; most have also become grandparents. Although being a grandparent is a familial role we associate with later life, most individuals enter grandparenthood while still in midlife, married, employed, and with one or more surviving parents and a child still living at home (Bengtson et al., 1990). For many women this means spending nearly one-half of her life as a grandparent. The timing of grandparenthood is, however, highly variable, depending in large measure on the age at which an individual bears their own children. Grandparenting can start as early as one's 30s if two generations in a row became adolescent parents; on the other hand, if multiple generations defer having children until age 30 or older, one may not become a grandparent until well into his or her 60s or even 70s (Burton, 1996). The vast majority of grandparents are in between these extremes.

Once entered, grandparenting is an enduring role, lasting until the grandparent's death. Grandparenting has expanded because of greater longevity, and more grandparents get to see their grandchildren grow up, graduate, marry, and even become parents themselves. Over this span, neither grandparents nor grandchildren remain static. But just what are the social roles (expected duties and rights) of grandparents? Given that only recently have large numbers of people lived long enough to spend much time as grandparents, the lack of clear social norms for this role is understandable. This cultural void gives families the chance to structure the role in a variety of ways, but it also provides them with few guidelines on how they *should* act as grandparents (Kennedy, 1990). Probably as a result, much of the early research on grandparenting

WE CAN'T MOVE IN WITH MY PARENTS. THEY'RE STILL LIVING WITH **THEIR** PARENTS...

focused on how adults view and structure these relationships with grandchildren. The role varies from a voluntary and intermittent one to holding major responsibility, serving in a parent-surrogate role in what has been dubbed a "grandfamily."

Voluntary Grandparenting in Middle-Class Families

One aspect of the research on grandparenting has focused on the varied styles and levels of involvement that reflect this less-structured family role. Early research, mostly on White middle-class grandparents, attempted to identify the *styles* of grandparenting, showing a wide variation in how the relationships operate (Roberto, 1990), including elements such as having fun and passing on family history and traditions. Relatively few clear-cut duties are mandated for grandparents because their roles typically are not critical to the survival of children. Less research has examined the relationship from the perspective of the grandchild. One study (Kennedy, 1990) asked more than 700 college students about their grandparents' roles. "Students tended to agree most strongly with items that described grandparents as being loving, helping and comforting, as providing role models, and sharing family history, as being persons who are important in the lives of young people and persons with whom they have fun" (Kennedy, 1990, pp. 45–46). Within the sample, female students emphasized the closeness of the relationships, and Black students described grandparenting as a more active role. With such limited expectations, there remains a wide range of ways in which grandparents could fulfill this role.

Relationships between grandparents and grandchildren are built within a larger context of family relationships. The middle generation plays a critical role, called the **lineage bridge**, linking the older and younger generations (Thompson & Walker, 1987). The nature of the relationships between the grandparents and parents, serving as lineage bridges, will inevitably shape the emotional closeness, geographic proximity, and frequency and types of interaction between grandparents and grandchildren. This linkage becomes critical in the case of divorce, where paternal grandparents may lose contact with grandchildren unless they maintain ties to their former daughter-in-law or exercise legal rights to visitation, which are available in some states (Roberto, 1990).

Surrogate Parenting and Grandfamilies

Beyond differences based on the respective ages of grandparent and grandchild, other factors that influence these bonds include economic status, race/ethnicity, and gender. According to estimates from the U.S. Census, 6.4 million U.S. children live in a household with at least one grandparent (Kreider, 2008); 1.6 million of these households had no parent present. These percentages have been growing over time. If neither parent is present or if the oldest generation is head of household, the situation is referred to as a *grandfamily* (Saluter, 1996; U.S. Census Bureau, 2003).

The percentages sharing a home across three generations are higher for Black than for White children. Almost 14% of Black children live with grandparents, and more than one-third of those children have neither of their parents living with them, creating a skipped-generation household. Nearly 6% of Black adults older than age 45 care for a grandchild, with more women than men, more disadvantaged than well-off, and more physically challenged individuals likely to have a grandchild in their care—including those who share a residence (Minkler & Fuller-Thompson, 2005). The percentage of Asian children living with grandparents is nearly as high (13.2%), but in these households the predominant pattern is for both parents to live there, creating a multigenerational family. Smaller but significant percentages of White (8.1%) and Hispanic grandchildren (11.5%) share a household with at least one grandparent (U.S. Census Bureau, 2008b). Exhibit 5.6 shows significant differences by race in the percentages of grandchildren who reside with their grandparents, showing the notable differences in the household composition. Most of these households are headed by grandparents.

In many cases, grandparents also serve as *surrogate parents,* undertaking the responsibilities of absent parent(s). Grandparents acting as surrogate parents take on short- or long-term responsibility for the care of grandchildren because of the problems of their adult children (including illness, job loss, drug abuse, homelessness, and incarceration) and because policy changes in the 1980s and 1990s supported "kinship care" when children needed to be placed in foster homes (Cherlin & Furstenberg, 1986; Hogan, Eggebeen, & Clogg, 1993; Minkler & Fuller-Thompson, 2005; U.S. Census Bureau, 1991a, 2003). This unexpected resumption of parenting responsibilities can be stressful for the grandparents, who may themselves be facing challenges associated with health or income (Burton & DeVries, 1995).

Families as Caregivers

As the number of very old adults in the population has grown, an incredible amount of research attention has focused on family caregiving. In examining this topic, one might conclude that caregiving is the major dimension of family relationships for older adults. But consider this issue further. Even if many individuals now live into their 80s or 90s, older adults do not suddenly

EXHIBIT   5.6

Percentage of Children Living in Households With Grandparents by Race/Ethnicity

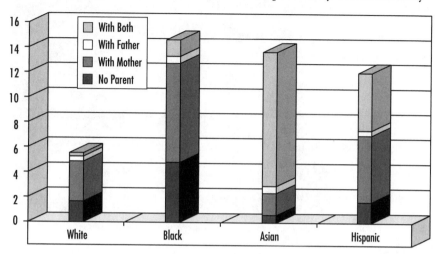

Source: U.S. Census Bureau, 2008b.

require support when they turn 65 or 70. Instead, any need for care is typically delayed to more advanced ages; for some individuals, death is sudden and preceded by little illness or dependency. In recent decades typical families have experienced many years with older relatives during which they have few dependencies across generations. Therefore, although caregiving is a challenge for some families and an issue in the larger society, it is not universal or a lengthy span for every family. More importantly, when caregiving needs arise, it is not a purely negative experience, as we explore in more detail later.

Context of Caregiving: Family Norms of Mutual Assistance

Families have always served both their members and the larger society by providing various types of support and assistance to their members (Cherlin, 2004). Caregiving has received considerable research attention because it is essential to dependent members, including children, disabled/disadvantaged adults, or frail elders. These supports vary across the life course; across class, culture, and ethnic groups; and historically. Within families support flows both within and across generational boundaries. Caregiving to elders should be understood as one aspect of the mutual support in families rather than as something "new" or "distinct" (Davey, Savla, & Janke, 2004). Wives and husbands, children, and parents continue to care for one another across the years. Sarah Matthews examined patterns of assistance toward parents older than age 75 and found that both gender and the history of family relationships are keys to understanding which child provides care, how it is shared among relatives, and how the older adult participates (Matthews, 2002). In other words, support is a natural, ongoing aspect of family relationships that shifts over time as needs and capacities of family members change.

Intergenerational Support

There is a 50-year research literature revealing ongoing patterns of exchange both within and across households of the modified extended family. Pioneering work by Reuben Hill (1970)

Our increasing life span allows more years to cherish spouses, children, grandchildren, great-grandchildren, and other family members. (Credit: E. J. Hanna and Mike Payne, courtesy of the Ohio Department of Aging)

examined the exchanges among three generation families in the 1950s. Hill found that family members in all generations of his sample's mostly White, middle-class families were involved in giving and receiving assistance, including care during illness, child care, financial aid, emotional support, and household management (see Exhibit 5.7). Hill's research found the middle (adult) generation to be the largest net givers of support—that is, they provided more types of help to both their elderly parents and their young-adult children than they received. Younger and older generations, in contrast, gave less and received more. Hill's analysis did not take into account issues such as the frequency with which each type of assistance might be given—for example, child care might be daily, whereas assistance during illness might occur only a few times each year—or the amount of time and energy each task demanded.

Amato, Rezac, and Booth (1995) replicated Hill's work in 1995 (see Exhibit 5.7). In Amato et al.'s study, young adult children, all of whom lived with their parents, were much more likely than Hill's sample to provide assistance with household tasks, and many more said they both gave and received advice. Fewer received child-care help than the earlier study, but most were not yet parents. Both studies confirm that active exchange patterns are normal in families.

Another study with a different sample (Hogan, Eggebeen, & Clogg, 1993) examined intergenerational support in a national sample of more than 5,000 adults who had both surviving parents and one or more children under 18 living at home. Four types of support were examined: financial, caregiving (to a child or parent), assistance with household tasks, and emotional support or advice. More than half (53%) of middle-generation adults were low exchangers, giving or receiving very little across generations, and 11% were high exchangers, typically both giving and receiving a variety of support with their aging parents. In this sample (and appropriately to the kinkeeper role) women were more active as exchangers. Black families were, contrary to the findings of previous research, *less* likely to be involved in intergenerational exchanges, a result explained by a shortage of resources within their families. This study also revealed another dynamic. When adult children had several siblings, each was less likely to receive support from their older parents, who had to divide their support and attention among several offspring. Older parents, on the other hand, improved the odds of being recipients of support with each additional adult child. Riley (1983) suggests that relatively low levels of assistance found in cross-sectional studies for any given point in time may mask a **latent kin matrix**, "a web of continually shifting linkages that provide the potential for activating and intensifying close kin

EXHIBIT   **5.7**

Percentage of Young Adults Receiving or Giving Intergenerational Support

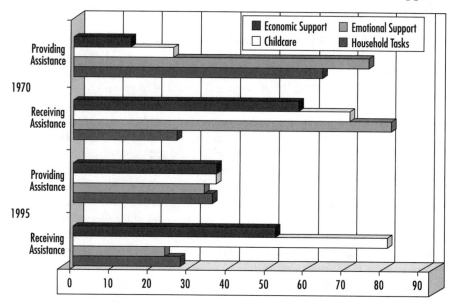

relationships" when and if they are needed (p. 441). Thus, current exchange and support (realized support) may be much more limited than the potential for exchange and support should greater need arise (anticipated or potential support).

Although this research continues to show that older adults receive considerable assistance from adult children, especially in crises, it would be erroneous to conclude that they are only the recipients of support. These studies also reveal the ongoing support of many types that older adults provide to their grown children and grandchildren (Walker, Martin, & Jones, 1992). As we saw in the earlier discussion of *grandfamilies,* most multigenerational households are created in response to the needs (economic, housing, child care) of adult children rather than the needs of older adults, as was once believed (Ward, Logan, & Spitze, 1992). Therefore, in considering the family exchanges of support, both giving and receiving assistance of various types is characteristic of a majority of older adults.

Family Members as Caregivers to Frail Elders

In times of illness or disability, a majority of older adults receive both emotional and practical assistance from kin. Turning to others for this support can be thought of as a means of compensating for physical or cognitive limitations. It is estimated that 70%–80% of informal care for frail and disabled elders is provided by *family caregivers,* rather than by paid caregivers or settings such as assisted-living or nursing homes (Dwyer, 1995; Wolff & Kasper, 2006). Adult children constitute approximately one-third of family caregivers, but their contributions are surpassed by those of older spouses (Stone, Cafferata, & Sangl, 1987). Other relatives (siblings, grandchildren, nieces/nephews) are also included among informal caregivers. Estimates also suggest that 5% to 10% of older adults receive help from non-kin, voluntary caregivers who are neighbors, friends, or community members. These other caregivers, who sometimes have lengthy personal relationships, provide significant support, including some cases where fictive kinship is established (Barker, 2002). Although family and other informal caregivers are sometimes limited in their skills in health care, for example, there are pressures toward placing more responsibility for skilled tasks in the hands of family or friends (informal caregivers) to control health care costs (Glazer, 1993). Older adults who lack these supportive ties are at greater risk for institutionalization when they can no longer care for themselves (see review by Antonucci & Akiyama, 1995).

Who Are Family Caregivers?

More than two decades of research on family caregiving has established that most adults receive much of the help they need from a single, *primary caregiver*. More than half of primary caregivers receive some level of assistance from one or more secondary caregivers (see review by Gatz, Bengtson, & Blum, 1990; Wolff & Kasper, 2006). The provision of care to older adults often follows a hierarchical pattern (Cantor, 1983; Horowitz, 1985), starting with available kin, with the role often falling first to an able spouse (Allen, Goldscheider, & Ciambrone, 1999). Because male marriage partners are generally older, more wives than husbands face being a primary caregiver (Chappell, 1990). Daily contact for care also requires proximity, ruling out adult children living at great distances. In some cases an unmarried child or one without her own children will be tapped as caregiver on the assumption that this person will face fewer role conflicts (Brody, 1985). It is unlikely that an adult child with a distant or conflicted relationship with the parent will undertake substantial caregiving unless there is no other alternative.

If the older person is widowed with multiple children, a decision must be made about which child undertakes primary responsibility or how duties are to be shared (Matthews, 2002; Stone et al., 1987). Elements including gender, residential proximity, marital status, and relationship quality influence the selection of a primary caregiver and the way support is shared among kin. The percentage of primary caregivers who are males is increasing (40% in 2004) (Gandel, 2009), but hours of care provided per week still vary by relationship and gender. Wives provided a median of 28 hours per week, husbands 15; daughters and sons differed less, with 13 hours for females and 10 for males (Center on an Aging Society, 2004). More male caregivers continue employment, limiting their time contributions (Gandel, 2009).

There are notable differences in how sons and daughters perform the caregiver role (Horowitz, 1985; Matthews, 2002), differing in the types of care they provided and their motivations. Aside from the emotional support commonly provided by both sons and daughters, more of the "hands-on" duty for transportation, household chores, meal preparation, and personal care fell to daughters. Daughters reported more stress in association with their caregiving duties, largely because of their greater commitment in time and task responsibility (Horowitz, 1985). Sons contributed via male gender-specific tasks (financial management, dealing with bureaucracies) or gender-neutral tasks, but spent less time and did fewer tasks than daughters. Most married sons also involved their spouses in caregiving, whereas fewer than half of daughters did so. Sons appear to be more motivated by norms of obligation, whereas daughters are more often motivated by the affection of the relationship, confirming the kin-keeping role of women in the family system (Silverstein, Parrott, & Bengtson, 1995).

Women in the Middle

As with kin-keeping, women provide the bulk of caregiving to elders, while providing ongoing services and care to members of their households (Center on an Aging Society, 2004). In a national study, about two-thirds of primary caregivers were women (Wolff & Kasper, 2006). Early research by Brody (1981) identified the risk of being a **woman in the middle** (also known as being in the **sandwich generation**). This phenomenon refers to those women who simultaneously have responsibilities for their offspring and for assisting frail parents or parents-in-law. Both increased longevity and decreased fertility (providing fewer potential adult-child caregivers) are thought to accentuate the problem (Gandel, 2009; Kinsella & He, 2009). Although this structural problem of being in the middle may be a serious one for those upon whose shoulders it falls (Brody, 2004), data suggest that the problem is not as common as once believed. First, the peak age for caregivers occurs between the ages of 45 and 64 (40% of 1999 caregivers, both spouses and children fell into this wide age range) (Wolff & Kasper, 2006). People ages 55 or older are typically in the final stages of childrearing; thus, at ages where parental disability becomes common, a shrinking subset of women face caregiving responsibility toward children (Rosenthal, Matthews, & Marshall, 1991). Second, as longevity increases and disability is delayed, the onset of caregiving responsibilities for a parent should occur at later ages, further reducing the potential for being "in the middle" (Cantor, 1995). Only 11% of informal caregivers to older adults were also caring for children under the age of 15 in their homes (Wolff & Kasper, 2006).

What the *woman in the middle* approach did not address was the other major role conflict, that is, being caught between employment and caring for an aged parent (Brody, 2004). Recent data suggest that nearly one in three caregivers is employed; almost half of them experience some conflict, reductions in their hours of work, or rearranging of their schedules to accommodate caregiving (Wolff & Kasper, 2006). The relatively low percentage of caregivers who are employed reflects the fact that the median age for caregivers is 62 and that 40% are spouses, who are similar in age to the care recipient (Wolff & Kasper, 2006). When the work/caregiver role conflict occurs (Matthews & Rosenthal, 1993), it may detract from effectiveness at work and sometimes results in quitting. Although family leave (without pay) is now available for limited time periods, the ongoing demands of care for a parent with chronic health problems often force choices between reducing or stopping work (with the attendant loss of income and savings or pensions) or purchasing care services. Therefore, the work/caregiving dilemma, especially for adult daughters, remains fraught with the potential for role conflict (Brody, 2004).

Caregiver Burden and Rewards

Families provide a wide array of assistance to kin with health limitations, most of it for routine tasks of everyday living (Chappell, 1990; National Alliance for Caregiving, 1997). Despite the obvious benefits to older adults, the stress experienced in providing such care may decrease the physical and psychological health of the caregiver (Center on an Aging Society, 2004; Schulz, Visintainer, & Williamson, 1990) or even have negative effects for their marriages (Bookwala, 2009). Caregivers sometimes experience stress and **caregiver burden** in conjunction with high level or prolonged duration of caregiving responsibilities. The experience of burden—a degree of strain reflecting lower life satisfaction, depression, and a decline in health—is highly variable, depending on the level and type of impairment and aspects of the familial relationship (Chappell, 1990). For example, adult children seem to be more prone to stress than caregiving spouses, perhaps because the high intensity of responsibility for an aged parent violates the norms of generational independence and creates the potential for role conflicts, as described previously. Caregivers to those with dementia and its associated behavioral problems (e.g., night wandering, agitation, and dangerous or embarrassing behaviors) also report greater caregiver burdens, due to the need for constant vigilance (Chappell, 1990).

Despite these burdens, research also reveals that caregivers report rewards and gains from their efforts (Kramer, 1997; Seltzer & Greenberg, 1999). In fact, it is quite possible for both strain/burden and rewards/gains to simultaneously characterize a caregiving experience (Lawton, Moss, Kleban, Glicksman, & Rovine, 1991). The literature on the positive aspects of reward/gain from caregiving is much less developed than that for burden (Long-Foley, Tung, & Mutran, 2002). This growing literature reinforces that caregiving, while often demanding, is not without some positive aspects for the caregiver.

Involvement of Older Adults in Their Care

Research on caregiving often characterizes older adults as passive objects toward whom care is directed—the great majority of research focuses on the givers rather than the recipients of care.

The study by Sarah Matthews of siblings and their age 75+ parents suggests that this passivity isn't always the case (2002). Examining the dynamics of care within these families, Matthews found that many older adults were active participants in arranging services for themselves, directing children regarding who should do what tasks, and retaining control by rejecting services or changes that violate norms of independence between the generations.

Matthews (2002) provides rich examples of instances where parents fought their children's well-intentioned efforts to start them on meals-on-wheels, resisted moves to their children's homes or senior housing settings, or dismissed their offers to manage their finances. Her research clearly shows that, except for the subset of parents who were extremely ill or cognitively impaired, the efforts of children are clearly shaped by older parents' wishes. Other studies that focuses on nursing homes or assisted-living settings confirm that service providers sometimes ignore the older adult, dealing instead with the adult child as the primary "client" or "consumer," and making the older adult "invisible" (Frank, 2002; Schumacher, Eckert, Zimmerman, Carder, & Wright, 2005).

Family Conflict: Elder Abuse and Neglect

Relationships with older family members, within or between generations, may have a history of stress and violence. As discussed earlier, growing older does not cure troubled family relationships or reduce tension and violence. Another manifestation of intrafamily stress is the **neglect and abuse** of older persons, particularly by those providing care to a frail or dependent individual (Steinmetz, 1988, 2005). There are multiple theories or explanations for elder abuse. One view is that abuse and neglect result from violations of the norms of independence and reciprocity, such as when an older person becomes very dependent on a relative, especially a child (Gelles & Cavanaugh, 2005). A second hypothesis, not yet thoroughly tested, is that violence is a product of reciprocity; that is, adult children who are violent toward a frail elderly parent are returning violence that they received as children. Indirect support for this argument comes from studies showing that children from violent families are themselves more likely to be violent toward kin (Wallace, 1996).

Finally, research has revealed that many of those committing abuse and neglect of older adults are *spouses,* rather than adult children. What remains unclear in these cases is whether this abuse began when the person reached later life (or became physically dependent), or whether this pattern of violence is a long-standing characteristic of the marriage (Vinton, 1991). Because not all couples experiencing violence get divorced, especially in today's older cohorts where divorce was less acceptable, one component of elder abuse may be "spousal violence grown old" (Harris, 1996). We relabel this behavior from spousal to elder abuse when the victim is age 65 or older, suggesting somehow that it is distinct from other familial violence. It is important, however, not to overestimate problems of neglect and abuse. In a national survey of 3,000 people age 57–85, only a small number (12) reported being victims of physical violence in the prior 12 months, a majority of which was perpetrated by someone other than a spouse/partner or child. Much more common were financial abuse (N = 152, taking money or property without permission) or verbal abuse (N = 398, insulting, disparaging talk); in both of these cases spouses/partners and children were less than half of those committing the abuse (Laumann, Leitsch, & Waite, 2008).

Social Changes and the Family's Future

Neither the family as a social institution nor individual families are static. They respond to changes in the larger society, and they contribute to, resist, or accelerate societal changes through their decisions and actions. Changes in the lives of young and mid-life individuals, such as earlier or later childbearing or a short supply of marital partners, carry forward through time, creating ripples of change as these cohorts move into later life. Given important changes that have taken place in recent decades (and doubtless continue to occur), we anticipate many changes for later-life families, intergenerational relationships, and family structures in the future. What predictions can we make about how families may age differently?

For example, there have been major changes in childbearing, including smaller family size and more nonmarital births. Studies on contemporary older women have connected greater risk of poverty with having been a single parent for 10 years or more. Does societal growth in single parenting portend greater female poverty in late life for future cohorts? Or are there other important differences (e.g., whether single parenthood is caused by divorce or widowhood vs. births outside marriage) that will change that connection in future cohorts (Johnson & Favreault, 2004)? Because multiple types of changes are taking place simultaneously, we are often unable to make a clear prediction from one cohort's experience to the next. Many other factors (i.e., women's increased education and labor force involvement) have also changed for these cohorts, further altering the equation of how earlier family events may influence well-being (e.g., poverty) in later life. Major social trends, including the growing rate of divorce and remarriage, shrinking numbers of children per woman, and legal changes regarding familial rights, portend major changes in the experiences with later-life families in the future. The next section describes some likely changes that may emerge that will differ from the experience of current cohorts of older adults.

Changes in Marriage

As mentioned previously, both the timing and the gender-related norms of marriage have shifted substantially over time. Age at first marriage has increased, although it remains unclear whether marriage is simply being delayed to later ages or whether there will be more adults moving through life unmarried—although perhaps not without a partner. Data on the population age 15 and older in the United States in 2008 showed 30% of them as "never married" (U.S. Census Bureau, 2008c). This is higher in part due to later ages of marriage, but some component is likely to include those who will never marry. Women in other Westernized countries, including Japan and Sweden, have lower rates of marriage—either reflecting delayed ages or diminishing rates of marriage. In some cases, including some Scandinavian countries, cohabitation seems to be replacing marriage as a normative pattern. How these changing patterns might reshape roles and responsibilities among these *families* over future decades remains unclear.

There are also gender-related changes in who is more or less likely to marry. While educated men have long had high odds of marrying, educated women lagged behind. As more women achieve college degrees and full engagement in the labor force, the odds of an educated, professional woman getting married have increased (Goldstein & Kenney, 2001). Rather than education and earnings enabling women to skip marriage and remain independent singles, as some theories had predicted, the opposite is happening—society is reworking the economic bargain in marriage to create new, more equal gender norms (Sweeney, 2002).

Changes in the Size and Shape of Families

Increased longevity has created the growing numbers of four-, five-, or six-generation families. In a **five- or six-generation family,** an individual can simultaneously be a grandparent and a grandchild, providing an even richer possible set of intergenerational family experiences. The possibilities for exchanges of support across so many generations raise many questions, such as whether all generations will feel some responsibility toward the oldest or youngest generations. Will sons and daughters who are themselves older adults be able to adequately assist their even older parents? What rights and duties, if any, does a great-grandparent have toward her offspring three generations removed?

As U.S. fertility rates have stabilized in recent years near replacement rate (just under two children per married couple), the shape of the family tree has also changed from the narrow base of one couple with many offspring across several generations (the familiar "family tree") (Kinsella & He, 2009). With fewer children, on average, there will be fewer grandchildren and cousins, resulting in a taller (more generations) but narrower structure, referred to as a **beanpole family** (Bengtson et al., 1990). As Exhibit 5.8 shows, the change between the shape of a family with a fertility rate of 3 to a fertility rate of 1.5 is dramatic because this alters the numbers of siblings, cousins, grandchildren, and great-grandchildren any individual is likely to have. It is unclear whether this altered family structure will be paralleled by changes in responsibilities across generations when fewer adult children are available as supporters to (relatively) more older kin in the beanpole family (Kinsella & He, 2009).

Future Changes in the Timing of Family Life Events

Major events of family life, such as marriage, birth of children, or child launching, occur at times that are dictated by social norms, ethnic and cultural traditions, individual decisions, and (sometimes) fate (East, 1998). Longer education pushes marriage and childbearing later, while teen births accelerate movement through the family life course. Lower fertility also shrinks the duration of parenthood, as shown in Exhibit 5.9.

Differences in timing of selected family events for females born between the 1920s and the 1950s (including early baby boomers) show fairly consistent timing of first marriage. During this time, however, life expectancy has expanded, and time spent parenting has shrunk, expanding the postparental stage. In the 1920s parenting spanned from ages 24–54, with only about a decade more of life; for women born in the early 1950s the postparental stage has grown to more than 20 years, on average (Schmittroth, 1991).

Growing Complexity of Family Relations

The percentage of ever-divorced persons will increase dramatically in future cohorts of older adults (Crown, Mutschler, Schulz, & Loew, 1993; Uhlenberg, Cooney, & Boyd, 1990).

EXHIBIT **5.8**

Family Structure and Size, High Versus Low Fertility

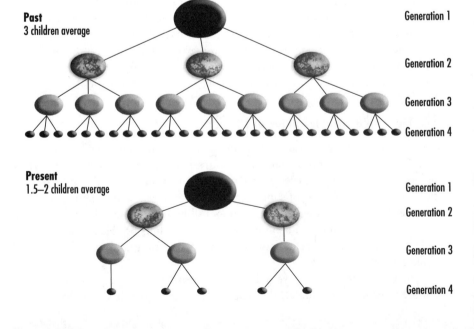

Past
3 children average

Generation 1
Generation 2
Generation 3
Generation 4

Present
1.5–2 children average

Generation 1
Generation 2
Generation 3
Generation 4

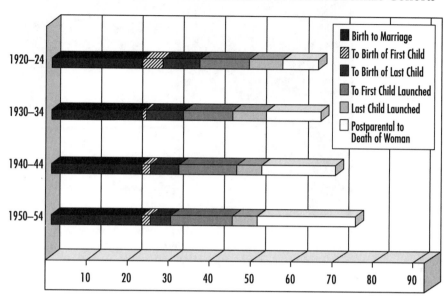

EXHIBIT 5.9

Life Event Timetables of Selected Female Cohorts

Source: Schmittroth, 1991.

Because the likelihood of remarriage after divorce diminishes rapidly for women as they age, given shorter male life expectancy and male remarriage to "younger" women, more women than men will enter later life in divorced status (Uhlenberg et al., 1990). In addition, more members of future aging cohorts will have experienced parental divorce or been divorced themselves and spent spans of their lives as a parent to stepchildren or having grown up with half- or stepsiblings. There are many unanswered questions about family relationships emerging from the complex families that arise in a society with substantial rates of divorce and remarriage. Will adult children feel strong filial obligation toward a biological parent, stepparent, or both? How enduring will relationships become between half- or stepsiblings as they grow older? Some research has confirmed a diminished support expected or received by fathers from adult children, particularly step-children, following divorce; a similar decline has not been confirmed for mothers, who more often have had custody (Amato et al., 1995; Cooney & Uhlenberg, 1990; Pezzin, Pollack, & Schone, 2008). In a study of sibling type, full siblings had more contact and higher-quality relationships as adults than stepsiblings, but having spent more time together in a household while growing up increased the amount of contact (White & Reidmann, 1992). Thus, divorce seems to alter traits of relationships that may be critical to well-being in adulthood and later life.

Summary

Family relationships are among the most enduring that people experience during increasingly long lives. Our roles as sons and daughters, wives and husbands, parents, siblings, and grandparents (and beyond) link many of us to a strong network of others with whom we share history, tradition, and responsibilities. Families provide considerable assistance and support to their members, with most of that assistance being viewed as routine or normal across the decades. Families take mutual assistance as a given in many family relationships.

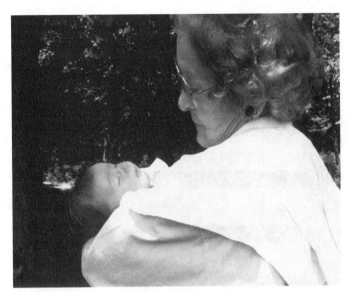

Great-grandparents and even great-great-grandparents are becoming more common as the average life span increases. (Credit: Mike Payne, courtesy of the Ohio Department of Aging)

It is difficult to talk about *family* as though it is a singular phenomenon because it varies across cohorts, race/ethnic groups, stages of the life course, and socioeconomic status, among other factors. We have seen throughout this chapter, for example, that the families of Blacks differ in some important ways from those of Whites, including more mutual assistance, closer sibling relationships, and a more active role for grandparents in rearing their grandchildren. Such differences are the products both of culture and of socioeconomic differences, creating a tradition encouraging greater reliance on kin networks.

The family as a social institution is a dynamic force within the larger society, both contributing to and responding to social changes in politics, the economy, and other social institutions. But families are also internally dynamic, experiencing ongoing change as new generational units are formed, adding members who mature and eventually pass from the scene as they age and die. Throughout this dynamism, however, are threads of continuity connecting the generations and patterns of family norms that are often passed down as part of familial heritage. The age-integrating family system is undoubtedly going to continue its pattern of change in the coming decades. Four- and five-generation families will be paired with sequential marriages to create intricate and complex family systems that may be more or less responsive to the needs of future older adults. As we all age, the families we build and the manner in which we enact family roles will help to shape the norms for this future and the place of the family within it.

Web Wise

Family Caregiver Alliance   http://www.caregiver.org/caregiver/jsp/home.jsp
A nonprofit organization founded in 1977, the Family Caregiver Alliance provides information and research, caregiving advice, and other information on its site, as well as being involved in programs and activities on behalf of caregivers and professionals. Their fact sheets and research/policy activities bridge knowledge and advocacy on this important topic. Caregivers can seek information about services in their area or learn more from online materials about what can sometimes be an isolating task.

Institute on Aging, University of Pittsburgh
http://www.aging.pitt.edu/family-caregivers/default.htm
This university-based site provides a wide variety of information, focusing on aging and caregiving. The "services" tab provides useful links on a variety of topics useful to aging families or caregivers. There is also a useful tab focusing on "aging myths" about aging, and the emerging realities of aging on topics as diverse as death and dying and interpersonal relationships.

National Center on Elder Abuse   http://www.ncea.aoa.gov/NCEAroot/Main_Site/Index.aspx
This site focuses on the issue of elder abuse. It provides basic information, legal and reporting aspects of elder abuse, and help to victims, professionals, and others in addressing this issue. The NCEA also collects state and national data on elder abuse as a clearinghouse of information and statistics on elder abuse and discussion of interventions.

Profile of Older Americans   http://www.aoa.gov/AoARoot/Aging_Statistics/Profile/index.aspx
AARP collaborates with the Administration on Aging and the U.S. Department of Health and Human Services to develop annual profiles on characteristics of the older population. Each year shows detailed tables on a range of characteristics of those age 65 and older, and several years' reports are available for comparisons through time on particular issues. Details on caregiving, marital status, and living arrangements are included.

Key Terms

beanpole family	five- or six-generation family	modified extended family
caregiver burden	generation	neglect and abuse
dependence	independence	norm of reciprocity
dyads	intimacy at a distance	obligation
family	kin-keeping	sandwich generation
family life cycle theory	latent kin matrix	surrogate family relationships
fictive kinship	lineage bridge	voluntarism
filial obligation	marital satisfaction	woman in the middle

Questions for Thought and Discussion

1. Do some genealogical sleuthing and map out the structure of your family tree. Examine such things as the number of siblings in various generations/historical periods and ages at marriage and at death. What larger social changes in the institutions of the family do you see reflected in the history of your own family?

2. Thinking about younger adults of today (in their 20s), what changes in the timing of family events, family norms, and individual behaviors are likely to differentiate their cohort experiences of family life from those of individuals in their 70s today?

3. Research to date suggests that marital satisfaction among older adults is high. Given social changes in expectations related to marriage and divorce, what predictions would you make regarding marital satisfaction and divorce rates among older adults in future cohorts?

4. When families provide care to an ailing or frail older relative, it provides both burdens and rewards. What new supports can you imagine that would promote caregiving to shift the balance toward greater rewards?

Work and Retirement in the Life Course

6

> *Aside from issues of war and peace and nuclear holocaust, the most important dramatic social, economic, and political issues and developments facing the societies with aging populations are those associated with the reduction of employment in the life span while the life span itself is extended.*
>
> (Matras, 1990, p. 75)

Employment as an Organizing Force in the Life Course

We may or may not agree with Matras quote that the changes in employment rank just under the possibility of nuclear holocaust on the list of compelling social issues. It is, however, difficult to argue with the centrality of employment to the structure of the larger economy and of individuals' lives. **Employment**—work for pay or being a worker—is one of the core roles around which we organize life in complex, modern economies. As societies age and longevity increases, we need to rethink employment and how it fits with the changing social context of longer lives and the macro-level needs of the labor market.

In this chapter we use the term *employment* more often than work because the latter concept also includes household, volunteer, and other unpaid activities of value, which, despite being essential to the survival of individuals, families, and society, are not paid or considered part of our calculations of economic productivity (Reskin & Padavic, 1994). The way in which *work* is defined, ignoring the unpaid contributions of people of all ages, renders some groups, notably children and older adults, as society's dependents in the eyes of some policies (Bass, 1995).

Modern economies (local, regional, national, or global) organize themselves around employment (Kinsella & Taeuber, 1993), so we focus the first portion of this chapter on age-related employment issues at multiple levels; we direct our attention to retirement and its importance in the second section of this chapter.

Dynamics of the Labor Force

Both the **market for labor**, the demand for employees (both in terms of numbers and skills), and the **labor force**, the supply of available employees with their particular skills and experience, are highly dynamic. Anyone encountering the major labor market shifts of the early 21st century economy recognizes that major employers, job locations, and needed skills shift dramatically, and in unexpected ways, over time; comparable dramatic changes occur in the supply of labor and its mix of skills and experience. Changes, such as outsourcing of jobs in the global economy and the opening of new jobs related to emerging technologies, continue to reshape the labor market; the pace of change in the labor market has exploded in the past 50 years.

In macro terms, labor resembles other commodities in the marketplace, except that communities cannot suddenly produce more workers if the local demand for labor builds, due to time required to prepare new cohorts of workers (i.e., to bear, raise, and educate children) (Cooperman & Keast, 1983). When shortages of labor occur, alternatives include bringing less active groups into the labor force (e.g., female homemakers during World War II), making each worker more productive through technology, attracting workers from other regions or countries, or keeping current employees on the job longer through incentives to delay retirement. When talented labor is difficult to find and keep, conditions become more advantageous for workers, who can bargain for better wages and benefits. When labor is abundant, however, employers can offer lower wages and benefits because workers are easier to replace (Reskin & Padavic, 1994).

Labor force participation rates describe the percentage of the population that is employed (or seeking employment) at a given time and, by extension, indicate the prevalence of retirement or other nonemployed statuses. In 2008, 25% of men and 16.6% of women over age 65 continued their participation in the labor force (U.S. Department of Labor [DOL], 2009). Exhibit 6.1 shows that while participation was declining slowly over 33 years for White men aged 55–59, their involvement remained the highest in 2008 of all four groups. Black men aged 60–64, with the lowest rate of participation over this time, also declined toward 40% participation. The two other groups demonstrated convergence by 2008. Older White men (60–64) dropped their involvement, and younger (55–59-year-old) Black males showed a jump in labor force participation rate in 1998, which was declining again by 2008. These trends show general decline in participation among men over age 60 and the long-established difference in labor force participation by race.

Black men and women more often experience physical disability resulting in exit from the labor force, a situation that reflects earlier economic and educational disadvantages (Bound, Schoenbaum, & Waidmann, 1996; Brown & Warner, 2008; Hayward, Friedman, & Chen, 1996). Despite this disability gap, Black men spend a greater percentage of their adult years in the labor force; although the number of working years is shorter, this group's lower life expectancy more than corrects for this (Hayward et al., 1996).

Trends in labor force participation for mature women show a sharp contrast with those for men, with growth over time instead of declines. As Exhibit 6.2 shows, during the decades when mature men were departing work earlier via retirement or disability, more women 55–64 remained active in the labor force, with higher participation by women of both races under age 60. This pattern is largely the result of increasing labor force involvement by sequential cohorts of American women during the second half of the 20th century. In each cohort since the 1950s,

EXHIBIT   *6.1*

Male Labor Force Participation 1975–2008 by Age and Race

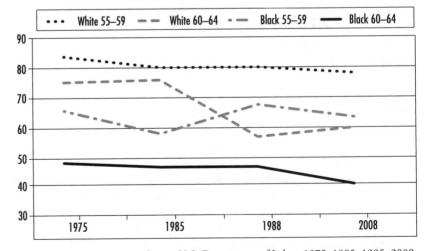

Source: U.S. Department of Labor, 1975, 1985, 1995, 2009.

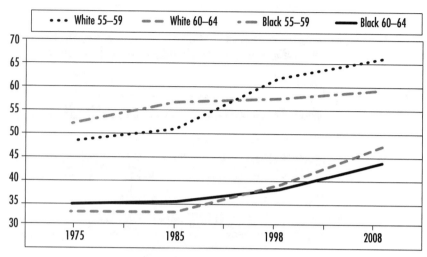

EXHIBIT *6.2*

Female Labor Force Participation 1975–2008 by Age and Race

Source: U.S. Department of Labor, 1975, 1985, 1995, 2009.

adult women have both had increasing participation and spent increasing percentages of their adult years in the labor force. While women are catching up to men in labor force involvement (i.e., note that the graph scale for the men goes to up 90% and for women only to 65%), there is no gap in labor force participation between unmarried men and women over age 50 (Ruhm, 1996). Further, during the economic recession that began in 2008, more men than women lost jobs, resulting in a higher percentage of women than men in the labor force for the first time in U.S. history.

Employment and Life Chances

Employment opportunities play a pivotal role in shaping the life chances of individuals. Employment opportunities develop in part from early **life chances**—resources including education, social class, good health care, and a strong family—and unfold over the life course with consequences such as differences in income, health status, and level of social prestige. The opportunities to which individuals are (or are not) exposed, and the resulting differences in the types of occupations they hold, are a key to understanding inequality throughout life. Critical choices and opportunities early in life, specifically education at the college level and beyond, have been shown to shape long-range outcomes for both women and men. *Winners* in the employment competition are those who, through good fortune or hard work, achieve advanced education relatively early in life. Those who leave education systems at high school or before and do not return to build their educational credentials suffer life-long disadvantage in competing for jobs and high wages (Elman & O'Rand, 2004). An intermediate-level benefit is conveyed to those who return later for education; by advancing their education later, they have fewer years to build the career and wage benefits available to those with a career "head start" (Elman & O'Rand, 2004).

Exhibit 6.3 presents information on gender and race inequality in earnings—often referred to as the wage gap. The statistics compare Black women and men and White women to the

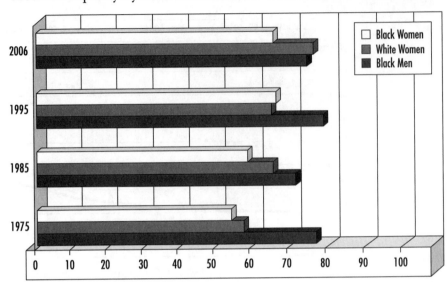

EXHIBIT   6.3

Income Inequality by Race and Sex, 1975–2006 (White Men = 100%)

Source: U.S. Census Bureau, 1997; Infoplease, 2003, 2007.

earnings level for White males (who are equal to 100% in each year of the chart). From 1975 to 2006, inequality of income has been reduced somewhat, but differences remain. Black and White women have largely caught up to the incomes of Black men, but all three groups still get significantly lower incomes than White males. Moreover, the gap in earnings has been reduced not because women workers and Black men are doing better, but rather because White males are doing relatively worse. It is important to remember, too, that White men, like all four groups, have considerable variation in earnings, job prestige, and other benefits that derive from employment.

Employment differences by sex and race/ethnicity continue to shape the working experience of adults, although differences in some areas are shrinking. Blacks and the growing Hispanic and Asian populations have continued lower access to good jobs (the wage gap for Hispanic men is 57.5% and for Hispanic women 51.7% of White men) (Infoplease, 2007); the better paying jobs are also those with employee benefits and pensions. Although we are progressing toward more equal opportunity in the labor force, differences persist in the occupations held by women and men and by White and other race/ethnicity workers (Wells, 1998).

Aside from the disadvantage to individuals, there is also a potential cost to society when jobs are segregated by race, sex, age, or other group characteristics. Taking a broad view, Reskin and Padavic (1994) argue that "society as a whole pays a price when employers use workers' sex (or other irrelevant characteristics such as age and race) to segregate them into jobs that fail to make the best use of their abilities" (p. 46). Even when new groups move into an occupation, they sometimes continue to be treated unequally. In a study of female engineers, when women broke into this nontraditional field (for women), a significant wage gap persisted. These gaps eventually diminish as more cohorts entered the field (Morgan, 1998), but women remain significantly underrepresented in the most well-paid fields, such as engineering and top management (Morgan, 1998; Reskin & Padavic, 1994). This occupational segregation leads to lower lifetime earnings and reduction of other opportunities (skill development, professional networking, or pension savings), which are directly related to life chances in older adulthood.

"SURELY YOU CAN EARN MORE THAN THIS! SOMEONE HAS TO SUPPORT MEDICARE AND SOCIAL SECURITY."

A pattern also persists in connection with the employment opportunities of racial and ethnic minorities in the United States. Although opportunities are improving in more recent cohorts, the employment experience of contemporary Black older adults was characterized by significant racial segregation of job opportunities. Jackson and Gibson (1985) show how limited life chances, resulting from both lower educational attainment and discrimination in jobs, cause disadvantage for Blacks throughout adulthood and into later life. In recent retiree cohorts, many Black workers left the labor force because of poor health, unemployment, or inability to find jobs. Many other older Blacks, even those in poor health, had to continue employment to maintain income and health insurance. In the past, a career as a day laborer or domestic, for example, often did not even carry the guarantee of Social Security and certainly lacked a pension, making continuing to work—as long as your health permitted—the only viable option. Jackson and Gibson also contend that an interrupted employment history might make retirement less meaningful as a concept to Blacks in the United States, who had experienced many unintended breaks in employment. Income differences during the working years are important because they are correlated with later-life economic well-being. In the later section of this chapter, we show how these occupational opportunities (or their absence) play out in terms of differences in retirement decisions and outcomes.

The Occupational Life Cycle

The patterning of employment in the lives of individuals is a taken-for-granted aspect of the life course to most of us. But, like many age-related phenomena, it is one that is socially constructed and subject to change. Most of us carry in our heads a socially constructed model of an occupational life cycle. The dominant model in U.S. culture reflects the typical employment pattern of middle-class males in the mid- to late-20th century. In this **occupational life cycle**, a worker, upon completion of education or training, lands an entry-level position with a corporation, government agency, or other employer. The worker, with the passage of time, advances upward through the ranks of that occupation, perhaps seeking additional training or changing employers along the way. The worker's earnings increase as he advances based on greater skill, experience, and responsibility, reaching a career plateau in middle- or late-middle age. At that point, advancement may slow or cease in anticipation of retirement, which comes with health benefits and a solid pension

(Doeringer, 1990). Research has demonstrated consensus among male workers regarding the ages at which promotions are most likely, with promotions less expected for workers beyond age 50 (Lashbrook, 1996). A random sample of Chicago-area adults confirmed that most people hold deadlines for completing school, entering full-time employment, settling on a career, and retirement, mirroring the ideas of the occupational life course (Settersten & Hagestad, 1996b).

Although quite informal, this socially accepted model regarding the occupational life cycle is so ingrained into our ways of thinking that many of us take it for granted and expect to follow this path in our employment. This model also translates into a macro-level expectation of how birth cohorts will transform into cohorts of workers for the labor market that enter and progress in predictable ways. We can see these expectations more clearly when we ask what would happen, for example, if older workers in large numbers chose not to retire from their senior positions in their organizations? Such a scenario, facing the baby boomers in the economic downturn of 2008, could squeeze opportunities for advancement of younger workers, violating one of the core elements of the career model—advancement. What if large numbers of young adults were to take time off after training before initiating a career? This violation of expectations could create a temporary shortage of new entrants to the labor force, perhaps prompting recruitment of nontraditional workers, importing workers from foreign countries, or improvement of wages, benefits, and working conditions to attract the labor they need. In short, our economy is built on the assumptions of the occupational life cycle.

Questions have been raised as to whether the occupational life cycle model has ever characterized the experience of a majority of workers. Further, many wonder whether this model is still viable even for the middle-class White males, upon whose lives it was based, in our changing economy. Layoffs from downsizing or corporate mergers, job automation via technology, or worker health problems may interrupt an orderly progression even among middle-class males expecting to follow the traditional steps of this model (Doeringer, 1990). In addition, there is ample evidence that this pattern has never fit the experiences of employed women, workers with limited education, or groups who have experienced segregation or discrimination in employment. First, women continue to encounter conflicting demands of family and career development (Moen, 1994); the years of career building are also prime years for childbearing. Second, jobs in the labor market that are occupied primarily by women have shorter career ladders, meaning that female workers have fewer opportunities to advance and attain higher wages, status, and benefits over time (Reskin & Padavic, 1994). Third, the working lives of women have been and continue to be more subject to interruption by family needs, such as caring for a parent or child with health problems or changing jobs to follow a husband's higher-earning career path. Such interruptions may diminish job and wage advancement significantly over time.

Similarly, the occupational life cycle model of the middle-class male does not fit other types of workers. How would it apply to migrant farm workers, who have no career ladder or guarantee of employment, minimal benefits, and no pension? How would the occupational life cycle model fit someone employed as an exotic dancer in a nightclub, as a technician repairing office machines, as a waitress in a diner, as a carpenter, or as a telephone sales representative for an online or catalog merchant? Clearly many jobs or companies, particularly in small businesses, do not offer the type of career trajectory that we generally associate with the traditional occupational life cycle model.

The changing nature of the labor market also limits the usefulness of the occupational life cycle model. In prior cohorts, career workers were predominantly full time and had incentives from pay and pension to remain with their employers (Henretta, 1994). Increasingly workers face careers where employer and occupation change over time are the norm, rather than the exception. Median years at the current job for male workers 55–64 has dropped in the past 25–30 years (Munnell & Sass, 2008), suggesting that job tenure is declining across the board. Changes in the U.S. labor market include the growth of smaller companies; less manufacturing, fewer labor unions, and more jobs in the service sector; outsourcing work to other countries; corporate mergers, takeovers, and downsizing; and the growth of what is called the **contingent labor force**. Contingent employees work on contracts for short spans of time (weeks or months to years), rather than being hired permanently. Contingent labor once was relegated to the lower rungs of the employment rankings, such as day labor in construction or crop harvesting, but it now extends all the way to the executive/consultant level.

The world of contingent work provides little continuity, career building, or benefits, such as health insurance or pension (Rupert, 1991). Hiring someone on a contract to complete a particular project is often more efficient for the company than making an open-ended employment commitment and avoids having to lay off workers when labor/expertise needs change. Estimates of contingent labor are difficult to determine and have ranged from 5%–20% of workers in the late 1990s (DOL, Bureau of Labor Statistics [BLS], 2001; Rupert, 1991). Not surprisingly, a majority of those categorized as contingent say they would prefer more traditional employment (DOL, BLS, 2001). It seems clear that the occupational careers of individuals will be much less predictable and orderly in the future. For example, median tenure in the current job among employed adults age 65 and older in 2006 was 10.2 years, far from the duration that we think of in a career job, and almost the same proportion of workers 55 to 64 (9.4%) had been in their current jobs less than 12 months (DOL, BLS, 2008c). Perhaps Riley's projection of adulthood as a shifting blend of education, leisure, and employment will become more realistic, with careers punctuated by breaks and returns to school for additional training or skill development (Riley & Riley, 1994). Eventually this expanding variability in the patterns of employment may change our age-structured notions of when it is appropriate to have a job or to be retired, leading to the final demise of the occupational life cycle model (Henretta, 1994).

One alternative in this new world of employment is for workers to anticipate **multiple careers**, in which an individual undergoes training and employment two or more times, potentially in very different fields. The idea of multiple careers seems to be premised on an undersupply of labor so that workers have choices about jobs and ample salary and benefits to prepare for periods of leisure and training between careers. Multiple careers theoretically reduce the risk of boredom for employees, accommodate changing labor market needs, and provide options to deal with skill obsolescence and a longer healthy life expectancy. It is as yet unclear whether there will be sufficient choices in future to make the multiple careers idea work for many people. And those undertaking careers requiring lengthy training and apprenticeship, such as medicine, might be discouraged from changing jobs and giving up their valuable experience and training investment. Downward mobility in earnings and prestige is likely to remain a risk in second-career jobs (Ruhm, 1990). However, with increasing healthy life expectancy, more of us should expect a future with multiple careers, possibly interspersed with periods of education or training (Myles & Quadagno, 1995).

Older Workers and the Dynamics of the Labor Force

Researchers and policy makers discuss a subset of those in the labor force referred to as **older workers**. Often this term is not clearly defined or is assigned varying ages of onset because there is little agreement on a chronological age at which a worker is deemed *older*. Workers may be considered older at a much earlier chronological age if they are bricklayers or professional athletes than if they are public school teachers or Wall Street portfolio managers. Both the demands of the job, physical or mental, and the ages at which workers in the occupation reach their peak on the career ladder in terms of promotion and performance may be keys to defining when older-worker status begins.

Also essential to understanding older workers are the views of employers. Workers may come to be defined as *older* when their employers start to treat them differently based on age—perhaps not considering them for promotions, training, or raises. When an employer stops investing in an employee because of age, the label of *older worker* has implicitly been assigned, even if the choice was seemingly made on individual criteria ("Walker isn't the 'go getter' she once was"). The fate of older workers in the labor force depends both on the overall level of demand for labor and on the views held by employers regarding the skills and productivity of older workers.

Workers over the age of 65, our socially constructed retirement age, work in different jobs than younger workers. They are concentrated among the self-employed (e.g., the self-employed accountant or acupuncturist), in fields where substantial experience is valued (e.g., engineering or construction supervisors, heads of government agencies), and in declining occupations, like auto manufacturing, where few younger people are being hired (Cooperman & Keast, 1983). In both developed and developing countries, older workers (generally those older than age 45 or 50) are more concentrated in agriculture (a declining occupation) and less often found in jobs in the service sector (where recent growth has occurred) than are younger workers (Kinsella & Taeuber, 1993). Is this pattern explained by individuals' moving out of clerical and service jobs and into agriculture as they age? For the most part, the answer is no. Again the key lies in the dynamics of the labor market and the changing distribution of job opportunities over time. Shrinking occupational fields, such as agriculture and manufacturing, attract relatively few entrants from younger cohorts because there are few opportunities. Entering cohorts turn instead to the growth sectors, such as service and new technology occupations. Such shifts in the labor market have marooned older workers in some fields that are in decline, further reducing their future employment options.

Skills and Employability of Older Workers

The jobs available to older workers depend in large measure on the overall supply of labor and the mix of workers' skills available relative to the demand. Specifically, the number of younger, prime-age workers (perhaps ages 25–45) influences whether older workers are in high or low demand. So could we simply project the future demand for older workers based on the size of younger cohorts entering the labor force in the next 10–30 years? This would be fairly straight-forward if the mixture of skills required and the number and kinds of jobs remained fixed over time. If job openings were stable, declining numbers of younger workers would simply signal an increasing demand for older workers. But social life is rarely so simple because both the numbers and the skills required shift constantly. The answer also depends on other factors, including the growth (or decline) of the overall economy and use of technology. Any given worker, young or old, faces a constantly changing array of opportunities in the marketplace for employment.

Another major influence on the demand for older workers is the perception of older people's competence and desirability as employees. Although it is true that a wide range of physical and mental capacities (speed, strength, visual acuity, reaction time) decline slightly with age, these changes are small until advanced ages and may be compensated for by greater experience, skill, or attention to the task (Shephard, 1999). As Robert Atchley (1994) argued more than 15 years ago, "A majority of older people continue to function physically and psychologically at a level well above the minimum needed for most adult performance" on the job (p. 280). In fact, as the physical demands of most U.S. jobs decline and general health of older worker improves, the physical barriers to continued employment, in particular, are diminishing (Steuerle, Spiro, & Johnson, 1999).

Also important are the attitudes of employers to hiring, retaining and promoting older workers. A 2006 study of 400 private sector employers (Munnell, Sass, & Soto, 2006) found that employers value the productivity of workers 55 and older, particularly those in white-collar jobs where experience pays benefits. These employers also saw strength in job knowledge and ability to interact with customers, but they gave more mixed responses for physical health/stamina and ability to learn new tasks. Seven of ten employers rated older job applicants as equally attractive compared to younger applicants, but ratings were more equal for "rank and file" workers, for larger companies and those with more older workers on staff, or if the responding employer was under age 55. While this sounds encouraging, other research suggests that employers are no less subject to ageism than anyone else in society.

Several studies, both old and new, suggest that managers' negative views remain an important influence on the hiring of older workers. In a classic survey, 1,600 middle- and top-level managers were asked to decide about hiring, promotion, and training one of two otherwise equivalent applicants—one young and the other older. These managers systematically favored

Older workers, like Richard Hoffman of the Ohio Department of Aging (ODA), often negate stereotypes by being among the most energetic, enthusiastic, and dependable employees in the workplace. Hoffman, pictured above, worked full-time at ODA until age 94. He started work there at age 66, after retiring from a full career in the aeronautics industry. (Credit: Mike Payne, courtesy of the Ohio Department of Aging)

the younger applicant over the older one. All voiced nondiscriminatory views about age, and older managers (over age 50) were more favorable toward the hypothetical older worker in hiring than the managers who were themselves younger than age 50 (Rosen & Jerdee, 1985). A recent Canadian study found both that employers failed to bring older applicants in for interviews and selectively offered second interviews to younger workers (Berger, 2006); in response, workers adapted their identities and profiles to obscure their ages through dying hair, using youthful slang, and removing select dates from work and educational histories (Berger, 2009). An AARP study of people 45–74 found that 80% of those seeking employment perceived age discrimination as a continuing problem (AARP, 2002).

In addition, the costs of providing job-based benefits are sometimes a barrier to hiring, retaining, or retraining older employees. Experienced senior workers have often achieved substantial salaries, causing employers to question whether the same work could be performed at lower pay by a younger employee. Federally mandated health benefit coverage has also added to the costs of employing older workers (Munnell et al., 2006; U.S. Senate Special Committee on Aging, 1991). Employers sometimes weigh these added costs and decide against selecting an older applicant for a job or against keeping their older employees, as we discuss further later on in this chapter.

Special Programs for Older Workers

At one time, the literature on employment of older workers contained exemplars of companies that hired older workers or rehired their own retirees to flexibly meet labor force needs (McNaught, 1994). The problem remains that few employers have considered options for using older workers—most companies have had no motivation to do so. In the late 20th century the greater concern of employers was how to reduce their labor force, often through early retirement incentives, rather than how to encourage older workers to return to work or stay on the job (Rix, 1991). Only recently, as the baby boomers approach retirement ages, have employers begun to discuss the labor force challenges they will face as these large cohorts in highly skilled positions consider retirement. A Web search of "baby boomer brain drain," the term that has become popular in business discussions of this issue, displays an active interchange of experts on the topic of companies losing large numbers of experienced knowledge workers. A tantalizing question remains—Will employers be forced by a shrinking pool of available and skilled labor to reconsider how they can make use of older workers, luring them back or keeping them working beyond traditional ages of retirement? Already research has shown that the self-reported likelihood of working past age 65 among boomer cohorts grew between 1992 and 2004 to 33%, suggesting an expectation of longer working lives (Mermin, Johnson, & Murphy, 2007).

Age Discrimination in Employment: Problems and Policies

In 2007 an age discrimination lawsuit involving 32 senior partners of a large law firm resulted in a $27.5 million award paid to those bringing the case (Elmer, 2009). The economic downturn, paired with the larger number of baby boomers now among the ranks of older workers, also caused a significant upturn in claims of age discrimination—24,580 such cases were filed with the Equal Employment Opportunity Commission (EEOC) in the fiscal year that ended September 30, 2008. This represented an increase of almost 30% from the year before (Elmer, 2009). Not surprisingly, most claims have to do with job termination (Neumark, 2008). From cases such as this one, we know that age discrimination in employment is far from a problem of the past.

Age discrimination occurs when an employer makes decisions on the basis of age that disadvantages their older workers in terms of hiring, promotion, training, wages, or other opportunities. Age discrimination, actions built upon stereotyped ageist attitudes, negatively influences the employment of older workers. The **Age Discrimination in Employment Act (ADEA)**, originally passed in 1967 and amended significantly afterward, prohibits the use of age in hiring, firing, and personnel policies for workers over age 40 (McConnell, 1983; Neumark, 2008). By 1986, amendments to the ADEA prohibited mandatory retirement in all but a few occupations; the percentages of workers facing mandatory retirement declined rapidly (Fields & Mitchell, 1984). The continued need for lawsuits in recent years and job losses among mid- or advanced-career workers in recent economic downturns highlight the ongoing need for the ADEA because mid- or late-career workers face greater challenges in finding new work compared to their younger peers, often described as "overqualified" for many available jobs (Berger, 2006).

Age discrimination is often subtle and difficult to prove in court; most cases that are initiated are never brought to court, and in a majority of the remainder, the employer wins the case (Neumark, 2008). If a supervisor selects a younger employee over an older one for a training program, is this action age discrimination? Not necessarily because the two employees undoubtedly differ on a variety of other work-related characteristics. But if the supervisor systematically selects younger workers over older workers, even when the qualifications of the older employee are equal or better, it is discrimination. Discrimination may be conscious or unconscious but is often predicated on negative assumptions concerning the attitudes and abilities of workers as they age. In defending such cases employers claim legitimate reasons for failing to hire, promote, train, or increase wages of one or more older employees. The burden of proving age-related reasons for such treatment falls to those bringing suit, a burden that can be lighter if multiple employees shared a common experience of discrimination (Neumark, 2008).

Even though most mandatory retirement is now prohibited by the ADEA, the law allows for exceptions. Those exceptions are specific occupations in which age is considered a **bona fide occupational qualification (BFOQ)**. Examples include airline pilots, air traffic controllers, and some public safety and law enforcement positions. For these jobs employers have convinced the courts that age has a predictable effect on one's ability to perform adequately, and the consequences of poor performance are potentially devastating. Some of these mandatory retirement ages have been increased in recent years in light of longer healthy life expectancy, including those of airline pilots (from age 60 to 65).

Age discrimination reflects our society's ambivalent feelings about older workers. These ambivalent views are reflected in the ideologies and underlying assumptions of two early theories attempting to describe retirement on the individual (micro) level.

Rocking Chairs or Rock Climbing: Disengagement and Activity Theories

Theories often mirror the values of their creators and the norms of their social/historical times, reflecting and reinforcing culturally dominant views of what *should be* the appropriate way to do things. The two theories contrasted here follow this pattern of reflecting and reinforcing social norms. Both disengagement and activity theories not only postulate how individuals' behaviors and orientations change with advancing age but also imply how they *should* change (specifying normative patterns of aging).

Disengagement theory, which was put forward by Cumming and Henry (1961), proposed that the process of **disengagement**—an inevitable, rewarding, and universal process of mutual withdrawal between the individual and society with advancing age—was normal and expected. This functionalist theory argued that it was beneficial (or functional) for both the aging individual and the society that such disengagement occur in order to minimize the social disruption caused at the older person's eventual death.

Cessation of work roles at retirement was a good illustration of this disengagement process, enabling the aging person to be freed of the daily responsibilities of a job, permitting the pursuit of other, more voluntary and flexible activities. Through disengagement, Cumming and Henry (1961) argued, society anticipated the eventual death of older people by removing them from essential employment and family roles, bringing new cohorts into full participation to replace them.

Although focused primarily at the individual level of analysis, disengagement theory also had significant implications for the overall society. Developed during the period when mandatory retirement was common, the theory provided a positive spin on retirement. On the side of the employer, the predictable withdrawal of older workers from various jobs meant they would be less likely to lose a critical employee

unexpectedly, and senior-level jobs would become open to younger workers seeking promotions and better pay.

Reaction to disengagement theory was swift and negative, however. To many of the activists and advocates at that time, disengagement theory represented a threat to their goal of promoting more positive roles and a fully engaged lifestyle for older persons (Kastenbaum, 1993). Although the original theory was not stated in these terms, it was quickly interpreted as a normative statement ("People should disengage") rather than as a description of reality ("As they age, people do disengage").

Disengagement theory has had mixed success as a theory. Some argue that it was successful because it stimulated discussion and research (Hochschild, 1975), a major function of any theory. Yet it has been widely criticized as being unfalsifiable, a major failing of any theory (Achenbaum & Bengtson, 1994; Hochschild, 1975). The theory states that disengagement is universal and inevitable but that its form and timing vary among individuals (Hochschild, 1975). Thus, if a person is not disengaged at age 85 or 95, it's not that they didn't disengage—only that they didn't disengage *yet*. Cumming and Henry also labeled some individuals who continued to be actively involved as unsuccessful disengagers, suggesting that being active and engaged was an improper, negative response to aging (Cumming & Henry, 1961; Hochschild, 1975). And, although we may be able to identify the loss of social roles as typical among individuals moving into advanced age, this change does not prove such change to be an inevitable or beneficial process.

Activity theory emerged, in part, in response to disengagement theory (Lemon, Bengtson, & Peterson, 1972). Activity theory also represents a normative view of aging—in this case arguing that individuals, in order to age well, must be active by maintaining social roles and interaction, rather than disengaging. "The essence of this theory is that there is a positive relationship between activity and life satisfaction and that the greater the role loss, the lower the life satisfaction" (Lemon et al., 1972, p. 511). The activity theory mandate for a retiree was, therefore, to locate some other engaging activity to substitute for loss of employment or family roles. In the case of employment, this activity chosen should substitute for nonfinancial goals, such as satisfaction and social contact, which the job fulfilled for the individual (Atchley, 1976).

The study by Lemon and colleagues (1972) examined key elements of activity theory in a cross-sectional sample of future residents of a retirement community. In contrast to the predictions of activity theory, their self-selected and economically advantaged sample showed little connection between activity levels and satisfaction with life. A central problem with activity theory is establishing causation, especially using a cross-sectional research design. If we find that more active people are more satisfied, does that mean that activity causes satisfaction, that satisfaction promotes activity, or that some other factors (such as good health or high education) enhance both activity and satisfaction? From cross-sectional data it is impossible to disentangle this causal puzzle.

Both activity and disengagement theories have fallen largely into disuse as theories, but they remain important guideposts regarding normative views on aging and examples of problems to avoid in creating theory. Activity theory remains a dominant ideology of successful or productive aging (Rowe & Kahn, 1998) and underlies the behaviors of individuals and groups that argue that active aging is successful aging.

Think about these two theories and how they might reflect your expectations about your future aging. Disengagement suggests that you should and will retire from employment, lose friends to death without replacing them, take a less central role in your family, and perhaps withdraw from community activities as you age. You should, in other words, move toward the rocking chair. Under the activity theory scenario, in contrast, you should maintain your active involvement in your family and community and replace lost activities or friends with new ones to maintain full involvement as you age. Rock climbing could replace the rocking chair, as long as good health persisted.

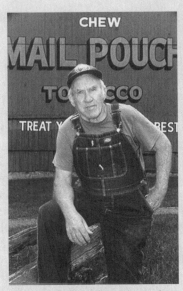

The late Harley Warrick, one of the last of the original Mail Pouch painters, defied disengagement theory by staying busier than ever painting and selling Mail Pouch birdhouses long after he climbed down the ladder from painting barns. (Credit: Mike Payne, courtesy of the Ohio Department of Aging)

Defining Retirement

Col. K. retired from the military after 30 years of service. She receives a military pension and has recently begun a full-time consulting business, based on her military expertise.

Mr. L., 70, receives a generous pension from the large accounting firm where he worked for 30 years. For 3 months of every year, Mr. L. is a full-time, self-employed tax preparer for long-time clients and family members. The remaining 9 months, he enjoys an active leisure lifestyle.

Ms. J., age 58, has had a spotty record of employment throughout her adult life, working temporary and part-time jobs when she could find them. Having more trouble in the past few years, she has given up looking for jobs and calls herself retired. She'd work again if she could find a job because money is scarce.

Would you categorize any or all of the above persons as retired? How do we decide? It is useful to establish some common boundaries defining retirement in order to develop both policies and research. As these examples show, even though the idea of retirement is familiar, defining it is not as simple as it first appears. Atchley (1976) described several ways in which we use the word **retirement**. It may refer to the event or ceremony marking departure from a job, a phase of the occupational life cycle preparatory to such a departure, the process of separation from employment, or a social role (the "retiree" role). We use the term *retirement* to refer to all of these diverse meanings. The central focus in this section is on retirement as a life stage and as a process of separation from employment.

Growing from this definitional problem we next turn to identifying when retirement begins and when an individual is considered retired. We can answer these questions in two ways: using self-definitions (answers to questions, such as "Are you retired?") or using standard indicators. Ekerdt and DeViney (1990) have outlined four indicators used by researchers to establish whether someone is retired: (1) receiving a pension, (2) total cessation of employment, (3) departure from the major job or career of adulthood, or (4) a significant reduction in hours of employment. As we saw in the cases described at the start of this section, many workers today do not make a clean break from employment by moving from full-time career jobs one day to no employment the next, which is our traditional view of how retirement occurred (Atchley, 1976). Instead of a clear-cut event, retirement has become somewhat more blurred as a life transition, so we may need more than one of these criteria to define retirement (Mutchler, Burr, Pienta, & Massagli, 1997). Although there is no overall agreement about these definitions, two criteria are part of most researchers' definitions: receipt of a pension (public or private) and diminished activity in the labor force at/after "retirement" age (Gendell & Siegel, 1992).

The Social Construction of Retirement

Where did retirement come from? Did it always exist? The fact that retirement is a social construct is easily seen by looking at historical information on employment and leisure. Retirement did not always exist and is still not common in many developing nations of the world (Kinsella & Phillips, 2005). Researchers date the start of large-scale retirement to the close of the 19th century in some developed economies (Quadagno, 1982).

Throughout most of history people of all ages and social classes were required to work in order to ensure the survival of themselves and their kin (Quadagno, 1982; Reskin & Padavic, 1994). Labor started early in life and continued until death or disability (Plakans, 1994). Even the wealthy nobility of Europe had duties to perform and could not do whatever they wished with their time. In fact, elders in many cultures have held responsibility as leaders or teachers to very advanced ages (see Amoss & Harrell, 1981, for examples). Historically speaking, however, the option of most people having a block of unstructured leisure time—including a source of income—at the end of the life cycle is relatively new. "Retirement in 'modern' society is unique only to the degree that it is associated with massive intergenerational income redistribution through a state bureaucracy. Retirement, itself, is not new" (Quadagno, 1982, p. 199).

Four social conditions set the stage for the emergence of retirement as a social institution (Atchley, 1976; Cooperman & Keast, 1983; Plakans, 1994; Quadagno, 1982). First, the society must produce an economic surplus (initially via industrial production) sufficient to support its nonemployed population. Second, there must be some mechanism in place (such as pensions) to divert that surplus to the needs of these nonemployed members of the society. Third, the culture must hold positive attitudes toward not working for pay as acceptable or desirable. Fourth, people must live long enough to accumulate an acceptable minimum of years of productive employment to warrant support during retirement (Atchley, 1976).

Following the growth of productivity in the Industrial Revolution, employer pensions first appeared in the late 1800s. Pension benefits to workers were considered a reward for merit and a gift from a magnanimous employer (Quadagno, 1982); there was no sense that employers owed their retirees any support. Initially few employers offered private pension options. In the post–World War II era, however, pension programs grew rapidly in a strong economy, expanding in the 1940s and 1950s to cover a wider range of occupations. Pension programs grew during periods when labor was in ample supply, as larger youth cohorts were continually entering the labor force (Cooperman & Keast, 1983). The availability of pensions continued to grow until the 1980s (Employee Benefit Research Institute, 2004). Analyses from various studies suggest that pension coverage has hovered around 50% between 1991 and 2003 (Sanzenbacher, 2006); approximately one in three individuals over age 65 were receiving private pension benefits in 2006 (McDonnell, 2008).

The first retirement programs in developed countries were regulated and highly structured; benefits were not available until reaching the minimum age of eligibility or the required years of service in the employer's plan (Kinsella & Phillips, 2005). When companies developed pensions, they paired them with mandatory retirement to have greater control over removing older workers and replacing them with younger ones. In less economically developed countries, however, where family-based business or agriculture dominate the economy, retirement remains less structured and pensions less common (Kinsella & Phillips, 2005).

Many older adults continue to work beyond typical retirement ages. (Credit: U.S. Census Bureau, Public Information Office [PIO])

The Institutionalization of Retirement in the United States

As the possibility of retirement grew from the first employer pensions through the first half of the 20th century (including the start of Social Security), worker attitudes toward retirement were slower to change. Atchley (1976) contends that sequential cohorts of workers have become more positive and accepting toward retirement. Initially, the idea of retirement had to contend with a strong work ethic, which suggested that the worth of an individual was tied to productivity, most specifically in the labor force. By the end of the 20th century, the idea of retirement as an expected and welcomed stage of life was widespread in developed economies of the world (Atchley, 1994). Retirement is now generally accepted as an appropriate stage of the adult life cycle and as a legitimate, earned privilege (O'Rand, 1990). This institutionalization of retirement, along with the legitimization of leisure, has a strong value basis—it is acceptable as long as retirees maintain a high level of personal activity and social involvement (Ekerdt, 1986). Nonetheless, retirement has never been as secure or available to less economically advantaged workers or women (Calasanti, 1996a; Jackson & Gibson, 1985). We turn now to two key forces enabling the institutionalization of retirement in the life course, and then we examine variations in retirement by gender, race/ethnicity, and social class.

The Role of Social Security

The creation of the Social Security program in 1935 enabled retirement to become a reality for the majority of U.S. workers (see Chapter 7 for further discussion of this program). Social Security has been important in helping to institutionalize and promote retirement in two related ways. Social Security (1) makes retirement socially legitimate as a transition and stage of the life cycle and (2) enables individuals to retire by providing benefits that are a reliable source of income to the vast majority of American workers. The percentage of people insured (covered for retirement/survivor benefits) by Social Security has increased dramatically—at the end of 2008 there were an estimated 203 million individuals insured by the Social Security program (Social Security Administration, 2008), more than 90% of men and women.

In the past Social Security encouraged full retirement by creating financial disincentives to continued employment. The key disincentive, called the **earnings test**, taxed earnings of workers over age 65 to recover some of the Social Security benefit dollars (e.g., in 1995 Social Security reduced benefit for those 65–69 years of age with earnings above $11,280 by cutting $1 of benefits for every $3 of earnings above this amount) (Social Security Administration, 1995). The earnings test has been changed so that it now applies only to workers taking early retirement (currently under age 66) with earnings over $12,000/year; those retiring at older ages face no earnings test. This change has substantially reduced Social Security's previous, negative influence on working at higher ages (Social Security Administration, 2004b).

Although Social Security was created to enable workers to retire, not all of its provisions clearly work in that direction. Social Security has started to encourage workers to stay in the labor force longer by raising the age of eligibility for full benefits. Though the age for full benefits is currently 66, only 18% of the public in a 2004 survey understood this change, leading to the possibility of poor decision making (Center for Retirement Research, 2004). Most still thought the full eligibility age was 65. Currently workers can take early (reduced) benefits between ages 62–66.

As Exhibit 6.4 shows, Social Security eligibility ages are important to the timing of retirement. In 1975 most workers waited to age 65; the surge in early retirement in the 1980s and 1990s has now started to change, with growth in the percentage taking retirement at age 65 or beyond. By 2027, a worker will have to be 67 (rather than 66) in order to retire with full Social Security benefits. The purpose of moving the age up was to control Social Security costs by shortening the number of years for which retirees receive benefits as life expectancy continues to expand. Raising the age for full benefits also increases the financial penalty for early retirement

EXHIBIT **6.4**

Age at Initial Receipt of Social Security, 1975–2007

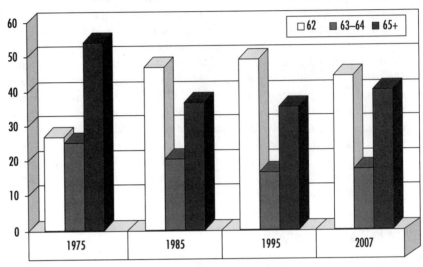

Source: Social Security Administration, 2004c, 2008.

because Social Security spreads out the same expected dollar amount of benefits over a longer span of years for early retirees. For example, benefits for taking retirement at age 62 will shrink from 80% of the full benefit amount (when the age was 65) to 70% (when full benefits age is 67).

In addition, incentives have been implemented to increase monthly benefits for those who work beyond the age of full eligibility, but researchers are unsure the degree to which this changing landscape of incentives will change the timing of individuals' retirements (Quinn & Burkhauser, 1990). Having people work even longer continues to be one of several alternatives under consideration to solve the fiscal problems facing Social Security and to reform the system (Center for Retirement Research, 2009; Espo, 2005).

The Role of Employer Pensions

For workers expecting pensions from their employers, the size and security of such benefits are central to retirement decisions (Bender & Jivan, 2005; Schultz, Morton, & Weckerle, 1998). Increasingly the stability of companies' promises to pay benefits through future decades have come into question as corporate mergers, bankruptcies, and other issues have resulted in dramatic cuts in pensions from some employers. The Pension Benefit Guarantee Corporation (PBGC), the government agency that works to insure pensions as the FDIC does for bank accounts, does not guarantee 100% coverage of expected pension benefits if a company's pension program goes into default (Pension Rights Center, 2005).

From the perspective of a worker, **employer pensions** have been thought of as compensation deferred from their working years or a reward for past productivity. From the viewpoint of an employer, however, pensions look very different (Burkhauser & Quinn, 1994). Employers see pensions as useful tools to modify their work force over time in two ways: (1) by building workers' loyalty during earlier spans of the career, and (2) by later enabling orderly departures (retirements) (Hardy, Hazelrigg, & Quadagno, 1996). In tight economies, when companies may need to reduce a work force suddenly, employers sometimes add incentives, making the pension more attractive and encouraging voluntary retirements (Hardy et al., 1996). The use of such incentives, called **early retirement incentive programs (ERIPs)**, flourishes during difficult economic times, when it is less costly for an employer to fund pension benefits (for which money may already be set aside) than salaries and benefits for higher-cost, mature workers. Using an ERIP is often costly in other ways, however, because employers must offer them to all eligible workers and may lose workers with critical skills and experience. ERIPs are viewed as more humane, better for the corporate image, and as causing fewer legal problems than layoffs while they target the more expensive workers.

The topic of employer pensions is incredibly complex, far beyond the scope of this chapter. However, it is important to understand recent changes, which indicate a shifting balance of power and the implied contract between workers and employers. As the supply of labor (including global labor) grows, workers are in a less powerful position to negotiate for generous wages and benefits, such as pension programs. When employees are scarce, employers must offer better wages and benefits to hire and retain skilled workers, including more generous pensions. To limit their costs and their long-term commitment to funding pensions, many employers have been switching to employee-funded and -directed pensions, called Defined Contribution (DC) pensions (e.g., 401k programs), over the past few decades (Quinn & Burkhauser, 1990).

In DC pensions, employees choose from several investment options and contribute, sometimes along with matching funds from their employers, to a pension "nest egg," which is really an investment in stocks and bonds outside the company's control (although company-based investments may be included). Advocates suggest that this change fits with the American ethic of individual responsibility. Individual workers own the fund, but they also undertake whatever risk arises from a downturn in the stock market or poor management (Quinn & Burkhauser, 1990). Only a modest percentage of workers who are eligible actually sign up for DC pensions available at their jobs because this reduces take-home pay when retirement seems a remote goal. Analysis of data on workers in the private sector showed that, while half of white collar and higher-income workers signed up for a DC plan, only one in five service sector workers, making lower wages, did so (Beckmann, 2006). In addition, employers who match all or part of worker contributions to DC plans often suspend these payments during times of financial stress, reducing the fund's growth over time. This change means that employers have less leverage over when their employees retire because they are not able to manipulate provisions of DC pensions

Retirement at early ages is declining in the United States. (Credit: E. J. Hanna)

to influence retirement timing (Quinn & Burkhauser, 1990). Movement away from early retirement and toward planning to work beyond age 65 have been connected to reduced amounts and perceived security of DC pension and other employer retiree benefits, such as health insurance (Mermin et al., 2007).

Gender and Retirement

Projections to 2016 from the Bureau of Labor Statistics (2008a) suggest that women will constitute 46.6% of the total labor force, essentially the same as 1996 and 2006, approaching half of all workers. Perhaps more significantly, however, an increasing proportion of women will be labor force participants during most of their adult lives, and nearly as many (60.7% versus 75.2% for men) work full time (DOL, BLS, 2008b). The legacy of presumed disinterest in employment among women that extended into the 1960s and 1970s has limited the study of retirement among women until fairly recently. Historical evidence from the 1800s (Quadagno, 1982) suggests that women then often continued employment into old age because of financial need, even if the jobs available to them were difficult or demeaning. Has the retirement situation improved for women since the early industrial era?

As labor force participation among women grew after World War II, married, middle-class women and mothers joined poorer and unmarried women in the labor force. Mothers of the baby boom, who are now among older cohorts, were the group that began this change, meaning that fewer older women today had lengthy or continuous careers compared to their daughters or granddaughters. These cohorts of working women were less likely to earn pensions or experience uninterrupted careers. As women have come to have working careers that more closely resemble those of men, we should also see cohort-based changes in how women enter and experience retirement. Already the average ages for retirement show a growing similarity across the sexes, as demonstrated in Exhibit 6.5. Both women and men participated in the trend toward early retirement, which has leveled off in recent decades. In 1996 50% of those contacted in a Gallup Poll planned to retire before age 65, and 15% planned to work beyond that age; in 2010 early retirement was expected by 29% and post-65 by 34% of those surveyed (Newport, 2010).

EXHIBIT **6.5**

Median Age at Retirement by Sex

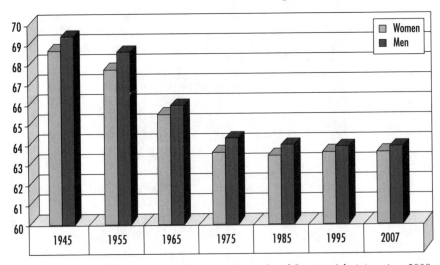

Source: Social Security Administration, 2008.

Consequently, retirement may encompass different social concerns and meanings in 2050 than it did in 1950, when the great majority of retirees were men. The world has indeed changed since Cumming and Henry (1961) declared, "Retirement is not an important problem for women, because . . . working seems to make little difference to them. Retirement is a man's problem" (pp. 144–145).

Race/Ethnic and Social Class Variations

How do life chances ultimately influence the choices workers face regarding retirement? Social class and race/ethnic diversity are important sources of variation in the conditions facing individuals approaching retirement. Those with sporadic employment histories or who became a part of the underground economy (i.e., worked off the books as day laborers, household help, or in illegal activities) are seldom covered by Social Security or employer pensions. Some of these workers are unaware that they have worked for years without building Social Security or Medicare eligibility for retirement. Exhibit 6.6 shows the percentages of three groups receiving income from several major sources, but not the amount of that income. Fewer Black and Hispanic retirees receive income from Social Security, employer pensions, or money generated by assets. Too poor to contemplate early retirement, many of these individuals continue employment as long as their health permits and opportunities are available, often at menial or physically difficult jobs (percentages receiving earnings are almost equal). Retirement, if it comes at all, arrives with the need to cease employment because of poor health or lack of a job and the acceptance of SSI (Supplemental Security Income) or similar welfare-type assistance. Exhibit 6.6 shows that only 3% of White American elders receive SSI, compared to 10% and 13% for older Blacks and Hispanics (Social Security Administration, 2010a). As this graph shows, it is important for us not to generalize about "the elderly" from the experience of middle-class individuals with pensions and other resources because not all adults have had equivalent opportunities through their working lives, upon which retirement income is based.

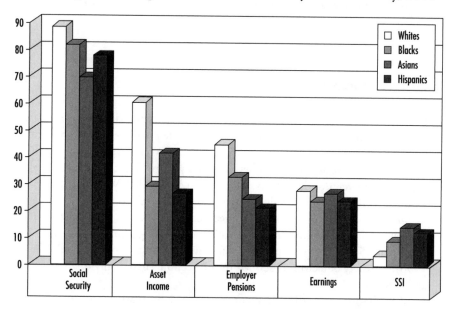

EXHIBIT *6.6*

Percentages Receiving Income From Sources by Race/Ethnicity, 2008

Source: Social Security Administration, 2010a.

The Deconstruction of Retirement?

As some of the expected security from traditional employer pensions disappears, due to corporate bankruptcies or mergers; as globalization shifts job opportunities around the world; and as concerns for the future funding for Social Security persists as a subject of political debate, studies of baby boomer cohorts suggest that the recently constructed life stage of retirement may be under reconsideration. Some have begun to speculate that we are now moving beyond the golden age of retirement (Scheiber, 2008), as fewer workers have pensions, as job insecurity grows, as employers try to control costs of pensions, and as life expectancy gradually extends. Both economic stresses at the individual, employer, and societal levels and the doubts about being able to afford retirement have raised the question of whether retirement as we have known it will persist. A recent study of 10 nations suggests that views of later life, including the place of retirement within it, are being rethought as economic conditions and life expectancy shift through time (HSBC/AgeWave, 2005). Ironically, while Americans now expect a span of time in retirement as a normative aspect of the life course, we may be entering an era where retirement comes into question.

The initial step, increasing the age of full benefits for Social Security gradually to 67, was begun in 1983, anticipating how the age-profile of the population of the United States and many other countries would be changing. The more recent changes in Social Security and pensions to promote working longer have created the context where workers may choose to work to later ages. Many countries besides the United States have passed legislation to raise the age of eligibility for benefits to minimize early retirement, including some where retirement was permitted at even earlier ages (e.g., 60). Data show that retirement at early ages is declining in the United States and slowing in European countries (Organisation for Economic Co-Operation and Development [OECD], 2000).

Further increases in age of full-benefits for Social Security may, however, have some repercussions. Such an increase would fall most harshly on workers who have had poorer life chances—women, minorities, and the less educated. Data on early (before age 66) retirees, for example, show that 20% of them have significant health problems, limiting their capacity to work (Leonesio, Vaughn, & Wixon, 2000). Raising the age of retirement would expand this percentage. If, on the other hand, economic cycles, technological change, and lower birth rates reduce the supply of labor, older workers may be encouraged by employers to continue employment. In sum, the future of retirement as a normative stage of the life course rests with social and economic dynamics beyond prediction today.

Individual Retirement

In addition to its importance to the economy, for corporations, and for the larger society on the macro level, retirement is also a key micro-level life cycle transition for individuals and couples. Because mandatory retirement is illegal (with a few exceptions), one might expect increasing variation in when and how workers withdraw from full-time career employment. For most workers, however, this decision is made within constraints. With the exception of the extremely wealthy, workers cannot decide at age 45 that they wish to retire and support themselves with income from public- or employer-funded pensions. Despite the normative nature of retirement as a part of the occupational life cycle today, a surprising number of workers at ages approaching retirement (51–61) have no plans for the transition or its timing (Ekerdt, DeViney, & Kosloski, 1996). A variety of factors, described in this section, shape individuals' decisions about whether and when to retire.

Orientations toward retirement are shaped by workers' attitudes as to personal goals, challenges, and gratifications expected in retirement years. Data from the 10-country study mentioned earlier found that while Americans focused on later life for spiritual fulfillment, positive attitudes, and private pensions, respondents in other countries differed significantly in their priorities (HSBC/AgeWave, 2005). Adults in Brazil focused on relaxation, religion, and support from children; Mexican respondents identified work, financial stability, and personal responsibility as priorities; and Japanese adults emphasized work, positive attitudes, and responsibility. Decisions about the purpose of retirement seem to be based, at least in part, in one's culture.

Determinants of the Retirement Decision

Often we think of retirement as determined by age; in fact an individual's age does play a role, both through social norms for timing for retirement and through eligibility for Social Security, Medicare, and employer pensions. The earliest research on retirement behavior in the 1940s focused on mandatory retirement policies and poor health as causes for male workers to retire (Quinn & Burkhauser, 1990), typically viewing retirement as a traumatic event in the life of the worker. A few decades later, attention turned to the critical role played by retirement income as an enabling factor in retirement. While economists continue to focus on pensions and Social Security benefits, many other factors—health status, job satisfaction, family responsibilities, and the retirement of a spouse—are considered key parts of retirement decisions today (Quinn & Burkhauser, 1990; Ruhm, 1996).

In thinking of the **retirement decision**, we assume that every worker approaching ages where retirement becomes more common periodically considers this array of factors to decide whether to retire this year, next year, 10 years in the future, or never. In fact, the process of reaching this retirement decision is probably not as orderly as researchers once presumed and may involve a variety of individual factors (how much they like their coworkers, the difficulty of their commute, changes in the cost of living or health care, what activities they anticipate during retirement, etc.) that remain largely unmeasured by researchers (Hardy et al., 1996; Weiss, 2005). Research has focused on more standard items, such as health, availability of pension and other retirement income, marital status, and employment history, which are available for secondary analysis in large national surveys (Quinn & Burkhauser, 1990).

Among the most highly researched topics are financial factors, which are often quite complex in their effects on retirement decision making (Fields & Mitchell, 1984). The size of a monthly pension benefit and its rules (e.g., based on age or years of service for eligibility), the monthly dollar value of Social Security benefits for retiring at various ages, and workers' expectations about the adequacy of these main sources of income over many future years of retirement help to shape the decisions individuals make regarding the timing of retirement. A worker might, for example, compare the value of current earnings and any added dollars to pension or Social Security benefits from another year of work against the value of those benefits now and leisure time sacrificed if she continues employment (Quinn & Burkhauser, 1990). It is unclear how well typical workers understand the economic intricacies involved, such as estimating the growth in cost of living over a 20–30 year retirement span, or how some expenses, such as health care costs, may grow faster than inflation over time.

Because it was not until the 1970s that researchers began to investigate retirement among women (Slevin & Wingrove, 1995), concerns have been raised that research using a "male model" of the retirement decision could overlook factors that influence women. Research on retirement decisions of women included factors that had been largely ignored for men, including family caregiving responsibilities and (for the married) their spouse's health (Weaver, 1994). For example, Ruhm (1996) found that married women with heavy caregiving responsibilities more often withdrew from employment, citing family responsibilities for their decisions; in some of these studies financial issues were less important than health and family characteristics in shaping the retirement decision for women (Weaver, 1994). Researchers also first considered the joint timing of retirement for married couples in studies of women

(Slevin & Wingrove, 1995). Wives were found to time their retirements to coincide with their husbands' when possible; many had to continue working longer, however, because they were younger than their husbands or were not yet pension-eligible. Some of these family-related and marriage-related issues have now begun to make their way into research on male retirement decisions, reflecting the less sex-segregated lives of recent cohorts approaching retirement.

Decisions on whether to retire and when to retire are also influenced by the availability of continued employment. Significant subsets of older adults continue employment beyond age 65 or 66 (Social Security Administration, 2004a), and there is a resurgent interest in both health and labor-market barriers to continued employment for workers over 65 (Quinn & Burkhauser, 1990). Many older workers say they would prefer to reduce their hours but keep the same hourly rate of pay, preferably in the same job. Employers seldom offer the same wages to part-time workers, however, so few workers can gradually retire from their long-term employer (Quinn & Burkhauser, 1990). This type of phased retirement is not yet common in most jobs (see Exhibit 6.7). Consequently, the retirement decision with one's career employer still usually requires an "either/or"—either continued full-time employment or complete withdrawal. Such a retirement may not be final, however, because many people become reemployed after retiring from a long-term job, as we discuss later in this chapter.

Our thinking about retirement may eventually evolve into a series of decisions on whether to seek a new job once the current job ends (Doeringer, 1990). Fields and Mitchell (1984) proposed a variety of possible models of retirement to substitute for the either/or retirement process, including intermittent work, gradual reduction of hours, and varying levels of part-time work after leaving a career (see Exhibit 6.7). Many experts project more varied patterns of movement out of the labor force in the future.

Employment After Retirement—Bridge Jobs

We continue to think of retirement as an abrupt transition, moving from full-time career employment one day to no employment the next (traditional pattern in Exhibit 6.7). In fact, today retirement is not so simple. A significant number of men and women also continue to participate in the labor force while receiving either Social Security retirement benefits or payments from a former employer's pension program. In addition, a growing percentage of older workers find their career jobs disappearing before they are ready to retire, requiring them to seek what are called **bridge jobs**—jobs to carry them over between a career job and full retirement, often with lower pay and fewer benefits (Burkhauser & Quinn, 1994; Doeringer, 1990; Quinn & Kozy, 1996). Such actions are most often seen among those who earn lower wages or are in jobs that do not provide pension coverage (Ruhm, 1990).

For some workers this involves retiring and then returning to employment, which has been dubbed *unretirement* (Maestas, 2004). One in four workers in the Health and Retirement Study unretired, and the rate was higher (37%) for those retiring at very young ages (in their early 50s). Most of those who unretired expected to do so, typically at substantially lower pay (Maestas, 2004). Therefore, it seems that workers retire from one job but, not having enough resources to meet expenses, continue some type of employment until Social Security and Medicare benefits are available, after which many more withdraw completely from employment. Some companies, such as McDonalds and Walmart, have tried to make use of those seeking bridge jobs, creating positions intended to attract retirees as part-time workers at low wages. This typically represents substantial downward mobility for a former manager or professional, but it may provide needed income for someone not yet eligible for full retirement benefits; such programs benefit employers, due to the greater reliability of older (versus teenage or young adult) workers. Additional bridge-job seekers find other jobs or construct self-employment options, such as being a consultant in an area of expertise (Quinn & Burkhauser, 1990). Growing use of bridge jobs or unretiring helps

EXHIBIT *6.7*

Alternative Retirement Patterns

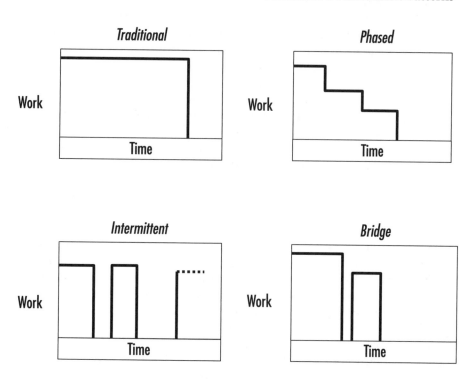

to explain the increasing number of people receiving pensions and paychecks at the same time. Ruhm (1990) describes job-stopping as increasingly similar to labor force entry, when a new worker holds several jobs on the way to a career job of longer duration. However, in this case it is a worker gradually stepping out of the labor force through a series of job changes or decreased hours of employment. Mutchler and her colleagues (1997) describe this newly recognized pattern as reflecting a "blurred" transition, rather than the "crisp" change characteristic of traditional retirement.

Retirement Consequences for Individuals and Couples

Early retirement researchers (in the 1940s and 1950s) studied the consequences of retirement with clear expectations. They anticipated, based on their orientations as middle-class males steeped in the work ethic, that all retirees would experience stress upon separation from employment and lose their core identities as male breadwinners. Because mandatory retirement was prevalent at the time, it was feared that workers were being unwillingly "put out to pasture" before they were socially, psychologically, or economically prepared. Research in recent years confirms that involuntary retirement, especially with insufficient financial resources, places retirees at greater risk of depression (Gallo et al., 2006). However, from the earliest research it was clear that most retired men were not unhappy or maladjusted (Atchley, 1976). Most early studies of retirement satisfaction showed that retirees were largely happy with their situations, not the stressed and roleless outcasts that had been expected (Atchley, 1976).

In more recent research, a longitudinal study of 800 workers found no change in self-esteem and less depression among those who retired (compared to those who kept working) (Reitzes, Mutran, & Fernandez, 1996); other studies suggest a honeymoon period of psychological health following retirement that lasts only a few years (Kim & Moen, 2002; Weiss, 2005). Research, using the Health and Retirement Study (HRS), reported that few individuals (7.5%) said retirement was not at all satisfying, with about 60% saying it was "very satisfying." Comparing to their prior lives, half reported that life was better than before (Bender & Jivan, 2005). Not surprising, individuals who faced pressures, such as poor health or being forced to retire, reported less satisfaction. Another study examined retirees' perceptions of whether their exits were voluntary or involuntary. Analyzing three waves of the longitudinal data, researchers learned that nearly one-third of retirees perceived that their retirements were forced by poor health, family caregiving, or job loss, bringing about retirement when it was not expected or desired. Retirees who were forced out were also in a more tenuous economic situation so that they felt insecure about retiring (Bender & Jivan, 2005; Szinovacz & Davey, 2005). Workers who chose to retire and the timing of retirement fare better than those forced to retire at a time not of their choosing (Hardy & Quadagno, 1995; Kim & Moen, 2002).

While negative outcomes have not emerged for the majority of male workers, the evidence for women is more mixed. Women are less satisfied than men in retirement, partly due to other major life events (illness of self or spouse, relocation, divorce, or widowhood) happening near the time of retirement (Szinovacz & Washo, 1992). A study of women's retirement outcomes (Szinovacz & Davey, 2004) shows that the women who retired abruptly due to spouse's disability experienced greater depression than men with similar experiences as caregivers, a result that seems to contradict gender-based expectations. These mixed findings may also be related to the poorer economic security of retiring women, especially if they are widowed (Calasanti, 1996a; Guy & Erdner, 1993). Women's satisfaction in retirement is shaped by both their less-advantaged experiences in the labor force in traditionally female jobs and their current health (Calasanti, 1996a). Using only the experiences of male workers (often middle-class, White male workers at that) gives an unrealistic picture of how the experience of retirement influences workers in other social groups.

Not all retirees enjoy retirement equally. Those who retire in good health, who have adequate income, and whose decision to retire was truly voluntary fare better, as do those with

The "busy ethic" has retirees approaching leisure in the same energetic, organized, and purposeful manner as they approached employment. (Credit: Mike Payne, courtesy of the Ohio Department of Aging)

strong social networks and activities planned during retirement. The work ethic, as we will see in an upcoming discussion of continuity theory, is transformed into the busy ethic of an active leisure in retirement for many of these advantaged individuals.

Rethinking Work and Retirement for the Future

Changes in Policies and Political Attitudes

As discussed earlier, the U.S. government has already taken steps (e.g., abolishing mandatory retirement and raising the age for full Social Security benefits) to encouraging employment to later ages. As businesses encounter financial stresses, however, they often try to address their problems through retiring senior workers; few currently encourage longer working lives or the flexible schedules preferred by older workers (Rix, 1991). Although well aware of the potential brain drain with retirement of the baby boomers and smaller worker cohorts to follow, society overall has not yet adequately responded to the age shift in the labor force (Kinsella & He, 2009).

Numerous proposals have identified ideas to address the changing age structure of society as it relates to employment and retirement. One involves further increasing the age of entitlement to Social Security beyond 67, as life expectancy expands—in essence keeping the length of retirement from growing (Chen, 1994). Other proposals simply suggest mandating 70 as the age of eligibility for full Social Security benefits, further penalizing early retirement financially and risking inequity toward those who become disabled early. In considering such changes, we should not underestimate the importance of programs like Social Security and Medicare in the decisions workers make to retire. Workers lacking financial support do not see retirement as a viable option if it would mean poverty! And dismantling or significantly altering what has now come to be an expected part of the life course will be far from simple.

Changes in the Economy and the Nature of Work

The productivity of the labor force depends on a number of factors, including the use of advanced technologies (e.g., computers, automated systems, and robotics), as well as the degree of fit between a job's demands and the skills and abilities of the worker filling it. Compared to a few decades ago, more jobs today require a high level of skill and continuous upgrading of training to remain up-to-date. Some other jobs are becoming deskilled as machines take over the tasks of workers (e.g., architects using design software), so a growing segment of workers simply service and maintain the equipment, rather than providing the skill. The servicing worker typically earns lower wages than the skilled predecessor and is more easily replaceable because training and knowledge so rapidly become obsolete (Auster, 1996). It is unclear how these changes will influence older workers or retirees' interests in full- or part-time employment in coming decades.

Employers are moving away from a system of lifetime employment for workers and from providing supports such as defined benefit pensions and retirement health benefits toward a more dynamic relationship. Consider contingent employment, discussed earlier in the chapter (Munnell & Sass, 2008). Employers like contingent workers; their use limits the employer's long-term investments in a worker, such as retraining, pension, or health benefits. It is unclear how prepared those pursuing careers as contingent workers will be to retire because they will only have as pensions money saved from their individual earnings (Quinn & Burkhauser, 1990). These changes also reflect the goals of large-scale business and industry as they compete in a global marketplace. Locking a business into long-term obligations with workers in one location limits its capacity to respond to lower wage rates or skilled labor elsewhere in the world. We have seen off-siting or off-shoring of many jobs, as communication- and knowledge-based jobs can be performed at home or in less-expensive office space halfway around the world. We should also

Continuity Theory and the Busy Ethic

A central tenet of Western cultures for centuries has been the importance of employment—the **work ethic**.

> The work ethic, like any ethic, is a set of beliefs and values that identifies what is good and affirms ideals of conduct. The work ethic historically has identified work with virtue and has held up for esteem a conflation of such traits and habits as diligence, initiative, temperance, industriousness, competitiveness, self-reliance, and the capacity for deferred gratification. (Ekerdt, 1986, p. 239)

Although sometimes attributed to the Puritans, the work ethic has a long cultural heritage from a time when labor by all was necessary to survival and pride in successful employment was central to identity (Plakans, 1994). The work ethic has long been viewed as a pivotal force, driving men (and more recently, women) to seek employment and job-related achievement as one basis of self-worth. But how do individuals adjust when retirement removes the status and achievement engendered by employment?

A partial answer to this question can be found in **continuity theory**, an individual-level theory spawned (along with activity theory) from the reaction to disengagement theory. Central to continuity theory is the idea that adults, in adapting as they age, attempt to preserve and maintain existing self-concepts, relationships, and ways of doing things (Atchley, 1989). Activity theory argues for equilibrium—replacing a lost activity or relationship with an equivalent one. "Continuity theory assumes evolution, not homeostasis, and this assumption allows change to be integrated into one's prior history without necessarily causing upheaval and disequilibrium" (Atchley, 1989, p. 183). Faced with change, aging adults select alternatives consistent with who they have been and what they have done in the past, sustaining the sense of self.

Consistent with this view, David Ekerdt (1986) posited a moral imperative for active involvement during retirement, which he calls the **busy ethic**. "Just as there is a work ethic that holds industriousness and self-reliance as virtues, so, too, there is a 'busy ethic' for retirement that honors an active life. It represents people's attempts to justify retirement in terms of their long-standing beliefs and values" (p. 239).

Ekerdt argues that people legitimate retirement and leisure by being highly occupied—keeping busy—much as they did during their years of employment. Rather than unlearning the work ethic, people transform it into the busy ethic, giving content to the retiree role, once considered devoid of expectations (a "roleless role"). Ekerdt argues that the busy ethic lets retirees approach leisure in the same organized and purposeful manner they used for employment. Retirees do not actually have to pursue constant busyness but should at least talk about their activities and plans to be busy in the future in activities such as volunteer work, socializing, and leisure pursuits. Busyness structures time in a much more socially acceptable and work-consistent manner, minimizing (according to the theory) the risks of disruption and distress.

Those planning activities for future cohorts of the elderly may want to keep the notion of continuity in the forefront. If continuity is important, then older adults who have retired will probably seek activities in which they can gain both the sense of busyness and the feelings of accomplishment formerly provided by employment. These needs may help explain why some adults eschew participation in today's senior centers, where chatting, arts and crafts, lunch, and bingo (un-worklike activities) often represent the core of the day. Rethinking senior centers to include meaningful volunteerism and opportunities for part-time employment could make them more relevant to future cohorts of retired Americans (Fitzpatrick & McCabe, 2008).

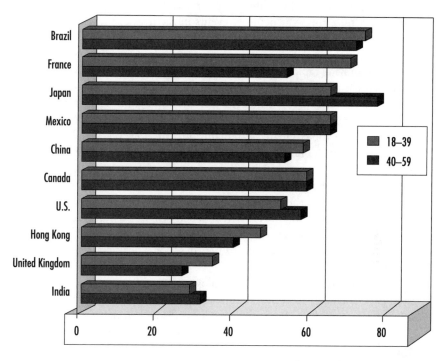

EXHIBIT 6.8

Percent Agreeing: Alternating Periods of Work and Leisure
Is the Ideal by Age and Country

Source: HSBC/Agewave, 2005.

keep in mind that a majority of U.S. workers are employed in smaller businesses; almost one in five (18.4%) worked in firms of fewer than 20 workers in 2004 and 36.4% in companies under 100 workers (U.S. Census Bureau, 2004); smaller firms have always had more difficulty offering benefits such as pensions to their workers, especially in economic downturns.

Attitudes about work and retirement seem to be moving in a direction supportive of a flexible view of moving into and out of the labor force in a less structured fashion. Exhibit 6.8 shows the percentages of working-age adults (18–39 and 40–59) in 10 countries supportive of going back and forth between periods of work, education, and leisure as the "ideal plan" (HSBC/Agewave, 2005). Support for this idea ranged from a low in India to a high in Brazil, with the United States among countries whose populations are less favorable to this possibility. There are age differences in these attitudes, but they are not systematic—sometimes the younger adults are more favorable, sometimes those closer to retirement. The study's authors suggest that this is part of a new vision for later life, which includes significantly more flexibility in social roles and their timing, including when—and whether—retirement is chosen by individuals.

Summary

By the year 2016 the U.S. labor force is anticipated to include 164 million individuals, an increase of 8% since its 2006 size (DOL, BLS, 2008a). At the same time, the composition of the

U.S. labor force will become more diverse as the Hispanic, Asian, Black, and female populations make up a growing proportion of workers (DOL, BLS, 2008a). The growth in the overall labor force is slower now than in recent decades, forcing society to consider how labor needs will be met. Regardless of the answers that emerge, the future will bring changes in how we view work and retirement as part of the life of society and the individual life course. Because employment helps to organize the sequencing of events in the lives of individuals on a micro level and the flow of cohorts into and out of the labor force at the macro level, any changes we devise will have substantial social and economic consequences. Our current concept of the occupational life cycle is moving rapidly into obsolescence, but new patterns of employment in the life course are not yet clear.

For the present we continue to face discrimination against older workers—a corporate mentality more interested in creating incentives to retire older workers than in developing them as a resource for the company. It remains unclear, however, whether the coming labor market will be an ally or the nemesis of older workers. As contingent labor grows, will more workers entering the labor force encounter lives as gypsy employees, moving regularly between jobs and risking a pension-less future? Individual, corporate, and societal decisions regarding the future of employment carry the potential for dramatically reshaping the way we organize the timing and sequencing of events in our lives. When science fiction writers speculate about possible futures, they often portray societies in which leisure abounds, thanks to the labor of robots and other technological advances. Others describe a future where workers might be scarce and highly valued.

While the particular nature of employment in the future is far from clear, we do expect the rapid pace of change to continue to re-form the occupational life cycle to something new and different, perhaps an individually specific pathway through family, employment, and educational roles. Options such as flexible job scheduling, working from home in a 24/7 world, and regularly retooling skills to remain competitive may also prompt us to think differently about how work fits with family needs, education, and employer needs. As policy discussions continue regarding the fate of Social Security (see Chapters 9 and 12), we face continuing questions regarding the future of retirement. As the break between employment and retirement becomes less clear, we may one day cease to celebrate this passage in the way we now do—with gold watches and parties—and simply bid farewell to workers of all ages as they move on to their next employment opportunity. Employment remains central to the life course, and the retirement remains normative; only future trends will reveal new and potentially more diverse pathways that may evolve to link personal lives and the economies of our communities, employers, and nations.

Web Wise

Center for Retirement Research (Boston College)   http://www.bc.edu/centers/crr/
The Center for Retirement Research, housed at Boston College, promotes research on current retirement issues from some of the leading scholars. It provides a range of publications focusing on current issues in work and retirement focuses on special topics, such as opportunities for older workers and state and local pension plans. Check out the *Social Security Fix-It Book* and the Retirement Game.

U.S. Department of Labor   http://www.dol.gov/
The U.S. Department of Labor (DOL), created by Congress in 1913, is responsible for securing the adequacy of workplaces in America, enforcing several key workplace and

employment laws such as the minimum wage. This comprehensive Web site offers information about DOL and its programs and an opportunity to explore department agencies. The link under the "Agencies" option links the user to access the BLS (Bureau of Labor Statistics) Web site described next. Press releases, the history of minimum wage, and current issues are profiled.

U.S. Department of Labor, Bureau of Labor Statistics (BLS)   http://www.bls.gov/
The Bureau of Labor Statistics (BLS) is a national agency within the United States Department of Labor that gathers, assesses, and disseminates data in the field of labor economics. The agency's Web site offers overviews of surveys on employment trends, productivity data, businesses, and projections surrounding the labor force, industries, and occupations. The current economy is profiled through these data in terms of labor force statistics, productivity, and price indexes; the option to view the data graphically is also available. This page provides opportunities to explore publications and research papers and examine detailed tables on a variety of topics.

Key Terms

activity theory	continuity theory	life chances
age discrimination	disengagement	market for labor
Age Discrimination in	early retirement incentive	multiple careers
Employment Act (ADEA)	programs (ERIPs)	occupational life cycle
bona fide occupational	earnings test	older workers
qualification (BFOQ)	employer pensions	retirement
bridge jobs	employment	retirement decision
busy ethic	labor force	work ethic
contingent labor force	labor force participation rates	

Questions for Thought and Discussion

1. Defining work as *paid employment* has implications for how society views other activity and rewards it (or fails to reward it). What consequences would arise and which groups would experience the most change if we broadened our definition of and recognition for work beyond the labor market to other productive activity?

2. Identify three social problems where the energies of retired adults might be put to good use to help society. Outline the kinds of programs that might attract these individuals to give back to their community, state, or country. What might these programs do, and what challenges would they face?

3. Employer pensions have been a cornerstone of enabling large numbers of people to fully withdraw from employment at retirement. As pensions become less reliable and baby boomers show some hesitancy to retire, consider whether they'll be able to find good quality employment, either bridge jobs or unretirement. What are the barriers and benefits for an employer?

4. David Ekerdt identifies what he views as a mainstream adaptation to retirement in his concept of the *busy ethic*. What constitutes a "good retirement," and does society currently enable all people opportunities to achieve a good retirement?

Ironies of Crime:
Silver-Haired Victims and Criminals

Older Persons as Victims of Crime

The conventional wisdom is that older people are frequently victims of crime, including violent confrontations. This notion permeates our culture, but is it realistic? Are older people more likely to be victims of crime than younger people? Data from the Bureau of Justice Statistics (Klaus, 2005) suggest that this image of widespread victimization is far from accurate. Persons over age 65 are substantially *less* likely than younger people to be victims of violent offenses, and this low rate has been true for many years. In a community-based sample, Lachs and his colleagues (2004) found that 29% of older adults had some contact with police in connection with a crime over a 10-year period (as a victim, perpetrator, witness, or in some other role), with only one in five victims being involved in a violent crime. In contrast, teens experience 25 times the risk of being victims of violent crime than people over 65. While many crimes that do occur against older adults involve property (burglary, auto theft, or other property theft) or money (fraud, purse snatching, or picking pockets), the age 65 and older group has the lowest rates of property crime of any age category (Jordan, 2002; Klaus, 2005).

Because older persons are more likely than younger victims to report crimes they experience to the police, this difference in the crime statistics is not an artifact of under-reporting by people over 65. Furthermore, both areas of crime (violent crime and property crime) have shown declines from the early 1990s, suggesting that our images of worsening crime do not apply, at least to those over age 65 (U.S. Department of Justice, 2008). This conclusion carries some important caveats. One has to do with the specific crime of purse/wallet snatching; older people are equally (but not more) likely to be victims of this particular crime as those in younger age groups. A second caution has to do with the implications of crime against the elderly. Elderly victims of crime involving physical contact of any type are more likely to suffer a serious injury than are younger victims, are more often victimized at or near their homes, more frequently face an assailant who is a stranger, and are (slightly) more likely to face an armed offender. Although smaller in number, the crimes perpetrated on older persons may be somewhat more dangerous or have more negative consequences (e.g., injuries) than those against more youthful victims.

Fear of crime among the elderly, on the other hand, is very high and has been so for decades. This fear has resulted in the so-called victimization/fear paradox, suggesting that older persons' irrational fear of crime (because it is largely based in myth) leads to overreactions in their behaviors. Most of the studies that have used cross-sectional data to compare fear of crime by age have shown dramatically higher levels of fear among older adults (Ferraro & LaGrange, 1992).

Fear of crime can be paralyzing to older persons and can have significant negative consequences for quality of life (Ferraro & LaGrange, 1992). Fear often leads elderly people to bar their doors and windows, avoid going out after dark, and experience high anxiety during any outing into the community surrounding their homes. What is responsible for these high levels of fear? No one is certain, but a variety of methodological weaknesses have been identified in research on fear of crime (Ferraro & LaGrange, 1992). Most of the fear of crime research has been based on single questions about level of fear. However, when people were questioned in more detail about fear of specific types of crime in other studies (such as being murdered or having your car stolen), it was found that older people were not more fearful than their younger counterparts of specific kinds of crime. Based on this more detailed measurement, younger people, the more likely victims, were more fearful of particular crimes than were older people (Ferraro & LaGrange, 1992).

Older Persons as Criminals

The other side of this image, less often seen in the media, involves the age of criminals held in local, state, and federal prisons. When we picture criminals, we generally imagine young or midlife adults (predominantly male), rather than people in their 70s and 80s, and this image is largely correct. Older persons are underrepresented in prison populations—of over 2.1 million prisoners at the federal, state, or local level, those over 65 number only 17,500. But those studying this topic consider older inmates to be ages 50 and older—expanding the overall number of older prisoners to 186,500, still 8.9% of the total (West & Sabol, 2009), less than their percentage in the larger population.

Why are older men and women incarcerated? Many of the older prisoners of today have life histories of crime, punctuated by alternating intervals of incarceration and freedom. Others are serving lengthy or life sentences for a single crime, such as murder (Aday, 2003; Gewerth, 1988). Some are first-time offenders, including perpetrators of violent crimes. Stricter sentencing laws, including "life without the possibility of parole" and "three strikes and you're out" rules, which make imprisonment a permanent status for serious criminals, will dramatically increase the older prisoner population in the future (Aday, 2003; Snyder, vonWermer, Chadha, & Jaggers, 2009). As crime has increased and public support for extended imprisonment has grown, criminals being sentenced in many jurisdictions today are facing all of their remaining years, including their old age and eventual death, behind bars.

This aging of the prison population creates some new issues. For example, crime by older persons without prior criminal records may result from cognitive impairments (such as Alzheimer's disease), a condition that law enforcement and prisons are not well suited to address (Aday, 2003; Snyder et al., 2009). Prison officials are scrambling to accommodate a growing population of older, increasingly physically frail individuals within facilities designed for youthful and midlife offenders (Aday, 2003). Prisons were typically not built to accommodate wheelchairs, nor are their medical facilities or staff equipped to manage some of the chronic conditions common in later life, such as arthritis and diabetes. Aged prisoners, in fact, pose the risk of dramatically increasing prison costs because of their needs for long-term health care and daily medications and their limited ability to work in prison industries and agricultural programs that help to defray the costs of prison systems in many states (Shatzkin, 1995; Snyder et al., 2009; U.S. Department of Justice, Federal Bureau of Prisons, 1989).

As society encourages courts to lock up violent offenders and "throw away the key," we are, over the long term, creating a geriatric prison population that has no precedent in history. This situation raises numerous questions that have yet to be answered. Do lengthy sentences rehabilitate prisoners? How do we assess the relative risk of recidivism (i.e., returning to crime) by a 70-year-old who murdered someone when he was 25 versus a 70-year-old who committed murder when he was 65? What will happen to criminals released after 40–50 years behind bars? Where will they go? Who will they know? How will they find a place in society? Who might provide housing and care for them if they become disabled or frail? What costs are we as a society willing to incur to maintain our resolve on "life without parole?" Is keeping older prisoners in jail, including costs of needed additional facilities to care for them, a judicious use of society's economic resources? These and many other questions have not yet been addressed by policy makers at the state and federal levels but will be a natural outgrowth of current, strict sentencing policies.

Economics and the Aging of Society

7

The future of old age is uniquely tied to the future history of our welfare state . . .
Politics, not demography, now determines the size of the elderly population and the
material conditions of its existence.

(Myles, 1989)

The Role of Economics in Aging

The economic structure of a society has a profound influence on the lives of its citizens. The economy affects, and is affected by, politics, social policy, employment, and family patterns. These interrelationships make it difficult to discuss one social institution without the others. As we explore the economics of aging, it is important to understand how our social policies relating to work, retirement, and income maintenance in later life at the macro level shape the economic circumstances of older people. This link between social policy and the economic situation of individuals and groups of older people is not unique to the United States. "Despite enormous national differences in social structure and political ideology, state-administered Social Security schemes are now the major source of income for the majority of elderly in all capitalist democracies" (Myles, 1989, p. 322). While an in-depth analysis of the intersections among ideologies, market economies, and the welfare state are beyond the scope of this book, we do need to acknowledge that political processes, power, and varied groups' agendas play a pivotal role in shaping the economic situation of older people.

Economic factors influence our lives as they unfold through time in many ways. In this chapter we examine both the economic status of the older population, primarily in the United States, and how older persons as a social group in turn influence the economy. We start by exploring the complex world of policies to provide income support to the older population and their implications for economic well-being.

Policy and the Economic Status of Older Adults

Income Maintenance Policies

In many countries of the world, older persons are protected by **income maintenance systems**—public, private, or combined systems for supporting the poor, ill, and elderly using public monies or funds generated through employment. The idea of providing income to maintain older persons in their later lives, after they are no longer involved in the labor force, grew from many roots. Central among these roots for the United States was the British system of Poor Laws, which were in force from the 17th century onward. Poor Laws defined older persons as among the **deserving poor**—citizens lacking the means to support themselves through no fault of their own. Poor older adults and other paupers who were considered deserving of society's support (those who had worked hard, tried to save, not drunk or gambled away their money) received either a modest pension or food and lodging in a workhouse or poorhouse run by the community (Quadagno, 1982). From this beginning has evolved a set of public and private programs in many countries of the world intended to maintain at least a minimal flow of income to older persons who have retired or become economically dependent (Kinsella & Phillips, 2005; Schulz & Myles, 1990).

Since its creation, the U.S. system to support the deserving poor kept changing between pensions to live in the community and poorhouses because of public concern that providing a cash income from public funds (called a pension) would discourage personal saving, undermine the duty of family to provide support, and ultimately increase the financial burden to the community. The poorhouse, a truly unattractive alternative, was believed by some to motivate personal and family responsibility compared to pensions (Schulz & Myles, 1990). As you may recognize, this debate about maintaining individual and family responsibility for the care of dependent elders and other deserving poor persons continues today. Western societies still struggle with the tension between individual and collective responsibility for providing for dependent populations. Concerns persist today that comfortable levels of government benefits will undermine the responsibility of individuals toward their families and their own financial support.

The interest of governments in establishing income maintenance policies is not purely altruistic. As Schulz and Myles (1990) point out, countries that develop industrial and post-industrial economies need ways to deal with those who are unable to participate as workers for reasons of poor health or advanced age. Having some income maintenance system, whether it involves benefits based on need (e.g., disability benefits from Social Security or Supplemental Security Income [SSI], discussed later in this chapter) or public/private pensions based in employment, enables governments to avoid upheavals from masses of disenfranchised and destitute persons. "Very simply, market economies need ways of providing for those who cannot participate in markets; labor markets need welfare states or people will die or revolt (or both!)" (Schulz & Myles, 1990, p. 401). Thus, as many countries industrialized and urbanized, moving away from a family-based economy, it was clear that income maintenance for these groups would need to be addressed.

Instead of general policies, many societies established separate programs of income maintenance for older persons, children, disabled adults, and other deserving groups. Until fairly recently, programs to support the elderly have been widely endorsed by both the public and politicians (Hudson, 1978). Support from the older population (and their family members) swells the constituency with an interest in seeing that income maintenance programs, such as Social Security, are continued. In recent years, however, income maintenance for older persons has become a more controversial issue in the United States and internationally, largely because the aging of populations worldwide raises the price tag for these programs.

Income Maintenance in the United States

Two distinct premises underlie the income maintenance system in the United States. The major programs of income maintenance are predicated on the idea that benefits are earned through prior productivity. Leading examples are Social Security retirement benefits and employer pensions, which are based directly on having made a significant contribution in the paid labor force (or being a dependent of such a contributor). By reaching a specified age (or number of years of employment), one becomes eligible for benefits—a system known as **age eligibility**. Additional programs, such as the Supplemental Security Income (SSI) program for poor and disabled older adults, are, in contrast, based on financial need. When individuals establish that their resources fall below a certain level, they receive benefits based on criteria of **need eligibility**.

Supplemental Security Income, or SSI, a major need eligibility program for income maintenance in the United States, supported just over 7 million beneficiaries in 2005 (about 2 million of them are 65 or older) with an average individual's monthly benefit of $436 (Social Security Administration, 2006a). Although SSI is administered by the Social Security Administration, it uses need eligibility criteria—in contrast to the age eligibility basis for retirement benefits—to determine who receives support. Because such need entitlement programs carry the stigma of welfare, they are embraced by neither taxpayers nor benefit recipients. In programs using age or need eligibility, the fundamental ideology behind income maintenance is that older people are economically dependent through age and (possibly) poor health and are deserving of public support, rather than being left to rely entirely on the family or their own resources to survive.

International Views on Income Maintenance

Although Americans tend to be most familiar with homegrown programs, such as Social Security, income maintenance for the elderly is a feature of social policy in most countries of the world (Smeeding & Sandstrom, 2005). In 1940 only 33 countries had retirement systems in place, but the number has grown to more than 177 as of 2008 (International Social Security Association [ISSA], 2008; Kinsella & Phillips, 2005). Most countries began with a minimal benefit, enabling workers to survive when health problems connected with aging or disability made them unable to earn a living. Percentages receiving coverage in these programs range from 90% or higher in some developed countries to coverage only for government workers in some developing countries (Kinsella & Phillips, 2005). The generosity of benefits also varies widely across countries and for women and men within these countries, with the U.S. programs doing worse than some other countries in keeping older adults out of poverty (Smeeding & Sandstrom, 2005).

Programs of the **social insurance** type (similar to U.S. Social Security) predominate among the industrialized nations (Schulz & Myles, 1990). Most social insurance programs share the traits of national coverage with compulsory participation, benefits related to earnings or length of employment, contributions from workers and employers, a benefit intended to meet minimum needs, and mechanisms to adapt this benefit to inflation (Smeeding & Sandstrom, 2005). Programs in less developed nations may take very different forms, such as mutual benefit societies among occupational groups (e.g., farmers or industrial workers) or compulsory savings programs, called provident funds, to meet a variety of needs including, but not limited to, retirement and disability (Schulz & Myles, 1990).

Income maintenance in the United States rests on a number of different programs and sources (Social Security, employer pensions, personal saving and IRAs, SSI, other benefits such as food stamps and housing subsidies) rather than on an integrated system of benefits, such as those used in some European countries. Many European countries have universal social insurance-type retirement pensions with relatively high minimum benefit levels. One recent comparison showed that, while older American women held more wealth in home ownership, they were relatively income poor compared to their peers in several countries in western Europe, which provide more generous and integrated systems of income support (Gornick, Sierminska, & Smeeding, 2009).

Sources of Income

The image used by the Social Security Administration in describing income maintenance for retired Americans is a **three-legged stool**. If any of the three legs is missing, it is impossible for the stool to provide support—it falls over. The three legs (or sources of income) are retirement benefits from Social Security, payments from employment-based pensions, and income from personal savings or **assets**. The device of the three-legged stool represents the view of Social Security's creators that it was not designed to provide an adequate standard of living by itself, but rather to serve as one component of a system of support. Exhibit 7.1 shows the percentage of older adults receiving income from leading sources in 2008 by race/ethnicity. In examining this chart, keep in mind that this does not reflect the amount of money coming from any source, but instead the percentage of people in each group who got *any* income from that source. Clearly the most common source is Social Security, and some of the remaining sources (e.g., assets, SSI) vary significantly across the groups. Higher percentages for Whites on the first four categories

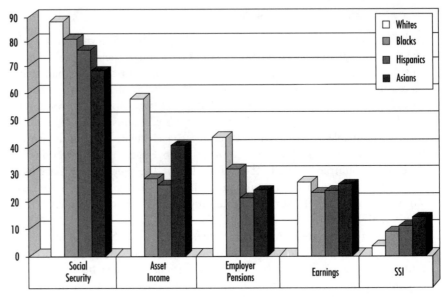

EXHIBIT   7.1

Percentages 65 and Older Receiving Income From Varied Sources
by Race/Ethnicity, 2008

Source: Social Security Administration, 2010a.

indicate that more of them experience a steady retirement income, with a stool having three or
even four legs.

Critics point out that this three-legged stool is quite precarious for many older persons because a majority of people have stools with only one or two legs (Borzi, 1993); that is, they lack
employer pensions, personal savings/assets, or both. In the aggregate these three components,
plus earnings (the more-recently added potential "fourth leg," providing income to about one-
fourth of older adult households), constitute the bulk of the income to households of older
persons (Social Security Administration, 2010a). This aggregate view of income can be quite
misleading, however, because there are striking differences in terms of who gets income from
what sources and in the amounts of income received from them in later life. Before examining
these inequalities let us take a closer look at the three original "legs" of the income maintenance
stool.

Social Security: Background and Contemporary Issues

Social Security, initiated in 1935, developed in the context of the Great Depression, with en-
couragement of the **Townsend Movement**—a 1930s social movement that advocated granting
$200 monthly pensions to older people and requiring the funds to be spent within 30 days to
stimulate the economy during the Great Depression (Quadagno, 1982). Many people supported both the Townsend movement and Social Security at its outset because older adults at
that time often relied on their kin for financial support. For families, the start of a public retirement program reduced their financial burden at a historically critical time, the depths of the
Great Depression.

The fundamental premise of the Social Security program is that of a social insurance program, in which society as a whole shares the risks of becoming economically dependent through
old age or disability. As with any insurance system, some participants benefit more than others;

Social Security's Redistributive Effects Based on Past Earnings
for Age-66 Retirees, 2009

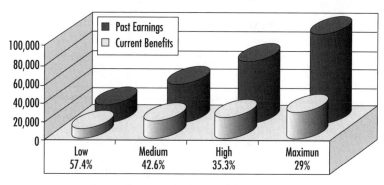

Source: Social Security Board of Trustees Report, 2009.

for Social Security this could be due to some groups receiving higher monthly benefits (from higher earnings while working) or by living longer (receiving benefits for more months). Alternatively, some individuals pay into Social Security through withholding and recoup few benefits because they die before or shortly after becoming eligible for benefits or receive minimum benefits.

A second critical aspect of Social Security is that it serves an **income redistribution** function, returning a higher percentage of prior income (called the replacement rate) to poorer individuals and a lower percentage to high-earning retirees, who are likely to have other income sources (Jones, 1996). This redistribution, shown as a comparison of prior earnings to current benefits in Exhibit 7.2, is important to reducing poverty because fewer individuals with low-earning or inconsistent employment histories have private pensions or savings to augment Social Security (Board of Trustees, 2009). This redistribution function is politically controversial because it is somewhat in conflict with the contributory basis of the program—the idea that benefits are linked to prior dollars contributed to the system. One of the proposed changes to Social Security would reduce this redistribution function, which would be harmful to less advantaged workers (e.g., minority or low-income workers) who rely more heavily on Social Security in later life.

Social Security is now a massive program, equal to 4.3% of the gross domestic product (GDP) in 2007 (Congressional Budget Office, 2009). The dollar amounts paid out as benefits by this program, which include the effects of inflation over many decades, have grown dramatically since the 1940s, as shown in Exhibit 7.3. Because of the huge number of recipients and the large dollar amounts involved, any changes that may be made in the program's provisions or funding will have a significant effect on this growth in the future, not just for individual retirees and other recipients (survivors, disabled, dependent children), but on the overall economy and the federal budget.

As you can see from Exhibit 7.4, retirees are not the only recipients of benefits from Social Security. At various points after the Social Security law's passage, dependents of workers (spouses, minor children), survivors of beneficiaries, and the younger disabled (pre-retirement age) were added so that now funds are distributed not only to retirees or the older population, but also to eligible younger people (Social Security Administration, 2008d). The largest component of dollars paid out by the program and the largest number of recipients, however, are still retired workers and their spouses.

EXHIBIT **7.3**

Growth in Social Security Payments: 1937–2008

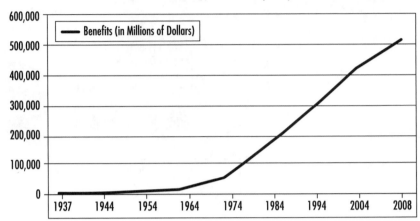

Source: Social Security Administration, 2009c.

EXHIBIT **7.4**

Types of Social Security Beneficiaries as of June 2009

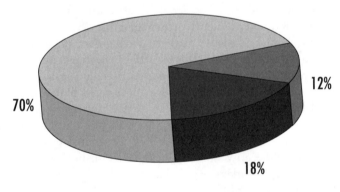

Source: Social Security Administration, 2009d.

Many experts agree that "Social Security style" programs have been highly effective in reducing poverty among the elderly both in the United States and in other countries. Data drawn from the Luxembourg Income Study of the United States and western European countries, displayed in Exhibit 7.5, show that Social Security–type benefits dramatically reduce the percentage of older adult population below 50% of the country's median national income, a standard employed here because there is no standardized poverty level across nations. The black bar shows the actual percentage of each country's older adult population below the country's median national income, and the gray extension to the bar shows what this percentage *would be* below that threshold

EXHIBIT 7.5

Population Below 50% of Median Income From Social Security Benefits

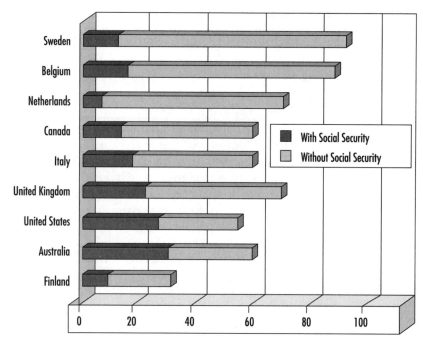

Source: Wu, 2005.

without the benefits from the country's Social Security benefit program (Wu, 2005). For example, while the percentage of older adults below this income would multiply several times over in Sweden without their Social Security system, it would double in the United States. Clearly many of these European countries have lower percentages of older adults falling into low-income or poverty ranges than the United States, and for many of these countries the public benefits received are substantially responsible for this success. This success in the United States has its limits, however, because there remain many older persons with incomes just above the poverty threshold (Shaw & Lee, 2005). In addition, certain groups continue to face higher risks of near-poverty or poverty-level incomes in later life than others, as we discuss later in this chapter.

Two areas of ongoing concern with Social Security center on the **adequacy of benefits** to support those relying on them and the **equity of benefits** across various groups. Under current provisions, monthly benefits to divorced and widowed women are often their sole source of income and are often well below the poverty level, raising the issue of adequacy (Burkhauser & Smeeding, 1994; Weaver, 1997). Many of these poor groups are in the one-third of recipients for whom Social Security is 90%–100% of their overall incomes (Munnell, 2004). Currently married couples, especially those with one high-earning worker, fare better in terms of Social Security benefit returns relative to contributions compared to unmarried people (Weaver, 1997). Proposals have been put forward to adjust the benefit amount for married couples downward to permit a more adequate benefit to widowed or divorced women without raising the total costs of Social Security (Burkhauser & Smeeding, 1994; Sandell & Iams, 1997); thus far the benefit structure has not been changed.

Concerns regarding equity of benefits—the degree to which fairness exists across groups—are also voiced for married women who have contributed as workers to Social Security, about half of whom receive benefits (as spouses) that are no larger than had the women never held jobs at all (Meyer & Herd, 2007). Under current policies, single-earner couples benefit more than do dual-earner couples or single persons because of the way benefits are calculated (Harrington Meyer, 1996). These inequities in the returns to beneficiaries compared to what they contributed reflect the now-outdated notion of the male breadwinner and economically dependent wife as the typical family pattern, which was more accurate when Social Security began. Although reforms have been discussed and researched for decades, the policies have not been modified substantially to address concerns about adequacy and equity of retirement benefits under Social Security (Herd, 2005).

Debates about the foundations of Social Security have escalated in the face of the large baby boom cohorts, now approaching and entering retirement. As these cohorts age, fears have escalated regarding the ability of smaller cohorts of future workers to provide the financial support needed to maintain funding for this system (Lee & Haaga, 2002; Munnell, 2004). What will the effects of societal aging be on the future of Social Security? The debate in recent years regarding Social Security is more fundamental than those in prior years, when modest adjustments, reflecting politically expedient compromises, adapted the program to changing societal needs. During the Presidency of George W. Bush, the debate included several issues fundamental to Social Security: the social insurance premise, using age as a basis for entitlement, redistribution of income, and the funding mechanism for the Social Security program (Munnell, 2004; Myles & Quadagno, 1995). We return to these issues later in the chapter.

Data from the Social Security Administration's projections show that the ratio of workers to beneficiaries will decrease from 3.2 in 2008 to 2.2 in 2030 and drop even lower by 2050 (Board of Trustees, 2009). Although the funding has been as a "pay as you go" system, with contributions by today's workers mostly going to support today's retirees, excess funds have always been kept in the **Social Security Trust Fund**. Changes enacted in 1983, the last major alteration of the Social Security System, mandated growth in the trust fund (via an increase in payroll deductions) in anticipation of the needs of the baby boom cohorts (Jones, 1996). As contributions are collected from paychecks and employers, extra monies are funneled into this trust fund, which will build up until about 2017. After that time, the retirement of baby boomers begins to deplete this surplus, and the trust fund, barring additional changes, is projected to run out of money around 2041 (Munnell, 2008). Depletion of the trust fund does not mean that Social Security will be bankrupt because it will continue to receive payments from current workers via FICA withholding dollars. As of now, the depletion of the trust fund means that Social Security will not be able to pay the full amount of benefits owed to retirees unless changes are made in some provisions of the program to close the gap.

This spending of the trust fund and reduction in the worker-to-retiree ratio will require either lowering benefits in some way (i.e., raising retirement age, changing formulas for benefit calculation), or increasing revenues (i.e., increasing economic productivity, increasing FICA deductions, or raising taxes on benefits received), or some combination of these approaches (Center for Retirement Research, 2007). Although the alarm has been raised in Washington about these issues for decades, political efforts to change the system have yet to result in any changes being enacted. Recent debates and publicity surrounding this issue have succeeded in raising national awareness of the Social Security issue and the challenges involved in its possible highly politicized restructuring. The most hotly debated suggestion during the Bush era focused on changing Social Security to permit some portion of contributions to be invested in stocks and bonds, which may yield higher returns than the government bonds used for the Trust Fund. These proposals were referred to as **privatization** or personal accounts, depending on your political leanings (Schulz & Binstock, 2006). Advocates then preferred the risks of the stock market to the lower returns of the current system, especially given the steady and prolonged rise in the stock market until the early 21st century. Moving toward privatizing Social Security would also reduce both the social insurance and redistribution aspects of the program (Rix & Williamson, 1998) and could have unknown effects on the stock market.

A number of developed countries around the world, facing population aging, attempted this type of privatization with limited success (Schulz & Binstock, 2006). In addition, enthusiasm for this alternative moderated substantially with the downturn in the economy and the stock market starting in 2008.

Critics of privatization point out two major concerns with privatizing some portion of the system. First, privatized accounts would provide no protection for individuals who, by seeking high returns, invest their money poorly or are swindled by con artists. Social Security and its Supplemental Security Income (SSI) program currently protect people against such risks. Second, the transition to a more privatized system could incur hidden costs, as one generation pays twice: once to finance their own future retirements and again to pay for the benefits owed to older adults already in the existing Social Security system (Myles, 2005; Starr, 1988). No resolution to this added near-term cost was ever identified.

Alternative scenarios for addressing the funding crisis include a number of adjustments that could, in combination, address the issue. These include increasing the ages for retirement (even slightly), increasing contributions through higher payroll (FICA) taxes, converting Social Security from an age entitlement to a need entitlement program, lowering benefits somewhat, or recovering benefits from high-income retirees through more taxation (Center for Retirement Research, 2009; Goss, 1997). Other proposed changes not receiving such public attention would change the rules about how benefits are adjusted for inflation, which amounts to an invisible reduction in benefits (Munnell, 2004). Most of these proposals face practical problems or political opposition, keeping them from adoption as solutions (Myles & Quadagno, 1995). For example, an increase in the retirement age could raise inequity to disadvantaged workers, who face higher rates of health problems limiting their employment and rely most heavily on Social Security as part of their later-life incomes (O'Rand, 2005). In 1983, Congress approved gradually raising the age of entitlement for full Social Security benefits to 67 (by 2027) and raising taxes on higher-income elders to recoup some of their Social Security benefits. Whatever plan emerges to remedy the expected gap in funding, which will endure for several more decades, will follow a lengthy and very political debate.

Attitudes about the Social Security System have also caused a political battleground. Although many younger people doubt that Social Security retirement benefits will be there for them when they retire (Borden, 1995), the program continues to enjoy considerable support from the public because most of us have at least one relative, neighbor, or friend receiving Social Security benefits (Day, 1993b). As the top bars of Exhibit 7.6 show, about half of younger adults are generally positive about Social Security, with approval increasing in higher age groups. Only about one-third of younger adults are confident of receiving benefits (second set of bars), compared to half of baby boomers and more than 80% of those 60 and older. Ironically, while younger adults were supportive of the idea of private/personal accounts, they also responded very positively to a question asking whether the Social Security system should be "protected, not privatized." Finally, younger adults admitted to being less knowledgeable regarding Social Security than their older counterparts, with the 60 and older group claiming to be most informed (AARP/Rock the Vote, 2005). What would families have to do if Social Security suddenly disappeared? Most people do not wish to contemplate the answer, and thus they support some version of the program.

Employer Pensions

Employer pensions—retirement income systems sponsored or organized (and often financed) by employers—represent a complex legal, fiscal, and policy area. The details of pension design and financing are beyond the scope of this chapter, and the magnitude of their importance in the overall economy is staggering. In 2009 pension expenses averaged $1.29 per employee hour worked, an amount totaling billions of dollars (Employee Benefit Research Institute, 2010). Paired with the vast accumulations from individual IRAs and other personal savings or

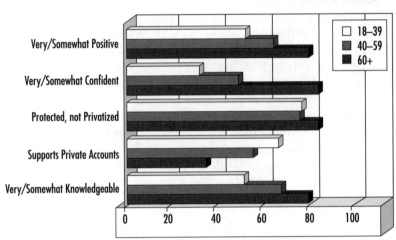

Source: AARP/Rock the Vote, 2005.

investments, these funds constitute a major component of financial capital in stock and bond markets. Because access to a private pension is often the difference between an economically secure old age and a more marginal lifestyle, both individuals and the larger society must be concerned about how pensions operate and their soundness.

Jobs usually come with or without pension coverage, so the type of occupation an individual undertakes influences the prospects for eventually receiving a pension. For some pension programs an individual must work a minimum number of years to become eligible, or **vested**, for eventual pension benefits. Therefore, not every worker covered by a pension will receive benefits if their job tenure is too short. The likelihood of being covered by a pension thus depends on a variety of factors, including occupation, education, union membership, frequency of job change, and gender. In 2008, 50.6% of adult workers in public or private sector jobs had an employer-sponsored pension program of some type; fewer (40.4%) participated in the plan (Copeland, 2009). Exhibit 7.7 shows the percentages of people in various groups with either type of pension plan (defined benefit [DB]/defined contribution or 401k-style plan, discussed later), based on a large national sample of older workers in 2008. Differences are great between low earners and high earners and across races, but gender differences have shrunk in recent years. Except for the higher earners and those approaching retirement ages, remaining groups have lower pension involvement, indicating a reason for concern about this leg of the three-legged stool for some time into the future.

Because employers generally seek to minimize pension costs, sometimes at the expense of the pensioners, the federal government passed legislation (the Employee Retirement Income Security Act of 1974, or **ERISA**) that controls how pensions are offered and funded. This law and its subsequent amendments mandate how funds must be collected and credited to employees, how employees become vested in pension plans, and how pension funds are managed. The legislation was prompted by the failure of a number of company pension funds, leaving the retirees without promised resources (Salisbury, 1993). ERISA also created protection for retirees through the Pension Benefit Guarantee Corporation (PBGC), much as the FDIC insures funds in banks. The PBGC, as we have discussed in Chapter 6, is under financial pressure due to a large number of corporate pension defaults during the economic downturn that began in 2008,

EXHIBIT 7.7

Pension Coverage of Workers, 2008

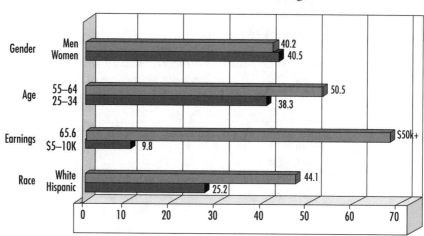

Source: Copeland, 2009.

and it is struggling to cover its obligations to thousands of pensioners from defined benefit plans (Pension Benefit Guarantee Corporation, 2009).

One basis of economic insecurity among older widows has to do with the rules for defined benefit pensions. Because pensions are earned by individual workers, in the past a pension often ended when that worker died. Because most pensioners in past cohorts were male and few wives were eligible for their own pensions, this major source of income would end abruptly for many widows, throwing them into poverty. In 1985 legislation was passed requiring all pensions to offer optional survivor benefits, as well as mandating that both spouses approve in writing the choice of either a single life or survivor option (Miller, 1985). If the survivor option is chosen, the monthly pension amount is decreased, saving funds to enable the pension to continue for the survivor after the pensioner dies. In fact, pensions are becoming such an important part of family wealth that they are increasingly viewed as jointly earned property, to be allocated like other property in divorce settlements (Women's Initiative, 1993). An analysis of data from the Health and Retirement Study regarding survivor benefits (Johnson, Uccello, & Goldwyn, 2005) found, however, that 28% of men and 66% of women decline survivor protection. Many of those making this choice, however, seem to have weighed the costs and benefits of their choices. As those authors point out, annuities such as those received from 401k-type programs are not covered by these laws, and such annuities may also disappear upon the death of its holder.

One major trend in pensions is away from what are called **defined benefit** systems. In a defined benefit pension system the employer controls a worker's pension. The employer funds and manages a common fund under rules defined by ERISA. Benefit amounts are guaranteed on a formula based on the number of years an individual has worked, salary level, and related factors (Smeeding, Estes, & Glass, 1999). Under such systems workers can know exactly what their pension amount will be as they approach retirement and whether the amount will grow with inflation or remain fixed. Issues may arise under defined benefit plans when the worker changes jobs because these programs are held and managed by employers—pensions may be frozen for those who leave after becoming eligible; often such benefits are forgotten and go unclaimed.

Growing more common are what is known as a **defined contribution** pensions, familiar to some readers as 401k plans. Defined contribution is a system where the worker, the employer, or both contribute to a fund (hence the name!) that is held by an independent financial entity; the money in this fund belongs to the worker immediately and contribution amounts help to determine a retiree's eventual benefit amount. Benefits at retirement are not guaranteed but depend on the trends in the stock and bond markets in which the employee chooses to invest, especially near the time of retirement (Smeeding et al., 1999). The economic and stock downturn in 2008 caused many individuals near retirement to reconsider their plans and continue to work due to the loss of value in their defined contribution investments (MacKenzie, 2008; Rainville, 2009). Payment from defined contribution pensions may come as a lump sum to be reinvested or as an annuity, which is paid over the life of the retiree and/or the spouse. Because the worker often has control over investment choices (and thus can take greater or lesser risks), benefits may grow or shrink depending on the vigor of the stock market and the worker's success at choosing investments (Gale, Iwry, Munnell, & Thaler, 2004). The risk and responsibility are shifted from the employer to the employees, whose level of financial literacy is, on average, very low (Hurd, 2009; Lusardi & Mitchell, 2009). Employers are not responsible for managing these funds, and DC pension systems also give the employer less control over the timing of workers' departures because they can't "tweak" benefits to encourage earlier or later retirements. Over the past 25 years, however, defined contribution plans have grown from supplemental programs to the only pension available to most workers (Gale et al., 2004).

Personal Savings/Assets

Savings and other assets accumulated during one's life are the third leg of income maintenance in retirement. As we saw in Exhibit 7.1, asset income is less available to Blacks, Asians, and Hispanics than to Whites over 65 (26%, 40%, and 23%, respectively, vs. 58% for Whites) (Social Security Administration, 2010a). Assets are all the resources people own that can be converted into money, including home equity, real estate, cash savings, IRAs, and stocks and bonds. Assets "provide housing, serve as a financial reserve for special or emergency needs, contribute directly to income through interest, dividends, or rents, and help to enhance the freedom with which individuals spend their income" (Schulz, 1992, p. 37). A majority of older persons have savings or assets of some type, although a large percentage of these assets do not generate income. Exhibit 7.8 shows the difference by age in overall assets held (also known as net worth). Clearly net worth increases with age—up to age 70. However, the great majority of this net worth at all ages is tied up in equity in a home, rather than representing savings, stocks and bonds, or other more liquid resources. This reflects the poor record of Americans at saving money at any age. In short, the great majority of net worth for those over age 65 does not generate income.

Like other resources discussed here, savings and assets are unequally distributed among the older population, and this inequality has grown in recent years (Smeeding & Sandstrom, 2005). Accumulation of assets is only possible by having a surplus of resources to save or invest, limiting the chances that low-income persons can develop independent assets to utilize in later life. In a few cases assets are inherited from kin, but most people who generate assets do so through their own productivity in the labor force. Thus, inequality in asset accumulation is a reflection of income inequality during the working years.

In summary, the three-legged stool of income maintenance for older people is a very shaky structure for a majority of older adults today, and it is significantly more wobbly for some groups than for others. Social Security is likely to face some adjustments in the future, private pensions are only available to some workers, and relatively few adults have substantial savings or assets beyond home equity to rely upon in their future retirements.

EXHIBIT   *7.8*

Median Net Worth by Age

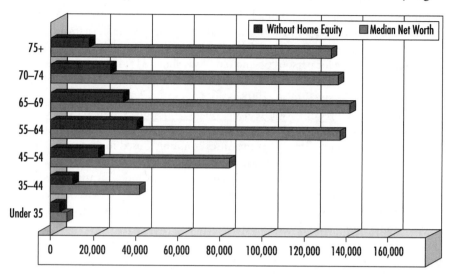

Source: U.S. Census Bureau, 2008f.

Economic Well-Being of Older Americans

So, how are older Americans doing economically? Armed with your understanding of the three legs of the income maintenance stool (and the newer, fourth leg—earnings), let us next consider the effectiveness and long-term impact of this income maintenance structure on the economic status of older people. The adequacy of our strategies and policies for maintaining economic well-being for older people is an important, complex, and multifaceted question. Given that many of us aspire to retire at some time in the future, these policies, any changes to them, will shape all of our economic futures.

As we have seen, groups in the older population vary widely in their sources of income. This heterogeneity plays an extremely important role in answering the question about the economic status of older people, and we will review major sources of, as well as explanations for, the variations in a later section. Another basic influence on our answers regarding the economic status of older Americans is the choice of definitions or measures we use to answer our question.

Alternatives for Measuring Economic Well-Being

Two measurement issues are involved in answering our question about how well or poorly older people are doing financially. First, there are many definitions of economic status, including current income, assets, and what is called in-kind income. Poverty level offers another kind of measure of economic well-being. In any measure, the number and nature of financial resources we include in our analysis influence our results. We will briefly review each of these measures and the sometimes conflicting conclusions they allow experts to draw about the economic status of older people. Second, the specific statistics we use to describe the economic well-being of older adults—such as means, medians, and measures of variability—will similarly shape any conclusions we draw.

Measures of Economic Status

Some economists have suggested that economic well-being encompasses not just income, but also broader economic responsibilities (such as family support and tax liabilities) and economic resources (such as home ownership and health insurance). Usually, however, economic status is measured more simply. One obvious way to assess people's financial situation is to find out about how much income they receive. Salaries and wages, interest and dividends, and income from public or private transfers (such as Social Security and unemployment compensation or child support payments) are traditionally included in definitions of income. When we compare older people to the younger population, we find that older people have lower incomes than younger adults and that people over age 75 have lower incomes than those 65–74. In 2007 the median household income for persons 65 and older was about $17,424; for people 75 and older, median income was only $16,054. This compares to $26,624 for households headed by anyone age 15 or older (U.S. Census Bureau, 2008d).

Income is only one measure of the financial resources available to people, and our picture of the economic status of older people is more complete and more complex when we consider these other indicators. Two other measures commonly used in discussing the financial situation of older people are assets and **in-kind income**. The first of these, assets, was discussed earlier in the chapter along with net worth. When assets are included in the consideration of economic well-being, a much more positive picture emerges than if we look only at income. As demonstrated earlier, this is primarily because so many older people own their homes and can count their home equity among their assets.

With all due caution regarding the variability among older adults, Smeeding (1990) reports an "impressive level of wealth among the older population" (p. 366). Home ownership by older persons is higher in the United States than in many equally developed European countries (Holtz-Eakin & Smeeding, 1994). Owning rental property, stocks, bonds, and mutual funds constitute about 20% of total wealth (U.S. Census Bureau, 2008d). Assets are important not just as a reserve; some can provide income through interest and dividends. Total median income for those receiving asset income after age 65 is twice as high ($35,510) compared to those with no income coming from assets ($15,600) (Social Security Administration, 2010a). Not surprisingly, those with the highest incomes also had the greatest store of wealth in assets (Federal Interagency Forum on Aging-Related Statistics, 2008).

Another element of economic well-being involves in-kind income. In-kind income includes noncash benefits that contribute to economic well-being by reducing expenditures. Publicly funded medical insurance (Medicare or Medicaid) is an example of in-kind income because it reduces expenses for participants. Subsidized housing and food stamps are other familiar examples of such noncash benefits. The inclusion of in-kind income in calculations of economic well-being has an enormous impact on the outcomes. In one study that used an "expanded income" measure (regular income plus some other cash and noncash benefits, including health insurance, capital gains, public housing subsidy value, and net equity), older people as a group were found to be as well-off as the nonelderly (Smeeding, 1990). This is quite a different conclusion from the one we would draw from the data on median personal income or assets exclusive of home equity. One dilemma of such inclusive measures has to do with the role of health benefits. When people are seriously ill, making heavy use of health care covered by Medicare or Medicaid, considering in-kind income would add the dollar value of this care to calculations of economic well-being. Even though no money comes to them, such seriously ill people appear wealthier because they receive high levels of in-kind health care. Such variations in how income is measured reinforce the need for caution in drawing conclusions about income unless you understand the definitions and measurements used to generate the results.

Rates of Poverty

While measures of financial resources answer one kind of question about economic well-being (How well off are older people?), poverty rates answer another kind of question about economic health: how large or small is the proportion of older people who are in serious financial jeopardy? Poverty rates tell us the proportion of the population living below a minimum level of income defined as necessary for survival. The poverty threshold is the income level below which people are categorically defined by the government as *poor*; this threshold is linked to eligibility for many of our nation's safety net (need eligibility) programs. For example, food stamps are available to people whose income is less than 130% of the poverty threshold. The poverty rate (the proportion living below the poverty threshold) is thus not a measure of how many resources individual people have, but of how many of them live in an untenable financial situation.

Researchers and policy makers often use poverty rates and trends to chart how effectively programs and policies address social ills, redistribute resources in ways society desires, and improve the financial situation of particular groups. The poverty among elderly Americans was 28.5% in 1966, compared to 9.7% in 2008, reflecting substantial improvement in the past several decades (Federal Interagency Forum on Aging-Related Statistics, 2008). Because of the many ways people use poverty statistics, and because of the many competing agendas that can underlie those uses, it is important to understand the way the U.S. government calculates poverty.

The original poverty level was based on the cost of food needed to meet minimal nutritional requirements. The cost of food was calculated using 1962 prices, when the index was initiated; and that food cost amount was multiplied by three (based on data from a 1955 survey that showed that food represented one-third of the average family's budget) to arrive at the official poverty threshold. The poverty threshold is now adjusted for inflation year-to-year for individuals and households of various sizes. Individuals or households whose incomes fall below the designated level qualify as poor. In 2005 the poverty threshold for a family of four was $20,144; by 2008 the equivalent figure had grown to $22,207—a slow growth related to inflation rates (U.S. Census Bureau, 2005b, 2008g).

The poverty threshold formula is open to serious criticisms. First, food costs are based on minimum nutrition and were originally developed for emergency periods; no one was expected to thrive on such a menu plan for a long time. Second, different food plans were developed for different kinds of households. The plan for a household in which the head of household is under 65 allows for higher food costs than if the household is headed by someone over age 65. The result of this difference is a lower poverty threshold for those 65 and older, meaning that older people have to meet an even lower income standard than younger people to be considered poor and to quality for need-based entitlement programs. For example, a single individual under age 65 had a poverty threshold of $11,201 in 2008, compared to $10,326 for a single individual aged 65 or older (U.S. Census Bureau, 2008g).

A final focus of criticism is the multiplier of three. The idea that food represents about a third of a family's budget, which was apparently the case for working class families in 1955, is quite unrealistic today. Most families require much more than three times their food budget to meet all of their other needs, including housing, utilities and transportation. Housing takes a much higher proportion of the budget and food a lower proportion than in 1955 (even though food costs are higher today). Moreover, families at different levels of living will have different expenditure patterns; for poor families, necessities such as housing and food will consume a higher proportion of the total budget than in middle-class families of the same size. The impact of the "food times three" approach to calculating the poverty threshold is to keep the amount artificially low, meaning that people have to be extremely poor in order to be categorized as living in poverty. Questions about how poverty is and should be calculated are receiving significant attention from researchers, policy analysts, advocates for older people, and the government agencies that produce poverty statistics (Pimpare, 2009).

Reflecting these concerns about the adequacy of the poverty threshold formula, poverty rates are now often reported including figures for 125% and up to 200% of the poverty line. Those falling within 100%–150% of the poverty threshold are often referred to as *near poor*.

Older adults vary in economic well-being; many today own their own homes. (Credit: U.S. Census Bureau, Public Information Office [PIO])

In 2006, 9% of all older people lived below the official poverty line; however, raising the poverty level to 199% of that threshold (just under $21,000 per year for an individual 65 and older) increased this percentage to 35% of adults over 65. Thus, hundreds of thousands of older people—more than one in three—who are not categorically poor according to the official poverty threshold are nonetheless economically vulnerable or *near poor* (Federal Interagency Forum on Aging-Related Statistics, 2008). Smeeding (1990) has termed the group between 100% and 200% of the official poverty level the *tweeners,* those not poor enough to qualify for safety net programs but too poor to be financially secure and meet ongoing needs.

Another study reinforces that we need to be cautious about concluding that poverty is not a serious problem for older adults. Rank and Hirschi (1999) examined not just the annual rate of poverty (a cross-sectional, snapshot view) but the likelihood that someone would experience an episode of poverty at some time in later life. In a large, longitudinal study the researchers followed individuals from age 60 and found that 35% experienced at least one episode of poverty by the time they reached 85. Some of the individuals in the study were at greater risk of becoming poor, especially those with less than high school education, those who were unmarried, and those who were Black. A married White male with more than high school education had a 14% risk of ever experiencing poverty by age 85; risks for a married Black man who did not graduate high school reached 60% and soared to 88% for his female counterpart (Rank & Hirschi, 1999). Once again, employing the life course perspective shows a different picture of the problem of poverty among the elderly than do snapshot cross-sectional views of current poverty rates.

These kinds of analyses underscore the complexity of answering questions about economic well-being. The very different conclusions that can be drawn—all of them supported by facts and figures—suggest that answers and conclusions can be easily shaped by ideology, vested interests, and political agendas. An 85-year-old widow subsisting on SSI in her modest house who appears to be economically secure because the benefits she received for a temporary nursing home visit are considered income suggests that we all need to develop a critical eye toward statistics on the economic well-being of the elderly. Data-based but ideologically motivated statements about the economic status of older people have stereotyped them as *greedy geezers,* responsible for the federal deficit and a drain on the welfare of children. You are now better prepared to be more informed as you examine such statements. Whatever definitions and measures we select, these discussions emphasize the importance of not generalizing about older adults as an economic category.

Economic Well-Being and Inequality Among Older People

Most researchers agree that there have been striking improvements in the economic well-being of the older American in the past 3 decades (Quinn & Smeeding, 1993; Social Security Administration, 2010a). Poverty rates among older Americans have fallen sharply since the advent of some familiar age-based entitlement programs. In 1959, 35.2% of older people lived below the poverty level; in 2008 the figure had dropped to 9.7%. This success, in turn, has provided support to those with political and social agendas seeking to reduce government entitlements to older people. However, despite the historical decline in poverty among older Americans, significant variation exists in the economic status of older adults, including pockets of severe economic distress in certain social groups (Quinn & Smeeding, 1993). Exhibit 7.9 shows the wide variation in levels of income and a persisting concentration of older adults in households at the low end of the income distribution (50.3% are under $25,000). You may be surprised to see that the modal (largest) income category is between $10,000 and $14,999 and that households over 65 with incomes over $75,000 constitute only 13.1% of older adults (Social Security Administration, 2010a); this data is far from the widespread notion of elder wealth.

These wide income variations are mirrored in the varying rates of poverty for different groups within the older population. Exhibit 7.10 shows that the overall poverty rate masks notable differences, with gray areas indicating poverty and black areas of the bars indicating those who are near poor. Black, Hispanic, unmarried, or female persons over 65 experience greater economic disadvantage, as indicated by the higher percentages of poverty/near poverty. The combined poverty and near poor rates for married people over age 65 (7.8%) are much lower than all other groups, and the combined poor/near-poor rates for older Black (29.9%) and Hispanic elders (31.3%) compares to 7.8% for older Whites.

EXHIBIT **7.9**

Income Distribution of the Population 65 and Older in 2008

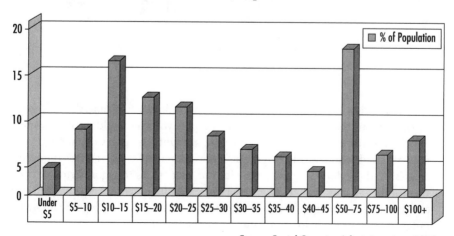

Source: Social Security Administration, 2010a.

EXHIBIT 7.10

Percent of Older Persons in Poverty by Marital Status, Sex, and Race/Ethnicity, 2008

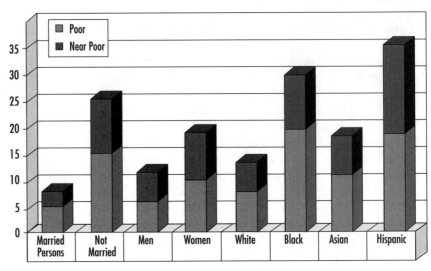

Source: Social Security Administration, 2010a.

EXHIBIT 7.11

Differences in Median Income by Age and Sex, 2008

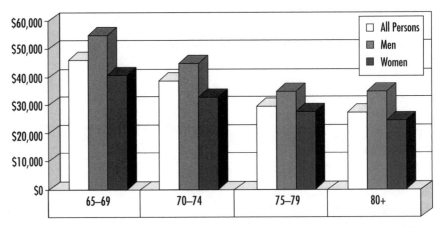

Source: Social Security Administration, 2010a.

In addition, older age is associated with diminished income. Exhibit 7.11 shows median income amounts by age and sex. As you compare younger to older cohorts across the lower axis, you find lower median household income amounts. Incomes of men are consistently higher than those of women as both groups report lower 2008 incomes as the respondent's age increases. And the difference in income for the "all persons" category across ages differs more than that for the incomes of men. How can this be? With differential mortality, more males are dying as age increases, meaning that the "all persons" person category is more influenced in upper age ranges by the generally lower income amounts of women.

As mature cohorts reach age 65 or retirement, each one in recent years has included a higher percentage of people with Social Security retirement benefits and income from pensions or assets. So when we state that the aggregate economic well-being of the older population has improved, it is mostly because poorer members of the oldest cohorts have died and been replaced by more affluent individuals moving into the 65 and older range (i.e., through cohort composition changes). It is generally not the case that the economic fortunes of specific persons have improved over time (Quinn & Smeeding, 1993), nor is it the case that individuals or couples, as they advance in age, necessarily move to lower levels of income. An analysis by McGarry and Schoeni (2005) found that nearly half of the differences in economic well-being between the married and widowed elders is due to economic conditions that predated the death of a spouse; remaining differences are due to high health costs in the last years of a spouse's life, loss of the spouse's income, and continuing high health costs for the surviving spouse. Some additional erosion of buying power is possible if income sources, such as employer pensions, do not adjust for inflation or if health or family problems require spending, or liquidating, assets that had been providing ongoing income. In interpreting cross-sectional data such as these, it is important to avoid the life course fallacy.

Effects of Population Aging on the Economy

So far we have considered the impact of aging (along with variations by gender, race/ethnicity, and marital status) on the economic well-being of older individuals. Another kind of question looks at the impact of societal aging on the economy of the nation as a whole. Population aging can have an effect on aggregate economic activity, the size and composition of the labor force, aggregate labor force participation rates, productivity, and the structure of demand and consumption (Matras, 1990). Here we consider some of these effects of societal aging on the economy.

Spending and Saving Over the Life Course

How will societal aging affect savings behavior in the United States and the pool of assets in pension funds and privately owned assets? If future cohorts behave like current ones, the already low level of savings by individual Americans could drop even more. However, we cannot necessarily predict the savings behavior of future cohorts from the activities of aging cohorts to date.

Economists posit what they call the **economic life-cycle hypothesis** of saving and spending. According to this hypothesis, rational economic planners (all of us, presumably) accumulate assets of various types, including personal savings, home equity, and pension wealth, in anticipation of a change in behavior in later life as we become less economically productive at retirement. The hypothesis argues that we defer some of our consumption (in pensions and IRA accounts) to support ourselves in later life, spending down these assets as we move through later life (Holtz-Eakin & Smeeding, 1994). A person who adapted perfectly to this economic life-cycle hypothesis would end up with absolutely no resources left at the time of death, but this outcome seldom occurs. Economically secure people often die leaving an estate, whereas some less advantaged may "outlive their money," requiring assistance to pay for basic needs and long-term health care before they die. Others start with significant resources, which can be quickly consumed by costs for health or long-term care services.

Research shows that the oldest age groups have fewer accumulated resources than do their younger counterparts over age 65, suggesting either that they are spending down their accumulated resources or that there is a cohort difference (i.e., they started out with fewer resources at age 65 than current cohorts). People certainly do spend down their resources with age, as they consume pensions and other resources, but not as quickly as the life-cycle

The Stratified Life Course and Economic Diversity

As we have seen, groups within the elderly population differ substantially in rates of poverty and on more positive measures of economic status, with married couples faring better than unmarried adults, and Whites better than Hispanics or Blacks. What brings about these systematic differences, which tend to appear regardless of the measure you use to evaluate economic well-being? The answer has to do with choices and opportunities available throughout the life course—described earlier as *life chances.*

These differences must be considered from a life-cycle perspective, as the consequence of differences in life chances over time (including education, health, family, and labor force experiences), consequent access to various types of resources in adulthood (income, family support, pensions, and assets), and ultimately the provision of income maintenance programs for later life (O'Rand, 1996). Thus, life chances, associated with earnings potentials and access to pensions, have long-term consequences for economic well-being in later life. Sociologists and economists have used the notions of **cumulative inequality** to describe this process, whereby individuals who have early opportunities for success (better life chances) most often build on that success to perpetuate their advantages through adulthood and into later life, while those with disadvantages also carry those disadvantages forward through sequential life stages, often resulting in economic security or poverty in later life (Ferraro & Shippee, 2009; O'Rand, 1996). Structural barriers to full employment in some groups within a society (women, minorities, those with less education) will inevitably result in their greater financial vulnerability in old age, barring income maintenance policies that correct for those disadvantages through income redistribution.

One interesting implication of a life cycle perspective is that, in the long run, the well-being of the elderly may be more efficiently served by concentrating on programs whose impact occurs long before old age-programs like education,

training or health . . . [Such programs] can have great impact on the income, assets, and health status of the elderly-to-be. (Quinn, 1993, p. 21)

As evidence of this argument, studies continue to confirm that women with children earn lower wages, even after differences of education, experience, and job type are taken into account (Sigle-Rushton & Waldfogel, 2007). This and similar life course events shape labor force choices, wages, savings, and a range of other behaviors over time. The tendency, then, is for those who have been advantaged in early stages of adulthood to continue that advantage into later life, with economic disadvantage also following persons as they age. Common exceptions to these patterns of continued advantage or disadvantage in later life are individuals whose resources are depleted suddenly by health problems and women who experience increased risks of impoverishment following widowhood (Quinn & Smeeding, 1993).

Both race and health influence the accumulation of wealth by affecting life chances: Blacks, Hispanics, and those with chronic health conditions generally have lower assets in later life than their more advantaged age peers (Shea, Miles, & Hayward, 1996). Older Blacks remain less likely to own homes or have high home equity amounts as they approach later life, giving them smaller assets for the future (Sykes, 2008). Life-course events, such as marriage, divorce, and childbearing, can also influence individuals' long-term economic status. For example, a study of preretirement-age women showed that those who had been divorced or widowed had significantly lower incomes and assets than those who remained in first marriages. Even if the divorced or widowed women had subsequently remarried, their economic well-being remained lower (Holden & Kuo, 1996).

Life chances and life course accumulation of inequality translate into various groups of older adults being more or less likely to have income from the major categories discussed earlier. Exhibit 7.12 compares the distribution of income across sources for older individuals in the highest one-fifth (or quintile) of the income distribution with those in the lowest 20% of that distribution. As the gray bars for the high income group show, people in this category rely much less on Social Security benefits than the low income group. For this group several sources are a much larger contributor to income, such as earnings; dollars generated by assets, such as stock, bonds, or rental property; as well as pensions. Clearly, those most economically secure in later life had earned incomes large enough to enable them to save and invest during their working years (Federal Interagency Forum on Aging-Related Statistics, 2008) and had a better chance of continued employment and pension coverage. Older persons in the lowest quintile of income receive 83% of their aggregate income from Social Security, with modest inputs from the other sources, including 8.5% from public assistance. Thus, the income sources, as well as the income amounts, of the most financially secure individuals differ substantially from those who are least economically secure.

Although life chances are associated with membership in particular social groups and categories, the system is not completely deterministic; individuals do "beat the odds" and do very well—getting excellent jobs, good incomes, and substantial pensions despite early disadvantages or membership in a group that fares poorly on average. The notion of life chances simply points out that, to date, individuals in different groups have had different odds of moving successfully through the events of the life course in ways that result in economic security in old age. These different odds—patterned by race, ethnicity, class, and gender—are the product of our history and social structure.

Differing life chances for economic security in later life is one kind of diversity among the older population, but diversity can have different meanings and implications. Is diversity a positive, negative, or neutral fact of life in our society? Should we promote diversity or seek to reduce it? Obviously the answer to that question depends on what kind of diversity and on the ideology of the people discussing it. In the case of economic status, a high degree of diversity may be a negative reflection on our society and may call for policies to reduce difference.

EXHIBIT **7.12**

Shares of Aggregate Income in Lowest and Highest Income Quintiles

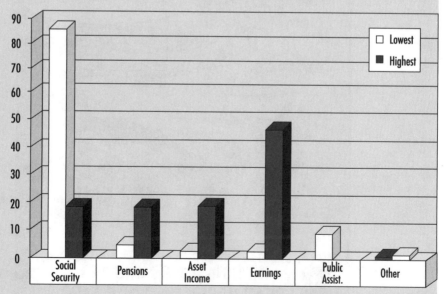

Source: Federal Interagency Forum on Aging-Related Statistics, 2008.

hypothesis suggests (Holtz-Eakin & Smeeding, 1994). While most people do not add much to their accumulated assets in later life, most work to hold onto the resources accumulated in earlier years to meet expected or unexpected needs (a new car, a health care emergency). If the life-cycle hypothesis is accurate for most people, the aging of society should reduce private assets, the stock of money in pension funds, and thus the capital available to the economy for investments in new business or research. While this sounds dire for the health of the economy, let us turn next to examining the somewhat-limited research on consumption patterns of older adults.

Consumption Patterns

Researchers have analyzed how patterns of saving, spending, and consuming vary by age, among other social variables. The amounts and types of spending by older adults may seem of little relevance to the rest of us. However, as the society ages and older consumers become more than one out of five Americans, the degree to which this group is able and chooses to consume desired goods and services (i.e., having discretionary income) will have a major impact on the overall vigor and size of the economy, indirectly influencing everyone. Spending by households headed by individuals over age 65 is lower than that of other age groups, averaging 73% of spending of all households (U.S. Department of Labor [DOL], Bureau of Labor Statistics [BLS], 2009). Studies have shown that, while older adults spent more on health care and made more charitable contributions, their spending in some other areas, such as housing and food, were similar to those of younger groups. Despite these lower spending levels, the choices made

by this growing consumer pool will also help to determine the mix of products and services available in the economy.

Early studies on the older population showed a significant percentage of their monthly incomes going for basics—food, health care, utilities, and housing—with discretionary spending on leisure and recreation varying substantially by income level (Goldstein, 1960). Poorer households could ill afford the travel or recreation consumed by the middle class; as with poor people of any age, nearly all of their incomes went for monthly necessities (food, shelter, and transportation). Other studies indicate that consumption patterns remain largely unchanged with advancing age for low- to moderate-income households. Fixed costs still constitute a major component of spending by older consumers. Data from the 2007 Consumer Expenditure Survey show age similarities and differences in spending patterns. Older and mid-life adults, for example, spent similar percentages of their total spending on necessities like housing and food, as well as on entertainment, even though total spending and household size were smaller for older study participants. While 45–54 year olds spent 4.8% of total dollars on health care, however, the percentage for older adults was 12.4% (DOL, BLS, 2009).

Differing opportunities for economic security in later life offer one kind of diversity among older persons. (Credit: E. J. Hanna)

Another analysis of the Consumer Expenditure Survey between 1984 and 1997 compares expenditures for "big ticket" items and recurring expenses for those 65–74 and 75 and older to determine whether preferences and behaviors changed over time (Paulin, 2000). While older consumers spent fewer dollars than those under 65 overall, the trends over time in spending for shelter, food, and other items did not change dramatically, with most age groups following parallel tracks through economic upturns and recessions. In general, trends and preferences in spending for these age groups did not change substantially over the 13-year period examined in this research.

One component of consumption that is not entirely predictable for individuals or families is costs related to health care. (See Chapter 8 for more detail on health care costs.) Those who can afford to do so seek to control this unpredictable cost by buying insurance that supplements Medicare, including an increasing share among those 65 and older (Paulin, 2000). More than half of the spending by adults over 65 in the health area is for insurance (DOL, BLS, 2009). One component of health care costs that has recently shifted, with the passage of Medicare Part D, is the cost for prescription drugs. Yin and colleagues (2008) report a modest reduction in out-of-pocket spending after the program began, but consumer research showed the average spending in households headed by an adult over age 65 remained high ($873 in 2007) (DOL, BLS, 2009). Concerns regarding the high cost of health care, and the potential for costly catastrophic illnesses, may prompt older adults to hold onto savings and suppress consumption in areas other than health care to retain a cushion just in case of a health emergency.

Experts disagree on whether consumption patterns will shift substantially in the next decades, as new cohorts with different saving/consumption experiences enter later life. Johnson and Williamson (1987) claim that the improved health and financial status of current and future retirees, as well as their potentially increased leisure time, will result in demand for new products and services targeted to this market. Their side of this debate suggests that specialized products and services (e.g., retrofitting a house with an elevator), as well as senior-oriented leisure, will be an expanding market as societal aging continues. For example, adults over age 60 made up almost a quarter (23%) of those taking a vacation cruise in 2007 (Cruise

Lines International Association, 2008). If that percentage remains constant as the population ages, shouldn't enterprising shipbuilders be preparing now for the growing number of customers?

On a less optimistic note, as more people survive to ages at which assistance is needed in household tasks and personal care, how much should home health care companies or assisted-living providers anticipate growing over the next several decades? Projecting the answer to this question is complicated further if each succeeding cohort has later onset of disability than its predecessors or differs in its consumer preferences. It remains unclear how quickly or vigorously such markets will shift, in part depending on the level of financial security of the older cohorts of the future.

On the other side of this debate, some researchers voice concerns regarding restricted consumption by the older population. As society ages, this group wonders whether the economy will slow if older consumers keep cars and durable goods (such as refrigerators) longer than do younger adults (Kneese & Cooper, 1993). Will the aging of society have a negative effect on overall consumerism? Again, the answer will turn on whether aging or cohort effects are more potent in these behaviors. Spending and consumption patterns of future aging cohorts may be based more on income levels and security and the choices available; we cannot assume that because a society ages, its rate of consumer spending automatically drops (Easterlin, 1996). Future cohorts may be more free-spending or more tight-fisted with their money, depending in part on their lifetime experiences with money and the state of the economy, their expectations about their futures, their levels of disposable income, and social policies in force at the times (e.g., potential limits to Social Security or Medicare/Medicaid benefits driven by high demand and insufficient funding).

One thing that is clear is that business and marketers have discovered the "gray/silver market" for products and services (Cutler, 2004–2005; Dennis, 2004–2005). This discovery has had the dual effects of recognizing and meeting the needs of this population, but it has also resulted in a focus on the affluent among the older population, downplaying the continuing economic marginality of some subgroups within the older population (Minkler, 1991b). Both the senior lobby and private corporations have contributed to the notion of the older population as a vast, untapped resource for marketing goods and services. The fact that we now see mature models in advertisements, even those for products not oriented only to older adults, is a signal that the older consumer market is no longer as marginalized by business (Dennis, 2004–2005; Minkler, 1991b). It remains important, however, for the marketplace to be responsive to the needs of a wide range of older consumers, not just the wealthiest.

Prospects for the Future Economic Status of the Elderly

Predicting the economic well-being of future cohorts of older persons involves many unknowns. Critical among these unknowns are the potential changes in public and private policies for income maintenance and the overall health of the economy. Under a worst-case scenario, the economy would face sustained growth in the elderly population, increases in the costs of care for this group (e.g., health care and personal assistance), a smaller working-age population, a less productive work force (dominated by older workers and less educated youth), and a stagnant level of economic growth (Szanton, 1993).

Although we know that the aging of society will likely proceed, barring an unexpected increase in fertility, many of the other elements in that worst-case scenario are hotly debated by experts and may deviate dramatically from current trends (Szanton, 1993). For example, the size and productivity of thee work force can vary depending on immigration policies, use of technology, and shifts toward higher average ages of retirement. How close we come to the worst-case scenario is yet to be determined.

Although we have seen improvement in the economic fortunes of recent cohorts, there is no guarantee that this improvement will continue for future cohorts. The cohort born in the 1920s has been dubbed the **"good times" generation** because of the way in which historical events have positively shaped their lives and their retirement incomes (Moon & Smeeding, 1989). The good times generation is a privileged cohort because members of this generation were in their prime working years during the economic boom following World War II, worked during the period in which private pension coverage was peaking, and benefited from the windfall of a dramatic increase in the value of real estate during their lives (Holtz-Eakin & Smeeding, 1994). The coincidence of so many favorable circumstances benefiting a cohort is unlikely to repeat so that future cohorts may fare worse on some economic indicators than their predecessors.

What also seems likely, however, is that inequality will continue to be problematic among the elderly. In contrast to many other countries, the piecemeal system of income maintenance in the United States leaves some individuals much less protected than others in old age. By attempting to create incentives early in life to work hard and achieve, our income maintenance policies mostly reward high achievers and do less for the unfortunate or unmotivated. As a nation, we will probably be revisiting several pieces of our income maintenance policies in the next decades, with the outcomes from those political processes shaping the economic well-being of all of us as we age.

Summary

Economic well-being is one area in which it is especially critical to avoid discussions of the average older adult. It is clear that economic well-being has improved on the average, but many sizable groups continue to experience high rates of poverty and economic marginality. Lifelong advantages or disadvantages embedded in the labor market and public and private policies of income maintenance result in individuals whose economic histories, for good or ill, follow them into later life to result in security or insecurity. In general, wealthy older people are not suddenly impoverished after retirement, nor are the poorest older persons likely to be in poverty for the first time as a result of retirement. As James Schulz eloquently put it, "The issue is not whether . . . we can have better pensions and services for the aged. The issue is whether we want a higher standard of living in our retirement years at the expense of a lower standard in our younger years. Whether we like it or not, the 'economics of aging' begins for most of us quite early in life" (Schulz, Visintainer, & Williamson, 1990, p. 201).

The choices of a graying consumer market regarding saving versus spending, and on what types of goods and services, will have a significant impact on the larger economy in years to come. The economy cannot afford to ignore such a large group of consumers and continue to gear merchandise for the youth market only. Whether consumption among older adults will be for necessities only or for leisure and optional goods will depend, to a great extent, on how much disposable income is provided by the public and private systems of income maintenance.

On the societal level, older persons constitute a growing percentage of the population. Income maintenance programs place large and growing demands on both the public and private sectors. We can undoubtedly anticipate some modifications of these policies that will affect future cohorts. The issues facing the United States and most other countries with aging populations are much the same. Can our economies support a growing number of economically dependent adults for increasingly lengthy periods of retirement and still survive in worldwide competition? These issues are likely to challenge political and economic leaders for years to come.

Web Wise

Social Security Administration Home page   http://www.ssa.gov
The Social Security Administration (SSA) provides a great deal of information on various topics including Social Security (SS) benefit information and forms, how to apply for services, direct online services, SS budget and planning, and SS laws and regulations. Linking to the research information (www.ssa.gov/policy) provides current data on programs (retirement, SSI) and SSA publications such as the biennial *Income of the Aged Chartbook*, cited widely in this chapter.

Center for Retirement Research, Boston College   http://crr.bc.edu/index.php
This Web site includes a number of reports relating to current economic issues related to retirement, with topics varying over time. In addition to the Center's usual publications, one key feature of interest is *The Social Security Fix-It Book*, which identifies the array of adjustments available to policy makers considering reforms to Social Security to make the trust fund last through the baby boomer cohorts. This colorful and clear booklet shows how putting together a solution to Social Security is not hard if we can put politics aside.

Key Terms

adequacy of benefits	economic life-cycle hypothesis	need eligibility
age eligibility	equity of benefits	privatization
assets	ERISA	social insurance
cumulative inequality	"good times" generation	Social Security Trust Fund
defined benefit	income maintenance systems	three-legged stool
defined contribution	income redistribution	Townsend Movement
deserving poor	in-kind income	vested

Questions for Thought and Discussion

1. Considering life chances and the pattern of cumulative advantage and disadvantage, what steps are you taking and what plans are you making in your current stage of your life that will influence your economic security in later life? In taking the long view, what are the major unknowns about how this will turn out? What choices have you already made, and what opportunities have been granted or withheld from you that will determine this outcome?

2. Social Security has for years battled to reach the goals of adequacy and equity, but they are sometimes inconsistent. Both reflect middle-class American values. Should one of these goals be more important than the other? Should they be weighted equally in policy changes? Explain why you think your choice is best.

3. Imagine yourself at a family gathering where your Uncle Charles asks about your classes this semester. When he hears that you are taking a course in aging, he lets you know in no uncertain terms that he thinks older people are selfish and a huge drain on the economy, living comfortably and demanding more than their fair share while giving back nothing. What response would you make to him?

4. Now that you know a little bit more about the social construction of poverty, do you think that the definition is adequate? Are the assumptions fair? What would be the advantages and disadvantages to changing the standards for measuring poverty for older and younger people?

E-Elders

The computer revolution and the exponential growth of the Internet are among the most recent in a long line of technological innovations that have touched the lives of current cohorts of older adults. The oldest old have seen the development of home electrification, air travel, interstate highways, "smart houses," portable recorded music, cell phones, and microwave ovens, to name only a few items. How are older adults responding to these major transformations of the social and electronic worlds? Do older adults embrace or reject the electronic revolution? Do the reactions of older adults to the emergent cyber-world support or refute stereotypes of older adults being resistant to learning about new innovations? While widespread cultural stereotypes in recent years show the degree of technological sophistication diminishing as age increases, are these stereotypes actually valid? Studies of older adults and the use of electronic technologies, most specifically personal computers, give us some clues.

Computer Use by Older Adults

National studies show that older adults increasingly have personal computers available in their homes and use them (Jones & Fox, 2009). In fact, the largest increase in users between 2005 and 2008 was among those ages 70–75, with 45% of that age group "online" by 2008. In short, the major gap that had existed across ages in use of computers and online services is closing rapidly (Administration on Aging, 2001; Jones & Fox, 2009). Books specifically addressed to older adult computer users are available, and technology specialists are attending to the myriad ways that computers may help older adults (see Burdick & Kwon, 2004). Older adults can and do learn to use these technologies (Morrell, Mayhorn, & Echt, 2004; Rogers, Mayhorn, & Fisk, 2004). However, neither training in computers nor amount of time spent surfing the Internet are associated with greater psychological or social well-being among older adults, according to a 12-month study (Slegers, Martin, vanBoxtel, & Jolles, 2008).

Computer Applications and Innovations

How do older people make use of home computers? In some ways, older people use computers just as younger people do—to stay in touch with friends, family, and their communities and to search for information, shop and bank, and locate needed information (Jones & Fox, 2009). While a stereotype existed for a while that older adults only used e-mail, increasingly they are downloading videos, participating in social networking sites, and employing computers in their employment (Jones & Fox, 2009). AARP's Web site provided a feature on social networking in early 2009, reflecting the dramatic growth in participation among adults over 55 in social networking sites (Stoudt, 2009). In the 1 year between 2009 and 2010, for example, Facebook users aged 55 and older grew by 923% (Corbett, 2010)! Clearly older adults of all ages are rapidly moving toward embracing the potential for computers to enrich their lives.

In addition to personal uses, in-home computers are increasingly being used as a means of providing services and support for older people, including high-tech health care. Older people with health conditions can certainly use the Web to access sources of information about health and treatments (Vastag, 2001). Increasingly, however, *telemedicine* allows health conditions and symptoms to be monitored at home, with results available to a supervising physician or nurse. Medication reminders can be conveyed, or a blood pressure monitor attached to a personal computer can easily keep a record of status with minimal effort (Tran, 2004). Web-cams can even permit a face-to-face medical consultation with a health provider for those whose mobility is limited. Using the Web can enhance autonomy among older adults in the community or in long-term care by linking people to information about services and organizations and by encouraging the creation or maintenance of social networks (Deatrick, 1997; Hunt, 1997; McConatha, McConatha, & Dermigny, 1994; Redford & Whitten, 1997; Setton, 2000).

Only recently have engineers, programmers, and Web site developers directed creative attention to the specific needs of older people for phones or computers. There is a growing thrust toward designing online devices, services, and products that are appealing to and accessible for older people. Web designers and advocacy groups have begun campaigns to make more online resources easily accessible through adapting visual aspects (e.g., larger fonts, more open layouts) (Benbow, 2004). During the end of 2005, for example, the Web became a primary source of information about the new Medicare prescription drug program (Part D). Future cohorts, including baby boomers, will doubtless enter later life much more computer savvy and ready to make use of the Internet, social networking, and all sorts of technological innovations yet to appear to enrich their lives and well-being.

Limiting Factors

Access to the world opened by the personal computer and the Internet may be hampered for older adults in two ways. First, physical or cognitive limitations may make computer technology and the Internet harder to use. Limited vision or hand dexterity due to arthritis or stroke, for example, makes use of standard computer keyboards difficult without additional modifications, such as voice recognition software. Handheld devices, such as cell phones, with small keys and screens, are even more challenging to use with such physical limitations (Scialfa, Ho, & Laberge, 2004). As to the effectiveness of learning new technologies, although older adults take more time to learn software and make more errors during training courses (White et al., 1999), most older adults are quite capable of learning computer skills (Morrell et al., 2004).

Second, the digital divide remains as a limiting factor in the use of computers among low income elders. While costs have decreased considerably, the expenses involved in getting connected are too high for some older adults with low incomes, a problem that may abate if costs for devices and services decrease. To help address the digital divide, many Senior Centers, libraries, and community programs have computers available to use at no cost. However, the best way for older adults to have meaningful access is not to hope for an open desktop at the Senior Center but to have a PC at home with Internet access. Economics and eyesight, not lack of interest or capacity to learn, remain the central barriers to broader use of computers and the Web by older adults.

Aging and Health: Individuals, Institutions, and Policies

8

We can have a dramatic impact on our own success or failure in aging. What we can do for ourselves, however, depends partly on the opportunities and constraints that are presented to us as we age—the attitudes and expectations of others toward older people, and on policies of the larger society of which we are a part.

(Rowe & Kahn, 1998, p. 18)

The **health** status of an older person is the result of many factors, including lifelong health habits (including diet and exercise), genetics, and exposure to occupational and environmental hazards. The quality and availability of health care throughout life also plays a role in health in later life. Many of these influences on individual health are, in large measure, socially shaped or constructed. As the chapter opening quote suggests, health behaviors are affected by societal values and by the practices and habits of the people in one's immediate social world, such as families and peers. For example, a person's food preferences and eating habits are clearly shaped by family experiences regarding food. Our growing awareness of the importance of exercise is another example of how societal values can influence individual values and behaviors. Your attitudes about exercise are probably quite different from those of your grandparents. This chapter explores the broad range of individual and social forces that influence health in later life. We will also examine the policies and practices within the U.S. health care system that shape access to and quality of health care for older adults, and thus their health status.

Physical Aging

Why do we grow old? What happens to health as we grow older? Is there an inevitable increase in illness and poor health that accompanies age? To answer these questions, we can compare the health status of older people overall to that of younger cohorts. However, we also need to look at variations within the older population. Indeed, the degree of diversity in health among older people suggests that age itself may not be a very strong predictor of health problems. Variations in health status across cultures provide further evidence for the idea that age is not the most powerful influence. For example, Americans experience a progressive age-related increase in blood pressure, but in Japan and China resting blood pressure changes very little well into old age (Alessio, 2001).

To set the stage for discussing these cultural and social variations in health, it is useful to know that there is extensive research on the physiology of aging. This specialized topic is beyond the scope of this book, but interested students can look to the numerous sources that

The timing of age-related decline and disability is highly variable, and some older persons demonstrate a great deal of strength and elasticity in their 70s, 80s, and beyond. (Credit: E. J. Hanna)

describe physical changes that accompany age and the array of biological theories that seek to explain how and why the human organism ages. An example of such a source is *Human Aging: Biological Perspectives* (DiGiovanna, 2000). An entire issue of *Generations* (Spring 2000) focused on genetics of aging, covering the genetic influence on disease, new research on telomeres and alleles (some of the mechanisms operating at the cellular level to influence the aging of an organism), cloning, and cell transplantation. The human genome project will have incredible implications for our understanding of the genetic basis for aging. Physician George Martin (2000) draws attention to the clinical, ethical, and social consequences of " 'new genetics' . . . the present explosion of information concerning the structure and function of the human genome" (p. 10).

(Credit: Mike Payne, courtesy of the Ohio Department of Aging)

Keep in mind that there are normal physical changes that accompany aging, such as a reduction in collagen that results in wrinkling of the skin and decreased elasticity of veins and arteries, which can reduce the ease and efficiency with which blood flows through the body. The timing and extent of such changes are highly variable among individuals, and they do not inevitably produce disease or disability. There are, however, diseases that become more common as we grow older, such as arthritis, heart disease, and Alzheimer's disease. Age can be a marker for physiological declines and increased risks of some diseases, but its role as a *cause* is not clear. As discussed in Chapter 1, Rowe and Kahn (1997) described this variability in their distinction among successful, usual, and pathological aging. This breakthrough changed our thinking about physiological aging, paved the way for "a new gerontology" (Blazer, 2006), and continues to generate considerable research. Recent refinements have focused on clarifying the multiple dimensions of **successful aging**, including the avoidance of disease and disability, engagement with life, and high cognitive and physical function (Rowe & Kahn, 1997). Other research examines the factors that predict successful aging (Depp & Jeste, 2006).

Obviously, we must be cautious not to assume that age-related patterns are solely or even primarily caused by age. Some older adults get certain of these diseases, others do not—so clearly age is not a cause, or almost everyone would get these diseases as they aged. Beyond this, the patterns of illnesses we see for older adults in the United States do not necessarily hold true for other cultures, as mentioned previously regarding high blood pressure. Compare, for example, the relative absence of breast cancer among Japanese women to its exponential increase with age among American women. In the United States in 2000, an average of 29.2 women per 100,000 died of breast cancer. The rates of this cancer mortality increase noticeably with age, from 59 per 100,000 women 55–64 to 151 per 100,000 for the 75 and older group. Based on these numbers, we might conclude that something about the passage of time—simply living a certain number of years—increases the likelihood of breast cancer. However, in Japan in 2000, only 14 women (of all ages) per 100,000 died of breast cancer (World Health Organization, 2006), less than half the U.S. rate for all women. The much lower breast cancer mortality in Japan is probably in part due to genetics because there is some heredity risk for the disease. But the overall difference between the United States and Japan also suggests that cultural factors—the context in which the passage of time is taking place—are at least as important as age.

Throughout this chapter we explore the health of the older population as a way to get a glimpse into what happens to the health of individuals as they age. It must always be recalled that these averages and patterns among the older population as a whole mask a great deal of individual variation. We can all think of examples of healthy, active 80 year olds, and frail, unhealthy 65 year olds. For any individual, health is a product of many factors—the genetics discussed previously, lifestyle choices related to exercise and diet, available medical and preventive care, and social characteristics such as gender, race, and social class. Because these latter characteristics reflect both individual characteristics and social forces, we use them as a way to disaggregate information about the entire older population. By presenting some information about groups within the older population, the variation among individuals becomes clear. The diagram in Exhibit 8.1 is a simple representation of the multiple forces that influence an individual's health.

The Health Status of Older People

To develop a profile of the health of older people, we need to clarify how health is defined and measured. Even though health includes more than the absence of disease, much national data focuses on diagnosed illnesses and impairments, chronic conditions, hospitalizations, and doctor visits. In fact, we typically measure the absence of health rather than health itself. Few national surveys include emotional, physical, spiritual, and social well-being, mirroring our emphasis on the **medical model** of thinking about health. Recently, however, there has been increased interest in positive health behaviors, such as prevention and health promotion activities, including good nutrition, exercise, and smoking cessation. Health promotion and disease prevention is the explicit goal of a major U.S. initiative called *Healthy People,* which seeks to reduce health disparities among social groups, address major risks to good health, and to improve quality of life and life expectancy for all Americans, emphasizing physical activity, healthy weight, mental health, and avoidance of tobacco (Healthy People 2010, 2006). This continuing initiative sets decennial goals for the health of the U.S. population, defines major indicators of health, and evaluates progress toward those goals. Even as the United States increases its focus on good health as more than the absence of disease, information on patterns of diseases and chronic conditions provide a useful foundation for understanding health in later life and for developing affirmative goals.

Prevalence Rates for Chronic Conditions

One of the most common measures of the health of the older population is the prevalence of chronic health conditions, such as diabetes and arthritis. **Chronic conditions** are health

EXHIBIT **8.1**

Factors Influencing an Individual's Health

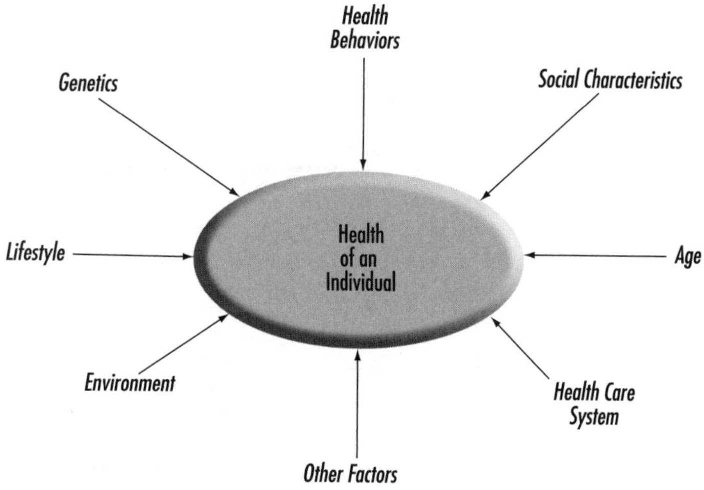

problems that last for an extended period of time and are not easily or quickly resolved. In contrast, an acute condition appears suddenly and changes quickly. Influenza is an example of an acute condition. Here we focus on chronic conditions because they become more common as we age. **Prevalence rates** indicate what proportion of a given group has a certain condition or diagnosis. These rates, which say something about how common a condition is, can be reported as percentages, telling us how many people per 100 have the condition. For health problems that are less frequent, prevalence rates are often reported per 1,000—how many people per 1,000 in the group of interest have the specified condition. Exhibit 8.2 shows the prevalence (expressed as a percentage) of several common chronic conditions among men and women ages 55 and older. Comparing the darker bars with the lighter bars in this chart shows that all four of these conditions become more common with age. In general, hypertension and hearing impairments are more common than heart disease and diabetes among older men and women.

There are also some interesting gender differences shown in Exhibit 8.2. Women have higher rates of hypertension and diabetes than men, but men have higher rates of heart disease—the number one cause of death in the United States among adults. This conclusion is consistent with the general observation that older men have higher rates of the most life-threatening conditions, but older women have higher rates of illness and disability overall. This pattern has been summarized (and probably oversimplified) in the statement, "Women get sick; men die," which reminds us of the life expectancy differences described in Chapter 3. Later in this chapter, we discuss a number of social forces, including gender differences in undertaking risky behaviors (e.g., drug use, high-speed driving), attention to bodily symptoms, and in seeking help for health problems that contribute to this pattern characterizing current cohorts of older adults.

Functional Ability

Another important indicator of the health status of older adults is the limitation in their ability to carry out activities of daily living (ADLs). Knowing about older people's health conditions is

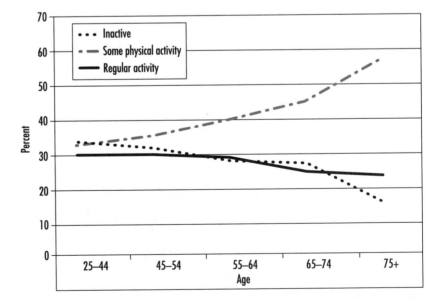

EXHIBIT 8.2

Leisure Time Physical Activity by Age, United States, 2003

Source: U.S. Department of Health and Human Services, 2005.

informative, but in order to plan meaningful and effective services, we need to know how these conditions affect people's lives. Measures of **functional ability** or functional limitation (these terms are used here interchangeably) serve that purpose. These measures evaluate an older person's' ability to get through the day by asking about what activities of daily life they are able to perform, how difficult a given activity is for them, and whether the help of another person is needed to accomplish a given task. The most common measures of functional ability are the Activities of Daily Living and Instrumental Activities of Daily Living (ADL/IADL) scales, developed by Katz, Downs, Cash, and Grotz (1970) and refined by numerous researchers (Freedman, Martin, & Schoeni, 2002; Glass, 1998; Kovar & Lawton, 1994; Lynch, Brown, & Harmsen, 2003). These measures assess the extent to which an individual needs help with basic personal tasks such as bathing, eating, and getting dressed and with household and independent living tasks such as preparing meals, shopping, and transportation. Some version of these measures of functional capacity are used for a wide range of purposes, including determining eligibility for services, evaluating the appropriateness of care plans for people receiving assistance, describing the health status of the older population, and projecting future challenges to the health care system.

Based on the ADL/IADL scale, Exhibit 8.3 shows the proportion of people at various ages having different levels of limits in functional ability: no disability, moderate disability, and severe disability. People were placed in these categories based on the kinds of activities for which they need assistance. The severe limitation category includes people who need help with the most basic activities, such as bathing, getting in and out of bed, and dressing. The moderate category includes people who need help with activities such as shopping, meal preparation, and walking. Even though the proportion of people who have severe disability goes up noticeably with age, the majority of older people under age 85 have little or no limitation in their ability to perform the personal and home management activities of daily life. At age 85, over half of older people have at least a moderate level of disability, requiring some assistance.

EXHIBIT **8.3**

Percentage of Adults Aged 65 and Above Who Had Some Difficulty With Physical Functions by Race and Ethnicity, United States, 2004–2007

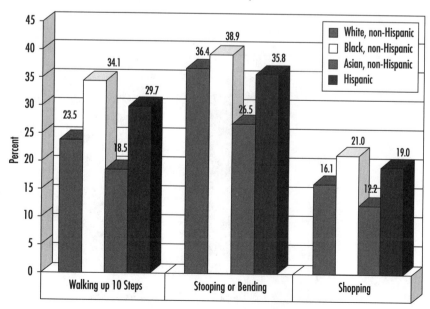

Source: Schoenborn & Heyman, 2009.

Such data on the prevalence of functional limitations have implications for the everyday lives of older people. While most people find ways to compensate for gradual loss of function, there comes a time when people who live long enough may need some kind of assistance. Most people get the help they need from family and friends for as long as possible. However, this informal assistance is only part of a complex and expanding system of long-term care. Thus, patterns of functional limitation in the older population have direct bearing on the issue of long-term care—special services and assistance provided on an ongoing basis (either in **nursing homes**, in specially designed living units, or in an individual's own home) to people who need help with the activities of everyday life.

Self-Assessment

Another way to measure the health of the older population is **self-assessed** (or self-rated) **health** status. With this subjective and straightforward indicator of perceived health, people are asked to rate their own health as excellent, very good, good, fair, or poor. It is an informative measure. First, it is quite useful to know how people view their own health situation because their views may influence their satisfaction and choices in other areas. Second, self-assessed health "is strongly associated with objective health status, such as physical exams and physician ratings" (Cohen & Van Nostrand, 1995, pp. 31–32). The fact that self-assessment is so closely connected with ratings by physicians is surprising to some people, but clearly older adults have a sense of how their bodies are working that goes beyond diagnoses or daily tasks.

Exhibit 8.4 displays variations in self-assessed health by age, race, and Hispanic origin. The majority of all older people in all groups rate their health as excellent, very good, or good. The proportion of people who rate their health as fair or poor goes up significantly with age, but the majority of those 65 and over still rate their health positively. There is a significant race/ethnicity pattern, suggesting that Whites have higher self-rated health than Blacks or Hispanics.

EXHIBIT   *8.4*

Self-Assessed Good to Excellent Health by Age Group, Race, and Ethnicity: U.S. Population 65 and Older, 2004–2006

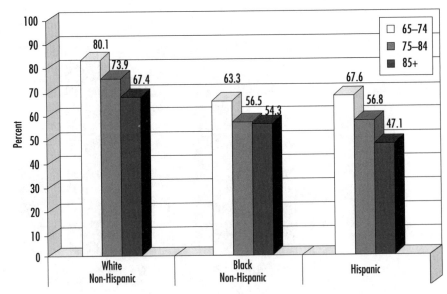

Source: Federal Interagency Forum on Aging-Related Statistics, 2008.

How does self-assessed health align with the prevalence of chronic conditions? Among the population age 75 and older a majority has at least one chronic condition; more than 50% have arthritis, 36% have heart disease, and 50% have hypertension (Schoenborn, Vickerie, & Powell-Griner, 2006). Given the high prevalence of major chronic conditions, how can older people rate their health as good, very good, or excellent?

Some researchers have suggested that older people rate their health positively because expectations about health change with age and because people tend to compare themselves with age peers (Cockerham, 1998). This explanation implies that people make mental adjustments in the reference point against which they judge their own health so that they see their health as better than they had expected for their age or better than others they know. An alternative explanation suggests that chronic conditions develop gradually so that older people are able to adapt to and compensate for them. Many of their health problems have minimal impact on their everyday functioning. "Physical decrements can be accommodated within their customary lifestyle, so that good health is a reality" (Atchley, 1997, p. 86). According to this view, positive self-assessments of health are not the result of altered expectations but are an accurate representation of the ability to perform daily activities.

Even though fairly high percentages of older people rate their health as good to excellent, there are significant differences among Blacks, Whites, and Hispanics on self-assessed health. Exhibit 8.4 shows that Blacks and persons of Hispanic origin are much more likely than Whites to rate their health as fair or poor at every age and much less likely to see their health as very good or excellent. These poorer self-assessments are not surprising, given the higher levels of illness and mortality among older Blacks compared to older Whites (see Chapter 3). They may also reflect cultural differences in defining categories such as good or poor.

Mortality

A final indicator of health status—or the ultimate lack of health—is mortality. **Mortality rates** reveal who dies, of what causes, and when (at what ages). Rates of death tell us how many people per 100,000 in a particular group died in a particular year. Not surprisingly, death rates go up significantly with age. But like most of the health measures discussed here, there is significant variation in mortality among the older population. Among people who are 65 and older, men have higher rates of death for heart disease, cancer, and lung disease; women have higher mortality rates for cerebrovascular disease (stroke) and Alzheimer's disease. For most of the causes on which comparisons can be made, Blacks have higher death rates than Whites, and Whites have higher rates of death than persons of Hispanic origin (Anderson & Smith, 2005). In 2002, for example, 605 of every 100,000 Black men ages 55 to 64 died of heart disease; for Black men 65 and older, that rate was more than 1,897 per 100,000.

Looking beyond general rates of mortality, we can consider causes of death. Exhibit 8.5 lists the leading causes of death by gender, race, and ethnicity for people 65 and older in the United States in 2006. Heart disease and cancer are the two leading causes of death for all gender and race/ethnicity groups ages 65 and over. There is more variability by gender and race among the less common causes of death. Alzheimer's disease is the fifth leading cause of death for White women 65 years and older, but it is not among the top 10 for Black men.

The cause of death rankings have implications for health policy and health promotion efforts, suggesting that such programs be tailored to meet the most pressing health needs of different groups. However, the largest number of deaths in a given year occurs to White males because Whites are the most numerous group in the United States, and males are more likely to die in a given year than females. Therefore, the experiences of White males have tended to set the agenda for public health efforts, including research, treatment, and prevention.

It is clear that illness and the timing of death are not evenly distributed across the population, either within a society or around the globe. The following section explores some of the individual, interpersonal, and cultural dimensions of mortality.

EXHIBIT 8.5

Cause of Death Ranking by Race, Hispanic Origin, and Gender: U.S. Population 65 and Older, 2006

Rank for total 65 and older population	Cause	Hispanic		Non-Hispanic Black		Non-Hispanic White	
		M	F	M	F	M	F
1	Heart disease	1	1	1	1	1	1
2	Cancer	2	2	2	2	2	2
3	Cerebrovascular disease	3	3	3	3	4	3
4	Chronic lower respiratory disease	5	6	5	7	3	4
5	Alzheimer's disease	9	5	—	6	6	5
6	Diabetes	4	4	4	4	5	7
7	Influenza and Pneumonia	6	7	7	9	7	6
8	Nephritis	7	8	6	5	9	9
9	Unintentional injury	8	9	10	—	8	8
10	Septicemia	—	10	8	8	10	10

Source: Centers for Disease Control, 2009a, 2009b.

The Social Context of Mortality: Death and Dying

How, when, and where we die and how we deal with death are further examples of social construction. While death is a physical event, it carries with it much social and cultural meaning, warranting our attention. Looking at the death rituals of any non-Western culture, or at our own culture in different historical periods, illustrates how differently we deal with death in the United States today than people have in other times and places. Death was handled very differently in early times in the United States than it is today. Helton (1997) provides an account of how death was handled in rural Kentucky during the early 20th century. Both family and community had central roles in carrying out funeral practices. Women prepared the body, cleaned house, and prepared food; men dug the graves and made the caskets. Body preparation included washing and dressing the body and trying to make the body look as good as possible by putting coins on the eyes to keep them shut and covering the face of the corpse with a washcloth soaked in baking soda to help preserve the color of the skin. Helton's description of the traditions and rituals in early 20th-century rural Kentucky is in direct contrast with impersonal and business-like approach to death that is common today. The United States even has drive-through funeral homes.

The majority of deaths in the United States occur in hospitals or nursing homes; only about 20% of people die at home (Edmonson, 1997). The place of death tells us something about our attitudes and approaches to death. Death has become highly medicalized and professionalized. Sustaining life and preventing death for as long as possible is a hallmark of the tremendous advances in our medical technology. However, our success at prolonging life has been accompanied by a reluctance to deal with death—as a physical reality or as an ethical and emotional reality. The emergence of end-of-life ethical debates among politicians and health providers about euthanasia and physician-assisted suicide reflects the fact that our technological ability to keep people alive has outpaced the development of clear societal values about humane death.

Just as we have come to rely on the medical system to prevent death, we have come to rely on other professionals to deal with death once it occurs. The funeral industry has become firmly established in the American way of death, offering products and services including funeral planning, casket selection, and body preparation. Turning these matters over to practitioners in the funeral industry is consistent with our professionalized and segregated approach to death. Moller (1996) argues that in the United States, "the movement away from ritual and community to bureaucratic management and medical treatment of dying patients is consistent with broader patterns of social life" (p. 25). In particular, he discusses bureaucratization—having rules and regulations about everything—and technological approaches to all kinds of problem solving, including dealing with death and dying. Social norms for how and how long we should grieve, which may be culturally or religiously specific, often reflect a societal emphasis on minimizing disruption and getting back to work and everyday routines. Many companies have policies about how long people can stay home from their jobs when there is a death in the family, even specifying what degree of kinship is required before any time off is allowed.

When people return to regular routines following the loss of a loved one, they are expected to control their emotions and get on with their lives. Crying and discussing the loss are not acceptable, except with close friends and family. While we would be sympathetic if a colleague began openly grieving during a meeting or a class, it would make most of us very uncomfortable. These rules about how long or under what social circumstances grieving can legitimately go on, where and how it can happen, and who can legitimately grieve reflect a unique set of historical and cultural values.

Doka (1989) offers the idea of **disenfranchised grief** to help explain the ways in which experiences surrounding death are socially constructed. He suggests that when a person experiences a sense of loss but does not have a socially acknowledged role or relationship with the deceased, the rights to grief are not recognized and thus the grief is disenfranchised (Doka, 1989). Clearly, the lack of social support and the lack of opportunity to participate in sanctioned, open mourning can make this process much more difficult. Homosexual relationships, divorced spouses, and assisted deaths defined as merciful (such as with advanced Alzheimer's disease) all can give rise to this disenfranchised grief (Doka, 1989). For example, the partner in a same-sex couple who is not accepted by the family might be excluded from participating in the funeral and related activities. People who are in relationships that are not sanctioned, in roles that are not clear, or in situations where the death is not recognized are likely to experience disenfranchised grief. Clearly, death is not a collective or community experience in our society but is highly restricted.

There is an extensive literature in both academic journals and the popular press about how people experience and adapt to loss. One of the best known approaches to understanding death and dying is the pioneering work of Elizabeth Kubler-Ross (1969), who identified five stages that dying patients go through: denial, anger, bargaining, depression, and acceptance. This model has also been applied to the experience of bereaved persons. Kubler-Ross developed her model out of her conversations with dying people. Clearly the model has validity; it summarizes the experiences of many people and helps both dying people and their loved ones to understand their experiences. The approach has been critiqued, however, for implying that there is a universal trajectory through the phases and for potentially imposing linear stages as the only appropriate way to deal with the intensely personal and complex phenomenon of dealing with death (Moller, 1996).

Perhaps in response to the imposition of a single right way to experience death and grief, and certainly in response to the medicalized, technological, impersonal, and individualized way of death in the United States today, some countervailing trends are emerging. The growing visibility and popularity of **hospice** care is probably the best example. The hospice movement emphasizes care, not cure; it uses liberal pain management to keep the person comfortable and takes a holistic approach to the dying person and his or her family and loved ones, including everyone in the experience and knowing the dying person as a whole person, not just as a medical patient. In addition, the ongoing debates about euthanasia (literally meaning "good death"), quality of life for the dying person, and control over the circumstances of one's own death suggest that we are trying to develop norms and values that will balance our awesome technological capacity to sustain life with elements making for a "good death" in this new age.

Mental Health and Aging

The foregoing discussion of health status has focused on physical health and mortality. The mental health status of the older population is an equally important issue. Parallel to the different ways in which physical health can be defined and measured, mental health also has different meanings. It can refer to emotional well-being in our everyday lives, but like physical health, most often the term is referenced negatively, as mental illness or mental conditions that are a departure from health. Mental illness includes cognitive, emotional, and behavioral problems, including Alzheimer's disease, depression, and anxiety disorders, among others. A thorough discussion of the comparative prevalence of mental disorders among older people, and of their causes, consequences, and treatment is beyond the scope of this book. However, a description of the overall mental health status of the older population will complete our picture of the health of older people.

Using a broad definition, about 15% of older people in the community and 25% of nursing home residents suffer from depression (Fogel, Gottlieb, & Furino, 1990). Major depression affects less than 1% of the total older population, but about 20% of the residents of nursing homes and 13.5% of older adults who are receiving long-term care services in their homes (Chapman & Perry, 2008). About 1 in 20 older people in the community have anxiety disorders (Burns & Taube, 1990). It is important to recognize that some older people who have mental health problems in later life have had those problems throughout their lives.

As with physical aspects of health, there is variation among groups in the prevalence of various mental conditions. Depression, for example, was found to be more common among Hispanic and Black older people than among Whites (Dunlop, Song, Lyons, Mannheim, & Chang, 2003). However, most of the racial/ethnic differences in depression disappeared when the researchers controlled for group differences in education, health insurance coverage, income, and physical health status. So it may not be so much the race/ethnic group as the other factors (like income or health insurance) that are connected both to these categories and to depression. In all groups, having physical health limitation is the strongest predictor of having major depression, more than doubling the odds (Dunlop et al., 2003). Another study showed that people with less education have higher rates of depression and that this difference grows even more pronounced with age (Miech & Shanahan, 2000). Education is linked to social advantage, especially economic advantage. The same disadvantage of low education in determining physical health and freedom from disability in later life affects mental health as well.

Cognitive impairment refers to the loss of mental capacity for higher-level mental functioning; memory loss, confusion, disorientation, and loss of ability to care for oneself are some of the symptoms of cognitive impairment, often referred to as **dementia**. The most common cause of severe cognitive impairment is Alzheimer's disease. About 13% of people age 65 and older have Alzheimer's disease, but the risk for the disease increases with age. By age 85, about 12% of men and 20% of women will have developed dementia (Alzheimer's Association, 2010). Cognitive impairments such as Alzheimer's disease are gradual, progressive deteriorations. In the early stages, people with Alzheimer's disease are very often cared for at home by family members. "For each [person with dementia] in a nursing home, there are two to three more in the community with equal levels of impairment who are cared for by some combination of family, friends, and paid caretakers" (Fogel et al., 1990, p. 4).

Positive mental health is an important aspect of one's overall health at all ages. (Credit: E. J. Hanna)

Estimates of the prevalence of other mental health problems vary, depending on whether the estimate includes all or some of the following: diagnosed conditions (for which individuals have been seen by health care professionals), diagnosable conditions (serious enough to be diagnosed if they are seen by physicians), and symptoms of conditions such as depression or psychological distress (they have signs of the disease, but not at the clinically diagnosable threshold). Many people of all ages have conditions that remain undiagnosed for many reasons, so typically mental health conditions, which carry more stigma than physical health problems, suffer from especially high rates of underreporting.

Explaining Gender and Race Variations in Health

On all of the measures of health we have reviewed, there are significant differences by race/ethnicity and gender. We have alluded to the various explanations for these differences. For both gender and race/ethnicity, there are two main categories of explanation for patterns of health difference: biological and social/behavioral. Here we look more systematically at some of those explanations.

Summing up the dynamics of gender differences in mortality, Nathanson (1990) points out that, while females outlive males in nearly all species, the nature and extent of the difference in human life expectancy vary across time and across cultures. That the differential persists across contexts provides some support for a biological basis for longer lives among females; its variation across historical and cultural context, however, also reinforces its social basis.

In Chapter 3, we discussed some of the biological bases for the female advantage in longevity, including the protective effects of estrogen. We also discussed the different health behaviors of males and females in our society. One of these differences is awareness of, and seeking help for, health problems. Women are more likely to attend to changes in their bodies (in part perhaps because of the emphasis placed on appearance and weight, and partly because of attention to changes that routinely happen during the menstrual cycle and maternity) and to visit physicians more regularly. One of the results of women's more frequent contact with health care providers is that they are diagnosed and diagnosed sooner than men for many health conditions. A related result is earlier treatment of health problems, which helps to explain women's greater longevity. Although this pattern of women's earlier and more frequent help seeking does not hold for all health problems, it is an important social factor in the gender difference in health and mortality.

Lifestyle risk factors for which men and women have been differently socialized also have an impact on risk for developing illness. For men in current older cohorts, these behaviors include more smoking, alcohol consumption, hazardous occupations, and fast driving; for women, stress related to competing demands on their time (e.g., work and family pressures) and emotional reactions to feeling stressed are two socially produced health risks. Gender differences in health in later life are thus a product of the cumulative effects of biology, lifestyle, and behavior; the latter two effects are strongly influenced by social forces.

Race/ethnicity differences in health are similarly created by a combination of biological and social forces. "Some conditions such as hypertension and sickle cell anemia have a genetic basis, but living conditions associated with poverty influence the onset and course of most physical health problems" (Cockerham, 1998, p. 52). The impact of biology on race/ethnicity differences in health is primarily limited to the genetic component of select diseases and conditions. The social forces that influence racial variation in health patterns are, as in the case of gender differences, both socioeconomic and cultural. In the United States there is a strong relationship between race and socioeconomic status, and there is a strong relationship between socioeconomic status and a range of health indicators, including prevalence of chronic conditions, obesity, lack of preventive health care, and early mortality. The historic link between race and poverty has meant that Blacks have poorer lifelong access to health care than Whites, greater health risks from hazardous jobs, poorer nutrition, and poorer prenatal care. The impacts of inadequate prenatal care are lifelong. In an interesting analysis of how health disparities are related to the complex intersection of race, ethnicity, socioeconomic status, and living environment, Murray and colleagues (2006) identified "eight Americas." Using county of residence as a way to measure income and risky environment (here defined by homicide rate), these researchers established eight race-county combinations of the U.S. population and compared life expectancies across these groups. Among these eight groups, the longest life expectancy was seen among Asian women, and the shortest life expectancy was among high-risk urban Blacks; the difference in life expectancy between these two groups was an astonishing 20.7 years.

Race and ethnicity can also operate through cultural factors that shape health behaviors related to diet, exercise, and willingness to seek the advice of a health care professional. An excellent example is the case of the Pima Indians. This group experienced almost no diabetes until, as a result of forced lifestyle changes, they began to lead more sedentary lives and to eat more processed foods high in simple sugars. Today almost half of all Pimas aged 35 and older have adult-onset diabetes (Alessio, 2001). The high rate of diabetes among these Native Americans clearly cannot be attributed to a biological predisposition.

To this point, we have emphasized that individual health outcomes, and the health status of any particular group of people, are the product of a variety of social and cultural factors. Another extremely important influence on patterns of health and illness is the health care system: how health care is financed, and what services are provided, when, how, where, and for whom.

Healthy aging is a blend of a number of social factors, including heredity, diet, lifestyle, and exercise. (Credit: E. J. Hanna)

The U.S. Health Care System

Health care is a large and fast-growing segment of the U.S. economy. In a comparison of the percentage of gross domestic product (GDP) spent on health care in 30 countries, the United States ranked first (Reinhardt, Hussey, & Anderson, 2004). In 2009, the United States spent an estimated $2.5 trillion (17.3% of its GDP) on health care (Truffer et al., 2010). Increases in health care expenditures are expected to outpace growth in the GDP over the next several years, and by 2018, national health expenditures are expected to reach $4.4 trillion (National Coalition on Health Care, 2009). A number of factors help to explain the growth in health care spending and the U.S. ranking on international comparisons. These factors include advanced medical technology of the United States, an aging population, cultural preferences for the very best (and often most expensive) care available, a medical model approach to solving health problems after they occur (which is discussed more thoroughly later), relatively high administrative costs for providing insurance and managing health services, and fee-for-service reimbursement, which has dominated the payment system for health care in the United States.

In **fee-for-service** (FFS) systems of care, doctors, hospitals, and other health care providers are reimbursed for all of the services they provide; the more they do, the more they are reimbursed. Because Americans tend to value the idea that everything medically possible is being done for them, their expectations as health care consumers reinforce the financial incentive for providers to do as much as possible. Spiraling health care costs result, in part, from this circular relationship among fee-for-service reimbursement, technological advances, and demands for the best possible treatment. Such a system encourages innovation, encourages consumer demand for high-tech services, and encourages providers to deliver costly services. The fee-for-service model is gradually, and to a limited extent, being replaced by a **prospective payment system**, in which standards set ahead of time determine which costs will be reimbursed in treating a given condition. This kind of payment system encourages more limited use of health care resources, especially expensive, high-technology care.

The high-tech, medical-model system of health care in the United States is a poor fit to the needs of an aging population. The most common conditions that older people have do not lend themselves to high-tech cures—or to cures at all, for that matter. The surgical or chemical treatments that are the foundation of the U.S. approach to fixing health problems simply are not appropriate for ongoing, chronic conditions, such as diabetes, arthritis, and heart disease. A system of care that is especially responsive to the health situations of older people would focus on the broader definitions of health, not just on the absence of disease. Managing rather than curing a condition and maintaining or enhancing an individual's ability to function in everyday life would be the major goals of a health care system matched to the needs of the older population. Instead, the health system in the United States is oriented toward curing illnesses, is biased toward care provided in institutions such as hospitals and nursing homes, and is financed in a very fragmented and uneven fashion.

The Medical Model of Health Care

Much of the approach to the provision of health care in the United States is derived from a medical model of health and illness. This model of health and health care focuses heavily on the diagnosis and treatment of disease within specific systems of the human body. As mentioned earlier in this chapter, when we summarize the health status of an individual or group, we tend to report the most common conditions or illnesses, the most common causes of death, and the success of various treatments for ill health. These statistics reflect the medical model emphasis. Although a focus on disease is certainly a central dimension of health, some important assumptions and limitations underlie this view of health.

First of all, the medical model implies that health is simply the absence of disease: if you are not sick, you are healthy. However, broader definitions of health include positive dimensions such as physical, psychological, and social well-being and the ability to function in and perform the tasks associated with everyday life. Health is not just the absence of something negative (disease), but rather the presence of positive mental and physical conditions.

Second, the medical model is founded on some assumptions that limit the perspective. Freund and McGuire (1999) identify several key aspects of the medical model. **Mind–body**

dualism is the assumption that there is a clear separation between physical functioning and psychological, spiritual, behavioral, and emotional dimensions of the person. One outcome of this view is a focus on disease as a purely physical process, with little attention to the complex interplay between the physical and the social, emotional, and spiritual aspects of existence. **Reductionism**, which is based on mind–body dualism, is the tendency to reduce any illness to a disorder of the physiological systems of the body of the afflicted individual.

The assumptions of the medical model (mind–body dualism and physical reductionism), as well as its limited definition of health as the absence of disease, have a strong impact on many aspects of the health care system and related health behaviors. The skills, training, and decisions made by physicians, the expectations of health care consumers, and what our health care insurance programs will pay for are all based on the medical model.

The implications of the medical model on health and illness are well illustrated by the discovery of diseases. Examples of discovered diseases from history include drapetomania, which caused slaves to run away from their masters; and onanism (otherwise known as masturbation), which allegedly caused stunted growth, impaired mental capacity, and a variety of other symptoms, including headaches, appetite problems, cowardice, and weakness in the back (Freund & McGuire, 1995). In the past, this deep-rooted focus of the medical model fostered the naming of troubling behaviors as diseases. Distance from the historical and social contexts that gave rise to the identification of these conditions allows us to see both the profound impact of social forces and, by extension, the limitations of the medical model.

The way in which menopause is commonly defined and treated in American society—as a medical condition—is another manifestation of the medical model. Current views about menopause have roots in some interesting, startling, and very reductionistic ideas about women's health. The primary assumption underlying the treatment of menopause as a disease was that a woman's reproductive organs define her essence. Giving a stark example of physical reductionism, a late 19th-century physician stated that the uterus is the "controlling organ in the female body; as if the almighty, in creating the female sex, had taken the uterus and built up a woman around it" (quoted in Ehrenreich & English, 1990, p. 277). The uterus and the ovaries were thought to be the source of any abnormality, from irritability to insanity.

This reductionism helped to pave the way for the medicalization of menopause. **Medicalization** is "the process of legitimating medical control over an area of life, typically by asserting the primacy of a medical interpretation of that area" (Freund & McGuire, 1995, p. 201). In the case of menopause, medicalization means that we focus on physical symptoms and biochemical processes, identify these symptoms as unpleasant and uncomfortable, and transform the very natural process of menopause into an estrogen deficiency disease. Defining menopause as a disease has several important implications. First, identifying something as a disease implies a course of treatment. In the case of menopause, the prescribed treatment has been hormone replacement therapy (HRT). Artificial hormones help to reduce hot flashes, vaginal dryness, and other symptoms of menopause but have been implicated in increased incidence of breast cancer. Recent research has found that HRT provides benefits that have nothing to do with menopausal symptoms—lower rates of heart disease and osteoporosis.

Focusing on menopause as a disease requiring physician intervention means that less attention is given to the subjective interpretations and meanings women give to their own experiences. Many women report very positive reactions to this phase of life, including a sense of physical and psychological freedom. Giving greater voice to the subjective social and psychological experiences of women going through menopause would provide a counterbalance to the medical model approach.

Analyzing this approach further, Estes and Binney (1991) suggest that the tendency to medicalize normal physical processes has resulted in the "biomedicalization of aging." They assert that our society has constructed aging as a medical problem, and numerous areas of professional practice (including a huge health care industry, policy efforts, and research agendas) have arisen to deal with this medical challenge. The growth of the aging industry (including increasing numbers of professionals involved in dealing with the medical problems of aging, and expanding opportunities for economic gains) is accompanied by an increasing social and economic investment in the medicalization of aging.

In a provocative challenge to the medical model, McKinlay and McKinlay (1990) suggest that traditional "medical care is generally unrelated to the health of populations" (p. 21). Using data on mortality trends following the introduction of major medical interventions, such as vaccines for polio, smallpox, and flu and treatments for pneumonia and typhoid, they conclude that "at most 3.5 percent of the total decline in mortality since 1900 could be ascribed to medical measures" introduced for those eight diseases (p. 21). Social factors such as improved nutrition, a rise in real income, and improved sanitation played a more significant role in improving the health of the American population than did the medical measures for treatment or prevention of disease. Although no one would argue against the value of medical measures at the individual level, McKinlay and McKinlay draw our attention to the contextual factors involved in population health and the limitations of the medical model.

The **biopsychosocial model** of health is a well-respected alternative to the purely medical model. This approach emphasizes a multidisciplinary and holistic view of health and health care and acknowledges that "complex problems of health and illness "are . . . inherently multidimensional in nature" (Schwartz, 1982, p. 1040). The biopsychosocial model advocates bridges across disciplines, redefinitions of health, and a general paradigm shift within medicine. It is an important alternative to the unidimensional, mechanistic views of health and illness of the medical model. Interestingly, this model of care sounds very much like the approach used by **geriatricians** (physicians who take additional training in caring for the health needs of older people). Geriatric medicine is distinguished by specialized training in conditions that affect older people; a holistic approach to understanding the interactions among aging, disease, mental health, and independence; and a focus on coordinated, interdisciplinary care that involves families and other caregivers important in the lives of older patients (American Geriatrics Society/Association of Directors of Geriatrics Academic Programs [AGS/ADGAP], 2005). Even though such an approach to health care for aging people seems like a better fit than the traditional medical model, the United States faces a severe shortage of physicians trained in the principles of geriatric medicine. There are currently fewer than 7,000 certified geriatricians in the United States; the gap between available and needed geriatricians is expected to reach 36,000 by 2030 (American Geriatrics Society Core Writing Group, 2005).

Geriatric medicine is distinguished by a holistic approach to understanding the interactions between aging, autonomy, mental health and disease. (Credit: E. J. Hanna)

Elements of the Health Care System

Access and Utilization

Even though the United States ranks first in the amount of money spent on health care, we have a growing number of people who do not have good access to this well-supported system. In 2004, 45.8 million Americans were uninsured, a significant increase compared to only 4 years prior when 39.8 million had no coverage (Center on Budget and Policy Priorities, 2005). Many of the uninsured are employed people or their families, whose employers do not offer health insurance. In eight states, 20% or more of working adults do not have coverage (Robert Wood Johnson Foundation, 2005). The Affordable Care Act, discussed in Chapter 9, will very likely change this statistic. Because the details of the new legislation and its implementation are being refined at the very time of the writing of this book, it is too early to predict the exact change that will occur in the proportion of Americans without health insurance coverage.

Older adults are less likely to be without medical insurance thanks to **Medicare**, which is discussed later in this chapter. However, individuals who enter their Medicare-eligible phase after years of no health insurance are likely to have some accumulated health deficits. National data show that high percentages of people without health insurance forego medical care and needed prescription drugs, are less likely than those with insurance to have a usual source of health care, and face large out-of-pocket expenditures for the care they do receive. Missed opportunities to receive health screenings and early interventions in diseases can have substantial consequences for health and functioning once people achieve Medicare eligibility. Exhibit 8.6 illustrates differences in utilization of health care by poverty status for adults in the United States. Poor and near poor people were less likely to have a usual source of health care, but more likely to have used the emergency room in the last year (probably for that reason). Poor women were much less

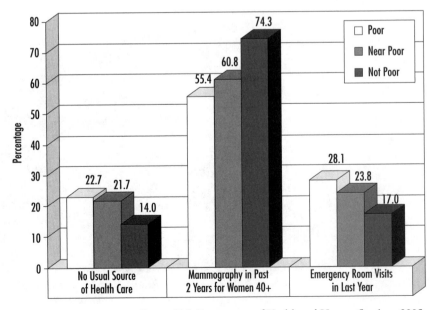

EXHIBIT **8.6**

Health Care Access by Poverty Status in the United States, 2002–2003

Source: U.S. Department of Health and Human Services, 2005.

likely than nonpoor women to have had a mammogram in the past 2 years. These differences in health care use can have lifelong consequences.

Even though virtually all older people have the benefit of Medicare coverage, differences in health care access persist throughout life, perhaps because of habits of health care use. For example, poor older people were significantly less likely than nonpoor older people to have gone to the dentist in 2004—37.1% compared to 67.8% (U.S. Department of Health and Human Services, 2005). Poor people are more than twice as likely to have lost all of their natural teeth than people who are not poor (Schoenborn et al., 2006).

Another illustration of unequal health care access and its implications comes from infant mortality data. Even though this example seems far removed from issues of aging, it is a powerful illustration of the effect of health care access, which has lifelong consequences for those lucky enough to survive. In 2003, the infant mortality rate for the United States overall was 6.9 per 1,000, but this rate masks important race differences. For White infants, the rate was 5.72 compared to 14.01 for Black infants (Hoyert, Heron, Murphy, & Kung, 2006). Low birth weight is the biggest risk factor for infant mortality. Although birth weight is related to individual factors such as the age of the mother and her health habits, the most powerful influence on birth weight is the adequacy of prenatal care. Access to adequate prenatal care is also linked to income and the availability of services in the mother's geographic area; these, in turn, are linked to race and ethnicity. In this way, an intensely personal outcome—the life or death of one's infant—is linked to larger social forces, such as social inequality. The connections among health outcomes (infant mortality), individual health behaviors (mother's nutrition), and macro-level societal forces (unequal access to prenatal care) operate throughout our lives.

Even for older people with good access to care, the structure of the current health care system presents some significant challenges. The system is fragmented and confusing. Acute care for short-term conditions that can be treated and resolved quickly is provided in one kind of location (doctors' offices and hospitals), while long-term care for ongoing chronic conditions and disabilities is provided in others (nursing homes, assisted-living facilities, or an older person's home). There is inadequate linkage among acute and long-term care services; older people often have to navigate the different systems of care on their own, or with the help of family and friends. The fragmented system reflects, in part, the way that health care for older people is financed.

Financing Health Care for Older Americans

Over the past 5 decades there has been a significant change in funding for health care for older Americans. In 1960, the system relied mostly on patient out-of-pocket payments. In 1960, just before Medicare legislation was passed, the government's share of the health care bill came to only 25%, including federal, state, and local sources. The remaining 75% of the nation's health care expenditures were paid for by private insurance or **out-of-pocket** (paid for by individuals). The story has changed considerably. The health care system now relies heavily on third-party private and government insurance programs. The transition occurred largely because of two important public policies for the financing of health care: Medicare and **Medicaid**.

Medicare and Medicaid are the major payers of the government's share of health care. These programs, along with other public sponsors of health care, including state-funded programs, accounted for 46% of the total health care dollars in 2007. Private sources, which include out-of-pocket expenditures and private health insurance paid for by individuals or businesses, sponsored 54% of health care spending (Kaiser Family Foundation, 2009).

The specific contributions made by Medicare and Medicaid to national health expenditures in 1994 and 2004, and the trends in their proportional contributions, are shown in Exhibit 8.7. The public and private proportions remained virtually the same (and are quite comparable to the 2007 figure), but Medicaid paid a slightly higher share of the public costs in 2004, and private health insurance paid slightly more in 2004 than in 1994.

The Political Economy of Health Care Access

The **political economy of aging** is a critical perspective that draws attention to the ways in which economic and political forces shape the policies, services, and experiences of an aging population. In particular, the political economy framework looks to the U.S. economic structure—capitalism—as an ideological and political force that shapes policies and services for older people. Estes (1999) suggests that a critical look at aging requires an examination of "the dilemmas and contradictions in maintaining both a market economy and democracy—that is, jointly advancing public interest in a democracy and private profit through capitalism" (p. 29). The profit motive of our health care system and universal protection of the rights of citizens are not always compatible.

This perspective often draws strong reactions because it calls into question the very foundations of U.S. society. However, it does provide a very important lens through which to look at some of the inequality in the U.S. health care system. Prior to the health care reform legislation of 2010, the United States did not have a universal health care system, one that would guarantee some degree of access to every citizen; the fact that more than 45 million people have no health insurance at all and the evidence provided on differential health care access and outcomes among the older population provide clear illustration of the lack of universal access to health care. In the United States, health care has been seen as a privilege, rather than a right of citizenship. That privilege was earned through certain kinds of employment, or through reaching Medicare eligibility at age 65. The Affordable Care Act will broaden access and options for all citizens, but the extent to which it will result in universal coverage remains to be seen as the legislation is implemented over the next several years.

The political economy perspective proposes that our lack of universal health care serves the economic purposes of those who profit from the current arrangement. In contrast, those who take issue with the political economists argue that the opportunity to make a profit from health care has driven the United States to be the best, most technologically advanced health care system in the world. In response, a political economy theorist might argue that there are actually two health care systems—the best in the world for those who have access to it through jobs or private resources, and one of the worst, for those who cannot get even minimum health care.

One of the most provocative challenges to our thinking about health care came from a 1987 book titled *Setting Limits: Medical Goals in an Aging Society*. Author Daniel Callahan argued that medical care should be rationed, especially expensive life-extending treatments, in order to spread health care resources among the greatest number of people. In a rationing system of this sort, older people would be unlikely to receive advanced and costly medical care, because the long-term benefits of such treatments for society and for the patient are limited. Callahan's work sparked extensive debate on a variety of fronts. One source of opposition came from those who were understandably concerned about the ageism implicit in an age-rationed health care system; others argued that rationing would produce a two-tiered system, one for people who can pay their own way and receive the best care possible, and another system for those who would only have access to services based on the rationed system. Political economists argue that we already have a two-tiered system of health care but that the rationing is based on social class and race, not age.

Callahan's (1987) proposal calls for an explicit formulation of principles to be used in a rationing health care. Because age would become a factor likely to limit access for older people, few gerontologists would support such a proposal. However, political economists of aging might see value in bringing to light the implicit rationing that already takes place. Acknowledging that we have had a two-tiered system was a necessary, if small, step toward declaring health care as a right of citizenship, rather than a privilege.

As health care reform unfolds, continued exploration of the tensions between market-driven advances in health care and universal access will be enlightening.

Medicare

Medicare is federal health insurance for people 65 and older; it also covers some younger disabled people, but older adults are the majority of its clientele. The legislation establishing Medicare passed in 1965, after decades of debate and concerns over whether it was the beginning of the slippery slope toward socialized medicine. This concern is especially problematic, given that it goes against U.S. norms and values regarding independence and self-reliance, which resurfaced in the 2009 debate on health care reform. Medicare is virtually universal for the older population, with about 97% of those over 65 insured by the Medicare program.

There are clear limits to what services are covered by Medicare, and some costs remain the responsibility of the individual. Medicare has two major sections: Part A and Part B. Part A, sometimes called hospital insurance, covers room, board, and nursing services in the hospital; it also covers up to 100 days of skilled nursing home care in a Medicare-approved facility, provided that certain conditions (such as a 3-day prior stay in a hospital) are met. Part A also covers hospice services and, to a very limited extent, home health care. There are copayments (a certain percentage that the insured must pay) and deductibles (an amount that the insured must pay before Medicare pays any part of the charges). The yearly deductible for hospitalization was $1,100 in 2010. There is no copayment required of a Medicare recipient for the first 60 days in the hospital. But, if someone stayed in the hospital for 61 to 90 days, they were charged $275 a day in 2010.

Part B, sometimes called supplementary medical insurance, covers doctors' fees, outpatient hospital treatment, lab services, and some limited home health care. For doctors' fees and special therapies, there is a deductible ($155 in 2010); Medicare then pays 80% of an approved

---

EXHIBIT **8.7**

Distribution of Health Expenditures by Source of Payment in the United States, 1994 and 2004

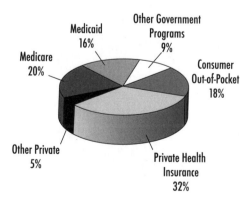

1994

Public 44.3%   Private 55.7%

Medicaid 16%
Other Government Programs 9%
Medicare 20%
Consumer Out-of-Pocket 18%
Other Private 5%
Private Health Insurance 32%

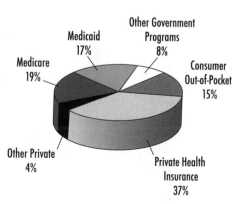

2004

Public 44.4%   Private 55.6%

Medicaid 17%
Other Government Programs 8%
Medicare 19%
Consumer Out-of-Pocket 15%
Other Private 4%
Private Health Insurance 37%

Source: Kaiser Family Foundation, 2006.

amount, and the insured is responsible to for paying the remainder. Part B is optional and carries with it a monthly premium. In 2010, the cost to the consumer was about $100 per month (Centers for Medicare and Medicaid Services, 2010).

Medicare has been a very successful program, providing nearly universal access to hospital care and reducing the cost of many routine health services for all older people. The major successes of the program include increased access to high-quality medical care, equality of treatment, and high levels of satisfaction reported by beneficiaries (Lave, 1996). There are challenges to the program as well. From the perspective of policy makers and budget analysts, the major concern with Medicare is its cost. Medicare program payments were estimated at $325 billion for 2005, accounting for 13% of the federal budget (Kaiser Family Foundation, 2005). More importantly, the Medicare fund currently faces short-term and long-term financial problems, like the trust fund for Social Security.

Other problems with Medicare include its acute-care focus and the lack of coverage for long-term care in nursing homes and for home-based health care. In addition, the copayments, deductibles, and gaps in Medicare coverage mean that many older people need to purchase gap-filler insurance, generically referred to as **Medigap** policies, or risk facing substantial out-of-pocket expenses. These private insurance policies, designed to cover the charges not covered by Medicare, are purchased by individuals or made available through employers. In 2008, 59% of the older population had some form of private health insurance policy (privately purchased or employment-based) to address gaps and copayments, as well as aspects of care not covered by Medicare at all (DeNavas-Walt, Proctor, & Smith, 2009).

The extra coverage provided by Medigap policies is not spread equally among all groups, as Exhibits 8.8 and 8.9 illustrate. The first chart shows that, among those ages 65 and older, non-Hispanic Whites are the most likely to have gap-filling insurance, and Hispanics are the least likely. Some of this differential is explained by employer-provided insurance. Whites are much more likely to be receiving employer-funded insurance than are any other group. Poverty status also has a strong relationship with having private insurance in later life, as shown in Exhibit 8.9. Individuals at or near the poverty level do not have sufficient disposable income to be able to afford gap-filling policies.

"HEY HONEY, NICE BONE DENSITY!"

EXHIBIT **8.8**

Percent of Adults in the United States Age 65 and Older With Insurance,
by Race and Ethnicity, 2003

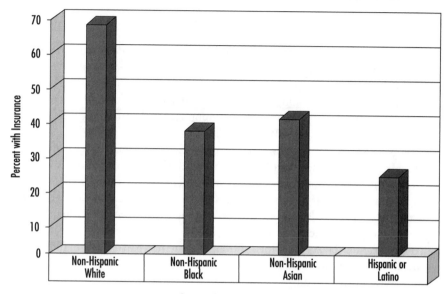

Source: Department of Health and Human Services, 2005.

EXHIBIT **8.9**

Percent of Adults in the United States Age 65 and Older With Private
Insurance by Poverty Status, 2003

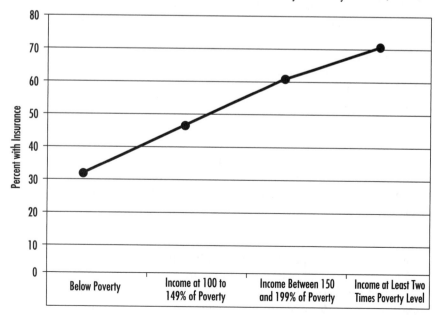

Source: Department of Health and Human Services, 2005.

While Medicare is a very significant benefit to older people, rising health care costs and gaps in coverage mean that individuals still have high out-of-pocket costs. The average older person paid $3,455 in 2003 for their health care; this amount represented 22% of the average older person's income (Caplan & Brangan, 2004). In addition, the program covers primarily acute care, not long-term care, which is the greatest health care need of the older population in general.

Medicare Part D

Prescription drugs are another major health care cost for older people. There are common stories about older people who cut pills in half or skip doses in order to make their prescription medicine last longer. Some media coverage has featured older adults with low incomes who skip their prescriptions because they could not afford them along with groceries or heat for their homes. Prescription drugs are one of the fastest growing components of national health care spending, increasing more than four-fold between 1990 and 2003 (Kaiser Family Foundation, 2005). In an effort to help older people with their prescription drug costs, Congress signed into law the Medicare Prescription Drug Improvement and Modernization Act of 2003, commonly known as Medicare Part D.

As with any major policy change, implementation has been challenging. As a result of the compromises necessary to make the coverage politically feasible and the costs of the program manageable, the legislation became a confusing mix of protection for those with very high or low drug expenses; there was also a so-called donut hole, representing a gap in the pharmaceutical coverage for those whose medication costs are not particularly high or low. Individuals who already had drug coverage through private or employer-based programs may decide not to enroll in Medicare Part D at all.

Medicare Part D enrollment opened in November of 2005, and coverage became available in January of 2006. Implementation of the program posed unusual challenges because the beneficiaries of the program (and/or their designees) had to sort through extensive and often confusing information about a very large number of possible plans from private companies, decide which plan to choose, and then take further steps to officially enroll in the program. Extensive media coverage showed consumers trying to understand the provisions of the new law and the nuances of complex program alternatives. Enrollment began at a much slower pace than anticipated. In the first years of implementation, a poll of Medicare beneficiaries showed that only 31% of the respondents had a favorable impression of the prescription drug program, and 61% said that they did not understand the program well or at all (Kaiser Family Foundation, 2005). Over the past few years, however, enrollments have increased gradually, and the overall goal of the legislation—to provide prescription drug coverage for Medicare beneficiaries who had no such coverage through other means—has largely been accomplished. In 2009, 90% of Medicare beneficiaries had prescription drug coverage of some kind; about 60% had coverage through Medicare Part D or a Medicare Advantage drug plan (Neuman & Cubanski, 2009).

Medicaid

Originally conceived as insurance for the acute health care needs of welfare recipients, Medicaid now plays a crucial role in financing health care for older people, most especially long-term care in nursing homes. Jointly funded by states and the federal government, Medicaid was created as the primary health insurance program for low-income individuals and families. Medicaid has always been available for low-income older people, but over the past few decades two important shifts have taken place. First, an increasing proportion of Medicaid expenditures have gone for health care for older people. Second, an increasing proportion of those expenditures have gone to long-term care rather than acute care. In 2001, older people represented about 11% of the Medicaid beneficiary population but 24% of Medicaid expenditures (Flowers, Gross, Kuo, & Sinclair, 2005). Medicaid benefits for older people are spent primarily on long-term care in nursing homes. Of the money that Medicaid spent on long-term care in 2004, 51% went to nursing homes (Kassner, 2006).

How did this shift occur? From the beginning, Medicaid coverage included nursing facility services. Older people who needed fairly extensive assistance with activities of daily living resorted to Medicaid-financed nursing home placement because they lacked other options. Most people with long-term care needs do not have the financial resources to stay at home and pay for long-term services out of their own pockets for very long. Because Medicaid originally covered long-term care only in institutions, older people who came to the end of their own and family financial resources often faced the dilemma of not having access to government assistance unless they went to a nursing home—using Medicaid funding.

For decades Medicaid provided almost no financing of community-based services, such as home health care. That situation has changed with the proliferation of **Medicaid waiver programs**. These programs allow states to waive (hence the term *waiver*) certain restrictions that typically apply to the delivery of services; in the case of long-term care, waiver programs allow Medicaid dollars to be spent on home- and **community-based care**, rather than just for institution-based (nursing home) care. Because average nursing homes cost about $6,700 per month in 2009 (MetLife

Even individuals with health limitations can volunteer to help at schools. (Credit: U.S. Census Bureau, Public Information Office [PIO])

Mature Market Institute, 2009b), and community-based services average less than one-half of that, the waiver programs are a potential source of cost savings. In addition, most people prefer to receive long-term care services in their own homes, rather than in institutions (Kane, Kane, & Ladd, 1998). Yet the availability of openings in state Medicaid waiver programs are often limited in number, and many states still spend a disproportionate amount of their Medicaid funds on nursing homes.

This potential for home- and community-based waivers to save money is of great interest to state and federal agencies that fund it. There is ongoing concern at many levels about the growth of Medicaid expenditures. In 1980, Medicaid state and federal spending totaled about $25.5 billion; by 2004, the total was $288 billion, growth that is far beyond the significant inflation of health care costs. The current Medicaid price tag, dramatic rates of growth, and the looming demand that baby boomers will place on the health care system combine to suggest that innovations and reform are necessary (Ku & Guyer, 2001).

In summary, Medicare and Medicaid provide the foundation for the financing of health care for older Americans. Because of the restrictions on what these programs will fund, they also play an important role in shaping how and where health care is delivered to older adults. The acute care (i.e., hospital) and institutional (nursing home) biases in these programs have helped to produced a delivery system that is not particularly responsive to the needs or preferences of the older population. The emergence of the Medicaid waiver programs signals a significant attempt to restructure the financing and delivery of some health care services to better fit the preferences and demands of an aging population.

Long-Term Care in the United States

One of the most important issues in health care for older people is long-term care. **Long-term care** is the system of services provided to assist people with long-term medical problems and limitations in their ability to complete the tasks of everyday life. It is fundamentally different from acute care in its focus. Rather than curing illnesses, long-term care is focused on managing chronic physical health conditions, such as severe arthritis, lung and heart disease, or cognitive conditions, such as dementia, while maintaining function for as long as possible. Long-term care provides people with assistance in the activities of daily living (ADLs) and instrumental activities of daily living (IADLs), briefly mentioned earlier in the chapter (e.g., help with bathing, dressing, meal preparation, and transportation). Some people also require medical care, including administration of medications that might be forgotten by someone with dementia, or medical treatments, like insulin injections. The diverse needs of older people for long-term care are met by a fragmented, complex array of programs and services (Kane et al., 1998).

The long-term care system includes a range of services (such as home care, adult day services, and home-delivered meals), locations where services are provided (such as senior centers, assisted-living facilities), consumers (including older adults and disabled or seriously ill people of all ages), and payers (government, insurance, and personal/family funds). However, as we discussed in Chapter 5, the vast majority of the day-to-day assistance that older people get is provided by family and friends in an informal system of support, without pay.

Although we often think of nursing homes as synonymous with long-term care, these services are provided in a range of settings—from an individual's own home to a specially designed congregate setting (such as assisted living), or in a more medically focused institution such as a nursing home. Some long-term care programs are designed to provide services to clients indefinitely for chronic or degenerative conditions from which recovery is not expected; others might be set up as a shorter-term solution to an immediate crisis, such as rehabilitation after major surgery or a serious health event. Finally, long-term care can be designed to improve an individual's functioning, to provide services to compensate for losses in functioning, or to prevent further decline in functioning; some systems claim all three of these goals (Kane & Kane, 1987, pp. 7–8). This diversity of services and programs that fall under the umbrella of long-term care thus includes paid and unpaid care, services provided in a person's home, services provided in specially designed housing, and services provided in a nursing home. In general, people in nursing homes have the highest level of need for assistance, followed by those in community housing with services, as shown in Exhibit 8.10. Next, we briefly discuss each of these components of the long-term care system. As is clear from the exhibit, older individuals living on their own in the community have the lowest average level of need for assistance.

Unpaid Long-Term Care

The vast majority of the day-to-day nonmedical help that older people receive comes from family and friends. The unpaid help that is provided by family members and friends can range from relatively infrequent help with a few activities and needs, such as shopping and transportation, all the way to a nearly constant level of daily assistance with more complicated personal needs (such as bathing, getting in and out of bed, and eating) and even medical treatments. A great many people are involved in providing these services. An estimated 21% of the U.S. population provides unpaid care to family and friends over age 18 (not all of whom are older people); the economic value of the care that is donated by family and friends has been estimated at more than $255 billion annually (Pandya, 2005). This astounding figure certainly challenges us to think about how long-term care should be provided and financed. Obviously those who pay for health care services (private insurers and various levels of government via Medicare and Medicaid) prefer that families continue this substantial contribution toward long-term care of their members.

Clearly, voluntary unpaid care is the economic, social, and personal foundation for the current system of long-term care. Families and friends generally want to continue to provide as much help as they possibly can for as long as they can, and caregiving has many rewards. However, extended intensive family caregiving can take a toll, as discussed in Chapter 5. In addition, caregivers who are employed face added costs. The working caregiver forfeits an estimated average of $660,000 over a lifetime in lost wages and reduced Social Security benefits because

EXHIBIT **8.10**

Percentage of Medicare Enrollees Age 65 and Over With Functional Limitations,
by Residential Setting, 2007

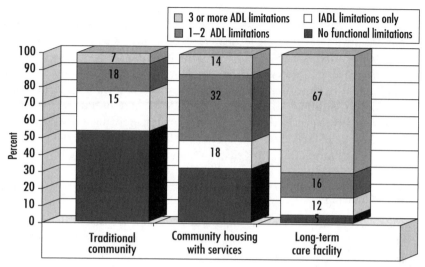

Source: Federal Interagency Forum on Aging-Related Statistics, 2008.

of missed days of work, unpaid leave, and reduction in work hours (Metlife Mature Market Institute, 2001). Because of the importance of informal caregiving to older people and to the long-term care system, increasing attention is being given to the development of services and employment policies that help to shore up the informal networks of support.

Nursing Homes

Nursing homes are a significant part of the formal system of long-term care today; however, they grew out of a much less formal system of care, in which families took other people from the community into their homes for care. This form of care expanded and became more formalized when additional sources of funding (notably Medicare and Medicaid) began to provide payment. Today nursing homes are highly regulated and strictly controlled by states, which oversee the number of homes that are built and monitor their compliance with state and federal guidelines. The federal government has national standards and strict guidelines regarding all aspects of nursing home operation for any facility that receives Medicare or Medicaid funding.

Much of the regulation of nursing homes has come about through cyclical discoveries over the decades of serious problems in some nursing homes—including abuse, inadequate nutrition or facilities, or insufficient medical treatment. As a consequence of the negative media coverage, most Americans carry very negative attitudes regarding nursing homes. Substantial resources are expended to try to avoid negative events in nursing homes through tight regulation, regular inspections, and training requirements of staff.

More recently, nursing homes have changed their orientation from caring for seriously ill or cognitively impaired older adults and disabled people of all ages to include more active rehabilitation and short-stay visits. One study of all nursing home residents in Ohio found that 57% stayed for 3 months or less; the majority of the short-stay residents were in the nursing home to receive rehabilitative services (Mehdizadeh, Nelson, & Applebaum, 2006). Some nursing homes also offer short stays (also known as *respite care*) so that family caregivers can have some respite in order to deal with their own health issues or take a break for a vacation from their nearly constant responsibility to oversee care. Nursing homes are serving an increasingly diverse range of needs, from short-stay rehabilitation or respite to long stays by older adults with complex health challenges; they are no longer simply the "last home for the aged" (Leiberman & Tobin, 1976).

Some nursing home providers are currently rethinking the way that nursing homes are run, including the physical environment, the amount of personal attention each resident receives, and other aspects of care. The "Eden alternative" and "Greenhouse" models of nursing homes, developed by Thomas (2004), are good examples of such innovative, person-centered, resident-empowering approaches. In both of these models, staff training, resident roles, and the physical environment of the facility are all based on the principle that elders, no matter where they live or what assistance they may need, have something unique and valuable to offer. As a result, long-term care services should be designed with this in mind. Such alternatives are at the leading edge of the culture change movement in nursing home care: bringing person-centered care and an improved quality of everyday life to those in nursing homes through innovations such as allowing pets in the nursing home, giving individuals with dementia more choice over how they spend their time, and creating entirely new physical designs for the living spaces of the nursing home, rather than shared rooms arrayed down long hallways.

Assisted Living

One major, new player in the long-term care sector is **assisted living**, which is generally considered to be a less medical setting, often featuring private efficiency apartments decorated with one's own belongings within a building that looks more like a hotel or apartment complex than a hospital. The philosophy of assisted living focuses on providing privacy, autonomy, and personal attention within a setting, where services to support ADLs are also available (Zimmerman et al., 2005). Much of the early development of assisted living was done by those in the hotel industry, who knew relatively little about the care needs of older adults who live there. Because most people prefer to remain in their own homes, individuals or couples choosing to move to assisted living do so because living at home is no longer feasible, often due to health or cognitive problems. Therefore, rather than just being a "cruise ship on land" that provides housing, housekeeping, and meals, developers quickly learned that residents with ADL or IADL limitations may require supervision in taking their medications, monitoring for falls, and assistance in dressing and bathing (Morgan, Gruber-Baldini, & Magaziner, 2001).

Assisted living is distinct from the nursing home environment in that most of the cost is paid for privately, by the residents or their families. A small percentage is paid for through Medicaid waivers or through long-term care insurance. Therefore, much of assisted living is not available to low-income individuals who cannot afford the monthly fees and instead still must choose between home and nursing home.

As time passes, the resident population of these assisted-living settings, which seldom provide extensive health care services, is becoming older and facing more health challenges. This forces decisions about whether to bring more services into assisted living or whether residents must move to a higher level of care, typically a nursing home. Some assisted-living facilities include specialized units to care for those with dementia, including a larger staff and locked doors (Sloane et al., 2005). As these progressions continue, some contend that assisted-living environments are becoming more like nursing homes without the same level of regulation. In response to negative events that have taken place in assisted living, all states have moved in the direction of regulating assisted living in ways that look a lot like a toned-down version of nursing home regulations (Mollica & Johnson-Lamarche, 2005). Nonetheless, their favorability compared to nursing homes among older adults and the population generally remains strong.

Community-Based Long-Term Care

The phrase *community-based long-term care* describes the assistance with daily activities that is provided in people's homes by community-based agencies. Options for community-based care began to expand in the 1970s. This expansion occurred because of the convergence of three factors: the sometimes inappropriate placement of individuals in nursing homes, the high costs of nursing home care, and the preferences of older adults to stay home, if possible. Even though home care was hotly debated at first (with strong opposition coming from the nursing home industry, expressed as concern that home care cannot be as well-regulated as care provided in an institution), this form of service delivery has been increasing increased steadily over the past 3 decades. Waivers programs have helped states to include home care as an option in their long-term care systems, albeit on a limited basis.

One of the recent innovations in community-based care is called **consumer direction**. The philosophy of consumer direction holds that consumers have the right and the ability to assess their own needs, determine how best to have those needs met, and evaluate the quality of the services they receive. Under this approach, health care consumers choose and hire their own workers, decide how and when services will be delivered, and provide feedback about how well the services are working. In practice, the most fully developed model of self-direction is embodied in the Cash and Counseling model. In this model, consumers are the legal employer of record—hiring and supervising their own care workers and managing their own services with professional support. But the key point is that the consumer, rather than someone else, is in charge of what happens and when. Based on the early successes and widespread diffusion of participant-directed service delivery models (Foster, Brown, Phillips, Schore, & Carlson, 2003; Kunkel & Nelson, 2005; Simon-Rusinowitz, Loughlin, Ruben, Garcia, & Mahoney, 2010), consumer direction is becoming part of the long-term care landscape. Consumer direction brings to long-term services greater flexibility, expanded options, and greater responsiveness to individual preferences.

Continuing Care Retirement Communities

A final option within long-term care is the **CCRC**, or continuing care retirement community. In this arrangement, housing and service options are combined and offered on a single campus. These communities typically offer independent living units (cottages, apartments, or houses), assisted-living units, and a health care facility or nursing home. There is often a steep entry fee to move into the community and monthly charges that vary, depending on where in the community the individual resides. In exchange for the entry fee and monthly charges, residents receive the promise of care that is tailored to their changing needs, all provided by the CCRC. Because of the high cost of CCRCs, this option is not affordable to all older people (Nelson, 2002).

Financing Long-Term Care

Through Medicare and Medicaid, the federal government is the largest purchaser of long-term care services. In addition, local programs, such as those funded by county tax levies or state subsidies, are becoming more common, but federal sources are still the primary payers of long-term care. Exhibit 8.11 shows the proportion of long-term care funded by various sources.

One alternative to expand the financial capacity of individuals to support whatever long-term care needs they may face is long-term care insurance. This option is widely discussed but still is not adopted by many people. These policies provide coverage for individuals who require long-term care services later in life, often including alternatives to enable them to receive care at home, if that is medically feasible. The low adoption rate of private long-term care insurance is probably linked to a general societal distaste for thinking about issues such as severe illness and end-of-life issues. We would rather gamble that we will not need long-term care than contemplate that possibility. In addition, the policies can be costly so that many people cannot afford to insure themselves against the prospect of a nursing home stay in their future.

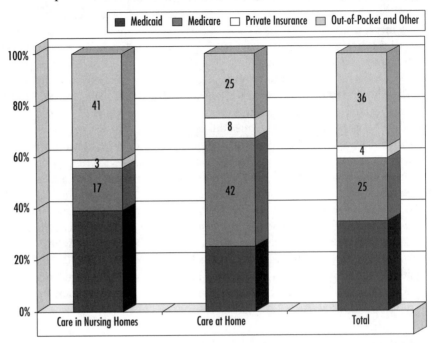

EXHIBIT **8.11**

Long-Term Care Expenditures for Older Americans by Source of Payment, 2004

Source: Congressional Budget Office, 2004.

CLASS Act

One of the most significant changes to our national health policy since Medicare and Medicaid is the Patient Protection and Affordable Care Act. One of the provisions within that legislation is the Community Living Assistance Services and Supports, or the **CLASS Act**. This is a voluntary public insurance program open to people who are currently employed. After a minimum of five years of enrollment (and paying premiums) in the insurance program, an enrollee is entitled to a cash benefit for long-term care, provided that they meet the disability criteria. The program is entirely financed by premiums paid by enrollees (Wiener, 2010). The details for this new long-term care financing option are still being ironed out at the time of this writing, but it already stands as a momentous addition to the long-term care portfolio for this nation, giving moderate income adults more of an opportunity to defray the risks of needing long-term care at an affordable cost.

Summary

The health status of older people—individually and collectively—is a product of lifelong forces: genetics, behaviors, lifestyles, and access to a particular kind of health care system. At the risk of oversimplification, we can reduce this array of factors affecting health to two primary categories: individual and societal. Individual influences include the decisions people make (e.g., about diet, exercise, and smoking) as well as one's genetic heritage. These individual factors interact with societal forces, including our health care system and social characteristics, such as education, income, gender, and race/ethnicity that create inequalities throughout the life course.

There are some optimistic trends in our health care system, including a growing emphasis on health promotion, increasing healthy life expectancy, and reducing health disparities. In stark contrast, however, increasing rates of obesity in our society will influence future cohorts, who have spent much of their lives eating more and exercising less than current older adults. Recent research suggests that obesity increases an individual's chance of disability but does not reduce life expectancy; thus, obesity may result in normal life expectancy but more years spent in disability (Reynolds, Saito, & Crimmins, 2005). This sobering prospect should encourage us to take stock of the individual and social forces that shape our individual health and the health of our older population, including our health care system.

The medical model has given rise to a system of health care not well suited to the needs of an aging population. It emphasizes acute care when the greatest need among older people is for long-term care for chronic health problems and functional limitations. The financing of health care for older people is fragmented, uneven, and biased toward care provided in an institution, rather than in the community or in people's homes.

Even if we can agree that a coherently financed, integrated, and accessible system of health care is the goal, the fundamental problem of paying for it remains unresolved. The cost of providing health care to an aging population has proved to be an enormous stumbling block in moving toward a better-designed system of care. The large portion of the federal budget currently spent on Medicare is the starting point for projections of an untenable financial burden posed by health care costs of the baby boom generation. Nonetheless, one should use a critical eye in considering the problems in the health care system and their potential solutions. Certainly the growing numbers of older people play a part in increasing health care costs to the nation. But the fees charged for health care services have increased also.

Blaming older people for rising health care costs is an example of what Robertson (1991) calls **apocalyptic demography**—"the social construction of catastrophe by suggesting that an increasing aging population will place unbearable demands on the health care system" (p. 144). Robertson goes on to suggest that the health care system focuses on the aging population as a growth market and responds by medicalizing many aspects of aging—"creating" diseases such as menopause or sexual dysfunction or aging itself (as described in the essay following this chapter), offering treatments for them, and receiving reimbursement for providing those services. This process—provider-induced increased demand for health care services for older people— and not the size of the older population may play the more significant role in increased health care costs.

The resolution of the health care financing crisis may well be on the horizon, even though debates about what care should be provided, to whom, under what circumstances, and by whom persist. We must come to terms with the question of whether health care is a right of citizenship (much as education and clean drinking water are) or a privilege (tied primarily to employment or economic resources). The importance we placed on individual responsibility, self-reliance, and independence had historically stood in the way of major health care reform; it was key to passage of the 2010 reforms that the legislation honors these values. Government responsibility is sometimes seen as damaging to private initiative, family responsibility, and independence. Momentous changes face us in the very near future, as we prepare for the aging of the baby boomers; the new health care reform legislation, including new provisions for long-term care, has framed those decisions.

Web Wise

Centers for Medicare & Medicaid Services   http://www.cms.hhs.gov
The Centers for Medicare & Medicaid Services (CMS) is the federal agency within the U.S. Department of Health and Human Services responsible for Medicare and Medicaid. The site

provides a description of the agency and information for consumers and professionals. Data on national health care expenditures, individuals covered by Medicare and Medicaid, and health care service utilization are also provided.

Healthy People 2010 and Healthy People 2020   http://www.healthypeople.gov/
This Web site includes leading health indicators and related data for the Healthy People initiative. Information and resources for people who are seeking to improve their own health, as well as data and publications related to the Healthy People 2010 goals can be accessed at this Web site. The proposed objectives for Healthy People 2020 are linked here. This site gives a thorough sense of the overall public health initiative for the United States, as well as the specifics for each decade of the program.

Kaiser Family Foundation: Medicare   http://www.kff.org/medicare/index.cfm
The Kaiser Family Foundation site contains a page focusing on Medicare, including policy issues, changes in the program, understanding how it works, and recent policy-based analyses. The site is useful for both understanding some of the complex issues of the program and supporting individuals in understanding their rights as participants in Medicare.

National Center for Health Statistics   http://www.cdc.gov/nchs
The National Center for Health Statistics (NCHS) is a part of the Centers for Disease Control and Prevention, United States Department of Health and Human Services. This Web site provides background information about NCHS, its products (publications and catalogs), current health-related news releases, and answers to frequently asked health-related questions. Information on NCHS data systems and national health surveys are offered. This site also presents various vital and health statistics, organized in tables from NCHS's warehouse. In addition, an opportunity to search chosen topics (older adults) as well as a list of other sites for health-related information and resources is available.

Key Terms

apocalyptic demography
assisted living
biopsychosocial model
CCRC
chronic conditions
CLASS Act
cognitive impairment
community-based care
consumer direction
dementia
disenfranchised grief

fee-for-service
functional ability
geriatricians
health
hospice
long-term care
Medicaid
Medicaid waiver programs
medical model
medicalization
Medicare

Medigap
mind–body dualism
mortality rates
nursing homes
out-of-pocket
political economy of aging
prevalence rates
prospective payment system
reductionism
self-assessed health
successful aging

Questions for Thought and Discussion

1. Picture two older people you know, one who is very healthy and active and one who is in poor health and quite frail. Can you explain why they are so different? What life circumstances, individual choices, or random events helped to influence their health today?

2. Consider the ways in which individual choices and behaviors affect health and the ways in which social and cultural conditions play a role. Can you give an example of an individual health behavior that is not influenced by social and cultural factors?

3. Look in your local telephone directory for physicians who specialize in geriatrics. Are there many of them compared to other specialties? Do you know an older person who sees a geriatrician? How does geriatric medicine better fit the needs of an older person than more traditional approaches?

4. What do you think are the most important health policy issues facing our aging nation? What are the most important health policy issues in older people's lives? What are the greatest challenges to our health care system?

Antiaging: Cosmetics and Aesthetics

Contributed by Mike Payne

"Vanity of vanities, all is vanity." It's hard to believe that observation came from the Old Testament (Ecclesiastics 1:2), thousands of years before the manufacture of facial creams, skin tucks, hair restoration, and liposuction. If they could only see us now.

Fittingly, the term *vanity* serves as a double entendre, with special application for aging. The word *vain* may be interpreted as excessive pride and preoccupation with one's appearance; the phrase *in vain* suggests the futility of battling the finiteness of human endeavors on earth.

What could be more ultimately vain, and in vain, than the human struggle against time and age? Not much. But, currently, as Hollywood and Madison Avenue universally assert, there seems to be little that is more important—or as lucrative. The American Society for Aesthetic Plastic Surgery (ASAPS) estimates that there were 11.7 million surgical and nonsurgical (e.g., BOTOX® injections) procedures performed in the United States in 2007; this number represents a 457% increase since 1997 (ASAPS, 2007).

Surgical procedures, almost all aimed at a more youthful appearance, climbed by 8% between 2006 and 2007, while nonsurgical procedures rose 1% during that year. ASAPS puts Americans' overall spending on cosmetic procedures in 2007 at $13.2 billion. The number of procedures performed on men grew 17% between 2006 and 2007; in 2007, men accounted for about 9% of the cosmetic procedures performed. Liposuction led the way of the most preferred surgical procedures (456,828). Eyelid surgery, a procedure directly related to a younger appearance, numbered 240,763. Among both surgical and nonsurgical treatments, BOTOX® injections (2.8 million) were by far the most favored (ASAPS, 2007).

But the money handed over for medical procedures pales in comparison to the amount Americans spent on antiaging products and remedies (such as antiwrinkle creams, antioxidants, and vitamins). Annual spending on these products was over $20 billion in 2004, with an annual growth rate of nearly 9%. At that rate, the antiaging market was expected to become a $30 billion industry by the year 2009 (Fredonia Group, 2006). Some estimates put the actual figure for 2010 much higher.

Interestingly, though, it is health maintenance products—most notably those relating to memory improvement, sharper vision, and sexual health—and not cosmetics related to a younger appearance that are expected to constitute the bulk of the gains in the years to come. Perhaps all is not vanity after all.

Americans are increasingly interested in not only looking younger, but feeling younger as well. The past 30 years have brought an increasing emphasis on physical health and put a spotlight on the "use it or lose it" approach to keeping both body and mind in sound condition as the years go by. As our average life span has risen from 47 to 77 years in the last century, we have become more aware of how much life—and the deeper, broader appreciation of it that often comes with age—holds for people still in good health well after the traditional time of retirement.

While a rapidly growing number of Americans are living to age 100 and beyond (from roughly 50,000 in 2000 to a projected 1 million by 2050) (Krach & Velkoff, 1999), the outer limit of the human life span has remained essentially constant for the past 100,000 years—at

roughly 120 years (Hayflick, 2001–2002). However, maybe because collagen and airbrushing cannot make a centenarian look 30, and all the antioxidants in the world will not make him or her feel it, most of us do not appear eager to reach those outer limits. An AARP study from the late 1990s found that only 27% of Americans surveyed hoped to live 100 years (Rostein, 1999).

But it might be just for the near future that 100 years of living brings with it undisguisable wrinkles, poor health, and a fading memory. Who knows what science may achieve in one of our final earthly frontiers—the human body. Some doctors and scientists in the field of aging expect to see humans routinely living beyond 120 years before the 21st century is over (Rostein, 1999).

Others, like Leonard Hayflick, Professor of Anatomy at the University of California, San Francisco, view the aging process and human life span as a predictable correlate of the brain-weight/body-weight ratio in primates so that a sudden jump in the human life span would be unnatural and improbable (Hayflick, 2000–2001). Such life extension might also be undesirable given the numerous social and ethical dilemmas an abrupt lengthening of the life span could unleash. For example, would only the wealthy, those now able to afford BOTOX®, facelifts and hair transplants, be able to afford the costly treatments leading to longer life? What would the new retirement age be if most people live to 130? How long would people stay in school? How many couples would celebrate their 100th wedding anniversaries?

Just this small sample of questions can seem daunting; certainly the technological and social challenges of significantly extending life expectancy are enormous and perhaps even overwhelming. But, we might take advice from some other scholars in the field who warn against being "gerontological Luddites," opponents of scientific change, when it comes to life extension (Moody, 2001–2002). The complexity of life extension and antiaging are summed up nicely by Cole and Thomson (2001–2002):

> Anti-aging is fueled by many elements: ancient yearnings for immortality; contemporary possibilities in genetic and clinical research; widespread fear of decline, dependency, and

death; a consumer culture eager to exploit this fear; and legitimate clinical care and self-help aimed at improving the quality of later life. (pp. 6–7)

It is important to question the underlying message of the many aspects of the antiaging movement. Promoting healthy long life is quite different from fighting physical signs of aging. We would be wise to question who benefits from antiaging medicine and products and what the burgeoning multibillion dollar industry implies about growing older in our society.

Politics, Government, and Aging in America

9

*Public policy reflects and reinforces the 'life chances' associated with each person's so-
cial location within the class, status, and political structures that comprise society.
The lives of each succeeding generation are similarly shaped by the extent to which
social policy maintains or redistributes those life chances.*

(Estes, 1991, p. 20)

In the realm of politics, members of the older population are both participants in and subjects
(collectively) of debate. The roles of older persons in politics extend from being voters and participants in programs such as Medicare and Social Security to holding high electoral office. As a
subject of political debate, the aging of the population focuses our attention upon the social ties
across age cohorts as well as the political interests that divide them. We have already begun to
discuss social policies (and the debates surrounding them) having to do with retirement, health,
and income maintenance. Here we continue and expand those discussions, focusing more directly on politics and the place of the older population in the political system.

Age-Based Government Policies

The Old-Age Welfare State

For the vast stretch of recorded history, older people (in relatively small numbers because life
expectancy was short) were the responsibility of their families or themselves. Governments and
leaders took no special note of the elderly as a category, often grouping the disadvantaged, frail,
or ill of other ages together with needy elders (recall the discussion of the British Poor Laws in
Chapter 7) (Quadagno, 1982). Only relatively recently, primarily during the 20th century, have
governments assumed any specific responsibility toward their older citizens by developing programs and laws focusing on the older age group. During the same time period, later life has been
identified as a unique and distinctive time of life, deserving of special attention and support via
social policies.

Robert Binstock describes American public policy in the middle of the 20th century (from
the 1930s through the 1970s) as the era of **compassionate ageism**. By ageism Binstock (1991a)
means "the attribution of the same characteristics, status, and just deserts to a heterogeneous
group that has been artificially homogenized, packaged, labeled, and marked as 'the aged'"
(p. 326). Compassionate ageism stereotyped older people as poor, lonely, neglected, in ill health,
and inadequately housed. Although founded to some degree on stereotypes, Binstock argues
that the approach was compassionate, intended to help those "deserving and needy" older people who were unable to provide adequately for themselves (Binstock, 1991b; Quadagno, 1982).
These views set the stage for policy makers to create a category of older persons and to develop
income, housing, and health policies to remedy their collective plight (Jacobs, 1990). Thus,
governments in the United States and in many other nations developed policies to address the
problems that were believed to generally afflict the elderly in their societies. Political support was
based on the view that the problems of the old were not their fault and that their needs followed

years of contribution to society (i.e., that they were deserving of help under standards of the Poor Laws). Thus it came to be accepted as appropriate for society to provide help collectively, rather than rely on individuals or their families to meet all needs (Binstock, 1991a). Exhibit 9.1 outlines the timing of selected social policy developments in the United States, with those during the era of compassionate ageism, many of which we have discussed in this book, shaded. As you can see, many of the cornerstone programs for older adults emerged during this era of compassionate ageism.

This definition of the aged as a distinct and especially deserving population has prompted policies to be enacted that would otherwise face potent political opposition. For example, despite ongoing, vigorous resistance in the United States to any national health insurance program, just such a program targeted to the elderly (Medicare) was passed by Congress in 1965. Programs and services for the elderly proliferated from the 1930s through the 1960s, and the popularity of helping older people rated alongside "old-fashioned family values" as reliable campaign issues.

Initiatives to assist older adults reached a peak of activity in the 1960s as part of Lyndon B. Johnson's "Great Society" (Estes, 1979). The deservedness of the older population in the 1960s, reflected in high rates of poverty, poor health, and inadequate housing, was unquestioned. Programs to help older adults expanded rapidly during this time (Binstock, 1991b). Legislation passed then led to an array of programs, services, and agencies at state and federal levels that has come to be called the **old-age welfare state** (Binstock, 1991a; Myles, 1983). The old-age welfare state had a clear purpose—to address the serious problems common in the older adult population at that time. Programs still operating today are evidence of this legacy.

Although we can talk about the network of programs in the old-age welfare state as a whole, its development was fragmented, leading to gaps and overlaps, such as those discussed in Chapter 8 for health care (Binstock, 2005). Programs were established on a piecemeal basis, with no single agency or group responsible for the overall well-being of the older population. "Existing social policies for older people include a vast array of fragmented, complicated but important agencies, services and benefits" (Torres-Gil, 1992, p. 37). "The system

EXHIBIT *9.1*

Enactment Timeline of U.S. Aging Policies

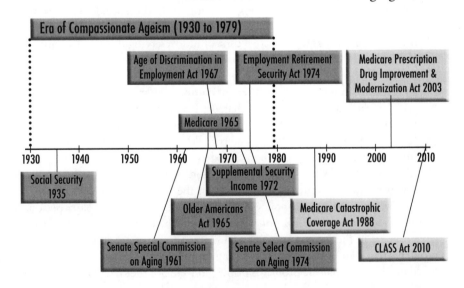

involves numerous administrative mandates, each with funds and authority over specific areas. Often, one agency knows nothing of what the others are doing. No single, overarching policy or agency wields responsibility for coordinating services or developing policy direction" (Torres-Gil, 1992, p. 58). In fact, Torres-Gil reports that there are programs related to the older population under the auspices of virtually every cabinet department serving the President. The largest concentration of programs is in the Department of Health and Human Services, including Social Security, Medicare, the Administration on Aging, and the National Institutes of Health (Torres-Gil, 1992). The largest program in terms of dollars of assistance each year is Social Security, described in Chapters 6 and 7. Social Security, Medicare, and Medicaid together accounted for 41% of all dollars expended in the 2010 federal budget (Kaiser Family Foundation, 2010).

The Older Americans Act

The **Older Americans Act** [OAA], designed to be the focal point of federal government policy on aging, established the Administration on Aging [AoA], a unit of the Department of Health and Human Services, to oversee the well-being of adults over age 60 (Torres-Gil, 1992). Passed with broad support in 1965, the OAA mandated a wide array of programs intended to deal with a comprehensive list of issues facing older adults: enhancing employment and housing, improving long-term care, and developing coordinated, comprehensive services to care for older adults with dependencies (Binstock, 1991b; McConnell & Beitler, 1991). The OAA, an age entitlement, was initially directed to assist all Americans aged 60 and older (Binstock, 1991a). The context for its passage included a booming economy, in which public funds seemed plentiful, and a relatively high social consensus favoring solutions to social problems through government programs (Binstock, 1991b).

The goals outlined in the OAA were lofty, but funding has never been adequate (Binstock, 1991b). OAA programs have been hindered by limited staff and budget over the past 40 years (Estes, 1979; Torres-Gil, 1992). Minimal initial funding for OAA was expanded in the early years, mostly as additional program responsibilities were added, but has shrunk since 1981 (Binstock, 1991b). Nonetheless, experts suggest that the Older Americans Act has had some successes.

> Its accomplishments, at the least, include (1) continuous and dynamic identification of needs of older persons; (2) creation and exemplification of strategies, programs, and services for meeting those needs; (3) provision of tangible and intangible help to innumerable older Americans; (4) development of a nationwide infrastructure for helping older persons, comprising 57 State Units on Aging, 670 Area Agencies on Aging, and about 25,000 associated service-providing agencies; and (5) recruitment and socialization of thousands of career professionals to the field of aging. (Binstock, 1991b, p. 11)

The programs offered under the auspices of the OAA have included senior citizen centers, nutrition programs, employment training initiatives, and a network of local and state agencies providing and coordinating services (Area Agencies on Aging). Successive commissioners of the Administration on Aging, faced with inadequate resources, have selected priorities for special attention during their administrations (Binstock, 1991b). As a result, the priorities under the OAA have shifted over time (Estes, 1979; Quirk, 1991).

In the past 20–25 years, the OAA has focused on serving subgroups of older adults in greatest need (low income, frail, and minority elders), moving away from its initial broader age entitlement to everyone over age 60. The OAA has also been a part of larger ideological debates regarding federal versus state or individual responsibility to meet the needs of vulnerable populations. Providing services at the state and local levels, the model utilized by the Administration on Aging is viewed as preferable by many politicians (Torres-Gil, 1998).

The Aging Enterprise

Some have viewed the development of initiatives to assist older persons with an uncritical eye—seeing them simply as helpful supports to a dependent group. In contrast, Carol Estes (1979) has pointed out that programs and services for older persons, like many social programs, have unanticipated consequences. The policies and programs established to ameliorate the problems of older adults have generated a system of agencies, service providers, and professionals that Estes refers to as the **aging enterprise**—"programs, organizations, bureaucracies, interest groups, trade associations, providers, industries, and professionals that serve the aged in one capacity or another" (p. 2). Included are both governmental and private organizations, most of which have grown up since the introduction of major aging legislation in the 1960s—notably, Medicare and the Older Americans Act. Over time, Estes argues, the aging enterprise has become a force in itself, with a vested interest in sustaining the dependency of the older population. According to Estes, "the age segregated policies that fuel the aging enterprise are socially divisive 'solutions' that single out, stigmatize, and isolate the aged from the rest of society" (p. 2). She argues that the programs themselves (and the people who implement them) reinforce stereotypic views of older people, foster dependency, and sustain a myopic "social problems" approach to dealing with what is today a highly diverse population of older adults to reinforce the need for their agencies and activities—and keep their jobs.

Many experts now question the viability of the old-age welfare state, as political ideologies have shifted to diminish the broad-based consensus that supported passage of many of these programs and as their costs rise (Binstock, 1991a; Cole, 1995). Given these changes, government deficits and the changing demographic profile of the population, questions arise regarding whether the programs and policies that originally created the aging enterprise will survive, be modified away from their original principles, or be eliminated entirely.

Aging and Politics

Age Norms and Rules for Political Participation

The U.S. Constitution includes legal age minimums for holding high federal office. Candidates must be at least 35 years old to run for the presidency, 30 to run for the Senate, and 25 to run for the House of Representatives (Office of the Federal Register, 1995). Presumably these rules were instituted in the belief that sufficient maturity and experience are necessary to fulfill these offices. Many states also have laws defining the minimum age for office seekers. States vary in whether they specify lower limits on age for governors, members of the legislature, or other offices. For example, the most commonly specified minimum age for governor is 30 (in 34 states), with 3 states allowing anyone over 18 to run and 6 states having no ages specified (Council of State Governments, 1994). Other offices, such as attorney general or lieutenant governor, less often have specific age limits, but almost all states have minimum ages for members of their legislatures. The most common is age 21 (22 states), with 14 other states specifying 18 and seven more requiring reaching ages 24 or 25 (Council of State Governments, 1994). One interesting point is that none of these laws, state or federal, imposes a maximum age for officeholders, a point to which we will return shortly.

Socially constructed age norms guide the timing of events in political careers, just as they do in families and in other occupations. For the ambitious politician, these norms include progress through adulthood from local or regional office to state and possibly national office. Generally the pattern involves expansion of responsibilities with maturation and proven ability, but the timing of political careers can vary widely. As an example, Exhibit 9.2 shows the distribution of ages at which individuals entered the highest elective office, as President of the United States.

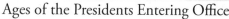
EXHIBIT **9.2**

Ages of the Presidents Entering Office

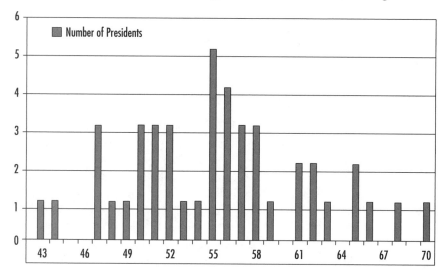

As you can see the range is quite broad, from the youngest entrant (Theodore Roosevelt) to the oldest (Ronald Reagan). The modal age for entry clearly is in the mid-to late 50s, with five Presidents inaugurated at age 55. Examining the trend showed no real pattern of age change over time. If we start with Teddy Roosevelt, the first president of the 20th century, the ages ranged from his low of 43 to 61; at the end of the 20th century and the start of the 21st century, we had Presidents entering office ranging from age 47 (the current incumbent) to 70 years of age. Although most are well past the Constitutional minimum age of 35, only a few (5) entered office past age 65.

Besides the formal rules that set legal age minimums, informal norms regarding age and office-holding sometimes become apparent. The media often point up instances in which individuals are violating implicit age norms by seeking public office at inappropriately young or advanced ages. Stories highlight newly elected members entering the House of Representatives at "only age 27," town mayors elected at 18, or veteran office-holders seeking re-election. In two recent presidential elections (1996 and 2008), the ages of candidates (Robert Dole and John McCain, both 73) were raised as an issue, questioning the candidates' health and vigor relative to the high demands of the office. The late Senator Strom Thurmond was the first person who serve in Congress until his death in 2003 at age 100! Critics questioned his capacity to complete the highly demanding duties of office at such an advanced age (Grove, 1996). Whether extremes of age actually hurt a candidate at the voting booth is unclear. The fact that the issue is raised suggests an implicit age norm for being either "too young" or "too old" to become President or to hold other high office. Reactions to extremes of age, in either direction, point out that our informal norms approve of individuals in the 50s–60s age range as most appropriate for high office in the United States.

Age, Period, and Cohort Effects on Political Behavior

Political behavior includes voting, participating in political activities (such as party organizations or campaigns), and running for office. One major topic of debate in the political life of any aging society is whether the changes related to population aging, period effects, or the flow of cohorts through the population over time influence any of these political behaviors. An extension of this debate has to do with the issue of political power among the aged. As populations in many countries age, is there a likelihood that the older population will take over the political process and control the direction taken by the government? The issue is important because political control determines who fashions the policies in any government. If younger people are politically active in large numbers, politicians in democratic societies will be responsive to their interests and agendas. If, on the other hand, older persons dominate the campaigns and ballot boxes, the political agenda could take a different path. Do aging, period, or cohort make a difference in how people engage in politics? What are the overall dynamics of these three forces in how individuals and demographic groups (based on age, gender, race, or socioeconomic status) interact with and react to the political institutions of society?

Period effects seem likely to be especially potent in the political domain. People of all ages are influenced by social and political events that shape their attitudes toward government, candidates, or specific public policies. It is therefore not surprising that major period events, such as the Watergate scandal in the 1970s or the Iraq war or economic downturn of the early 21st century, can have significant effects on attitudes toward government and toward political parties across age groups (Kahn & Mason, 1987; Pew Research Center, 2009b). Such events may also selectively (by age, social class, etc.) influence people's attitudes and confidence in the political institutions that govern them (Peterson & Somit, 1994). According to Jacobs (1990), cohort effects do appear. "Distinct political and economic experiences may separate generations and have lasting impact" (p. 350). Sometimes trends are difficult to see unless data are examined over long spans of time. For example, the General Social Survey and other polling data suggest increases in the public's favorability toward government spending for social programs between 1975 and 2006, despite periods of political conservatism (Beaulier, Boyes, & Mounts, 2008). Recent studies by the Pew Research Center (2009a) show important cohort differences, with younger people (born after 1977) expressing more support for a strong, active government and equal opportunity in society and less support for a socially conservative agenda compared to older cohorts, including Gen X-ers, baby boomers, and those born earlier than 1946. The amount of difference varies across time, however, with some periods where attitudes are closer across cohorts than is the case now.

Answering our questions about the effects of age on political activity and orientation reflects our earlier debate about the relative influence of aging vs. cohort experience. As discussed in earlier chapters, Mannheim (1952a, 1952b) hypothesized that, during a formative period in late adolescence and early adulthood, core attitudes and orientations (including political ideas) are set, changing relatively little with advancing age (Alwin & Krosnick, 1991; Silverstein, Angelelli, & Parrott, 2001). If Mannheim's hypothesis is true, young people's political attitudes are shaped by political socialization within their families and by the political attitudes of the times in which they mature. Thus, if Mannheim is correct, political behaviors and orientations in society should change slowly, as succeeding cohorts with differing attitudes move through the age structure of society (Alwin & Krosnick, 1991). If, however, events (period effects) can modify political attitudes and behaviors at any age, then Mannheim's view would not be supported, and political change could occur at a more rapid pace.

Fortunately, politics is an area with a fairly long history of data collection, enabling us to examine how age groups voted, affiliated themselves with political parties, and participated in other ways in the political system. Using these data resources, we can develop fairly sound answers to our questions about age, period, and cohort.

Voting and Activism: The Potential for Old-Age Political Power

There is a long tradition of political involvement and activism among older adults in the United States.

Since the Townsend Movement of the 1930s, senior citizens have strongly influenced public policies and political decisions. Their political activism pressured Franklin

Roosevelt to pass Social Security, and their alliance with President John Kennedy, labor unions, and the Democratic Party helped establish Medicare and Medicaid. (Torres-Gil, 1992, p. 75)

Political activism can take many forms, from voting or volunteering in campaigns to contributing to political causes, running for office, or simply following political issues in detail in the media. Research data going back to the 1940s suggest that young adults are consistently less likely to be politically active by contacting their elected representatives or belonging to political organizations than are members of older age groups (Foner, 1973). Older individuals also demonstrate more interest in political campaigns and public affairs debates (Torres-Gil, 1992). Torres-Gil argues that both high voting rates and membership in advocacy organizations continue to empower older citizens politically.

One of the most consistent findings in the study of age and political behavior is the higher rates of voter registration and participation among older adults (Foner, 1973; Jacobs, 1990). The percentage of eligible voters who cast ballots has been higher among older voters for several decades, suggesting a potential aging effect for this type of political behavior. This gives relatively greater power to older adults in two ways. First, there are fewer younger people registered to vote, and second, a lower percentage of those young adults who are registered actually cast ballots in the election. The percentage of adults who are registered to vote rises consistently as age increases, with a clear progression upward until we reach those 75 and older (see Exhibit 9.3). While this age gap in voting had been growing over time due to diminishing voting among young adults (Torres-Gil, 1992), the gap declined for the 2008 presidential election, with noteworthy involvement among young adults through online activity (e.g., Facebook) and initiatives like Rock the Vote (U.S. Census Bureau, 2009). In addition, a recent survey shows that young adults (under 30, 61%) are catching up to older age groups (71%) in considering voting a duty; this is a major jump from 2007 where only 46% of those under 30 said voting was a duty (Pew Research Center, 2009a).

EXHIBIT *9.3*

U.S. Citizen Voter Registration by Age and Sex, 2008

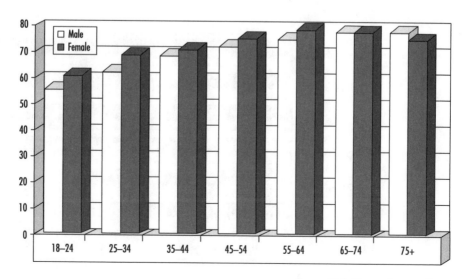

Source: U.S. Census Bureau, 2009.

Several explanations have been offered for why younger people vote less often. They may have less political experience or feel less party attachment; they also relocate more frequently, requiring frequent re-registration to be eligible to vote (Foner, 1973). Strate, Parish, Elder, and Ford (1989) suggest that age is related to voting behavior through a variety of forces that increase social integration with advancing age. According to the Strate's **civic development hypothesis**, young people are neither well socialized into political processes nor do they have completely developed connections with family, community, and employment (social integration), which foster voting among more mature adults (Strate et al., 1989).

Studying the effects of aging on behaviors such as voting is complicated by factors that are related to both. For example, Exhibit 9.4 shows that among men and women 65 to 74, those with the most education are also most likely to vote. Therefore, we cannot simply group people by age and have all of our answers. Many experts predict that the political activism of the older population will increase further with the rising educational levels and previous experience of political activism among baby boomers entering later life (Peterson & Somit, 1994; Rosenbaum & Button, 1992). Among younger cohorts today, females outpace males in voter registration (see Exhibit 9.3); this situation is reversed in the cohorts beyond age 75, perhaps as a residue of earlier cohort experiences (recall the Nineteenth Amendment women voters from Chapter 2). Thus, voting among older women—the majority of the older population—will likely become even more common in the next cohorts, possibly further increasing voting rates of those 65 and older.

Individuals from higher socioeconomic status (SES) backgrounds vote more regularly than their less advantaged counterparts (Peterson & Somit, 1994; Wallace, Williamson, Lung, & Powell, 1991). They also tend to live longer (Rogot, Sorlie, & Johnson, 1992), meaning that, as age increases, the composition of the older population shifts more toward the more high-voting, higher-SES individuals (Riley, 1987). So, if voting increases with age, it may be that part of this increase is due to the cohort composition effect discussed in Chapter 2.

As you are already well aware, the size of the older population (both in absolute terms and as a percentage of the population) is growing. Through high voter turnout, the population over

EXHIBIT **9.4**

2008 Election Voting of 65–74 Year Olds by Education and Sex

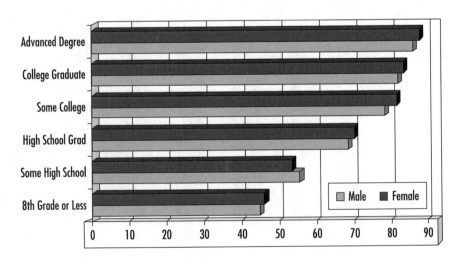

Source: U.S. Census Bureau, 2009.

65 wields proportionally more influence than their actual percentage of the population. In short, if current patterns hold, the older population seems likely to continue to exercise substantial political influence in the future. Candidates and issue campaigns—those focused on passing referendums or voter initiatives—already recognize this potential voter power as they seek favor with older voters (Torres-Gil, 1992; Wallace et al., 1991). Candidates often visit senior centers and develop "sound bites" on issues that are thought to appeal to older voters, who are also more likely to watch the television news campaign coverage than are younger voters. Strategists discuss capturing groups, such as "soccer moms" and "older adults," as though they were homogeneous in their interests and political behavior (Jacobs & Burns, 2005; Schulz & Binstock, 2006). The remaining question is whether the pool of older voters ever has or ever will act as a voting bloc?

For cohorts or age groups to act according to age-based or generational interests requires some degree of **age identification**—whereby individuals label themselves as part of an age cohort or generation. Age identification has been studied for some time, and the findings are consistent; majorities of study participants who are chronologically over 65 do not identify themselves as older adults or accept other, similar labels—selecting instead the label of middle-aged (Day, 1990). If individuals reject being labeled as part of any age group, including the socially devalued older population, it is less likely that they will join age-based organizations or vote (or make other political choices) based on age (Day, 1990; Gilleard & Higgs, 2009; Weiss, 2002). Instead, they may use other identifications (occupation, gender, religion, region, social class, or party) that seem to have greater relevance and have been used throughout their lives to make political choices (Gilleard & Higgs, 2009; Schulz & Binstock, 2006).

Turning to how people vote for specific candidates or on issues, age differences appear selectively. The 2008 Presidential election differs from earlier elections in terms of age differences in voting (Binstock, 2009). Specifically, election-day exit polls (with a national sample of almost 18,000 voters) showed age differences, with 66% of voters under age 30 supporting President Obama. Comparable percentages for those 30 and older ranged from 54% (30–39) to a low of 45% (65 and older) (Binstock, 2009; CNN, 2008). These age differences are also shaped by the lower race/ethnic diversity in the over 65 population relative to younger groups, as well as their cohort experience of being raised during the presidency of Republican Dwight Eisenhower (Binstock, 2009).

In most prior elections, attitudes toward particular issues, such as the Medicare drug benefit, have been less important than political party affiliation in voter choice so that age 60 and older voters acted much like the rest of the electorate, rather than like a voting bloc (Jacobs & Burns, 2005). Although age identification among those over 65 has not coalesced, some predict that it could in the future, based in part on greater longevity; Torres-Gil (1992) refers to the baby boomers as the "most age-segregated generation" (p. 129) and hints at the potential for strong age identification among its members in later life. Certainly we might wonder whether the baby boomers, identified throughout their lives as a distinct (albeit highly heterogeneous) generation, will be more likely to act politically in later life on this basis of their experience as an age-identified group (MetLife Mature Market Institute, 2009a; Morgan, 1998). However, neither in the United States nor in European countries have older adults yet voted as a bloc or identified with political parties based on age (Gilleard & Higgs, 2009).

A related concern in aging societies is the possibility of **gerontocracy**—a society ruled by the elderly (Schulz & Binstock, 2006). Some nations today could be considered gerontocracies. In the decades after its Communist revolution, for example, China saw the age of its governmental leadership, drawn from the revolutionary cohorts, steadily increase as revolutionary leaders took turns in leadership. Now that those leaders are mostly gone, new and more youthful leadership from the postrevolutionary cohorts has emerged. This has coincided with major changes in the focus of policies in China toward Western-style market economies, but drawing any direct causal connection between the two changes is risky.

When can we say that a gerontocracy exists? One piece of evidence is the domination by older people of positions of power and authority in the political and economic realms. We have already looked at U.S. history, where the modal age of presidents at election is 55—hardly old (see Exhibit 9.2) (Kane, 1993). The seniority system in both houses of Congress means that members, as they accumulate years in office, grow in power to head major committees and shape the legislative agenda. However, although members of Congress in 2009 ranged in age from one member under 30 to a notable number (75) who were age 70 or older, the bulk of members (67%) were between ages 50 and 69 ("Congressional Demographics," 2009)—again, not very old.

A second way to evaluate the possibility of a gerontocracy is to examine whether economic power and wealth are concentrated in the hands of older people. Exhibit 9.5 shows the age distribution of the Fortune 400 wealthiest individuals in 2008. The group includes both "self-made" and inherited wealth (only 19 of 400 were listed as fully or partly based on "inheritance") with some of the top names (Bill Gates) familiar to most of us. The exhibit shows relatively few wealthy individuals under age 35, with the highest concentrations in the age range from 65–74 and a declining number at higher ages, in part due to mortality thinning the ranks even of the wealthiest. Almost half are under age 65, including many individuals who have made their own fortunes ("Special Report," 2008). In sum, neither political office-holding nor the resources of wealth are so concentrated in the hands of those over age 65 or 70 as to warrant concluding that a gerontocracy exists in the United States.

Attitudes and Party Affiliation

Sears (1983) defines two types of political attitudes or orientations. The first, symbolic attitudes, are items such as liberal/conservative orientation and party affiliation. Sears argues that such symbolic political attitudes are deeply rooted in the individual's sense of self and less subject to the effects of short-term political events or change with aging. Following the Mannheim (1952a, 1952b) hypothesis on cohorts, Sears believes that these symbolic attitudes are formed in youth and persist across the life course. Other, more specific attitudes—such as those toward the budget deficit, gun control, or particular policy initiatives or candidates, which he calls

EXHIBIT   *9.5*

Age Distribution of Forbes Richest 400 Americans: 2008

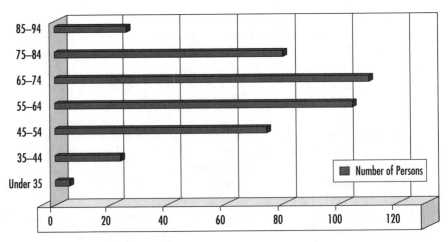

Source: Forbes, 2008.

nonsymbolic—Sears contends are more subject to the influence of period effects or aging.

Using a life cycle approach, Dangelis, Hardy, and Cutler (2007) examined the stability of nonsymbolic attitudes, indirectly testing the Mannheim hypothesis that would lead us to expect more fixed attitudes among older age groups. Employing 30 years of national data from the General Social Survey, this study found that, rather than becoming more rigid in their attitudes, older cohorts shifted their views somewhat more than their younger counterparts toward issues such as privacy, historically disadvantaged groups, and civil rights. These findings suggests that older adults remain open to external influences, such as broad changes in society; in short, the results do not support Mannheim's suggestion that ideas, including attitudes on politics, persist throughout life once set in youth (Dangelis et al., 2007). In another study, Silverstein and his colleagues (2001) focused specifically on an age-related topic, attitudes regarding whether Social Security benefits should be increased, maintained, or decreased. They found that there was a general shift in this nonsymbolic attitude over time, with the most dramatic shift (toward decrease) happening among those approaching old age, who might have been expected to more actively defend the system due to their proximity to getting benefits. In addition, the youngest individuals studied were most swayed by the public questioning of entitlement programs, such as Social Security, early in the Bush administration (a period effect) (Silverstein et al., 2001), suggesting that cohort effects remain important in understanding political attitudes and choices.

Political participation in the later years may take many forms beyond voting. At age 90, Doris Haddock (aka Granny D) finished her 3,200-mile walk across the country, from Pasadena, California, to Washington, DC, to advocate for campaign finance reform. (Credit: Mike Payne, courtesy of the Ohio Department of Aging)

Turning now to symbolic political attitudes, early discussions of the political attitudes of older persons proposed an **aging-conservatism hypothesis**, suggesting that people become more politically conservative as they age—a variation, perhaps, of the "old people are set in their ways" stereotype (Dobson, 1983). Research conducted in the late 1960s confirmed that older people espoused more conservative political views than did their younger counterparts, which seemed to support such a notion. These cross-sectional results, however, overlooked the complexity of aging, period, and cohort. In essence, research conducted since the 1960s shows that liberal or conservative orientation, a symbolic attitude, does not change in any systematic fashion with aging, supporting Mannheim's hypothesis. Instead, individuals maintain a fairly high level of continuity in their general political orientations, with the intervention of period effects likely to have an impact across all age groups (Alwin & Krosnick, 1991). In fact, the political leanings of the older and younger portions of the population are constantly shifting as cohorts age and period effects influence attitudes. Cohorts born between 1928 and 1946 have become less conservative in their overall views between 1987 and 2009, with baby boomers changing much less during that time, reducing age differences between these two groups and younger adults (Pew Research Center, 2009a). As different cohorts move into the ranks of those in later life, the political profile of that age group changes via shifts in cohort composition and life course experience.

In a similar vein, aging was thought to affect political party affiliation, a related symbolic attitude. Early cross-sectional data established that as age increased, affiliation with the Republican Party grew larger. As an outgrowth of the aging-conservatism hypothesis, maturing individuals were thought to become more attuned to the Republican agenda. Careful analysis of cohorts, however, proved this conclusion to be mistaken. Although comparisons of the elections from 1946 to 1958 seemed to show higher percentages of Republicans among the oldest categories, when cohorts were followed across time Cutler (1969–1970) found that party af-filiation did not change systematically with aging. That finding was reinforced starting in the 1980s, when older people began voting for the candidates of, and were more often affiliated with, the Democratic Party in comparison to the young (Jacobs, 1990; Pew Research Center, 2003). And, young adults, who are voting in larger numbers, have increased their affiliation with the Democrats from 46% in 1992 to 58% in 2008, suggesting yet another swing in party affiliations of the 65 and older category when this group enters later life (Keeter, Horowitz, & Tyson, 2008).

Instead of systematic age-related changes in party affiliation, both family socialization toward political parties and the effects of major events (such as major electoral victories or political scandals) are more potent forces in shaping how, when, and whether individuals se-lect a particular party or remain independent voters (Jacobs, 1990). In an earlier study by Alwin and Krosnick (1991), stability of party affiliation among various age groups over time was a particular focus. Because they followed various age groups over time in two separate de-cades, it became possible to test more directly the aging-versus-cohort issues regarding party affiliation. The results indicate that stability of party affiliation, unlike some other attitudes, increases slowly with age through most of adulthood (Alwin & Krosnick, 1991). The inten-sity of party identification also increases with age from rather weak to stronger, but decreases slightly in the oldest age group. People tend to keep their party affiliation as they age, with the intensity of partisanship increasing in the older groups—perhaps partly explaining higher voting rates.

The bulk of research fails to demonstrate that political party affiliation changes in systematic ways as individuals age (Schulz & Binstock, 2006). Instead, the effects of cohort flow through age categories cause gradual change in the distribution of political affiliations and attitudes. Exhibit 9.6 shows the changes over 50 years in party affiliation, grouping those who say they are "strong" or "weak" identifiers with the two major parties or independent, including those saying they "lean" toward one party or another (American National Election Studies, 2005). What is noteworthy is the overall convergence among the three groups over time, largely as a result of decline growth of independents, largely at a cost to Democrats. Surprising, perhaps, is the relative stability of identification among the Republican segment over time; Democrats and Independents changed much more (Pew Research Center, 2007). Remember, however, that this effect is not driven by many individuals changing their party through the life course, but rather the changing composition of voters as new cohorts enter the scene, others leave, and the fortunes of each party and their agendas shift over historical time. So the most recent shift of younger adults toward the Democrats may start yet another change in the profile shown in Ex-hibit 9.6. Political or governmental events (period effects), such as the 9/11 attacks, the invasion of Iraq, and the 2008 Presidential election, have been shown to create inflections (either upward or downward) in the public's satisfaction with government, with results that differ based on the survey respondent's political affiliation and which party is in power at the time. Between 2001 and 2007, for example, while events influenced how positive people were toward government, Republicans were more positive at each survey than Democrats (Pew Research Center, 2007). The most recent of the series of Pew surveys, discussed previously, showed a major attitudinal shift among younger cohorts; as a group they are less cynical about the government, more so-cially progressive in their attitudes, and believe more in voting (Pew Research Center, 2009a). These shifts may portend a long-term political trend that will follow this age group throughout their lives.

Working the Political System: Age-Based Advocacy

An interesting and diverse set of organizations advocate for and provide services to the older population. Most of the advocacy organizations for age-related issues were created after the ad-vent of the major governmental programs to assist older people (Binstock, 1995), during the

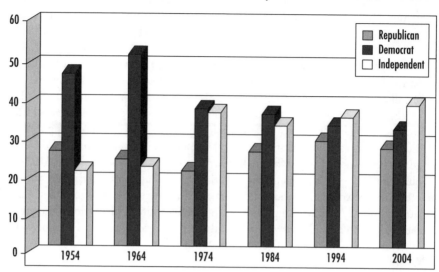

EXHIBIT *9.6*

Party Identification 1954–2004

Source: American National Election Studies, 2005.

era of compassionate ageism. A few earlier movements, such as the Townsend movement that predated Social Security, were critical in the creation of these policies (Torres-Gil, 1992), but most of the major organizations of today have been created since the middle of the 20th century. Wallace and his colleagues (1991) argue that much of the influence that older adults have exerted politically has been through these organizations and via older individuals' participation in **power elites**—formal or informal groups that build policy and sway public opinion. Numerous age-based organizations have been party to shaping policies on the federal and state levels for many years, regardless of whether or not they represent the full range of older adults. These groups are not organized and run only by older people but often include and rely upon the work of younger people on behalf of the older population. A range of issues specific to groups, such as older women (Older Women's League), race/ethnicity (National Association for Hispanic Elderly), those involved with particular illnesses (Alzheimer's Disease Association), industry organizations (American Association of Homes and Services for the Aged), and groups advocating on issues related to existing government programs such as Social Security abound in Washington. One of the largest of these organizations, which began in the 1950s, is AARP (formerly American Association of Retired Persons).

AARP and Capitol Hill

One of the major political advocacy groups of recent years has been AARP, the current name for the organization that was founded as the American Association for Retired Persons. AARP, which has expanded its mandate to include the vast numbers of baby boomers aged 50 and older, boasts 40 million members, an apparently formidable support group for any candidate or issue (Binstock, 1995; Schulz & Binstock, 2006). The organization, founded in 1958, has grown rapidly in the past few decades as the population has aged (Jacobs, 1990). Membership over-represents White, middle-class individuals, many of whom would be considered among the "young old" (Day, 1990). Exploration of their Web site shows active advocacy in multiple areas.

It is important to point out that memberships are initiated and continued primarily for benefits and discounts available to members (e.g., travel and health insurance programs), rather than specifically in support of the political advocacy that the AARP pursues (Binstock, 1995). AARP employs a professional staff to provide member services and to sustain its reputation for political clout in Washington (Binstock, 1995), but the organization has sometimes taken moderate positions on key age-related policy issues (Schulz & Binstock, 2006).

There is some question as to whether AARP can deliver votes of its millions of members for particular candidates or causes and whether its diverse membership supports (or even is aware of) all of the positions taken by the organization during policy battles in Washington (Binstock, 1991a). AARP has been accused of using what Binstock calls the **electoral bluff**. This bluff occurs when organizations of this size implicitly threaten to churn up support for or against a candidate or proposal, pressuring legislators or policy makers to vote in favor of AARP's legislative goals (Binstock, 1991a). No one knows, in most cases, whether the AARP can deliver on this bluff. Such large membership organizations wield much of their power through high levels of access to elected officials and policy makers, drawing legitimacy from their size when taking positions publicly and working through the media to make their views known. On Capitol Hill, the AARP and its lobbyists vigorously advocate its priorities (which can be viewed on the AARP Web site) on major issues affecting older adults.

Recent Legislation: Medicare Part D and Health Care Reform

The pace of age-related legislation has slowed since the era of compassionate ageism. Nonetheless, legislation continues to be proposed—and some passed—addressing topics pertinent to older adults. Two more recent efforts to augment federal programs involving services to the older population show how the political environment has shifted since the era of compassionate ageism. The first was the most recent addition to age-based programming, coverage for prescription drugs of older adults, referred to as Medicare Part D. Growing costs of prescriptions drugs had been long identified as a challenge for low- and moderate-income groups of older adults, with multiple periods where Congress discussed but failed to respond to this issue (Oliver, Lee, & Lipton, 2004). But the combination of budget surpluses, support from the powerful lobbyists for the pharmaceutical industry (who saw the potential for increased profits) and AARP, as well as strong perceived public need created a context where a bill could successfully be crafted (Oliver et al., 2004). Political compromises were required, however, to make the program fiscally affordable and politically acceptable in a Congress dominated by Republicans (Waller, 2006). The resulting legislation controls the burden of out-of-pocket pharmaceutical costs for older adults with either relatively low drug expenses and those with very high expenses, but left a major gap in coverage for those in the middle (the so-called donut hole) (DeNatale, 2007). Subsidies are in place for enrollees in low-income groups, with significant costs to the federal budget. After its passage, the public was not pleased with the bill, and both parties thought they could make it into a political issue for the 2004 elections (Oliver et al., 2004).

Medicare Part D's startup in 2006 involved a frenzy of media attention to the challenges older adults encountered in understanding and making choices among multiple detailed prescription plans, as well as no small number of glitches and problems in funding and reimbursement (DeNatale, 2007; Waller, 2006). There were other concerns about the modest numbers of eligible people enrolling in this voluntary program at its inception because this type of initiative relies upon large enrollment numbers to make it work (Heiss, McFadden, & Winter, 2006; Waller, 2006).

This program represents another example of shift in government's approach to providing for the needs of older adults. "The chief legacies involved in the design of the new program are that participation is voluntary and that the costs will be shared by the Medicare beneficiaries and taxpayers, rather than borne entirely by the beneficiaries themselves. In addition, policy-makers went to great lengths to ensure that the new prescription drug benefits will be administered principally by private companies and not by the federal government" (Oliver et al., 2004, pp. 289–290). Rather than adding another traditional entitlement program, the law reflected the newer political realities of paying for programs as you approve them and using private companies to provide services.

The second example, the most recent policy shift affecting older adults, is the passage of legislation creating a major health care reform during 2010. The legislation, the Patient Protection and Affordable Care Act (PPACA), was finalized after long and partisan political debate, with most of the debate focusing on issues other than health care for older adults, such as whether or not to have a "single payer" (i.e., government-based) insurance program and how to finance the costs associated with coverage for the millions of Americans who were uninsured. One debate topic related to Medicare because the bill's provisions included reducing payments to "Medicare Advantage" programs, which are operated through private insurance companies and provide more extensive (and expensive) benefits than regular Medicare. But the legislation includes a wide variety of other provisions pertaining to services to older adults, including decreasing the impact of the "donut hole" in Medicare part D; expanding programs to encourage care at home rather than in nursing homes; instituting a modest, voluntary program of national long-term care insurance; enhanced programs to address elder abuse; and increasing initiatives to grow the large workforce needed to meet the health and service needs of the coming baby boom cohorts, among others. Despite these provisions, the legislation is not widely thought of as a bill for older adults. The CLASS Act, legislation that was under development prior to the health care reform but eventually included within it, addresses long-term care provided either in nursing home/assisted-living settings or in one's home. It was not subject of much public attention or political debate, despite its numerous innovations (Manard, 2010).

As a strong priority for the new Obama administration, health care reform quickly became a focal point for vigorous partisan debate, with final voting on the bill clearly along party lines. Widespread political activism, including the emergence of the Tea Party conservatives to oppose the legislation, marked a new height of conflict politics in Washington. Opponents attempted to woo older voters to their side with arguments that the bill would undermine Medicare benefits (through discontinuing Medicare Advantage), while at the same time opposing the single-payer system, another government-run entitlement program—but, in this case, for people of all ages. The PPACA largely maintains the distinctions between the systems of health care for people under age 65 from those of older adults, rather than breaking down this barrier. As with Medicare Part D, under PPACA private companies will likely continue to cover most people for health insurance, and the legislation works to cover new costs through limiting the growth in health care costs in the future and through controlling costs of publicly funded programs, such as Medicare and Medicaid.

Generational Politics: Conflict and Consensus

Many of the recent battles over policies relating to older adults, such as Social Security and health care reform, are based in deep, ideological differences that relate to party politics and differing views of the roles of government. These differences focus on the extent to which the government (versus the individual/family or the private marketplace) should be responsible for solving problems in society, including the challenges faced by older people. Whether and how best to maintain a safety net for older persons who are poor or infirm are questions that reflect the schism between conservative and liberal ideologies. The **liberal agenda**, championed during the ascendance of compassionate ageism and appearing again at the start of the Obama administration, focused on government programs to address problems affecting large numbers of adults in later life. That role has been challenged consistently by the **conservative agenda**, which argues that individual responsibility should be the norm, with people responsible to find their own solutions within the family or the marketplace, thereby reducing the role of government in peoples' lives. These battles that seem to be about age-related policies are actually about core political ideologies that apply more broadly to all aspects of government. Our current array of age-based policies arose from divided political opinion within the country on both the meaning and the consequences of old age and on the role of government with regard to the welfare of older adults (Ekerdt, 1998; Torres-Gil, 1992)—a debate that, based on the arguments about health care reform, cannot be readily settled.

In the United States families and state governments are responsible for much of the support needed by dependent children (e.g., families for most things, the state for public education); in contrast, more of the support directed toward older adults is provided through public systems, mostly at the federal level (Achenbaum, 1992). Our current system expends more *federal* dollars (but not necessarily state dollars) on programs for the older population than it does on programs for children. It was not until the late 1970s that politicians and advocates for the elderly recognized the growing costs of benefits for older citizens from existing entitlement programs. Hudson (1978) called this process the **graying of the federal budget** (see also Binstock, 1991a). This "graying" refers to the growing percentage of the federal budget each year allocated to entitlements for the older population, including the dollars spent on Medicare, Medicaid, and Social Security. Exhibit 9.7 shows the increase in the percentage of the federal budget allocated to these entitlements over a 40-year period, with the gray portion of the bars moving closer to half of total federal expenditures by 2008, even before the baby boomers retire.

In the next sections, relating to this challenge of aging societies worldwide, we discuss three, interrelated debates that have emerged in recent decades as we have moved into our new era of politics and aging.

The Debate on Age and Need Entitlements

Most programs developed during the era of compassionate ageism share a basis in age entitlement. As described in Chapter 6, individuals become eligible for age entitlement programs on the basis of chronological age. Usually the legislation includes age limits, such as the original

EXHIBIT **9.7**

Percentage of Federal Spending Devoted to Entitlements: 1968–2008

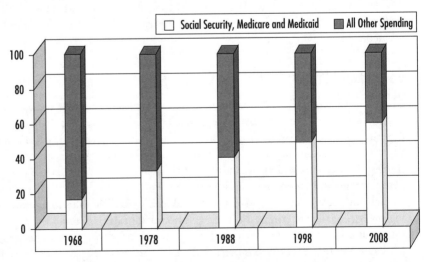

Source: Senior Journal, 2005; U.S. Census Bureau, 1975, 1976, 1995, 2008a.

40–70 age range in the Age Discrimination in Employment Act or the age 65 minimum for Medicare benefits (Quadagno, 1996). Pure age entitlement means that all individuals are eligible for benefits, with only proof of age required. Because of this, age entitlement programs are fairly simple to administer because most people can establish their ages easily. Other programs, such as Social Security, pair age eligibility with other requirements, such as having a sufficient work history, to qualify for benefits.

Age entitlements are based on two somewhat contradictory goals: adequacy and equity. "The adequacy goal seeks to protect those most needy by assuring a minimum standard of living and granting special benefits to the disadvantaged. The equity goal seeks to reward individualism and self-reliance by basing government benefits on the amount contributed individually during the working years" (Day, 1990, p. 121). When one goal (either adequacy or equity) is met, the other necessarily cannot be fully met, challenging policy makers to decide on a balance between the two goals. The focus of age entitlement during the period of compassionate ageism was more on adequacy than equity. As we shall see, the current debates have turned attention more toward the equity goal.

Age entitlement contrasts with need entitlement—a system of providing benefits or services based on need, such as low income, poor health, or inadequate housing (Quadagno, 1996). Need entitlement results in fewer individuals receiving benefits (thus saving money), but requires more effort to establish who is (and who is not) eligible, raising the program's administrative costs. Need entitlement programs for older adults in many countries, often referred to as welfare-type programs, have been subject to pressures to reduce funding when governmental budgets are tight (Hoskins, 1992). Because need-based programs unintentionally suggest that their recipients are "different from the rest of us," such programs are more politically vulnerable; they lack broad-based, bipartisan support from those not needing or using such benefits. It is often said that "programs for the poor become poor programs," due to the social stigma and negative public opinion toward welfare benefits. This makes need entitlements for any group, including elders, more vulnerable in terms of public support and funding for programs that return no direct benefits to those whose taxes support it (Kingson, 1994).

To reduce expenditures, conservative politicians have suggested changing some current age entitlement programs, such as Social Security or Medicare, to include need criteria for eligibility (Quadagno, 1996). This push is evident in the incremental changes that have already occurred in some age entitlement programs. For example, the 1983 Social Security Reform Act began this trend by introducing taxation of Social Security benefits for higher income older persons, in effect recapturing some benefit dollars going to those with greater economic security (Binstock, 1994). Similar changes have been built into other legislation, instituting sliding scales for taxes or services based on the level of need of the older person. Thus, as Binstock (1994) reports, "a substantial trend of incremental changes has firmly established the practice of combining age and economic status as policy criteria in old-age benefit programs" (p. 728).

Since the late 1970s, when the Era of Compassionate Ageism ended, both the stereotypes of the elderly and the political popularity of programs for them have changed dramatically. The conservative political trend from the 1980s onward focused on growing government deficits and diminished confidence that government programs could successfully resolve social problems (Torres-Gil, 1992). One key question is whether age is a good proxy for needing services/benefits. If we examined the circumstances of older persons in the early 1960s, we would discover that many of them were poor, inadequately housed, unable to afford needed medical care, and discriminated against in employment. In other words, by directing social policy interventions at this age group, Congress was fairly certain to hit most of those in need of assistance, and relatively few who were not, while keeping administration of the programs simple and inexpensive. Therefore, during the era when many of the programs were established, age was a fairly good proxy for need.

Ironically, it is the very successes of these programs in alleviating problems such as poverty (Social Security) and inadequate health care (Medicare) that bring about lower percentages of the older population living in want. This improving situation in the aggregate makes the public and political support of policies to assist "the elderly" more tenuous (Hudson, 1996). It is important to remember, however, that aggregate improvement does not mean that any individual's circumstances have improved. As conditions in the population over 65 have become more varied, age becomes a less adequate proxy for needing assistance. The change is reflected in the political rhetoric, which has shifted the stereotype of older Americans from the "deserving poor" to "greedy geezers" (Binstock, 2005; Ekerdt, 1998). Under the new stereotype, the older population is incorrectly seen as mostly affluent (see Chapter 7) and as a strong, unified political force (as discussed in this chapter), voting in self-interested ways to protect their age entitlements (Binstock, 1991a; Hudson, 1996). Although ageism has survived, according to Binstock and others, the compassion has evaporated. The new stereotype of affluent, healthy, and politically savvy elders has altered the prior political value of supporting causes for the older adult population (Torres-Gil, 1992).

The Battle Over Social Security

Social Security was a political battleground before its passage in 1935 and has served as the focus of policy and partisan debate many times in its 70+ year history. Debates about reforming Social Security are not new, nor are such discussions occurring only in the United States (Hoskins, 1992). In the early 1990s, most nations of the world with aging populations faced increasing economic pressures that prompted them to examine whether they had the fiscal capacity to meet their obligations for public pensions and health entitlements to growing populations of older persons. In other cases, countries in Eastern Europe that have recently moved to capitalist economies have experienced both economic recession and dramatic political changes, rendering their former system of old-age pensions inappropriate (Hoskins, 1992). They lack the resources to pay full pensions that were expected by older adults resulting in negative political reactions and protests.

The United States has seen regular political and ideological battles over Social Security, including notable battles surrounding major changes to the program in 1977 and 1983. Prior to his election Ronald Reagan proposed deep cuts to the program, which were formalized as part of his first budget proposal in 1981. A tremendous public uproar followed, chastening the Reagan Administration into steadfast support of Social Security (Jacobs, 1990). Like Reagan,

other politicians have learned of the dangers of tampering with Social Security. Social Security is a program with a very large and interested constituency, comprising not just those receiving benefits but also those expecting to receive benefits in the future and those whose family members currently receive benefits (Day, 1993a), making it a high-risk target for change by politicians.

Following the abortive Reagan reform proposal, a range of political groups have entered the battle over the future of the U.S. Social Security System, including the political parties, a variety of "think tank" advocates, and the mainstream aging organizations (Day, 1990). After being re-elected in 2004, President George W. Bush began a major push to change significant aspects of Social Security, including the addition of private accounts and reduction in the redistributive formula for benefits, despite the fact that Social Security ranked only at the middle of a list of issues of concern to the public (Blendon et al., 2005). After a prolonged publicity campaign, however, the effort seemed to lose steam in the face of strong campaigns from other groups, other events (the war in Iraq and Hurricane Katrina), and the continued belief by the public that there is no fiscal crisis in Social Security (Blendon et al., 2005).

The Generational Equity Debate

Politicians and the media have paid attention to one specific aspect of generational conflict in recent decades: the generational equity debate. The United States, like a variety of other nations throughout the world, transfers resources between individuals who are economically productive and those who are not (dependent children, disabled adults, and older persons). We often take these transfers for granted; we tax local property owners to finance public schools, and we tax wages to pay for Social Security and Medicare. The growth of the older population has prompted politicians, economists, and sociologists to examine the fundamental assumptions behind such transfers through government entitlement programs (Cornman & Kingson, 1996). The generational equity debate is clearly an extension of the long-standing debates about age vs. need entitlement and the campaign to fundamentally alter provisions of Social Security.

Alarms have sounded in some circles as the baby boom cohorts approach old age and life expectancy continues to increase. This alarmist view, commonly conveyed in the media, encourages us to "Picture retiring boomers, with inflated economic expectations and inadequate nest eggs, voting down school budgets, cannibalizing the nation's infrastructure, and demanding ever-steeper hikes in payroll taxes" (Peterson, 1999, p. 209). The generational equity argument holds that demography, combined with the ongoing commitment to pay for these entitlements in future generations, should lead us to conclude that the economy can ill afford the current set of old-age entitlements (Cornman & Kingson, 1996). This is a debate with many assumptions that are seldom examined in detail. A major part of this debate has focused upon the future financing of Social Security, Medicaid, and Medicare. Surprisingly, some countries with populations older than the United States have not encountered public resistance to paying the costs of age entitlement programs (Myles, 1996). A clear example of a group focused on this issue is the Concord Coalition, a bipartisan organization whose mission is "dedicated to educating the public about the causes and consequences of federal budget deficits, the long-term challenges facing America's unsustainable entitlement programs, and how to build a sound foundation for economic growth" (Concord Coalition, 2009).

Advocacy groups from the 1980s onward, responding to the entitlement alarm and to a broader political agenda, argued that we should look at whether age should be the basis for entitlement to benefits. Pointing to the improved economic well-being of the older population (the lower rate of poverty) and increasing rates of poverty among children, some posited a causal connection—that society is throwing excessive resources at older people that would be better spent to support future cohorts (Minkler, 1991a; Quadagno, 1991). An approach referred to as generational accounting advocated examining the potential burden on resources of coming generations of the entitlement costs of the baby boomer cohorts for programs like Social Security and Medicare, an issue that remains under debate (Herd & Kingson, 2005; Kotlikoff, 1992; Myles, 2005). Several groups have advocated moving away from age entitlements to need entitlements, eliminating cost-of-living increases in these programs, raising the retirement age for Social Security, and using tax policies to encourage private old-age or long-term care insurance (Quadagno, 1991).

Holstein (1995) points out, however, that reducing entitlements for older people in no way guarantees that those resources would be redistributed to assist children. Quadagno's strongest complaint with the argument is its contention that increases in childhood poverty are caused by greater entitlements to the older population. She points instead to other significant social changes during the time that child poverty has increased (i.e., more single parents, changes in labor market) that have contributed to childhood poverty. In spite of such critiques, there has been success in altering the nature of the debate about age entitlements from its prior focus on adequacy and equity of benefits to a single dimension of equity—specifically, intergenerational equity (Ekerdt, 1998; Quadagno, 1989).

At first glance, Exhibit 9.7 seems to provide support for the generational equity argument. According to research, the largest increase in entitlement spending occurred after the enactment of Medicare in 1965 (Quadagno, 1996). Yet using standard economic measures for the costs of programs, neither Social Security nor overall entitlements to the elderly have grown much in real terms since the early 1970s. Instead, other changes have contributed to the growing percentage of gray programs in the government's budget. For example, as Congresses in the late 1990s cut spending in other areas (e.g., defense) and reduced some taxes on individuals and corporations, old-age entitlements became a larger percentage of overall spending, creating an exaggerated impression of the growth in these entitlements (Quadagno, 1996). Quadagno concludes that the entitlements crisis has been socially constructed through careful rhetoric to advance a political agenda of shrinking government programs.

Marmour, Mashaw, and Harvey (1990) have argued that Social Security has become "a scapegoat for anxieties engendered by a distressingly volatile economic environment" (p. 127). Quadagno (1991) concludes that a major change to a need entitlement system simply shifts economic support functions back to families and would most hurt those individuals who rely primarily on Social Security for income—those lacking private pensions from their employers. This group is disproportionately composed of women and minorities. As a consequence, she argues, many of these most disadvantaged individuals would need to continue working in low-wage jobs into advanced old age because they have inadequate finances to retire on reduced Social Security benefits (Quadagno, 1991).

It is apparent that supporters of the generational equity debate have been quite effective in getting its political message out. Many popular magazines and other media now use the rhetoric of "greedy geezers" and sound the alarm regarding financing of entitlements in the future. In contrast, Achenbaum (1992) argues that it is necessary to make manifest the transgenerational benefits of programs like Social Security to ensure their political survival for the future. Cornman and Kingson (1996) point out that we invest resources in children in anticipation of their future contributions to society and assist the elderly in reciprocity for their prior contributions, evening out the balance sheet over the life course. It is only if we freeze the picture at one point in time and define entitlements as a zero-sum game that the old and the young seem like competing drains on society.

By some measures, the programs of the old-age welfare state have been successful in dealing with the problems they were created to address. As Chapter 7 discussed, overall poverty has been greatly reduced by the presence of Social Security benefits. The housing and health of the older population have improved, albeit only partly through the efforts of federal government programs (Quirk, 1991). Some aging advocates argue that these programs are now victims of their own success. Because the condition of the overall group of older people has improved significantly in recent decades, there is less momentum to maintain the age entitlements that have helped to bring about (and to maintain) that success. In addition, there remain a substantial number of older persons, primarily widowed women, who are poor and receive little help from this safety net. It is a major failing of the old-age welfare system that it leaves behind some severe pockets of disadvantaged people (Binstock, 1991a).

While some researchers have spent considerable time forecasting conflict between the generations over entitlements and policies, others have begun to speculate about the possibility of intragenerational conflict (Day, 1993a). Intragenerational conflict—conflict among members of the same generation or age group—might be predicated on socioeconomic status, with many analysts predicting increasing distance between the "haves" and the "have nots" among elderly of the future (Torres-Gil, 1992). It is already overly simplistic to discuss advocacy on behalf of "the elderly" because that population includes so many diverse constituencies and interests. Such diversity may promote more intragenerational conflict in the future and serve as a hedge against formation of a voting bloc based on age.

The Potential for Generational Conflict

Analysts disagree regarding the prospect of **intergenerational conflict** (between generations) over the distribution of government resources or on the basis of other social attitudes and values (see Binstock, 1991a; Wynne, 1991). Advocates of generational equity argue that such conflict is inevitable if current policies and entitlements remain unchanged; others claim that cross-cutting allegiances pull people into groupings organized on bases other than age (recall the discussion of the absence of age identification) (Day, 1990). Although conflict between cohorts or generations is often discussed, scant evidence exists for it today or in the past.

This issue of political conflict between generations came into public awareness in the late 1960s, during the era of youthful political activism by the oldest baby boomers during the Vietnam War. The issue boils down to whether the fundamental goals and interests of young and old are sufficiently different as to make them natural adversaries in the political arena. Under a scenario of age-based political conflict, groups would solidify for political action based on age identification. Young people might want more funding for college while older adults might want more support for Medicare, for example. In times of scarce fiscal resources, as this argument goes, the old and the young may splinter along age lines, with each group promoting its own age-based political agenda. For example, evidence from exit polls during the 1996 presidential election suggests that Medicare, used as an issue by both sides in that campaign, was not effective in gaining such a response from voters (Binstock, 1997). Wallace and his associates (1991) claim that when older adults have been effectively mobilized to act on an issue, it has been more on the basis of economic interests than on age.

The potential for age identification and age-based political action rests on people's interests and how narrowly self-centered they are. For example, questions have often been raised about whether older adults vote in support of bond issues for schools, which affect neither themselves nor their grown children. Ecology advocates wonder whether older voters care about (and vote to support) pollution-abatement programs to benefit unborn generations of the future (Kneese & Cooper, 1993). Although there is some evidence of lower support for school bond issues among older adults (see Button, 1992), the evidence for this sort of generational schism is far from comprehensive, and voting on issues varies only slightly by age (Campbell, 2005).

In Chapter 5 we discussed reciprocity within the context of the family. It is also useful to consider reciprocity on a societal level, including across age cohorts. In this larger context, Social Security can be considered a form of reciprocity—support provided for the elderly in return for their contributions in earlier years to building both the economy and their successor cohorts (Wynne, 1991). Wynne argues for expansion of the concept of reciprocity within the larger society, encouraging civic involvement among young and old for the betterment of society. Under this macro-level version of reciprocity, the age strata of society can be seen to have mutual interests and goals, with exchange among them a natural occurrence (Kingson, Hirshorn, & Cornman, 1986). Generations are pulled together by this reciprocity, rather than pulled apart. Day's study (1990) concludes that "the lines that divide Americans on the issue of government benefits for the elderly are not generational, but economic and partisan" (p. 60).

The fact that the older population will be growing more racially and ethnically diverse as current cohorts age may further dilute the odds of an older adult coalescence against younger people (Torres-Gil, 1992). Torres-Gil projects that activism and organizations may become more focused and specialized, addressing the needs, for example, of disadvantaged older women rather than the economic issues of the elderly as a whole. Age, he argues, may be less compelling as an organizing force than as a common interest when the older population is so diverse. Given this focus on diversity and heterogeneity in the older population, it is useful to revisit a theory we have alluded to before, age stratification theory.

Rethinking Age-Based Policies?

As we move forward in the new millennium, some experts have raised questions regarding why we persist in organizing services, including health care, by age, rather than in some other way. The recent health care debate reopened discussion in this area—why separate health systems for young and old? While legislation on health care reform excluded the single-payer, universal systems for health services found in many countries of Europe, any major reconfiguration of health care brings forward questions as to whether our current systems (notably the very large and underfunded Medicare and Medicaid programs) should continue as they have since the 1960s (Moon, 2005; Schulz & Binstock, 2006). These debates take many approaches, including altering Medicare to a need-based entitlement program to unifying programs to provide health care across all age groups. While the U.S. system of providing health care through employers has its pros and cons, it nonetheless has consistently left out older adults—a group in n eed of regular health care services.

One other approach to removing age as a focus for some policies relates to combining programs and services for younger, disabled people with those serving older adults. Right now programs for the disabled under age 65 operate under separate legislation from those for older adults in terms of providing income (Social Security's distinct retirement benefits versus its disability benefits). In addition, programs such as in-home health care and personal care services, specialized transportation services, and other programs that might work equally well for both groups are separately funded and operated because they were created at different times by distinct legislation. Each has its own established organizations (like those described for the Older Americans Act) and may be hesitant to reorganize (Estes, 1979). Advocates for continued separation suggest that "one size doesn't fit all" and that younger disabled people (as members of different cohorts) have expectations and preferences that do not match well with those of older adults, despite using many similar services.

Some experts predict that transgenerational alliances (e.g., the alliance between older people in frail health and younger disabled people) focused on specific issues such as health care, housing, or income may make the politics of age obsolete (Day, 1990). For example, in 1996 the House of Representatives passed legislation that would enhance criminal penalties for crimes of violence against both the elderly and children. Because efforts at policy change can drag on for years or suddenly "catch fire" and move very quickly, only time will tell whose predictions are correct.

Age Stratification Theory

Age stratification theory posits that we divide the population into strata (or layers) that are ranked hierarchically. As in other stratification systems focusing on social class, race, or gender rather than age, the population is divided into groups; age stratification substitutes age as the criterion upon which individuals are divided. In age stratification, age is used to cluster groups of people together (into age strata or, in the term we have used most often, *cohorts*) and to differentiate among people on the basis of the age stratum to which they belong (Dowd, 1980). We can determine, for example, whether someone belongs to the teenage or old old age stratum and, on that basis, make some educated guesses about the person. These guesses are based on the assumption that people in the same stratum have significant social characteristics in common and that members of different strata are different in critical ways, much as we discussed earlier in relation to cohort differences. To visualize the idea of age strata you need look no farther than the layers of the population pyramids presented in Chapter 3.

Age stratification systems are straightforward in a sense because chronological age allows us to readily order individuals into groups and rank them hierarchically as having more or fewer accumulated years of life. In contrast, class stratification systems require considerable effort to define the boundaries and characteristics of strata and the placement of individuals within them. In age stratification, it is clear that someone who is 35 is older, and therefore in a different stratum, from someone who is 15. The question remains, however, whether the distinction between those two chronological ages is socially meaningful. And because age strata usually include several chronological ages (such as the 65–74 range used in Exhibit 9.2), the boundaries dividing strata may be arbitrary rather than inherently meaningful.

What about stratification based on stages of the life course? Once we attempt to develop stratification based on life-course stages, the strata become even less clear and distinct (O'Rand, 1990). What criteria must one meet, for example, to be considered an adult? Using life-course events, people might be considered adults when they married, got a full-time job, left their parents' home, had children, or some combination of these events (Hogan & Astone, 1986). It is much simpler, although not necessarily always equally meaningful, to use chronological ages in some cases; for voting eligibility, for example, you are an adult when you become 18 years of age.

Age stratification theory goes beyond the recognition that societies divide their populations by ages or into cohorts, and examines how societies offer different rewards and opportunities to members of different age strata. According to Dowd (1981), "both age strata and social classes may be defined by their differential possession of valued resources and differential access to the means of acquiring these resources" (p. 158). People in the 35–55 age stratum as a rule hold more socially valued resources and are given more opportunities to augment those resources than someone who is 15 or 85. Age, like many other bases for stratification, serves as a basis of structured social inequality (Foner, 1973). Riley, Johnson, and Foner (1972) point to the opportunities for (or requirements placed on) individuals to be enrolled in educational institutions at certain ages and limited access to other activities (such as marrying, voting, or holding office) until a certain age has been achieved. Informal norms and sanctions that go with them also encourage people to "act their age," performing in ways that are consistent with the expectations associated with their location in the stratification system (Riley et al., 1972). The hierarchy of age stratification is not as easily grasped as the system of class stratification, however, because those higher in the age stratification system do not benefit as a group from greater resources than those in the middle, as is the case with social class. Therefore, the concept of age stratification

In times of scarce government resources, the young and old may flex muscles for their own specific agendas. (Credit: E. J. Hanna)

is less clear-cut in terms of social inequality (Cain, 1987).

Another element of age stratification that differentiates it from stratification by social class has to do with **social mobility**. *Social mobility* refers to the movement of an individual between levels of the stratification system. In stratification systems based on gender or race, such mobility is extremely limited; most of us are stuck with our race and gender. In the case of social class, mobility between strata is quite possible—for example, when a young person from a poor background seeks an advanced education and achieves a high-level professional career, thereby moving to a higher social class. In age stratification, mobility through the age stratification system is automatic and unavoidable—you cannot avoid growing older (Riley et al., 1972). In fact, according to Riley, aging can be considered a type of social mobility. Simply by virtue of surviving, individuals and cohorts are upwardly mobile in the age stratification system; but upward age mobility, unlike upward social class mobility, does not necessarily mean an improvement in one's social prestige or economic situation. In social class stratification, higher is better; in age stratification, older may or may not be better.

Although we are introducing age stratification theory in a more complete manner here, we have already used elements of age stratification theory throughout this book, especially in discussions of cohorts and their movement through the society. Age stratification also has roots in modernization theory, described further in Chapter 10. Modernization theory includes consideration of the relative status of older age groups (compared with younger adults) in more and less developed societies, positing that as societies modernize, people in higher age strata lose the foundations that gave them power and prestige in less developed economies (O'Rand, 1990). Although modernization theory has been heavily criticized, it nonetheless directs attention to age stratification systems.

Age stratification theory is flexible, enabling us to look at movement of individuals through age-related roles and expectations on a micro level or focus attention on the flow of cohorts through social institutions on the macro level, adding the important element of inequality among strata (O'Rand, 1990). Age stratification theory also reflects elements of the life course perspective in that it focuses our attention on the issues that age cohorts have in common—how society structures both opportunities and expectations based on the age of the individual (or life stage). O'Rand (1990) points out that in the 20th century the state has imposed more standardization on the lives of the youngest and oldest in society—for example, creating regulations requiring school attendance and institutionalizing retirement age via Social Security provisions. In this way governments define the civil rights and responsibilities of individuals in these age strata. You have doubtless felt the restrictions of age boundaries already in your life—being "too young" or "too old" to participate in certain activities—and you may have celebrated passing a milestone birthday as you experience mobility through the age stratification system.

To focus attention on age stratification in no way diminishes the importance of other systems of stratification. It is often informative to use multiple systems of stratification—for example, examining age strata and then, within age strata, looking at variations by gender, social class, or race to see how these stratification systems augment or diminish opportunities and disadvantages for individuals within their ranks. Stratification theory—using age, class, gender, or other criteria—encourages using the sociological imagination and taking a more macro-level view of social inequality.

The fundamental question today for age stratification is its usefulness, given the growing fuzziness of boundaries and definitions of age strata (recall the discussion of blurred retirement transitions), the expectations of increasing diversity in the older population of the future (Torres-Gil, 1992), and the importance of other dimensions of stratification intersecting with age. Will age really matter more than social class, educational background, gender, or race and ethnicity in understanding the social placement and life chances available to individuals in various groups? The answer may be no, but as long as age-based restrictions on opportunities in society continue, there is some utility in using an age stratification framework to examine social and political issues.

Summary

As we have seen in earlier chapters, there is every reason to expect that the political experience of future cohorts will differ from those of contemporary cohorts of older Americans. For example, the boundaries of later life and the inclusiveness of an elderly constituency might change (O'Rand, 2005). Those past 65 who are employed, in good health, and with 20 or more years of future life expectancy might not consider themselves part of the interest group of older adults (Torres-Gil, 1992), and might behave accordingly.

Will old age continue its relevance as a focal category for social policy, or will crosscutting issues such as social class, health, or race/ethnicity prove more politically powerful as the foci for societal intervention (Schulz & Binstock 2006)? Analysts disagree about the future of both advocacy and policy relative to old age. Torres-Gil (1992) expects a different future of old-age politics, where social class (and need entitlement) will become the basis for government programs, and the strong advocacy network for old-age issues will self-destruct. Not everyone agrees, arguing that the baby boomers, by their sheer numbers and education, will be a political force to be reckoned with for many years (Cornman & Kingson, 1996; Schulz & Binstock, 2006). What seems apparent is that the pressure of the baby boomers has brought many of these policy discussions into sharp focus, even though the cohorts that immediately follow them will be smaller in size. As policy is formulated, we need to ask whether the decisions make sense not only for the baby boomers, but also for those smaller cohorts who will follow them into later life (Myles, 2005).

Should age become less salient as a criterion for policy, disadvantaged elders could find themselves vying with younger poor persons for limited societal resources. Although concerns regarding "demography as destiny" have driven debates about and changes in age-based policies and entitlements in many aging societies, the issues are much more complex than just the growing old-age dependency ratio. Political commitments and public attitudes, which have largely favored societal attention to the needs of older adults, are potent forces in shaping how collective resources are allocated. With regard to intergenerational politics and issues, Moody (1992) suggests, the "political argument comes down to a matter of confidence and legitimization: a feeling that institutions of intergenerational transfer—whether Social Security or the public schools—can be counted on to do their job and remain reliable for successive cohorts" (p. 239).

Web Wise

Administration on Aging/Older Americans Act   http://www.aoa.gov/
One of the major pieces of legislation establishing the "aging network" was the Older Americans Act (OAA), found under the "about AOA" tab. The Administration on Aging, the governmental agency charged with fulfilling the mandate of the OAA, describes the legislation and how it has been implemented in the aging network and a range of programs. Information provided focuses on home and community based services, elder rights protection and other programs offered under this legislation, as well as the very useful "Profile of Older Americans."

Senior Law   http://www.seniorlaw.com/index.htm
This site, which is maintained by attorneys Goldfarb, Abrandt, Salzman, & Kutzin specializing in Senior Law, provides information for seniors and their advocates, as well as for attorneys, on issues in the area of "elderlaw." They provide significant resources for attorneys and non-specialists as well, providing answers to frequently asked questions, links to articles on issues of Medicare and Medicaid, wills, guardianship, Social Security, nursing homes, and a variety of other elder law topics. If you are seriously interested in the law, you may wish to check out their "resources for professionals," which includes topics reaching well beyond senior law.

American National Election Studies   http://www.electionstudies.org/
This site includes data from the ongoing series of American National Election Studies, whose goal it is to better understand why America votes as it does on Election Day. Conducting pre- and post-election surveys during Presidential elections since 1948, this site offers data, as well as data showing changes over time in voting behavior, political affiliation, and attitudes on issues. For the latest statistics on voting, this site holds a wealth of information.

HealthCare.gov   http://www.healthcare.gov/law/introduction/index.html
This site was created by the federal government to provide citizens information on the massive, new health reform legislation signed in early 2010. The law includes a wide variety of changes, including changes for older adults, which will gradually be coming into use during the next few years, barring further legislative action. The site describes the provisions and the timelines for their implementation and is a good resource to learn more about this major legislation.

Key Terms

age identification
age stratification theory
aging-conservatism hypothesis
aging enterprise

civic development hypothesis
compassionate ageism
conservative agenda
electoral bluff
gerontocracy
graying of the federal budget

intergenerational conflict
liberal agenda
old-age welfare state
Older Americans Act
power elites
social mobility

Questions for Thought and Discussion

1. Period effects are thought to influence both individuals' political party affiliation and their confidence in social institutions, such as the government. Thinking about your life and about past history, what are some of the events that you might expect would have a significant effect on these political views?
2. Think about or discuss with others the reasons people choose to vote or not to vote (including reasons not to register). What are the major themes that appear to be

central for young adults compared to people of other ages? Can you identify any strategies that might accomplish what political parties have tried in recent decades—to get out the "youth vote?" What are the implications for public policy if fewer young than older people continue to vote in upcoming elections as the population ages?

3. Proponents of generational equity contend that the United States should move toward need-based entitlements, rather than age-based ones. What major programs would this influence? How would changes in these programs to need-based entitlement influence your neighbors, family, and friends?

4. Does it make sense to have minimum ages mandated for running for political offices? Would you suggest that we have maximum ages for holding high office? If so, what age would you suggest, and why would it be the relevant one to choose?

Global Aging

With J. Scott Brown

There is a need to raise awareness about not only global aging issues but also the importance of rigorous cross-national research and policy dialogue that will help us address the challenges and opportunities of an aging world. Preparing financially for longer lives and finding ways to reduce aging-related disability should become national and global priorities.

(NIA, NIH, HHS, & Department of State, 2007, p. 1)

Global Aging and Regional Economies

The phenomenal pace at which global aging is occurring was introduced in Chapter 3, along with some of its far-reaching impacts within countries, across regions, and around the world. Recall that the world's elderly population is increasing by about 880,000 persons *per month!* (Kinsella & He, 2009). We looked at examples of countries (including Nigeria, India, Italy, Japan, and China) in which the proportion of population that is aged 65 and above will more than double between 2000 and 2050. Other countries will have even higher growth; India's proportion aged will nearly triple, and Kuwait will experience a nine-fold increase in the proportion of its population that is 65 or older during those 50 years.

The aging of the world's population, and the issues that each nation is facing as its aging citizens increase in number are receiving increasing attention from the media, government, and policy-making officials; international organizations such as the United Nations; and researchers around the world. The growing numbers of older people in developed nations is especially noteworthy. Today, more than 60% of all people 65 and older live in developing nations (a term discussed in detail later); that proportion will exceed 75% by 2040 (Kinsella & He, 2009). These figures may seem surprising given the relatively low proportions aged today in many of these countries, as well as lower life expectancies and median ages. But consider that about 82% of the world's total population in 2010 lives in the developing nations of the world (Population Reference Bureau, 2010a). Take India as an example. Even though only 5% of India's population is currently aged 65 or above, with a population of more than a billion people, that 5% adds up to a very large number of older people. Because so much of the world's population is concentrated in these developing nations, and because these regions are beginning to experience rapid population aging, a very high proportion of the world's older people will be living in these areas in only a few decades.

Population aging in developing nations (such as India, Thailand, Kenya, Chile, and Guatemala) poses unique challenges to the governments, families, and individuals in those countries. Their populations are aging quickly, but they are less likely to have in place programs, policies, or health care systems that are prepared to meet the needs of older people. This structural lag in the development of options to deal with coming older populations in those nations can be explained by a combination of factors including relatively poor economies without revenues to invest in new programs or services; pressing concerns about nutrition and maternal and child health; traditional value systems that emphasize norms of family care; and the very rapid pace of demographic and health transitions, giving countries little time to adjust to the new realities of an aging population. Many nations in the developing regions of the world are simultaneously dealing with relatively high fertility, problems of poverty and hunger, population aging, and the emergence of need for chronic disease care among the growing older adult population as a substantial demand in the health care system.

Although of quite a different nature, the **more developed countries** around the world, such as the United States, Japan, and Germany, face significant challenges relating to aging populations as well. In particular, existing pension programs and formal long-term care systems in such countries are already inadequate, or likely to become so, as the proportions of older people continue to grow. At the risk of oversimplifying a complex situation, the general pattern is that nations in the less developed regions of the world are faced with the dilemmas of devising new programs, policies, and services for aging populations; more developed regions are dealing with the problems of funding, adapting, or expanding existing policies and programs. It has been said that developing nations get old before they get rich, while today's developed nations got rich before they got old (World Health Organization, 2010b).

The intersection of demography, culture, politics, and economics comes into play as countries around the world plan for and adapt to their aging populations. Each nation is unique in its configuration of these social, economic, and cultural factors, and this chapter describes the specific situation of a few countries as examples of this diversity. However, it is also useful (and common in the global aging literature) to compare across regions of the world. Because many of those comparisons are based on the categorization of more, less, and least developed regions, a discussion of those designations is warranted here.

More, Less, and Least Developed Designations

While classifying countries or regions is complicated, the categorization is generally based on the area's level of economic development. The United Nations Statistics Division cautions that such designations should be understood as a "statistical convenience" rather than a judgment, and that there is no single, established standard for classification (United Nations Statistics Division, 2010). For our purposes, think of the designations as the result of a two-step process. First, the World Bank calculates a gross national income per person for each country, and then places each into one of four categories: low income, lower middle income, upper middle income, and high income. In the next step, high income countries are defined as **developed countries**, and all remaining (low and middle income) countries are classified as **developing countries**. As a point of reference, the threshold for high income (developed) countries in 2010 was $12,196 gross national income per person (in U.S. dollars); at the other end of the continuum, low income countries were at or below $995 per person, with the other groups in between (World Bank, 2010). Even though these categorizations are only "statistical conveniences," they do provide a general sense of the level of resources available in a country to address important needs, including those related to having an aging population.

The United Nations currently designates all of Europe and Northern America, plus Australia, New Zealand, and Japan as more developed countries; all others are **less developed countries** (or sometimes referred to in shorthand as "developed" and "developing"). Within the group of less developed countries is a special designation for **least developed countries** (LDCs). Three criteria are used to distinguish the nations in that category: very low income per person, economic vulnerability, and poor human development indicators (population nutritional status, mortality, literacy, and education). LDCs currently include 33 African nations, 15 Asian countries, and Haiti (United Nations Office of the High Representative for Least Developed Countries, 2010). For our exploration of global aging, these designations help to differentiate countries and regions of the world on a number of dimensions, including the current age of the country. More developed countries currently have a much higher proportion of older people than do less or least developed countries. However, the populations of the less developed nations are aging much faster than developed nations did. Consequently, the nations in these categories differ in the kinds of challenges they face related to population aging. Each of these issues is explored in greater depth throughout this chapter.

Demographic Overview of Global Aging

The nature, scope, and importance of global aging far exceed simple descriptions of economic or demographic patterns. However, such information sets the stage for—and is an integral part of—a deeper discussion of social and cultural changes associated with global aging. For example, the concept of the **demographic divide** captures some significant patterns in population aging and social change. The demographic divide, briefly mentioned in Chapter 3, refers to the distinction between countries with low birth rates and high life expectancies (aging populations with slow or no growth) and those with high birth rates, significant growth, and comparatively young populations. This divide is defined by demographic patterns, but it coincides with the more/less/least developed designations discussed previously.

The less developed nations, characterized by high fertility and young populations, will contribute virtually all of the population growth that will take place in the world over the next four decades (Haub, 2007). They will also contribute the vast majority of older people because life expectancy is increasing, in some cases rapidly, in most of the less developed countries. Some of these societies will be addressing the challenges of nearly simultaneous population growth and population aging. The countries already on the old side of the demographic divide are, in contrast, facing labor force pressures that arise from low birth rates and low fertility, resulting in little or no population growth. These countries may not have enough workers to sustain economic productivity or to sustain the support programs for the older population, as discussed in Chapter 8. The demographic divide is one of many ways to think about global patterns of aging and how those patterns are related to the economic and social challenges of population aging.

Exhibit 10.1 provides some information about the three major regions of the world (developed, less developed, and least developed) on the indicators related to the demographic divide: life expectancy, fertility, and proportion 65 and older. The information on fertility helps to illustrate how countries on the young side of the demographic divide—those in less developed regions—will contribute virtually all of the growth in the world's population. It is easy to see that, with an average fertility rate of 2.7 children per woman and a 2010 population of more than 5.5 billion people, the less developed region of the world will be contributing a much higher proportion of new global citizens. In contrast, the more developed region has low fertility, longer life expectancies, and older populations. This indicates that, while today we have a wide array of age profiles when we look across the two sides of the demographic divide, that gap is going to be closing very quickly—making aging a worldwide challenge, not simply an issue for the developed countries of the world. It may be a challenge that the less/least developed nations will face without adequate resources, leading to risks of serious, negative outcomes across the globe.

Speed of Population Aging

Aging is occurring much more rapidly in less developed regions than it did in the United States and other already-aging countries. This pattern may seem counterintuitive because you know that developing regions have much higher fertility and younger populations than the developed nations. How is it possible that they can grow older so much faster? The major explanation is

EXHIBIT **10.1**

Population Data for Regions of the World

Region	Mid-year population in 2010 (in millions)	Total fertility rate	Percent of population 65 and older	Life expectancy at birth
World	6,892	2.5	8	69
More developed	1,237	1.7	16	77
Less developed	5,656	2.7	6	67
Least developed	857	4.5	3	56

Source: Population Reference Bureau, 2010a.

that the improvements in mortality (i.e., the extension of life expectancy that is part of the demographic transition) happened more slowly in the developed nations, and typically followed a decline in fertility. Contemporary developing nations are slower to decrease fertility than was the case in Europe and the United States but are more quickly getting control over mortality. The medical and public health advancements necessary to reduce mortality, such as immunizations and cleaner food and water, became more quickly available to the developing world than they had been in today's developed nations. For example, it took France 115 years for the proportion of its population 65 and older to increase from 7% to 14%; Sweden took 85 years for this change; and in the United States, this increase will be completed in 59 years. For Thailand, this same doubling of the proportion of older population will take place in only 22 years, and in South Korea it will take only 18 years (Kinsella & He, 2009).

Exhibit 10.2 shows the speed of population aging for selected countries and the time period during which the transformation it has taken/will take to move the population from 7% to 14% older people. France completed its 115-year transition by 1980; the United States will have reached the 14% mark by 2013. South Korea only began its aging transformation in 2000, but will have completed the change by 2018, only 5 years after the United States! It is easy to imagine the magnitude of the challenges facing countries whose populations will age so rapidly. Systems to serve the unique health, housing, social and economic needs of older people continue to be at issue in countries such as the United States, which have had a considerably longer time to prepare for this change. The less developed countries are having or will have significantly less time and fewer resources to faces these challenges, making the development of culturally appropriate adaptations even more difficult.

Demographic Dividends

As you know from Chapter 3, the demographic transition (changes in fertility and mortality that produce population growth and, eventually, population aging) is proceeding at varying pace in different countries around the world. All countries are experiencing, or on the cusp of, significant demographic shifts as part of population aging. In contrast to the challenges of the demographic divide, the **demographic dividend** is a different and interesting perspective on these changes. As the name implies, this term refers to the positive economic impacts and potential benefits a nation might experience during the demographic transitions. During the

EXHIBIT **10.2**

The Speed of Population Aging in Selected Countries

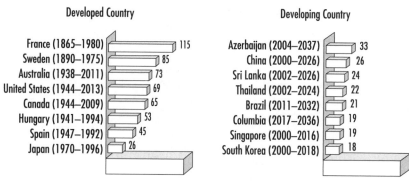

Developed Country		Developing Country	
France (1865–1980)	115	Azerbaijan (2004–2037)	33
Sweden (1890–1975)	85	China (2000–2026)	26
Australia (1938–2011)	73	Sri Lanka (2002–2026)	24
United States (1944–2013)	69	Thailand (2002–2024)	22
Canada (1944–2009)	65	Brazil (2011–2032)	21
Hungary (1941–1994)	53	Columbia (2017–2036)	19
Spain (1947–1992)	45	Singapore (2000–2016)	19
Japan (1970–1996)	26	South Korea (2000–2018)	18

Source: Kinsella & He, 2009.

demographic transition, fertility rates decline, and the young people already born are very likely to survive to become part of the adult labor force—a change that may enhance progress toward economic development. At this stage, the older population remains relatively small because changes in fertility and mortality have not yet produced the longer term results, an increasing older population. Therefore, not only is the labor force larger than the younger population that depends upon it (that is, a favorable youth dependency ratio), the old age dependency ratio is also low. At this point, "the labor force grows more rapidly than the population dependent on it, freeing up resources for investment in economic development and family welfare" (Lee & Mason, 2006, p. 1). Thailand and Vietnam are examples of countries currently in the midst of this phase in their transitions (Goldstein, 2009; Wongboonsin, Guest, & Prachuabmoh, 2005). Whether the shifting age structure, resulting in a large labor force and low dependency ratios, will produce a positive impact on economic development in any particular country depends on a host of factors, including policies about the larger economy (e.g., wages and taxation rates), as well as social norms about consumer spending and saving (Kinsella & He, 2009).

Some scholars postulate a second demographic dividend, as countries move into later stages of the demographic transition. As a society ages, the population becomes concentrated in the older working ages, as is the case today in the United States and many western European countries. Because these older workers (people in their 50s and 60s) can look forward to a long life after retirement, they have strong incentives to save and invest for their later years. These savings, in turn, contribute to individual economic well-being (which can encourage both mid-life investment and later-life spending, both of which benefit the economy) and to total national income. As with the first demographic dividend, whether the shifting age structure will result in the full potential gains depends on complex economic and policy factors, including tax incentives and disincentives for work and for investment, policies about mandatory retirement, and patterns of consumption across the life cycle (Lee & Mason, 2006).

For the study of global aging, the potential for demographic dividends illustrates important connections among changes in fertility and mortality, shifting population age structures, and implications of population aging for all aspects of social life, including the vigor of the economy. The quiz in Exhibit 10.3 covers some additional information about the demographic and social manifestations of global aging. This chapter should provide answers to all of these questions, or should give you the tools to make good guesses. If you cannot wait, go to Exhibit 10.7 at the end of the chapter to see how you scored on the quiz.

EXHIBIT **10.3**

Ten Questions About Global Aging

1. True of false? The world's children under age 5 outnumber people aged 65 and over.

2. The world's older population (65 and over) is increasing by approximately how many people each month in 2008?

   a. 75,000
   b. 350,000
   c. 600,000
   d. 870,000

3. China has the world's largest total population (more than 1.3 billion). Which country has the world's largest older population?

   a. China
   b. Germany
   c. Russia
   d. India

4. True or false? More than half of the world's older people live in the industrialized nations of Europe, North America, Japan, and Australia.

5. Which country has the world's highest percentage of older people in 2008?

   a. Sweden
   b. Japan
   c. Spain
   d. Italy

6. True or false? Today, average life expectancy at birth is less than 45 years in some countries.

7. There are more older widows than widowers in virtually all countries because:

   a. Women live longer than men.
   b. Women typically marry men older than themselves.
   c. Men are more likely to remarry after divorce or the death of a spouse.
   d. All of the above.

8. What proportion of the world's countries have a public old-age security program?

   a. All
   b. Three-fourths
   c. One-half
   d. One-fourth

9. In which country are older people least likely to live alone?

   a. The Philippines
   b. Hungary
   c. Canada
   d. Denmark

10. True or false? In developing countries, older men are more likely than older women to be illiterate.

Source: Kinsella & He, 2009.

Cultural Traditions, Population Aging, and Social Change

To place the demographic trends of global aging into broader context, we offer three case studies that describe countries with quite different demographic, cultural, and social situations related to population aging: China, Germany, and Kenya. These examples illustrate the intersections of population aging with social change and cultural traditions within each unique context. You can also compare each case study to what you have learned about aging in the United States to inform your understanding of the specific dynamics that have shaped aging here, and recognize the distinctive influences of different societies and cultures.

China: One-Child Policy

As we saw in Chapter 3, population pyramids provide a great deal of information about population aging; comparisons of pyramids, either across different countries or across time for the same country, reveal significant demographic shifts and hint at the social changes that accompany such shifts. Given your experience in interpreting them, you can now knowledgeably examine a very distinct population pyramid, that of contemporary China. Exhibit 10.4 reveals a very unique age structure for China in 2010. This structure is the result of China's well-known "one-child policy," implemented in 1979 to stem a very high and unsustainable rate of population growth in favor of long-term economic development and improved standards of living for China's people. The impact of the one-child policy can be seen in the much smaller size of the base of China's population pyramid in 2010. As a result of this very rapid decrease in fertility, combined with low mortality, the proportion of China's population 65 and older is increasing very rapidly. China has, through policy, accelerated the normal decline in fertility that is part of the demographic transition. The population pyramid for 2050 illustrates this reality; the base of the pyramid (children) is much smaller than all of the other age strata except for the very oldest (80 and above). By 2050, the first generation of parents who were affected by the one-child policy will be in their 60s and 70s; these cohorts will be significantly larger in number than those just behind them—including their children. In a culture that highly values traditions of respect, care, and honor from children to parents and grandparents, this age structure will be culturally and socially challenging.

Another notable challenge to the traditional systems of kin support of elders is the migration of young and middle-aged Chinese citizens from rural areas to cities, where economic prospects are better. For the upcoming generations of older people, the combination of very small family size and migration patterns will challenge the traditional system of norms and expectations about the responsibilities of children to provide care for elders. "The huge transient labor force renders a severe blow to the traditional Chinese type of family support for the elderly," as do unresolved issues regarding how one-child families should support parents (Du & Yang, 2009, p. 146). A single married couple, for example, would share the responsibility for up to four aging parents, with no siblings to share that obligation.

Aging and changes to family structure pose another challenge to China because of its limited infrastructure for programs and services to older people. Even though the traditional family system for care is vulnerable to demographic changes, there is a shortage of facilities and trained professionals ready to step in to provide formal care. For example, China is only now developing nonfamily alternatives for long-term care needs of older adults. It has been suggested that this lack of a formal care system essentially "pushes the burden of long-term care back to the family" (Du & Yang, 2009, p. 154). Because of the limitations in the availability of family caregivers and the growth of the older population, scholars who study aging in China are calling for the development of a formal long-term care system that is supported by public funding and overseen via government regulation (Du & Yang, 2009; Flaherty et al., 2007). Changes in social structures and public policies have not kept pace with the rapid transformation of China's age structure. Retirement is also an emerging institution in China, with few norms or opportunities for meaningful use of time after retirement. The mandatory retirement age for men is 60, and for women 55, ages that are not a problem now for a nation with a large workforce. However, with increasing longevity, these retirees face decades of life without work and, at the moment, without meaningful alternatives to work. In addition, the Chinese pension system is inadequate to provide income security for the majority of its retirees (Population Reference Bureau, 2010b). The public pension system is funded in the same way as the U.S. Social Security system (pay-as-you-go) and faces the same fiscal challenges of too many retirees and too few workers in the very near future. Shifting age structures require some change to the pension financing mechanism. Just as in the United States, China faces hard choices—either an increase in taxes, a decrease in outlays, an exception to the strict pay-as-you-go model to allow accumulation of funds today

EXHIBIT   *10.4*

Population Pyramids for China, 2010 and 2050

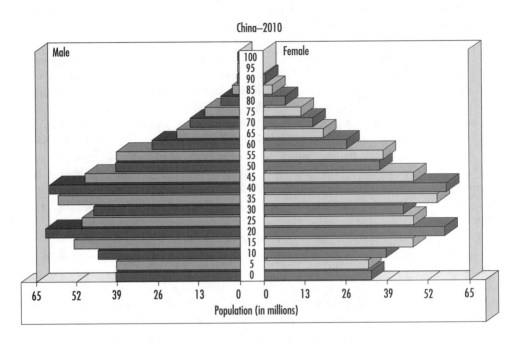

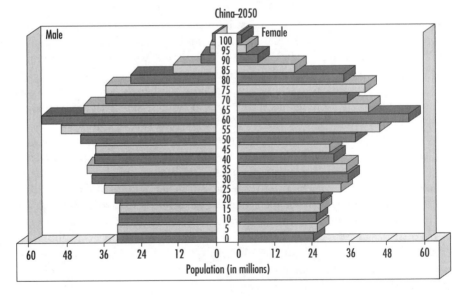

Source: U.S. Census Bureau International Data Base, 2010.

(while the numbers of people paying into the system is still relatively high) to be used in the future (when the number of workers paying in will be much lower and beneficiaries will be numerous), or some combination of these strategies.

China's health care system will also be adapting away from a focus on maternal/child health and infectious diseases toward inclusion of care for chronic conditions and health care needs of older population; this change requires retraining health professionals. The challenge is great, but the health care system clearly needs to adapt in many ways. "By 2030, older adults will account for two-thirds of the total disease burden in China" (Population Reference Bureau, 2010b, p. 4).

Germany: Inverted Pyramid

Germany's population pyramids for 2010 and 2050 show the classic pattern for developed nations with little population growth. Evidence of a baby boom in the 1950s and 1960s is seen in the large numbers of people between the ages of 40 and 55 in 2010; by 2050, that bulge will have moved upward in the pyramid, and its weight will rest on smaller numbers of young people. Germany has had sustained low fertility (about 1.4 births per woman) for several decades and has enjoyed high life expectancy for many decades. The projected result of these trends is an inverted population pyramid, as illustrated in Exhibit 10.5.

One of the obvious (and previously discussed) results of such an age structure is a shrinking labor force. As we saw in the discussion of the demographic divide, labor force declines are a hallmark of countries on the old side of the divide. Decreasing size of the working-age population has implications for the aged dependency ratio, the sustainability of pension programs, and simply filling jobs to keep the economy vibrant. Germany, Japan, and Italy have the worst aged dependency ratios in the world—three working age people for every person age 65 and older (Population Reference Bureau, 2010a). The viability of Germany's well-established and generous pension program is already threatened by the inverted pyramid. At present, Germany spends about 13% of its gross domestic product on the pension system, one of the highest percentages in the world (Kinsella & He, 2009). The proposed solutions to the public pension problem in Germany include increasing the tax rate or the age at which a person is eligible to receive the pension, and extending further immigration from other countries. The political and economic viability of any of these solutions is under heated debate (Haub, 2007), just as they are in other nations.

In addition to a long-standing public pension program, Germany has a well-developed system of services and programs for older people, including formal long-term services offered in institutions and in the community. Even so, the significant size of the older population poses challenges for the future. Germany's response to, and planning for, these challenges reflects basic cultural values, as illustrated in a recent national report on aging policies. These values include a shared responsibility and solidarity, old age as a driving force for innovation, generational equity, lifelong learning, and disease prevention (Kruse & Schmitt, 2009). In its focus on promoting healthy, active aging, and lifelong opportunities for learning and civic engagement, Germany is very similar to the United States. Developed nations in general have the luxury of such a focus while their economies permit sufficient funding, but may find them challenged when the population pyramids are inverted. In contrast to this picture, some developing nations are struggling with poverty and significant health challenges, even without an aging population. Kenya is an example of such a country.

Kenya: Health Challenges

Kenya's population pyramid for 2010 was used in Chapter 3 as an example of a young society, with a true pyramid shape. By 2050, however, that shape will change dramatically, getting thicker in the middle and growing noticeably broader at the top—signs of the demographic transition. That altered age structure is illustrated in Exhibit 10.6. Between 2000 and 2050, the proportion of Kenya's population that is 65 and older will triple—from 2.8% to 8.6%. While still low in comparison to other nations, Kenya's circumstances reflect those of a number of countries in the less developed category.

Kenya's story is not simply one of development and aging because other health-related events are contributing to the challenges it faces. As Kenya anticipates its growing aging population over the next decades, there are already pressing realities for older people today. The HIV/

EXHIBIT   *10.5*

Population Pyramids for Germany, 2010 and 2050

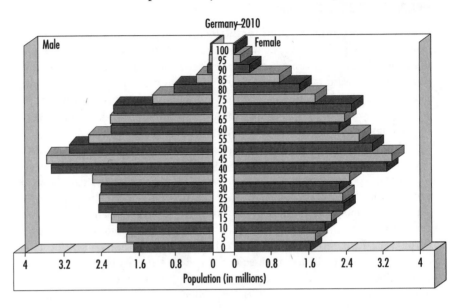

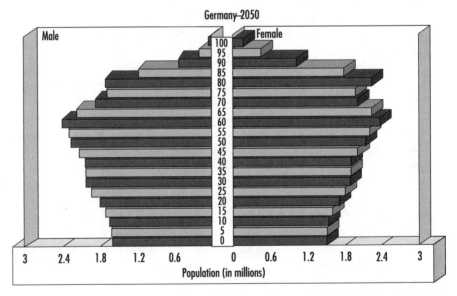

Source: U.S. Census Bureau International Data Base, 2010.

AIDS epidemic has "eroded hard-won progress in health and mortality, and has led to a decline in life expectancy from 59 years in the 1980s to 53 years in 2007" (Yin & Kent, 2008, p. 2). However, this added mortality is not affecting the older population as much as adults in their prime years of productivity. For many older people, the HIV/AIDS epidemic translates into loss of their adult children and the necessity to care for their orphaned grandchildren. The HIV/AIDS epidemic in Africa is a broad-based epidemic, involving both women and men. This means that both marital partners may get the disease, and without expensive (and sometimes unavailable) medications, die from it. While the majority of older people in Kenya live with family, some are now living in **skipped-generation households**, with the middle generation missing and grandparents acting as surrogate parents. Africa has the highest proportion of elders living in such a situation (12.2%), which, in contrast to varied reasons in the United States, is most often related to HIV/AIDS mortality of the middle generation (United Nations Department of Economic and Social Affairs, 2005).

In addition to the vast implications of HIV/AIDS mortality, elders in Kenya face problems with poverty, illiteracy, poor nutrition, limited housing options, lack of income security, and few social service programs (Mwangi, 2009). As in many nations across Africa, the Kenyan legal system has not specifically recognized the rights of elders and does not provide them with much protection from age discrimination, including inheritance and property laws, and lack of equal access to health care, social services, and income security (HelpAge International, 2008).

Kenya has recently adopted a national policy on ageing and older persons, which identified priority areas consistent with the problems listed previously. The policy focuses on health, nutrition and food, income security, poverty reduction, and healthy family culture. Financial support for the most vulnerable elders and small retirement benefits were authorized in this 2008 legislation, one of the first steps in Kenya's development of government support for older people (Mwangi, 2009). Eligibility for Kenya's old age pension is 55; however, life expectancy at birth is just 56. About one-third of African countries that offer some old age insurance benefit have life expectancies lower than the pensionable age (NIA et al., 2007).

Though challenged significantly by a relatively low level of economic development, Kenya is currently seeking to amend its constitution to guarantee the rights of its elders to protection from discrimination, life with dignity and respect, and reasonable care and assistance from family and the government (Mwangi, 2009).

These three countries—all with old or aging populations—illustrate a wide range of demographic, cultural, and social characteristics. How are these countries planning for and responding to their aging populations? Clearly there are many cultural, economic, demographic, and political forces at work in shaping the responses in these countries. To understand the development of

EXHIBIT *10.6*

Population Pyramid for Kenya, 2050

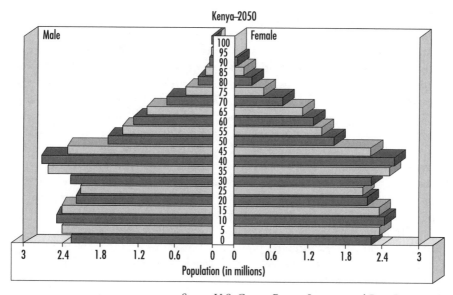

Source: U.S. Census Bureau International Data Base, 2010.

public policies and programs in particular, the concept of the **welfare state**, discussed in Chapter 9 for the United States, is a useful framework.

Aging and the Welfare State

In the United States, the term *welfare* usually connotes the safety net programs for citizens who, for a variety of reasons, require public support for basic necessities such as income, food, and health care. However, the welfare state is much broader than just a system of safety net programs. The concept is most often thought of as the collection of social assistance policies and programs provided by a nation state that take the place of support traditionally provided by the family or by religious institutions. Such policies often include public pensions, health care programs, family allowances, sickness and maternity/birth benefits, and unemployment compensation. Policies and programs that focus specifically on the needs of the older population comprise an **old-age welfare state**; Chapter 9 discussed the development of such a system in the United States. Though most industrialized nations have fairly well-developed welfare states, there is considerable variability in how policies are applied across countries. Many developing nations, like Kenya, are at the early stages of forming national policies for aging populations. Exploring how, when, and why welfare states originally emerged provides important context for our later discussions of the differences across nations today in the extent of policies and programs for older people.

History of the Welfare State

As you will see in the "analyzing theory" section on modernization later in this chapter, population shifts related to economic development, industrialization, and urbanization produce social conditions that no longer mesh with traditional sources of social and economic support, namely the family and religious institutions. As these traditional social institutions become less able to address the needs of these groups in a rapidly changing social environment, people in many countries have looked to the nation state for help with the challenges of assisting dependent persons and groups. Thus, the emergence of the welfare state unfolded across the 19th and 20th centuries in countries of Western Europe and the United States, with other countries following in subsequent years.

More specifically, industrialization, through its need for large concentrations of workers for factories, induced a substantial migration in various nations from rural farmland to urban areas. This migration introduced a new way of life, where individuals were separated from the land and frequently from their extended families. Whereas rural farmers often had kin for neighbors, ensuring others nearby who could provide social and economic assistance when necessary, urban dwellers typically found themselves amidst strangers, separated from their traditional social support networks. This new social living condition required some mechanism to replace that lost family support, and this mechanism became the welfare state. This process that unfolded for Western Europe and the United States in the late 19th and early 20th centuries is similar to what is happening in the developing nations of the world today. As we saw in the case of China, the migration of young people to cities in search of better jobs, and the resulting isolation of older people in rural areas, is one factor that is undermining the traditional system of family care.

Though some systems comparable to the welfare state existed even prior to the industrial revolution (e.g., Britain's poor laws and various military pension programs dating as far back as the Roman Empire) (c.f. Cowen, 2008), the first modern welfare state emerged in Germany in the 1870s and 1880s. Under Otto von Bismarck's state socialism, a collection of programs was established to provide for the social and economic welfare of German workers (Fay, 1950). These included policies on health insurance, accident insurance, and old age and disability pensions. The next 6 decades witnessed the spread of such programs across many European nations as well as to several industrialized former European colonies, including the United States. This expansion meant that, by 1950, almost all industrialized nations had well-established welfare programs in place for older people (Esping-Andersen, 1990).

The post-1950 period also included a new diffusion of the welfare state into developing nations. The 30 years following 1950 witnessed the rapid formation of new nation states from former colonial holdings, especially in Africa, parts of Asia, as well as among the island colonies in the Caribbean and the Pacific (Brown, 2005). These new nations, however, often had only limited industrialization, and thus, their experience with welfare programs was quite different than that of the developed world. In particular, policies were frequently in place "on paper," but never fully implemented. Commonly, welfare state benefits in these developing contexts were available only to government employees or to individuals residing in major urban areas, or were phased into existence in stages across different economic sectors; an example of the latter is the implementation of a universal pension system in Zimbabwe. In some cases, welfare policies were official law, but the programs to fulfill these policies were not established or funded for several years, if ever. For example, Cameroon enacted public pension legislation in 1969, but the program was not implemented until 1974 (Social Security Administration, 2005). As is the case in less developed nations today, the evolution of a welfare state does not always follow the western model.

Rapid global aging came to dominate welfare state issues among developed countries in the latter half of the last century. Public pensions were among the first types of welfare state programs. In these countries, by the 1970s, public pensions were easily the most widespread social assistance programs across all nations. This breadth of policy adoption, coupled with the rapid aging of many national populations, resulted in the overwhelming majority of welfare state spending across the globe (about 70%) being devoted to public pension programs, such as our Social Security system, by the 1980s (Pampel & Williamson, 1989). More recently, health care programs are beginning to consume increasing proportions of welfare state spending in some developed nations, such as the United States and the United Kingdom. In many nations, increases in the size of the aged population, as well as increases in longevity, have heightened demand for medical care programs that are part of the welfare state. These changes have, in many developed nations, been accompanied by increasing health care expenditures due to costs of pharmaceuticals and the availability of advanced, and expensive, medical technology. Population aging and higher health care costs each contribute, albeit differently in different countries, to overall expenditures; the result is that the annual costs of health care programs rival or exceed those of public pension systems. This shift has not occurred in every nation but is likely to become a policy challenge for many. China is already facing dramatic increases in health care costs and a public health care system that has been weakened as a result of a shift to a market-oriented health care system that relies on private funding (Kaneda, 2006).

Beginning in the 1980s, the increased financial burden of these programs created by population aging resulted in financial crises in many developed nations. At this time in many democratic nations, fiscally conservative governments were elected and efforts to reform welfare state programs to reduce costs were undertaken, with mixed success (Liebfried & Obinger, 2000). You recall the discussion in the early years of the 21st century of altering Social Security to "save" it from fiscal ruin or burdening future generations. Similar issues arose in countries like the United Kingdom and the Netherlands, where welfare states ceased expansion of funding for programs, and in many cases, actually began to contract. Often, changes to social insurance programs resulted in significant reductions in benefit levels, more stringent program eligibility rules, and higher age for eligibility (Hinrichs, 2000). As we saw earlier, these are the options that Germany and other developed nations are debating in response to growing numbers of people drawing on the system and decreasing labor pools contributing.

The reworking of a program sometimes resulted in a significantly more privatized and individualized approach to social welfare, which is a fundamental change in a public, shared approach to dealing with an issue like population aging via the welfare state. Chile was the first country (1980) to alter its public pension system, toward one of government-mandated, individual retirement accounts, managed by government-approved financial firms—similar to some recent proposals to "privatize" the U.S. Social Security system (Kinsella & He, 2009). In the late 1990s several European nations (e.g., Sweden) introduced privatized public pension systems (essentially government mandated savings accounts) that replaced their previously universal pension system that had paid a flat-rate benefit to all citizens. In other words, the responsibility for funding and managing pension funds moved from the responsibility of the government to the hands of individuals and families, as has been happening in the United States with private pensions. This process of welfare state contraction is often referred to as *retrenchment,* and it is still occurring today as populations continue to age and old-age welfare programs continue to encounter financial crises.

Program Types and Eligibility

Variation across countries today in welfare state programs and in who qualifies for these programs is considerable. Even though almost 75% of all countries have some sort of old age income security program, the proportion of citizens who are covered by such programs varies. In developed nations, 90% of the work force is covered by some kind of mandatory public pension program, but in developing countries the fraction is much smaller and is often restricted to a few categories of workers, such as military personnel and civil servants (Kinsella & He, 2009).

Public pensions, given their commonality across nations, can also illustrate other ways that nations have varied in their provision for old age via the welfare state. Public pensions vary internationally in how they are financed, who is covered, and when those who are eligible can begin to receive benefits. First, public pensions vary considerably across countries in terms of how the programs are funded. Looking across the globe, public pensions are funded in varying proportion by workers, employers, and the government itself. For each of these three categories variation in these proportions is substantial, ranging from 0% to 100%, depending on which nation one is examining. Workers in nations such as The Netherlands (19%) and Egypt (13%) make much higher contributions, for example, than those in Finland (4.5%) and Iran (7%); employer contributions also vary for these countries (The Netherlands, 5.7%; Egypt, 17%; Finland, 17%; and Iran, 20%) (Social Security Administration, 2010b). Second, public pensions vary across the globe according to how people become eligible for program benefits; that is, whether an individual has a "right" to use a particular program and, eventually, to receive benefits. Many Scandinavian countries have had universal programs, whereby all citizens, and even long-term noncitizen residents, may be eligible for pensions. This is often referred to as **citizenship entitlement**. In the United States, on the other hand, entitlement to Social Security depends on having been a worker (who has paid into the system) for a minimum period of time or on one's relationship to such a worker (e.g., a spouse, widow, or minor dependent). This system is termed an **earnings-related entitlement**. And, as noted previously, in many developing nations not all kinds of employment are covered by the public pension system (e.g., only covering government workers), so simply working at any job may not guarantee you a public pension.

Entitlement to participate in a program is one difference across countries; in addition, the specific requirements to eventually receive a benefit also differ. Two types of eligibility dominate social policies: age eligibility and need-based eligibility. As you recall from Chapter 9, a U.S. citizen is entitled to a Social Security benefit based on having accumulated a minimum number of "quarters" of workforce participation, during which time the worker paid taxes into the program's trust fund. Actually receiving Social Security benefits, however, is also based on reaching a certain age—62 years for reduced (early retirement) benefit and (soon) 67 years for standard benefits. While age eligibility is fairly straightforward, the age one must reach varies greatly across nations. Public pensions may be received as early as 55 years in Kenya, Cuba, and Venezuela, while in the United States, Norway, and Iceland, countries on the other side of the demographic divide, age eligibility approaches 70 years (Social Security Administration, 2010b).

Chapter 9 also pointed out that need-based eligibility programs often have income thresholds that are set at or near poverty level, with programs intended as a form of poor relief. So one must both be eligible and meet income or resource requirements to receive benefits. However, some exceptions exist to the typical poverty level standard. For example, Australia's need-based eligibility for public pension benefits has an income threshold that is set so much higher than their poverty level that the overwhelming majority of its aged citizens are eligible for public pension benefits.

Pension programs are but one dimension of the welfare state. Health insurance, unemployment benefits, coverage for long-term care, and compensation for workplace injuries are other aspects of the welfare state that relate to the needs of older adults in many countries. In light of global aging, the current status and future development of welfare state programs and policies are topics of great interest to researchers, advocates, and decisions makers working in the realm of public policy and aging. From our earlier discussion of the different situations in China, Kenya, and Germany, it should be clear that welfare state programs develop as part of a whole fabric of social change, including both shifting cultural values and economic development. Advising caution when making international comparisons of social security systems, a recent report notes that all such systems "are embedded in economic and demographic realities and in cultural expectations about who cares for the elderly" (Population Reference Bureau, 2009, p. 3). No single model of the welfare state, or even for a particular aspect of the system, would work well or be culturally appropriate across the diverse set of aging nations in the world.

If one model would fit every country, it would be reasonable to expect a **welfare state convergence**, in which the welfare state programs in all nations would mirror each other as each country modernizes and their economies become more developed. This assumption is problematic for many reasons, including lack of evidence for such convergence, and the Western-dominated perspective that underlies it. One study of the convergence hypothesis provides ample evidence to question it. Among 18 countries in one study with advanced economies (including Germany, Italy, Japan, Netherlands, and Australia), the United States provided an example of a notable exception toward convergence: it lacked a national health policy (Montanari, 2001). While the very recent health care legislation in the United States may negate that exception, there is every reason to question the path and destination of old-age welfare state evolution, especially in the developing world. Just as the demographic transition is unfolding differently for those countries, so too will the welfare state emerge in distinctive, culturally shaped patterns.

Welfare State and the Role of the Family

As we think about the evolution of the welfare state in developing nations, the role of the family deserves particular attention. The definition of the welfare state at the beginning of this section suggests that such a system emerges when societies develop economically and their social structures modernize. The assumption within that description is that government-sponsored programs and policies are necessary to supplant, or at least complement, some of the roles that had traditionally filled by families in earlier times. While this general pattern—in which a welfare state accompanies economic growth—has been well-documented for currently developed nations, it is dangerous to make dogmatic predictions about what will happen in today's developing nations. As noted previously, such changes are the result of social change, economic development, *and* cultural values. We cannot easily predict that a welfare state will replace the role of the family in the lives of older adults in all currently developing regions, as it did in developed nations of the past.

Cultural values play an extremely important role. As you saw in Chapter 5, the U.S. value of independence in family relationships across the life cycle translates into patterns such as "intimacy at a distance" and older adults not wanting to "be a burden" on children. This value is reflected in contemporary living arrangements. As in other developed nations, the most common living arrangement for older people in the United States is alone or with a spouse. In contrast, coresidence of multiple generations is the most common living situation for older people in most developing nations, where norms of family caretaking are strong (Kinsella & He, 2009).

China's strong tradition of filial piety is a clear example of such family norms. According to Charlotte Ikels (1993), China's traditional culture of the early 20th century (pre-Communism) was based on Confucianism, "an ethic of familism that not only served as the standard to guide proper family organization for many centuries but was also codified into law" (p. 124). This system emphasized vertical family ties—those between the generations—as more important than horizontal ties, such as those between spouses, which were viewed primarily as a means by which to continue the lineage (or vertical line) through offspring. It is unlikely that this deeply rooted value system will be completed replaced by an old-age welfare state in China, even in the face of formidable demographic pressures. Can China somehow integrate these values into its need to adapt to a rapidly aging population, widespread migration, and the high levels of pressure on younger generations with large numbers of elders, for whom a cultural sense of responsibility continues? Over the next several years, research on the evolution of China's welfare state will surely provide insights into how rapidly aging countries manage to balance public programs, traditional values, shifting family patterns, and the needs of an unprecedented number of older people.

In a study of old-age homes in India—another developing nation that strongly endorses coresidence and family caregiving—Liebig (2003) surveyed managers, supervisors, and board members of nearly 50 old-age homes and day care centers for older adults. Responses to questions about the proper role of old-age homes reveals three, diverse perspectives: (1) government involvement in meeting such needs for elders will erode the family responsibility, (2) such care options should be seen as a last resort for elders who have no family support, and (3) old-age housing is necessary because elders sometimes fall through the safety net of family care (Liebig, 2003). This range of responses nicely captures the tension between a desire to preserve traditional, family-based systems of care and the pressure to recognize that those systems may be increasingly less viable because of changes in family structure and growing numbers of older people who need assistance. This tension between traditional values and modernization embodies the transition to some kind of welfare state.

Public pensions, government-sponsored old-age homes, and other aspects of the welfare state will continue to emerge in some form in developing nations; both the growing size of the older population and changing family structures in many of these countries seem to demand some government response. However, cultural values will play a crucial role in the development of public policies in these nations. Families provide the vast majority of long-term care in many nations throughout the world (just as in the United States) and are quite likely to do so in the future as well. The balance of traditional values against changes in economic structure, availability of kin, and population aging in vastly different cultures is not likely to produce welfare state convergence. An overview of modernization theory may help provide a context for the possible divergence of societal responses to population aging.

The Study of Global Aging

The information discussed in this chapter is part of an exploding literature on global aging. To sort through the growing number of reports and research articles on this topic, it is useful to consider that the study of global aging actually encompasses three different categories of investigation. First are broad questions about the aging of the globe as a whole. The focus for this kind of descriptive **global patterns research** is on macro-level, aggregated depictions of major demographic, economic, and social trends across the world. The preceding discussions of global and regional trends are an example of this category of exploration. Two very good examples of this kind of research on global aging are *Why Population Aging Matters* (NIA et al., 2007) and *An Aging World: 2008* (Kinsella & He, 2009). Both of these publications describe important trends related to population aging, such as increasing life expectancy, increasing burden of chronic rather than infectious diseases, and living arrangements among older people in a wide range of countries and regions of the world.

This type of research on global aging relies on international data sets, or a compilation of national data sets, on demographic, health, economic development, and human development indicators. You have already seen references to numerous data sets available from the United Nations, including the study of living arrangements of older people around the world (United Nations Department of Economic and Social Affairs, 2005). The Luxembourg Income Study is another example. This data set provides standardized income, poverty, and inequality data from 30 countries around the world, enabling researchers to easily draw comparisons. Some countries have participated for 30 years or more, also permitting comparisons over time for developing or developed nations (Luxembourg Income Study, n.d.).

A second area within the study of global aging focuses on questions about aging *within* a country, a set of countries, or a culture. This kind of scholarship contributes to the literature on global aging by illuminating the policies, social structures, cultural practices, and experiences of older people in countries from around the world. Examples of **single-nation global aging research** include a study of health and living arrangement transition among China's oldest-old (Zimmer, 2005), an analysis of the productivity of older women and men in rural Bangladesh (Cameron, Kabir, Khanam, Wahlin, & Streatfield, 2010), and an investigation of the prevalence and portrayal of older adults in prime time television in Taiwan (Lien, Zhang, & Hummert, 2009). These in-depth explorations of aging within a culture or within a nation are growing in number, as are the outlets for such publications, pointing to the increasing prominence of this component of **global aging research**. This kind of research that focuses on aging within a particular culture or society relies on the same range of methods that are described in Chapter 2, and those used by social scientists in general. The articles mentioned previously as examples of within-nation research used interviews, surveys, and secondary analysis of national data, such as information collected by some other countries' censuses. These articles follow the same rules of conceptualization, measurement, sampling, and analysis already familiar to you.

Global aging research also includes a third category, **comparative research**, which analyzes similarities and differences across two or more countries on topics related to aging such as pension plans and family caregiving. While descriptive global aging research (the first category) includes information from specific countries to illustrate patterns or trends, comparative research typically explores one topic in greater depth across two or more countries or cultures. For example, four recent issues of *Journal of Cross-Cultural Gerontology* (volume 25, nos. 1 & 2, and volume 24, nos. 3 & 4) included the following comparative studies: satisfaction with intergenerational communication in Bulgaria and the United States; hospice development in Japan, South Korea, and Taiwan; meaning and measurement of social support across four ethnic groups; and comparison of self-perceptions of aging in France and Morocco. This kind of research presents unique challenges and opportunities to understand the complex interactions of policies, cultures, economic development, and other unique aspects of nations being compared.

Comparative Methods

One of the first decisions in this type of comparative research is about the unit of analysis: are we comparing countries, cultures, or different cultures within a country? The answer to this question immediately raises another: what are the boundaries of the units to be compared? For countries, recognized geographic boundaries are generally appropriate, but those boundaries are sometimes political and contested. Boundaries may divide a single cultural group into the populations of two

Modernization Theory

The basic premise of classic **modernization theory** is that the status of older people declines as a society modernizes—or, in terms we discussed previously, as it moves from less to more economically developed. The theory contends that changes such as urbanization, technological advancement, health advances, and population growth combine to erode the position of honor, prestige, and respect accorded to older people in less developed societies. Thus, the theory argues that "with increasing modernization the status of older people declines" (Cowgill, 1972, p. 124). In the least modern (or less developed) societies, the theory contends that older people supposedly enjoy high status, and family members are economically and culturally bound to meet their elder relatives' physical and emotional needs. Families, according to the theory, require society's assistance only when modernization disrupts the traditional (mostly agrarian) family's economic and social structures. Based on modernization theory, we would expect that in most rural, agrarian developing countries the elderly enjoy high status and that their needs are routinely met by family members, rather than by paid services or government programs.

Modernization theory has a great deal of intuitive appeal and some (but not universal) empirical support from cross-cultural research. However, it has been criticized for using unclear and inconsistent definitions to assess the social status of older adults, oversimplifying the processes of modernization, and ignoring intervening variables, such as ideology and cultural value systems.

Perhaps the most significant assumption made by modernization theory is that the extended family in all developing societies fully integrates its older members, eliminating the need for pensions, senior housing, and other older adult services familiar to us. According to Tout (1989), "in some instances, reliance on the traditional extended family may not be the normally acceptable panacea, but may for the old person be a gruesome and cruel experience of dependence, deprivation, and degradation" (p. 300). The traditional situation of widows in India is one clear example of this less than idyllic circumstance of family integration. In today's Indian society, most widows do not throw themselves on their husband's funeral pyre, as tradition once mandated; instead, the widow is supported with housing and other essentials by her husband's family. However, she holds very low status in his family, is often viewed as a burden, and is sometimes the victim of verbal and physical abuse (Stein, 1988).

In a review of family demography in developing nations, Martin and Kinsella (1994) provide further grounds upon which to question the stereotypical model of multigenerational households providing for elders in traditional, less developed societies. They found that multigenerational households are declining in many developing countries, and there is a trend toward more independent living arrangements, which was also observed in a more recent study (United Nations Department of Economic and Social Affairs, 2005). Martin and Kinsella found that the likelihood of sharing a residence diminishes as age increases—the oldest adults are least likely to occupy extended family households. In addition, multigenerational households were as likely to be based on the needs of sons and daughters as on the needs of older family members. If the needs of elders were the primary motivation for sharing households, we would expect the prevalence of coresidence to increase with advancing age. Instead older adults who share a household with descendents are more often supporting others than being supported by them.

Some, though not all, of the developing nations studied by Martin and Kinsella (1994) are still characterized by an extended family structure. Nepal is one example. Based on this criterion, we might expect the status of the elderly in Nepal to be high. However, research conducted by Goldstein and Beall (1983) in both rural and urban Nepal found that equating membership in an extended family with high status, security, and satisfaction for the elderly person is misleading. They found that economic factors (unemployment, low wages, and inflation) and social factors (less property as a result of the division of the familial inheritance and migration of eldest sons to urban areas) had affected the nature and quality of relationships within the family, often leaving the elderly as relatively powerless dependents on younger family members. Findings from the study indicated that, instead of a cultural tradition of high regard and duty, the status of older people in the family depended on the elders' ability to control property and income. These researchers conclude that, given the socioeconomic conditions of most developing societies and the inability of governments to provide substantial social service programs, there are likely to be increasing numbers of elderly adults without property, pension, or savings in their old age—in short, without a safety net. Current research is providing a more varied picture of aging in developing nations, but this image from Goldstein's classic study—older people exchanging promises of economic reward for receipt of care in later years—was among the first to force Western scholars to rethink idealized visions of life in developing nations with traditional value systems that call for support of elders. While the premise of modernization theory has a lot of appeal, it is not a uniform pattern of development across societies everywhere. Nor does it adequately take into account the role of social insurance policies and programs in supporting elders in some developing countries—the welfare state, described earlier in this chapter.

countries being compared, for example. In the case of a cross-cultural analysis, operationalizing the definitions of culture and the geographic boundaries of "place" you wish to compare is essential.

Another step in comparative research, as in any other research, is to decide what variables to include in the study. What is the dependent variable, and what are the independent variables? Comparing across nations or cultures assumes that some specific features have an especially important impact on the dependent variable of interest. For example, a researcher might be interested in the factors that determine labor force participation of older men and women in two different countries. This study might include variables related to cultural values about economic participation, degree of economic development of the country, and gender roles. The researchers would then look at the influence of these factors on labor force participation and compare these interrelationships across the two countries. The special challenge in comparative research is to find or devise measures that are meaningful across cultures and across languages, or to find existing data sets from the countries of interest that include variables defined and measured in the same way in each place.

Some have argued that cross-national or cross-cultural comparative research is more a general approach to research than one specific method. Indeed, the overall goal of comparative research is the same as any research with multiple groups: to compare two or more identifiable items (e.g., age groups, people who participated in a program to those who did not, countries, points in time) to learn something about the similarities and differences of those being compared. Are they the same or are they different? What are the sources of differences or similarities? In the case of comparative research on aging, what are the implications of any variations we discover for aging or the older population? Even though comparative research is indeed guided by universal standards for rigorous research, there are unique challenges to making comparisons across cultures and across nations.

Beyond the "Exotic Other"

As we think about examining the experience of aging in different countries, or comparing across countries, a word of caution against a tourist approach to the study of global aging is required.

Careful investigation of global aging requires thinking beyond an interest in the **exotic other**. This concept derives from a rich tradition in anthropological research that seeks to understand other cultures from a wholly authentic point of view, not reducing people who live in other societies to cultural objects. It can be argued that a fascination with the exotic other is preferable to disdain for anyone different from us; however, a deeper understanding of the meanings and experiences of aging around the world requires commitment to seeing realities of aging deeply woven into an entire fabric of history, culture, and social structures from the point of view of those within that culture. What makes aging in another culture interesting and important is not that it is different from our own experiences, but that there are commonalities, patterns, and uniqueness to uncover.

International Initiatives on Aging

In recognition of the many complex and momentous issues, opportunities, and challenges raised by the aging of the globe, the United Nations convened the First World Assembly on Ageing in Vienna in 1982. This congress, attended by representatives from countries around the world, resulted in the first international document intended to guide research, planning, and policies related to aging: the Vienna **International Plan of Action on Aging**. The plan sought to strengthen government and community commitments and capacities to address the needs of older people, their ability for continued growth and development, and their right to such opportunities. More than 60 recommendations were included in the plan, covering issues related to health and nutrition, income security, employment, and housing. The Vienna conference action plan generated a series of other international initiatives, including the International Year of Older Persons in 1999. In 2002, a Second World Assembly on Ageing convened in Madrid, with participation from 156 countries, to review progress and challenges that had occurred since the 1982 World Assembly and to refine the original plan of action. One of the most important features of the Second World Assembly on Ageing was the focus on, and involvement of, developing nations. At the time of the First World Assembly, "many developing countries did not consider the issue of ageing to be a pressing concern" (Huber, 2005, p. 3). In contrast, the second world meeting emphasized the rapid aging occurring in less developed nations and the challenge for those nations to simultaneously address issues of poverty as well as aging. The implementation plan resulting from the Second Assembly—the Madrid International Plan of Action on Ageing (MIPAA)—addresses concerns and contributions of older people around the world. MIPAA emphasizes full participation of older people in every society, as did the first action plan. However, MIPAA placed this goal in the context of overall economic development goals; the plan notes that societal participation of older people rests on the assurance that basic necessities of an adequate income and access to health care are provided. On top of this foundation, nations were called to provide opportunities for fulfillment, well-being, and empowerment of older people to participate in all aspects of society. Summing up the ideology that is the foundation of the International Plan of Action, the Madrid World Assembly offered that, "A longer life provides humans with an opportunity to examine their lives in retrospect, to correct some of their mistakes, to get closer to the truth, and to achieve a different understanding of the sense and value of actions. This may well be the most important contribution of older people to the human community" (United Nations, 2003, p. 1).

Progress toward the specific goals of these international action plans is monitored via periodic reports to the Secretary-General of the United Nations. The 2010 follow-up report provides a snapshot of a wide range of efforts by individual nations to move toward these goals. Initiatives undertaken in support of MIPAA include: a program in Mexico providing tax incentives to employers who hire older workers; a government-sponsored program in Thailand in

EXHIBIT **10.7**

Answers to Global Aging Quiz

1. **True.** Although the world's population is still aging, children still outnumber older people as of 2008. Projections indicate, however, that in fewer than 10 years, older people will outnumber children for the first time in history.

2. **d.** The estimated change in the total size of the world's older population between July 2007 and July 2008 was more than 10.4 million people, an average of 870,000 each month.

3. **a.** China also has the largest older population, numbering 106 million in 2008.

4. **False.** Although industrialized nations have higher percentages of older people than do most developing countries, 62% of all people aged 65 and over now live in the developing countries of Africa, Asia, Latin America, the Caribbean, and Oceania.

5. **b.** Japan, with 22% of its population aged 65 and over, has recently supplanted Italy as the world's oldest major country.

6. **True.** In some African countries (e.g., Malawi, South Africa, Zambia, and Zimbabwe) where the HIV/AIDS epidemic is particularly devastating, average life expectancy at birth is less than 45 years.

7. **d.** All of the above.

8. **b.** As of 2004, 167 countries/areas of the world (74%) reported having some form of an old age/disability/survivals program. In many cases, program coverage is limited to certain occupational subgroups.

9. **a.** The Philippines. The percentage of older people living alone in developing countries is usually much lower than that in developing countries; levels in the latter may exceed 40%.

10. **False.** Older women are less likely to be literate. For example, data from China's 2000 census revealed that 26% of older women could read and write, compared to 66% of older men.

Source: Kinsella & He, 2009.

which volunteers are paid a small stipend to take older people to health clinics and make sure that they receive the proper medication at home; a long-term care insurance policy adopted into law in the Republic of Korea; and a meals program for older people in Ecuador. Kenya's new constitutional provision for the protection of the right of older people (mentioned earlier) was another highlight of the 2010 follow-up on the Second World Assembly on Ageing, as was the U.S. Patient Protection and Affordable Care Act (United Nations General Assembly, 2010).

Summary

The demographic realities of global aging are undeniable; clearly the aging of a society is accompanied by, and is a catalyst for, enormous social change. These changes are part and parcel of a set of "trends that represent a transformation of the world" (NIA et al., 2007). In addition to the changing patterns of fertility and mortality, global aging is associated with changing family structures, changes in work and retirement patterns, shifting burdens of disease away from infectious to chronic illness, new economic challenges, and the development of social welfare systems. Global trends in longevity and population aging are heralded as a success story, but the challenges posed are also widely acknowledged (Kinsella & Phillips, 2005). How these issues play out in specific countries or major regions of the world varies, depending upon a host of factors including demographics, economics, and cultural values.

Each region and each nation faces the promise and the challenge of aging societies. There has never been a clearer mandate for the role of gerontology education and research. In response to this mandate, gerontology programs are beginning to appear in countries around the world. In some places, such as the United States and Germany, gerontology is a well-developed discipline, with credentials offered at several levels of higher education. In others, gerontology is a specialty within other professional programs such as medicine, nursing, and social work. In still others, gerontology education is offered primarily as training for direct care workers. In recognition of the need for data about aging populations, many national and cross-national efforts are underway. Examples of such research initiatives include a survey of aging, health, and well-being conducted in Argentina, Mexico, Barbados, Uruguay, Chile, and Brazil; a longitudinal study of aging in India; the Survey of Health, Ageing, and Retirement in Europe (SHARE); and the World Health Organization longitudinal study of global ageing and adult health. These are but a few examples of the educational and research efforts underway in acknowledgement of the challenge and the promise of global aging.

Web Wise

HelpAge International   http://www.helpage.org/Home
HelpAge International is a global network of not-for-profit organizations with a mission to work with, and for, disadvantaged older people worldwide to achieve a lasting improvement in the quality of their lives. Their Web site provides the reader with access to a vast array of reports about aging around the world, and information about current projects that HelpAge is working on, research and policy, and news. You can watch videos, view photos, retrieve reports, and hear stories from older people around the world. It also provides an in-depth overview of worldwide emergencies and helpful resources. HelpAge has organizational affiliates in 50 countries around the world.

United Nations Programme on Aging   http://www.un.org/esa/socdev/ageing/
The United Nations has a multifaceted agenda to promote dignity, independent, and security for older persons around the world, as embodied in their slogan, "Towards a Society for All Ages." This Web site describes the major initiatives, such as the "Policy Framework for a Society for All Ages." The site includes a wide variety of other resources, including the list of UN Principles for Older Persons, a summary of the Madrid International Plan of Action, and a document that describes links to other sites on a range of topics related to global aging, including links to publications about population aging, income transfer programs, older person's rights, retirement, civic engagement, and a toolkit for practitioners and policy makers interested in implementation of the International Plan of Action on Ageing policy reports from countries and regions around the world.

World Health Organization: Ageing and Life Course   http://www.who.int/ageing/en/
In their "WHO Active Ageing" agenda, the World Health Organization emphasizes the positive contributions that older people can contribute to make to their communities up until the

very ends of their lives. Their approach focuses on strategies for prevention of chronic disease, access to age-friendly primary health care, and creation of age-friendly environments (including age-friendly cities). This Web site describes the WHO strategies and provides links to information and resources relates to these initiatives, as well as resources and general information about aging and the life course.

Key Terms

citizenship entitlement
comparative research
demographic divide
demographic dividend
global aging research
global patterns research
developed countries
developing countries

earnings-related entitlement
exotic other
International Plan of Action
 on Aging
least developed countries
less developed countries
modernization theory
more developed countries

old-age welfare state
single-nation global aging
 research
skipped-generation households
welfare state
welfare state convergence

Questions for Thought and Discussion

1. What would you list as the most important aging issues facing developing nations? What would be the issues on your list for developed nations? Why?
2. What lessons can the United States learn from other nations with respect to programs and services for older people?
3. The idea that there is a demographic imperative that can compel political and policy solutions to population aging was presented (and criticized) in Chapter 3. Economic, political, and cultural factors play a role in any decisions or plans that might be considered. As you think about the demographics of global aging, what role do you think such information does and should have in planning for aging societies?
4. Pick one country that you are especially interested in, and find out what kinds of policies or programs are in place for older people in that country. Who is eligible for the programs? Does the welfare state play a dominant role? Would the welfare state come in to conflict with the traditional values of the country you are studying?

Baby Boomers and the Changing Landscape of Aging

The boomers in old age will represent complete realization of the institutional standing older people have come to assume in American life over the past half-century. No longer a marginal presence, seniors today (and certainly tomorrow) are demanding and receiving recognition of their new prominence.

(Hudson, 2009, p. viii)

The oldest baby boomer turned 65 on January 1, 2011. Baby boomers—people born between 1946 and 1964—make up the largest **cohort** in our history. Because of its sheer size, this group has had an effect on every social institution as they have moved through. New schools had to be built and educational approaches were modified to accommodate larger classes than ever before. Family dynamics changed, with more siblings in the average household than before. Baby boomers entering the job market faced more competition than their predecessors. As they enter later life, baby boomers are having an effect on the health care system, politics, work, families, education, and retirement.

Within all of these social institutions, baby boomers certainly present challenges to current social systems and policies; but as we meet these challenges, a "new aging" is emerging. Because baby boomers do not fit neatly into prior images of aging, just as they did not fit into the schools that were too small for them, our society is making adaptations—to structures, expectations, and opportunities for older people. Recall our discussion in Chapter 3 of the baby boom moving through the population pyramid of the United States (the "pig in a python" image); this is, to some extent, a good analogy for thinking about how the baby boom is changing aging. As this very large cohort moves into and out of social structures, such as education and work, those structures must adapt to accommodate not only the numbers of boomers, but also their values, preferences, and characteristics. One straightforward example is the adjustment to Social Security that we discussed in Chapter 6. To accommodate the large number of baby boomers who will be eligible to receive benefits, and to compensate for the smaller post-boomer cohorts who will make up the work force that pays into Social Security, the age of eligibility for full benefits is increasing. Another way that baby boomers are changing aging is in the growth of volunteering and **civic engagement** for older people. This increasingly common role is an opportunity for older people to remain actively involved in their communities, and it is a way to make up for the loss of such a large portion of the labor force when baby boomers retire. We discuss this in detail later in this chapter, but it serves as another example of new opportunities, roles, and expectations for older people that are emerging as baby boomers moving through our social institutions.

But let us be clear: just as with any other social change, alterations to the realities and variations of aging experiences are the product of a host of economic, political, and cultural forces—not just the demographics of one very large aging cohort. And this is where the "pig in the python" analogy becomes less useful. The python is designed to be able to digest the pig, but societies are not so singularly focused or organic in function. Ultimately, the changes that societies make to respond to the aging of the population are human decisions. As we saw in Chapter 3, demography is not destiny. Political, economic, and historic forces play a major role in shaping the specific responses of any society to its aging population. The quote at the beginning of this chapter clearly illustrates that baby boomers are entering an old age that is the culmination of decades of social change; and they will contribute to further change. Cohorts of aging people—their characteristics, behaviors, and values—are part of the complex set of factors that change aging. In fact, every past and future cohort of older people has helped or will help to modify the stage of later life.

Cohort Flow and Changing Aging

The idea of **cohort flow**, mentioned in chapters 2 and 4, helps to illustrate the process by which any cohort will change an **age stratum** (or age category) as it moves through that stage because of its unique demographic characteristics, generational values, and responses to social change. In their groundbreaking work on age stratification discussed earlier, Riley, Johnson, and Foner (1972) defined a cohort as a group of people who were born in the same time interval and who age together. Each cohort enters a particular age category containing most of the people it will ever have; the only way that new members can be added to a birth cohort is if they migrate into the society. Some members of the cohort will be lost (due to mortality or, for a much smaller number, migration out of the society) as the cohort moves into the next stratum; the surviving group then has a different composition than it did previously (i.e., cohort composition effects). In addition, each cohort is different from other cohorts, as we shall see when we compare baby boomers to other generations. Intercohort differences are partly due to the social and historical circumstances they encountered throughout their lives. "Since their respective life spans cover different periods of history, each cohort encounters a unique sequence of social and environmental events" (Riley et al., 1972, p. 9).

Distinctive cohort characteristics mean that each age stratum (or age category, such as 65 and older) is altered by the flow of successive cohorts through that stratum. This may seem like a complicated way to describe a straightforward observation: being 75 in 2010 is not the same as it was 30 years earlier, in 1980. But it is important to understand the role of cohorts in bringing about changes in the experience of aging. The world has changed, and each unique cohort that moves through the later stages of life brings with them their own histories, including the social changes that they have experienced; as they react to the circumstances of aging, they also alter them for future generations of older people. Our colleague Millie Seltzer described the phenomenon of cohort flow and social change using an analogy to escalators in a department store (personal communication to S. Kunkel, 1993). An age cohort starts up the escalator, getting off at each floor and spending some time there. In Seltzer's example, the floors of the department store are age strata. While on the adolescence floor, for example, a particular cohort or **generation** will buy certain things, reject others, and demand new and different items than their predecessors. When that cohort moves on to the next stage, the next age cohort follows them onto the adolescence floor, which now looks quite different than it did before the preceding cohort changed things. And the preceding cohort made its changes based on their unique character, stemming from the social and historical events they had experienced. Using more sociological language, Ryder (1965) described the intersection of cohort flow and social change in this way: "The capacity for societal transformation . . . [is aided by] the continual emergence of new participants in the social process, and the continual withdrawal of their predecessors" (p. 844).

While cohort flow through the age structure of a society is a universal phenomenon, it is certainly the case that baby boomers, based on sheer size of the cohort, will have a larger impact than previous generations on the experience of aging and on societal responses to the older population. Exhibit 11.1 shows the numerical impact of baby boomer aging: dramatic growth in the numbers of older people during the next few decades, with the steepest part of the growth occurring between now and 2050.

If you are in doubt about the impact of baby boomers, do a quick Google search; the term baby boomers generates more than 12 million hits, with an astonishing range of sites,

EXHIBIT **11.1**

Population Growth, United States, 1980–2050

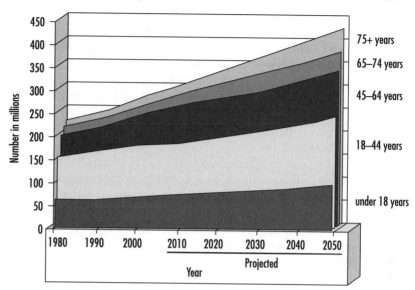

including credible research on health and retirement, nostalgic reminiscence about the 1960s and 1970s, political rhetoric, and vendors that sell everything an aging baby boomer might want (such as travel packages, financial planning, insurance, music of the '60s, active adult communities, and dietary supplements). Every aspect of social life—from politics to the marketplace—is responding to the wave of baby boomers entering later life. Some have called this wave the silver tsunami, predicting a disaster for our nation's economy, health care, labor force, and Social Security. Others predict that the growth of silver industries, business opportunities targeting the wants and needs of this larger population of older adults, will be the drivers of the new economy (O'Neill, 2009). As we discuss throughout this chapter, the baby boomers do represent the new aging; their numbers are impressive, and the landscape of aging will never be the same. However, none of these statements necessarily guarantees either of doom or prosperity.

Who Are the Baby Boomers?

You are by now well aware that baby boomers were born between 1946 and 1964. During those years, the total fertility rate increased from 2.19 per woman in 1940 to 3.58 in 1957, usually considered the peak of the boom (Weeks, 2005). The number of babies born in each year of the baby boom was higher than ever before, topping 4 million in several years; the count for 1945 (the year just before the start of the baby boom) was 2.8 million, compared to 3.47 million just one year later.

While the demographic beginning and end of the baby boom have been well-researched and documented, there is also recognition that the earliest and latest boomers are different from each other. They are, after all, 18 years apart in age, and therefore likely to have been affected differently by the major historic and social events or trends. Some contend that the two groups may, in fact, be different cohorts! For example, the so-called **"leading edge" boomers** (defined generally as those born 1946 to 1954) were very much affected by the Vietnam War, while the

"trailing edge" boomers (born 1955 to 1964) were, due to their younger ages during that period, less embroiled in antiwar causes. These younger baby boomers, for example, entered college after both the military draft and the war had ended. **Leading edge boomers** can all tell you where they were when John F. Kennedy was shot in 1963; the very youngest boomers were not yet born. In short, even within this group, which is widely discussed as an identified cohort, there are notable differences in the historic experiences of the oldest and youngest members. Boomers, like many other social groups, demonstrate considerable variation among members (MetLife Mature Market Institute, 2010).

An extensive discussion of this distinction is beyond the scope of this chapter. Suffice it to note that much of the demographic, sociological, and economic research on the baby boomers segments the baby boomers in order to better understand their varying experiences, interests, values, and behaviors. For example, Easterlin, Schaeffer, and Macunovich (1993) were interested in the economic fate of baby boomers, comparing them to their parents with respect to income, wealth, and family circumstances over the life course. While their general (and highly simplified here) finding is that baby boomers are doing better economically than their parents were at the same stage of their lives, they found notable variation within the boomer cohort. **Trailing edge boomers** have less advantage than leading edge boomers on several measures of economic well-being, including home ownership and income (Easterlin et al., 1993). This finding can be interpreted in light of Easterlin's cohort size theory, described in Chapter 2, which posits that life chances are better for members of smaller cohorts. The leading edge boomers immediately followed, and perhaps shared life chances with, the relatively small Veterans generation. Trailing edge boomers joined the largest cohort in our history, and thus would have faced the disadvantages suggested by Easterlin's hypothesis: greater competition and more obstacles in achieving success.

These differences between leading and trailing edge baby boomers also point us to another important caveat before we begin describing baby boomers in more detail. Within this cohort, there is significant variability by race, ethnicity, social class, gender, and region of residence, among other factors. This variability warrants a reminder about the dangers of overgeneralization. Throughout this book we have attended to some of these sources of difference in the experience of aging, and we do so again here. You know that all older people are not alike; neither are all baby boomers alike. In fact, Hudson (2009) identifies the high degree of within-cohort (or intracohort) variability as one of many challenges researchers, marketers, and policy makers face in understanding the impact of this large group. We do not know, according to Hudson, how singularly this group will behave in later life, nor whether their generational identity will be significant in the future. We saw in Chapter 9 that the potential voting power of older people has not been harnessed into an age-based coalition, partly because of the identities other than age that divide individuals when they cast their votes. This reminder about the differences among members of the baby boom cohort is worthwhile as we begin to explore their distinctive cohort-based characteristics.

Characteristics of the Baby Boomer Cohort

The purpose of describing baby boomers on the cusp of later life is to show how they are different from older generations before them and to understand something about the unique aspects of the aging experience for this cohort. We also want to reinforce that your experience of aging will differ from that of your parents and grandparents in ways that we may not be able to predict. Each generation is distinctive because of what its members bring with them to this phase of life, such as their access to health advances, and their level of education. We can observe this information on boomers from historical trends on immunizations and education attainment. But we can also gain insight about the aging baby boomers by looking at projections of the older population. Keep in mind that the oldest baby boomers turned 65 in 2011, and the youngest baby boomers will not turn 65 until 2029, so projections about

EXHIBIT *11.2*

Age of Birth Cohorts in 2010, 2030, and 2040

Birth Cohorts	Age in 2010	Age in 2030	Age in 2040
1956–1965 Younger Boomers	45–54	65–74	75–84
1946–1955 Older Boomers	55–64	75–84	85–94
1936–1945	65–74	85–94	95–104
1926–1935	75–84	95–104	105 and older
1910–1925	85–100	105+	

the older population in the year 2030 are telling the story of baby boomer aging. When we look at projections that take us out to the year 2040 and 2050, we are still talking about surviving baby boomers in the older age ranges, but we are also including new cohorts of older people from the post–baby boomer era. As you can see in Exhibit 11.2, in 2040, baby boomers will all be in the 75 and older age category. By 2050, all baby boomers will be 85 and older. At that point, the older population (those 65 and older) will be made up primarily of post-boomer cohorts.

So, how do we make sense of these historical trends and projections? We can do so with the concept of cohort flow and its intersection with social change, of course. Our concern with the topic of baby boomers is partly based in the importance of cohort flow in general. But there is no doubt that the sheer size of the baby boom cohort magnifies its impact on the meaning, experiences, and social structures related to aging. To know what aging will be like in the future, it makes sense to see what the new, boomer-driven landscape of aging looks like and the kinds of changes the baby boomers will leave in their wake.

Predicting the future is a notoriously difficult (and risky) process, especially for those with some allegiance to the rules of science. Given the large number of unknown factors, what can we really say about the future and what the older population will be like in the year 2020 or 2050? It is perhaps easier than it seems because the people who will be part of the over-65 population in those years are already born. We can examine these cohorts and identify ways in which they are similar to and different from current cohorts above the age of 30, 60, or 70. Based on these differences from their predecessors, we can speculate about how boomers may age differently. Let us first examine a few of the differences we can quantify for baby boomers and later speculate about other social changes and cohort experiences likely to make these cohorts very distinct as they age from today's older population.

Education

There are clear cohort differences in educational attainment. During the last century, "formal schooling expanded to dominate childhood and adolescence" (Carlson, 2009, p. 5). As a result, each successive cohort thus far has a higher level of educational attainment than the previous cohorts. Comparing younger cohorts to older cohorts shows that more and more people are completing high school, attending or completing college, or going on to advanced degrees. Between 1940 and 2000, the proportion of people age 25 or older who had completed high school increased from only 24.5% (to 80.4%) (U.S. Census Bureau, n.d.). Between 1960 and 2002 the proportion of high school graduates who were enrolled in college during the year following graduation increased from 45.1% to 65.2% (U.S. Census Bureau, 2005a).

EXHIBIT **11.3**

Percentage of the Population Age 25 Years and Over With a High School Diploma
or More by Race, United States, 1940–2000

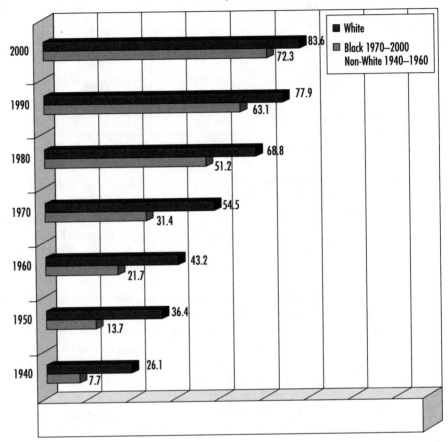

Source: U.S. Census Bureau, n.d.

This overall pattern of increase is consistent for men and for women, and for Whites and Blacks, though there are some interesting variations. By 2000, there was no difference in the proportion of men and women with at least a high school diploma. Exhibit 11.3 shows the increase in education by race (using the two major race categories tracked over this period of time). Both groups show a marked increase in the proportion of adults who have a high school diploma or beyond. The dramatic gap between Blacks and Whites has narrowed considerably since the 1940s and 1950s, reflecting significant social and policy change, but it has not disappeared.

Baby boomers would have been included in the "25 and older" group starting in 1971, at which time the overall proportion of adults with high school or beyond was 52%. By the time the youngest boomers joined the ranks of the 25 and older group, about 75% had achieved that level of education (U.S. Census Bureau, n.d.). As a consequence of this long-term trend toward higher educational attainment, the educational profile of the adult population is shifting, as members of older, less educated cohorts die out and younger, more educated cohorts, including baby boomers, move into later life.

Sharing Lives and Households

Marital status, nonmarital relationships, and living arrangements in later life are the product of a lifetime of opportunities and decisions, some not under the control of the individual.

Will the later-life outcome of these major life choices and events differ markedly for baby boomers? Major social changes have continued to sweep through the institution of the family, mirrored in sometimes dramatic changes in the lives of individuals of different cohorts. An example is marriage. In 1970 about 36% of women ages 20–24 and 11% aged 25–29 had never married; by 2008 the comparable figures for women were 87.3% and 58.8%, indicating both the possibility of delayed marriage (with ramifications for the later timing of other family events) or the increased likelihood of never marrying at all (Saluter, 1996; U.S. Census Bureau, 2008c). Men also experienced dramatic changes; 9% of men 30–34 (leading edge baby boomers) had not married in 1970, compared with 30.3% in 2008. In other words, these trends were starting to occur as baby boomers were moving through marriageable ages. Exhibit 11.4 shows projections of the marital status of the female population over 65 through 2050, assuming that current trends hold (Hobbs & Damon, 1996). Among women, who constitute the majority of the older population (and whose marital futures differ substantially from those of men), we can expect a substantial increase in the percentage divorced, a slight increase in the percentage who remain single, and corresponding declines in the widowed population. The percentage of the female population over age 65 who are expected to be married remains remarkably stable across this time period (Hobbs & Damon, 1996).

These projections represent the current marital status of women 65 and over, not their marital histories. Given the higher levels of divorce among baby boomers, more individuals will approach later life having lived as single persons, perhaps having experienced one or more marriages or long-term relationships along the way. Because being stably married over many decades historically has provided certain advantages in later life, the smaller percentage of adults who will approach old age having experienced a continuous marriage, with its expectations of substantial mutual support and economic security, may have significant implications for issues such as economic security or caregiving. One neglected area is the potential for companionship and social support provided by nonmarital couple relationships with either same- or opposite-sex partners (Kimmel, 1993). Researchers have, until recently, paid attention to whether or not someone is married, but not to other, nonmarital forms of partnering that may be meaningful and may be more openly practiced by future cohorts. Given the cohort experience of the baby boomers, it is likely that a higher proportion of older adults will have lived in such nonmarital relationships in the future.

EXHIBIT *11.4*

Trends in Marital Status for Women 65 and Older: 1980–2050

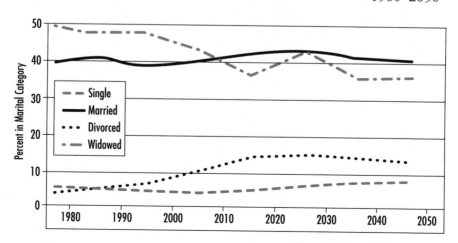

Source: Hobbs and Damon, 1996.

Researchers have recently begun to study one such trend in nonmarital relationships: living apart together, or **LAT**. This term is used to describe a relationship in which the partners define themselves as a couple, and perceive that their close social network defines them as a couple, but each lives in her/his own home (Karlsson & Borrell, 2002; Levin, 2004). According to research based in several European countries, LATs are becoming more common; this new pattern is partly attributable to more flexible norms about marriage that began to change during the youth of baby boomers, allowing nonmarital forms of long-term relationship to emerge. The prevalence of LAT relationships among unmarried, noncohabiting adults in Sweden increased from 6% in 1993 to 12% in 1998 (Levin, 2004). For aging boomer cohorts in the United States, LAT may be an attractive option, especially following divorce or widowhood. There are a host of reasons that people might choose such an arrangement. Some would prefer to cohabit, but have other responsibilities such as family care or jobs in different locations, making living in their own homes more practical. Others choose to live apart while in a committed relationship in order to maintain some degree of an independent lifestyle, or to continue residence in a preferred and familiar household of many years (Levin, 2004). Gender and age are important factors in the choice of a LAT relationship. For the repartnered adults in de Jong's (2004) study, being older at the dissolution of the previous relationship predicted a higher likelihood of entering a LAT relationship; being younger increased the likelihood of remarriage. Karlsson and Borrell suggest that "women rather than men . . . are the driving force behind the choice to live as LAT-partners" (2002, p. 16); women ranked as important having a home of one's own and being able to maintain one's own habits. Men and women equally valued the emotional support they derived from their relationship. The authors conclude that "LAT relationships can offer older [people] a fulfilling intimate relationship, but they can also ensure . . . a significant degree of autonomy, [which is] of particular importance to women" (p. 23). Researchers point out that we do not have appropriate language yet to describe nonmarital, committed relationships among adults. We often use youth-oriented terms such as *dating* or *boyfriend* and then qualify the term to relate it to later life decisions and situations (Karlsson & Borell, 2002). Because baby boomers pioneered cohabitation and may be pioneers in later-life LAT arrangements, it is very likely that we will be learning more—including new language—about the flexible living arrangements becoming more common among older adults in the United States.

Health

Baby boomers have benefited in their lifetimes from an accumulation of public health achievements, including medical advances in the diagnosis and treatment of heart disease and cancer, widespread childhood immunization against infectious disease, and an overall decrease in smoking. Baby boomers have higher life expectancies than cohorts preceding them. Life expectancy at birth has increased from 57.1 in 1929, to 65.9 in 1945, to a projected 78.3 in 2010 (U.S. Census Bureau, 2010c). In Chapter 3 we discussed different measures of life expectancy: at birth, and at a particular age. The trends in life expectancy at birth tell us something about the advantages baby boomers have over earlier cohorts. The biggest gains in life expectancy at birth came from our ability to control infectious diseases and maternal and infant mortality. More recent medical advances have helped to add years of life expectancy at higher ages. Exhibit 11.5 graphs the trends in life expectancy for people ages 65 and 85 between 1900 and 2006. We can see that the greatest gains in additional expected years of life for older people occurred since the 1950s and 60s and that the rate of increase is beginning to slow, especially for people 85 and above.

Perhaps even more important than additional years of life expectancy is the question of how those years will be spent. New measures referring to **healthy life expectancy**, active life expectancy, and disability-free life expectancy are helping us to set new goals for

EXHIBIT *11.5*

Life Expectancy at Ages 65 and 85, by Sex, Selected Years 1900–2006

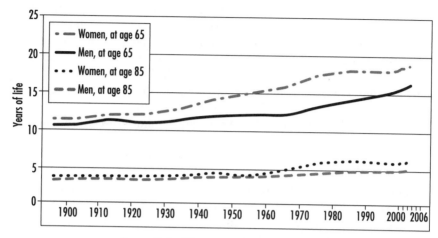

Source: Federal Interagency Forum on Aging-Related Statistics, 2008.

EXHIBIT *11.6*

Percentage of the Population Age 65 and Over Who Are Obese, by Sex and Age Group, Selected Years 1988–2008

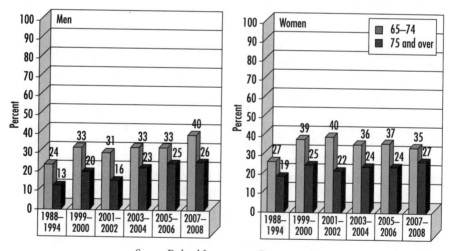

Source: Federal Interagency Forum on Aging-Related Statistics, 2008.

improvements in the health of our aging population. Instead of simply living longer, the goal is to live longer in good health. Whether the additional years of life enjoyed by aging baby boomers (and the cohorts that follow) will be healthy years depends on a number of factors. One of the greatest public health concerns in the United States today is obesity, which is on the rise for people of all ages. The rates of obesity among older people are shown in Exhibit 11.6, which indicates a recent substantial increase in obesity among 65- to 74-year-old men in particular.

The consequences of obesity are significant, including increased risk of diabetes, heart disease, mobility limitations, and other chronic conditions. Rising prevalence of obesity, combined with the fact that we have not seen significant increases in levels of regular physical activity, will have a negative impact on healthy life expectancy; there is some concern that it will also have a long-range effect on life expectancy itself for upcoming generations (Olshansky et al. 2005). A recent study that compared the negative effects of obesity to the positive effects of decreased smoking on the health of our population concluded that unchecked increases in obesity will outweigh the health gains of lower rates of smoking: "Failure to address continued increases in obesity could result in an erosion of the pattern of steady gains in health observed since early in the 20th century" (Stewart, Cutler, & Rosen, 2009, p. 2252). For baby boomers, the rise in obesity and lack of improvement in activity levels could reduce healthy life expectancy relative to earlier cohorts, even if overall life expectancy is not affected.

Adding to the mixed message about the health status of aging baby boomers is the research on substance abuse and illicit drug use among this cohort, all pointing to an increasing public health problem stretching into later life. A recent national report on illicit drug use predicts that the number of persons 50 and older needing treatment for substance abuse will double very quickly—by 2020 (Substance Abuse and Mental Health Services Administration [SAMHSA], 2009). Not only are the numbers of mature/older adults seeking treatment likely to increase, patterns of abuse are different. The proportion of overall admissions for treatment of alcohol abuse declined from 84.6% in 1992 to 59.9% in 2008; admissions for primary heroin abuse more than doubled during this time period, and the proportion of admissions involving cocaine abuse (not necessarily as the primary substance of abuse) increased from 8.6% to 26.8% (SAMHSA, 2010). Duncan, Nicholson, White, Burr, and Bonaguro (2010) also analyzed these changing patterns of drug abuse in the older adult population, calling for more research on the growing varieties of abuse within the older population. This is especially critical because the national drug use and treatment data sets categorize people 50 and above as "older adults," thereby including significant numbers of baby boomers in their data. These authors note that we cannot assume "that adults aged 50 to 54 consume the same drugs at the same rates, with the same consequences as . . . [prior older age groups]. We cannot assume homogeneity of use and effectiveness of treatments" (Duncan et al., 2010, p. 246). Echoing the importance of cohort and age differences, the 2009 SAMHSA report suggests that recent differences in substance use across age groups may reflect cohort differences. The current 65 and older cohort, comprised of non–baby boomers, was significantly less likely to have any illicit drug use than the other age groups in the study. Not only do types of substance abuse differ, but also rates of abuse. From 2006 to 2008, the percentage who used illicit drugs was 1.2% among those 65 and older, compared to 9.3% for baby boomers age 50 to 54 (SAMHSA, 2009). Age and cohort patterns are beginning to converge: the large size of the baby boomer cohort, their high rates of lifetime drug use, and the increased possibility that older adults will have complex interactions between illicit drugs, prescription, and over-the-counter medications are creating an unprecedented demand for substance abuse prevention and treatment aimed at older adults. The convergence of these patterns also suggests that training for medical personnel, including pharmacists, should include drug interactions.

Diversity

One final area of population projection that bears careful examination is the growing racial/ethnic diversity within the older population in the United States. As the baby boomers enter old age, they will be part of an aging population that is more diverse than before. In 1990, non-Hispanic Whites made up 86.7% of the older population in the United States (Hobbs & Damon, 1996). By 2010, that proportion decreased to 80%. However, the most dramatic increase in diversity is yet to come. As we saw in Exhibit 3.10, the proportion of the older population that is non-Hispanic White will decrease to 58.5% by 2050.

The issue of increasing diversity is an interesting illustration of population dynamics at work. While we are focusing in this chapter on the aging of the baby boomers, the increasing diversity in the older population is not attributable simply to the aging of the baby boom. Our more diverse population is largely explained by patterns of immigration. The United States saw an increase in migration, primarily from Asia and Latin America, starting in the 1970s, as baby boomers were coming of age. Many of these new immigrants were young adults, joining the ranks of the native-born baby boomers (Mutchler & Burr, 2009). Thus, these immigrants also migrated into, and augmented the size and diversity of, the baby boom cohorts, as well as those that follow.

Exhibit 11.7 shows the growth in the proportion *of each racial and ethnic group* that is 65 and older. This graph tells us something different from Exhibit 3.10, which displayed the proportion *of the older population* who belong to different racial and ethnic groups. Looking

EXHIBIT *11.7*

Percentage of the Population Age 65 and Over by Race and Hispanic Origin for the United States: 2010, 2030, and 2050

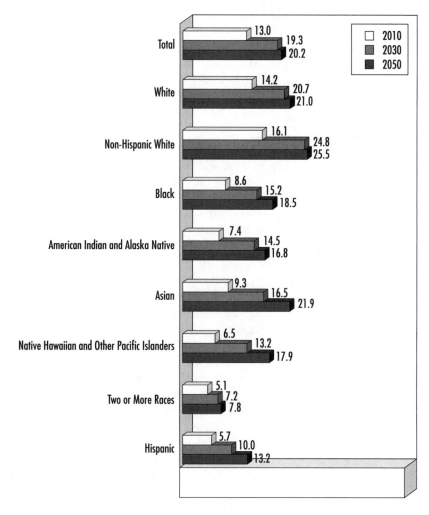

carefully at the numbers in the chart, we can see that in 2010, the Hispanic population in the United States is not very old; only 5.7% are 65 and older. But by 2050, 13% of Hispanics will be 65 and older. As the Hispanic population ages over the next 4 decades, they will contribute proportionally more to the composition of the older population. Non-Hispanic Whites, who are already an old group (14.2% of them were 65 and over in 2010), will be joined in the 65 and older category by younger counterparts from other racial and ethnic groups. Thus, the diversity within the older population will increase dramatically due to immigration flows and the aging of racial and ethnic groups. In short, when the baby boomers reach their later years, their racial and ethnic composition will gradually come to reflect the diverse faces we see today among children and younger adults.

Summary of Demographic and Health Characteristics

Baby boomers are entering old age with higher education, higher life expectancy, greater ethnic and racial diversity, and more diverse family lives than preceding generations of older people. Their health status is a mixed picture; they have lower rates of mortality for most major causes of death, but obesity is an increasing problem. There has been no significant change between 1997 and 2008 in the proportion of people age 45 or older who report regular physical activity (Federal Interagency Forum on Aging-Related Statistics, 2010). All of these factors will come into play as baby boomers move into the later stages of life. We will see the effects of this generation on the opportunities and meanings associated with aging because people are living longer and some of those extra years are healthy years. We will also see effects of this group on major social policies such as Social Security, Medicare, and from the new Affordable Care Act. The size of the cohort commands attention, but the diversity among the baby boomers must always be part of our discussions of the impact of this group. With all due caution about the dangers of overgeneralization in mind, let us consider some of the characteristics of the baby boomers as a generation and how those shared characteristics are changing aging.

Generational Characteristics

If you think back to Chapter 1, you will notice that *cohort* and *generation* are not the same thing, even though the terms are often used interchangeably. Up to this point, we have been discussing the baby boom cohort, referring to one thing that this group has in common: they were born during the same general time period. Generation is a much more complex concept, and it is used in many different ways. It is sometimes used to refer to a birth cohort, to describe kinship lineage (e.g., to designate how many family generations separate one person from an ancestor or offspring), to designate a life stage (such as "the older generation"), or to reference a historical period ("the Great Depression generation") (Kertzer, 1983). To further complicate matters, some of these meanings of the term *generation* intersect. For example, being part of a particular birth cohort is related to current age, life stage, and to the historical period in which the group members grew up. Mannheim's (1952b) conceptualization of cohort captures all of these dimensions. In Chapter 1, we summarized Mannheim's description of *generation* as a category of people born within a specific historical era and characterized by common world views that distinguish them from other generations. These shared world views develop from being exposed to the same kinds of experiences and historical events in a common social and political environment, and a resulting shared consciousness with age peers. According to Mannheim then, belonging to a generation is a combination of a state of mind, age grouping, and shared history, all contributing to **generational characteristics**.

Taking a demographic perspective, Carlson (2009) argues that cohort size and normative characteristics, such as typical family structure, average household size, and where people lived as children, all contribute to the distinctive character of each cohort. These demographic factors intersect with the economic and political climate, major historical events, and societal shifts in norms and values to shape the identity of a generation. Each demographically unique generation reacts to their social and historical time; sharing these experiences gives each generation a unique "character," regardless of whether they share a strong collective identity. Some of the defining aspects of life for baby boomers have included economic prosperity, participation in or opposition to the Vietnam War, the political Watergate scandal, growth of suburbia, increasing involvement in dual income households, and national and international human rights movements (Lancaster, 2004).

Certainly the popular literature on generations refers to the values, attitudes, behaviors, and "character" shared by a birth cohort (e.g., Gen Xers, Boomers, or Millennials). There is no agreement about the birth years that divide the population into generations, or what to call them, but one common categorization of today's adult population is into these four generations: Veterans or Traditionalists, born between about 1925 and 1945; Baby Boomers, born between 1946 and 1964; Generation X (1965 to 1980); and Generation Y, Nexters, or the Millennials, born after 1980. There are numerous variations on these labels and the years used to bound them. You might have also heard the terms in the media including Silent Generation, Lost Generation, and Greatest Generation.

The often-used Veterans/Boomers/Gen X/Millennials categorizations were used in research done by the Society for Human Resource Management (SHRM) and are the foundations for much of their writing and consulting focus on "generations in the workplace." The SHRM survey, completed by a random sample of human resource professionals, covered a host of questions about generational characteristics of workers (Burke, 2004). According to the study, some of the traits most frequently attributed to baby boomers in the workplace include the willingness to give maximum effort, being results-driven, and planning to stay with the organization long-term. A trait that was *not* thought to be characteristic of baby boomers, however, was respect for organizational hierarchy. The most common attributes of the Millennials (your generation, perhaps) included technologically savvy, learning quickly, and favorable views of workplace informality (Burke, 2004). Beyond the SHRM, the baby boom generation has been described as competitive, work-centric, independent, poor at waiting for gratification and rewards, and comfortable with confrontation. Millennials have been described as seeking a balance between work and family, team-oriented, needing information, and craving feedback (Cox, 2004).

But Are They Happy?

How the life experiences, demographic realities, and values of a generation come together to create a generational mood is an interesting question. In spite of the numeric power of the baby boomer cohort, and its well-documented impact on social institutions and norms, some are suggesting that they are not very happy or optimistic. In a 2005 study, boomers (who were then age 41 to 59) were less likely than people 60 and older to say that their generation, compared to their parent's or children's generation, will enjoy old age the most (Pew Research Center, 2005). Boomers were pessimistic about their own financial futures and the general economic outlook. Of three age groups (adults aged 18 to 42; baby boomers 43 to 62; adults 63 and above), baby boomers were much more likely to say that it is harder to get ahead now compared to 10 years ago and that it is more difficult to maintain their current standard of living compared to 5 years ago. They were also more likely to say that they are financially worse off than their parents at the same age (Cohn, 2008). In contrast, members of the millennial generation, born after 1980, express confidence about their futures. In spite of the difficult economy, 90% of these young adults say that they currently have enough money or will eventually be able to fulfill their financial goals (Pew Research Center, 2010). Why would the boomers be so negative, especially because we know from research cited previously that they are generally doing better financially than their parents were at the same age? Yang (2008), who found that baby boomers had lower levels of happiness than other cohorts, suggested that the size of their cohort meant that boomers faced greater competition for jobs and schooling, supporting Easterlin's hypothesis that this competition created stress and insecurity about the future.

Avoiding Stereotypes

Of course, as we have discussed throughout this book, it is important to exercise great caution in applying labels or ascribing attributes to everyone in a particular generation or age group. Overgeneralization can lead to stereotyping members of a generation, and, by extension, individuals within that age group. Many comparisons of generations today make reference to how they are different with respect to the use of technology and social media. While Gen X and the Millennials are often described as highly tech savvy, that attribute is one that is quite unlikely to be ascribed to Boomers and Veterans (Burke, 2004). However, you might be surprised to learn that 40% of American adults age 50 and over are very or extremely comfortable using the Internet, and among those who use the Internet, more than one-third (37%) use social media, especially Facebook (AARP, 2010). The essay on e-elders earlier in this book pointed out that there has been a 900% growth in Facebook participation for the 50 and older group. In addition, the proportion of video game players who are baby boomers is about equal to their percentage in the overall population, and women over 40 are the fastest growing gamer population (Pearce, 2008).

In some ways, the use of technology by baby boomers is one more example of their ability to challenge old expectations and attitudes about aging. It is likely that they will take a different attitude into later life that is more welcoming toward use of technology to assist them in their daily lives and pursuits. While not all baby boomers are alike, as a group, they have brought about shifts in society throughout their lives. Social institutions were altered because of them at nearly every stage of their lives. They grew up during, and were part of, powerful social changes: civil rights, rapid increase in women's labor participation, war protests, higher educational attainment, and youth-oriented political activism. Given their size, the social times during which they grew up, and the changes they have brought with them, it is not surprising that the baby boomers are changing the landscape of aging as well.

New Landscapes of Aging

It is certainly clear by now that the aging of baby boomers is receiving a lot of attention, as the marketplace, service delivery network, and political system try to anticipate the needs and preferences of this group of unprecedented size and purchasing power. Millions of Web sites are offering baby boomer nostalgia, travel packages, educational opportunities, financial planning services, or seeking to rouse political support for one side of an issue or another. More and more silver industries will arise to provide products and services targeted to this group. In short, businesses and entrepreneurs have noticed, and are making efforts to respond to, the needs of this large group. Boomers will continue to have far-reaching impacts on all aspects of society as they move into—and through—the span of later life. In the next sections we discuss some of the significant changes in the world of aging that have already begun. These changes can all be understood as significant shifts in the age-based organization of society. The number of stages in our life course is expanding, and the strict segregation of education, work, and leisure into narrow age ranges is gradually disappearing.

The Third Age: A New Phase of the Life Course

In the discussion of the life course in Chapter 4, we described the emergence of a new stage: the **third age**. Laslett (1991) first described this new period of life, in which people—although chronologically older—are healthy and independent, free of the obligations of child-rearing and employment. In short, this is the postretirement span, characterized today (and probably for the baby boomers) as one of health, activity, and engagement. It is the image of later life to which our culture directs us to aspire—healthy, busy, and independent (Ekerdt, 1986). The third age ends when the fourth age—characterized by declining health and loss of independence—begins. The emergence of this new life phase was driven by demographic and ideological changes: longer life, better health, some measure of financial security, a more positive attitude about aging, and more flexible attitudes about meaningful use of time. It is part of rethinking and elaborating what was once an undifferentiated span of later life to reflect new realities. While Laslett argued that the third age is a time of personal fulfillment because people can leave the workforce and have opportunities for leisure, other scholars suggest that continuing to work can be a meaningful option in the third age (James & Wink, 2006). Defining, measuring, understanding, and analyzing the experiences of the third age are setting a new agenda for gerontology research. Baby boomers are already entering this phase of healthy postretirement. But, as you can imagine, marking the beginning and end of the third age remains quite a challenge. Should we consider physical health, functional independence, retirement status, age, or some combination of these or other characteristics to identify the start and end of the third age? While such questions are essential to research on this topic, for our purposes, it is important to understand that the concept of a new phase of life—the third age—is part of the new terrain and language of aging. For example, you will see later in this chapter that higher education is undertaking a national initiative to "reinvest in the third age," by bringing older learners into the classroom, including the electronic classroom.

One of the important dimensions of the third age, as it has been defined so far, is the capacity for an individual to make continued contributions to the community, either through paid work, volunteering, or other forms of civic engagement. Time and good health (personal resources), along with opportunities to contribute to society, are the fundamental requirements for another widely discussed emergent concept in gerontology: **productive aging**.

Productive Aging: Expanded Opportunities, Altered Expectations

For people who survive to age 65, life expectancy is age 83 and rising. Because many of those years are expected to be healthy, active years, there is a growing concern about what people can, should, and will do after they retire from full-time paid employment. This concern has become particularly acute as the large cohorts of the baby boom expand the percentage of our overall population in the 65 and older years of life. Attitudes regarding employment and retirement may be critical to deciding how individuals allocate this time. As we discussed in Chapter 6, the values of maintaining activity in retirement dominate U.S. cultural views of what constitutes a good and productive later life (Ekerdt, 1986). One way of addressing the devaluation of nonworking status (i.e., being retired) is to rethink and broaden our definitions of work and productivity. Doing so permits us to create a variety of options for continued, meaningful activity that builds a broader societal benefit than undertaking a hobby, for example.

On a macro-social level, one of the great dilemmas facing developed and aging societies is the large and growing amount of unstructured time provided by retirement. Various scholars and aging advocacy groups have questioned whether it is beneficial to enable individuals to have this time without expectations for utilizing at least some of it for the social good. The growth of leisure industries, intended to provide enjoyable activities for those able to retire in good financial and physical health, does not confer the social status, build the social integration, or support the self-esteem we derive from more work-like activities, like employment and volunteering. Nor does it address the pressing social problems of most societies. As baby boomers enter the third age in record numbers, the availability of meaningful opportunities for this postretirement period has become a pressing issue. Many experts view this population as an essential "untapped resource" (Freedman, 2002).

Researchers, policy makers, community leaders, and advocates are now considering how to tap the productive potential of baby boomers. *Productive aging* refers to both a social movement in which the potential for older people to contribute to society increases and to a particular set of activities undertaken by older adults. According to Caro, Bass, and Chen (1993), "productive aging is any activity by an older individual that produces goods or services, or develops the capacity to produce them, whether they are to be paid for or not" (p.6). This definition includes paid and unpaid work, including volunteer and familial work, but excludes activities undertaken primarily for personal enrichment or growth. The productive aging approach also identifies existing structural barriers to full use of the productive capacity of older people. Factors such as ageism and age-based eligibility rules may foster inactivity for individuals who otherwise could be more productive (Caro et al., 1993).

In Chapter 6, we discussed the growing number of options for continued employment in later life. It is also important to point out that older persons already contribute vast numbers of hours in volunteer work for their families and communities, work that gains little recognition in society (Commonwealth Fund, 1993). Examining unpaid activities including family caregiving, informal volunteer activities, and formal volunteer work, one estimate suggests that *per person* voluntary efforts by persons 55 and older would (if paid) be valued at $2,700 per year (Johnson & Schaner, 2005). About 70% of people 55 and older did some form of volunteer work; those who were not employed volunteered for more hours (Zedlewski & Schaner, 2006). Surveys show that many are interested in contributing more (Commonwealth Fund, 1993).

In coming decades society is likely to depend more on these contributions as the size of the working age population decreases and the retirement-age population grows. Productive aging is a movement that will continue to expand meaningful opportunities for older people and, at the same time, will expand the numbers of people available to the paid and unpaid labor markets. In doing so, this productive effort may counteract ageist stereotypes that have prevented older people from remaining connected and contributing as members of their communities. Whether productive aging is a positive statement about the value of older adults or an effective way of mobilizing a bigger labor pool, or both, "we can ill afford to squander the resources of age" (Achenbaum, 2009, p. 58).

Civic Engagement: Productive Aging for the Public Good

Productive aging is a broad concept, expanding meaningful options for older people to contribute more to society at many different levels, including paid and unpaid (volunteer) activities. Civic engagement is a particular subset of productive aging. It also includes paid and unpaid options but is focused on a specific range of activities and behaviors, those that contribute to community well-being and public affairs. Some research has focused on three major categories of civic engagement, each with several indicators: (1) civic activity, including volunteering for a nonelectoral organization, community problem solving, and participation in fundraising; (2) electoral activity, including regular voting, persuading others, volunteering for political organization; and (3) political voice, including contacting public officials, canvassing, or signing petitions (Lopez et al., 2006). While this list is helpful in specifying the kind of work that can be considered civic engagement, the activities listed are not equivalent in intensity or involvement; signing a petition is not the same as volunteering in a soup kitchen, for example. Chapter 9 pointed out that older adults have traditionally been involved with electoral activity through voting; there are mixed results to date on other forms of civic engagement. Advocates suggest that baby boomers in particular could give back more actively than they have done within their communities, through broadening their involvement in civic engagement activities particularly after retirement.

There is widespread acknowledgement within gerontology that we still do not have a precise and shared definition of civic engagement for older people. A related concern is that civic engagement is too often simply equated with volunteering (Kaskie, Imhof, Cavanaugh, & Culp, 2008). Even though there are different definitions of civic engagement—sharing only the idea that the activity is connected to benefits for the larger public—this concept has reached new heights of attention in recent years, with particular attention given to the potential impact that baby boomers can have in improving their communities.

A pioneering report on civic engagement identified the mismatch among the need for continued contributions by older people, the lack of structured opportunities for such contributions, the promise that boomers hold (given their numbers, higher levels of education, and healthier longer lives compared to previous generations of aging adults), and boomers' track record to date for lower involvement than their parents' generation in all types of civic engagement (Center for Health Communication, Harvard School of Public Health, 2004). To correct this imbalance, new cohort-based norms about volunteering must emerge, and these opportunities will need to be incorporated into individual planning for retirement. In addition, national and local community organizations have a role in creating a wide range of meaningful opportunities, as well as in recruiting and retaining boomer volunteers.

While there is considerable momentum in the civic engagement movement, it does have critics. For example, Martinson and Minkler (2006) point out that the push for civic engagement coincides with significant decreases in government funding for the very kinds of community organizations in which older adults would be encouraged to volunteer. They and others cite the coincidence between "the desperate economic need to fill gaps in services and systems now vacated or severely underfunded by government" (Martinson & Minkler, 2006, p. 320). Other criticisms of civic engagement point to the fact that not every aging baby boomer will have the health, education, or inclination to participate; if civic engagement becomes an expectation, individuals who do not participate may be marginalized.

While civic engagement may not be a feasible or desirable option for all aging baby boomers, it does seem to be a logical fit between societal needs—for a renewed sense of connection and community, not just getting the work done—and the right of aging baby boomers to have meaningful opportunities for continued engagement in the life of their society. In so doing, it also reframes later life away from older ideas of solitude and leisure to a more socially engaged phase; this reframing reflects broader societal values that may, in turn, reduce ageism.

Employment and Productive Aging

Many boomers want or need to continue working past the typical retirement ages. Seventy percent say they want to continue working on some basis after retirement (AARP, 2003). Robert Kahn (1994) has suggested a rethinking of how we define and organize work. He concurs that the concept of productive aging should be expanded to include activities such as family and household duties and volunteerism but that options for continued employment should be part of the broadened set of options. Given the preferences many baby boomers have for part-time jobs, Kahn also suggests that we re-engineer work time into 4-hour work modules that can be flexibly combined into full- or part-time options. This more flexible approach would avoid a false dichotomy between the 35- to 40-hour full-time status and any other type of schedule (i.e., part-time/retired) that now seems to be built into the thinking of many employers. It is this type of innovative thinking that may give us clues to how productive engagement for older adults may evolve into an entirely new, socially constructed pattern in the future where work, education, and leisure are variably combined through time, much like Riley's (1994) rethinking of the age-integrated life course discussed in Chapter 4.

Workplace adaptations—flexible policies and practices designed to retain older workers and support employed caregivers—are part of the restructuring of the age-segregated life course. Some industries will lose up to 30% of their work force in the next 10 years due to retirements. While retirement has been seen as a positive option for workers and their employers, changing demographics and the new realities of aging suggest that the workplace will be impoverished by the loss of older workers. Fitting the workplace to the needs, preferences, and contributory value of older workers is essential for a nation on the brink of unprecedented numbers of older workers. The workplace, in general, has not been well-positioned to value, retain, and accommodate aging workers. Aging baby boomers are heightening the awareness of employers and policy makers to the necessity of such accommodations. Businesses are beginning to develop strategies to recruit and retain older workers, as we discussed in Chapter 6. These strategies include bridge jobs and more work structure options such as flex jobs and phased retirement (Rix, 2009). Management practices are also being adapted to the retention of the aging workforce, including age diversity training, succession planning, and talking with employees about their retirement plans (Piktialis, 2009).

For the millions of employed baby boomers who are also caregivers, conflicts between caregiving and paid work often require individual adjustments in the workplace, including taking time off, reducing work hours, and sometimes giving up work entirely (Gonyea, 2009). In order to reduce the burden of such pressures for employees to individually adapt their work lives to the demands of caregiving, some employers offer flexible work options and assistance programs, which provide information, referral, and planning support. Because we will increasingly require their involvement in the labor force, addressing the needs of employed caregivers and the workplace needs and desires of aging baby boomers is essential.

Encore Careers

Building on some of the same trends that underlie productive engagement, societal need for the contributions of aging baby boomers, workplace adaptations, and civic engagement, the concept of **encore careers** has recently emerged. The term describes workforce re-entry into jobs that combine continued income with a desire to contribute in a meaningful way. Freedman and Segal (2008) describe encore careers as "a livelihood and a lifestyle . . . for people who have found a way to do work that matters in the second half of life, work that they want to do and that society needs doing" (p. 4). Based on a set of questions about their current employment, about 9% of the respondents in a recent survey of people age 44 to 70 were considered to be in encore careers; the majority of these respondents worked in education, health care, government, and other nonprofit organizations. Another 45% expressed interest in working during retirement and in pursuing encore careers (Hart Research Associates, 2008). As with civic engagement opportunities, expanding the option for encore careers will take a combination of altered expectations, individual planning, and workplace flexibility in policies and practices. Whether encore careers will become more common as more baby boomers enter retirement remains to be seen. But this option is an interesting synergy of several trends—including the burgeoning number of experienced baby boomers who might seek meaningful and flexible employment after retirement. Encore careers are one more example of transformation of the nature and meaning of work across the life course.

Workforce Needs for an Aging Society

In addition to the need for the workplace to adapt to aging workers, aging baby boomers pose an additional workforce challenge: the need to build a workforce that will be prepared to meet the needs of the growing number of older people. In particular, the health and long-term care systems require significant expansion in personnel. Comparing projections of the aging population with the current status of the health care workforce clarifies the upcoming shortage. For example, by 2020 we will have only about one-third of the number of geriatric social workers that we will need (Institute of Medicine, 2008), and the number of physicians certified in geriatric medicine is currently declining, rather than increasing to meet this need (Harahan & Stone, 2009). There is an especially acute shortage in the direct care workforce, those trained to work with older people to provide personal care and assistance that is nonmedical. This mismatch between growth of the older population and current status of the health care workforce creates a compelling case for retooling: enhancing the geriatric skills of the overall health workforce; stronger recruitment and retention for direct care workers; and improving the links among good training, good care, and financial rewards (Institute of Medicine, 2008).

Lifelong Learning

As discussed elsewhere in this book, there is a growing trend toward education beyond traditional ages, sometimes referred to as adult education, continuing education, or **lifelong learning** (an increasingly common phrase). Data have often reflected the out-of-date expectation that little additional education occurs beyond approximately age 25. Educational institutions were clearly age-segregated in the past, enrolling children and young adults. Since the 1970s, however, enrollments have grown dramatically, with more mature students, including those returning to school after many years of involvement in work, family, or both. Baby boomers are likely to expand these enrollments even further. Increases in adult education rates for all ages continued during the 1990s, but the trends were strongest in older adults (Hamil-Luker & Uhlenberg, 2002). In 2004 to 2005, 23% of adults over 65, 41% of those 51 to 65, and 48% of those 41 to 50 had been enrolled in some sort of formal course in the prior 12 months (U.S. Census Bureau, 2010d).

The increasing involvement of older adults in formal education portends a gradual transition of education to an age-integrated, rather than age-segregated, social institution (Riley & Riley 1994), a transition that the education-oriented baby boomers will help to bring about. The very phrase *lifelong learning* speaks volumes about the integration of education across the life course. A variety of lifelong learning opportunities have emerged over the past 2 decades. Elderhostel (now called Exploritas) and the Institute for Learning in Retirement may be familiar names to you, but the opportunities for lifelong learning take many forms. They can be vocationally oriented programs or focused primarily on intellectual stimulation and fellowship; age-segregated or intergenerational; peer-led or based on a teacher-led continuing education approach (Manheimer, 2009, p. 101).

Higher education institutions are developing strategies to meet the needs and desires of aging baby boomers. Colleges and universities face the challenge that the traditional college-age population will decline for some time; at the same time, baby boomers are seeking to retool for the ever-changing job market and to expand their intellectual horizons. For higher education, baby boomers are an attractive new market; for baby boomers, higher education options that are designed with their needs, preferences, and learning styles in mind can be an attractive and meaningful product. A 2-year national study of higher education and older adults explored the factors that draw older people into higher education, as well as the barriers (e.g., cultural barriers and structural factors like scheduling and programs offered) that keep them away. This project also highlighted the role that higher education can play in mobilizing the potential of the baby boom generation to meet labor force needs. Quite appropriately, one of the reports from this project noted that older adults and the higher education system are simultaneously "discovering ways to reinvest in the third age" (Lakin, Mullane, & Robinson, 2007, p. 24).

Whatever form lifelong learning may take, "the cohort reaching retirement age in the next twenty years will regard opportunities for continued learning as not a privilege but a given, a natural and valued part of the new retirement lifestyle" (Manheimer, 2009, p. 100). If education continues to become more integrated throughout adulthood, we may find it less relevant to distinguish among students of traditional ages and those augmenting their education in other stages of life—being a student may become an ageless" role, and the linear progression from education to work to retirement may become increasingly irrelevant.

Summary

The flow of cohorts or generations through the age structure of society is one significant aspect of social change. The baby boomers, with their unprecedented size, demographic characteristics, and unique generational character, are changing the landscape of aging as they move into the later stages of life. To be sure, it is not only the aging of the baby boomers that is changing aging. Other changes have been taking shape for decades: longer life, health improvements, well-established welfare state policies for income security and health insurance for older adults, historical improvements in educational attainment, an ideological shift to the concepts of successful and productive aging, and widespread challenges to conventional negative stereotypes about growing older. The demographics of the large boomer cohort and smaller succeeding cohorts certainly come into play in the size of the labor market and the viability of programs such as Social Security, which are funded through payroll taxes. But boomers are galvanizing these demographic and social trends and are making their mark on the stages of later life. The tripartitioned life course in which education, work, and leisure are segregated into narrow age ranges no longer fits as well as it once did. Baby boomers are entering later life marked by a new life stage—the third age. They are facing new opportunities for lifelong learning; unique work options including bridge jobs, flex jobs, and encore careers; and higher expectations for their continued contributions to society.

This chapter has described some of these changes that are already taking place in the expanding life course. However, the extent of these changes, and their impact on future generations of older people, are yet to be determined. If employment policies do not change to dramatically increase older adults' involvement in paid jobs, societies must ask themselves how they can both integrate those individuals into the society and effectively harness the skills, experience, and energy to improve their communities and nations. Will the civic engagement movement be successful in encouraging norms of and opportunities for volunteerism so that healthy and willing retirees give a significant portion of their time to fighting poverty, illiteracy, teen pregnancy, environmental problems, or other social issues? Such norms, and the social policies supporting them, would have implications for income maintenance policies (would such work be paid or unpaid?), the marketplace for leisure activities (would purveyors of cruises and golf equipment suffer?), and family life (would there be less support available from older to younger generations?). If civic engagement and encore careers become an established part of the third age of life, will these opportunities be equally available to all baby boomers who choose to pursue them? Or will participation in such activities be dictated by patterns of education, race, ethnicity, and social class, thus reinforcing existing inequalities?

In summary, the United States is in the midst of dramatic social change as a new phase of the life course, the third age, and a more age-integrated life course take shape. The baby boomers are responding to the changes that have come before them and are creating new realities of aging as they move through this life stage. What will later life be like in the future as the baby boomers vacate that age stratum and younger cohorts move into it? Are the changes that are taking place in the experiences, expectations, and opportunities of later life for baby boomers going to fit well with the demographic and generational characteristics of the next cohorts of older people? Does the new landscape of aging fit with what you imagine you and your age peers will need and want when you grow older?

Web Wise

Reinventing Aging http://www.hsph.harvard.edu/chc/reinventingaging/
Sponsored by the Harvard School of Public Health and the MetLife Foundation on Retirement and Civic Engagement, this Web site describes the civic engagement initiative and features well-known political and entertainment figures who are encouraging boomers to "Share What You Know." The site includes a long list of volunteer resources and opportunities and links to other sites that provide information about aging, dispel ageist ideas about growing older, and promote civic engagement.

ChangingAging http://www.Changingaging.org
This multifaceted, highly interactive Web site provides links to news stories, conferences, YouTube videos, and articles related to new images of aging and new approaches to providing care for elders. Articles, blogs, and newsfeeds challenge traditional, stereotypical, and negative attitudes about aging. Dr. Bill Thomas, the geriatrician who is the driving force behind the concept of changingaging.org, promotes positive attitudes and alternative approaches to aging. You can learn more about the Eden Alternative and the Green House models for nursing home care, participate in blogs, and link to very current news stories related to positive aging.

Metlife Generational Profiles of Americans Born in the 1900s
http://www.metlife.com/mmi/research/generational-profiles.html
This Web site offers profiles of older, middle, and younger boomers, as well as Gen X and Gen Y (Millennials); includes demographic information about each generation such as racial and ethnic composition; average household expenditures on food, education, entertainment, health care, and apparel; and median household income. Significant historical and social events that took place in the teen years of each generation, and a list of well-known members of each generation are included.

Age and Generations Study
http://www.bc.edu/research/agingandwork/projects/generations.html
The Sloan Center on Aging and Work at Boston College conducted a two-phase study of multigenerational work teams at nine U.S. workplaces. Reports available through this site describe the experiences of different generations in the workplace, the effect of the economic downturn on workers at various life stages, and the impact of workplace flexibility on the employment experience of workers of different generations.

Key Terms

age stratum   generation   lifelong learning
civic engagement   generational characteristics   productive aging
cohort   healthy life expectancy   third age
cohort flow   LAT   trailing edge boomers
encore careers   leading edge boomers   workplace adaptations

Questions for Thought and Discussion

1. Your college or university very likely has a policy that allows older people (usually age 60 and above) to audit classes at no charge. Have you had an over-60 student in any of your classes? What were your reactions? If you have not yet had this experience, how do you imagine you would react?

2. Given how many of them there are, you probably know some aging baby boomers. Do they challenge the stereotypes you may have had about aging? Think of some specific examples of baby boomers that you have read about, seen in the media, or know personally who help to dispel negative myths about aging.

3. What generation do you belong to? What are the characteristics that are typically ascribed to your generation? Do you think that these attributes fit you and your age peers well? Do you have any negative reactions to being classified as a member of a particular generation, such as Gen X or the Millennials?

4. College campuses are increasingly emphasizing service learning for students, in which coursework is supplemented with active engagement with the community in a project that does public good. Does this seem to be the same as civic engagement for older people? Do you think that such expectations are fair, reasonable, and beneficial? How important to you and to your community is your involvement in the public and political life? Should baby boomers be required to participate in civic engagement?

The Dynamics of Aging in Our Future

12

The traditional categorization of the aged population as 65 and older is arbitrary and, at best, now obsolete.

(O'Rand, 2005, p. 109)

The preceding chapters have described the processes of aging and the social contexts that structure and give meaning to aging in society. There are many things we can predict about the large and diverse cohorts of the baby boom. But what will aging be like in the more distant future, as cohorts—including yours—move into later life? Will science fiction predictions of immortality become real? Advances in technology, efforts at health promotion, and changes in our attitudes about aging (among many other unpredictable social changes) will all contribute to a changed experience of aging for you . . . and your children.

As examples of this new world of aging, in recent years a woman in her 60s gave birth to her first child with the assistance of a fertility clinic; the first President George Bush celebrated his 85th birthday in 2009 by skydiving; and former Senator John Glenn of Ohio, the first American to orbit the globe as an astronaut in the early 1960s, returned to space in his late 70s to study the effects of weightlessness on an aging body. These examples, as well as the growing buzz about antiaging medicine, brain health programs, and genetic breakthroughs, push us to consider the rapidly changing world of our aging society. The repercussions of an aging world will be widespread, complicated, and influential in many aspects of everyday social life, as suggested by the title of a 2006 book, *The Futures of Aging*. The authors argue that aging will not simply create a larger and more diverse population of older adults but will also reshape the economy, government and policy, family, and living arrangements for everyone—leading to multiple futures of aging (Vincent, Phillipson, & Downs, 2006).

While the future holds promise for many types of change, our collective attitudes toward later life in the United States today continue to be largely negative, despite the positive reports we get from older people regarding their well-being and satisfaction with life (Abramson & Silverstein, 2004; George, 2010). Older people themselves do not see a picture of their lives that is nearly as negative as our stereotypes portray. Exhibit 12.1 shows selected (the 4 highest, 2 lowest) responses to a national survey of adults age 18 and over regarding the problems faced by older adults. This chart shows the gap between what older adults reported as problematic for themselves (shown by the lightest bars) in contrast to what respondents ages 18–64 and respondents 65 and older believed to be serious problems for older Americans in general (shown by the gray and black bars, respectively). In every case, the lightest bar, which shows the proportion of older people who say they have a particular problem, is considerably shorter than the darker bars (what people believe to be true). This gap clearly shows that both age groups, including survey participants who themselves were over age 65, believed these problems to be much more prevalent among older adults than they really are. The most common serious problems reported by the older survey respondents were not having enough money to live on (21%) and fear of crime (19%). In contrast, 62% of 18–64 year olds and 45% of adults over 65 think that not having enough money is a serious problem for older adults generally; 46% and 44% (respectively) thought fear of crime was a serious problem for people 65 and older (compared to the 19% reported by those 65 and older). Reported experiences of problems by older adults were consistently (and often significantly) lower than what the general population, including older

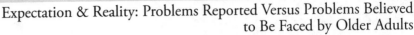

EXHIBIT   *12.1*

Expectation & Reality: Problems Reported Versus Problems Believed
to Be Faced by Older Adults

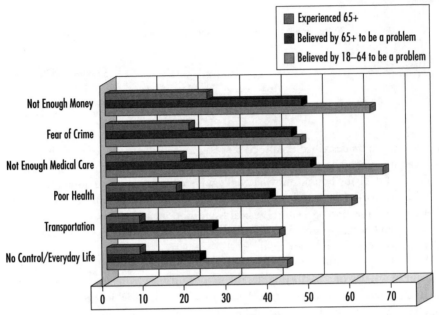

Source: Abramson & Silverstein, 2004.

adults, believes to be the typical experience at this stage of life (Abramson & Silverstein, 2004).
Half of the remaining items were reported by only 6%–8% of older adults as being a serious
problem to them. Older adults, according to this study, do not find later life a stage of endless
problems, worry, and decline. Nonetheless, even older people thought later life was problematic
for their age peers. In short, we tend to think things are much tougher for people over 65 than
older people say they actually are. It will be interesting to see if this gap between today's experiences and expectations will narrow as the older population grows in size and as baby boomers
continue to challenge long-standing stereotypes about older people.

In the remainder of this chapter we summarize some key points about understanding aging
in this dynamic social context, consider how time and place will shape cohorts beyond the baby
boomers, and think about our own aging selves within our social and cohort contexts in this
new millennium.

Aging in a Changing Social World

Rethinking Old Age and the Life Course

Clearly we need to reconsider our ideas about what aging means and move beyond outdated
stereotypes of age and the life course. Some scholars propose that we will shift many of our current assumptions about aging (see Angela O'Rand's quote at the start of this chapter) as more of
us survive to ages approaching or passing on the century mark. Carstensen (2009) suggests that
we (both as individuals and as a society) face a major challenge in figuring out how to utilize the
added decades of life in ways that benefit individuals, groups, and society—a need that will be
much more urgent in the future.

In looking to the future it is important to recall that age and stages of the life course are so-cial constructs, which have been generated, given meaning, and taught to us; each of these con-structs are specific to one historic time and sociocultural context (Cornman & Kingson, 1996). The life stages we take for granted today did not always exist. In addition, not all cultures have distinguished childhood from adulthood or adulthood from later life in the ways that we do today (Aries, 1962; Cole, 1992). Being both socially constructed and culturally-based, the stages of life and the boundaries of later life are very likely to change in the future. Many forces are pushing toward reconsideration of these stages and, in particular, what later life means, when it begins, and the social roles available to older people. The age-shift in the population may itself prompt changing attitudes about aging, turning old age from a negative to a neutral or even a positive stage of life, breaking it into multiple stages, or pushing up its lower age limit.

As we have seen, categorizing people purely on the basis of chronological age presents many problems. The first problem is that 65 and older is not a meaningful category. It is very difficult to see meaningful physical, social, or psychological commonalities between those who have just reached age 65 and those in their later 90s, but both groups are currently referred to simply as *older adults*. In earlier eras, when most people died before what we call middle age today, it was less important to consider differences between 65 year olds and centenarians because there were few survivors of either age. The second problem is that chronological age overall is already be-coming less relevant as a marker of human life and its connected social roles, particularly during adulthood (O'Rand, 2005; Vincent et al., 2006; Zepelin, Sills, & Heath, 1986–1987), suggesting that the life course no longer fits as neatly into discrete stages. The United States adopted age 65 as the policy-based start of later life by setting Social Security retirement benefits and Medicare eligibility at this age. We have already changed the eligibility age for full retirement benefits under Social Security. Although this change was based largely on actuarial calculations, moving such a social marker also raises far-reaching questions about the onset of later life—would it start at retirement, at a particular age, or based on some other criterion? Such policy steps may gradually shift our socially accepted definition of when old age/later life begins.

Just as chronological age is less useful as a marker for old age, current stages of the life course are a poor fit for the realities of later life. As people spend, on average, more time in the later phases of the life course, we find ourselves pulled toward making finer distinctions, creat-ing more stages along the path of the life course. Researchers and practitioners are dissatisfied with the over-generalizations of *old age,* sometimes substituting other, more detailed terms, such as *young old* versus *old old* or distinguishing the *third age* of healthy postretirement years (discussed in Chapter 11) from the *fourth age,* reflecting a period of greater frailty and depen-dence toward the end of life (James, Wink, & Schaie, 2006; Laslett, 1991). The idea that there are different issues and opportunities for 67 year olds and 94 year olds increasingly pushes to-ward reconsideration of our current, limited system of stages for the end of the life course. If we have expanded childhood into several, more specialized stages, could we and should we do the same for later life?

A second important reason to reconsider the life course is related to a consistent theme throughout this book—the extent to which aging is constituted differently for various gender, class, race, or ethnic groups. In future cohorts of aging individuals (including ourselves as we grow older), some individuals and subgroups will still require considerable assistance to meet daily needs. These individuals may experience poor health, inadequate housing or income, lack of informal support from kin, or other disadvantages as a result of the cumulative inequality. Di-versity among older adults is expanding, not contracting; this reinforces our need to avoid gen-eralities about older adults. Older adults are not uniformly poor, unhealthy, or isolated, nor are they uniformly wealthy, socially engaged, "greedy geezers." Older adults exist at both extremes of the advantage/disadvantage continuum and everywhere in between. But advantage and dis-advantage are patterned, suggesting that an overly generalized depiction of the life course will be a poor fit for different gender, race, ethnicity, and social class groups.

Continued differences in life expectancy across racial and ethnic groups, for example, may produce varied ideas about stages of life, such as when one is *middle-aged* or *old.* Higher rates of physical disability result in more early retirement among Blacks; if being retired is a marker of old age, then disadvantaged Blacks may reach that benchmark chronologically sooner than others (Jackson & Gibson, 1985). For working-class individuals, careers begin and plateau at earlier ages than do those of middle-class workers, and families are usually started and grown at earlier ages. As a result, working class individuals may engage in the social roles generally reserved for middle age (e.g., grandparenthood) at earlier chronological ages than those in the middle class, where work and family may be delayed for further education. From these few examples, it is clear that not all groups move through life-course stages in chronological lockstep, even if they are all members of the same birth cohort. To the extent that these differences continue or even expand, today's life course stages may be less useful for researchers or for all of us, as participants in a more age-diverse society.

Another question about the life course can also shed light on possible future changes in the life course. Do major biological and psychological developments correspond meaningfully to today's socially constructed stages of life? Perhaps not! Physical development sometimes outpaces and at other times lags behind the social stages that societies have today. Age at puberty has been declining in the United States, so it occurs long before society encourages marriage or reproduction. Retirement typically occurs at ages when a majority of individuals are quite capable of continued productivity on the job. In sum, what happens to us in biological development and social development are often out of synch.

Taking into account all of these important trends (the relative inadequacy of chronological age as a meaningful marker, the variability in the life course for different groups within U.S. society, and expanding stages within the life course), it is reasonable to speculate that change in age-based structures of our society is inevitable. Consider the area of employment. Currently we have roles temporally structured in the life course in such a way that young adults face the pressures of attempting to succeed in jobs at the same time that they are parenting small children. Yet it is still difficult to defer childbearing beyond the years of advanced education and career building, especially for women. As another example, knowledge is now becoming obsolete more quickly, suggesting that restricting the timing of education to the span of life before employment will become less useful as careers span 50 and older years. Multiple careers, with individuals taking a midlife sabbatical for updating their knowledge in a field or even changing careers entirely, might make more sense. Simultaneous employment with continuing education could also become much more common. We already see evidence of more education taking place beyond the traditional ages of schooling among baby boomers (Hamil-Luker & Uhlenberg, 2002). All of these trends may be indicators of a less age-structured (and more age-integrated) view of lives in the future.

Long-Term Changes in Aging: Beyond the Boomers

While we prepare now for the impact of the aging cohorts of baby boomers, another issue has largely escaped the attention of the public and policy makers. The changes that occur as a result of continuing population aging in many societies, including the United States, are likely to be permanent. That is, the challenges that are now being attached to (or blamed on) baby boomers will become persistent features of many developed societies, barring unexpected demographic changes, such as a dramatic increase in fertility. So the issues and challenges driven today by the impending boomer growth in the ranks of the 65 and older population will not simply fade away after the boomers depart the population. Instead, societies like ours are facing major changes that are likely to require us to permanently adapt major social institutions and policies and modify the daily lives of everyone.

This section deals with some of the altered aspects of social structure, which will continue to reshape how the life course and aging will unfold through additional, coming cohorts—including yours. Multiple changes can influence aging and the life course in the future. First, there are gradual social, economic, or political changes that eventually alter fundamental aspects of social life, including

Contradictions to the stereotypes of aging are all around us.
(Credit: E. J. Hanna)

aging. These might include conservative or liberal political tides, shifts in gender roles, technological or medical innovations, or shifting views of race/ethnicity or of age itself. These trends typically unfold slowly, giving us previews of likely alterations in the social aspects of aging and later life. But other changes are sudden and less predictable. The second type of change comes from period effects of several types, both intentional and unplanned—a technological breakthrough that changes work or health, or major change in policies impacting later life. Period effects can suddenly and dramatically alter aspects of our social world in unexpected ways, with positive, negative, or mixed consequences.

Growth and Change: The Aging of the Older Population

This book has emphasized the impact of the growing older population on society and on the lives of individuals. Just how significant is that growth? The federal government routinely makes projections of future sociodemographic characteristics for the purpose of planning. According to Easterlin (1996), "Projections of population in developed countries over the next half century consistently assume that the rate of childbearing will remain low, total population size will stabilize or decline, and the proportion of the older population will rise markedly" (p. 73). For instance, projections assume that there will not be another span of high fertility, such as occurred during the baby boom, nor will there be major breakthroughs that will significantly extend average life expectancy. Should these or other major changes occur, the projections will be off, either underestimating or overestimating the size or composition of the future population. With that caveat in mind, let us examine what we are expecting to see in the next several decades.

Exhibit 12.2 shows population trends and projections for those over 65. Several things are readily apparent from a quick examination of these trends. First, the growth in the population over age 65 will continue to be a major social phenomenon, with the size of the U.S. population over 65 more than doubling between 2000 and 2050. Second, the growth will be rapid for those between 75 and 84, but fastest among those above age 85, who will have grown from near invisibility in the 1940s to more than 20% of the over 65 population by 2050 if current assumptions hold true (Vincent & Velkoff, 2010). In contrast, the size of the young old population (ages 65–74) is expected to grow quite slowly during this time period (Day, 1996; Hobbs & Damon, 1996).

The growth of the population over 65 will not be matched by growth among the population aged 64 and under, according to population projections. Therefore, the median age of the

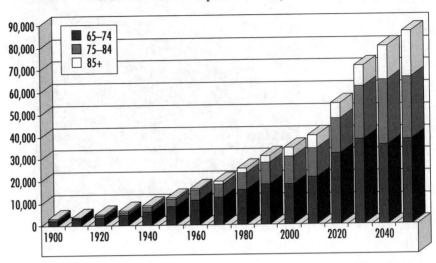

EXHIBIT 12.2

Middle Series Population Projections (in Thousands)

Sources: Day, 1996; Hobbs & Damon, 1996.

society (the age marker with 50% of the population older and 50% younger) will also increase. Past history shows the effect of the birth rate on the median age, with the lowest point showing the effects of large numbers of children and teenagers just after the end of the baby boom. Exhibit 12.3 shows three projections for median age of the U.S. population to 2050, with the intermediate projection demonstrating an increase to around 38 years before a slight downturn. In 2010, the median age in the United States was 36.5, on track with the middle projections (U.S. Central Intelligence Agency, 2010). Keep in mind that the median age is shaped by both mortality and fertility (and sometimes by migration). The dotted lines indicate projections with either higher or lower fertility assumptions, which might result in either an older society or a younger society, as indicated by the median age (Day, 1996).

Another way to look at projections of the changing age structure of U.S. society is in terms of the dependency ratio, as described in Chapter 3. Exhibit 12.4 divides the dependent population into its two components, those under age 18 and those 65 and over. Clearly there have been dramatic historical changes in the overall dependency ratio during the 20th century, and we can expect continuing drama in the first 50 years of the 21st century. The level of dependency is expected to increase until about 2030 (during the baby boomer era), and then essentially level off. By 2050 children and older adults are almost even in their contribution to the total dependency ratio. Even with the growth of the older population, however, total dependency in the next several decades is not expected to exceed the levels of the peak years of childhood dependency during the baby boom era (see Exhibit 12.4).

Centenarians

Embedded within these projections is a notable growth in **centenarians** (persons age 100 and older) in the United States and in many other countries. The United States has even seen an increase in the number of **supercentenarians** (those age 110 and older). Thomas Perls and his colleagues at the New England Centenarian study have been investigating centenarians and their families to understand how some individuals live to such advanced ages, including some who do so with no dementia and little or no diagnosable disease (New England Centenarian Study, 2010).

EXHIBIT **12.3**

Projected Median Age of the U.S. Population to 2050 Under Varied Assumptions

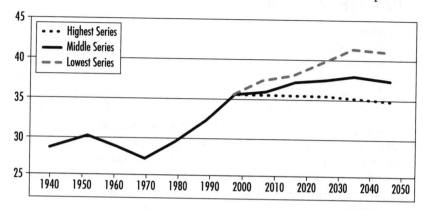

Source: Day, 1996.

EXHIBIT **12.4**

Dependency Ratios: History & Projections to 2050

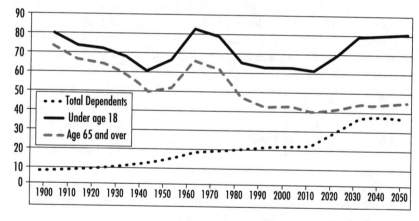

Source: Day, 1996.

In 2010 there were an estimated 10,000 centenarians, about 85% of whom are women. There appears to be some familial connection to such long lives, whether genetic or social in nature. Many of those living to advanced ages either delay the onset of or escape altogether many of the health problems experienced by others as they age, leading the researcher to conclude that "the older you get, the healthier you've been" (Hitt, Young-Xu, & Perls, 1999). The growing ranks of centenarians and supercentenarians, whose longevity approaches what is believed to be the maximum life span of our species, has pointed to the future potential for **exceptional longevity** in growing numbers of people across a wide array of social groups (Perls, Kunkel, & Puca, 2002).

The knowledge being gained from studying these exceptionally long-lived individuals may enable us to age better—learning ways to delay the diseases that are the focus of our culture's negative views of aging. The growing ranks of centenarians may also encourage us to think further about the timing of the life course because ending productivity during one's 7th decade of life is a true waste of talent and potential for those remaining vigorous for several more decades.

Changing Family Structures

As an example of a social trend that gradually unfolds, consider expectations regarding how family-based shifts will play themselves out differently in future cohorts of older adults, well beyond the baby boomers. Dramatic changes within families over the past several decades will influence the economy, the educational system, as well as housing and services in varied ways that may shape quality of life for older adults of the future. Achievement of a 50% female labor force, particularly with growth in full-time female workers, portends a significant reduction in the availability of informal family caregivers for older adults compared to today (National Alliance for Caregiving, 2009), raising the questions of whether and how that care gap will be filled. In addition, lower fertility means that future older cohorts have fewer adult children who might serve as potential caregivers. Who will undertake caregiving for the growing percentage of childless people or those with children geographically or emotionally distant from them?

We also have yet to realize the full ramifications of *serial monogamy* (sequential divorces and remarriages) on family relationships in later life. The impacts of these complex and sometimes temporary kinship bonds on parent/child as well as sibling relationships remain unclear. Will having six, eight, or even more biological and step-grandparents be advantageous to a child; or will none of them take on a meaningful grandparenting role (Cherlin & Furstenberg, 1986)? How will step-parents relate to children who may have lived with them only a few years, during one of a series of marriages? Taking a pessimistic view, we might find that such families may relinquish their current roles as providers of caregiving support to frail relatives; on the other hand, the relationships that persist across the shifts in these complex kinship relationships may be even stronger than those engendered through only a sense of duty, enforced by social norms (Pezzin, Pollack, & Schone, 2008). New familial or quasifamilial social norms may also emerge to generate alternative caregivers, as the traditional patterns of family care become less prevalent in society.

In addition to current, formal (paid) systems of providing services via the aging network, private businesses and industries are gearing up to provide for the needs and wants of a growing market of older adults able to pay for goods and services. The major boom over the past 30 years in independent or semi-independent senior housing (e.g., active adult, assisted-living facilities, cohousing options) marks an early effort in the for-profit sector to meet the anticipated market demand for housing options. In continuing care retirement communities, for example, independent elders may have their own condos or apartments, but may move to more supportive environments (e.g., on-site assisted living) as needed (Newcomer & Preston, 1994). Clearly these private housing alternatives, some of which provide personal care and health services, are restricted to middle- to upper-income clients able to afford them, leaving only family care or nursing home placement as options for those unable to afford these newer alternatives. Some provisions of the 2010 federal health care reform may assist those with moderate incomes to afford community-based or housing-based services through a public system of long-term care insurance. If the family's role in caregiving diminishes with these changes and social programs do not fill the gap, society also faces the following question: what type of negative fallout (such as inadequate care, unnecessary suffering, or premature deaths) is the society willing to accept?

In addition, family relationships will be even longer-lasting than today. As life expectancy grows, siblings may commonly spend 80 or more years together. And, survival of more generations brings other possibilities. For example, a newspaper story chronicling the birthday celebration of a 115-year-old Maryland woman will soon not warrant coverage as special as the number of centenarians grows. In that story, the mentally intact and healthy 115-year-old woman was visited in her nursing home daily by her 92-year-old daughter and less often by a 70-year-old grandson. Three generations of this one family were all receiving Social Security and Medicare! All six generations of this family, including a 2-month-old great-great-great-granddaughter, were present for the woman's birthday celebration (Vitez, 1995). Although many of us will probably not achieve the century mark, having the potential for a century of fairly healthy life warrants a serious rethinking of how, and when in life, we enact particular roles, including key roles within the family.

Changes in Health: Incremental Changes and Breakthroughs

It is difficult to anticipate the nature and extent of changes in areas such as health, disability, and life expectancy. Improvements in life expectancy (and in healthy life expectancy) in recent decades have been gradual and incremental. Better and earlier diagnosis, expanded treatment options, and improved preventative health care and nutrition have led to gradual pushing of both frailty and mortality to later and later ages. However, some experts see few longevity-increasing innovations remaining other than solving the fundamental puzzle of what causes aging. Nonetheless, we continue to innovate in health care, nutrition, and prevention in ways that are likely to extend healthy lives in the future.

The prospect of a major breakthrough in understanding the biological mechanisms of aging, which might enable a dramatic extension of life expectancy, remains under debate. Other options, such as growing replacement organs for those that are failing, or using stem cells to repair the effects of aging, are also being addressed by researchers. Any major change would raise important ethical questions regarding access to potentially costly life-extending technologies that have, until only recently, been the subject of science fiction. Who would be able to afford extensive medical procedures? Might a small, wealthy elite be able to double their lives, even as most people aged and died on timetables we see today? How could health insurance companies or government programs hope to afford such extensive (and expensive) care for others without wealth? Might a two-tier system of life expectancy that is even more pronounced than today result in social unrest?

Nor can we predict what small changes in everyday health practices and preventive care will mean for health or longevity. For example, dietary changes from 1970 to 1994 included an average of 15% per-person decline in consumption of red meat, 20% reduction for distilled liquor, but increases of 25% consumption for fruits and 33% for the healthiest vegetables (U.S. Census Bureau, 1996). We are doing better on getting necessary nutrients, but not all changes are positive. Continuing data collected by the U.S. Department of Agriculture shows we now consume more calories overall (including a lot from soft drinks), but fewer of those are calories from fat, moving closer to dietary recommendations (Tippett & Cleveland, n.d.). In short, there is a complex set of nutritional changes over time. These changes have influenced the long-term health and functioning of cohorts alive during these time periods, perhaps for the remainder of their lives. Will more recent changes in dietary habits and patterns of inactivity have a negative influence on longevity and health in later life, as current research on obesity suggests? Will widespread fluoridation of water, which began in the middle of the 20th century, mean that future elders routinely retain all of their teeth and therefore get more satisfactory nutrition in their later years? How have childhood immunizations (or avoidance of them due to fears of side effects) and flu shots for adults altered acute and chronic disease over the life course? How will the countervailing trends toward more exercise and more sedentary jobs and leisure (watching television, surfing the Web) influence long-term health prospects? Will the recent trends of drinking more water or lower rates of cigarette smoking have long-term benefits for health and longevity? How will earlier diagnoses for health conditions, such as high blood pressure or diabetes, and increasingly effective treatments influence the trajectories of health for people with these conditions? The changes are so numerous (with potential interactions among them) that it is difficult to isolate the single effects of any one. Nonetheless, the cumulative effect of these changes will, without any doubt, influence life expectancy; physical, cognitive, and emotional well-being; and ultimately, the types and ages of onset of illness/disability in future cohorts of elders.

While many scientists continue to seek an overall cure for aging at a cellular or genetic level, there is widespread and long-standing debate about the probability of locating some useful biomarker or treatment that enables us to cease or dramatically slow the biological aging process. If such a breakthrough came, how might society be impacted when people live much longer and in good health? Would adults continue to have children through a presumably longer period of fertility, expanding the population? Could our planet sustain such growth, as each of us remains in the population longer? Or would such a breakthrough spur exploration and colonization of other planets? It is clear that nobody can fully imagine the impact of such a re-engineering of the human life course.

The Risks of Prediction

The predictions outlined here must be considered in the context of unanticipated changes that will reshape the lives of future cohorts of older adults. As an example of such an unexpected change, life expectancy for individuals with developmental disabilities has expanded significantly, far beyond what had been the case just a few decades ago. As Ansello (2004) notes, "In less than 20 years, the median life expectancy for someone with Down's syndrome has nearly doubled, to almost 50 years" (p. 3). In earlier eras parents typically outlived their developmentally disabled children and were often able to personally provide for their care. The policy and service communities were not prepared for the growing group of aging individuals with these lifelong disabilities (Ansello, 2004); policies and programs for people with these disabilities (and some other types of disabilities) have historically been distinct from programs serving older adults. Ironically, "For the disabilities system, aging is a success. For the aging network, [the occurrence of] disabilities are a failure" (Ansello, 2004, p. 4).

Currently we have some seemingly parallel programs, one set serving adults with physical or intellectual disabilities and another set focused on aging adults. Numerous analysts and commentators have pointed to the need to rethink this parallel structure for providing services, and some experiments in collaboration are underway (Kane, 2004). This pattern is starting to change. The CLASS Act, one part of health care reform that deals with long-term care and services, grew from joint effort among Senator Ted Kennedy and advocates from both aging and disability communities (Manard, 2010), and would apply to both groups.

In another area of change, most children, teens, and adults use computers—many text, tweet, and use social media in percentages that are still higher than those for older adults (Jones & Fox, 2009). If utilizing new technologies is a cohort-based phenomenon, we should expect continued growth in the proportion of older adults who utilize the Internet, social networking sites, and other online services as newer, tech-savvy cohorts enter later life. Innovators are already finding ways to make use of these technologies for providing in-home services and conducting research. But cost may continue to be a factor in access. If reductions in pensions or Social Security benefits limit the disposable incomes of future cohorts of older adults, technology-related costs may limit users to those who are most economically secure.

While we are in the midst of many changes, we cannot anticipate what the "next big thing" will be that will reshape aging within our social world. Will some dramatic reorganization of family life, employment, values, or politics make our understood ways of doing things, including growing older, less relevant? Will social attitudes about age and life stages change dramatically so that age and experience are valued and older adults hold meaningful roles in their communities and society? These possibilities are only a few of the endless alternatives. It is an exciting time to be a student of gerontology. Given the pace of social and technological change, major and currently unanticipated historical changes, generating period and cohort effects and further changing the impact of age itself will certainly come.

The older population of the future will be more diverse in many ways. (Credit: U.S. Census Bureau, Public Information Office [PIO])

The Uniqueness of Aging in Each Cohort

One of the challenges in predicting the future of aging is that each cohort comes to the experience with their own unique characteristics and enters stages of later life that have been evolving constantly during their lives. What we know about aging and later life today is drawn from the experience of a limited number of cohorts of older people, and thus does not provide a sufficient basis for predicting how your aging will unfold. We have informed you about the profile of older adults today and described some of the key changes that will likely emerge with the aging of baby boomers. This dynamic nature of aging means that we should not expect our own aging to follow the path of today's elders, or those of prior cohorts. In short, thinking about how your grandparents experienced later life is not likely to be a good guide for what you will experience when you arrive in later life.

Consider the "good times generation," born early in the 20th century. The demographic profile of this group, as well as the particular mixture of social, economic, historic, and political conditions they encountered through their lives, led them to a relatively healthy and secure later life. Demographically less diverse than younger cohorts, this group experienced the Great Depression of the 1930s, World War II, the strong family values and traditional gender roles of the 1950s, and raised the baby boomers. This group built careers during an era of high employment, job security, and strong pensions; they were lucky to see the values of their suburban homes skyrocket during the 1970s. With many stable marriages and careers, large families (by today's standards), and relatively high rates of home ownership, this group approached later life with resources well beyond those of their predecessors, albeit with less advantaged subgroups embedded within this larger cohort.

Their children, including many members of the baby boom, face dramatically different prospects as they approach later life. Many entered their working years in a stagnant economy, where job security and pensions were evaporating at the same time as the Watergate scandal reduced their confidence in the political system. Their children, in turn, are moving toward maturity in the age of computers, as a global economy alters employment with more contingent work and "outsourcing" jobs to far-flung countries, and the Social Security trust fund appears to be endangered. As these three groups age, their outlooks, expectations, and well-being can be expected to differ substantially.

As discussed in several previous chapters, the social meanings, norms, and history of a society shape the landscape of aging, and each new cohort entering later life brings about further change because of its unique characteristics. Those characteristics are, in turn, shaped by the historical and social context in which they have grown up and older. As a consequence, not only must we think about diversity in terms of race, class, ethnicity, gender, education, and similar social structural variables but also in terms of age cohorts (Gibson, 1996). At any given point in time, 66- and 96-year-old birth cohorts have experienced different slices of history and been differentially shaped by historical events.

Challenges and Opportunities for the Field

Throughout this book we have outlined what we know about aging and, just as important, what we do not know about aging today and in the future. The sociology of aging, and social geron-tology, are obviously still young areas, with growing pains evident over recent decades. In this section we discuss some of the issues facing the study of aging and some key opportunities for enhancing our understanding of this dynamic social process.

Throughout the earlier chapters, we have pointed to distinctions in the perspectives used to study aging, the level of analysis along the micro/macro continuum, and the subject matter under consideration. The critical message to remember is that everything about aging is con-nected. Although we have divided material into categories for purposes of clarity in presentation (health, demography, politics, etc.), in the real world of aging individuals and societies, complex interactions blur many of the distinctions we have drawn. Politics influences families; economics influence health; individual choices influence social change; and social trends reshape the way a society constructs the life course (Settersten, 1999). Age, the life course, and how cohorts experi-ence their particular, shared movement through time are constantly demonstrating the dynamic changes that make what we study truly a moving target.

Disciplinary Frameworks

Many people who study aging or work with older adults approach their tasks from a specific dis-ciplinary framework—they look at things as a physician, a social worker, a political scientist, or a psychologist. Each of the many disciplines used to study aging has information and insights to offer, if we seek to understand the process of aging in all of its complexity. In fact, anyone trained in the study of aging would be very unlikely to argue for the usefulness of just one discipline to the exclusion of all others in addressing the puzzle of human aging in social context. A recently published work, for example, connects the concept of cumulative inequality (as discussed in Chapter 7) to biological indicators of health and well-being in older adults, reflecting the broad biopsychosocial perspective (Ferraro, Shippee, & Schafer, 2009). The growing acceptance of the biopsychosocial framework to study aging and the increased emphasis on building bridges between basic, clinical, and applied fields suggests that many people trained in disciplines now accept that disciplinary boundaries are fuzzy at best. Ideally, these boundaries should become in-visible in the service of broader-based understanding of the complex processes of human aging.

Kenneth Ferraro encourages all of us interested in aging to apply the gerontological imagi-nation in our work. "The gerontological imagination is an awareness of the process of human aging that enables one to understand the scientific contributions of a variety of researchers studying aging" (Ferraro, 2007, p. 327). Among the elements of the **gerontological imagina-tion** are recognizing that changes that come with aging are often *not* caused by aging; seeing aging as a multifaceted dynamic of change over time, not simply biological or social; and recog-nizing and honoring the heterogeneity and diversity that characterizes human aging within and across societies. This requires that we move beyond the narrow focus of disciplines like econom-ics, sociology, or biology to understand all that aging entails.

Applied aging research often occurs in such a truly interdisciplinary fashion, with research-ers from numerous disciplines, including history, epidemiology, economics, biochemistry, and physiology, coming together to address a research question or policy issue. Even research that is more basic often crosses boundaries in identifying both pertinent theory and research techniques to best address its question. This interdisciplinary approach strengthens, rather than weakens, the research process because the physical, psychological, and social aspects of aging are all simultaneously interactive at the micro (person) and macro (societal) levels. In fact, biologists, sociologists, psychologists, and those in other disciplines have a lot to teach each other about the process of aging for individuals, groups, communities, organizations, or nations.

Micro/Macro Distinctions: Implications for Policy and Practice

Although distinctions among disciplines are instructive but somewhat arbitrary, the range from micro to macro in studying aging represents a clearer continuum. On numerous occasions we have identified questions or issues that have serious implications on multiple levels, from the individual to the group, community, and society. The example of longevity is a handy one. Any significant extension of human life expectancy would certainly raise important questions for aging individuals. How would the extended years of life be used? Would longer-lived humans demand more of a role for themselves in the later years than they do today? On a midlevel (meso level) of this continuum, we could think of how increased life expectancy would influence family relationships, the world of employment, and other social groups and institutions. On a macro level, using the widest lens possible, we would confront the issues of societies that are already aging, or some that might need to restrict births in order to avoid overpopulation, and others that are altering their economies to manage dependency in later years created by the current system of retirement.

Questions on these various levels are relevant to researchers and also link to the worlds of practice and policy. For example, as people are living longer, we begin to examine whether policies based on chronological age have appropriate age limits. Should age discrimination laws use age 40 as the appropriate definition of an older worker? Many programs (the Older Americans Act and even Social Security) have moved away from eligibility based solely on age to a combination of age and need as the older population has grown larger and more economically diverse. Service providers, such as geriatric nurse practitioners, faced with a growth in the demand for their services in an aging society, must remain attuned to the policy issues because policies determine who is or is not eligible for services and, consequently, the security of/demand for their employment. The changes on one level reverberate in the others. For this reason, we encourage consideration of how changes at the individual level, the group/organizational level, and the societal level of the micro/macro continuum are intricately connected.

On the micro level of the individual, connections between these domains are fairly easy to see. As individuals move through the life course, the family shapes their initial socioeconomic status, thereby influencing their life chances and opportunities for education and occupation. Early health care and habits, taught by the family, will have long-range repercussions on health and disability into advanced old age. Attitudes taught by and experiences in the family are also likely to have some influence on political orientation and party affiliation, as well as religious values and activities. The schooling and part-time jobs of youth provide a springboard toward higher or lower levels of success in future career pursuits. Throughout adulthood, employment patterns, economic status, and health are likely to have mutual influences; persons in poor health cannot be as competitive in work, and those who are poorer or work in less advantaged jobs are less likely to have health care coverage or pensions. For women especially, jobs may influence their involvement in family life, and their family responsibilities may, without further growth of child-care alternatives, continue to shape women's likelihood of pursuing high-powered, full-time careers.

As the life course perspective reminds us, opportunities available, actions undertaken, and choices made in early and midlife have clear repercussions on later-life well-being. Today's working poor, for example, are less likely to have pensions, good health, or complete choice about when to retire, resulting in their continued vulnerability into later life (Meyer & Greenwood, 1997). Seldom do those who are economically marginal at earlier stages find themselves in a financially comfortable old age; generally those in excellent health or poor health find those statuses the starting point for whatever changes they experience in self-sufficiency and functioning with advancing age. Those intervening to assist physically frail or poor elders would do well to look beyond the initial problems (such as poor health, or poverty) to examine other issues, such as the availability of family support or adequacy of housing, in developing their strategies to provide assistance.

Employers have altered their retirement programs for workers in response to both government mandates and the economic pressures of the world economy. Currently, the government encourages people to work longer and is looking ahead to possibly raising further the age of entitlement to full Social Security benefits, while the private sector may sometimes still offer incentives for early retirement, especially during temporary economic downturns or company crises. Families may constrain their childbearing in response to the need for two incomes to meet their needs. Societies cannot develop new (and perhaps badly needed) programs to assist the elderly or any other group unless both economics and political opinion are on their side. In short, the macro- and micro-level processes influencing aging are intricately interwoven.

Firming Our Theoretical Foundations

Among the problems that have slowed progress of the study of aging is that much of the research done in the past was not clearly directed by theory (Bengtson, Burgess, & Parrott, 1997; Hendricks, Applebaum, & Kunkel, 2010). Theoretical developments in aging have, according to many experts, lagged behind that of other, established disciplines (Passuth & Bengtson, 1988). Until recently the field had generated a lot of testable hypotheses and specific conceptual models (what Linda George calls theory with a small "t"), rather than examining "broad views of fundamental processes underlying social structure and social life," or theory with a capital "T" (George, 1995, p. S1). The development of theory in the study of aging has sometimes been slow and parochial, generating specialized, small-scale theories relating to specific points of data. In a study of published research in eight leading social-gerontological journals from 1990 to 1994, Bengtson and his colleagues (1997) concluded that 80% of the articles lacked a theoretical framework for their research findings.

However, recent years have seen a renewed emphasis on development and application of theories. A replication of the study by Bengtson et al. (1997), this time focusing on research between 2000 and 2004, found that articles lacking theory had dropped from 80% to 61% (Alley, Putney, Rice, & Bengtson, 2010). In addition, a recent handbook of theories of aging shows noteworthy expansion of theories relating to varied dimensions of aging in the past few years, including both theories drawn from disciplinary orientations and those that bridge multiple disciplines or the basic/applied research divide (Bengtson, Gans, Putney, & Silverstein, 2009).

Perhaps some of the earlier reluctance to theorize arose from the field's early experience with disengagement theory. Highly controversial when it was introduced, disengagement theory was immediately attacked, including some rather hostile reactions (Achenbaum & Bengtson, 1994). Attacks were based both on scientific criteria and on implicit value positions of researchers, oriented toward activity as the successful mode of adaptation to later-life changes. That first major theoretical effort may have dissuaded theoretically minded individuals from putting forward theoretical orientation, fearing a similar fate (Achenbaum & Bengtson, 1994). Another barrier to the development of theory has been the applied origins of the field. Theorizing was considered by some to be a waste of valuable time that could be spent problem solving.

What is lost when we lack (or do not use) theories to organize our knowledge? In the absence of theory, research provides a set of unrelated bits of knowledge that fail to build a larger picture, support effective interventions, or predict how future cohorts will age differently. Results of research not driven by theory become an array of factoids—what Seltzer (personal communication to S. Kunkel, 1993) calls "itty-bitty" gerontology—which fail to contribute to our understanding of the underlying process of aging. Theories help us by creating meaningful frameworks for understanding the complexities of the social world in which we operate. As Bengtson and his colleagues (1997) note, "A policymaker would have difficulty supporting a program that does not have clearly stated goals and a plan for how they will be achieved. And it is intellectually irresponsible for a program of research to proceed without a similar set of statements—in short, a theory" (p. S73). They conclude that there is nothing as practical as a good theory!

Addressing Diversity in Policy and Practice

As previous chapters have emphasized, the older population is becoming more diverse; in sociological terms, the older population is more differentiated by structural factors, such as age, race, ethnicity, social class, and cohort (Calasanti, 1996b). Even though it has always been problematic to discuss "the elderly," it will become increasingly critical to focus on which components of the older population are under consideration. As discussed in Chapter 9, formulating policy specifically targeted to an older group as a single category may be a thing of the past (Torres-Gil, 1992). The life experiences, and hence the later-life trajectories, of various social groups differ in ways that are obvious but also in more subtle ways.

Can we expect, for example, that a Black woman, aged 85, with a large network of family but little income will have much in common with a newly retired, White professional man who has remained single and childless? Not only do their objective circumstances of aging differ, but perhaps more important, they may interpret their situations and even the meaning of later life very differently. For example, retirement for the man just described may mean free time, with opportunities to pursue new hobbies, travel, and participate in community service; for the woman, retirement may mean moving from two jobs (one in the home and one for pay) to one, paired with a dramatic reduction in income (Calasanti, 1996a)—clearly not the same meaning at all.

We have already emphasized the changing racial/ethnic profile of the older population. Those planning future social policy or preparing interventions overlook the growth in diversity among older adults, especially among Hispanic and Asian groups, at their own peril. Even a local seniors' nutrition program will need to recognize the diverse palates of the people it is serving and be responsive to the distinct dietary and cultural needs of these groups (Kayser-Jones, 2002).

In the face of this growing diversity, we need to reconsider the standard traditionally used as the reference group for older adults: married, middle-class, White males. Because men face shorter life expectancies, divorce is increasing, and ethnic diversity is growing, it will be increasingly unrealistic to use males of the majority culture as our benchmark for how various groups are doing as they age (Gibson, 1996). This tendency to use male experience as the norm casts other groups into the role of "the other," being compared with a standard. Instead, no group should be considered the standard against which all other groups are compared.

Transforming Knowledge to Inform Policy and Practice

Research on aging grew from a tradition of identifying and ameliorating the problems of aging individuals within societies. Now we recognize that not only individuals but entire societies face challenges as their populations grow older. Effective response to these challenges requires high-quality information. More than ever before, those formulating policy need to have accurate information, not only on current cohorts in later life but also on the differences to be expected in future cohorts.

The policy process often focuses on immediate problems, without much consideration of the long-term view as new and different cohorts move through the age structure of society. Since the 1990s came to a close, for example, members of Congress have been struggling with ways to modify both Social Security and Medicare to secure their trust funds into the future. Decisions regarding the best way to reform these and other policies should, in the best of all possible worlds, consider the likely needs of individuals just born, not just those already receiving benefits or the cohorts of the baby boom.

Researchers, too, have a critical role to play in making research results accessible to the public and to those making policy. As the research process has become more sophisticated and technical, it often becomes more difficult to translate the results of research into language easily comprehensible by nonscientists. Many researchers studying aging are hesitant, given the complexities of the connections among aging, period effects, and cohort differences, to make definitive statements about trends and recommendations to intervene in the most effective fashion. The National Institutes of Health (2006) has made the goal of translating research, from laboratory bench to bedside and on to community and to policy, a priority for its researchers. It is incumbent on both scientists and policy makers to work toward better understanding of the complexities of the others' work and make their own work more accessible.

Your Future Aging Self

You are an aging person. Most of us easily conceptualize aging on an individual level—the physical and social changes that we have observed in others as they move through various ages/stages of the life course. It is, however, sometimes difficult to visualize *ourselves* as older adults because of persistent ageist views we have learned and see reinforced in society. Beyond the level of the person, however, it remains challenging to grasp the complex implications of population aging on a more macro level (Vincent et al., 2006). This raises some fundamental questions. For example, is aging simply an individual process to be addressed by personal choices (regarding employment, family, financial planning) and positive behaviors (building a history of good nutrition and exercise and a strong network of social support)? Or is the aging of the population a collective issue to be addressed by the larger society through adaptation of social institutions and the provision of needed services and opportunities to include or respond to an older population? Clearly the answer is both.

As individuals we age within constantly changing social contexts that dramatically influence us in many ways, both positive and negative. This socially constructed, culturally and cohort specific context not only defines the opportunities available to us based on age (and other characteristics), but also defines the ways in which we identify ourselves and others as young, middle-aged, or old. As the cartoon suggests, our thinking about aging is shifting; this shift is also reflected by sayings such as "60 is the new 40." Often, however, we do not look forward to ourselves as older adults

"Here's our new retirement plan: at age 65,
we'll get divorced then marry other
people who planned better."

because of the stereotypes, stigma, and ageism that our society teaches us. Clearly the fortunate among us will approach later life with good health, strong family and friendship networks, a secure financial future, and opportunities to contribute to society in ways we define as meaningful.

On the positive side, frailty, loss, and disadvantage do not define later life. Certainly some older persons experience these problems over time, but at any given time most older adults live autonomously in the community, are financially independent, and, despite some chronic health conditions, successfully fend for themselves. Older adults make contributions to their families and communities on a daily basis and have ongoing relationships and meaningful lives. Recent evidence strongly suggests that many dimensions of the quality of life, from age of onset of disease and disability to economic well-being and social engagement, could improve in coming cohorts, in part through positive lifestyle choices of individuals at all ages (Rowe & Kahn, 1998). We are, to some extent, agents in shaping our aging selves through our decisions. Aging is not a spectator sport; choices we each make every day will bear fruit over the long haul in terms of health, housing, economic status, and social networks. So a choice to exercise daily through adulthood significantly shifts the odds against early disability compared to those for an obese "couch potato." Our choices, however, remain limited by tradition, expectations, policy, and social structures surrounding us. They also are limited by external events, such as economic trends, wars, and natural disasters that can thwart the best-laid plans.

You may want to start now to consider the steps you choose to take to create a path through life that will lead you in the best directions for both the near-term and the long-term. Research presented here certainly provides some clues as to what types of choices and behaviors have, to date, led to positive outcomes in later life. Carstensen's (2009) book, translating research findings about aging into advice for building a successful later life, also debunks some popular myths, such as the idea that genetics determines longevity, that older people are lonely, and that we age alone. Caring for your health, planning for your career, creating positive relationships, and planning financially for your future all are elements. Actively including later life in thinking about your future, rather than presuming medicine will have cured it or that somehow you are going to escape aging, may help all of us think more positively about aging—it's about "us" and our families, not about "those people." One day, if each of us survives that long, we will be one of "those people." Think now about how you want to be treated in that future part of your life course, and make choices today for yourself, and toward others, that reflect those goals.

Summary

The process of aging is not just an individual journey; it is also a societal force developing within a political/historical/economic context that both shapes individuals and their cohorts and, in turn, is shaped and altered by the passage of those age cohorts through the society (Riley, 1987, 1994). The study of aging is the attempt to capture an ever-changing process that affects us all as we move through our individual lives, through the domains of family, work, and the political world. Your aging will not be like that of your parents or your grandparents. The dynamic interplay between social change and the aging of cohorts, including your cohort, guarantees that the only thing we can count on is that aging in the future will be different socially, economically, and (to some degree) physically. Predicting the form that those differences will take, however, is a much riskier task.

Even if age is a socially constructed phenomenon, and thought by some people therefore to be "unreal," we must recall W. I. Thomas's (1972) wisdom that any phenomenon, if perceived as real, is real in its consequences. We have constructed as part of our social world a complex understanding of aging that extends far beyond the physical parameters and changes experienced by individuals through time. We organize much of our social lives based on age, with access to opportunities and relationships among individuals constrained by the formal and informal rules of age stratification systems. This reality, which we share as part of our culture, comes to be a system by which society organizes itself and through which individuals develop their lives. Social construction is a powerful force. Just recall the next time someone encourages an individual to "act their age"—regardless of whether that age is 6 or 66—that you are seeing the power of age as a social construct in operation.

It is not simply for individuals, however, that age is significant. Social life would be chaotic if we lacked some rules and orderliness of events and relationships imposed by the social construct of age. We all rely on the rules and build them into our personal planning in complex ways. There seems to be little likelihood that a completely "age irrelevant" society is on the horizon. Nonetheless, many of the distinctions we make today, between someone who is 16 and 18 or between 63 and 66, for example, are subject to serious question.

We must recognize the power of aging as a concept. Individual and larger-scale planning, as we face an aging society, must include flexibility. Social scientists do not have a very good track record of predicting trends far into the future, and the aging of society is one of the most potent trends we face today. One goal of any planning is certain: if you plan, you must plan for change. The future of aging is uncertain; only the fact that we are all aging is firmly guaranteed.

Web Wise

Association for Gerontology in Higher Education Student Page   http://www.aghe.org/
The Association for Gerontology in Higher Education, the national association for educational institutions in gerontology and geriatrics, has a page of resources for students, accessible from its home page. It includes information on a database (with tailored searches available for a modest fee for students) to identify specific types of educational programs in gerontology/geriatrics nationwide, information on scholarships and fellowships for advanced study in aging/gerontology, and information on careers in aging for the potential professional.

Road Scholar/Elderhostel   http://www.roadscholar.org/
Elderhostel, recently adding the new name Road Scholar, has been a source of social activity, travel, and education for older adults for decades. Recently changing its mission from travel and learning for older adults/retirees to all adults, it offers a wide array of programs for the United States and abroad. A visit to their Web site demonstrates the richness and diversity of education/travel programs they offer. Although courses do carry costs and primarily cater to a middle-class clientele, some scholarships are available, supported by donations.

Senior Net   http://www.seniornet.org/php/default.php
Senior Net is a nonprofit organization of computer-using adults ages 50 or above. The goal is to enhance the lives of those in later life and to share useful knowledge. This lively site holds a lot of information and many links to other useful sites related to active, engaged maturity.

Senior Women Web   http://www.seniorwomen.com
Senior Women Web is a site focusing on issues of specific concern to women. It includes news stories, sections on art, leisure, politics, fitness and media, including links to other woman-oriented Web sites.

Key Terms

centenarians

exceptional longevity

gerontological imagination

supercentenarians

Questions for Thought and Discussion

1. If you were working for a service provider planning for the future needs of the elderly, what steps would you recommend right away based on what we know about changes in the older population? What specific changes are going to be most important to those planning for service needs?

2. Do we have too many life cycle stages, too few, or just the right number? Because these are socially constructed, it is possible to change them. As the average life expectancy grows, does that mean we should have more stages, or should we move toward making age irrelevant to more aspects of society?

3. Now that you are more educated about the complexities of aging, what steps can you take right now to maximize a "good old age" for yourself, including the avoidance of "pathological aging"? Answering this question requires you to consider what makes for successful aging according to your value system.

4. Speculate on the likely changes to later life that may be brought by the large cohorts of the baby boom. What have their cohort experiences suggested about this large age group that may transform later life?

References

AARP. (2002). *Staying ahead of the curve: The AARP work and career study.* Washington, DC: Author.

AARP. (2003). *Staying ahead of the curve 2003: The AARP working in retirement study.* Washington, DC: Author.

AARP. (2005). *Reimaging America.* Retrieved from http://www.2030.org.fr990719.html/

AARP. (2010). *Social media and technology use among adults 50+.* Washington, DC: Author.

AARP/Rock the Vote. (2005). *Public attitudes toward Social Security and private accounts.* Washington, DC: AARP Public Policy Institute. Retrieved from http://assets.aarp.org/rgcenter/post-import/soc_sec_pr_acc.pdf

Abramson, A., & Silverstein, M. (2004). *Images of aging in America 2004: A summary of selected findings.* Washington, DC: AARP and University of Southern California.

Aboderin, I. (2004). Decline in material family support for older people in urban Ghana, Africa: Understanding processes and causes of change. *Journals of Gerontology: Social Sciences, 59,* S128–S137.

Achenbaum, W. A. (1992). With justice for all? Social Security, symbolic politics, and generational equity. *In Depth, 2*(3), 13–36.

Achenbaum, A. (2009). A history of productive aging and boomers. In R. Hudson (Ed.), *Boomer bust? Economic and political issues for the graying society* (Vol. 1). Westport, CT: Praeger.

Achenbaum, W. A., & Bengtson, V. L. (1994). Re-engaging the Disengagement Theory of aging: On the history and assessment of theory development in gerontology. *The Gerontologist, 34*(6), 756–763.

Aday, R. H. (2003). *Aging prisoners: Crisis in American corrections.* Westport, CT: Praeger.

Adelman, R. C. (1995). The Alzheimerization of aging. *The Gerontologist, 35*(4), 526–532.

Administration on Aging. (2001). *Profile of older Americans, 2001.* Washington, DC: Department of Health and Human Services. Retrieved from http://aoa.gov/prof/Statistics/profile/2001/2001profile.pdf

Administration on Aging. (n.d.). *Minority aging: Statistical profiles.* Retrieved from http://www.aoa.gov/AoARoot/Aging_Statistics/Minority_Aging/index.aspx

Administration on Aging. (2010). *A profile of older Americans: 2009.* Retrieved from http://www.aoa.gov/AoARoot/Aging_Statistics/Profile/2009/docs/2009profile_508.pdf

Agree, E. M., Biddlecom, A. E., Chang, M., & Perez, A. E. (2002). Transfers from older parents to their adult children in Taiwan and the Philippines. *Journal of Cross-Cultural Gerontology, 17,* 269–294.

Ajrouch, K. (2008). Introduction to a special issue of *Research in Human Development:* Aging families in global context. *Research in Human Development, 5*(1), 1–5.

Alessio, H. (2001). Physiology of human aging. In L. A. Morgan & S. Kunkel (Eds.), *Aging: The social context* (2nd ed., pp. 107–137). Thousand Oaks, CA: Pine Forge.

Allen, S., Goldscheider, F., & Ciambrone, D. (1999). Gender roles, marital intimacy, and nomination of spouse as primary caregiver. *The Gerontologist, 39*(2), 150–158.

Alley, D. E., Putney, N. M., Rice, M., & Bengtson, V. L. (2010). The increasing using of theory in social gerontology: 1990–2004. *Journal of Gerontology: Social Sciences, 65B*(5), 583–590.

Almost half of U.S. domestic spending in 2002 for Social Security, Medicare, Medicaid. (2005). Retrieved from http://www.seniorjournal.com/NEWS/Features/3–06–4almost.htm

Alwin, D. F., & Krosnick, J. A. (1991). Aging, cohorts, and the stability of sociopolitical orientations over the life span. *American Journal of Sociology, 97*(1), 169–195.

Alzheimer's Association. (2010). Alzheimer's disease: Facts and figures. In *Alzheimer's and Dementia* (Vol. 6). Retrieved from http://www.alz.org/documents_custom/report_alzfactsfigures2010.pdf

Amato, P., Rezac, S., & Booth, A. (1995). Helping between parents and young adult offspring: The role of parental marital quality, divorce, and remarriage. *Journal of Marriage and the Family, 57*(2), 363–374.

American Geriatrics Society/Association of Directors of Geriatrics Academic Programs (AGS/ADGAP). (2005). *Geriatric medicine: A clinical imperative for an aging population.* Retrieved from http://www.americangeriatrics.org/WrittenReport.pdf

American Geriatrics Society Core Writing Group of the Task Force on the Future of Geriatric Medicine. (2005). Caring for older Americans: The future of geriatric medicine. *Journals of the American Geriatrics Society, 53,* S245–S256.

American National Election Studies. (2005). *The ANES guide to public opinion and electoral behavior.* Retrieved from http://www.electionstudies.org/nesguide/toptable/tab2a_1.htm

American Society for Aesthetic Plastic Surgery. (2007). *Quick facts: Highlights of the ASAPS 2007 statistics on cosmetic surgery.* Retrieved from http://www.surgery.org/sites/default/files/statsquickfacts.pdf

Amoss, P. T., & Harrell, S. (Eds.). (1981). *Other ways of growing old: Anthropological perspectives.* Stanford, CA: Stanford University Press.

Anderson, R. N., & Smith, B. L. (2005). Deaths: Leading causes for 2002. *National Vital Statistics Reports, 53*(17).

Ansello, E. F. (2004). Public policy writ small: Coalitions at the intersection of aging and lifelong disabilities. *Public Policy and Aging Report, 14*(4), 1, 3–6.

Antonucci, T. (1990). Social supports and social relationships. In R. H. Binstock & L. K. George (Eds.), *Handbook of aging and the social sciences* (3rd ed., pp. 205–226). San Diego, CA: Academic Press.

Antonucci, T., & Akiyama, H. (1987). Social networks in adult life and a preliminary examination of the convoy model. *Journals of Gerontology, 42,* 519–527.

Antonucci, T., & Akiyama, H. (1995). Convoys of social relations: Family and friendships within a life-span context. In R. Bleiszner & V. H. Bedford (Eds.), *Handbook of aging and the family* (pp. 355–371). New York: Greenwood Press.

Arias, E. (2010). United States life tables, 2006. *National Vital Statistics Reports, 58*(21). Hyattsville, MD: National Center for Health Statistics.

Aries, P. (1962). *Centuries of childhood: A social history of family life.* New York: Vintage.

Association of Reproductive Health Professionals. (2002). *Mature sexuality clinical proceedings: Who's doing what?* Retrieved from http://www.arhp.org/healthcareproviders/cme/onlinecme/maturecmecp/whosdoingwhat.cfm?ID=45

Atchley, R. C. (1976). *The sociology of retirement.* New York: Schenkman.

Atchley, R. C. (1989). A continuity theory of normal aging. *The Gerontologist, 29*(2), 183–190.

Atchley, R. C. (1994). *Social forces and aging* (7th ed.). Belmont, CA: Wadsworth.

Atchley, R. C. (1997). *Social forces and aging* (8th ed.). Belmont, CA: Wadsworth/Thompson Learning.

Atchley, R. C. (2004). *Social forces and aging* (10th ed.). Belmont, CA: Wadsworth/Thompson Learning.

Auster, C. (1996). *The sociology of work: Concepts and cases.* Thousand Oaks, CA: Pine Forge Press.

Barker, J. C. (2002). Neighbors, friends, and other non-kin caregivers of community-living dependent elders. *Journal of Gerontology: Social Sciences, 57B*(3), S158–S167.

Bass, S. A. (Ed.). (1995). *Older and active: How Americans over 55 are contributing to society.* New Haven, CT: Yale University Press.

Beaulier, S. A., Boyes, W. J., & Mounts, W. S. (2008). The influence of economists on public attitudes toward government. *The American Economist, 52,* 65–71.

Becker, G. (1993). Continuity after a stroke: Implications of life-course disruption in old age. *The Gerontologist, 33*(2), 148–158.

Beckmann, A. (2006). *Access, participation, and take-up rates in defined contribution retirement plans among workers in private industry, 2006.* Washington, DC: U.S. Department of Labor. Retrieved from http://www.bls.gov/opub/cwc/cm20061213ar01p1.htm

Beedon, L., & Wu, K. (2005). Women age 65 and older: Their sources of income. *AARP Research Report publication ID: DD126.* Retrieved from http://www.aarp.org/research/socialsecurity/benefits/dd126_women.html

Benbow, A. E. (2004). Increasing access to reliable information on the World Wide Web: Educational tools for web designers, older adults, and caregivers. In D. C. Burdick & S. Kwon (Eds.), *Gerotechnology: Research and practice in technology and aging* (pp. 86–96). New York: Springer Publishing.

Bender, K. A., & Jivan, N. A. (2005). *What makes retirees happy?* (Issue Brief #28). Boston, MA: Center for Retirement Research at Boston College.

Bengtson, V. L., Burgess, E. O., & Parrott, T. M. (1997). Theory, explanation, and a third generation of theoretical development in social gerontology. *Journal of Gerontology: Social Sciences, 52B,* S72–S88.

Bengtson, V. L., Cutler, N. E., Mangen, D. J., & Marshall, V. W. (1985). Generations, cohorts, and relations between age groups. In R. H. Binstock & E. Shanas (Eds.), *Handbook of aging and the social sciences* (2nd ed., pp. 304–338). San Diego, CA: Academic Press.

Bengtson, V. L., Gans, D., Putney, N. M., & Silverstein, M. (2009). *Handbook of theories of aging.* New York: Springer Publishing.

Bengtson, V. L., Rosenthal, C., & Burton, L. (1990). Families and aging: Diversity and heterogeneity. In R. H. Binstock & L. K. George (Eds.), *Handbook of aging and the social sciences* (3rd ed., pp. 263–287). San Diego, CA: Academic Press.

Bennett, A. (2006). Punk's not dead: The continuing significance of punk rock for an older generation of fans. *Sociology, 4,* 219–235.

Berger, E. D. (2006). "Aging" identities: Degradation and negotiation in the search for employment. *Journal of Aging Studies, 20,* 303–316.

Berger, E. D. (2009). Managing age discrimination: An examination of the techniques used when seeking employment. *The Gerontologist, 49*(3), 317–332.

Berger, P. L., & Luckmann, T. (1966). *The social construction of reality.* Garden City, NY: Anchor Books.

Bernburg, J. G. (2003). *State reaction, life course outcomes and structural disadvantage: A panel study of the impact of formal criminal labeling on the transition to adulthood* (Doctoral dissertation). Albany, State University of New York.

Binstock, R. H. (1991a). Aging, politics, and public policy. In B. B. Hess & E. W. Markson (Eds.), *Growing old in America* (4th ed., pp. 325–340). New Brunswick, NJ: Transaction.

Binstock, R. H. (1991b). From the Great Society to the aging society—25 years of the Older Americans Act. *Generations, 15*(3), 11–18.

Binstock, R. H. (1994). Changing criteria in old-age programs: The introduction of economic status and need for services. *The Gerontologist, 34*(6), 726–730.

Binstock, R. H. (1995). A new era in the politics of aging: How will the old-age interest groups respond? *Generations, 19*(3), 68–74.

Binstock, R. H. (1997). The 1996 election: Older voters and implications for policies on aging. *The Gerontologist, 37*(1), 15–19.

Binstock, R. H. (2005). The contemporary politics of old age policies. In R. B. Hudson (Ed.), *The new politics of old age policies* (pp. 265–293). Baltimore: Johns Hopkins University Press.

Binstock, R. H. (2009). Older voters and the 2008 election. *The Gerontologist, 49*(5), 697–701.

Birren, J. E., & Schaie, K. W. (Eds.). (2006). *Handbook of the psychology of aging* (6th ed.). San Diego, CA: Academic Press.

Blackmar, F. W. (1908). *The elements of sociology.* New York: Macmillan.

Blazer, D. G. (2006). Successful aging. *American Journal of Geriatric Psychiatry, 14*(1), 2–5.

Blendon, R. J., Brodie, M., Benson, J. M., Neuman, T., Altman, D. E., & Hamel, E. C. (2005). American's agenda in aging for the new congress. *Public Policy & Aging Report, 15*(1), 1, 20–23.

Board of Trustees. (2009). *The 2009 annual report of the Board of Trustees of the Federal Old-Age and Survivors Insurance and Federal Disability Insurance Trust Funds.* Washington, DC: U.S. Government Printing Office. Retrieved from http://www.ssa.gov/OACT/TR/2009/tr09.pdf

Bookwala, J. (2009). The impact of parent care on marital quality and well-being in adult daughters and sons. *Journal of Gerontology: Psychological Sciences, 64B*(3), 339–347.

Borden, K. (1995). Dismantling the pyramid: The why and how of privatizing Social Security. *Social Security privatization.* Washington, DC: The Cato Institute.

Borzi, P. C. (1993). A congressional response to pensions reform. In R. V. Burkhauser & D. L. Salisbury (Eds.), *Pensions in a changing economy* (pp. 111–112). Washington, DC: Employee Benefit Research Institute.

Bound, J., Scheonbaum, M., & Waidmann, T. (1996). Race differences in labor force attachment and disability status. *The Gerontologist, 36*(3), 311–321.

Brody, E. M. (1981). Women in the middle. *The Gerontologist, 21,* 471–480.

Brody, E. M. (1985). Parent care as normative family stress. *The Gerontologist, 25,* 19–29.

Brody, E. M. (2004). *Women in the middle: Their parent care years.* New York: Springer Publishing.

Brown, J. (2005). Examining the adoption of old-age security programs in the developing world. *Sociological Perspectives, 48*(4), 505–529.

Brown, T. H., & Warner, D. F. (2008). Divergent pathways? Racial/ethnic differences in older women's labor force withdrawal. *Journal of Gerontology: Social Sciences, 63B,* S122–S134.

Brubaker, T. H. (1990). *Family relationships in later life.* Newbury Park, CA: Sage.

Burdick, D. C., & Kwon, S. (2004). *Gerotechnology: Research and practice in technology and aging.* New York: Springer Publishing.

Burkhauser, R. V., & Quinn, J. F. (1994). Changing policy signals. In M. W. Riley, R. L. Kahn, & A. Foner (Eds.), *Aging and structural lag* (pp. 237–262). New York: Wiley-Interscience.

Burkhauser, R. V., & Smeeding, T. M. (1994). *Social Security reform: A budget neutral approach to reducing older women's disproportionate risk of poverty* (Policy Brief No. 2/1994). Syracuse, NY: Syracuse University Center for Policy Research.

Burke, M. E. (2004). *Generational differences survey report.* Alexandria, VA: SHRM Research Department.

Burns, B. J., & Taube, C. (1990). Mental health services in general medical care and in nursing homes. In B. S. Fogel, A. Furino, & G. Gottlieb (Eds.), *Mental health policy for older Americans: Protecting minds at risk* (Chapter 4, pp. 63–84). Washington, DC: American Psychiatric Press.

Burton, L. M. (1996). Age norms, the timing of family role transitions and intergenerational caregiving among aging African American women. *The Gerontologist, 36*(2), 199–208.

Burton, L., & DeVries, C. (1995). Challenges and rewards: African-American grandparents as surrogate parents. In L. Burton (Ed.), *Families and aging* (pp. 101–108). Amityville, NY: Baywood.

Butler, R. N. (1989). Dispelling ageism: The cross-cutting intervention. *Annals of the American Academy of Political and Social Sciences, 503,* 138–147.

Button, J. W. (1992). A sign of generational conflict: The impact of Florida's aging voters on local school and tax referenda. *Social Science Quarterly, 73*(4), 786–797.

Byrd, M., & Breuss, T. (1992). Perceptions of sociological and psychological age norms by young, middle-aged, and elderly New Zealanders. *International Journal of Aging and Human Development, 34*(2), 145–163.

Cain, L. D. (1987). Alternative perspectives on the phenomena of human aging: Age stratification and age status. *The Journal of Applied Behavioral Science, 23*(2), 277–294.

Calasanti, T. M. (1996a). Gender and life satisfaction in retirement: An assessment of the male model. *Journal of Gerontology: Social Sciences, 51B*(1), S18–S29.

Calasanti, T. M. (1996b). Incorporating diversity: Meaning, levels of research, and implications for theory. *The Gerontologist, 36*(2), 147–156.

Callahan, D. (1987). *Setting limits: Medical goals in an aging society.* New York: Simon & Schuster.

Callis, R. R. (2003). Moving to America—moving to homeownership: 1994–2002. In *Current Housing Reports H21/03–1.* Washington, DC: U.S. Census Bureau.

Cameron, L. J. H., Kabir, Z. N., Khanam, M. A., Wahlin, A., & Streatfield, P. K. (2010). Earning their keep: The productivity of older women and men in rural Bangladesh. *Journal of Cross-Cultural Gerontology, 25*(1), 87–103.

Campbell, A. L. (2005). The non-distinctiveness of senior voters in the 2004 election. *Public Policy & Aging Report, 15*(1), 1, 3–6.

Campbell, R. T. (1988). Integrating conceptualization, design, and analysis in panel studies of the life course. In K. W. Schaie, R. T. Campbell, W. Meredith, & S. C. Rawlings (Eds.), *Methodological issues in aging research* (pp. 43–69). New York: Springer Publishing.

Campbell, R. T., & O'Rand, A. M. (1985). Settings and sequences: The heuristics of aging research. In J. E. Birren & V. L. Bengtson (Eds.), *Handbook of aging and the social sciences* (pp. 58–79). New York: Springer Publishing.

Cantor, M. H. (1983). Strain among caregivers: A study of experience in the United States. *The Gerontologist, 23,* 597–604.

Cantor, M. H. (1995). Families and caregiving in an aging society. In L. Burton (Ed.), *Families and aging* (pp. 135–144). Amityville, NY: Baywood.

Caplan, C., & Brangan, N. (2004). Out-of-pocket spending on health care by Medicare beneficiaries age 65 and older in 2003. *Data Digest.* AARP Public Policy Institute. Retrieved from http://assets.aarp.org/rgcenter/health/dd101_spending.pdf

Carlson, E. (2009). 20th century generations. *Population Bulletin, 64*(1).

Caro, F. G., Bass, S. A., & Chen, Y. P. (1993). Introduction: Achieving a productive aging society. In S. A. Bass, F. G. Caro, & Y. P. Chen (Eds.), *Achieving a productive aging society* (pp. 3–25). Westport, CT: Auburn House.

Carstensen, L. L. (2009). *A long bright future: An action plan for a lifetime of happiness, health, and financial security.* New York: Broadway Books.

Cash and Counseling Program. (2006). Cash and Counseling homepage. Retrieved from http://www.cashandcounseling.org

Center for Health Communication, Harvard School of Public Health. (2004). *Reinventing aging: Baby boomers and civic engagement.* Boston, MA: Harvard School of Public Health.

Center for Retirement Research. (2004). *Most people don't know the Social Security retirement age is rising.* Boston, MA: Center for Retirement Research at Boston College. Retrieved from http://www.bc.edu/crr

Center for Retirement Research. (2007). *The Social Security fix-it book.* Retrieved from http://crr.bc.edu/special_projects/the_social_security_fix-it_book.html

Center for Retirement Research. (2009). *The Social Security fix-it book.* Retrieved from http://crr.bc.edu/special_projects/the_social_security_fix-it_book.html

Center on an Aging Society. (2004). *Caregivers of older persons data profile: A decade of informal caregiving.* Washington, DC: Georgetown University. Retrieved from http://ihcrp.georgetown.edu/agingsociety/pubhtml/caregiver

Center on Budget and Policy Priorities. (2005). *The number of uninsured Americans continues to rise in 2004.* Retrieved from http://www.cbpp.org/8–30–05health.htm

Centers for Disease Control. (2009a). *Deaths, percent of total deaths, and death rates for the 15 leading causes of death in selected age groups, by Hispanic origin, race for non-Hispanic population, and sex, United States, 2006.* Retrieved from http://www.cdc.gov/nchs/nvss/mortality/lcwk6.htm

Centers for Disease Control. (2009b). *Deaths, percent of total deaths, and death rates for the 15 leading causes of death in selected age groups, by race and sex, United States, 2006.* Retrieved from http://www.cdc.gov/nchs/nvss/mortality/lcwk3.htm

Centers for Medicare and Medicaid Services. (n.d.). *National health expenditures by sponsors 2008 summary and tables.* Retrieved from http://www.cms.gov/NationalHealthExpendData/downloads/bhg08.pdf

Centers for Medicare and Medicaid Services. (2010). *Medicare and you: 2010.* Retrieved from http://www.medicare.gov/Publications/Pubs/pdf/10050.pdf

Chapman, D., & Perry, G. (2008). Depression as a major component of public health for older adults. *Preventing Chronic Disease, 5*(1). Retrieved from http:www.cdc.gov/pcd/issues/2008/jan/07_0150.htm

Chappell, N. L. (1990). Aging and social care. In R. H. Binstock & L. K. George (Eds.), *Handbook of aging and the social sciences* (3rd ed., pp. 483–454). San Diego, CA: Academic Press.

Chen, Y.-P. (1994). Equivalent retirement ages' and their implications for Social Security and Medicare financing. *The Gerontologist, 34*(6), 731–735.

Cherlin, A. J. (2004). *Public and private families.* Boston: McGraw-Hill.

Cherlin, A. J., & Furstenberg, F. (1986). *The new American grandparent.* New York: Basic Books.

Clarke, E. J., Preston, M., Raksin, J., & Bengtson, V. L. (1999). Types of conflicts and tensions between older parents and adult children. *The Gerontologist, 39*(3), 261–270.

Clawson, M. A. (1999). When women play the bass: Instrument specialization and gender interpretation in alternative rock music. *Gender & Society, 13,* 193–210.

CNN. (2008). *Local exit polls: Election center 2008.* Retrieved from http://www.cnn.com/Election/2008/results/polls/

Coale, A. (1964). How a population ages or grows younger. In R. Friedman (Ed.), *Population: The vital revolution* (pp. 47–58). Garden City, NY: Anchor Books.

Cockerham, W. C. (1998). *Medical sociology* (7th ed.). Upper Saddle River, NJ: Prentice-Hall.

Cohen, R. A., & Van Nostrand, J. (1995). Trends in the health of older Americans: United States, 1994. National Center for Health Statistics. *Vital and Health Statistics, 3*(30).

Cohler, B. J. (1983). Autonomy and interdependence in the family of adulthood: A psychological perspective. *The Gerontologist, 23,* 33–39.

Cohler, B. J., & Altergott, K. (1995). The family of the second half of life: Connecting theories and findings. In R. Blieszner & V. H. Bedford (Eds.), *Handbook of aging and the family* (pp. 59–94). Westport, CT: Greenwood Press.

Cohn, D'Vera. (2008). *Baby boomers: The gloomiest generation.* Retrieved from http://pewresearch.org/pubs/880/baby-boomers-the-gloomiest-generation

Cole, T. R. (1992). *The journey of life: A cultural history of aging in America.* New York: Cambridge University Press.

Cole, T. R. (1995). What have we "made" of aging? *Journal of Gerontology: Social Sciences, 50B*(6), S341–S343.

Cole, T. R., & Thomson, B. (2001–2002). Introduction: Aging is going out of style. *Generations, 25*(4), 6–8.

Coleman, M., Ganong, L. H., & Rothrauff, T. C. (2006). Racial and ethnic similarities and differences in beliefs about intergenerational assistance to older adults after divorce and remarriage. *Family Relations, 55*(5), 576–587.

Commonwealth Fund. (1993). *The untapped resource: Final report of the Americans Over 55 at Work Program.* New York: Author.

Concord Coalition. (2009). Mission statement. Retrieved from http://www.concordcoalition.org

Congressional Budget Office. (2009). *Long-term budget outlook: December, 2007.* Retrieved from http://www.cbo.gov/ftpdocs/88xx/doc8877/Frontmatter.1.3.shtml

Congressional Demographics. (2009). Congress.com. Retrieved from http://www.congress.org/congressorg/directory/demographics.tt?catid=all

Condie, S. J. (1989). Older married couples. In S. J. Bahr & E. T. Peterson (Eds.), *Aging and the family* (pp. 143–158). Lexington, MA: Lexington Books.

Cooney, T., & Uhlenberg, P. (1990). The role of divorce in men's relations with their adult children after mid-life. *Journal of Marriage and the Family, 52,* 677–688.

Cooperman, L. F., & Keast, F. D. (1983). *Adjusting to an older work force.* New York: Van Nostrand Reinhold.

Copeland, C. (2009). *Employment-based retirement plan participation: Geographic differences and trends 2008.* Washington, DC: Employee Benefit Research Institute. Retrieved from http://www.ebri.org/pdf/briefspdf/EBRI_IB_11–2009_No336_Ret-Part.pdf

Corbett, P. (2010). *Facebook demographics and statistics report 2010.* Retrieved from http://www.istrategylabs.com/2010/01/facebook-demographics-and-statistics-report-2010–145-growth-in-1-year/

Cornman, J. M., & Kingson, E. R. (1996). Trends, issues, perspectives, and values for the aging of the baby boom cohorts. *The Gerontologist, 36*(1), 15–26.

Council of State Governments. (1994). *The book of the states* (1994–1995 ed., Vol. 30). Lexington, KY: Author.

Cowen, D. (2008). *Military workfare: The soldier and social citizenship in Canada.* Toronto: University of Toronto Press.

Cowgill, D. (1972). A theory of aging in cross-cultural perspective. In D. Cowgill & L. Holmes (Eds.), *Aging and modernization* (pp. 1–13). New York: Appleton-Century-Crofts.

Cox, R. (2004). *When generations collide: How to solve the generational puzzle at work* (Management forum series). Retrieved from http://www.executiveforum.com

Crown, W. H., Mutschler, P. H., Schulz, J. H., & Loew, R. (1993). *The economic status of divorced older women.* Waltham, MA: Policy Center on Aging, Brandeis University.

Cruise Lines International Association. (2008). *2008 Cruise market profile study.* Retrieved from http://www.cruising.org/cruisenews/news.cfm?NID=355

Cumming, E., & Henry, W. H. (1961). *Growing old: The process of disengagement.* New York: Basic Books.

Cutler, N. E. (1969–1970). Generation, maturation, and party affiliation: A cohort analysis. *Public Opinion Quarterly, 33,* 583–588.

Cutler, N. E. (2004–2005). Silver industries: Introduction. *Generations, 28,* 6–7.

Cutler, S. J. (1995). The methodology of social scientific research in gerontology: Progress and issues. *Journals of Gerontology: Social Sciences, 50B*(2), S63–S64.

Dangelis, N. L., Hardy, M., & Cutler, S. J. (2007). Population aging, intracohort aging, and sociopolitical attitudes. *American Sociological Review, 72,* 812–830.

Dannefer, D. (1988). What's in a name? An account of the neglect of variability in the study of aging. In J. E. Birren & V. L. Bengtson (Eds.), *Emergent theories of aging* (pp. 356–384). New York: Springer Publishing.

Davey, A., Savla, J., & Janke, M. (2004). Antecedents of intergenerational support: Families in context and families as context. In M. Silverstein (Ed.), *Intergenerational relations across time and place. Annual Review of Gerontology and Geriatrics* (Vol. 24, pp. 29–54). New York: Springer Publishing.

Day, C. L. (1990). *What older Americans think.* Princeton, NJ: Princeton University Press.

Day, C. L. (1993a). Public opinion toward costs and benefits of Social Security and Medicare. *Research on Aging, 15*(3), 279–298.

Day, C. L. (1993b). Older Americans' attitudes toward the Medicare Catastrophic Coverage Act of 1988. *Journal of Politics, 55,* 167–177.

Day, J. C. (1996). *Population projections of the United States by age, sex, race and Hispanic origin 1995–2050* (U.S. Census Bureau, Current Population Reports, P25–1130). Retrieved from http://www.census.gov/prod/2004pubs/04statab/pop.pdf

Deatrick, D. (1997). Senior-med: Creating a network to help manage medications. *Generations, 21*(3), 59–60.

de Jong, G. (2004). Remarriage, unmarried cohabitation, living apart together: Partner relationships following bereavement or divorce. *Journal of Marriage and the Family, 66*(1), 236–243.

DeNatale, M. L. (2007). Understanding the Medicare Part D prescription program: Partnerships for beneficiaries and health care professionals. *Policy, Politics & Nursing Practice, 8*(3), 170–181.

Dennis, H. (2004–2005). The evolution of the link between business and aging. *Generations, 28,* 8–14.

DeNavas-Walt, C., Proctor, B., & Smith, J. (2009). *Income, poverty, and health insurance coverage in the United States: 2008* (Current Population Reports, P60–23). Washington, DC: U.S. Government Printing Office.

Depp, C., & Jeste, V. (2006). Definitions and predictors of successful aging: A comprehensive review of larger quantitative studies. *American Journal of Geriatric Psychiatry, 14*(1), 6–20.

DiGiovanna, A. G. (2000). *Human aging: Biological perspectives.* New York: McGraw-Hill.

Dillaway, H., & Byrnes, M. (2009). Reconsidering successful aging: A call for renewed and expanding academic critiques and conceptualizations. *Journal of Applied Gerontology, 28.* Retrieved from http://jag.sagepub.com/content/28/6/702.full.pdf+html

Dobson, D. (1983). The elderly as a political force. In W. P. Browne & L. K. Olson (Eds.), *Aging and public policy: The politics of growing old in America* (pp. 123–144). Westport, CT: Greenwood Press.

Doeringer, P. B. (1990). Economic security, labor market flexibility and bridges to retirement. In P. B. Doeringer (Ed.), *Bridges to retirement: Older workers in a changing labor market* (pp. 3–19). Ithaca, NY: Cornell University Press.

Doka, K. J. (1989). *Disenfranchised grief: Recognizing hidden sorrow.* New York: Lexington Books.

Dowd, J. J. (1980). *Stratification among the aged.* Monterey, CA: Brooks/Cole.

Dowd, J. J. (1981). Age and inequality: A critique of the age stratification model. *Human Development, 24,* 157–171.

Du, P., & Yang, H. (2009). China. In E. Palmore, F. Whittington, & S. Kunkel (Eds.), *International handbook on aging: Current research and developments* (pp. 145–158). Santa Barbara, CA: Praeger.

Duncan, D., Nicholson, T., White, J., Burr, D., & Bonaguro, J. (2010). The baby boomer effect: Changing patterns of substance abuse among adults ages 55 and older. *Journal of Aging & Social Policy, 22*(3), 237–248.

Dunlop, D. D., Song, J., Lyons, J. S., Mannheim, J. M., & Chang, R. W. (2003). Racial/ethnic differences in rates of depression among preretirement adults. *American Journal of Public Health, 93*(11), 1945–1952.

Duvall, E. M., & Miller, E. C. (1985). *Marriage and family development* (6th ed.). New York: Harper and Row.

Dwyer, J. W. (1995). The effects of illness on the family. In R. Blieszner & V. H. Bedford (Eds.), *Handbook on aging and the family* (pp. 401–421). New York: Greenwood Press.

East, P. L. (1998). Racial and ethnic differences in girls' sexual, marital, and birth expectations. *Journal of Marriage and the Family, 60*(1), 150–162.

Easterlin, R. A. (1987). *Birth and fortune: The impact of numbers on personal welfare* (2nd ed.). Chicago: University of Chicago Press.

Easterlin, R. A. (1996). Economic and social implications of demographic patterns. In R. H. Binstock & L. K. George (Eds.), *Handbook of aging and the social sciences* (4th ed., pp. 73–83). New York: Academic Press.

Easterlin, R., Schaeffer, C., & Macunovich, D. (1993). Will the baby boomers be less well off than their parents? Income, wealth, and family circumstances of the life cycle in the United States. *Population and Development Review, 19*(3), 497–522.

Edmonson, B. (1997, April). The facts of death. *American Demographics, 19*(3), 46–53.

Ehrenreich, B., & English, D. (1990). The sexual politics of sickness. In P. Conrad & D. Kerns (Eds.), *The sociology of health and illness: Critical perspectives* (pp. 270–284). New York: St. Martin's Press.

Ehrlich, R. (Ed.). (2000). *Civic responsibility and higher education.* Phoenix, AZ: Oryx Press. Retrieved from http://www.nytimes.com/ref/college/collegespecial2/

Ekerdt, D. J. (1986). The busy ethic: Moral continuity between work and retirement. *The Gerontologist, 26*(3), 239–244.

Ekerdt, D. J. (1998). Entitlements, generational equity, and public-opinion manipulation in Kansas City. *The Gerontologist, 38*(5), 525–536.

Ekerdt, D. J., & DeViney, S. (1990). On defining persons as retired. *Journal of Aging Studies, 4*(3), 211–229.

Ekerdt, D. J., DeViney, S., & Kosloski, K. (1996). Profiling plans for retirement. *Journal of Gerontology: Social Sciences, 41B*(3), S140–S149.

Elder, G. H. (1974). *Children of the great depression.* Chicago: University of Chicago Press.

Elder, G. L., Johnson, M. K., & Crosnoe, R. (2007). The emergence and development of life course theory. In J. T. Mortimer & M. J. Shanahan (Eds.), *Handbook of the life course* (pp. 3–19). New York: Kluwer Academic/Plenum Publishers.

Elman, C., & O'Rand, A. M. (2004). The race is to the swift: Socioeconomic origins, adult education, and wage attainment. *American Journal of Sociology, 110*(1), 123–160.

Elmer, V. (2009). Age discrimination claims by workers reach record high. *AARPBulletin Today.* Retrieved from http://bulletin.aarp.org/yourmoney/work/articles/age_discrimination_claims_by_workers_reach_record_high.html?CMP=KNC-360I-GOOGLE-BULL&HBX_OU=50&HBX_PK=age_discrimination

Elwert, F., & Christakis, N. A. (2008). Effect of widowhood on mortality by the causes of death of both spouses. *American Journal of Public Health, 98*(11), 2092–2098.

Employee Benefit Research Institute (EBRI). (2004). *Databook.* Retrieved from http://www.ebri.org/pdf/publications/books/databook

Employee Benefit Research Institute (EBRI). (2008). *Databook.* Retrieved from http://www.ebri.org/publications/books/index.cfm?fa=databook

Employee Benefit Research Institute (EBRI). (2010). *EBRI databook on employee benefits: Employer costs for employee compensation.* Retrieved from http://www.ebri.org/pdf/publications/books/databook/DB.Chapter%2003.pdf

Epstein, J. S. (1994). *Adolescents and their music: If it's too loud, you're too old.* New York: Garland.

Erikson, E., Erikson, J. M., & Kivnick, H. (1986). *Vital involvement in old age: The experience of old age in our time.* London: Norton.

Esping-Andersen, G. (1990). *The three worlds of welfare capitalism.* Princeton, NJ: Princeton University Press.

Espo, D. (2005, June 16). Senators consider boosting Social Security retirement age to 69. *The Detroit News.* Retrieved from http://www.detnews.com/2005/politics/0506/16/0pols-217281.htm

Estes, C. L. (1979). *The aging enterprise.* San Francisco: Jossey-Bass.

Estes, C. L. (1991). The new political economy of aging: Introduction and critique. In M. Minkler & C. L. Estes (Eds.), *Critical perspectives on aging: The political and morale economy of growing old* (pp. 19–36). Amityville, NY: Baywood.

Estes, C. L. (1999). Critical gerontology and the new political economy of aging. In M. Minkler & C. L. Estes (Eds.), *Critical gerontology: Perspectives from political and moral economy* (pp. 17–36). Amityville, NY: Baywood.

Estes, C., & Binney, E. (1991). The biomedicalization of aging: Dangers and dilemmas. In M. Minkler & C. L. Estes (Eds.), *Critical perspectives on aging: The political and moral economy of growing old* (pp. 117–134). Amityville, NY: Baywood.

Fay, S. (1950). Bismarck's welfare state. *Current History, 18,* 1–7.

Federal Interagency Forum on Aging-Related Statistics. (2008). *Older Americans 2008: Key indicators of well-being.* Retrieved from http://www.agingstats.gov/Agingstatsdotnet/Main_Site/Data/2008_Documents/OA_2008.pdf

Federal Interagency Forum on Aging-Related Statistics. (2010). *Older Americans 2010: Key indicators of well-being.* Retrieved from http://www.agingstats.gov/agingstatsdotnet/Main_Site/Data/2010_Documents/Docs/OA_2010.pdf

Ferraro, K. F. (2007). Afterword. In K. F. Ferraro & J. Wilmoth (Eds.), *Gerontology: Perspectives and issues* (pp. 325–343). New York: Springer Publishing.

Ferraro, K. F., & LaGrange, R. L. (1992). Are older people most afraid of crime? Reconsidering age differences in fear of victimization. *Journal of Gerontology: Social Sciences, 47*(5), S233–S244.

Ferraro, K. F., & Shippee, T. P. (2009). Aging and cumulative inequality: How does inequality get under the skin? *The Gerontologist, 49*(3), 333–343.

Ferraro, K. F., Shippee, T. P., & Schafer, M. H. (2009). Cumulative inequality theory for research on aging and the life course. In V. L. Bengtson, D. Gans, N. M. Putney, & M. Silverstein (Eds.), *Handbook of theories of aging* (pp. 413–434). New York: Springer Publishing.

Fields, G. S., & Mitchell, O. S. (1984). *Retirement, pensions, and Social Security.* Cambridge, MA: The MIT Press.

Finch, J. F., & Graziano, W. G. (2001). Predicting depression from temperament, personality, and patterns of social relations. *Journal of Personality, 69,* 27–55.

Finley, N. J., Roberts, M. D., & Banahan, B. F. (1988). Motivators and inhibitors of attitudes toward aging parents. *The Gerontologist, 28*(1), 73–78.

Firebaugh, G., & Chen, K. (1995). Vote turnout of Nineteenth Amendment women: The enduring effect of disenfranchisement. *American Journal of Sociology, 100*(4), 972–976.

Fitzpatrick, T. R., & McCabe, J. (2008). Future challenges for senior center programming to serve younger and more active baby boomers. *Activities, Adaptation & Aging, 32*, 3–4.

Flaherty, J. H., Liu, M. L., Ding, L., Dong, B., Ding, Q., Li, X., & Xiao, S. (2007). China: The sleeping giant. *International Health Affairs, 55*(8), 1295–1300.

Flowers, L., Gross, L., Kuo, P., & Sinclair, S. (2005). *State profiles 2005: Reforming the health care system.* Washington, DC: AARP Public Policy Institute.

Fogel, B. S., Gottlieb, G., & Furino, A. (1990). Minds at risk. In B. S. Fogel, A. Furino, & G. Gottlieb (Eds.), *Mental health policy for older Americans: Protecting minds at risk* (Chapter 1). Washington, DC: American Psychiatric Press.

Foner, A. (1973). The polity. In M. W. Riley, M. Johnson, & A. Foner (Eds.), *Aging and society, Vol. 3: A sociology of age stratification* (pp. 115–159). New York: Russell Sage Foundation.

Foner, A. (1996). Age norms and the structure of consciousness: Some final comments. *The Gerontologist, 36*(2), 221–223.

Foster, L., Brown, R., Phillips, B., Schore, J., & Carlson, B. (2003, March 26). Improving the quality of Medicaid personal assistance through consumer direction. *Health Affairs Data Watch: Medicaid.* Retrieved from http://content.healthaffairs.org/content/early/2003/03/26hlthaff.w3.162.citation

Frank, J. B. (2002). *The paradox of aging in place in assisted living.* Westport, CT: Bergin & Garvey.

Fredonia Group. (2006). *Anti-aging products to 2009.* Retrieved from http://www.biz-lib.com/ZFR69320.html

Freedman, M. (2002). Civic windfall? Realizing the promise of an aging America. *Generations, 26*(11), 86–89.

Freedman, M., & Segal, P. N. (2008). *When purpose is front and center: A Metlife Foundation/Civic Ventures Encore Career Survey.* San Francisco: Civic Ventures.

Freedman, V. A., Martin, L. G., & Schoeni, R. F. (2002). Recent trends in disability and functioning among older adults in the United States: A systematic review. *Journal of the American Medical Association, 288*(24), 3137–3146.

Freund, P. E., & McGuire, M. B. (1995). *Health, illness, and the social body.* Englewood Cliffs, NJ: Prentice-Hall.

Freund, P. E., & McGuire, M. B. (1999). *Health, illness, and the social body* (3rd ed.). Englewood Cliffs, NJ: Prentice-Hall.

Friedland, R. B., & Summer, L. (1999). *Demography is not destiny.* Washington, DC: National Academy on Aging, Gerontological Society of America.

Friedland, R. B., & Summer, L. (2005). *Demography is not destiny, revisited* (Georgetown University Commonwealth Publication No. 789). Washington, DC: Center on an Aging Society.

Gale, W. G., Iwry, M., Munnell, A. H., & Thaler, R. H. (2004). *Improving 401(k) investment performance* (Center for Retirement Research Issue Brief No. 26). Boston: Boston University.

Gallo, W. T., Bradley, E. H., Dubin, J. A., Jones, R. N., Falba, T. A., Teng, H-M., et al. (2006). The persistence of depressive symptoms in older workers who experience involuntary job loss: Results from the Health and Retirement Study. *Journal of Gerontology: Social Sciences, 61B,* S221–S228.

Gandel, C. (2009). The new face of caregiving: Male caregivers. *AARP Bulletin.* Retrieved from http://bulletin.aarp.org/yourhealth/caregiving/articles/the_new_face_of_caregiving.html

Gatz, M., Bengtson, V. L., & Blum, M. J. (1990). Caregiving families. In J. E. Birren & K. W. Schaie (Eds.), *Handbook of the psychology of aging* (3rd ed., pp. 404–426). San Diego, CA: Academic Press.

Gendell, M., & Siegel, J. S. (1992). Trends in retirement age by sex, 1950–2005. *Monthly Labor Review, 115*(7), 22–29.

George, L. K. (1995). The last half-century of aging research and thoughts for the future. *The Journal of Gerontology: Social Sciences, 50B*(1), S1–S3.

George, L. K. (1996). Missing links: The case for a social psychology of the life course. *The Gerontologist, 36*(2), 248–255.

George, L. K. (2003). What the life course perspectives offer the study of aging and health. In R. Settersten (Ed.), *Invitation to the life course: Toward new understandings of later life* (pp. 161–188). Amityville, NY: Baywood.

George, L. K. (2010). Still happy after all these years: Research frontiers on subjective well-being in later life. *Journal of Gerontology: Social Sciences, 65*(3), 331–339.

Gerontology Research Group. (2006). Home page. Retrieved from http://www.grg.org/

Gewerth, K. E. (1988). Elderly offenders: A review of previous research. In B. McCarthy & R. Langworthy (Eds.), *Older offenders: Perspectives in criminology and criminal justice* (pp. 14–31). New York: Praeger.

Giarrusso, R., Feng, D., & Bengtson, V. L. (2004). Charting the intergenerational-stake over historical and biographical time. In M. Silverstein (Ed.), *Intergenerational relations across time and place. Annual Review of Gerontology and Geriatrics* (Vol. 24, pp. 55–76). New York: Springer Publishing.

Gibson, D. (1996). Broken down by age and gender: "The problem of old women" redefined. *Gender & Society, 10*(4), 433–448.

Gilleard, C., & Higgs, P. (2009). The power of silver: Age and identity politics in the 21st century. *Journal of Aging & Social Policy, 21,* 277–295.

Gitlin, L. (2003).Conducting research on home environments: Lessons learned and new directions. *The Gerontologist, 43*(5), 628–637.

Glaser, B. G., & Strauss, A. L. (1967). *The discovery of grounded theory: Strategies for qualitative research.* Chicago: Aldine Publishing.

Glass, T. (1998). Conjugating the "tenses" of function: Discordance among hypothetical, experimental, and enacted function in older adults. *The Gerontologist, 38*(1), 101–112.

Glazer, N. Y. (1993). *Women's paid and unpaid labor.* Philadelphia, PA: Temple University Press.

Glick, P. C. (1977). Updating the life-cycle of the family. *Journal of Marriage and the Family, 39*(1), 5–13.

Goffman, E. (1969). *The presentation of self in everyday life.* London: Allen Lane.

Goldstein, C., & Beall, C. M. (1983). Modernization and aging in the third and fourth world: Views from the rural Hinterland in Nepal. *Human Organization, 1,* 48–49.

Goldstein, J. (2009). How populations age. In P. Uhlenberg (Ed.), *International handbook of population aging* (Vol. 1, Part 1, pp. 7–18). Retrieved from http://www.springerlink.com/content/x40621714xhwt753/fulltext.pdf

Goldstein, J. R., & Kenney, C. T. (2001). Marriage delayed or marriage forgone? New cohort forecasts of first marriage for U.S. women. *American Sociological Review, 66*(4), 506–519.

Goldstein, S. (1960). *Consumption patterns of the aged.* Philadelphia: University of Pennsylvania Press.

Gonyea, J. (2009). Multigenerational bonds, family support, and baby boomers: Current challenges and future prospects for elder care. In R. Hudson (Ed.), *Boomer bust? Economic and political issues for the graying society* (Vol. 2, pp. 213–232). Westport, CT: Praeger.

Gornick, J. C., Sierminska, E., & Smeeding, T. M. (2009). The income and wealth packages of older women in cross-national perspective. *Journal of Gerontology: Social Sciences, 63*(3), 402–414.

Goss, S. C. (1997). *Comparison of financial effects of advisory council plans to modify the OASDI Program.* Retrieved from http://www.ssa.gov./search97cgi/

Goyal, R. S. (1989). Some aspects of aging in India. In R. N. Pati & B. Jena (Eds.), *Aged in India: Sociodemographic dimensions* (pp. 19–36). New Delhi, India: Ashish Publishing House.

Gross, C. P., Anderson, G. F., & Powe, N. R. (1999). The relation between funding by the National Institutes of Health and the burden of disease. *New England Journal of Medicine, 340,* 1881–1886.

Grove, L. (1996, April 8). The 100-year-old senator? Some fans, foes say quit. Strom Thurmond says no. *The Washington Post.*

Gupta, G. R. (1976). Love, arranged marriage, and the Indian social structure. *Journal of Comparative Family Studies, 7,* 75–85.

Guy, R. F., & Erdner, R. A. (1993). Retirement: An emerging challenge for women. In R. Kastenbaum (Ed.), *Encyclopedia of adult development* (pp. 405–409). Phoenix, AZ: Oryx Press.

Hagburg, B. (1995). The individual's life history as a formative experience to aging. In B. K. Haight & J. D. Webster (Eds.), *The art and science of reminiscing* (pp. 61–76). Washington, DC: Taylor & Francis.

Hagestad, G. O. (2003). Interdependent lives and relationships in changing times: A life course view of families and aging. In R. Settersten (Ed.), *Invitation to the life course: Toward new understandings of later life* (pp. 135–160). Amityville, NY: Baywood.

HSBC/AgeWave. (2005). *The future of retirement in a world of rising life expectancies.* Retrieved from http://www.hsbc.com/public/groupsite/retirement_future/en/

Hamil-Luker, J., & Uhlenberg, P. (2002). Later life education in the 1990s: Increasing involvement and continuing disparity. *Journal of Gerontology: Social Sciences, 57B*(6), S324–S331.

Hamilton, B., Martin, J., & Ventura, S. (2010). Births: Preliminary data for 2008. *National Vital Statistics Reports, 58*(16), 1–6.

Hammill, G. (2005). Mixing and managing four generations of employees. *FDU Magazine.* Retrieved from http://www.fdu.edu/newspubs/magazine/05ws/generations.htm

Han, H.-R., Choi, Y. J., Kim, M. T., Lee, J. E., & Kim, K. B. (2008). Experiences and challenges of informal caregiving for Korean immigrants. *Journal of Advanced Nursing, 63*(5), 517–526.

Harahan, M. F., & Stone, R. I. (2009). Who will care? Building the geriatric long-term care labor force. In R. Hudson (Ed.), *Boomer bust? Economic and political issues for the graying society* (Vol. 2, pp. 233–252). Westport, CT: Praeger.

Hardy, M. A., Hazelrigg, L. E., & Quadagno, J. (1996). *Ending a career in the auto industry: Thirty and out.* New York: Plenum.

Hardy, M. A., & Quadagno, J. (1995). Satisfaction with early retirement: Making choices in the auto industry. *Journal of Gerontology: Social Sciences, 50*(4), S217–S228.

Hareven, T. K. (1994). Family change and historical change: An uneasy relationship. In M. W. Riley, R. L. Kane, & A. Foner (Eds.), *Aging and structural lag* (pp. 130–150). New York: Wiley-Interscience.

Hareven, T. K. (1995). Historical perspectives on the family and aging. In R. Blieszner & V. H. Bedford (Eds.), *Handbook of aging and the family* (pp. 13–31). Westport, CT: Greenwood Press.

Harrington Meyer, M. (1996). Making claims as workers or wives: The distribution of Social Security Benefits. *American Sociological Review, 61,* 449–465.

Harris, S. B. (1996). For better or for worse: Spouse abuse grown old. *Journal of Elder Abuse & Neglect, 8*(1), 1–33.

Hart Research Associates. (2008). Executive summary. In *A Metlife Foundation/Civic Ventures Encore Career Survey* (p. 8). San Francisco, CA: Civic Ventures. Retrieved from http://www.civicventures.org/publications/surveys/encore-career-survey.cfm

Harvard School of Public Health. (2004). *Reinventing aging: Baby boomers and civic engagement.* Retrieved from http://www.hsph.harvard.edu/chc/reinventingaging/Report.pdf

Hatch, S. L., Feinstein, L., Link, B. G., Wadsworth, M. E. J., & Richards, M. (2007). The continuing benefits of education: Adult education and midlife cognitive ability in the British 1946 birth cohort. *Journal of Gerontology: Social Sciences, 62B,* S404–S414.

Haub, C. (2007). Global aging and the demographic divide. *Public Policy & Aging Report, 17*(4), 1–6.

Hayflick, L. (2001–2002). Anti-aging medicine: Hype, hope, and reality. *Generations, 25*(4), 20–25.

Hayslip, B., & Glover, R. J. (2008). Traditional grandparents' views of their caregiving peers' parenting skills: Complimentary or critical? In B. Hayslip & P. Kaminsky (Eds.), *Parenting the custodial grandchild: Implications for clinical practice* (pp. 149–164). New York: Springer Publishing.

Hayslip, B., & Kaminsky, P. (Eds.). (2008). *Parenting the custodial grandchild: Implications for clinical practice* (pp. 149–164). New York: Springer Publishing.

Hayward, M. D., Friedman, S., & Chen, S. (1996). Race inequalities in men's retirement. *Journal of Gerontology: Social Sciences, 51B*(1), S1–S10.

Hazelrigg, L. (1997). On the importance of age. In M. A. Hardy (Ed.), *Studying aging and social change* (pp. 93–128). Thousand Oaks, CA: Sage Publications.

He, W., Sengupta, M., Velkoff, V., & DeBarros, K. (2005). *65+ in the United States: 2005* (Current Population Reports, P23–209). Washington, DC: U.S. Government Printing Office.

Healthy People 2010. (2006). Home page. Retrieved from http://www.healthypeople.gov/

Heiss, F., McFadden, D., & Winter, J. (2006). Who failed to enroll in Medicare Part D and why? Early results. *Health Affairs, 25,* 344–354.

HelpAge International. (2008). *Protecting the rights of older people in Africa.* Retrieved from http://www.helpage.org/publications/?ssearch=Protecting+the+Rights+of+Older+People+in+Africa&adv=0&topic=0&region=0&language=0&type=0

Helton, D. R. (1997, April). A look at how Kentuckians in Knox County once treated the dead. *Kentucky Explorer,* 34–39.

Hendricks, J. (1992). Generations and the generation of theory in social gerontology. *International Journal of Aging and Human Development, 35*(1), 31–47.

Hendricks, J., Applebaum, R., & Kunkel, S. (2010). A world apart? Bridging the gap between theory and applied social gerontology. *The Gerontologist, 50*(3), 284–293.

Hendricks, J., & Cutler, S. (2003). Leisure in life course perspective. In R. Settersten (Ed.), *Invitation to the life course: Toward new understandings of later life* (pp. 107–134). Amityville, NY: Baywood.

Henretta, J. C. (1994). Social structure and age-based careers. In M. W. Riley, R. L. Kahn, & A. Foner (Eds.), *Age and structural lag* (pp. 57–79). New York: Wiley-Interscience.

Herd, P. (2005). Ensuring a minimum: Social Security reform and women. *The Gerontologist, 45*(1), 12–25.

Herd, P., & Kingson, E. (2005). Reframing Social Security: Cures worse than the disease. In R. B. Hudson (Ed.), *The new politics of old age policy* (pp. 184–204). Baltimore: Johns Hopkins University Press.

Hess, B. B., & Waring, J. H. (1978). Changing patterns of aging and family bonds in later life. *Family Coordinator, 27,* 303–314.

Hill, R. (1970). *Family development in three generations.* Cambridge, MA: Schenkman.

Hillier, S., & Barrow, G. (1999). *Aging, the individual, and society* (7th ed.). Belmont, CA: Wadsworth Press.

Hinrichs, K. (2000). Elephants on the move: Patterns of pension reform in OECD countries. *European Review, 8*(3), 353–378.

Hitt, R., Young-Xu, Y., & Perls, T. (1999). Centenarians: The older you get, the healthier you've been. *Lancet, 354*(9179), 652.

Hobbs, F. B., & Damon, B. L. (1996). *65+ in the United States* (Current Population Reports, P-23, No. 190). Washington, DC: U.S. Government Printing Office.

Hochschild, A. R. (1975). Disengagement theory: A critique and proposal. *American Sociological Review, 14*(5), 553–569.

Hogan, D. P., & Astone, N. M. (1986). The transition to adulthood. *Annual Review of Sociology, 12,* 109–130.

Hogan, D. P., Eggebeen, D. J., & Clogg, C. C. (1993). The structure of intergenerational exchanges in American families. *American Journal of Sociology, 98*(6), 1428–1458.

Holden, K. C., & Kuo, H.-H. D. (1996). Complex marital histories and economic well-being: The continuing legacy of divorce and widowhood as the HRS cohort approaches retirement. *The Gerontologist, 36*(3), 383–390.

Holstein, M. (1995). The normative case: chronological age and public policy. *Generations, 19*(3), 11–14.

Holtz-Eakin, D., & Smeeding, T. M. (1994). Income, wealth, and intergenerational economic relations of the aged. In L. G. Martin & S. H. Preston (Eds.), *Demography of aging* (pp. 102–145). Washington, DC: National Academy Press.

Horowitz, A. (1985). Sons and daughters as caregivers to older parents: Differences in role performance and consequences. *The Gerontologist, 25*(6), 612–617.

Hoskins, D. D. (1992). Developments and trends in Social Security, 1990–1992: Overview of principal trends. *Social Security Bulletin, 55*(4), 36–42.

Hoyert, D. L., Heron, M. P., Murphy, S. L., & Kung, H. C. (2006). Deaths: Final data for 2003. *National Vital Statistics Report, 54*(13), 1–7.

Hu, Y., & Goldman, M. (1990). Mortality differentials by marital status: An international comparison. *Demography, 27*(2), 223–250.

Huber, B. (2005). *Implementing the Madrid Plan of Action on Aging.* United Nations Department of Economic and Social Affairs. Retrieved from http://www.un.org/esa/population/meetings/EGMPopAge/EGMPopAge_21_RHuber.pdf

Hudson, R. (1978). The "graying" of the Federal budget and its consequences for old-age policy. *The Gerontologist, 18,* 428–440.

Hudson, R. (1996). The changing face of aging politics. *The Gerontologist, 36*(1), 33–35.

Hudson, R. (2009). Preface. In R. Hudson (Ed.), *Boomer bust? Economic and political issues for the graying society* (Vol. 1, pp. vii–xii). Westport, CT: Praeger.

Hudson, R. B. (2005). *The new politics of old age policy.* Baltimore, MD: Johns Hopkins University Press.

Hunt, G. G. (1997). Cleveland free-net Alzheimer's forum. *Generations, 21*(3), 37.

Hurd, M. (2009). *Life cycle spending after retirement and adequacy of preparation for retirement.* Washington, DC: Brookings Institution. Retrieved from http://www.mrrc.isr.umich.edu/publications/other/pdf/Financial%20Literacy%20Proceedings.pdf

Huyck, M. H. (1995). Marriage and close relationships of the marital kind. In R. Blieszner & V. H. Bedford (Eds.), *Handbook of aging and the family* (pp. 181–200). Westport, CT: Greenwood Press.

Ikels, C. (1993). Chinese kinship and the state: Shaping of policy for the elderly. In G. L. Maddox & M. P. Lawton (Eds.), *Annual Review of Gerontology and Geriatrics: Focus on kinship, aging, and social change* (Vol. 13, pp. 123–146). New York: Springer Publishing.

Infoplease. (2007). *The wage gap by gender and race.* Retrieved from http://www.infoplease.com/ipa/A0882775.html

Infoplease. (2009). *Median age at first marriage 1890–2007.* Retrieved from http://www.infoplease.com/ipa/A0005061.html

Institute of Medicine. (2008). *Retooling for an aging America: Building the health care workforce.* Washington, DC: Author.

International Social Security Association (ISSA). (2008). *Social Security country profiles.* Retrieved from http://www.issa.int/aiss/Observatory/Country-Profiles

Jackson, J. S., & Gibson, R. C. (1985). Work and retirement among the black elderly. In Z. S. Blau (Ed.), *Work, retirement, and social policy* (pp. 193–222). Greenwich, CT: JAI Press.

Jacobs, B. (1990). Aging and politics. In R. H. Binstock & L. K. George (Eds.), *Handbook of aging and the social sciences* (3rd ed., pp. 349–361). San Diego, CA: Academic Press.

Jacobs, L. R., & Burns, M. (2005). Don't lump seniors. *Public Policy & Aging Report, 15*(1), 7–9.

James, J. B., & Wink, P. (2006). The crown of life: Dynamics of the early post-retirement period. In *Annual Review of Gerontology and Geriatrics* (Vol. 26). New York: Springer Publishing.

Jarrett, W. H. (1985). Caregiving within kinship systems: Is affection really necessary? *The Gerontologist, 25*(1), 5–20.

Johnson, C. L. (1995). Cultural diversity in the late-life family. In R. Blieszner & V. H. Bedford (Eds.), *Handbook of aging and the family* (pp. 307–331). Westport, CT: Greenwood Press.

Johnson, E. S., & Williamson, J. B. (1987). Retirement in the United States. In K. S. Markides & C. L. Copper (Eds.), *Retirement in industrialized societies* (pp. 9–41). New York: John Wiley and Sons.

Johnson, R. W., & Favreault, M. M. (2004). Economic status in later life among women who raised children outside of marriage. *Journal of Gerontology: Social Sciences, 59B*(6), S315–S323.

Johnson, R. W., & Schaner, S. G. (2005). Value of unpaid activities by older Americans tops $160 billion per year. In *Perspectives on productive aging.* Washington, DC: The Urban Institute. Retrieved from http://www.urban.org/publications/311227.html

Johnson, R. W., Uccello, C. E., & Goldwyn, J. H. (2005). Who forgoes survivor protection in employer-sponsored pension annuities? *The Gerontologist, 45*(1), 26–35.

Jones, S., & Fox, S. (2009). *Generations online in 2009.* Pew Internet & MetLife Mature Market Institute. Retrieved from http://www.pewinternet.org/~/media//Files/Reports/2009/PIP_Generations_2009.pdf

Jones, T. W. (1996). Strengthening the current Social Security system. *The Public Policy and Aging Report, 7*(3), 1, 3–6.

Jordan, L. (2002, May). Law enforcement and the elder: A concern for the 21st century. *FBI Law Enforcement Bulletin,* 20–23.

Juster, F. T., & Suzman, R. (1995). An overview of the health and retirement survey. *The Journal of Human Resources, 30,* 7–56.

Kahn, J. R., & Mason, W. M. (1987). Political alienation, cohort size, and the Easterlin Hypothesis. *American Sociological Review, 52*(2), 155–169.

Kahn, R. (1994). Opportunities, aspirations, and goodness of fit. In M. W. Riley, R. L. Kahn, & A. Foner (Eds.), *Aging and structural lag* (pp. 37–53). New York: Wiley-Interscience.

Kahn, R. (2002). On successful aging and well-being: Self-rated compared with Rowe and Kahn (Guest editorial). *The Gerontologist, 42*(6), 725–726.

Kaiser Family Foundation. (2005). *Medicare fact sheet: Medicare at a glance* (Publication No. 1066–08). Retrieved from http://www.kkf.org

Kaiser Family Foundation. (2009). *Trends in health care costs and spending.* Retrieved from http://www.kff.org/insurance/upload/7692_02.pdf

Kaiser Family Foundation. (2010). *Fast facts: Medicare spending as a share of total federal outlays, FY2010.* Retrieved from http://facts.kff.org/chart.aspx?ch=378

Kalton, G., & Anderson, D. W. (1989). Sampling rare populations. In M. P. Lawton & A. R. Herzog (Eds.), *Special research methods for gerontology* (pp. 7–30). Amityville, NY: Baywood.

Kane, J. N. (1993). *Facts about the presidents.* New York: H. W. Wilson.

Kane, R. A. (2004). Coalitions between aging and disability interests: Potential effects on choice and control for older people. *Public Policy and Aging Report, 14*(4), 15–18.

Kane, R. A., & Kane, R. L. (1987). *Long-term care: Principles, programs, and policies.* New York: Springer Publishing.

Kane, R. A., Kane, R. L., & Ladd, R. C. (1998). *The heart of long-term care.* New York: Oxford University Press.

Kaneda, T. (2006). *China's concern over population aging and health.* Population Reference Bureau. Retrieved from http://www.prb.org/Articles/2006/ChinasConcernOverPopulationAgingandHealth.aspx

Karlsson, S. G., & Borell, K. (2002). Intimacy and autonomy, gender and ageing: Living apart together. *Ageing International, 27*(4), 11–26.

Kaskie, B., Imhof, S., Cavanaugh, J., & Culp, K. (2008). Civic engagement as a retirement role for aging Americans. *The Gerontologist, 48*(3), 368–377.

Kasl, S. V. (1995). Strategies in research on health and aging: Looking beyond secondary data analysis. *Journal of Gerontology: Social Sciences, 50*(4), S191–S193.

Kasper, J. D., Ensminger, M. E., Green, K. M., Fothergill, K. E., Juon, H.-S., Robertson, J., et al. (2008). Effects of poverty and family stress over three decades on the functional status of older African American women. *Journal of Gerontology: Social Sciences, 63B*, S201–S210.

Kassner, E. (2006). Medicaid and long-term services and supports for older people. *Research Report*. Washington, DC: AARP Public Policy Institute.

Kastenbaum, R. (1993). Disengagement theory. In R. Kastenbaum (Ed.), *Encyclopedia of adult development* (pp. 126–130). Phoenix, AZ: Oryx Press.

Katz, S., Downs, T., Cash, H., & Grotz, R. (1970). Progress in the development of the Index of ADL. *The Gerontologist, 10*(1), 20–30.

Kayser-Jones, J. (2002). The experience of dying: An ethnographic nursing home study. *The Gerontologist, 42*(3), 11–19.

Keeter, S., Horowitz, J. M., & Tyson, A. (2008). *Gen Dems: The party's advantage among young voters widens.* Pew Research Center. Retrieved from http://pewresearch.org/pubs/813/gen-dems

Kennedy, G. E. (1990). College students' expectations of grandparent and grandchild role behaviors. *The Gerontologist, 30*(1), 43–48.

Kertzer, D. (1983). Generation as a social problem. *Annual Review of Sociology, 9,* 125–149.

Kim, J. E., & Moen, P. (2002). Retirement transitions, gender, and psychological well-being: A life-course, ecological model. *Journal of Gerontology: Psychological Sciences, 57B*(3), P212–P222.

Kimmel, D. C. (1993). The families of older gay men and lesbians. In L. Burton (Ed.), *Families and aging* (pp. 74–79). Amityville, NY: Baywood.

Kingson, E. R. (1994). Testing the boundaries of universality: What's mean? What's not? *The Gerontologist, 34*(6), 736–742.

Kingson, E. R., Hirshorn, B. A., & Cornman, J. M. (1986). *Ties that bind: The interdependence of generations.* Washington, DC: Seven Locks Press.

Kinsella, K., & He, W. (2009). *An aging world: 2008* (Current Population Reports P-95-09-1). U.S. Census Bureau. Washington DC: U.S. Government Printing Office. Retrieved from http://www.census.gov/prod/2009pubs/p95–09–1.pdf

Kinsella, K., & Phillips, D. R. (2005). Global aging: The challenge of success. *Population Bulletin, 60*(1), 3–42.

Kinsella, K., & Tauber, C. M. (1993). *An aging world II.* Washington, DC: U.S. Census Bureau.

Kinsella, K., & Velkoff, V. (2001). *An aging world: 2001* (U.S. Census Bureau Series P95/01–1). Washington, DC: U.S. Government Printing Office.

Klaus, P. (2005). *Crimes against persons age 65 or older, 1993–2002* (Special report). Bureau of Justice Statistics. Retrieved from http://www.ojp.usdoj.gov/bjs/abstract/cpa6502.htm

Kneese, A., & Cooper, C. L. (1993). Demography, resources, and the environment: Further considerations. In *Aging of the U.S. population: Economic and environmental implications* (pp. 61–68). Washington, DC: American Association of Retired Persons.

Kochanek, K. D., Murphy, S. L., Anderson, R. N., & Scott, C. (2004). Deaths: Final data for 2002. *National Vital Statistics Reports, 53*(5).

Kohli, M. (1994). Work and retirement: A comparative perspective. In M. W. Riley, R. L. Kahn, & A. Foner (Eds.), *Aging and structural lag* (pp. 80–106). New York: Wiley-Interscience.

Kohli, M. (2007). The institutionalization of the life course: Looking back to look ahead. *Research in Human Development, 43*(4), 253–271.

Kotlikoff, L. J. (1992). *Generational accounting: Knowing who pays, and when, for what we spend.* New York: The Free Press.

Kovar, M. G., & Lawton, M. P. (1994). Functional disability: Activities and instrumental activities of daily living. In *Annual Review of Gerontology and Geriatrics: Focus on assessment techniques* (Vol. 14). New York: Springer Publishing.

Krach, C., & Velkoff, V. (1999). *Centenarians in the United States* (Current Population Reports P23–199RV). Washington, DC: U.S. Government Printing Office.

Kramer, B. J. (1997). Gain in the caregiving experience: Where are we? What next? *The Gerontologist, 37,* 218–232.

Krause, N. (2001). Social support. In R. Binstock & L. George (Eds.), *Handbook of aging and the social sciences* (5th ed., pp. 273–294). San Diego, CA: Academic Press.

Krause, N., & Rook, K. S. (2003). Negative interaction in late life: Issues in the stability and generalizability of conflict across relationships. *Journal of Gerontology: Psychological Sciences, 58B,* P88–P99.

Kreider, R. M. (2008). *Living arrangements of children: 2004* (Current Population Reports, P70–114). Washington, DC: U.S. Census Bureau.

Kruse, A., & Schmitt, E. (2009). Germany. In E. Palmore, F. Whittington, & S. Kunkel (Eds.), *International handbook on aging: Current research and developments.* Santa Barbara, CA: Praeger.

Ku, L., & Guyer, J. (2001). *Medicaid spending: Rising again, but not to crisis levels.* Center on Budget and Policy Priorities.

Kubler-Ross, E. (1969). *On death and dying.* New York: Macmillan.

Kuhn, T. S. (1996). *The structure of scientific revolutions* (3rd ed.). Chicago: University of Chicago Press.

Kunkel, S., & Applebaum, R. A. (1992). Estimating the prevalence of long-term disability for an aging society. *Journal of Gerontology: Social Sciences, 47*(5), S253–S260.

Kunkel, S., & Atchley, R. C. (1996). Why gender matters: Being female is not the same as not being male. *American Journal of Preventive Medicine, 12*(5), 294–295.

Kunkel, S., & Nelson, I. (2005). Consumer direction: Changing the landscape of long-term care. *Public Policy & Aging Report, 15,* 4, 13–16.

Kunkel, S., & Subedi, J. (1996). Aging in south Asia: How "imperative" is the demographic imperative? In V. Minichiello, N. Chappell, H. Kendig, & A. Walker (Eds.), *Sociology of aging* (pp. 459–466). Melbourne: International Sociological Association, Toth Publishing.

Kunkel, S., & Wellin, V. (2006). *Consumer voice and choice in long-term care.* New York: Springer Publishing.

Lachs, M., Bachman, R., Williams, C., Kossack, A., Bove, C., & O'Leary, P. (2004). Older adults as crime victims, perpetrators, witnesses, and complainants: A population-based study. *Journal of Elder Abuse & Neglect, 16*(4), 25–40.

Lakin, M., Mullane, L., & Robinson, S. (2007). *Framing new terrain: Older adults and higher education.* Retrieved from http://www.acenet.edu/Content/NavigationMenu/ProgramsServices/CLLL/Reinvesting/Reinvestingfinal.pdf

Lashbrook, J. (1996). Promotional timetables: An exploratory investigation of age norms for promotional expectations and their associations with job well-being. *The Gerontologist, 36*(2), 189–198.

Laslett, P. (1991). *A fresh map of life: The emergence of the third age.* Cambridge, MA: Harvard University Press.

Laub, J. H., Nagin, D. S., & Sampson, R. J. (1998). Trajectories of change in criminal offending: Good marriages and the desistance process. *American Sociological Review, 63,* 225–238.

Laumann, E. O., Leisch, S. A., & Waite, L. J. (2008). Elder mistreatment in the United States: Prevalence estimates from a nationally representative study. *Journal of Gerontology: Social Sciences, 63B,* S248–S254.

Lave, J. (1996). Rethinking Medicare. *Generations, 20*(2), 19–23.

LaViest, T. A. (1995). Data sources for aging research on racial and ethnic groups. *The Gerontologist, 35*(3), 328–339.

Lawrence, B. S. (1996). Organizational age norms: Why is it so hard to know one when you see one? *The Gerontologist, 36*(2), 209–220.

Lawton, M. P. (1986). *Environment and aging.* In Classics in Aging Reprinted Series 1 (Vol. 1). New York: Center for the Study of Aging.

Lawton, M. P., & Herzog, A. R. (1989). Introduction. In M. P. Lawton & A. R. Herzog (Eds.), *Special research methods for gerontology* (pp. v–viii). Amityville, NY: Baywood.

Lawton, M. P., Moss, M., Kleban, M. H., Glicksman, A., & Rovine, A. (1991). A two-factor model of caregiving appraisal and psychological well-being. *Journal of Gerontology: Psychological Sciences, 46,* P181–P189.

LeBlanc, A., Sims, W., Silvola, C., & Obert, M. (1996). Music style preferences of different age listeners. *Journal of Research in Music Education, 44*(1), 49–59.

Lee, G. R. (1988). Marital satisfaction in later life: The effects of nonmarital roles. *Journal of Marriage and the Family, 50*(3), 775–783.

Lee, R., & Haaga, J. (2002). Government spending in an older America. *Population Reference Bureau Reports on America, 3*(1).

Lee, R., & Mason, A. (2006). What is the demographic dividend? *Finance and Development, 43*(3), 1–9.

Leiberman, M. A., & Tobin, S. S. (1976). *Last home for the aged.* San Francisco: Jossey-Bass.

Lemon, B. W., Bengtson, V. L., & Peterson, J. A. (1972). An exploration of the activity theory of aging: Activity types and life expectation among in-movers to a retirement community. *Journal of Gerontology, 27,* 511–523.

Leonesio, M. V., Vaughn, D. R., & Wixon, B. (2000). *Early retirees under Social Security: Health status and economic resources.* Washington, DC: Social Security Administration. Retrieved from http://www.ssa. gov/policy/docs/workingpapers/wp86.pdf

Levin, I. (2004). Living apart together: A new family form. *Current Sociology, 52*(2), 223–240.

Levine, R., Sato, S., Hashimoto, T., & Verma, J. (1995). Love and marriage in eleven cultures. *Journal of Cross-Cultural Psychology, 26,* 554–571.

Liang, J., & Lawrence, R. H. (1989). Secondary analysis of surveys in gerontological research. In M. P. Lawton & A. R. Herzog (Eds.), *Special research methods for gerontology* (pp. 31–61). Amityville, NY: Baywood.

Liebfried, S., & Obinger, H. (2000). Welfare state futures: An introduction. *European Review, 8*(3), 277–289.

Liebig, P. (2003). Old-age homes and services: Old and new approaches to aged care. *Journal of Aging & Social Policy, 15*(2/3), 159–178.

Lien, S., Zhang, Y. B., & Hummert, M. L. (2009). Older adults in prime-time television dramas in Taiwan: Prevalence, portrayal, and communication Interaction. *Journal of Cross-Cultural Gerontology, 24*(4), 355–372.

Linton, R. (1942). Age and sex categories. *American Sociological Review, 7,* 589–603.

Litwak, E. (1960). Geographic mobility and extended family cohesion. *American Sociological Review, 25,* 385–394.

Litwak, E. (1965). Extended kin relations in an industrial society. In E. Shanas & G. Streib (Eds.), *Social structure and the family: Generational relations* (pp. 290–323). Englewood Cliffs, NJ: Prentice-Hall.

Long-Foley, K., Tung, H., & Mutran, E. J. (2002). Self-gain and self-loss among African American and white caregivers. *Journal of Gerontology: Social Sciences, 57B*(1), S14–S22.

Longino, C. F., Jr. (1990). Geographical distribution and migration. In R. H. Binstock & L. K. George (Eds.), *Handbook of aging and the social sciences* (3rd ed., pp. 45–63). San Diego, CA: Academic Press.

Lopata, H. Z. (1979). *Women as widows: Support systems.* New York: Elsevier.

Lopez, M., Levine, P., Both, D., Kiesa, A., Kirby, E., & Marcelo, K. (2006). *The 2006 civic and political health of the nation: A detailed look at how youth participate in politics and communities.* Retrieved from http://www.civicyouth.org/PopUps/2006_CPHS_Report_update.pdf

Lueschler, K., & Pillemer, K. (1998). Intergenerational ambivalence: A new approach to the study of parent-child relations in later life. *Journal of Marriage and the Family, 60*(2), 413–425.

Lund, D. A., Caserta, M. S., Diamond, M. F., & Shaffer, S. K. (1989). Competencies, tasks of daily living, and adjustments to spousal bereavement in later life. In D. A. Lund (Ed.), *Older bereaved spouses* (pp. 135–152). New York: Hemisphere.

Lusardi, A., & Mitchell, O. S. (2009). *Financial literacy, retirement planning, and retirement well-being: Lessons and research gaps.* Washington, DC: Brookings Institution. Retrieved from http://www.mrrc.isr. umich.edu/publications/other/pdf/Financial%20Literacy%20Proceedings.pdf

Luxembourg Income Study. (n.d.). Home page. Retrieved from http://www.lisproject.org/

Lynch, S. M., Brown, J. S., & Harmson, K. G. (2003). The effect of altering ADL thresholds on active life expectancy estimates for older persons. *Journals of Gerontology, Social Sciences, 58,* S171–S178.

Machemer, R. (1992). *The news in the biology of aging: The good, the bad, and the confusing.* Paper presented at annual meeting of the Association for Gerontology in Higher Education, Baltimore, MD.

Macionis, J. J. (1997). *Sociology.* Upper Saddle River, NJ: Prentice Hall.

MacKenzie, S. (2008). The impact of the financial crisis on older Americans. *Insight on the Issues, 19,* 1–18. AARP Public Policy Institute. Retrieved from http://www.aarp.org/research/economy/trends/ i19_crisis.html

Maddox, G. L. (1968). Retirement as a social event in the United States. In B. L. Neugarten (Ed.), *Middle age and aging* (pp. 357–365). Chicago: University of Chicago Press.

Maddox, G. L., & Lawton, M. P. (1988). Varieties of aging. In *Annual Review of Gerontology and Geriatrics* (Vol. 8). New York: Springer Publishing.

Maestas, N. (2004). *Back to work: Expectations and realizations of work after retirement* (Working paper 2004–85). Ann Arbor, MI: University of Michigan Retirement Research Center. Retrieved from http:// www.mrrc.isr.umich.edu/publications/papers/pdf/wp085.pdf

Manard, B. (2010). Dueling talking points: Technical issues in constructing and passing the CLASS Act. *Public Policy & Aging Report, 20*(2), 21–27.

Manheimer, R. (2009). Gearing up for the big show: Lifelong learning programs are coming of age. In R. Hudson (Ed.), *Boomer bust? Economic and political issues for the graying society* (Vol. 2). Westport, CT: Praeger.

Mannheim, K. (1952a). *Essays on the sociology of knowledge* (P. Kecskemeti, Ed.). New York: Oxford University Press.

Mannheim, K. (1952b). *Ideology and utopia.* New York: Harcourt, Brace & World.

Markides, K. S., Liang, J., & Jackson, J. S. (1990). Race, ethnicity, and aging: Conceptual and method-ological issues. In R. H. Binstock & L. K. George (Eds.), *Handbook of aging and the social sciences* (3rd ed., pp. 112–129). San Diego, CA: Academic Press.

Marmour, T. R., Mashaw, J. L., & Harvey, P. L. (1990). *America's misunderstood welfare state: Persistent myths, enduring realities.* New York: Basic Books.

Martin, G. M. (2000). Genetic influences on late-life diseases. *Generations, 24*(1), 8–11.

Martin, L., & Kinsella, K. (1994). Research in the demography of aging in developing countries. In L. Martin & S. Preston (Eds.), *Demography of aging.* Washington, DC: National Academic Press.

Martin, P. J. (1995). *Sounds and society: Themes in the sociology of music.* Manchester, UK: Manchester University Press.

Martinson, M., & Minkler, M. (2006). Civic engagement in older adults: A critical perspective. *The Gerontologist, 46*(3), 318–324.

Matras, J. (1990). *Dependency, obligations, and entitlements: A new sociology of aging, the life course, and the elderly.* Englewood Cliffs, NJ: Prentice Hall.

Matthews, A. M., & Rosenthal, C. J. (1993). Balancing work and family in an aging society: The Cana-dian experience. In G. L. Maddox & M. P. Lawton (Eds.), *Annual Review of Gerontology and Geriatrics: Focus on kinship, aging and social support* (pp. 96–119). New York: Springer Publishing.

Matthews, S. (2002). *Sisters and brothers/daughters and sons: Meeting the needs of old parents.* Bloomington, IN: Unlimited Publishing.

McAuley, J. (1987). *Applied research in gerontology.* New York: Van Nostrand-Reinhold.

McConatha, D., McConatha, J. T., & Dermigny, R. (1994). The use of interactive computer services to enhance the quality of life for long-term care residents. *The Gerontologist, 34*(4), 553–556.

McConnell, S., & Beitler, D. (1991). The Older Americans Act after 25 years: An overview. *Generations, 15*(3), 5–10.

McConnell, S. R. (1983). Age discrimination in employment. In H. S. Parnes (Ed.), *Policy issues in work and retirement* (pp. 159–196). Kalamazoo, MI: W. E. Upjohn Institute.

McDonnell, K. (2008). *Retirement annuity and employer-based pension income among individuals age 50 and over: 2006.* Retrieved from http://www.ebri.org/pdf/notespdf/EBRI_Noptes_01–2008.pdf

McFalls, J. A. (1998). Population: A lively introduction. *Population Bulletin, 53*(3). Washington, DC: Population Reference Bureau.

McGarry, K., & Schoeni, R. F. (2005). Widow(er) poverty and out-of-pocket medical expenditures near the end of life. *Journal of Gerontology: Social Sciences, 60B*(3), S160–S168.

McKinlay, J., & McKinlay, S. (1990). Medical measures and the decline of mortality. In P. Conrad & R. Kerns (Eds.), *The sociology of health and illness: Critical perspectives* (pp. 10–23). New York: St. Martin's Press.

McKinsey Global Institute. (2008). *Talkin' 'bout my generation: The economic impact of aging US baby boomers.* Retrieved from http://www.mckinsey.com/mgi/reports/pdfs/Impact_Aging_Baby_Boomers/MGI_Impact_Aging_Baby_Boomers_executive_summary.pdf

McNaught, W. (1994). Realizing the potential: Some examples. In M. W. Riley, R. L. Kahn, & A. Foner (Eds.), *Aging and structural lag* (pp. 219–236). New York: Wiley-Interscience.

Meara, E., Richards, S., & Cutler, D. (2008). The gap gets bigger: Changes in mortality and life expec-tancy, by education, 1981–2000. *Health Affairs, 27*(2), 350–360.

Mederios-Kent, M., & Haub, C. (2005). Global demographic divide. *Population Bulletin, 60*(4). Wash-ington, DC: Population Reference Bureau.

Mehdizadeh, S. A., Nelson, I. M., & Applebaum, R. A. (2006). *Nursing home use in Ohio: Who stays, who pays?* (Scripps Gerontology Center Brief Report). Retrieved from http://casnov1.cas.muohio.edu/scripps/publications/NHUse.html

Mermin, G.B.T., Johnson, R. W., & Murphy, D. P. (2007). Why do boomers plan to work longer? *Journal of Gerontology: Social Sciences, 62B,* S286–S294.

Metlife Mature Market Institute. (2001). *Toward a national caregiving agenda: Empowering family caregiv-ers in America.* Metlife Research Center. Retrieved from http://www.metlife.com

MetLife Mature Market Institute. (2009a). *Boomer bookends: Insights into the oldest and youngest boomers.* Retrieved from http://www.metlife.com/mmi/?WT.mc_id=vu1243

Metlife Mature Market Institute. (2009b). *Market survey of long-term care costs.* Retrieved from http://www.metlife.com/assets/cao/mmi/publications/studies/mmi-market-survey-nursing-home-assisted-living.pdf

Meyer, J. A., & Greenwood, D. (1997). Back to the future: Poverty among the elderly in the twenty-first century. *The Public Policy and Aging Report, 8*(1), 1, 17–20.

Meyer, M. H., & Herd, P. (2007). The business of retirement. In M. H. Meyer & P. Herd (Eds.), *Market friendly or family friendly? The state and gender inequality in old age* (pp. 65–94). New York: Russell Sage Foundation.

Miech, R. A., & Shanahan, M. J. (2000). Socioeconomic status and depression over the life course. *Journal of Health and Social Behavior, 41*(2), 137–161.

Miller, B., McFall, S., & Campbell, R. T. (1994). Changes in sources of community long-term care among African-American and white frail older persons. *Journal of Gerontology: Social Sciences, 49*(1), S14–S24.

Miller, D. (1985). The Economic Equity Act of 1985. *Washington Social Legislation Bulletin, 29,* 61–64.

Mills, C. W. (1959). *The sociological imagination.* New York: Oxford University Press.

Minkler, M. (1991a). "Generational Equity" and the new victim blaming. In M. Minkler & C. L. Estes (Eds.), *Critical perspectives on aging: The political and moral economy of growing old* (pp. 67–80). Amityville, NY: Baywood.

Minkler, M. (1991b). Gold in gray: Reflections on business discovery of the elderly market. In M. Minkler & C. L. Estes (Eds.), *Critical perspectives on aging: The political and moral economy of growing old* (pp. 81–93). Amityville, NY: Baywood.

Minkler, M., & Fuller-Thompson, E. (2005). African American grandparents raising grandchildren: A national study using the Census 2000 American Community Survey. *Journal of Gerontology: Social Sciences, 60B*(2), S82–S92.

Mitchell, J., & Register, J. C. (1984). An exploration of family interaction with the elderly by race, socio-economic status, and residence. *The Gerontologist, 24*(1), 48–54.

Moen, P. (1994). Women, work and family: A sociological perspective on changing roles. In M. W. Riley, R. L. Kahn, & A. Foner (Eds.), *Aging and structural lag* (pp. 151–170). New York: Wiley-Interscience.

Moen, P., Dempster-McClain, D., & Williams, R. M. (1989). Social integration and longevity: An event history analysis of women's roles and resilience. *American Sociological Review, 54,* 635–647.

Moller, D. W. (1996). *Confronting death.* New York: Oxford University Press.

Mollica, R., & Johnson-Lamarche, H. (2005). *State Residential and Assisted Living Policy: 2004.* Portland, ME: National Academy for State Health Policy. Retrieved from http://aspe.hhs.gov/daltcp/reports/04alcom.htm

Montanari, I. (2001). Modernization, globalization, and the welfare state: A comparative analysis of old and new convergence of social insurance since 1930. *British Journal of Sociology, 52*(3), 469–494.

Moody, H. R. (1992). *Ethics in an aging society.* Baltimore, MD: Johns Hopkins University Press.

Moody, H. R. (1993). Overview: What is critical gerontology and why is it important? In T. R. Cole, W. A. Achenbaum, P. L. Jakobi, & R. Kastenbaum (Eds.), *Voices and visions of aging: Toward a critical gerontology* (pp. xv–xli). New York: Springer Publishing.

Moody, H. R. (2001–2002). Who's afraid of life extension? *Generations, 25*(4), 33–37.

Moody, H. R. (2004–2005). Silver industries and the new aging enterprise. *Generations, 28*(4), 75–79.

Moon, M. (2005). Sustaining Medicare as an age-related program. In R. B. Hudson (Ed.), *The new politics of old age policies* (pp. 205–218). Baltimore, MD: Johns Hopkins University Press.

Moon, M., & Smeeding, T. M. (1989). Can the elderly really afford long term care? In S. Sullivan & M. E. Lewin (Eds.), *The care of tomorrow's elderly: Encouraging initiatives and reshaping public programs* (pp. 137–160). Washington, DC: University Press of America.

Moore, P. (1985). *Disguised.* Waco, TX: Word Books.

Morgan, D. L. (1998, Spring). Facts and figures about the baby boom. *Generations,* 10–15.

Morgan, L. A. (1984). Changes in family interaction following widowhood. *Journal of Marriage and the Family, 46*(2), 323–332.

Morgan, L. A. (1991). Economic security of older women: Issues and trends for the future. In B. B. Hess & E. W. Markson (Eds.), *Growing old in America* (4th ed., pp. 275–292). New Brunswick, NJ: Transaction.

Morgan, L. A., Gruber-Baldini, A. L., & Magaziner, J. (2001). Resident characteristics. In S. I. Zimmerman, P. D. Sloane, & J. K. Eckert (Eds.), *Assisted living: Residential care in transition* (pp. 144–172). Baltimore, MD: Johns Hopkins University Press.

Morrell, R. W., Mayhorn, C. B., & Echt, K. V. (2004). Why older adults use or do not use the internet. In D. C. Burdick & S. Kwon (Eds.), *Gerotechnology: Research and practice in technology and aging* (pp. 71–85). New York: Springer Publishing.

Munnell, A. H. (2004). *A bird's eye view of the Social Security debate* (Center for Retirement Research Issue Brief No. 25). Boston: Boston College.

Munnell, A. H. (2005). *Social Security's financial outlook: The 2005 update and a look back.* Boston: Center for Retirement Research, Boston University.

Munnell, A. (2008). *Social Security's financial outlook: The 2008 report in perspective.* Boston: Center for Retirement Research, Boston University. Retrieved from http://crr.bc.edu/briefs/social_security_s_fi nancial_outlook_the_2008_update_in_perspective.html

Munnell, A. H., & Sass, S. A. (2008). *The decline of career employment.* Boston: Retirement Research Center, Boston College. Retrieved from http://crr.bc.edu/briefs/the_decline_of_career_employment.html

Munnell, A. H., Sass, S. A., & Soto, M. (2006). *Employer attitudes toward older workers: Survey results.* Boston: Center for Retirement Research, Boston College. Retrieved from http://crr.bc.edu/images/stories/ Briefs/wob_3.pdf?phpMyAdmin=43ac483c4de9t51d9eb41

Murray, C., Kulkarni, S., Michaud, C., Tomijima, N., Bulzacchelli, M., et al. (2006). Eight Americas: Investigating mortality disparities across race, counties, and race-counties in the United States. *PLoS Med, 3*(9), e260. Retrieved from http://www.plosmedicine.org/article/info:doi/10.1371/journal. pmed.0030260

Mutchler, J., & Burr, J. (2009). Boomer diversity and well-being: Race, ethnicity, and gender. In R. Hudson (Ed.), *Boomer bust? Economic and political issues for the graying society* (Vol. 1). Westport, CT: Praeger.

Mutchler, J. E., Burr, J. A., Pienta, A. M., & Massagli, M. P. (1997). Pathways to labor force exit: Work transitions and work instability. *Journal of Gerontology: Social Sciences, 52B*(1), S4–S12.

Mutran, E. (1985). Intergenerational family support among blacks and whites: Responses to culture or to socioeconomic differences. *Journal of Gerontology, 40*(3), 382–389.

Mwangi, S. (2009). Kenya. In E. Palmore, F. Whittington, & S. Kunkel (Eds.), *International handbook on aging: Current research and developments.* Santa Barbara, CA: Praeger.

Myles, J. F. (1983). Conflict, crisis, and the future of old age security. *Millbank Memorial Fund Quarterly/ Health and Society, 61,* 462–472.

Myles, J. F. (1989). *Old age and the welfare state: The political economy of public pension* (2nd ed.). Lawrence: University Press of Kansas.

Myles, J. F. (1996). Social Security and support of the elderly: The western experience. In J. Quadagno & D. Street (Eds.), *Aging for the twenty-first century* (pp. 381–397). New York: St. Martin's Press.

Myles, J. (2005). What justice requires: A normative foundation for U.S. pension reform. In R. B. Hudson (Ed.), *The new politics of old age policies* (pp. 42–64). Baltimore: Johns Hopkins University Press.

Myles, J. F., & Quadagno, J. (1995). Generational equity and Social Security reform. *Aging Research & Policy Report, 3*(5), 12–16.

Nathanson, C. A. (1990). The gender-mortality differential in developed countries: Demographic and sociocultural dimensions. In M. Ory & H. Warner (Eds.), *Gender, health and longevity: Multidisciplinary perspectives* (pp. 3–24). New York: Springer Publishing.

National Alliance for Caregiving. (1997). *Family caregiving in the U.S.: Findings from a national survey.* Bethesda, MD: Author and AARP.

National Alliance for Caregiving. (2009). *Family caregiving in the U.S. 2009.* Retrieved from http://assets. aarp.org/rgcenter/il/caregiving_09_fr.pdf

National Archive on Computerized Data on Aging (NACDA). (2010). *About us.* Retrieved from http:// www.icpsr.umich.edu/icpsrweb/NACDA/

National Center for Health Statistics. (2010). *Health, United States, 2009: With special feature on medical technology.* Hyattsville, MD: Author.

National Coalition on Health Care. (2009). *Health care costs.* Retrieved from http://nchc.org/sites/default/ files/resources/Fact%20Sheet%20-%20Cost.pdf

The National Election Studies. (2004). *The NES Guide to public opinion and electoral behavior.* Ann Arbor: University of Michigan, Center for Political Studies. Retrieved from http://www.umich.edu/~nes/nes guide/nesguide.htm

NIA, NIH, HHS, & Department of State. (2007). *Why population aging matters: A global perspective.* Retrieved from http://www.nia.nih.gov/researchinformation/extramuralprograms/behavioralandsocialre search/globalaging.htm

National Institutes of Health. (2006). *NIH roadmap for medical research: Translational research.* Retrieved from http://nihroadmap.nih.gov/clinicalresearch/overview-translational.asp

Nelson, I. M. (2002). Continuing care retirement communities. In D. Ekerdt (Ed.), *Encyclopedia of aging.* New York: Macmillan.

Nesselroade, J. R. (1988). Sampling and generalizability: Adult development and aging research issues examined within the general methodological framework of selection. In K. W. Schaie, R. T. Campbell, W. Meredith, & S. C. Rawlings (Eds.), *Methodological issues in aging research* (pp. 13–42). New York: Springer Publishing.

Neugarten, B. L., & Datan, N. (1973). Sociological perspectives on the life cycle. In P. B. Baltes & K. W. Schaie (Eds.), *Life-span developmental psychology* (pp. 53–71). New York: Academic Press.

Neugarten, B. L., Moore, J., & Lowe, J. (1965). Age norms, age constraints, and adult socialization. *American Journal of Sociology, 70,* 710–717.

Neugarten, B. L., Moore, J., & Lowe, J. (1968). Age norms, age constraints, and adult socialization. In B. L. Neugarten (Ed.), *Middle age and aging* (pp. 22–28). Chicago: University of Chicago Press.

Neuman, P., & Cubanski, J. (2009). Medicare Part D update: Lessons learned and unfinished business. *New England Journal of Medicine, 361*(4), 406–414.

Neumark, D. (2008). *Reassessing the Age Discrimination in Employment Act.* Washington, DC: AARP Public Policy Institute. Retrieved from http://assets.aarp.org/rgcenter/econ/2008_09_adea.pdf

New England Centenarian Study. (2010). *Why study centenarians? An overview.* Retrieved from http://www.bumc.bu.edu/centenarian/overview/

Newcomer, R., & Preston, S. (1994). Relationship between acute care and nursing unit use in two continuing care retirement communities. *Research on Aging, 16*(3), 280–300.

Newport, F. (2010). *Americans' projected retirement age continues to creep up.* Gallup Poll Analysis. Retrieved from http://www.gallup.com/poll/

Nihtila, E., & Martikainen, K. (2008). Institutionalization of older adults after the death of a spouse. *American Journal of Public Health, 98*(7), 1228–1234.

O'Brien, R., Stockard, J., & Isaacson, L. (1999). The enduring effects of cohort characteristics on age-specific homicide rates, 1960–1995. *American Journal of Sociology, 104*(4), 1061–1095.

Office of the Federal Register. (1995). *The United States Government manual 1995/1996.* Washington, DC: U.S. Government Printing Office.

Oliver, T. R., Lee, P. R., & Lipton, H. L. (2004). A political history of Medicare and prescription drug coverage. *The Millbank Quarterly, 82*(2), 283–354.

Olshansky, J., Passaro, D., Hershow, R., Layden, J., Carnes, B., Brody, J., et al. (2005). A potential decline in life expectancy in the United States in the 21st century. *New England Journal of Medicine, 352*(11), 1138–1145.

O'Neill, G. (2009). The baby boom age wave: Population success or tsunami? In R. Hudson (Ed.), *Boomer bust? Economic and political issues for the graying society* (Vol. 1). Westport, CT: Praeger.

O'Rand, A. M. (1990). Stratification and the life course. In R. H. Binstock & L. K. George (Eds.), *Handbook of aging and the social sciences* (3rd ed., pp. 130–148). San Diego, CA: Academic Press.

O'Rand, A. M. (1996). The precious and the precocious: Understanding cumulative disadvantage and cumulative advantage over the life course. *The Gerontologist, 36*(2), 230–238.

O'Rand, A. (2005). When old age begins: Implications for health, work, and retirement. In R. B. Hudson (Ed.), *The new politics of old age policies* (pp. 109–128). Baltimore: Johns Hopkins University Press.

Organisation for Economic Co-Operation and Development. (2000). *Employment outlook 2000.* Paris, France: OECD.

Palmore, E. (1989). Medical records as sampling frames and data sources. In M. P. Lawton & A. R. Herzog (Eds.), *Special research methods for gerontology* (pp. 127–135). Amityville, NY: Baywood.

Palmore, E. (2005). Three decades of research on ageism. *Generations, 29*(3), 87–90.

Pampel, F., & Williamson, J. (1989). *Age, class, politics, and the welfare state.* New York: Cambridge University Press.

Pandya, S. (2005). *Caregiving in the United States.* AARP Policy Institute. Retrieved from http://www.aarp.org/research/

Panel Study of Income Dynamics. (2009). *Frequently asked questions.* Retrieved from http://psidonline.isr.umich.edu/Guide/FAQ.aspx

Parker, R. G. (1995). Reminiscence: A continuity theory framework. *The Gerontologist, 35*(4), 515–525.

Parsons, T. (1959). The social structure of the family. In R. Anshen (Ed.), *The family: Its function and destiny* (2nd ed., pp. 241–274). New York: Harper and Row.

Parsons, T., & Bales, R. F. (1955). *Family socialization and process.* New York: Free Press.

Passuth, P. M., & Bengtson, V. L. (1988). Sociological theories of aging: Current perspectives and future directions. In J. E. Birren & V. L. Bengtson (Eds.), *Emergent theories of aging* (pp. 333–355). New York: Springer Publishing.

Paulin, G. D. (2000, May). Expenditure patterns of older American, 1984–97. *Monthly Labor Review, 123,* 3–28.

Pavalko, E. K., & Elder, G. H., Jr. (1990). World War II and divorce: A life-course perspective. *American Journal of Sociology, 95*(5), 1213–1234.

Pearce, C. (2008). *The truth about baby boomer gamers. A study of over-forty computer game players.* New York: Sage.

Pension Benefit Guarantee Corporation [PBGC]. (2009). *News and highlights.* Retrieved from http://www.pbgc.gov/

Pension Rights Center. (2005). *The pension underfunding "crisis": Should you be worried?* Retrieved from http://www.pensionrights.org/

Perls, T., Kunkel, L., & Puca, A. (2002). The genetics of exceptional human longevity. *Journal of the American Geriatrics Society, 50,* 359–368.

Peterson, P. G. (1999). *Gray dawn: How the coming age wave will transform America—and the world.* New York: Times Books.

Peterson, S. A., & Somit, A. (1994). *The political behavior of older Americans.* New York: Garland Publishing.

Pew Research Center. (2003). *Evenly divided and increasingly polarized: 2004 political landscape.* Washington, DC: The Pew Research Center for the People and the Press. Retrieved from http://people-press.org/reports/display.php3?PageID=750

Pew Research Center. (2005). *Baby boomers approach age 60: From the age of Aquarius to the age of responsibility.* Retrieved from http://pewresearch.org/assets/social/pdf/socialtrends-boomers120805.pdf

Pew Research Center. (2007). *Trends in political values and core attitudes: 1987–2007.* Washington, DC: Author.

Pew Research Center. (2009a). *Independents take center stage in Obama era.* Retrieved from http://people-press.org/report/?pageid=1523

Pew Research Center. (2009b). *Gen next squeezed by recession, but most see better times ahead.* Retrieved from http://pewresearch.org/pubs/1245/gen-next-squeezed-recession-most-see-better-times-ahead

Pew Research Center. (2010). *Millennials: A portrait of generation next.* Retrieved from http://pewsocialtrends.org/assets/pdf/millennials-confident-connected-open-to-change.pdf

Pezzin, L. E., Pollack, R. A., & Schone, B. S. (2008). Parental marital disruption, family type, and transfers to disabled elderly parents. *Journal of Gerontology: Social Sciences, 63*(B), S349–S355.

Piktialis, D. S. (2009). Redesigning work for an aging labor force: Employer and employee perspectives. In R. Hudson (Ed.), *Boomer bust? Economic and political issues for the graying society* (Vol. 2). Westport, CT: Praeger.

Pillemer, K., & Suitor, J. J. (2004). Ambivalence in intergenerational relations over the life-course. In M. Silverstein (Ed.), *Annual Review of Gerontology and Geriatrics* (Vol. 24). New York: Springer Publishing.

Pimpare, S. (2009). The failures of American poverty measures. *Journal of Sociology & Social Welfare, 36*(1), 103–122.

Pineo, P. C. (1961). Disenchantment in the later years of marriage. *Marriage and Family Living, 23,* 3–11.

Plakans, A. (1994). The democratization of unstructured time in western societies: A historical overview. In M. W. Riley, R. L. Kahn, & A. Foner (Eds.), *Aging and structural lag* (pp. 107–129). New York: Wiley-Interscience.

Plassman, B. L., Langa, K. M., Fisher, G. G., Heeringa, S. G., Weir, D. R., Ofstedal, M. B., et al. (2007). Prevalence of dementia in the United States: The Aging, Demographics, and Memory Study. *Neuroepidemiology, 29,* 125–132.

Population Reference Bureau. (2009). Social security systems around the world. *Today's Research on Aging,* 15.

Population Reference Bureau. (2010a). World population highlights: Key findings from PRB's 2010 world population data sheet. *Population Bulletin, 65*(2).

Population Reference Bureau. (2010b). China's rapidly aging population. *Today's Research on Aging, 20.* Retrieved from http://www.prb.org/pdf10/TodaysResearchAging20.pdf

Preston, S., Elo, I., & Rosenwaike, I. (1996). African-American mortality at older ages: Results of a matching study. *Demography, 33,* 193–209.

Quadagno, J. (1982). *Aging in early industrial society.* New York: Academic Press.

Quadagno, J. (1989). Generational equity and the politics of the welfare state. *Politics and Society, 17,* 353–376.

Quadagno, J. (1991). Generational equity and the politics of the welfare state. In B. B. Hess & E. W. Markson (Eds.), *Growing old in America* (4th ed., pp. 341–351). New Brunswick, NJ: Transaction.

Quadagno, J. (1996). Social Security and the myth of the entitlement "crisis." *The Gerontologist, 36*(3), 391–399.

Queen, S., Pappas, G., Harden, W., & Fisher, G. (1994). The widening gap between socioeconomic status and mortality. *Statistical Bulletin, 75*(2), 31–35.

Quinn, J. F. (1987). The economic status of the elderly: Beware the mean. *Review of Income and Wealth, 33,* 63–82.

Quinn, J. F. (1993). *Poverty and income security among older persons: Overview of proceedings.* Syracuse, NY: National Academy on Aging.

Quinn, J. F., & Burkhauser, R. V. (1990). Work and retirement. In R. H. Binstock & L. K. George (Eds.), *Handbook of aging and the social sciences* (3rd ed., pp. 307–327). San Diego, CA: Academic Press.

Quinn, J. F., & Kozy, M. (1996). The role of bridge jobs in the retirement transition: Gender, race, and ethnicity. *The Gerontologist, 15*(3), 363–372.

Quinn, J. F., & Smeeding, T. M. (1993). The present and future economic well-being of the aged. In R. V. Burkhauser & D. L. Salisbury (Eds.), *Pensions in a changing economy* (pp. 5–18). Washington, DC: Employee Benefit Research Institute.

Quirk, D. (1991). An agenda for the nineties and beyond. *Generations, 15*(3), 23–26.

Rainville, G. (2009). *AARP Bulletin survey on employment status of the 45+ population.* Retrieved from http://www.aarp.org/research/work/employment/bulletin_jobs_09.html

Rank, M. R., & Hirschi, T. A. (1999). Estimating the proportion of Americans ever experiencing poverty during their elderly years. *Journal of Gerontology: Social Sciences, 54B*(4), S184–S193.

Redford, L. J., & Whitten, P. (1997). Ensuring access to care in rural areas: The role of communication technology. *Generations, 21*(3), 19–23.

Reinhardt, U. E., Hussey, P. S., & Anderson, G. F. (2004). U.S. health care spending in an international context. *Health Affairs, 23*(3), 10–25.

Reitzes, D. C., Mutran, E. J., & Fernandez, M. E. (1996). Does retirement hurt well-being? Factors influencing self-esteem and depression among retirees and workers. *The Gerontologist, 36*(5), 649–656.

Reskin, B., & Padavic, I. (1994). *Women and men at work.* Thousand Oaks, CA: Pine Forge Press.

Reynolds, S. L., Crimmins, E. M., & Saito, Y. (1998). Cohort differences in disability and disease presence. *The Gerontologist, 38*(5), 578–590.

Reynolds, S. L., Saito, Y., & Crimmins, E. M. (2005). The impact of obesity on active life expectancy in older American men and women. *The Gerontologist, 45,* 438–444.

Riley, M. W. (1983). The family in an aging society: A matrix of latent relationships. *Journal of Family Issues, 4,* 439–454.

Riley, M. W. (1987). On the significance of age in sociology. *American Sociological Review, 52,* 1–14.

Riley, M. W. (1994). Aging and society: Past, present, and future. *The Gerontologist, 34*(4), 436–446.

Riley, M. W. (1996). Discussion: What does it all mean? *The Gerontologist, 36*(2), 256–258.

Riley, M. W., Johnson, M., & Foner, A. (1972). *Aging and society: Vol 3: A sociology of age stratification.* New York: Russell Sage Foundation.

Riley, M. W., Kahn, R. L., & Foner, A. (Eds.). (1994). *Aging and structural lag.* New York: Wiley-Interscience.

Riley, M. W., & Riley, J. (1994). Age integration and the lives of older people. *The Gerontologist, 34,* 110–115.

Rix, S. E. (1991). Making resourceful aging a reality. In *Resourceful aging: Vol. IV: Work/second careers* (pp. 85–91). Washington, DC: American Association of Retired Persons.

Rix, S. E., & Williamson, J. B. (1998). *Social Security reform: How might women fare?* Washington, DC: AARP Public Policy Institute.

Roberto, K. A. (1990). Grandparent and grandchild relationships. In T. H. Brubaker (Ed.), *Family relationships in later life* (2nd ed., pp. 100–112). Newbury Park, CA: Sage.

Robertson, A. (1991). The politics of Alzheimer's disease: A case study in apocalyptic demography. In M. Minkler & C. Estes (Eds.), *Critical perspectives on aging: The political and moral economy of growing old* (pp. 135–152). Amityville, NY: Baywood.

Robert Wood Johnson Foundation. (2005). *Working but uninsured.* Retrieved from http://rwjf.org/newsroom/newsreleasesdetail.

Rogers, W. A., Mayhorn, C. B., & Fisk, A. D. (2004). Technology in everyday life for older adults. In D. C. Burdick & S. Kwon (Eds.), *Gerotechnology: Research and practice in technology and aging* (pp. 3–17). New York: Springer Publishing.

Rogot, E., Sorlie, P. D., & Johnson, N. J. (1992). Life expectancy by employment status, income, and education in the National Longitudinal Mortality Study. *Public Health Report, 107,* 457–461.

Rosen, B., & Jerdee, T. H. (1985). *Older employees: New roles for valued resources.* Homewood, IL: Dow Jones-Irwin.

Rosenbaum, W. A. & Button, J. W. (1992). Perceptions of intergenerational conflict: The politics of young vs. old in Florida. *Journal of Aging Studies, 6*(4), 385–396.

Rosenmayr, L., & Kockeis, E. (1963). Propositions for a sociological theory of action and the family. *International Social Science Journal, 15,* 410–426.

Rosenthal, C. J., Matthews, S. H., & Marshall, V. W. (1991). Is parent care normative? The experiences of a sample of middle-aged women. In B. B. Hess & E. Markson (Eds.), *Growing old in America* (pp. 427–440). New Brunswick, NJ: Transaction.

Rosow, I. (1985). Status and role change through the life cycle. In R. H. Binstock & E. Shanas (Eds.), *Handbook of aging and the social sciences* (2nd ed.). New York: Van Nostrand-Reinhold.

Rossi, P. H., Lipsey, M. L., & Freeman, H. E. (2004). *Evaluation: A systematic approach* (7th ed.). Thousand Oaks, CA: Sage.

Rostein, G. (1999, July 6). The promise of longer life grows, but eternal youth remains out of reach. *Pittsburgh Post-Gazette.*

Rowe, J. W., & Kahn, R. L. (1997). Successful aging. *The Gerontologist, 37*(4), 433–440.

Rowe, J. W., & Kahn, R. L. (1998). *Successful aging.* New York: Pantheon Books.

Ruhm, C. J. (1990). Career jobs, bridge employment, and retirement. In P. B. Doeringer (Ed.), *Bridges to retirement: Older workers in a changing labor market* (pp. 92–107). Ithaca, NY: Cornell University Press.

Ruhm, C. J. (1996). Gender differences in employment behavior during late middle age. *Journal of Gerontology: Social Sciences, 51B*(1), S11–S17.

Rupert, P. (1991). Contingent work options: Promise or peril for older workers. In *Resourceful aging: Vol. IV work/second careers* (pp. 51–53). Washington, DC: American Association of Retired Persons.

Russell, A., & McWhirter, N. (1987). *1988 Guinness book of world records.* New York: Bantam Books.

Ryder, N. B. (1965). The cohort as a concept in the study of social change. *American Sociological Review, 30,* 843–861.

Salisbury, D. L. (1993). Policy implications of changes in employer pension protection. In R. V. Burkhauser & D. L. Salisbury (Eds.), *Pensions in a changing economy* (pp. 41–58). Washington, DC: Employee Benefit Research Institute.

Salthouse, T. (2006). Theoretical issues in the psychology of aging. In J. Birren & K. W. Schaie (Eds.), *Handbook of the psychology of aging* (6th ed., pp. 3–13). San Diego, CA: Academic Press.

Saluter, A. F. (1996). Marital status and living arrangements: March 1994. *U.S. Census Bureau, Current Population Reports, Series P-20,* No. 484. Washington, DC: U.S. Government Printing Office.

Sandell, S. H., & Iams, H. M. (1997). Reducing women's poverty by shifting Social Security benefits from retired couples to widows. *Journal of Policy Analysis and Management, 16*(2), 279–297.

Sanderson, W., & Scherbov, S. (2008). Rethinking age and aging. *Population Bulletin, 63*(4), 3–16.

Sankar, A., & Gubrium, J. (1994). Introduction. In J. Gubrium & A. Sankar (Eds.), *Qualitative methods in aging research* (pp. vii–xvii). Thousand Oaks, CA: Sage.

Sanzenbacher, G. (2006). *Estimating pension coverage using different data sets.* Boston: Center for Retirement Research, Boston College. Retrieved from http://crr.bc.edu/briefs/estimating_pension_coverage_using_different_data_sets.html

Schachter-Shalomi, Z., & Miller, R. S. (1995). *From age-ing to sage-ing: A profound new vision of growing older.* New York: Warner Books.

Schaie, K. W., & Herzog, C. (1982). Longitudinal methods. In B. B. Woman (Ed.), *Handbook of developmental psychology* (pp. 91–115). Englewood Cliffs, NJ: Prentice-Hall.

Scheiber, S. J. (2008). *Beyond the golden age of retirement: Policy Brief.* Ann Arbor: University of Michigan Retirement Research Center. Retrieved from http://www.mrrc.isr.umich.edu/publications/policy/

Scheidt, R., & Windley, P. (2006). Environmental gerontology: Progress in the post-Lawton era. In J. Birren & K. Schaie (Eds.), *Handbook of the psychology of aging* (6th ed., pp. 105–125). Amsterdam: Elsevier Academic Press.

Schmittroth, L. (1991). *Statistical record of women worldwide.* Detroit, MI: Gale Research, Inc.

Schoenborn, C., Vickerie, J., & Powell-Griner, E. (2006). Health characteristics of adults 55 years of age and over: United States 2000–2003. *Advance Data from Vital and Health Statistics, 370.*

Schoenborn, C., & Heyman, K. (2009). Health characteristics of adults aged 55 years and over: United States, 2004–2007. *National Health Statistics Reports, No. 16.* Hyattsville, MD: National Center for Health Statistics.

Schulz, J. H. (1986). Voodoo economics and the aging society. *Of Current Interest from the Policy Center on Aging, 6* (2).

Schulz, J. H. (1992). *The economics of aging* (5th ed.). New York: Auburn House.

Schulz, J. H., & Myles, J. (1990). Old age pensions: A comparative perspective. In R. H. Binstock & L. K. George (Eds.). *Handbook of aging and the social sciences* (3rd ed., pp. 398–414). San Diego, CA: Academic Press.

Schulz, J. H., & Binstock, R. H. (2006). *Aging nation: The economics and politics of growing older in America.* Baltimore: Johns Hopkins University Press.

Schulz, R., Visintainer, P., & Williamson, G. M. (1990). Psychiatric and physical morbidity effects of caregiving. *Journals of Gerontology, 45,* 181–191.

Schultz, K. S., Morton, K. R., & Weckerle, J. R. (1998). The influence of push and pull factors on voluntary and involuntary early retirees' retirement decision and adjustment. *Journal of Vocational Behavior, 53,* 45–57.

Schumacher, J. G., Eckert, J. K., Zimmerman, S., Carder, P., & Wright, A. (2005). Physician care in assisted living: A qualitative study. *Journal of the American Medical Directors Association, 6,* 1, 34–45.

Schuman, H., & Scott, J. (1989). Generations and collective memories. *American Sociological Review, 54*(3), 359–381.

Schutt, R. K. (2004). *Investigating the social world* (4th ed.). Thousand Oaks, CA: Pine Forge Press.

Schwartz, G. E. (1982). Testing the biopsychosocial model: The ultimate challenge facing behavioral medicine? *Journal of Consulting and Clinical Psychology, 50*(6), 1040–1053.

Scialfa, C. T., Ho, G., & Laberge, J. (2004). Perceptual aspects of gerontechnology. In D. C. Burdick & S. Kwon (Eds.), *Gerotechnology: Research and practice in technology and aging* (pp. 18–41). New York: Springer Publishing.

Scrutton, S. (1995). Ageism: The foundation of age discrimination. In J. Quadagno & D. Street (Eds.), *Aging for the twenty-first century* (pp. 141–154). New York: St. Martin's Press.

Sears, D. O. (1983). The persistence of early political predispositions: The roles of attitude object and life stage. In L. Wheeler (Ed.), *Review of personality and social psychology* (Vol. 4, pp. 79–116). Thousand Oaks, CA: Sage.

Seltzer, M. M., & Greenberg. J. S. (1999). The caregiving context: The intersection of social and individual influences in the experience of family caregiving. In C. D. Ryff & V. W. Marshall (Eds.), *The self and society in aging processes* (pp. 362–397). New York: Springer Publishing.

Settersten, R. A. (1999). *Lives in time and place: Problems and promises of developmental science.* Amityville, NY: Baywood.

Settersten, R. A. (2003). Propositions and controversies in life-course scholarship. In. R. Settersten (Ed.), *Invitation to the life course: Toward new understandings of later life* (pp. 15–45). Amityville, NY: Baywood.

Settersten, R. A. (2005a). Toward a stronger partnership between life-course sociology and life-span psychology. *Research in Human Development, 2*(1 & 2), 25–41.

Settersten, R. A. (2005b). Linking the two ends of life: What gerontology can learn from childhood studies. *Journal of Gerontology: Social Sciences, 60B*(4), S173–S180.

Settersten, R. (2007). The new landscape of adult life: Road maps, sign posts, and speed lines. *Research in Human Development, 43*(3–4), 239–252.

Settersten, R. A., Furstenberg, F. F., & Rumbaut, R. G. (Eds.). (2005). *On the frontier of adulthood.* Chicago: The University of Chicago Press.

Settersten, R. A., & Hagestad, G. O. (1996a). What's the latest? Cultural age deadlines for family transitions. *The Gerontologist, 36*(2), 178–188.

Settersten, R. A., & Hagestad, G. O. (1996b). What's the latest? II: Cultural age deadlines for educational and work transitions. *The Gerontologist, 36*(5), 602–613.

Setton, D. (2000). Cyber granny. *Forbes, 165*(12), 40–41.

Shanahan, M. J., Porfeli, E. J., Mortimer, J. T., & Erickson, L. D. (2005). In R. A. Settersten, F. F. Furstenberg, & R. G. Rumbaut (Eds.), *On the frontier of adulthood* (pp. 225–255). Chicago: The University of Chicago Press.

Shanas, E. (1967). Family help patterns and social class in three countries. *Journal of Marriage and the Family, 29*(2), 257–266.

Shanas, E. (1979a). Social myth as hypothesis: The case of family relations of old people. *The Gerontologist, 19,* 3–9.

Shanas, E. (1979b). The family as a social support system in old age. *The Gerontologist, 19,* 169–174.

Shatzkin, K. (1995, October 22). Twilight behind bars. *The Baltimore Sun.*

Shaw, L. B., & Lee, S. (2005). Growing old in the U.S.: Gender and income equity. *Feminist Economics, 11,* 174–186.

Shea, D. G., Miles, T., & Hayward, M. (1996). The health-wealth connection: Racial differences. *The Gerontologist, 36*(3), 342–349.

Shephard, R. J. (1999). Age and physical work capacity. *Experimental Aging Research, 25,* 331–343.

Shuey, K., & Hardy, M. (2003). Assistance to aging parents and parents-in-law: Does lineage affect family allocation decisions? *Journal of Marriage & the Family, 65,* 418–431.

Sigle-Rushton, W., & Waldfogel, J. (2007). Motherhood and women's earnings in Anglo-American, continental European, and Nordic countries. *Feminist Economics, 13,* 55–91.

Silverstein, M. (2006). Intergenerational family transfers in social context. In R. H. Binstock & L. K. George (Eds.), *Handbook of aging and the social sciences* (6th ed., pp. 166–181). Burlington, MA: Academic Press.

Silverstein, M., Angelelli, J. J., & Parrott, T. M. (2001). Changing attitudes toward aging policy in the United States during the 1980s and 1990s: A cohort analysis. *Journal of Gerontology: Social Sciences, 56B*(1), S36–S43.

Silverstein, M., Conroy, S. J., Wang, H., Giarrusso, R., & Bengtson, V. L. (2002). Reciprocity in parent-child relations over the adult life course. *Journal of Gerontology: Social Sciences, 57B*(1), S3–S13.

Silverstein, M., Parrott, T. M., & Bengtson, V. L. (1995). Factors that predispose middle-aged sons and daughters to provide social support to older parents. *Journal of Marriage and the Family, 57*(2), 465–475.

Simmons, C. H., Vom Kolke, A., & Hideko, S. (1986). Attitudes toward romantic love among American, German, and Japanese students. *The Journal of Social Psychology, 126*(3), 327–336.

Simon-Rusinowitz, L., Loughlin, D., Ruben, K., Garcia, G., & Mahoney, K. (2010). The benefits of consumer-directed services for elders and their caregivers in the cash and counseling demonstration and evaluation. *Public Policy and Aging Report, 20*(1), 27–31.

Singer, B. H., & Ryff, C. D. (Eds.). (2001). *New horizons in health: An integrative approach.* Washington, DC: National Academy Press.

Slegers, K., Martin, P. J. van Boxtel, & Jolles, J. (2008). Effects of computer training and internet usage on the well-being and quality of life of older adults: A randomized, controlled study. *Journal of Gerontology: Psychological Sciences, 63B,* P176–P184.

Slevin, K. F., & Wingrove, C. R. (1995). Women in retirement: A review and critique of empirical research since 1976. *Sociological Inquiry, 65*(1), 1–21.

Sloane, P. D., Zimmerman, S., Williams, C. S., Reed, P. S., Gill, K. S., & Preisser, J. S. (2005). Evaluating the quality of life of long-term care residents with dementia. *The Gerontologist, 45*(1), 37–49.

Smeeding, T. M. (1990). Economic status of the elderly. In R. H. Binstock & L. K. George (Eds.), *Handbook of aging and the social sciences* (3rd ed., pp. 362–381). New York: Academic Press.

Smeeding, T. M., Estes, C. L., & Glasse, L. (1999, August). Social Security in the 21st century: More than deficits: Strengthening security for women. *Gerontology News,* (special insert), 1–8.

Smeeding, T. M., & Sandstrom, S. (2005). Poverty and income maintenance in old age: A cross-national view of low income older women. *Feminist Economics, 11,* 163–174.

Snyder, C., van Wormer, K., Chadha, J., & Jaggers, J. W. (2009). Older adult inmates: The challenge for social work. *Social Work, 54*(2), 117–124.

Social Security Administration. (n.d.). *Thinking of retiring? Information insert to those 55+.* Retrieved from http://www.ssa.gov/mystatement/insert55+.pdf

Social Security Administration. (1995). Fast facts and figures about Social Security. *SSA Publication # 13–11785.* Washington, DC: Department of Health and Human Services.

Social Security Administration. (2004a). *Income of the aged chartbook 2002.* Retrieved from http://www.ssa.gov/policy/docs/chartbooks/income_aged/2002/iac02.pdf

Social Security Administration. (2004b). *Exempt amounts under the earnings test.* Retrieved from http://www.ssa.gov/OACT/COLA/rtea.html

Social Security Administration. (2004c). *Annual statistical supplement.* Retrieved from http://www.ssa.gov/policy/docs/statcomps/supplement/2004/6b.pdf

Social Security Administration. (2004d). *SSI federal payment amounts.* Retrieved from http://www.ssa.gov/OACT/COLA/SSI.html

Social Security Administration. (2005). *Social Security Programs Throughout the World: Africa, 2005.* Washington, DC: Author.

Social Security Administration. (2006). *Social Security/SSI information fact sheet.* Retrieved from http://www.ssa.gov/legislation/2006FactSheet.pdf

Social Security Administration. (2006b). *Income of the aged chartbook.* Retrieved from http://www.ssa.gov/policy/docs/chartbooks/income_aged/2004/index.html#toc

Social Security Administration. (2008). *Annual statistical supplement,* 2008. Table 4.c1. Washington, DC: author. Retrieved from http://www.socialsecurity.gov/policy/docs/statcomps/supplement/

Social Security Administration. (2009c). *Social Security and Medicare benefits. Actuarial Publications.* Retrieved from http://www.socialsecurity.gov/OACT/STATS/table4a4.html

Social Security Administration. (2009d). *Number of Social Security beneficiaries.* Retrieved from http://www.ssa.gov/OACT/ProgData/icpGraph.html

Social Security Administration. (2010a). *Income of the aged chartbook.* Retrieved from http://www.ssa.gov/policy/docs/chartbooks/income_aged/#toc

Social Security Administration. (2010b). *Social Security throughout the world.* Retrieved from http://www.socialsecurity.gov/policy/docs/progdesc/ssptw/

Special Report: The 400 richest Americans. (2008). *Forbes Magazine.* Retrieved from http://www.forbes.com/2008/09/16/forbes-400-billionaires-lists-400list08_cx_mn_0917richamericans_land.html

Starr, P. (1988). Social Security and the American public household. In T. R. Marmour & J. L. Mashaw (Eds.), *Social Security: Beyond the rhetoric of crisis* (pp. 119–148). Princeton, NJ: Princeton University Press.

Steffenmeier, D. J., Allan, E. A., Harer, M. D., & Streifel, C. (1989). Age and the distribution of crime. *American Journal of Sociology, 94*(4), 803–831.

Stein, D. (1988). Burning widows, burning brides: The perils of daughterhood in India. *Pacific Affairs, 61*(3), 465–485.

Steinmetz, S. K. (1988). *Duty bound: Elder abuse and family care.* Newbury Park, CA: Sage.

Steinmetz, S. K. (2005). Elder abuse is caused by the deviance and dependence of abusive caregivers. In D. R. Loeske, R. J. Gelles, & M. M. Cavanaugh (Eds.), *Current controversies in family violence* (2nd ed.). Thousand Oaks, CA: Sage Publications

Steuerle, E., Sprio, C., & Johnson, R. W. (1999). *Can Americans work longer?* Washington, DC: Urban Institute. Retrieved from http://www.urban.org/UploadedPDF/Straight5.pdf

Stewart, S., Cutler, D., & Rosen, A. (2009). Forecasting the effects of obesity and smoking on U.S. life expectancy. *New England Journal of Medicine, 361*(123), 2252–2260.

Stone, R., Caffertata, G. L., & Sangl, J. (1987). Caregivers of the frail elderly: A national profile. *The Gerontologist, 27*(5), 616–626.

Stoudt, A. (2009). Socially networked: How teens, parents and grandparents are all online and linked. *AARP Bulletin.* Retrieved from http://bulletin.aarp.org/yourworld/yourhome/articles/_socially_networked.html

Strate, J. M., Parish, C. J., Elder, C. D., & Ford III, C. (1989). Life span civic development and voting participation. *American Political Science Review, 83*(2), 443–464.

Strawbridge, W., Wallhagen, M., & Cohen, R. (2002). Successful aging and well-being: Self-rated compared with Rowe and Kahn. *The Gerontologist, 42*(6), 727–733.

Substance Abuse and Mental Health Services Administration. (2009). *The NSDUH report: Illicit drug use among older adults.* Rockville, MD: Author.

Substance Abuse and Mental Health Services Administration. (2010). *The TEDS report: Changing substance abuse patterns among older admissions: 1992 and 2008.* Rockville, MD: Author.

Suitor, J. J., Pillemer, K., Keeton, S., & Robison, J. (1994). Aged parents and aging children: Determinants of relationship quality. In R. Blieszner & V. H. Bedford (Eds.), *Handbook of aging and the family* (pp. 223–242). Westport, CT: Greenwood Press.

Sussmann, M. B. (1985). The family life of old people. In R. H. Binstock & E. Shanas (Eds.), *Handbook of aging and the social sciences* (2nd ed., pp. 415–449). New York: Van Nostrand Reinhold.

Sussmann, M. B., & Burchinal, L. (1968). Kin family network: Unheralded structure in current conceptualizations of family functioning. In B. L. Neugarten (Ed.), *Middle age and aging* (pp. 247–25). Chicago: University of Chicago Press.

Sweeney, M. M. (2002). Two decades of family change: The shifting economic foundations of marriage. *American Sociological Review, 67*(1), 132–147.

Sykes, L. L. (2008). Cashing in on the American dream: Racial differences in housing values 1970–2000. *Housing, Theory & Society, 25,* 254–274.

Szanton, P. (1993). Implications of an aging population: predictions, doubts, and questions. In *Aging of the U.S. population: Economic and environmental implications* (pp. 69–76). Washington, DC: American Association of Retired Persons.

Szinovacz, M. E., & Davey, A. (2004). Retirement transitions and spouse disability: Effects on depressive symptoms. *Journal of Gerontology: Social Sciences, 59B*(6), S333–S342.

Szinovacz, M. E., & Davey, A. (2005). Predictors of perceptions of involuntary retirement. *The Gerontologist, 45*(1), 36–47.

Szinovacz, M. E., & Washo, C. (1992). Gender differences in exposure to life events and adaptation to retirement. *Journal of Gerontology: Social Sciences, 47*(4), S191–S196.

Thomas, W. H. (2004). *What are old people for?* Acton, MA: Vander Wyk & Burnham.

Thompson, L., & Walker, A. (1987). Mothers as mediators of intimacy between grandmothers and their young adult granddaughters. *Family Relation, 36,* 72–77.

Thompson, W. S., & Whelpton, P. K. (1933). *Population trends in the United States.* New York: McGraw-Hill.

Tippett, K. S., & Cleveland, L. E. (n.d.). *How current diets stack up: Comparison with recommended dietary guidelines.* Retrieved from http://www.ers.usda.gov/publications/aib750/aib750c.pdf

Tornstam, L. (1997). Gerotranscendence: The contemplative dimension of aging. *Journal of Aging Studies, 11*(2), 143–154.

Tornstam, L. (2005). *Gerotranscendence: A developmental theory of positive aging.* New York: Springer Publishing.

Torres-Gil, F. M. (1992). *The new aging; Politics and change in America.* Westport, CT: Auburn House.

Torres-Gil, F. M. (1998). Policy, politics, aging: Crossroads in the 1990s. In J. S. Steckenrider & T. M. Parrott (Eds.), *New directions in old-age policies* (pp. 75–88). Albany: State University of New York Press.

Tout, K. (1989). *Aging in developing countries.* New York: Oxford University Press.

Townsend, P. (1968). The emergence of the four-generation family in industrial society. In B. L. Neugarten (Ed.), *Middle age and aging* (pp. 255–257). Chicago: University of Chicago Press.

Tran, B. Q. (2004). Technologies to facilitate health and independent living in elderly populations. In D. C. Burdick & S. Kwon (Eds.), *Gerotechnology: Research and practice in technology and aging* (pp. 161–173). New York: Springer Publishing.

Treas, J. (1995). Older Americans in the 1990 and beyond. *Population Bulletin, 50*(2), 2–46.

Truffer, C., Keehan, S., Smith, S., Cylus, J., Sisko, A., Poisal, J., Lizonitz, J., et al. (2010). Health spending projections through 2019: The recession's impact continues. *Health Affairs, 29*(3), 1–9. Retrieved from http://nchc.org/sites/default/files/resources/PPM136_2009–1074_final.pdf

Turner, R. (1956). Role-taking, role standpoint, and reference group behavior. *The American Journal of Sociology, 61*(4), 316–328.

Uhlenberg, P. (1996). Mutual attraction: Demography and life-course analysis. *The Gerontologist, 36*(2), 226–229.

Uhlenberg, P., Cooney, T., & Boyd, R. (1990). Divorce for women after midlife. *Journal of Gerontology: Social Sciences, 45*(1), S3–S11.

United Nations. (2002). *World population ageing: 1950–2050.* Department of Economic and Social Affairs, Population Division. Author.

United Nations. (2003). *International Plan of Action on Ageing.* Retrieved from http://www.un.org/esa/socdev/ageing/ageipaa1.htm.

United Nations Department of Economic and Social Affairs. (2005). *Living arrangements of older persons around the world.* New York: United Nations.

United Nations Department of Economic and Social Affairs. (2009). *World population ageing.* New York: United Nations.

United Nations General Assembly. (2010). *Follow-up to the Second World Assembly on Ageing: Report of the Secretary-General.* Retrieved from: http://daccess-dds-ny.un.org/doc/UNDOC/GEN/N02/439/32/PDF/N0243932.pdf?OpenElement

United Nations Office of the High Representative for the Least Developed Countries. (2010). *Criteria for identification of LDCs.* Retrieved from http://www.unohrlls.org/en/ldc/related/59/

United Nations Statistics Division. (2010). *Composition of macro geographical (continental) regions, geographical sub-regions, and selected economic and other groupings.* Retrieved from http://unstats.un.org/unsd/methods/m49/m49regin.htm

U.S. Census Bureau. (1975). *Statistical abstract of the United States, 1975.* Washington, DC: U.S. Government Printing Office.

U.S. Census Bureau. (1976). *Historical Statistics of the United States, Colonial Times to 1970.* Bicentennial Edition. Washington, DC: U.S. Government Printing Office.

U.S. Census Bureau. (1991a). Marital status and living arrangements: March 1990. *Current Population Reports,* P-20, No. 450. Washington, DC: U.S. Government Printing Office.

U.S. Census Bureau. (1991b). *Global aging: Comparative indicators and future trends.* Washington, DC: U.S. Department of Commerce.

U.S. Census Bureau. (1992). Voting and registration in the election of November 1992. *Current population reports,* Series P20–466. Retrieved from www.census.gov/population/socdemo/voting/history/vot04.txt—3k—Supplemental Result

U.S. Census Bureau. (1995). *Statistical Abstract of the United States.* Washington, DC: U.S. Government Printing Office.

U.S. Census Bureau. (1996). Population projections of the United States by age, sex, race and Hispanic origin: 1995–2050. *Current Population Reports.* P-25, No. 1130. Washington, DC: U.S. Government Printing Office.

U.S. Census Bureau. (1997). *Statistical abstract of the United States.* Washington, DC: U.S. Government Printing Office.

U.S. Census Bureau. (2003, March). *Annual Demographic Survey.* Retrieved from http://pubdb3.census.gov/macro/032004/pov/new01_100_01.htm

U.S. Census Bureau. (2004). *Statistics of U.S. businesses: 2004.* Retrieved from http://www.census.gov/epcd/susb/2004/us/US—.HTM

U.S. Census Bureau. (2005a). *Statistical Abstract of the United States 2004–2005.* Retrieved from http://www.census.gov/prod/2004pubs/04statab/socinsur.pdf

U.S. Census Bureau. (2005b). *Poverty thresholds 2005.* Retrieved from http://www.census.gov/hhes/www/poverty/threshld/thres05.html

U.S. Census Bureau. (2008a). *Press release on 2008 Federal budget.* Retrieved from http://www.census.gov/Press-Release/www/releases/archives/governments/013997.html

U.S. Census Bureau. (2008b). *Grandchildren under 18 living with their grandparents.* Retrieved from http://www.census.gov/population/www/socdemo/hh-fam.html#ht

U.S. Census Bureau. (2008c). America's families and living arrangements: 2008. *Current Population Reports.* Retrieved from http://www.census.gov/population/www/socdemo/hh-fam.html

U.S. Census Bureau. (2008d). *Annual social and economic supplement: 2007.* Retrieved from http://www.census.gov/hhes/www/poverty/poverty/html

U.S. Census Bureau. (2008e). *Voting and registration in the election of November 2008.* Retrieved from http://www.census.gov/population/www/socdemo/voting/cps2008.html

U.S. Census Bureau. (2008f). *Net worth and assets of households 2002.* Current Population Reports P70–115.

U.S. Census Bureau. (2008g). *Poverty thresholds 2008.* Retrieved from http://www.census.gov/hhes/www/poverty/threshld/thresh08.html

U.S. Census Bureau. (2009). *Voting and registration in the election of November 2008.* Retrieved from http://www.census.gov/population/www/socdemo/voting/cps2008.html

U.S. Census Bureau. (2010a). *Facts for Features: Older Americans Month 2010.* Retrieved from http://www.census.gov/newsroom/releases/archives/facts_for_features_special_editions/cb10-ff06.html

U.S. Census Bureau. (2010b). Marital status of the population by sex and age, 2008. *2010 Statistical Abstract.* Retrieved from http://www.census.gov/compendia/statab/cats/population/marital_status_and_living_arrangements.html

U.S. Census Bureau. (2010c). Expectation of life at birth and projections. *2010 Statistical Abstract.* Retrieved from http://www.census.gov/compendia/statab/cats/births_deaths_marriages_divorces/life_expectancy.html

U.S. Census Bureau. (2010d). *Statistics abstract of the United States: 2010* (129th ed.). Retrieved from http://www.census.gov/compendia/statab/2010/tables/10s0294.pdf

U.S. Census Bureau. (n.d.). *United Stated educational attainment of the population 25 years and over: 1940 to 2000.* Retrieved from http://www.census.gov/population/socdemo/education/phct41/US.pdf .

U.S. Census Bureau International Data Base. (2010). Retrieved from http://www.census.gov/ipc/www/idb/informationGateway.php

U.S. Central Intelligence Agency. (2010). *World Fact Book.* Retrieved from https://www.cia.gov/library/publications/the-world-factbook/geos/us.html

U.S. Department of Health and Human Services. (n.d.). *HHS: What we do.* Retrieved from http://www.hhs.gov/about/whatwedo.html

U.S. Department of Justice. (2007). *Crime in the United States.* Retrieved from http://www.fbi.gov/ucr/cius2007/arrests/index.html

U.S. Department of Justice. (2008). *Reported crime in the United States—Total (1960–2006).* Retrieved from http://bjsdata.ojp.usdoj.gov/dataonline/Search/Crime/State/statebystaterun.cfm?stateid=52

U.S. Department of Justice, Federal Bureau of Prisons. (1989, January). Looking ahead—The future BOP population and their costly health care needs. *Research Bulletin,* 1–5.

U.S. Department of Labor. (2009). *Employment status of the civilian non-institutionalized population by age, sex and race, 2008.* Retrieved from http://ftp.bls.gov/pub/special.request/lf/att3.txt

U.S. Department of Labor, Bureau of Labor Statistics. (1975). *Employment and Earnings, 22*(3), 21.

U.S. Department of Labor, Bureau of Labor Statistics. (1985). *Employment and Earnings, 32*(11), 10–11.

U.S. Department of Labor, Bureau of Labor Statistics. (1995). *Employment and Earnings, 42*(11), 21–22.

U.S. Department of Labor, Bureau of Labor Statistics. (2000). *Spending patterns by age.* Retrieved from http://www.bls.gov/opub/ils/pdf/opbils41.pdf

U.S. Department of Labor, Bureau of Labor Statistics. (2001). *Contingent and alternative employment arrangements, February 2001.* Retrieved from http://www.bls.gov/news.release/conemp.nr0.htm

U.S. Department of Labor, Bureau of Labor Statistics. (2004). *Economic and employment projections: 2002–2012.* Retrieved from http://www.bls.gov/news.release/ecopro.nr0.htm.

U.S. Department of Labor, Bureau of Labor Statistics. (2008a). *Employment projections: 2006–2016.* Retrieved from ftp://ftp.bls.gov/pub/special.requests/ep/labor.force/emplab01.txt

U.S. Department of Labor, Bureau of Labor Statistics. (2008b). *Work experience of the population by sex and full- and part-time status, selected years 1970–2006.* Retrieved from http://www.bls.gov/cps/wlf-table22–2008.pdf

U.S. Department of Labor, Bureau of Labor Statistics. (2008c). *Employee tenure summary.* Retrieved from http://www.bls.gov/news.release/tenure.nr0.htm.

U.S. Department of Labor, Bureau of Labor Statistics. (2009b). *Consumer expenditure survey: Table 3.* Retrieved from http://www.bls.gov/cex/tables.htm

U.S. Senate Special Committee on Aging. (1991). *Aging America: Trends and projections.* Washington, DC: U.S. Department of Health and Human Services.

Vaillant, C. O., & Vaillant, G. A. (1993). Is the u-curve of marital satisfaction an illusion? A 40-year study of marriage. *Journal of Marriage & Family, 55*(1), 230–239.

Van Eijck, K. (2001). Social differentiation in musical taste patterns. *Social Forces, 79,* 1163–1184.

Vastag, B. (2001). Easing the elderly online in search of health information. *Journal of the American Medical Association, 285*(12), 1563–1564.

Velkoff, V. (2000). Centenarians in the United States, 1990 and beyond. *Statistical Bulletin, 81*(1), 2–9.

Vincent, G., & Velkoff, V. (2010). The next four decades. The older population in the United States: 2010 to 2050. *Current Population Reports,* P25–1138. Washington, DC: U.S. Bureau of the Census.

Vincent, J. A., Phillipson, C. R., & Downs, M. (2006). *The futures of old age.* London: Sage Publications.

Vinton, L. (1991). Abused older women: Battered women or abused elders? *Journal of Women and Aging, 3*(3), 5–19.

Vitez, M. (1995, November 29). Ripeness is all, in centenarians as in cheeses. *The Baltimore Sun.*

Wahl, H., & Weisman, G. (2003). Environmental gerontology at the beginning of the new millennium: Reflections on its historical, empirical, and theoretical development. *The Gerontologist, 43*(5), 616–627.

Waldron, I. (1993). Recent trends in sex mortality ratios for adults in developed countries. *Social Science and Medicine, 36*(4), 451–462.

Walker, A. J., Martin, S., & Jones, L. L. (1992). The benefits and costs of caregiving and care receiving for daughters and mothers. *Journal of Gerontology: Social Sciences, 47,* S130–S139.

Wallace, H. (1996). *Family violence: Legal, medical and social perspectives.* Needham Heights, MA: Allyn and Bacon.

Wallace, S. P., Williamson, J. B., Lung, R. G., & Powell, L. A. (1991). A lamb in wolf's clothing? The reality of senior power and social policy. In M. Minkler & C. L. Estes (Eds.), *Critical perspectives on aging: The political and moral economy of growing old* (pp. 95–114). Amityville, NY: Baywood.

Waller, D. (2006, January 22). Health: Take two aspirin and read this now. *Time.*

Ward, R., Logan, J., & Spitze, G. (1992). The influence of parent and child needs on coresidence in middle and later life. *Journal of Marriage and the Family, 54*(1), 209–221.

Weaver, D. A. (1994). The work and retirement decisions of older women: A literature review. *Social Security Bulletin, 57*(1), 3–24.

Weaver, D. A. (1997). The economic well-being of Social Security beneficiaries, with an emphasis on divorced beneficiaries. *Social Security Bulletin, 60*(4), 3–17.

Weeks, J. (2005). *Population: An introduction to concepts and issues.* Belmont, CA: Wadsworth.

Weiner, J. (2010). What does health reform mean for long-term care? *Public Policy and Aging Report, 20*(2), 8–15.

Weishaus, S., & Field, D. (1988). A half century of marriage: Continuity or change? *Journal of Marriage and the Family, 50*(3), 763–774.

Weiss, M. J. (2002). Chasing youth. *American Demographics, 24,* 35–41.

Weiss, R. S. (2005). *The experience of retirement.* Ithaca, NY: Cornell University Press.

Wells, T. (1998). *Changes in occupational sex segregation during the 1980s and 1990s.* Madison: Center for Demography and Ecology, University of Wisconsin.

West, H. C., & Sabol, W. J. (2009). *Prison inmates at midyear 2008—Statistical tables.* Bureau of Justice Statistics, U.S. Department of Justice. Retrieved from http://www.ojp.usdoj.gov/bjs/pub/pdf/pim08st.pdf

White, L., & Peterson, D. (1995). The retreat from marriage: Its effect on unmarried children's exchange with parents. *Journal of Marriage and the Family, 57*(2), 428–434.

White, L. K., & Reidman, A. (1992). When the Brady Bunch grows up: Step/half- and full sibling relationships in adulthood. *Journal of Marriage and the Family, 54,* 197–208.

White, H., McConnell, E., Clipp, E., Bynum, L., Teague, C., Navas, L., et al. (1999). Surfing the net in later life: A review of the literature and pilot study of computer use and quality of life. *Journal of Applied Gerontology, 18*(3), 358–378.

Wiley, D., & Bortz, W. (1996). Sexuality and aging—usual and successful. *Journals of Gerontology, 51A,* M142–M146.

Winship, C., & Harding, D. (2004). *A general strategy for the identification of age, period, cohort models: A mechanism based approach.* Retrieved from http://www.qmp.isr.umich.edu/ASAMConference/Papers/WinshipHardingAPC.pdf

Winship, C., & Harding, D. J. (2008). A mechanism-based approach to the identification of age–period–cohort models. *Sociological Methods & Research, 36*(3), 362–401.

Wolff, J. L., & Agree, E. M. (2004). Depression among recipients of informal care: The effects of reciprocity, respect, and adequacy of support. *Journal of Gerontology: Social Sciences, 59B,* S173–S180.

Wolff, J. L., & Kasper, J. D. (2006). Caregivers of frail elders: Updating a national profile. *The Gerontologist, 46,* 344–356.

Women's Initiative. (1993). *Women, pensions and divorce: Small reforms that could make a big difference.* Washington, DC: American Association of Retired Persons.

Wongboonsin, K., Guest, P., & Prachuabmob, F. (2005). Demographic change and the demographic dividend in Thailand. *Asian Population Studies 1*(2), 245–256. Retrieved from http://pdfserve.informaworld.com/707869__727239124.pdf

World Bank. (2010). *How we classify countries.* Retrieved from http://data.worldbank.org/about/country-classifications

World Health Organization (WHO). (2006). *World Health Organization mortality database.* Retrieved from http://www3.who.int/whosis/mort/table1_process.cfm.

World Health Organization. (2010a). *WHO Age-Friendly Environments Programme.* Retrieved from http://www.who.int/ageing/age_friendly_cities/en/index.html

World Health Organization. (2010b). *Older people and primary health care.* Retrieved from http://www.who.int/ageing/primary_health_care/en/index.html

Wu, K. B. (2005). *How Social Security keeps older persons out of poverty across developed countries.* Washington, DC: AARP Public Policy Institute. Retrieved from http://www.aarp.org/ppi

Wynne. E. A. (1991). Will the young support the old? In B. B. Hess & E. W. Markson (Eds.), *Growing old in America* (4th ed. pp. 507–623). New Brunswick, NJ: Transaction Books.

Yang, R. (2008). Social inequalities in happiness in the United States, 1972 to 2004: An age-period-cohort analysis. *American Sociological Review, 73,* 204–226.

Yaukey, D. (1985). *Demography: The study of human population.* Prospect Heights, IL: Waveland Press.

Yin, S., & Kent, M. (2008). *Kenya: The demographics of a country in turmoil.* Retrieved from http://www.prb.org/Articles/2008/kenya.aspx

Yin, W., Basu, A., Zhang, J. X., Rabbani, A., Meltzer, D. O., & Alexander, G. C. (2008). The effect of the Medicare Part D Prescription Benefit on drug utilization and expenditures. *Annals of Internal Medicine, 148,* 169–177.

Zedlewski, S. R., & Schaner, S. G. (2006). Older adults engaged as volunteers. Urban Institute: *Perspectives on Aging #5.* Retrieved from http://www.urban.org/UploadedPDF/311325_older_volunteers.pdf

Zepelin, H., Sills, R. A., & Heath, H. W. (1986–1987). Is age becoming irrelevant? An exploratory study of perceived age norms. *International Journal of Aging and Human Development, 24*(4), 241–256.

Zhang, Z., Gu, D., & Hayward, M. D. (2008). Early life influences on cognitive impairment among oldest old Chinese. *Journal of Gerontology: Social Sciences, 63B,* S25–S33.

Zimmer, Z. (2005). Health and living arrangement transitions among China's oldest-old. *Research on Aging, 27*(5), 526–555.

Zimmerman, S., Sloane, P. D., Eckert, J. K., Gruber-Baldini, A., Morgan, A. L., Hebel, J. R., et al. (2005). How good is assisted living? Findings and implications from an outcomes study. *Journal of Gerontology: Social Sciences, 60B*(4), S195–S204.

Index